# WITNESS
# TO THE
# HOLOCAUST

# WITNESS
# TO THE
# HOLOCAUST

**AZRIEL EISENBERG**

The Pilgrim Press

NEW YORK

THE PILGRIM PRESS
132 West 31 Street
New York, N.Y. 10001

**Library of Congress Cataloging in Publication Data**
Main entry under title:

Witness to the holocaust.

    Includes bibliographical references.
    1.    Holocaust, Jewish (1939–1945)—Personal narratives.    2.    Refugees, Jewish—Biography.
I.    Eisenberg, Azriel Louis, 1903–
D810.J4E17    1981        943.086        80-25961
ISBN 0-8298-0432-3

Printed in the United States of America

# ACKNOWLEDGMENTS

For permission to reprint the selections in this volume, grateful acknowledgment is made to those named below and on the following pages which constitute an extension of the copyright page. Every reasonable effort has been made to obtain appropriate permission to reproduce the copyrighted materials included in this volume. If notified of errors or omissions, the editor and the publisher will make the necessary corrections in future editions.

    "Tell the World," "Dr. Mengele's Criminal Laboratory," "Farewell to Life" and "Revolt in Auschwitz" from *Auschwitz* by Miklos Nyiszli; copyright© 1960 by Miklos Nyiszli. By permission of Frederick Fell Publishers, Inc.
    "Becoming a Jew At Last" by Beth Durchschlag. By permission of the *Courier-Post*, Camden, N.J.
    "Lamentations" by permission of the poet, Menachem Z. Rosensaft. Reprinted with permission from *Midstream*, May 1975.
    "Portrait of a German Family" from the Foreword by Carl Binger to *Human Behavior in the Concentration Camp* by Elie A. Cohen; copyright© 1966. By permission of W.W. Norton and Co. Inc.
    "Nazi Headmaster" from *The Germans: An Indictment of My People* by Gudrun Tempel, translated by Sophie Wilkins; copyright© 1963 by Gudrun Tempel. By permission of Random House Inc. and Rowohlt Taschenbuch Verlag GmBH.
    "Around the Fires of the Solstice Festival," "The Changed Tempo of Life," "The Fuehrer

Dedicated
to all those
who have committed themselves
never to forget

# PREFACE

I express my thanks to Yad Vashem—the Martyrs and Heroes Remembrance Authority in Jerusalem, and to the Ghetto Fighters' House in memory of Itzhak Katznelson, both of which helped guide me in my work during my visits to Israel. They also courteously permitted me to reprint several selections from their publications in this book.

In this, as in my other works, I leaned heavily on the resources of five Jewish libraries in New York City for my research. They are the libraries of YIVO—the Yiddish Scientific Institute; the Zionist Library; the New York Public Library, Jewish Division; Hebrew Union College-Jewish Institute of Religion; and the Jewish Theological Seminary. I am grateful to their librarians for their ever-ready services; for this book in particular I single out Ms. Dina Abramovitch of the YIVO library, to whom I am especially beholden.

I wish to thank Sam E. Bloch, director of the Department of Publications of the World Zionist Organization, American Section, who has extended himself to assist me whenever I have called on him; Dr. Harry H. Shapiro, Professor of Political Science, Rutgers University, for reading the manuscript and for his helpful suggestions; and Ed Cone for technical assistance.

## Preface

I am indebted to Messers Larry Werbel and David M.L. Olive-
stone for the help that they extended to me in preparing the
manuscript. They too have been committed to the affirmation
that the Holocaust shall never be forgotten.

Finally, as in all my works, I acknowledge my profound appreciation to my wife, Rose, who, for over five decades, has not only
borne with me in my preoccupation as writer and editor, but has
also distinguished herself as critic and superb proofreader. May
she, with God's help, continue in these capacities for many years
to come.

Azriel Eisenberg

New York City
January 1981

# CONTENTS

Contents

# Contents

# Contents

xix

# Contents

# 1. | A CRIME WITHOUT EQUAL

Gideon Hausner, Israel's prosecuting attorney in the Eichmann trial, once told an audience about an experience he had at an airport. He was chatting with a woman survivor of a death camp. It was summer, and she wore a sleeveless dress. On her forearm was a number tatooed in blue. Nearby, he noticed some agitation among a family group. The wife, followed reluctantly by her husband and shame-faced children, came over to Mr. Hausner's companion. She apologized profusely and said, "That *is* a camp-tatooed number on your arm, isn't it? Please forgive us. If you do not mind very much, we would like our children to see it. They just don't believe the Holocaust atrocities really happened." The lady graciously complied with the request.

*Witness to the Holocaust* has been an agonizing book to prepare—and it will be agonizing to read. But we must study the Holocaust; the deaths of six million Jews have charged us to live, to learn, to remember, and to tell the world. To forget is to make Hitler triumphant.

*Witness to the Holocaust* is the story of the hunted, persecuted, and murdered; but it is also the story of the heroic Jewish resistance, and of courageous acts of humanity by individual non-Jews. It describes a "society"—a highly developed, supposedly civilized nation, in the very heartland of Europe—that regarded genocide as one of its main goals, and made the mass murder of millions into a routine, mechanical process.

This state of horror continued for twelve years (1933–45) and enveloped all of Nazi-occupied Europe. The genocide operation was swift and was over before the world could grasp its enormity. Of the approximately 8,300,000 Jews in Nazi Europe, 6,000,000 perished—2,000,000 of the

1

dead were children. Of every four Jews, one survived; hunted, bereaved, homeless—an empty shell.

The term most commonly used in describing this tragedy is "Holocaust." It is derived from the Greek word for a sacrificial offering that is consumed entirely by flames. More commonly, it is used to define a total or widespread destruction by fire. For our purposes the term is inadequate and inappropriate, but it is the best we have. Interchangeably with "Holocaust" I shall use the popular Hebrew word *Shoah,* which means "destruction," or "disaster," as well as "tragedy" and "catastrophe," words that are all too familiar in Jewish history.

Jews have lived through severe persecution and suffering in the past; for example—the Crusades (1096–1300), the Spanish Inquisition (1483–1650), the Chmielnicki massacres (1648–58), and the Czarist pogroms (1882–1906). However, the number of six million killed during the Nazi Holocaust exceeds the combined total of all these catastrophes.

The focus in this book is on the Jews, but in point of fact, precious human beings of other nationalities, faiths, and ideologies were also annihilated by the millions—among them Gypsies, Czechs, Yugoslavs, Poles, Russians, and French. However, it was the Jews that were singled out for *total* destruction. From its very beginnings in 1933, Nazi Germany carefully defined who was a Jew. As the Nazi armies overran Europe, Jews were immediately hunted down, transported, and liquidated. The whole Nazi war machine, even when overtaxed and facing certain defeat, was bent on destroying them. The "Final Solution" received topmost priority, and had Nazi Germany triumphed, World Jewry might have been destroyed. What happened to European Jewry would have happened everywhere.

One people that shared the fate of the Jews were the Gypsies. They, too, had been persecuted through the ages, and like the Jews, the Gypsies were isolated and liquidated, country by country. Unlike the Jews, however, they left almost no records of the atrocities committed against them, which were no less horrible than those recorded in this book. When the bloodbath was over, only pitiful remnants were left alive. The world hardly knew of their sufferings, nor is it fully aware today of their disappearance. Except for the few survivors, a whole people, unique in its life-style, language, culture, and art, was wiped off the face of the earth. There are no memorials to their dead or commemorations of their tragedy. The death of the Gypsy nation was more than physical; it was total oblivion.[1]

We must always remember that the massacres of the Jews would also have fallen into oblivion, and the conscience of the world would have languished and abated, had the records not been preserved. World-

[1] Read Kenrich Donald and Puxon Grant, *The Destruction of Europe's Gypsies,* Columbia Centre Series (England: Chatto-Heinemann, Sussex University Press, 1972).

stirring trials like those in Nuremberg, the Eichmann Case, the Dering Case, the ongoing Nazi criminal trials, and the outlawing of genocide by the United Nations were made possible, in part, by the records left by Jewish martyrs like Emanuel Ringelblum, Shimon Huberband, Moshe Flinker, and Anne Frank; by the unrelenting pursuit of Nazi criminals by individuals like Simon Wiesenthal, Tuviah Friedman, and Beate Klarsfield; by the writings of survivors like Elie Wiesel and André Schwarz-Bart; and by the labors of historians like Leon Poliakov, Philip Friedman, Mark Dworzhetsky, Isaiah Trunk, Raul Hilberg, Jacob Robinson, Gerald Reitlinger, Lucy S. Dawidowicz, Nora Levin, and others. Commemorations such as Warsaw Ghetto Day, institutions like Yad Vashem and the Ghetto Fighters' House in Israel, the Memorial to the Unknown Jewish Martyr in Paris, and organizations like the World Federation of Bergen–Belsen Associations help keep memories fresh and consciences alert.

Repeatedly, those who went to their deaths left behind documents and testimonies for posterity. In the face of death, they put aside the paralyzing prospect of what lay ahead and recorded their experiences. They wrote their memoirs in many languages, especially in Yiddish, Hebrew, German, Polish, and Hungarian. But the full story of their suffering will take years to tell. They wrote *for* us and *to* us. The memory of their lives must be bound with our lives so that their deaths will not have been in vain. It is our moral obligation, and our responsibility to our consciences, to humanity, and to future generations, to remember them. Too often we are shocked to hear how many people have been and still are ignorant of this incomparable crime.

We must be prepared to challenge the prevarications and downright falsifications expressed in books, movies, and plays by dodgers of guilt. Efforts are being made to minimize and even obliterate the Jewish tragedy as such. In this book, you will read about Babi Yar, and the efforts of the Soviet government to wipe out the memory of the Jews who were martyred there. A similar policy has been adopted by Poland. In April 1973, the Association of Polish Jews in Great Britain accused the Polish government of trying to falsify history with regard to the Warsaw Ghetto Uprising and Jewish resistance. They charged that the Polish authorities "are deliberately misrepresenting the events of that era, and especially the events relating to Jewish resistance." They also charged that "pressure has been brought to bear upon the Jewish Historical Institute in Poland to present the revolt in the Warsaw Ghetto not as a heroic act of the Jews of the ghetto, but merely as an episode within Polish resistance to German occupation."

Furthermore, a proper study of the tragedy will supply the information necessary to refute those who espouse the Nazi viewpoint—the Norwegian author Knut Hamsun, winner of the Nobel Prize in literature, the American poet Ezra Pound, and others.

But there are other valid reasons to study the *Shoah*. It gives perspective to the miracle of Israel reborn; as in the vision of the Valley of the Dry Bones (Ezekiel 37), the dry bones of the *She'erit Hapletah* (the Surviving Remnant) sprang to life. The events in Israel since 1948 constitute that important sequel to the *Shoah*—the State of Israel—and afford our generation a sense of deep pride in the vitality of the Jewish people and of faith in its future. The intensity of that faith, however, is dependent on our thorough comprehension of the history of the period.

A study of the past through the eyewitness accounts in this book must fill us with sorrow and anger. We must be angry at the passivity of the family of nations in the face of human suffering. During the early years of the catastrophe (1933–39), the civilized world responded with a deafening silence. Governments looked on and did very little to alleviate the tragedy. Very few countries opened their doors to even limited immigration. During the years of the Final Solution (1940–45), only one country, Denmark, resisted valiantly. Its bravery will never be forgotten. All the Slavic lands (except Bulgaria to a limited degree) collaborated, more or less, in the slaughter. We must be angry at the democracies, including our own country, which could have saved hundreds of thousands if only they had responded in time.

We should be angry with leaders and organizations who did not do enough to shake the foundations of society during 1933–45. We should be angry with ourselves for not relating more intimately to the sufferings of the victims. We should be furious at our peers who are apathetic and to whom this catastrophe is irrelevant in their daily lives. We must commit ourselves to keep the memory of the *Shoah* alive, so that mankind shall always be alert and concerned.

There is yet another purpose for studying the tragedy: self-preservation. The *Shoah* cries for some kind of rational explanation; yet there is none. It is incomprehensible; it defies all parallels. Still, we always face the unthinkable possibility that it may again happen. Indeed, today at more than one demonstration, American Nazis celebrate Hitler's birthday and espouse Hitlerism. They have paraded such slogans as "Gas the Jews" and "Finish Hitler's Job." Synagogues have been smeared with swastikas, and many Jewish cemeteries have been desecrated.[2] In 1948, 1956, 1967, and again in 1973, the Arab leaders threatened a new massacre of the people of Israel. Hitler and Goebbels' "Destroy the Jews" propaganda is still being disseminated widely in the Near East, in Latin America, and in our very midst. The inherent evil in man, and the inhumanity released by Hitler, can easily reappear, given certain conditions. We must not be lulled into a mood of passive tranquillity.

This is not just another book on a heart-rending chapter of modern history; it is a scroll of agony and heroism. As such, it must be studied

[2]Read Saul Carson, *165 Temples Desecrated* (New York: Popular Library, 1971). Also *Swastika 1960*, a brochure published by the Anti-Defamation League of B'nai B'rith.

4

with awe and reverence. As we read it, we should take to heart the words of the prophet Joel: "Listen to this, you who are old; hear this, all you inhabitants of the land! Has the like of it ever been in your day or in the days of your fathers? Tell it to your children, and your children to their children, and their children to the coming generation" (1:2–3). The lessons of the Holocaust must be transmitted as a legacy to future generations.

You will not find much, if anything, about this tragedy in the usual textbooks used in schools. In fact, historians generally neglect to write about Gentile-Jewish relations in textbooks. To most historians, Jews, as such, do not exist. They are viewed as members of an economic class in any particular country, not as members of an ethnic, religious group. With a few notable exceptions, historians have not made known to the world the great tragedy of the exterminated Jews as *Jews*. Where mention is made, it is capsulized into a kind of statistical abstract, giving the number killed, mentioning the names of a few death camps, and concluding with a few moralistic phrases. Rarely is graphic documentation of the Holocaust, such as pictures, maps, charts, or quotations from primary sources, included to impress the facts on the mind of the reader. One example is the University of Michigan's well-known eighteen-volume modern history series, *History of the Modern World* (one of the editors was the distinguished historian Allan Nevins). The volume on Germany was written in 1961, by Marshall Dill, Jr. The persecution of the Jews is discussed in but five paragraphs; the extermination of the Jews in one. Another example is the book *Soviet Partisans in World War II* (University of Wisconsin Press, 1964), edited by John A. Armstrong; the role of the Jewish partisans is hardly mentioned.

As you study the record, you will experience vicariously, and begin to understand, the enormity and gravity of the ignorance and indifference to the *Shoah*—and how, today, many ill-informed people succumb to the repulsive Soviet and Arab propaganda that likens Zionism to Nazism. We must fight this perversity. We should also protest the casual application of such concepts as "Auschwitz" and "genocide" to other world crimes. The Holocaust was unique.

The *Shoah* cannot be intellectualized. To validate this contention, readers are invited to test their emotional reactions to the introductions of the chapters in this book as compared to the first-hand accounts that follow them. To establish any kind of meaningful tie with Auschwitz, the Warsaw Ghetto, the partisans, the martyrs, and the survivors, we must share in their experiences. For this reason, the heart of this book is a compilation of authentic, first-hand, personal, and eyewitness accounts. They will affect your innermost being. I have tried to present selections of the most effective, relevant, and representative writings on the tragedy, the great majority of which have not appeared in any other anthology to date. To supplement and complement the various aspects, I have pro-

5

vided introductions for each section with background information, as well as cross-references. In addition, I have included concise prefatory comments, where necessary, and selected bibliographical references to guide students in the continuation of their studies.

Generally, I refer the reader to books I have personally read. The books on the *Shoah* are overwhelming in number; as new studies appear, our knowledge of the *Shoah* grows, and errors, as well as inaccuracies, are corrected. I have endeavored to include the latest significant data which appeared before this book went to press.

Finally, this book continues beyond the ugly finale of Nazidom. It gives witness to the fact that there was no repatriation for the *She'erit Hapletah* to their former homes, and that persecutions did not abate in the Slavic lands. It gives testimony to the fact that the DPs had to fight their very liberators to find haven and home in *Eretz Yisrael*. It documents how mankind, shaken by the stark crimes, brought, and is still bringing, the criminals to justice before world tribunals. It provides commentary on conditions in postwar Germany, which are also integral to this study. And in closing this volume, I have included a discussion on the lessons of the tragedy and an overview on how mankind and World Jewry have been memorializing the *Shoah* in the community, synagogue, and home.

It is my sincere hope that young and old will try fervently to relate to the *Shoah*, that they will commit themselves to memorializing the six million martyrs in their own personal lives, and that they will take to heart the lessons of the *Shoah* for our time and all time. Remember!

# Tell the World

*Last of the large European communities deported to Auschwitz (450,000) were the Hungarian Jews, a year before Germany's defeat (1945). Their end was the swiftest and weirdest of all. Among the victims was Dr. Miklos Nyiszli, who, to stay alive, served as chief physician of the Auschwitz death factories . . .*

Next door to the SS living quarters . . . was a carpenter's shop, where three carpenters plied their trade, fulfilling any and all requests that were sent to them. For the moment they were busy filling a "private order." Oberschaarführer Mussfeld, taking advan-

From *Auschwitz, A Doctor's Eye Witness Account* by Dr. Miklos Nyiszli.

tage of the opportunity, had ordered the carpenters to make him a sort of double bed that could also serve as a large sofa . . .

It was no easy job, but in the crematoriums there was no such word as "impossible" when an order was given. The carpenters had salvaged the necessary wood from among the construction materials scattered about the crematorium grounds. The springs had come from the easy chairs that certain deportees had brought with them to make the journey more comfortable for their ailing parents . . .

I had followed all phases of its construction and seen it completed. I had watched them install the springs and cover them with elegant tapestries. Two French electricians had installed a bed lamp and arranged a niche for a radio. After it had been varnished it was quite handsome . . . the sofa was to be sent to Mussfeld's home at Mannheim. There it would wait till the victorious *Ober,* back from the trying wars, could use it to rest his weary bones.

One day . . . I was in my room and saw a half dozen silk pajamas—a natural supplement for the sofa—waiting to join the package. They were of fine imported silk and would certainly have been unobtainable on the outside, where ration tickets were needed for even the most essential items . . . In the undressing room the goods were there waiting to be taken. It only took one point per item, a point of flame from the *Ober's* gun, sending a bullet into the back of the owner's neck.

In exchange for these "points" (i.e., the killings) the SS officials received jewelry, leather goods, fur coats, silks and fine shoes. Not a week went by without their sending some packages home . . .

As I watched, day by day, the final phases of its construction, an idea began to take shape in my mind. Little by little the idea transformed itself into a project. In a few weeks the Sonderkommando[1] would be a thing of the past. We would all perish here, and we were well aware of it. We had even grown used to the idea, for we knew there was no way out. One thing upset me however. Eleven Sonderkommando squads had already perished and taken with them the terrible secret of the crematoriums and their butchers. Even though we did not survive, it was our bounden duty to make certain that the world learned of the unimaginable cruelty and sordidness of a people who pretended to be superior. It was imperative that a message addressed to the world leave this place. Whether it was discovered soon afterwards, or years later, it would still be a terrible manifesto of accusation. This message would be signed by all the members of number one crematorium's Sonderkommando, fully conscious of their impending death. Carried beyond the barbed wires in the sofa, it would remain for the time being at Oberschaarführer Mussfeld's home at Mannheim.

[1]The special command in charge of burning the dead.

7

The message was drafted in time. It described in sufficient detail the horrors perpetrated at Auschwitz from the time of its founding until the present. The names of the camp's torturers were included, as well as our estimate of the number of people exterminated, with a description of the methods and instruments utilized for extermination.

The message was drawn up on three large sheets of parchment. The Sonderkommando's editor, a painter from Paris, copied it in beautifully written letters, as was the custom with ancient manuscripts, using India ink so that the writing would not fade. The fourth sheet contained the signatures of the Sonderkommando's 200 men. The sheets were fastened together with a silk thread, then rolled up, enclosed in a specially constructed cylindrical tube made of zinc by one of our tinsmiths, and finally sealed and soldered so as to protect the manuscript from air and humidity. Our joiners placed the tube in the springs, among the wool floss of the upholstering.

Another message, exactly the same, was buried in the courtyard of number two crematorium.

# Becoming a Jew at Last

*Johnny Montanti, age six, told me the marriage was definitely off.*

*"You're a Jew," he explained, matter-of-fact and all that, as he passed the mud pie.*

*Ten minutes later I was in my mother's lap, my five-year-old heart shattered.*

*"It's part of being a Jew," her worldwise voice whispered; her heart was breaking too.*

Fourteen years later she was dead, and I had escaped what had become the awful heritage of self-inflicted segregation.

\* \* \*

It was the Jewish New Year and my friends and I had gone to services. Afterwards, we gathered in an off-campus apartment to complain about the rabbi's sermon—another "Remember the Six Million Dead" harangue.

We could not relate to the six million, we decided. We hadn't lived

---

By Beth Durchschlag. From the *Courier –Post*, Camden, N.J.

8

through it and could not feel it. We were born at the same time as Israel and so, for us, there had always been dynamic proof of Jewish permanence.

We must forget about being Jewish and remember that we're only human beings. We must assimilate.

\* \* \*

It is Sunday, April 23, 1972, in Trenton's Holiday Inn. I have come to be amused at the sight of 50 men celebrating the birth of Adolf Hitler. They will be harmless fools, I expect, outdated in their hatreds and beliefs. They will be pathetic and I will have a good laugh.

*There were the swastikas. A jolt, a nerve touched that I had not known I had. There were the brown shirts, the storm trooper uniforms. They shuffled around the Capitol Ballroom in the inn, looking for the cameras they had been instructed to smash.*

\* \* \*

I ask for Frank Drager, who has made the party reservations.

"You're a Jew," Drager says as we meet, neither a smile nor a frown on his husky face.

My affirmation is surprisingly intense, even to me.

"Let's get on with the interview. I'm a very busy man," he says. "Adolf Hitler expounded a philosophy that could be acceptable to all white people on this earth. I personally don't believe he was a mass murderer."

Tell that to my father, I think, who liberated the concentration camps. To the uncles and aunts I have never met or known or loved, whose bones lie crumbled under Auschwitz.

*"I'm not saying that they (the murders) won't take place in America. It'll be worse than whatever happened in Germany," he continues.*

*He is drunk, I think, as the beer breath invades my nostrils. He is not drunk, I know.*

\* \* \*

"They've stopped the gentiles from competing in America. The Jews have taken over our economy.

The Jews, they are the scum of the earth."

Yes, it is the Holiday Inn in Trenton and on the top floor people are dining and laughing as the revolving restaurant goes 'round.

Here on the bottom floor it is a very different world.

If I think about it, even now, I will cry.

"We have a stockpile of artillery and weapons, an arsenal. I'm a street-fighter and we will go into the streets. I'm not an intellectual. I'm a *dummkopf,* a fighter."

9

"I'll assign a guard to you. You'll need it; you're a Jew," he concludes, signalling to three armbanded youths. But he does not tell them my heritage.

*I need a drink and, shaking, I ask the bartender for anything. He hands me a beer and I take two sips before realizing I am not thirsty.*

\* \* \*

I give the beer to Mike, who is one of my guards, and tell him it is going to waste. He ponders and then says, "Well" . . . and takes it. It would not be unpleasant if he would die then, I muse, poisoned by the lips of a Jew.

He drinks and he doesn't die and my hysteria subsides, then grows, as he describes how he murdered a man in Canada and then slipped across the border to America. I cannot tell if he is lying.

He was 11 when he became a Nazi, he says, and now is "on parole for as many jobs as Carter has liver pills."

"The Jews . . . the Jews . . . the Jews," he goes on, his hate as intense as my fear.

He's talking about me and he doesn't know it. How can he hate me and not know it?

*Finally, a three-hour film tribute to Hitler—the highlight of the celebration— is ready. We go to the banquet room, my three Nazis around me. An honor guard stands surrounded by Nazi and American flags, flown together.*

\* \* \*

But I am not in America, I am in some miserable state that these men have somehow achieved.

I drop a cigarette in my seat, which is next to the door, and Mike reaches for it, his fingers settling for a moment on my leg.

You are touching the leg of a Jew, you maniac, I realize that is what I am—a Jew—and that it is Mike who has made me what my parents couldn't.

I am afraid Drager is going to let the cat out of the bag. The men of the audience, Mike tells me, have guns and brass knuckles and knives with them and are listening to the word "Kill!" I do not know if he is lying.

"Adolf Hitler started with seven men," the next speaker begins. Here is what it is all about: the hate, the vengeance, the cold, slicing eyes of men who feel they've been cheated.

*"I see nothing wrong with destroying millions,"* the speaker continues, his syllables staccatoing into German gutturals. *"He—the Jew—must not exist."*

The terror comes from all sides, now. I breathe deeply and my scare is temporarily over. I look around at the Aryan polyglot of people—fat ones, thin ones, tall ones, sharp-nosed, straight-nosed, blonds, brown-

10

haireds. They are losers, I decide. They do not have what it takes and so they blame . . . the scapegoat.

It is pre-war Nuremberg on the movie screen and the crowds are bathing Hitler with their love. They knew what they were doing . . .

"Sieg Heil!" It is the room in New Jersey, U.S.A., which is exploding with the cry. I am electrified, petrified.

The chant surrounds me, crawls inside me. It is 1972 and I am still their enemy and they are mine.

# *Lamentations*

*and even if a million dying children*
*did not destroy Creation*
*there will be another*
*already forgotten*
*universe*
*over which God will have to cry*
*those tears*
*that should have extinguished*
*the fires of Auschwitz*

From *Midstream,* May 1975, by Menachem Z. Rosensaft.

# Readings and Anthologies on the Holocaust

*The Final Solution: The Attempt to Exterminate the Jews of Europe 1939–1945* by Gerald Reitlinger (Beechurst Press, 1953), describes the search for and the implementation of the "Final Solution."

*The Yellow Star* by Gerhard Schoenberner, edited, written, translated into English (1969), and published by Transworld Publishers, London, was compiled originally in German for the Germans. Basically a black and white picture book, it contains over 100 documentary pictures accompanied by appropriate text; it is unsparing, comprehensive, and frank. Recommended as a visual resource. Also available in a smaller Bantam paperback.

*The War Against the Jews: 1933–1945* by Lucy S. Dawidowicz (Holt, Rinehart and Winston, 1975), is a complete, authoritative, and definitive history on the subject.

*Harvest of Hate* by Leon Poliakov (Jewish Publication Society, 1954), is an excellent account of the Nazi program for the destruction of European Jewry.

*Encyclopedia Judaica* (Keter Pub. Co.) contains authoritative articles on the Holocaust and its various aspects. Especially recommended is Dr. Jacob Robinson's impressive presentation of the subject in volume VIII. The reader may follow up each item marked with an asterisk for further study.

*Documents of Destruction: Germany and Jewry 1933–1945* (Quadrangle Books, 1971), edited with commentary by Raul Hilberg. An impressive collection of fifty documents.

*The Holocaust* by Nora Levin (Crowell Pub., 1969), is a comprehensive historical presentation of the destruction of European Jewry (1933–1945) including photographs and maps. (Also available in paperback by Schocken Books.)

*Holocaust* (Keter Books, 1975), a concise anthology culled from the authoritative articles of *Encyclopedia Judaica*.

*Out of the Whirlwind,* edited by Albert H. Friedlander (Union of American Hebrew Congregations, 1968), includes fictional, philosophical and documentary materials.

*Anthology of Holocaust Literature,* edited by Jacob Glatstein, Israel Knox, and Samuel Margoshes (Jewish Publication Society, 1968), includes eyewitness and personal accounts, translated from Yiddish sources.

*The Root and the Bough,* edited by Leo W. Schwartz (Rinehart, 1949), was the first significant anthology of the Holocaust.

*The Destruction of the European Jews* by Raul Hilberg (Quadrangle Books, 1967), is a detailed comprehensive book on the Tragedy. Putting aside the author's indictment of the Jews for not resisting enough, this book serves as an exhaustive reference work on the history of the Holocaust.

*The Jewish Catastrophe in Europe,* edited by Judah Pilch (American Assoc. for Jewish Education, 1968), affords an overview of Jewish life in Europe between the two world wars (1919–1939), the Tragedy, and the literature of the Holocaust. The latter is especially recommended.

*The Jews of Germany: A Story of Sixteen Centuries* by Marvin Lowenthal (Jewish Publication Society, 1936), is recommended reading to obtain a bird's-eye view of the Jewish settlement of the Germanic lands until the rise of the Third Reich.

# A Crime Without Equal

*Legal References and List of Documents relating to the Persecution of the Jews,* Vol. 1, pp. 1008–1022, in *Nazi Conspiracy and Aggression* (Office of the United States Counsel for Prosecution of Axis Criminals, U.S. Government Printing Office, Washington, 1946, eleven volumes).

# 2. | GERMANY GOES NAZI

## BACKGROUND

Totalitarianism and dictatorship were common during the period following World War I. In Europe, South America, and Asia, countries formerly ruled by monarchies and long-established ruling dynasties turned to dictatorships and military juntas. Without experience in self-government, with a tradition of disciplined obedience and dependence on a ruler, these nations seemed to welcome dictatorship and its "easy" solutions to the overwhelming postwar problems and conflicts that threatened even well-established democracies. Dictatorship appealed to the simple, conservative peasant, to the small businessman, to the civil servant, as well as to those seeking power. Totalitarian government galvanized the energies of people seeking national identification by making national pride paramount. To achieve solidarity, the masses were incited against a common enemy, imaginary or real. The postwar attempts to form viable democratic, constitutional governments were unsuccessful, and charismatic figures emerged who took advantage of their country's insecurity: Hitler in Germany, Lenin and later Stalin in the USSR, Horthy in Hungary, Mussolini in Italy, Metaxas in Greece, Franco in Spain, Kemal Atatürk in Turkey, etc. The new order in each country dictated the social, economic, and moral life-styles. It perpetuated itself and ruthlessly suppressed any opposition.

Viewed from this perspective, the rise of Nazism in Germany was not unique—but there was one fundamental difference. Fascist countries like Italy and Spain did not contest the role of the Church in the lives of their people; Nazism, however, claimed man in his entirety. It was more than a political commitment, it was an uncompromising faith and a total way of life. It monopolized the individual—his external daily behavior as well

14

as his inner self, his conscience. It was supreme and brooked no other allegiance, whether religious, spiritual, or ethical. Another unique feature was Hitler's rise to overriding power so quickly and with no sustained resistance, in a country with a rich political, industrial, and cultural heritage.

The hideous form of Hitler's Nazism emerged from conditions resulting from the First World War. After occupying a prominent position and enjoying the world's respect for its culture, its power, and its predominance as a modern industrialized state, imperial Germany was forced to surrender unconditionally after having engaged twenty-three nations, with the help of Austria-Hungary and Turkey, in a devastating world conflict. Germany found the terms of the Versailles Treaty (June 28, 1919) harsh and humiliating. It was stripped of its army and navy, fined an indemnity of thirty-two billion dollars, and forced to surrender valuable territories to France, Denmark, and Poland, though Germany itself remained virtually intact.

After the war, Europe was hit with an economic depression which, in turn, spurred political upheavals and social unrest. Germany was devastated by a terrible inflation that wiped out savings, life insurance, pensions, and everything of monetary value. Depression and unemployment, affecting almost 25 percent of the laboring class, ravaged the country. Just when the situation began to improve, the world depression hit hard and conditions worsened. When Germany failed to deliver the goods specified under the Versailles Treaty, such as lumber and coal, France occupied the rich Ruhr Valley. This not only helped strangle the German economy further, since the Ruhr produced most of Germany's coal and steel, but also aroused extreme nationalism, over and above the economic loss. The occupation of Reich territory was considered an insult to national honor.

Another source of resentment and humiliation was the stipulation in the peace treaty that called for the disarmament of Germany and the dissolution of its mighty army—the pride and glory of the Fatherland. Only a volunteer army of 100,000 (called the Reichswehr) was permitted; the navy was abolished, and so was the General Staff. To keep alive the old army traditions, hundreds of "sport" and "athletic" associations sprang up everywhere, engaging in camouflaged military drills. Army officers were trained secretly in the Soviet and Japanese armies. As economic and political conditions worsened, these groups engaged in mischievous and terroristic acts in order to intimidate the people, especially liberals, socialists, and Jews, who were blamed for Germany's plight. These groups were the spawning ground for the Nazi movement, which came to power during these catastrophic years.

The shame of "national humiliation" rankled deep in the German soul. Defeat had been inconceivable and was unacceptable. Thus the myth

15

arose that the invincible German army must have been betrayed into defeat. This "stab in the back," as the "betrayal" was labeled, was allegedly caused by the desertion from the battlefield of leftists, socialists, and liberals, who were aided and abetted by collaborators in the enemy camp. The alleged saboteurs of the war effort were called "November criminals," because the armistice had been signed on November 11, 1918.

Such was the propaganda dinned into German ears and used to explain the hard times which followed defeat. The "they" who "caused" all the trouble were identified with the most convenient scapegoat—the Jews; and anti-Semitism, ever lurking under the surface, flourished. The myth was amplified to involve a world Jewish conspiracy, which threatened not only Germany but all of Western civilization.

Unfortunately, a published version of the conspiracy myth was readily available to the public, entitled *Protocols of the Elders of Zion*. This vicious document purported to describe a scheme by a secret Jewish international government to subjugate the world. Exposed as a fraud time and time again, the *Protocols* were, nevertheless, exploited to the full by the Nazis, who claimed they had documented, researched, and validated them.

The *Protocols* were translated into many languages. In the United States, during the 1920s, Henry Ford helped spread the *Protocols* far and wide. In 1938 Father Charles E. Coughlin, an American Catholic priest, also assisted the Nazi propagandists by reprinting the *Protocols* in his magazine, *Social Justice*, which was read by millions. The *Protocols* were circulated in many editions throughout the world; some were even luridly illustrated and accompanied by commentaries. Today this fraudulent work is still being distributed widely, especially in the Moslem world and by Arabs residing in Latin American countries. One French historian, Henri Rollin, surmised that the *Protocols* was "probably the most widely distributed book in the world (after the Bible), and was a potent factor in the shaping of world history."[1]

Certainly, Hitler and the Nazi leaders made opportunistic use of the myth that everything that happened for the worse in economic, political, and social affairs was caused by the "Jewish Elders." Thus, in the poisonous atmosphere of economic catastrophes, political strikes, ultranationalism, fear of communism, governmental and judicial corruption, and the impotence of the League of Nations and the Western powers, the Nazi plague took seed, sprouted, and flourished.

[1]Norman Cohn, *Warrant for Genocide* (New York: Harper & Row, 1966), p. 170. Cohn recounts the fantastic story of the *Protocols* with documents, careful research, and illustrations.

## ROOTS OF ANTI-SEMITISM AND GROWTH OF RACISM

Hitler's domination over sixty-six million people did not spring from a vacuum. The hatreds and prejudices he activated were deeply rooted, not only in his own consciousness, but in the German national psychology as well. Throughout the dark Middle Ages in Catholic Europe, the Jew was regarded as Satanic, an anathema, a source of contamination. He was persecuted everywhere, hounded, forced into ghettos, and expelled from many European countries. The attitude of the Church was clear-cut: convert to Christianity, leave, or die.

Martin Luther (1483–1546), the German religious reformer who broke with Catholicism, changed his pro-Jewish sentiments near the end of his life. He attacked the Jews ". . . because of their refusal to accept Christ, and urged that either they be deported to Palestine, or their synagogues be burned, their books be taken away from them, and they be forbidden money-lending and be compelled to earn their livelihood by tilling the soil." (Latourette's *A History of Christianity*). Generations of Germans were raised on books and pamphlets such as those of Luther that went beyond the realm of religion. The terminology of Hitler's rantings against the Jews were, thus, familiar to most Germans from their infancy.

The poison of Jew-hatred was not restricted to the religious domain. It infected so-called scholarly circles. In the middle of the nineteenth century, a few "intellectuals" began to expand the popular notions about Jews with pseudoscientific trimmings. Count de Gobineau was the first. His book, *The Inequality of the Human Race* (1853) was one of the earliest glorifications of the white race as compared to the yellow and the black. He claimed that the growing tendency to "mix bloods" would lead to the decadence of the superior white race. The French, by and large, ignored his teachings; not so the Germans, who were introduced to his ideas some forty years later.

A greater influence on the Germanic people was Houston Stewart Chamberlain's *The Foundations of the Nineteenth Century* (1899). He blended Gobineau with the German philosopher Friedrich Nietzsche's concept of the superman. He preached the idea of Teutonic (Germanic) racial superiority and its antithesis, the inferiority of the Jew. These and other anti-Semitic works were absorbed and spewed forth in *The Myth of the Twentieth Century* (1930), by Alfred Rosenberg, the chief ideologist and intellectual exponent of the Nazi Party.[2]

---

[2]For a full discussion of anti-Semitism in modern Germany, read Lucy S. Dawidowicz, *The War Against the Jews, 1933–1945* (New York: Holt, Rinehart & Winston, 1975), chap. 2.

Emerging side by side with the onslaught of anti-Semitism on the political and economic scene was the worship of the state and a manic pride in the Teutonic tradition. Otto von Bismarck (1815–98), the Iron Chancellor, had popularized the nationalistic doctrines of German imperialism. Prussian political leaders justified the Pan-Germanic drive with the idea that Germans were a superior people; Germany's astonishing progress during the Industrial Revolution, as well as the pressure of its growing population, produced the incentives for territorial expansion.

Thus, anti-Semitism and chauvinism were an integral part of German culture. Even the basis for a systematized, political, anti-Jewish program had long existed. In fact, the first International Anti-Semitic Congress had been held in Germany in 1881, and three years before Hitler's birth, a member of the Reichstag was elected on an out-and-out anti-Semitic platform.

Hitler exploited anti-Semitism, combining it with the idea of "race." From the Middle Ages to the rise of Hitler, a Jew could "escape" by converting to Christianity, but escape by conversion became an impossibility after 1933. Judaism was considered a biological inheritance; a Jew could never be other than a Jew. Hitler isolated the Jew from the rest of the Germans, branding him an "internationalist," and thus a traitor to the Fatherland. (Ironically, German Jews had been the most acculturated of all European Jews and were very proud of their German nationality.) Anti-Jewish slogans and catchwords became deeply imbedded in the German heart and mind, and they influenced patterns of feeling and behavior toward the Jew.

Organization, precision, consistency, and methodical persistence are reputed to be German characteristics. As Nazism grew, it made use of these traits by fostering their application in every avenue and walk of life. Hitlerism reached in all directions, organizing Nazi associations of men, women, children, professionals, workers, and peasants. Nazism became a total way of life. Books were rewritten, and history was altered, to achieve the complete degradation of the Jews.

Nazi racial science was taken seriously, and it was very thorough in its methods and application. Everything in which Jews participated was purged, whether science, art, literature, or music. Statues of famous Jews were destroyed and reduced to rubble or scrap iron; Jewish books and musical scores were burned in festive bonfires; paintings were defaced or confiscated. The "Jewish influence" was savagely stamped out.

Nazi racial anti-Semitism portrayed the Jew as a grotesque creature. His facial characteristics were depicted as hideous, his gestures, diction, and speech were stigmatized as repulsive. A leading Nazi, Julius Streicher, published *Der Stuermer,* a newspaper which featured caricatures of Jews with long, crooked noses, greedy eyes, grasping hands, pot bellies, and cunning, deceitful smiles—altogether depraved and corrupt.

Thus, a vicious stereotype of the Jew was created to be used as visual "proof" that Jews had to be branded, quarantined, and done away with, so as not to contaminate society.

Nazism was also made attractive and lucrative to the professional classes, and to university and scientific circles. Courses in "racial science" sprang up in the leading universities to research the biology, psychology, and anthropology of the Jew, e.g., the measurements of his skull, the length of his nose, and other physical characteristics. They engaged in exploring the "Jewish question" in the world, and in investigating the conflicts between "Aryan" and "non-Aryan" cultures. Under the guise of scholarship, conferences were called, papers read, and German culture was prostituted.[3]

The goal was clear: anti-Semitism was to serve as "one of the foundations of National Socialism [Nazism] and at the same time its most important propaganda weapon." The theories of German superiority, slave races, aggression, and the need to subjugate Eastern Europe, including Russia, prepared the ground for the Final Solution of the Jewish problem, which, in simple terms, meant total extermination.

Racism also led to other refinements. In articles, monographs, and books, Darwin's law of "survival of the fittest" was promulgated as the uncontested law of nature and it became a basic tenet of Nazi "racial science." If necessary, the "unfit" must be helped to "disappear." The unfit meant, of course, the Jews, the mentally deficient, the Gypsies, the Slavs, the Negroes, and the "unsocials" (political opponents of Nazism). Leading biologists brought evidence from animal breeding that inferior animals produced degenerate stock while superior animals produced superior stock. Therefore, inferior individuals should be sterilized as an act of humaneness; on the other hand, an elite must be produced by a program of "breeding," as in the case of horses, cattle, and dogs.

In view of expanding populations and limited land space and resources, the "unfit" were to be wiped out to make room for the "fit." This idea was used to necessitate preparations for war in order to expand Germany's borders to provide *Lebensraum* (living space). The lands of Eastern Europe were considered ripe for the plucking, and an elaborate plan was worked out to repopulate them with settlers from Germany proper and with Polish, Ukrainian, and other East European nationals of German origin (known as ethnic Germans). To make this possible, fifty million people would be resettled in Siberia.[4] All this, of course, was to take place after the Soviet Union was conquered.

Each step of the Nazi program was carefully planned, and the "scien-

[3]Read *Hitler's Professors* (New York: YIVO, 1946).
[4]Read Robert L. Koehl, *RKFDV: German Resettlement and Population Policy; 1939–1945* (Cambridge: Harvard University Press, 1957).

tific" theories "justifying" it were published before and after the action. Thus the invasion of Poland was preceded by studies on the relationship of Germany to Poland, "proving" that it and other lands to the east were once ruled by Germans, and that the Third Reich was therefore righting a historic wrong against Germany. The "scientific" rationalization for the occupation of Czechoslovakia was given in a publication entitled *The Germans and Czechs*. The new "science" was a potent weapon and was used both to initiate conquest and to present "evidence" that Nazism was not ruthless barbarism but an expression of the needs, not only of Germany, but of the society of "Aryan" nations as a whole.

# Portrait of a German Family

I once lived with a German family in Heidelberg. They were sentimental, good people who made a great to-do about Christmas. They had suffered severely during the inflation period and were convinced, even in 1928, that it was the Jews who had been their economic undoing. The father of the household was a bearded dictator, a sentimental man whose children trembled at his frown and rushed to bring him his slippers and his smoking jacket. His wife was a domestic slave. She hurried to fulfill her husband's whims and took great pains not to anger him. Once he asked her, in my presence, to go upstairs and bring down the mirror out of the bathroom and, to my amazement, I saw her stagger down a steep flight of steps trying to carry a heavy framed pier glass as large as herself. This same man thought it entirely just and fitting for the Germans to have shot Edith Cavell.[1] His wife constantly held a threat over her children of reporting them to Father for any infraction of rules. The children were good and obedient and polite. Even the little ones sat up late at night doing their lessons. They lived in terror of their teachers and of their parents whom they loved very much, just as their father was in terror of his employers. This sounds like a caricature of German family life, but it is true. Out of this competitive bullying came the Nazi Schrecklichkeit (horror).

[1]British Red Cross nurse shot by the Germans during World War I (Oct. 11, 1915) because she was suspected of espionage.

From *Human Behavior in the Concentration Camp* by Dr. Elie A. Cohen (Foreword by Carl Binger).

# Nazi Headmaster

The school I went to was renamed for Karin Göring.[1]
My troubles there began one day when I was about eleven. During a
Hitler's Birthday celebration in the auditorium, a Jewish girl, Lore
Wassermann, did not raise her right arm during the Horst Wessel
Song,[2] nor did she sing with the rest of us. Someone informed against
her and, because I had stood next to her, I was summoned to the
headmaster's office. From sheer pigheadedness—I did not have political views at eleven—I lied, insisting that she *had* sung and, for the sake
of plausibility, freely added that she had sung badly out of tune at that.
The girl was not expelled, but I had attracted the headmaster's attention, and he did not forget.

Like so many other eminent Nazis, this headmaster had previously
been a failure in his profession and a bit of a crook. He had bilked the
parents of his private pupils by charging fees for lessons he never gave,
and had been expelled from the Teachers' Guild. As a supporter of
Hitler he was appointed headmaster of the school which had justly
fired him. He spent his vacations as relief officer for the commandants
of concentration camps! . . .

Most Germans enjoyed life under Hitler until the war, and since they
had not taken part in politics previously, they never missed the political
choices that, one by one, were being taken from them. . . . The apple
[of illusion] looked particularly splendid during the Olympic Games of
1936[3]. Hardly anyone in Germany could feel tempted to break it open
for the dubious reward of discovering the rottenness inside.

Hitler contrived to make every German feel important in some way.
. . . Everyone was therefore deeply gratified by the illusion of individual
significance conferred upon him in his role of farmer, fisherman,
stoker, long-distance runner, at the great rallies in Nuremberg . . . One
would see a thousand and one organizations, each in its special uniform, and there were always magnificent "circuses."

There was some facet to attract nearly everyone. My father, a most
retiring sort of man and usually deeply suspicious of anything done by

---

[1]Hermann Göring's wife.
[2]See p. 49.
[3]The anti-Jewish signs were removed and the Nazis were on their best behavior during
the Olympics.

---

From *The Germans: An Indictment of My People* by Gudrun Tempel.

Hitler, had tears of joy in his eyes when the long-desired *Anschluss*—Austria's "joining" of the Reich—was announced. He had not the faintest notion of the means by which this had been brought about. How could he? Ours was a country without a free press, without a parliamentary opposition to ask disagreeable questions. He simply loved the Austrians and had never quite understood the need for a border at all.

If you tell the mother of a whore what her daughter is doing, she will probably deny it because it is something she cannot face, and she will hate you for telling her. This precisely describes the situation of the Germans under Hitler—at least until the days of Stalingrad. When the mother sees her daughter kneeling in church, or when the German sees the "good deeds" of his Führer, both forget everything else.

My headmaster, Dr. Horbach, looked so impressive in his uniform, he was so energetic, so efficient, so neat, so punctual that no one could possibly think of him as anything but the very model of an excellent headmaster. He could, therefore, pursue his prey to the kill without fear that anyone might interfere. His prey happened to be blond girls, especially those who resisted his wishes. He had been married to three blond women, one after the other, all of whom had mysteriously committed suicide. . . .

The fact that my father sent a monthly check to my grandfather—who after losing his professorship was not even allowed to continue his sculpting privately—sufficed to place me on a special list. For a time I was saved from expulsion by my prize-winning essays, ski championships, and medals for fencing and horseback riding. My picture appeared in the local papers, and the school was proud of me. But from that day when at age eleven I had shielded Lore Wassermann, there was a cross after my name on every list circulating through the school.

When the headmaster canceled our traditional Christmas singing, on the grounds that Christ was a Jew, I defied him by collecting names on a petition, and the interdict was lifted for two years. As long as I was an outstanding student and kept collecting those sports prizes, he had to be content with an occasional summons to his office to tell me that my parents were swine because they continued to support my grandfather. I could not transfer to another school, or get an education elsewhere; this was his power over me. When he challenged me to become a leader of the BDM,[4] I refused on the grounds of poor health and I had to bring him a medical certificate to prove it.

Then the struggle between us sharpened. He began to interrogate me systematically, at first once a month, then almost daily, calling me

[4]Hitler Youth organization for girls.

out of class in person or sending the porter for me. By the time I was just over fourteen he could see that I was breaking down and he intensified the torture. When we were sent to farms during the summer vacation, to help with the harvesting for the war effort, I was of course assigned to the worst place; my petitions for a transfer were ignored.

Every morning at 4 A.M. we drove out to the fields in the dark and we gathered rocks. Every night at 10 P.M. I was on duty, cooking potatoes. Once I fainted from exhaustion. Afterward I telephoned to my mother and she went to the headmaster. When she called back, she was dissolved in tears. He had threatened to send her and my father to a concentration camp if I fell ill or left the farm—and we all knew that he meant it.

Back at school in the fall, I wanted only to die; within six months my grades dropped from the top of the class to the bottom. In class I would sit as if paralyzed, waiting for the headmaster's steps outside in the corridor, his brisk entrance, the shout of "Heil Hitler!" which greeted him from the class, then the long walk to his office, the wait under the hideous picture of Hitler in a steel helmet—a widely distributed glorification of Hitler as the Unknown Soldier of World War I, which made me shudder.

In many respects Dr. Horbach was the Eichmann type—there is a distinctive Eichmann type, and not only in Germany. He carefully took down in shorthand every word I uttered, writing on large sheets of paper, sometimes underlining with a large wooden ruler engraved with the words "Blood and Honor." If it had not been so genuinely menacing it might have been a farce: a twentieth-century witch hunt against an ordinary school girl shaking under the constant threat that her parents would be killed.

What particularly stoked the headmaster's fury was that I was close to being the ideal type of born leader believed in by so many besides Boy Scouts, militarists, and Nazis. I was physically hardy, resourceful in danger, a winner at sports, a good organizer, and all the rest of it. In addition, I had something of the utmost importance to the Nazis— golden blond hair and a narrow, fine-boned "Aryan" face. What, then, was wrong with me?

I hate being organized relegated, ordered about—and I am a clown by nature. I cannot help laughing at the absurd, no matter how threatening the context. . . . Yet to laugh or even smile at a person who is proposing to kill you is an unforgivable affront; you are supposed to shake visibly in your shoes. There was something in the nature of the true Nazi which did not tolerate being laughed at. There he sat, this Dr. Horbach, always dressed in boots and SS uniform, wearing spurs—of all things, when I knew that he had never sat on a horse in his life. The man was a farce, in the same sense in which we all know today that

Eichmann was a farce—a mediocre, overly tidy, middling, bureaucratic intelligence, a genuine nobody. But this nobody had power over my life and over the lives of my family, and he enjoyed playing with it. . . .

My struggle with the headmaster was known to the whole school, but no one could take it really seriously, least of all myself at this moment. When Dr. Horbach told me what fine children I would bear for the Führer, I couldn't help retorting that I would like to marry a coal-black Negro. Horbach's face turned pale with rage.

On another occasion he suggested that I leave my parents, since they were obviously "unfit to bring up children at all. They are completely weak and degenerate. . . ."

When it became obvious to my mother and me that I could no longer bear the strain, we went to the Ministry of Education. A high-ranking woman official listened horrified to our story and, picking up the receiver to speak to the Minister himself, turned to us for a final check: "What did you say his name was?" "Horbach," said my mother, "Dr. Armin Horbach." The official's face turned to stone. "I am sorry," she said, got up and showed us to the door. "You must be mistaken."

And so the day came when, during my interview with Horbach, I broke down completely. In a last gesture, trying for a glimpse of the sky, I looked out of the window at the horse chestnut trees—and burst out laughing. That was the end. With two strides Dr. Horbach came from behind his big desk and began to strangle me. Perhaps I screamed—I can't remember—for suddenly our hunchbacked school secretary stood at the door. Horbach released me. I left that room and the school.

Shortly thereafter my parents received a letter telling them I had been expelled, and that I was unworthy of serving the Führer in the BDM or the Labor Service (the year of compulsory labor that followed graduation). After this, people often avoided being seen with me. No one, not even my mother, quite believed everything I had told them—until after one day in 1953.

That day an English friend and I fell into conversation with a stranger on the train to Rotterdam. We discovered that we had lived not far from each other in Saxony. He said that throughout the war he had been in a concentration camp and had nearly died there. Since he was not a Jew, I asked him why.

"Well, you'll never believe this," he began. "The headmaster of the school my daughter attended was an SS officer. He kept calling her in for a kind of interrogation. My daughter is a light blond, and incredibly pigheaded. We finally became so uneasy about it that we sent her off to an aunt in Holland. Then they came and picked me up."

My English friend had been listening to him with mounting amazement—she knew *my* story. Suddenly she shouted: "And his name was Horbach!"

"How did *you* know that?" he said.

When I explained, he was almost beside himself with relief.

"You know, I thought so often I would go out of my mind. You see, no one believed me, and often I thought I must have dreamed the whole thing; yet I *knew* it really happened."

I told him then that Dr. Horbach had been shot by the Russians. As the train entered the Rotterdam station, where his wife was waiting for him, he leaned out of the window and shouted to her joyfully, "He is dead, he is dead! Horbach is dead!"

Only now the story became a nightmare for me, which it took years to shake off. I had managed to force it out of my memory as a cruel, improbable fantasy, but now, once more, I knew that it had all really happened to me.

# Around the Fires of the Solstice Festival

. . . The events of the last days have filled me with such a great enthusiasm that despite the late hour I take up my beloved diary in order to write in it what has so deeply stirred me. It was cloudy and overcast when I set out for the Rhine yesterday with my Hitler comrades, men and women. Nevertheless, we paid no attention to the unfavorable weather. Our hearts flamed with a glowing enthusiasm and a great joy. The lutes played and our song-happy lips never rested. Men and women party comrades boarded the train at almost every station and brought even more cheer to the frolicsome group. Time flew by so quickly with all the singing and jingling and jangling and before we were aware of it Germania was already greeting us from the Niederwald. Upon arriving in Bingen, we were still undecided whether we should go by ferry in order to travel up the other side of the Rhine by train or whether we should proceed to our destination by steamboat on the German Rhine. (The weather decided for us. An opaque black mass of clouds had formed in the skies. The clouds were riveted together like iron chains.) While we were looking up at the skies pondering alternatives, a violent storm began to rage and pound the waves of the Rhine with terrible force. Then we were all seized by a

From *Nazi Culture* edited by George L. Mosse.

yearning for wild waves, stormy wind and rain. We boarded the steamer and clambered to the upper deck, to let the storm wind blow through us and to lift our heads to the elements. How loudly our hearts pounded and how proudly waved our swastika flags and pennants in the storm wind. . . . Unnumbered bands of Brownshirts marched with their blood-red flags to assembly on the banks of the Rhine. Roaring shouts of "Heil!" greeted us, echoing back and forth. We were met by a wonderful panorama when we entered the town. The streets were a regular forest of flags. From every house waved the glorious German banners. Garlands and a profusion of flowers decorated the streets. There was liveliness everywhere. SA men hurried past us, carrying out the orders of their leaders. From every side we could hear stirring tunes of Prussian military marches. And then I saw something I had never seen before: women and girls in the brown Hitler uniform. They sold us badges for the solstice celebration. This touched me in a wondrous way, and a desire began to burgeon and to burn within me, to be permitted to help, like these women and girls, in the great work of our leader Adolf Hitler. A torch had been thrown into my heart and continued to flame and blaze. There was no place for any other thought within me.

Almost in a trance, I followed my girl comrades to our quarters. I no longer heard or saw what was happening around me; I just sat on my cot and wondered how I could become a helper in the reconstruction of the Fatherland. I was still lost in thought when one of my girl comrades found me and took me to the open-air concert of the SA. Deep inside I was annoyed that I had been disturbed in my thoughts. But outwardly, of course, I gave no indication and acted as though I were in high spirits. But in spite of the eager talk of the other girls, I was soon lost in my thoughts again, not at all aware of the fact that I was already beginning my work for the Hitler movement. As we approached the square, we heard the last few bars of the Petersburg March, and then there was a pause in the music program. I soon lost my comrades in the press of people. I went along a stretch of the Rhine promenade and suddenly found myself before the statue of our great Blücher. I stood on the spot where, on New Year's night in 1814, the Prussian army led by Blücher had crossed the Rhine. My thoughts rushed back to that memorable night and, fully occupied with meditation on this great deed of the courageous Prussians, I just stood there. I was torn out of my thoughts when I heard a man's voice beside me and I saw an SA man standing in front of me. He said to me: "Pardon me, are you a party comrade?" "Yes, of course," I answered. "Heil and greetings." I looked up and saw before me a weather-browned manly face with a pair of strikingly large and sunny eyes. He looked at me questioningly. "Wouldn't you like to help the movement a bit by selling some cards?" "With pleasure," I responded, and received a stack of cards from his hands. With joy I rushed toward the mass of people that surrounded the band. In only a quarter of an hour I had sold all the relief cards and joyfully delivered the money to the SA man for the movement. He was overjoyed and thanked me by shaking my hand. He told me his name, Wolfgang Jensen. I told him my name in return. We exchanged a few more words and then I hastened to rejoin my comrades to tell them about my card selling.

In the evening, at ten o'clock, there was a great assembly before the Blücher monument. We had bought torches from the SA men and now we took our place in the ranks of the Hitler legions. Countless people stood in formation. SS and SA men, Hitler Youth, National Socialist women and girls' groups, Stahlhelmer, Pfadfinder, Wandervögel, and thousands of others formed the endless ranks of the participants in the solstice festival. In the van stood the standard-bearers with their blood-red swastika flags, and countless pennants waved between the ranks in the evening breeze. We stood like that in rank and file for more than two hours. At twelve-fifteen finally came the great moment. The order came to march off and the torches were lighted. We marched with joyful song, accompanied by lutes, through the streets of the little town. After a short time we were in top marching form. As we entered the market square, there was a roar of "Heil!" There stood Flight Captain Hermann Göring, his hand raised in the Hitler salute, and he reviewed the long line of marchers, while shouts of "Heil!" echoed in the square. After we left the town, the road led us up into the mountains toward the solstice fire. It was a splendid sight. The road led to the mountain in serpentine twists and turns. From the top we could look back on the long marching columns. The brilliant glare of the torches in the night was glorious. It was an overwhelming sight. My words are too poor to portray this experience. For a long time we let this picture enter our thirsty souls to their uttermost depths until our eyes were focused on one mighty flaming fire. It was our solstice celebration. We were received by the tunes of Prussian military marches. Then . . . the inspiring festival began. Heads were bared. With folded hands we listened devoutly to the solemn melody: "We come to pray before the righteous God . . ."

Toward the end Hermann Göring rose again to deliver a flaming address. In his call to battle for Germany's freedom the rustle of the Rhine sounded like a prayer for redemption from foreign despotism. In the deep darkness of the night, the iron words of Ernst Moritz Arndt[1] sounded forceful and thundering on Hermann Göring's tongue: "The Rhine, Germany's river, but not Germany's border."

After singing the national anthem, we all sat down around the great fire and sang our songs. Göring stepped into the circle and remained

---

[1]Ernst Moritz Arndt (1769–1860), a patriotic Romantic poet.

27

standing, proud and upright. It was a glorious picture, the great air hero standing there, surrounded by the light of the solstice fire. But his face remained somewhat in the dark, since the dying flames did not reach that far. I had the luck to sit directly behind him. With a sudden decision I jumped up and held my torch over his shoulder, and now his face, too, radiated a great glow. Then came a great, eventful moment for me. He turned and nodded thankfully to me. Who could have been happier than I? . . . Again, the main speaker addressed us in imperative and flaming words and stepped out of our midst, accompanied by roaring shouts of "Heil!" Our eyes followed him for a long time until he vanished in the dark night. I thought that I would not see him again for a long time. I had not noticed that meanwhile an SA man had stepped to my side. I turned around only after I heard myself addressed by name, and encountered the manly face of SA man Jensen. He shook my hand and asked about my impressions of the solstice celebration. I began to tell him in my stormy and elated state of excitement. He looked at me with joyful and shining eyes, sharing my enthusiasm and joy. After I had expressed all my feelings about the solstice celebration, we both fell silent. I noticed that his facial expression had changed. A deadly seriousness was on his face. He looked at me silently for a long time and then he asked how long I had been a follower of Hitler and what had prompted me to become a National Socialist. He did not turn his eyes from me, but continued to look at me, steadfast and probing. I felt his eyes in the deepest corner of my heart and it would have been impossible for me to make a secret of anything that he wanted to know of me. I answered his question and explained clearly and simply when and why I had become a National Socialist. He was silent for a while, turned his head, and looked thoughtfully into the flames of the solstice fire. Slowly he turned his face to me, looked deep into my eyes, and, shaking my hand, said in all seriousness: "You have truly grasped what National Socialism is!" Meanwhile the fire was banking. Some threw their torches into the flames. Wolfgang Jensen said admonishingly, almost solemnly, to me: "Don't ever forget the solstice fire. Let it flame in your heart and let its rays reach out to your racial comrades. Then you will truly help in the great work of Adolf Hitler."

# The Changed Tempo of Life: The City of Herne: A Case Study

The life of the citizens had changed. Even old familiar streets now had other names. Thus Rathausplatz was now called Adolf-Hitler-Platz, Bebelstrasse became Hermann-Göring-Strasse, Otto-Hue-Strasse became Schlageterstrasse,[1] Neustrasse became Franz-Seldte-Strasse,[2] Rathenau-Platz became Josef-Wagner-Platz (when Gauleiter Wagner fell into disgrace it was renamed Hans-Schemm-Platz[3]), and so on.

. . . The citizens got used to the new names as they got used to everything else. It was a bad time for individualists, because the party and the state reached out their hands for all people. Anyone who was looking for a job or needed a passport, or even merely wanted to join a club, had to present his genealogical chart. Thus marriage-license bureaus and the parish rectories were kept quite busy. If two people wanted to get married they had to present a letter from the public health authorities stating that they were suitable for marriage. If there were certain illnesses in the family, this created enormous difficulties and led to investigations in accordance with the Law of July 14, 1933, for the prevention of hereditary diseases among the rising generation. New courts were set up, such as the Hereditary Health Court . . . and the Entailed Estates Court at Herne, where the twenty-one entailed farmers who were still left over in Herne ultimately had to file appeals in cases dealing with their farms. The work book was an essential personal document in many professions. New authorities were called into being, such as the Draft Board and the District Army Command . . . as a result of the establishment of the Wehrmacht, and the Reich Labor Service. On October 1, 1935, the first age groups of young people eligible for labor service were called up and the first age group eligible for military service moved out on November 1, 1935. At the same time, those born in 1913 and 1916 were mustered for labor and military service respectively on November 13.

[1] Name of a popular Nazi play.
[2] Nazi Minister of Labor, formerly the leader of the Stahlhelm veterans' organization.
[3] Leader of Nazi teachers' union and Bavarian Minister of Education.

From *Nazi Culture* edited by George L. Mosse.

The party itself displayed great inventiveness in interfering in all spheres of life. It simply controlled everything through its secondary organizations: no welfare activity could be conducted without the interference of the National Socialist Public Welfare Organization, no cultural event could take place without the Strength Through Joy.[4] New notions and slogans were always being coined in order to organize and to levy financial contributions, for such purposes as thanks offerings to the nation, National Labor Days, tributes to the prolific German families, thanks offerings to the workers of Germany, excursions for old party members, the banner of the DAF[5] National Socialist Model Factory . . .

There were always new organizations and institutions, such as the Country School for Mothers, the Mother and Child Welfare Organization, Childrensland Camps, the Food-Supply Welfare Organization. Further: Winter Aid, the one-dish meal on Sunday, National Solidarity Day . . .

And orders constantly rang out: "Display the flag!" and only the swastika banner was allowed to be displayed; the old Reich colors—black, white, and red, much used at first—were soon prohibited. There was always a reason for celebration, marches, and demonstrations. The course of the year took on a new rhythm. A cycle of festivities was arranged which was always being repeated. And the racial experts of the party already spoke reverently about renewing the myth. The traditional festivals had to take a back seat. Christmas developed into a feast of the winter solstice. The Hitler Youth no longer sang Christian Christmas carols, but "High Night of Clear Skies." All the while the propaganda machines went on working briskly, and the great hubbub and eternal thundering, the constant repetition of slogans (the one-dish meal on Sunday required at least six impressive admonitions in the newspaper) which accompanied this must not be forgotten. And in fact the events did unfold obtrusively and noisily and a plain sober description of them cannot give a proper idea of the fuss and fanfare that accompanied them.

[4]Organization of the DAF for leisure time activities.
[5]The German Workers' Front.

# Readings

William L. Schirer's *Rise and Fall of the Third Reich* (Simon and Schuster, 1960), presents an authoritative first-hand account of the history of Nazi Germany, from the rise of Hitler to the end, as seen by an outstanding American journalist and radio commentator who lived and worked in Germany until 1942. Excellent.

*The Nazi Years, A Documentary History* by Joachim Remak (Prentice-Hall, 1969). Excellent.

*The Burden of Guilt* by Hannah Vogt (Oxford Univ. Press, 1964) was originally published in German. It is a short history of Germany from 1914 to 1945, objectively written by an insider for the younger generation of Germans. It reveals the attitude of young Germany to the Nazi generation.

*Nazi Culture* by George L. Mosse (Grosset & Dunlap, 1968), provides insights into the Nazi mind by a skillful compilation of selections which reflect the thinking, feeling, practices, education, and experiences of Nazis of all ages and in all walks of life, particularly the young. Excellent.

*The German Dictatorship* by Karl Dietrich Bracher (Praeger, 1971), is a study for more advanced readers on the rise of Nazism and an analysis of its regime.

*The Twelve Year Reich* by Richard Grunberger (Holt, Rinehart and Winston, 1971), is a social history (1933–45) portraying the everyday life of the Germans during the Nazi reign—how they lived, worked, relaxed. Excellent.

*The Myth of the Master Race: Alfred Rosenberg and Nazi Ideology* by Robert Cecil (Dodd Mead, 1972), is a full-length study of the chief exponent of the Nazi ideology.

*Sex and Society in Nazi Germany* by Hans Peter Bleuel (J. B. Lippincott, 1973), discusses sexual ethics and relationships, the roles of males and females in the Third Reich, as well as the function of woman as the child-bearing "machine."

*Film in the Third Reich: A Study of the German Cinema* by David Stewart Hull (Univ. of California Press, 1970), presents a documented study of the subject and particularly the production of anti-Semitic films.

# 3. | ADOLF HITLER

## PERSONALITY AND CHARACTER

Adolf Hitler was born in Austria, near the German border, on April 20, 1889; his father was an Austrian customs official. After dropping out of high school and failing to gain admission to an art school in Vienna, Hitler wandered around aimlessly in Vienna, where he absorbed the anti-Semitic and fascist ideas which he later activated. During these years he was engaged in odd jobs and was frequently helped along by Jews and Jewish institutions. When World War I began, Hitler volunteered to join the German army. While serving as a dispatch runner, he was wounded in the leg; promoted to lance-corporal, he returned to the front. During a gas attack he was temporarily blinded (in addition, his vocal chords were permanently affected). By the time he recovered, the war was over.

After being mustered out of the army, Hitler was appointed a political instructor in the postwar Reichswehr, the limited army of 100,000. He settled in Munich, which was to be the base of his operations until he became Chancellor of the Reich and moved to Berlin. In fact, he did not become a German citizen until the eve of his becoming Chancellor.

In September 1919, Hitler joined a minuscule party which later became the National Socialist German Workers Party, or Nazi Party for short, of which he became the Fuehrer (leader) in 1921. He soon achieved prominence because of his energy, his ability as a political leader, his effectiveness as a mob orator, and his fixed ideas of: (1) Jew-hatred, (2) contempt for democracy, (3) extreme nationalism, (4) racism, (5) the expansion of Germany's borders, (6) aggressive war as an instrument for the evolution of the "super race," and (7) the principle of the Fuehrer and Fuehrer State.

Between 1933 and 1945 Hitler was the central figure in world events.

32

# Adolf Hitler

There is no question that he was instrumental in launching the greatest catastrophe in the history of mankind.

Winston Churchill once described Hitler as the "embodiment of . . . soul-destroying hatred." Hitler, for his part, regarded the British and French leaders as "little worms." He condemned the French as "degenerate Negroes,"[1] the Czechs as "Slavic swine," the Russians as "filthy mongrels," and the Gypsies as "subhuman." Above all, he hated the Jews, claiming they were communists, capitalists, traitors, internationalists, destroyers of culture, the enemy of the human race, pacifists, and instigators of war. To Hitler the Jew symbolized all evil.

Sickly looking, medium sized, stooped, with a brown cowlick perpetually falling over a sloping forehead, small eyes, ugly nose, and a Charlie Chaplin mustache, Hitler would have passed unnoticed in a crowd. When he spoke in public his dull, opaque eyes glowed; he threw tantrums, he screamed hysterically, his face swelled with fury. He spit curses at those who were against him, at the powerful and the common man alike; sometimes he even foamed at the mouth and fell to the ground as if he were in a fit. He exercised a hypnotic influence on his audiences and swayed them with the force of his personality. His orations were simple, primitive, and explosive. After a major speech he was soaking wet and had lost several pounds.

Hitler was an eccentric, a vegetarian; he abstained from coffee, beer, liquor, and tobacco. No one dared smoke in his presence. Many questions have been raised about his relationships with women. The facts are that he married Eva Braun, his common-law wife, the day before he committed suicide, and that his writings, speeches, and actions are indicative of serious sexual disturbances and obsessions. He was a believer in astrology and in faddish medical treatments. He was also a mystic and relied on hunches. He believed that the will to win and the relentless pursuit to achieve one's ends were supreme; knowledge and reason were unimportant. He declared, "I shall give a propagandist reason for the starting of war; no matter whether it is plausible or not. The victor will not be asked afterward whether he told the truth or not."

Hitler glorified the "big lie." In his book, *Mein Kampf,* he wrote, "The [people] more readily fall victims to the big lie than the small lie." Thus he proclaimed his love of peace again and again. "I know what war is like," he thundered, "I would be insane if I ever wanted war again. Only our enemies want war." But even as he was speaking, he was preparing for and planning total war. And every time he overran another country, he pledged that it was the last. To further Nazi conquest he would stop at nothing: sign treaties, give guarantees, form alliances—he would use any means to dupe, and deceive, in order to achieve his goals.

[1]This insult stemmed from the fact that many of the French soldiers occupying the Rhineland after World War I were colonial troops from Africa.

33

Hitler was consumed with the concept of racism and the theory that race was transmitted by blood. He was convinced that the Aryan[2] or Nordic, race was superior to all others; that it alone was the creator of culture, while the other races were destroyers of culture. Aryans were typified as tall, blond, blue-eyed, slim, large-boned—everything that he himself was not.

Hitler's maniacal anti-Semitism and fanatical racial principles also led to his assaults on Christianity, both as a religion and as a system of ethics and morals. He assaulted its doctrines, which favored the weak, the poor, and the lowly; its emphasis on mercy, love, and the equality of man; its teachings of universalism and of peace on earth; and its roots in Judaism. To him God and conscience were Jewish inventions, "a blemish like circumcision." He wanted to create a German national church with Aryan clergy, ideology, and ideals. He demanded to be viewed as the new Messiah, to replace the cross with the swastika, and to make race, blood, and soil the sacred tenets of a new German religion. He resurrected the mythology of the Teutonic gods and the Nordic sagas, and created a mystical new paganism preaching a religion of fire and sword.

Hitler cunningly played on the weaknesses of others: the German people's feelings of anger and frustration, the army's humiliation after Versailles, the British and French fear of communism, Stalin's fear of the West, the European fear of war, and so on. He betrayed and murdered many friends who had helped him rise to power. He had no roots, no conscience, no loyalties of any kind.

## HITLER'S *MEIN KAMPF*

During the evening of November 23, 1923, in a Munich beer hall, Hitler mounted a rebellion against the Bavarian state government. He had been impressed by Mussolini's easy success in overthrowing the Italian government the previous year. Once in control of Bavaria, he hoped to march on Berlin as Mussolini had marched on Rome. The "Beer-hall Putsch" ended in a fiasco; Hitler and the other conspirators got off with five-year prison terms for this act of high treason. (That Hitler was released after nine months is evidence of the compliance of the judicial and police officials.) Treated as a VIP in prison, Hitler wrote the first volume of *Mein Kampf* (My Struggle), which became the Nazi bible.[3]

*Mein Kampf,* a two-volume book of some eight hundred pages, was written in the white heat of hatred and was a passionate claim to Hitler's supreme leadership. The book became a sacred household object, second in popularity only to Luther's Bible. By 1933 it had sold 5,450,000

[2]The Aryans were an ancient people who idealized war and conquered India and surrounding lands. Their name comes from a Sanskrit word meaning "master" or "noble."
[3]Read Konrad Heiden's introduction to Ralph Manheim's translation of *Mein Kampf* (Boston: Houghton Mifflin, 1943).

copies; by 1942, 9,840,000. Had the leaders of the world read it carefully and taken it seriously, they would have learned exactly what Hitler had in mind for Germany, Europe, and the world. They would have become aware that he planned to destroy democracy with its own instruments. The family of nations would have been forewarned that his fanatic racism and belief in Germany's destiny as the Fuehrer State meant that he would rule the world and make all nations and peoples vassals to Nazism. In short, *Mein Kampf* was a blueprint of the actual tragedy as it unfolded later step by step. Hitler was brutally frank. He hid nothing. No one can deny that he gave full warning of what he intended when he came to power. Why, then, did he get away with it? Perhaps because his program was so preposterous and grotesque that it was utterly inconceivable. Even when the blueprint began to take on reality, his victims, including the Jews, continued in their delusion that it just could not happen.[4]

In the prison at Landsberg, where Hitler had the leisure to contemplate and map out his strategy, he determined that if he was to seize power it would have to be through legal means, *within* the framework of the democratic process and of the constitution of the Weimar Republic, as the successor to the prewar imperial German state was known. A direct attack like the one in Munich, he realized, would be opposed by the Germans, who were used to discipline and orderliness. In the years that followed, despite the opposition of his army of revolutionary storm troopers, who were anxious to move faster, Hitler pursued his policy of destroying democracy by its own "legal" means. Again and again, he and his men proclaimed this aim, which he pursued openly. As early as 1928, Joseph Goebbels wrote that the Nazi deputies elected to the Reichstag would paralyze it with its own weapons. He taunted the Weimar Republic, declaring, "We come as enemies . . . as the wolf breaks into the fold . . . "[5] He derided the democratic powers for being stupid enough to provide the tools to destroy themselves.

And the Weimar government *was* stupid. It simply looked on while Hitler used every means in the democratic process to terrorize, spread panic, and deceive both his allies and his opponents. Growing numbers of the "republic-weary" electorate were blinded by the Nazi slogan of "national awakening." They wanted to give Hitler "a chance," because they thought that the Nazi Party served the goals of the "national revolution."

The second principle of his program was to build up a full government apparatus to take over the nation. "We recognize," he declared, "that it is not enough to overthrow the old state. A new state must previously have been built up."

[4]For a study of this book in depth, read Werner Maser, Hitler's "Mein Kampf": An Analysis, trans. R. H. Barry (London: Faber & Faber, 1970).
[5]Read Karl Dietrich Bracher, The Road to Dictatorship: Germany, 1918 to 1933, trans. from the German by Jean Steinberg (New York: Praeger), chap. 4.

# HITLER'S SWIFT ADVANCE TO POWER

An outside sequence of events helped Hitler gain power: the relentless attacks on the Weimar Republic from both the right (nationalists and the army) and the left (socialists and communists), the widening gulf of a "house divided," the economic disasters, the senility of President Hindenburg, the fear of communism, the ineffectiveness of a docile, compliant world, America's isolationism, and the admiration of the "strong man" by world statesmen and renowned personalities like Lloyd George, Charles Lindbergh, and others.

Hitler dazzled his countrymen with visions of a great Germany, a strong military force, a powerful centralized state, and a rich harvest of booty and plunder. He promised benefits of all kinds of young and old, to the poor and the middle class. He assured industrialists that he would throttle the labor unions; he promised the unions that the workers would share in the nation's prosperity. All thrilled to his slogans: "One People, One Government, One Leader!" and "Today Germany, Tomorrow the World!"

To win over the Prussian gentry (the *Junkers*), Hitler polished their tarnished prestige. Although he wiped away the hereditary aspect of their tradition, he nevertheless gained their support and wealth, as well as the allegiance of the army officers when they realized that he would restore their commands.

The leading industrialists and capitalists also backed Hitler: Alfred Hugenberg, czar of the propaganda empire; Fritz Thyssen, the steel king who ruled over 170,000 workers; Hjalmar Schacht, the leading banker; and the giant firms of I. G. Farben, Krupp, and others. Hitler's promises to scrap the Versailles treaty and to rearm Germany were welcomed by the industrialists, the army, the patriots, and the masses, who still smarted from their defeat. And to the workers, rearmament meant work and real wages after having suffered through depression, unemployment, and inflation. Thus, step by step, Hitler muted clashing interests. He played on both capital and labor, landowners and farmers, nobility and middle class, producers and consumers. His intimidations and early bloodless conquests exhilarated Germany. Teachers, clergymen, and university professors, instead of teaching freedom and peace, rhapsodized on the splendors of the glorious Germany emerging under the Fuehrer. Germans saw in Hitler a man of the people, the "unknown soldier" of World War I, who had risen to greatness.

On the international scene, Hitler used the tactics of deceit. He was continually on the move, never giving his opponents any rest, dealing with the countries of Europe one at a time. In October 1933, he brusquely withdrew from the League of Nations and the disarmament conference. In January 1934, he signed a treaty with Poland renouncing any claims to Polish territory. In June 1935, he concluded a naval agreement with

England. In October 1935, when Italy invaded Ethiopia, he created an alliance with Mussolini which led to the Berlin-Rome Axis. In July 1936, he signed an agreement with Austria affirming its sovereignty. In November 1936, he concluded the Anti-Communist International Pact with Japan. And on November 5, 1937, Hitler revealed his top secret to the top leadership—his irrevocable decision for an all-out war. Surprise was his favorite gambit in politics, diplomacy, and later, in war.

## THE TECHNIQUES OF HITLER'S MASS APPEAL

Hitler knew and exploited the value of a "good show" and of symbols that would stir his followers. He understood the effectiveness of decorations, pins, uniforms, medals, impressive parades, and ceremonies in uniting the masses. He played on the desire of the individual to lose himself in the crowd, to be part of an identifiable group. To the detached observer, the goose-stepping, stiff-armed, Heil Hitler—saluting marchers looked like an army of robots. To the German soul it was a disciplined, moving expression of mass devotion.

The staging of the mass rallies was spectacular. They were meticulously planned to arouse the imagination to the great possibility of Teutonic mastery. An overpowering array of flags and banners displayed the swastika. Torches lit up the darkness. Loud martial music, blaring trumpets, fifes, and thundering drums conjured up the mythology of the primitive pagans. Goose-stepping, jack-booted thousands marched like a gigantic machine with stiff, outstretched arms, and rhythmic shouts of "Heil Hitler" stirred the participants and cast a hypnotic spell. The climax came when, in a blaze of light, *he* emerged before the crowd. The crowds were spellbound and intoxicated. Foreign listeners were repelled and frightened.

As part of the ceremonies and public display, Hitler created new festivals. He gave his people no rest. There were holidays commemorating red-letter days of the Nazi movement, such as his birthday and German victories. Pagan festivals like the summer and winter solstices were revamped, and new rituals were created, symbolizing the marriage between party and people.

In between festivals, collection campaigns were staged; for instance, the winter relief (from October to March) and the monthly "one-pot-meal day." Demonstrations against Jews, "Marxist scum," Poles, etc., were triggered at the drop of a hat. To cap it all, it became the obligation of every German to use the Heil Hitler salutation in place of "good morning" or "good night" and at the end of all personal and business correspondence. It was a potent conditioning device and the best indicator of the greeter's enthusiasm or lack thereof for the Fuehrer.

Day and night the radios blared the Nazi propaganda line. Communal listening was a matter of obligation in every factory, office, restaurant, cafe, and town square. Some three-quarters of the German populace owned radios—but they were so constructed that no foreign broadcasts could be heard. Hitler once remarked that without radio and sound films, the victory of Nazism would not have been possible.

Inherent in Hitler's appeal was the belittling of intellectualism and the disparagement of the intellectual, despite all the "scientific" panoply of theories, studies, and experiments. The peasant and the common man were idealized. They were favored because they reacted with emotion rather than with reason. Nazi education was directed to educate "character," i.e., to condition behavior.

In brief, Hitler was the dominant force in Germany during the 1930s and the early 1940s. He exercised an uncanny influence in activating the evil that made the twelve years of his Third Reich the most horrendous chapter in world history.

---

# "The Prince of Darkness . . . A Monstrosity"

*The Prussian aristocrat Reck-Malliczwen was a violent anti-Nazi. He recorded the horrors of the Nazi period in his diary. He was shot in Dachau early in 1945.*

I saw Hitler last in Seebruck, slowly gliding by in a car with armor-plated sides, while an armed bodyguard of motorcyclists rode in front as further protection: a jellylike, slag-gray face, a moon-face into which two melancholy jet-black eyes had been set like raisins. So sad, so unutterably insignificant, so basically misbegotten is this countenance that only thirty years ago, in the darkest days of Wilhelmism,[1] such a face on an official would have been impossible. Appearing in the chair of a minister, an apparition with a face like this would have been disobeyed as soon as its mouth spoke an order—and not merely by the higher officials in the ministry: no, by the doorman, by the cleaning women!

And today? I hear that Hitler recently ended a report—by Wilhelm Keitel, the Army commander—which had given him reason for dissatisfaction, by throwing a bronze vase at the head of the general. Isn't this

[1] Kaiser Wilhelm's Era.

From *Diary of a Man in Despair* by Friedrich P. Reck-Malleczewen.

38

the kind of thing that happens when a people is sinking in the cesspool of its own disgrace? . . .

I am neither an occult nor a mystic, I am a child of my time despite all forebodings, and I hold strictly to what I see. But there is a frightful riddle here, and I come back again and again to what appears to me to be the only answer to it:

What I saw gliding by there, behind the fence of his mamelukes, like the Prince of Darkness himself, was no human being.

That was a figure out of a ghost story.

I have met him a few times—not at any of his meetings, of course. The first time was in 1920, at the home of my friend Clemens von Franckenstein . . . According to the butler, one of those present was forcing his way in everywhere, had already been there a full hour. It was Hitler. He had managed an invitation to Clé's house under the guise of being interested in operatic scenic design . . . Hitler very likely had the idea that theatrical design was connected with interior decorating and wallpaper-hanging, his former professions.

He had come to a house, where he had never been before, wearing gaiters, a floppy, wide-brimmed hat, and carrying a riding whip. There was a collie, too. The effect, among the Gobelin tapestries and cool marble walls, was something akin to a cowboy's sitting down on the steps of a baroque altar in leather breeches, spurs, and with a Colt at his side. But Hitler sat there, the stereotype of a headwaiter—at that time he was thinner, and looked somewhat starved—both impressed and restricted by the presence of a real, live Herr Baron; awed, not quite daring to sit fully in his chair, but perched on half, more or less, of his thin loins; not caring at all that there was a great deal of cool and elegant irony in the things his host said to him, but snatching hungrily at the words, like a dog at pieces of raw meat.

Eventually, he managed to launch into a speech. He talked on and on, endlessly. He preached. He went on at us like a division chaplain in the Army. We did not in the least contradict him, or venture to differ in any way, but he began to bellow at us. The servants thought we were being attacked, and rushed in to defend us.

When he had gone, we sat silently confused and not at all amused. There was a feeling of dismay, as when on a train you suddenly find you are sharing a compartment with a psychotic. We sat a long time and no one spoke. Finally, Clé stood up, opened one of the huge windows, and let the spring air, warm with the föhn, into the room. It was not that our grim guest had been unclean, and had fouled the room in the way that so often happens in a Bavarian village. But the fresh air helped to dispel the feeling of oppression. It was not that an unclean body had been in the room, but something else: the unclean essence of a monstrosity.

I used to ride at the Munich armory, after which I liked to eat at the

Löwenbräukeller: That was the second meeting. He did not need to worry now that he might be put out, and so he did not have to smack his boots continually with his riding whip, as he had done at Franckenstein's. At first glance, the tightly clenched insecurity seemed to be gone—which allowed him to launch at once into one of his tirades. I had ridden hard, and was tremendously hungry, and wanted just to be let alone to eat in peace. Instead I had poured out over me every one of the political platitudes in his book. . . .

With his oily hair falling into his face as he ranted, he had the look of a man trying to seduce the cook. I got the impression of basic *stupidity*, the same kind of stupidity as that of his crony, Papen—the kind of stupidity which equates statesmanship with cheating at a horse trade. . . .

The third time, I saw him in a courtroom accused of creating a disturbance at some political meeting: By then, he was known outside the Munich city limits. . . . And then I observed him in Berlin, entering his hotel, already a celebrity. In court, he looked like he was begging for a kind word from the small and very low-ranking official who was in charge of the hearing: the look of a man who has been in jail a number of times. . . .

Notwithstanding his meteoric rise, there is absolutely nothing that has happened in the twenty years since I first saw him to make me change my first view of him. The fact remains . . . that he basically hates himself, and that his opportunism, his immeasurable need for recognition, and his now-apocalyptic vanity are all based on one thing—a consuming drive to drown out the pain in his psyche, the trauma of a monstrosity.

There are additional details—Erna Hanfstaengl, who knows him better than I do, says he is becoming increasingly afraid of ghosts. She believes that this fear of the spirits of those he has murdered drives him on continually, and does not allow him to stay for long in any one place. . . . Quite in accord with this is that he has taken to spending his nights in his private projection room, where his poor projectionists have to show sex films for him, night after night. . . .

I saw him once more at close range. This was in the fall of 1932, as the fever began to take hold of Germany. Friedrich von Mücke and I were dining at the Osteria Bavaria in Munich when Hitler entered and crossed the restaurant to the table next to ours—alone, by the way, and without his usual bodyguard. There he sat, now a power among the Germans . . . sat, felt himself observed by us, and critically examined, and as a result became uncomfortable. His face took on the sullen expression of a minor bureaucrat who has ventured into a place which he would not generally enter, but now that he is there demands for his good money "that he be served and treated every bit as well as the fine gentlemen over there. . . ."

There he sat, a raw-vegetable Genghis Khan, a teetotaling Alex-

40

ander, a womanless Napoleon, an effigy of Bismarck who would certainly have had to go to bed for four weeks if he had ever tried to eat just one of Bismarck's breakfasts. . . .

I had driven into town, and since at that time, September, 1932, the streets were already quite unsafe, I had a loaded revolver with me. In the almost deserted restaurant, I could easily have shot him. If I had had an inkling of the role this piece of filth was to play, and of the years of suffering he was to make us endure, I would have done it without a second thought. But I took him for a character out of a comic strip, and did not shoot.

It would have done no good in any case: in the councils of the Highest, our martyrdom had already been decided. If Hitler at that point had been taken and tied to railroad tracks, the train would have been derailed before it got to him. But when his hour strikes, the end will come down upon his head from every possible direction, and from places, even, that were never thought of. There are many rumors of attempts to assassinate him. The attempts fail, and they will continue to fail. For years (and especially in this land of successful demons) it has seemed that God is asleep. But, to quote a Russian proverb:

"When God wills it, even a broom can shoot!"

(August 11, 1936)

Three years later . . . in front of the Reich Chancellery, packed into the mob, deafened by the crash of drums, cymbals, and tubas of the marching troops, I witnessed the festivities. I heard the clamor, saw the enraptured faces of the women, saw, also, the object of this rapture.

There he stood, the most glorious of all, in his usual pose with hands clasped over his belly, looking, with his silver-decorated uniform and cap drawn far down over his forehead, like a streetcar conductor. I examined his face through my binoculars. The whole of it waggled with unhealthy cushions of fat; it all hung, it was all slack and without structure—slaggy, gelatinous, sick. There was no light in it, none of the shimmer and shining of a man sent by God. Instead, the face bore the stigma of sexual inadequacy, of the rancor of a half-man who had turned his fury at his impotence into brutalizing others.

And through it all this bovine and finally moronic roar of "Heil!" . . . hysterical females, adolescents in a trance, an entire people in the spiritual state of howling dervishes.

I went back to the hotel with Clemens von Franckenstein, whom I met accidentally today. We talked about my observations yesterday, and he reminded me that the German peerage register is full of listings of families like the von Arnims, Riedesels, von Kattes, von Kleists, and Bülows, with members holding positions such as "Group Leader" and similar offices under this criminal. . . . These honors are accepted without a thought of the disgrace they thereby bring to the famed old names they bear, and to their forefathers. And I reflected again on this thick-witted mob and its bovine roar; on this failure of a Moloch to whom this crowd was roaring homage; and on the ocean of disgrace into which we have all sunk.

No, the much-maligned generation of the Wilhelms never quite reached this point of adoration of a Chosen One. In this case, it is really true that yesterday's sins were not as bad as today's. No, these are filth! These ceremonials are not anything to be seen and grasped. Satan has loosed his bonds, a herd of demons is upon us. . . .

This people is insane. It will pay dearly for its insanity. The air of this summer is full of foreboding, and fire and iron must heal what no physician can any longer cure. . . .

# Hitler at the Olympic Games (1936)

*Bella Fromm was a well-known journalist and socially prominent personality in Berlin. She kept a diary . . .*

Olympic games. I attended a couple of times. Everything is colossal. The swastika is everywhere, and so are the black and brown uniforms.

The lack of sportsmanship of Germany's First Man is disgusting and at the same time fascinating. He behaved like a madman, jumping from his seat and roaring when the swastika was hoisted, or when the Japs or Finns won a victory. Other champions left him cold and personally offended at their victories over their Nordic contestants.

The manner in which Hitler applauds German winners is an orgasmic frenzy of shrieks, clappings, and contortions, is painful proof that the whole idea of the Olympic games is far too broad for his single-track mind. This is *his* show, and *his* Germans are supermen. That the whole world must admit. He has said some remarkable things.

"The American Negroes are not entitled to compete," he said, for example. "It was unfair of the United States to send these flat-footed specimens to compete with the noble products of Germany. I am going to vote against Negro participation in the future."

From *Blood and Banquets, A Berlin Social Diary* (August 15, 1936) by Bella Fromm.

He means it, too. Although it is his policy to bid every winner to his box, to congratulate him and shake hands, he has repeatedly snubbed and ignored the colored American representatives. Whenever one of the tall, graceful, perfectly built dark-skinned athletes scored a triumph, Hitler left his seat hurriedly and returned only when the signal for the next event was sounded. "The American team leader should complain," said the Swedish Minister.

# "Terror Is the Most Effective Political Instrument" . . . "The Most Horrible Warfare Is the Kindest"

*Hermann Rauschning, a German leader of Danzig who resigned as president of its Senate and fled abroad in 1936, recorded his meetings and conversations with Hitler during 1932–34. The following is a record of a meeting after the Reichstag Fire . . .*

Complaints as to the horrors of the concentration camps had begun to reach Hitler. I remember a particular instance in Stettin, where, in the empty engine-rooms of the former Vulkan docks, respected citizens, some of them of Jewish parentage, were brutally maltreated. Vile things were done in an unmistakable enjoyment of brutality for its own sake. The matter had been brought to Göring's attention, and he had been unable to evade an investigation. In one case, reparation was made.

In those days the routine excuse was that a revolution was taking place in Germany which was extraordinarily bloodless and lenient. It was not justifiable, we were told, to draw general conclusions from a few isolated cases. But the truth was very different. The cruelty, of a nature increasingly refined, dealt out then and later by the SS and the SA to political opponents was part of a definite political plan. The selection of asocial, abnormal types to guard the concentration camps was carried out with conscious purpose. I had occasion to see some-

From *Voice of Destruction* by Hermann Rauschning.

43

thing of this myself. Notorious drunkards and criminals were selected from the military organizations of the party and placed in special sub-divisions. It was a typical example of specially selected sub-humans for definite political tasks.

I happened to be present when Hitler's attention was called to the Stettin incident and other similar occurrences. It was entirely character-istic that Hitler was by no means indignant, as one might have expected, at the horrible excesses of his men, but on the contrary roundly abused those who "made a fuss" about these trivial matters.

The occasion was my first experience of Hitler's paroxysms of rage and abuse. He behaved like a combination of a spoilt child and an hysterical woman. He scolded in high, shrill tones, stamped his feet, and banged his fist on tables and walls. He foamed at the mouth, panting and stammering in uncontrolled fury: "I won't have it! Get rid of all of them! Traitors!" He was an alarming sight, his hair disheveled, his eyes fixed, and his face distorted and purple. I feared that he would collapse, or have an apoplectic fit.

Suddenly it was all over. He walked up and down the room, clearing his throat, and brushing his hair back. He looked round apprehen-sively and suspiciously, with searching glances at us. I had the impres-sion that he wanted to see if anyone was laughing. And I must admit that a desire to laugh, perhaps largely as a nervous reaction to the tension, rose within me.

"Preposterous," Hitler began in a hoarse voice. "Haven't you ever seen a crowd collecting to watch a street brawl? *Brutality is respected.* Brutality and physical strength. The plain man in the street respects nothing but brutal strength and ruthlessness—women, too, for that matter, women and children. The people need wholesome fear. They *want* to fear something. They want someone to frighten them and make them shudderingly submissive. Haven't you seen everywhere that after boxing-matches, the beaten ones are the first to join the party as new members? Why babble about brutality and be indignant about tortures? The masses want that. They need something that will give them a thrill of horror."

After a pause, he continued in his former tone:

"I forbid you to change anything. By all means, punish one or two men, so that these German Nationalist donkeys may sleep easy. But I don't want the concentration camps transformed into penitentiary institutions. Terror is the most effective political instrument. I shall not permit myself to be robbed of it simply because a lot of stupid, *bourgeois* mollycoddles choose to be offended by it. It is my duty to make use of *every* means of training the German people to severity, and to prepare them for war."

Hitler paced the room excitedly.

"My behavior in wartime will be no different. The most horrible

44

warfare is the kindest. I shall spread terror by the surprise employment of all my measures. The important thing is the sudden shock of an overwhelming fear of death. Why should I use different measures against my internal political opponents? These so-called atrocities spare me a hundred thousand individual actions against disobedience and discontent. People will think twice before opposing us when they hear what to expect in the camps . . ."

# Readings

*Hitler—A Study in Tyranny* by Alan Bullock (Harper and Row, 1962), is a carefully researched authoritative study.

*Mein Kampf* by Adolf Hitler, is the two-volume book (*A Reckoning* and the *National Socialist Movement*) in one. Translated by Ralph Manheim (Houghton Mifflin, 1943).

*Der Fuehrer* by Konrad Heiden (Victor Gollancz, 1951), was eyewitness to Hitler's rise covering a period of twenty-three years and ending with the blood purge of Roehm.

*Hitler: An Anthology*, edited by George H. Stein (Prentice-Hall, 1968), comprises the following: Hitler Looks at the World; The World Looks at Hitler; Hitler in History.

*Adolf Hitler, His Family, Childhood and Youth* by Bradley F. Smith (Stanford University, 1967), is a record of the early years of the Fuehrer.

*The Mind of Hitler* by Walter Langer (Basic Books, 1972), is a psychological analysis prepared in 1943 for the American O.S.S. and the Allies, and released in 1972.

*Warrant for Genocide* by Norman Cohn (Harper and Row, 1966), is a comprehensive study of the Protocols of the Elders of Zion, the undying myth of the so-called Jewish world conspiracy.

*The Life and Death of Adolf Hitler* by Robert Payne (Popular Library Paperback, 1973), is one of the latest biographies. Recommended. Contains illuminating letters from Hitler and Eva Braun's Diary.

# 4. THE NSDAP, SS, AND GESTAPO: STATE WITHIN A STATE

## THE NSDAP (NAZI PARTY)

The National Socialist German Workers Party was organized by Hitler as a state within a state. It was a closed, "strait-jacketed" conglomeration of people with its own rules, its distinct ways of life, festivals, and norms. At the first assembly in Munich (January 22, 1921), it already had a membership of three thousand and had launched its program, which may be summarized as follows:

1. The political state is supreme. The individual's thoughts, feelings, ambitions, desires, and happiness are not important. He exists to serve the state.
2. The state is to be ruled by a Fuehrer. In a democracy the mass overwhelms the elite. Not so in a Fuehrer-State, where the leader is absolute and infallible. Only he is endowed with "mystic" qualities; only he knows what is best and how to achieve the ultimate good for "his" people.
3. The Fuehrer's subordinates are the instruments of his will. Their authority is derived from him. They are the elite selected by him as extensions of his "genius" to fulfill the special destiny of the Fuehrer-State. There is to be no free exchange of thought between the leader and the masses. The "flow" is in a downward direction only, from the topmost authority to all who are below him.

4. None but persons of pure German blood may be members of the German nation.
5. The ideas of German superiority and the Fuehrer principle are the "religion" of Nazidom, replacing the "weak and obsolete" Christian faith and doctrines.
6. As a consequence, Nazism and its revolutionary teachings provide a new code of morality that negates the ethics and morals of Christianity and the Western world. Nothing is wrong or immoral if it advances the Nazi cause.
7. Germany must have *Lebensraum,* ample living space for its people, its civilization, and its revolutionary philosophy.
8. Nazism is destined to conquer the world.

The vanguard and muscle of the party were the SA, the brown-shirted storm troopers, and the elite—the black-shirted SS. The country was divided into thirty-two administrative regions *(Gaue),* each headed by a leader—the *Gauleiter*—appointed by Hitler. Each region in turn was divided into subregions, local groups, cells, and blocks. Each had its own leader who was responsible to his superiors.

The party was a perfect machine, tightly knit, clear in its aims. It recruited members and propagandized for votes on a year-round basis, not only prior to elections. Its annual party congresses in Nuremberg were national, even world spectacles. After Hitler assumed power they became the platform from which new decrees were pronounced.

The party organized and implemented associations at all age levels, and embraced all avenues of life. Between 1928 and 1932, its membership rose from 108,000 to 1,500,000 and by 1934 to some 4,500,000. In one way or another, it touched the lives of every one of Germany's 66,000,000 citizens, as well as the millions of German nationals and Volksdeutsche (German ethnic populations) in neighboring countries and overseas.[1]

## THE SA AND ERNST ROEHM

Ernst Roehm was one of those who had preceded Hitler as a member of the party's executive committee in Munich. A former army officer, he was a burly, ruthless, brutish homosexual. Like many of his ilk, he headed a group of rowdies who later called themselves *Sturmabteilung* (SA), or storm troopers. They copied the fashion of the black-shirted Fascists in Italy, choosing brown for their uniforms. They were trained in street brawls, beating up Jews as well as communists, liberals, and other political opponents. Roehm and his strong-arm squad were Hitler's first mainstay and striking force. They became the laboratory in which the Nazi scourge was tested and "refined." Around the SA there gathered an

[1]Read Dietrich Orlow, *The History of the Nazi Party,* 2 vols. (Pittsburgh: University of Pittsburgh Press, 1969).

assortment of "old timers"—fanatics, bullies, and veterans who gloried in military pomp and grandeur.

Typical of the SA was a Berlin member named Horst Wessel. The son of a Protestant clergyman, he left his home and family to live with pimps and prostitutes. He engaged in street fighting with communists and others and built a reputation for himself with the SA. He was killed in a street brawl and might have been forgotten were it not for the fact that he had written a song which became the Nazi "anthem"—even superseding the German national anthem, and Goebbels's propaganda created a heroic legend around him.

The lawless acts of the SA were treated leniently by the police and courts. Indeed, political Germany was rife with contradictions. The law-makers were democratic; the law-enforcers, i.e., the courts and the police, were anti-democratic. This explains why Hitler and his cohorts were treated with silk gloves. The civil service and the judiciary were at one with the officer corps and the SA; and with them went along most of the university professors and the clergy, Protestant and Catholic.

And so the Weimar Constitution, aided by the law-enforcement agencies, permitted the development of a party that functioned as a state within a state, or better yet, a state outside a state, with its own foreign, agricultural, and defense departments. The SA became a private "shadow" army, and the SS, an elite guard. They provided Hitler with manpower to spy and inform on the opposition; to plot against, terrorize, cripple, and assassinate opponents; and to recruit workers and voters at the polls.

Between Hitler and the head of the SA, Roehm, there was a fundamental disagreement. Hitler wanted the SA to be a kind of police body, the strong-arm branch of the party, to intimidate the opposition and browbeat the populace. Roehm, on the other hand, hated the army and wanted the SA to take it over, oust the Junker officers, and become a people's army. Hitler, however, needed the backing of the regular army, which, in turn, was backed by big business, finance, President Hindenburg, and the conservatives. The SA quickly grew to four million, twenty times the size of the army. Naturally, the army, the moneyed class, and Hindenburg's people were disturbed. They prodded Hitler to purge Roehm and his clique or else they would declare a state of martial law, giving complete power to the army. Hitler realized that if Roehm had his way, his plan to succeed the senile Hindenburg would go to pieces. Forced to make a choice in 1934, Hitler liquidated Roehm and took the opportunity to kill off other opposition leaders in the party and settle old accounts with other personal enemies.

## THE SS AND HEINRICH HIMMLER

Black-uniformed, wearing a death's-head badge (skull and bones), and bound to Hitler in eternal allegiance, the SS was a law unto itself. The initials came from the word *Schutzstaffel*, which is German for "staff-guard" or "protective troops." The SS was made a distinct autonomous body in 1934, in recognition of its services in the purge. They were the real rulers of Hitler's empire; they murdered millions of Jews, Gypsies, Slavs, and "unsociables." They penetrated the police force and the secret service, and they manned the key positions in agriculture, health services, scientific affairs, racial policies, and the diplomatic corps.

The SS was a privileged fraternity, inflexible, mysterious and sinister, impervious to human emotions, and contemptuous of "inferiors." These traits were carefully cultivated and added to its fearful reputation. The members gloried in the terror they caused with the mere appearance of their black uniforms and ominous insignia.

Although the SS later became a motley group, in the early 1930s its members came from professional and academic circles, the army, and even the nobility. They were carefully selected on the basis of their physical, racial, and political background. They were fully indoctrinated with Hitler's ideas and hatreds, and considered themselves the lords of creation. Their proud slogans were "My honor is my loyalty," which was displayed on their buckles, and "Blood and Honor," on their daggers.

At their head was Heinrich Himmler, a slight, sickly, squeamish schoolmaster and former chicken breeder, who looked the exact opposite of the tall, robust knights of the new German order. Himmler feared Hitler and could not easily gain his favor because Hitler considered him an unintelligent subordinate, albeit diligent and loyal. To attain his desire of building an empire over which he would be supreme, Himmler had to move carefully, plotting and taking advantage of all available opportunities to increase his power. The one area in which he could exercise a free hand was the Final Solution. And Himmler fully exploited this opportunity. Although every branch of the Nazi Party and the German government had a hand in Jewish affairs, it was Himmler and his assistants, Heydrich, Eichmann, and Müller, of the Gestapo, who in the end decided the fate of the Jews.

## THE GESTAPO

Immediately following Hitler's rise to power, the Berlin police force was purged of two-thirds of its men. These "unreliables" were replaced by picked Nazis, selected on the basis of their brutality. Thus was born the Gestapo (a combination of three words meaning "secret state police").

The Gestapo were plainclothes men. Apart from that, they were affiliated with the SS Black Order, and their overall chief was Heinrich Himmler. Their immediate head was Reinhard Heydrich, son of a prominent family, an ideal Aryan, talented, cultured, musical, athletic, and ruthless. He could call on the facilities of both the party Security Service,

50

which he headed, and the Gestapo, which was presumably a state agency. The state was the party, and the party the state. The tasks of the Gestapo were to eliminate all opposition and any and all critics. The party had gathered a list of such "enemies." Millions of files on individuals were at its disposal, and it made full use of them. The Gestapo was a dreaded, sinister body, with eyes and ears everywhere. No one was exempt from surveillance, from the top officers of the army to the leaders of the party.

The prisons soon became overcrowded, so Himmler set up his own concentration camps. The first was Dachau, which served as a model for those that followed. It was run on army-camp lines, but with one difference; it was sadistic and inhuman in the extreme. It was a training ground in terror and dehumanization for Himmler's SS administrators of slave labor. The SS reigned supreme in the scores of camps established after the war began. It recruited irregular SS battalions made up of criminals who had been imprisoned for years, *Volksdeutsche,* and outcasts from society. At the Nuremberg trials, the SS was declared guilty as a body of the "persecution and extermination of Jews and others . . . of murder of prisoners of war . . . and various other atrocities."

## THE HITLER YOUTH

It may be said that among Hitler's first victims were the children of Germany itself. He fired them with the intense flame of his fanaticism and hates and hammered out their characters and personalities on the anvil of a thorough Nazi indoctrination. He twisted their souls and brutalized them, so that they became inflamed with his passions against the immediate enemy—"Jewish Bolshevism." Communist Russia was far away; he would come to grips with her later. But right at home, the Jews were conspicuous in the press, theater, cinema, radio, music, in the shops and offices, and on the main streets. And they were vulnerable and defenseless—a convenient target.

Habituated at home to severe discipline and male domination, and seduced by the flair of the Hitler youth movements, the young people of Germany became hypnotized, hysterical devotees of their Fuehrer, and absorbed the patriotic fervor he generated. In 1932 the Hitler youth movement numbered thirty-five thousand; in 1935, about six million, inclusive of the *Volksdeutsche* (people of German origin) in fifty-three foreign countries.

Orientation began in the formative school years. Six- and seven-year-olds were enrolled in the movement, playing soldier, marching, saluting, drilling, singing, "living it up," eager to be promoted to the next exciting level. From ten years of age and up, boys and girls were organized in clubs which met in churches, and in athletic groups. Their military exercises, disguised as sports activities, became more intense and wide-

51

ranging. They were always directed by fanatical leaders, who carefully screened their films and radio programs, drilled them at rallies, and accompanied them on their hikes and trips. Slogans such as "Strength Through Joy" and "Tomorrow the World" were coined to inflame the young. They were taught to be tough and strong, to suppress pity, to hate as Hitler hated. They were imbued with Hitler's ideas and ambitions. They became non-individuals, a dehumanized pack moved by regimented savage instincts which were kept at a high pitch.

Initiation ceremonies were highly colorful, full of ritual and panoply; they were conducted at all age levels. The first award of recognition was the brown shirt. After passing more advanced tests of physical prowess and further exposure to the Nazi arsenal of ideas, songs, myths, and slogans, the "brown shirt" was next awarded a dagger. At the age of fourteen, after still more physical training, such as wrestling, boxing, inflicting and accepting pain, the teenager was given a red swastika armband. Now he reached the distinction of being counted as a junior storm trooper, a member of the SA, directly subject to Hitler's will and blindly obedient to his program. Once, at a large rally in Munich, Hitler thundered, "This young generation will realize and fulfill what today we can only prophesy and see in our dreams."[2]

And so a whole generation was molded, single-minded in purpose, automated, indifferent to pain, even cheerful when inflicting injury and death on others. Youth leaders who excelled in these traits were selected for special training to become the Nazi elite, the glorified SS. Every teacher and professor took a direct oath to Hitler that he would train his students to grow up "in the direction set by your will." Laws were passed to regulate the lives of all students from the pre-school to the postgraduate and professional levels. Early marriages were encouraged by special subsidies because the state needed to produce armies of Nazis. Girls were prepared for motherhood, whether married or not, and were mated with selected young men at special retreats. Some fifty thousand children were bred in this way, who were raised by the state and belonged to the Reich. Young people were also conscripted for labor services to work on farms and factories. The Hitler net was all-embracing.

What sacrifices did the youth bring to the altar of Nazism? They gave up the ability to reason, the instinct to love and raise a family (marriage and care of infants and children were secondary to the reproduction of little Nazis), the development of curiosity, discernment, the adventures of the mind, the qualities of the heart, the cultivation of their individual talents—in short, all the human characteristics that a free society encourages. They became blind idol worshipers of the Fuehrer and the Fuehrer State.

The new Germany was male-centered; females were merely instruments for reproduction. Mother love was spurned, youth was hard and

[2]Dorothy Macardle, *The Children of Europe* (London: Victor Gollancz, 1951), p. 23.

52

cruel, tenderness was extirpated. Dueling, which had previously been prohibited, again became fashionable. Jew-baiting and persecutions of ingenious kinds became a sport through which the young generation sharpened their fangs for future brutality. Speaking of the ideal youth, Hitler exclaimed to Hermann Rauschning, who published a record of his conversations (*Hitler Speaks*), "In my *Ordensburgen* [the top training schools for Nazi leaders] a youth will grow up before which the world will shrink back. A violently active, dominating, intrepid, brutal youth . . . indifferent to pain . . . no weakness or tenderness . . . in its eyes the gleam of pride and independence of the beast of prey."[3]

And so Hitler robbed the German youth of their natural endowments in their very bloom of life and ripened them for murder and as cannon fodder. Those who broke under the strain, the oversensitive and the delicate, were ostracized and scorned by society and by their peers. Many committed suicide. The tough, the "fittest," who survived to ruin Europe and other large areas of the world, were the supreme "lords of creation." Ultimately their blood soaked the snows of Stalingrad, the sands of North Africa, and the battlefields of Europe.

---

# Nazi Party Rally, Nuremberg 1936: An Outsider's View

The celebrations were bigger and brighter than ever before, and Hitler now gave his messages, not to Germany alone, but to the whole world. At this Rally he launched two new campaigns—the Four Year Plan for economic self-sufficiency and a crusade against "the powers of disorder" led by Russia.

His *Ehrengäste*[1] were a curious assortment, including an official delegation of Italian Blackshirts; a few lone Japanese waving their national flag so that they could be identified; Hungarian Fascists and Scandinavian publicists; many German Americans; English peers, parliamentarians, writers, and publishers . . . , French authors and Croix de Feu[2] representatives, and isolated Britons from as far afield as Australia and British Guiana.

The Rally opened in the huge Congress Hall, where 60,000 people

[3]Quoted in *The Children of Europe*, p. 27.
[1]honored guests.
[2]Fascist French organization.

---

From *The House that Hitler Built* by Stephen Roberts.

gathered to listen to Hitler's proclamation on his achievements of the last three years. Hundreds of swastika banners filed in, to the impressive music of the *Song of the Standards,* and formed a solid mass of red and gold at the back of the stage. Every device of music and coloured light was used to keep the atmosphere tense, and the spotlight that played on the giant swastika behind the banners exerted an influence that was almost hypnotic.

Victor Lutze, head of the Brownshirts, solemnly read the name of every Nazi who had died for his cause. There were over four hundred of them . . .

Adolf Wagner, the ruler of Munich, next read Hitler's proclamation, ostensibly because his voice is almost exactly that of Hitler himself, even to the hoarseness and breaking. I shall not easily forget the roars that went through those crowds when Wagner dramatically declared that "within four years Germany must be independent of foreign raw supplies."

The atmosphere was most strained and unreal. The speakers deliberately played on the feelings of the people. At intervals, when something particularly impressive was read out, a curious tremor swept the crowd, and all around me individuals uttered a strange cry, a kind of emotional sigh that invariably changed into a shout of *"Heil Hitler".* It was a definite struggle to remain rational in a horde so surcharged with tense emotionalism. . . .

The rest of the week consisted either of lavish displays or of meetings at which Party leaders spoke. The German excels in mass meetings. Not an hour of the day or night was quiet, and, when the official functions ended, zealous Nazis formed impromptu torchlight processions of their own. One day 160,000 men of the popular Labour Service Corps filed past, with their dark-brown uniforms and bright-polished shovels, and, on a bitterly cold morning, many thousands of them stood stripped to the waist for hours, listening to official speeches. On another day, a still larger number of Hitler Youth and Maidens and groups of the sea-scouts crowded a huge arena to listen to Hitler and von Schirach. On still another day, the Brownshirts and Black Guards formed a solid mass of humanity in the Leopold Arena—160,000 of them. One of the most striking ceremonies took place. Before addressing them, Hitler solemnly marched up to the sacrificial fires that paid homage to those who had died for the movement. It was the only moment of quietness in the whole week. For what seemed an interminable time, three men—Hitler, Himmler, and Lutze—strode up the wide path that clove the brown mass in twain and, after saluting the fire, as solemnly marched back. It was a superbly arranged gesture. Those three men represented individualism as against the solid anonymity of the massed Brownshirts; they stood for leadership as against the blind obedience of the people. The silence became almost unendur-

54

able, and it was a relief when Hitler returned to the presidential stand and broke into one of his impassioned speeches that "the Brown Army must march again, as it has marched in the past, if Bolshevism raises its challenging head in Germany or on Germany's frontiers." The meeting closed with still another ritual—the consecration of rows of new banners by the touch of Hitler and the "Blood Banner" of 1923.[3]

That Sunday afternoon every Brownshirt and every Black Guard in Nuremberg filed past Hitler in the central square of the town. For five and a half hours they marched in columns of twelve, and the whole time Hitler stood erect, punctiliously acknowledging every salute and never showing fatigue. Göring obtained relief by leaning against the side of Hitler's car, and the standard-bearers had to be relieved every half-hour, but Hitler went on to the end—and then dashed away to other lectures and a round of committee meetings. Anybody doubting his physical strength need only look at his list of engagements that day.

The files seemed interminable . . . . old Storm Troopers from all over Germany, the new Kraftwagen Corps with sinister black helmets (like figures from a future mechanical world), the permanent soldiers of the Brownshirt staff corps . . . and S.S. men in their striking black uniforms. All of them goose-stepped past Hitler, the younger men with military precision, their elders more raggedly. . . .

On the last day came the eagerly expected military display, the second of its kind. Ordinary Germans bought tickets for anything up to forty marks each, and the supply was exhausted days before the Rally commenced. Six hundred aeroplanes zoomed down to Hitler's box with deafening roars (but none engaged in any stunts or aerobatics), and then the great silver Zeppelin dipped its front in salute and rested motionless over the stadium. Mock aerial fights took place, the aim being to demonstrate the efficiency of the new anti-aircraft guns. Then a review was held of all ranks of the army, and with almost unpleasant realism a prolonged battle took place in the arena, to show how the new mechanized divisions could storm a defended post. The noise was deafening, the fight terribly real. . . . For hours that afternoon, Nuremberg had all the experience of war, except for the ambulances and the burying-squads. A rally has no time for that side of war.

So the week closed—a triumph of organization and showmanship. A million and a quarter visitors were crammed into a town of 400,000 people, and every man—indeed, every guest—was moved about as if he were under orders. In fact, it was said that, amongst its many purposes, the Party Rally was a miniature mobilization. As a display of mass organization and as a colourful spectacle, the Rally could scarcely be surpassed; but, as one left Nuremberg with Hitler's closing speech against the Bolsheviks ringing in one's ears, one wondered about many

[3] Beer Hall Putsch banner.

things. One felt deadened by the endless reiteration of a few simple motives. Everything was hammered in at a relentless pace, until one craved for solitude and quietness. Undoubtedly this was a new Germany one was seeing, with a new kind of patriotism; but the values, clad with mysticism and pseudo-religious ceremonies though they were, made one conscious of an impassable mental gulf between Nazi Germany and the outside democracies. But Hitler is so certain of his movement that he has renamed Nuremberg "the City of the Rallies," and decreed in 1933 that the *Partei-Tag*[4] was to be held there for all time. . . . Nuremberg, with its fantastic medieval survivals, goes back to the beginnings of Germany; Hitler plans to make it the permanent visible expression of the Party Rally. This linking of past and future is typical of the movement.

# A Nazi Views the Nuremberg Rally, 1936

. . . We have witnessed many great march-pasts and ceremonies. But none of them was more thrilling, and at the same time more inspiring, than yesterday's roll call of the 140,000 political wardens, who were addressed by the Fuehrer at night, on the Zeppelin Meadow which floodlights had made bright as day. It is hardly possible to let words describe the mood and strength of this hour.

Twilight covers the Zeppelin Meadow as we enter the grandstand. It is only on the outer limits of the field that a sea of light envelops the walls formed by the flags of the movement, which extend and shine for miles into the dark evening. Twenty straight columns cut across the square of the Zeppelin Field; they are the 140,000 political wardens, who have formed ranks in rows of twelve. Innumerable swastika flags flutter in the light evening breeze, torn from the darkness by the floodlights, and providing a sharp contrast to the pitch black nocturnal sky. The Zeppelin Field proves to be too small. The stands will not hold the vast stream of people who are moving in without pause.

The students of Castle Bird Song[1] march in. The popular name for

[4]Annual Nazi Party Day.
[1]*Ordensburg Vogelsang:* these castles, named and patterned after those of the medieval Teutonic order, were élite schools for training future Nazi leaders.

From *The Nazi Years, A Documentary History* edited by Joachim Remak.

them is the bird singers. They are perfectly in step; alignment and general bearing are flawless. Then these very best of the party's new generation take up their position in front of the grandstand.

A distant roar becomes stronger and comes even closer. The Fuehrer is there! Reich Organizational Leader Dr. Ley[2] gives him the report on the men who are standing in parade formation. And then, a great surprise, one among many: as Adolf Hitler is entering the Zeppelin Field, 150 floodlights of the Air Force blaze up. They are distributed around the entire square, and cut into the night, erecting a canopy of light in the midst of darkness. For a moment, all is deathly quiet. The surprise still is too great. Nothing like it has ever been seen before. The wide field resembles a powerful Gothic cathedral made of light. Bluish-violet shine the floodlights, and between their cone of light hangs the dark cloth of night. One hundred and forty thousand people—for it must be that many who are assembled here—cannot tear their eyes away from the sight. Are we dreaming, or is it real? Is it possible to imagine a thing like that? A cathedral of light? They do not have much time to pursue such thoughts, for a new spectacle is awaiting them. It is perhaps even more beautiful and compelling for those whose senses can embrace it.

Dr. Ley reports the march-in of the colors. Nothing is to be seen yet. But then they emerge from the black night—over there, on the southern edge. Seven columns of flags pour into the spaces between the ranks. You cannot see the people, you do not recognize the bearers of the flags. All you can see is an undulating stream, red and broad, its surface sparkling with gold and silver, which slowly comes closer like fiery lava. You sense the dynamics contained in this slow approach, and receive a small impression of the meaning of these sacred symbols. Twenty-five thousand flags, that means 25,000 local, district, and factory groups all over the nation who are gathered around this flag. Every one of these flag bearers is ready to give his life in the defense of every one of these pieces of cloth. There is not one among them to whom this flag is not the final command and the highest obligation.

The last flag has entered the field. The 140,000 are submerged in a sea of glistening tips, which resemble a dense abatis; to penetrate it can bring nothing but death.

The song that contains the oath rises up into the infinite cone of light. It is sung by the Castle students. It is like a great devotion, for which we are all met here, to collect new strength. Yes, that is what it is. A devotional hour of the Movement is being held here, is protected by a sea of light against the darkness outside.

The men's arms are lifted in salute, which at this moment goes out to

[2] In addition to heading the German Labor Front, Robert Ley was the organizational director of the Nazi party.

57

the dead of the Movement and of the War. Then the flags are raised again.

Dr. Ley speaks: "We believe in a Lord God, who directs us and guides us, and who has sent to us you, My Fuehrer." These are the final words of the Reich Organizational Leader; they are underlined by the applause that rises from the 150,000 spectators and that lasts for minutes. . . .

# The Making of an SS Man[1]

*The memoirs of an ex-Waffen SS provides a characteristic example of the military training . . .*

There was a special method of humiliating a man. If anyone, while filling cartridges into a charger, let a cartridge fall to the ground, he had to pick it up with his teeth. I made up my mind that I would not do that. They can do what they like with me, I said, but I will not pick up a cartridge with my teeth; I shall use my hand. Naturally I took care not to let the situation arise and determined to do everything I could not to let a cartridge fall to the ground. One day of course it happened. On these occasions no one gives an order; the N.C.O.[2] simply turns down his thumb and the man concerned knows what he has to do. In my case of course he turned down his thumb—and I bent down and picked the cartridge up with my hand. He rushed at me like a wild animal, stuck his face close up to mine so that there was hardly an inch between his nose and mine and bellowed whatever came into his head. Of course I could not understand a word because he was bellowing so loud that he was choking. Eventually I gathered that he was yelling: "Have you forgotten what to do?" When he had finished bellowing he handed me over to the deputy section commander who made me do a ten-minute "showpiece". That's a long time when you're at the double all the time. And it's embroidered with all the usual well-known "additions". After such a chasing your shirt is wringing wet. Then the deputy commander handed me back to the commander himself. His first order was: "Chuck that cartridge away." I was not

[1]The SS was an exceedingly complex organization exercising supreme authority over police, criminal, and secret service; complete control over the concentration camps, and they were also soldiers in the German armies. The latter were known as the Waffen SS (armed forces).
[2]commanding officer.

From *Anatomy of the SS State, Part III, Command and Compliance* by Hans Buchheim.

ready for that. I was practically all in. I threw the cartridge away; it fell some six feet away from me—and he turned his thumb down once more. I hesitated for a second. Seeing this he came up to me. I was almost at the stage of picking it up with my teeth. But then—I just wasn't thinking and I don't know why—again I picked up the cartridge with my hand. That was it! He went scarlet, bellowed out something unintelligible, handed the section over to his deputy and took me on himself. He began with fifty "knees-bend" with rifle held out at arm's length. I had to count out loud. I was fairly fit and I had got used to anything here, but to be asked to do fifty knees-bend with your rifle held out in front of you, following ten minutes "showpiece" which has left you little better than a jelly—that's a tall order. I'm not saying that it's physically impossible. The only question is whether one is ready for it mentally. And this was what happened. After twenty knees-bend I stopped counting. I just couldn't go on. I did one more knees-bend and then I lowered my rifle and stood up. I can't say that I thought this out; I just knew that I was all in. I heard him bellowing all over again but that left me cold because suddenly I could control myself no longer. I felt I had to weep although I knew that it was neither manly nor soldierly. I couldn't answer his questions because I was so shaken with sobbing that I couldn't speak. I was not in a rage and I was not in pain. I had just had enough. When he saw that he bellowed: "Look at this!" and then: "Mollycoddle! Mother's little darling! Crybaby! Who's ever heard of an SS man blubbering! All our dead will turn in their graves! Is this what we're trying to take to war—etc. etc." Then "assembly" was blown and the training period ended. He ordered me to clean out all the first floor latrines for a week and then report to him so that he could inspect them. And straightaway he ordered: "Chuck this cartridge away." I did so and then without even waiting or looking to see whether he had turned his thumb down I picked it up with my teeth.

# The Fuehrer Bequeathed to Me by the Lord

The new God, in which German youth were to believe, manifested himself in these "invocations" which children in Cologne were instructed to recite at the children's lunch program:

From *Nazi Culture* edited by George L. Mosse.

Before Meals:

> *Fuehrer, my Fuehrer, bequeathed to me by the Lord,*
> *Protect and preserve me as long as I live!*
> *Thou hast rescued Germany from deepest distress,*
> *I thank thee today for my daily bread.*
> *Abideth thou long with me, forsaketh me not,*
> *Fuehrer, my Fuehrer, my faith and my light!*
> Heil, mein Fuehrer!

After Meals:

> *Thank thee for this bountiful meal,*
> *Protector of youth and friend of the aged!*
> *I know thou hast cares, but worry not,*
> *I am with thee by day and by night.*
> *Lie thy head in my lap,*
> *Be assured, my Fuehrer, that thou art great.*
> Heil, mein Fuehrer!

---

# "O, To Be Part of the Hitler Youth Movement!"

---

One morning, on the school steps, I heard a girl from my class tell another: "Hitler has just taken over the government." And the radio and all the newspapers proclaimed: "Now everything will improve in Germany. Hitler has seized the helm."

For the first time politics entered our lives. Hans at that time was fifteen years old; Sophie was twelve. We heard a great deal of talk about Fatherland, comradeship, community of the Volk, and love of homeland. All this impressed us, and we listened with enthusiasm whenever we heard anyone speak of these things in school or on the street. For we loved our homeland very much . . . And every square foot of it was well known and very dear to us. Fatherland—what else was it but the greater homeland of all who spoke the same language and belonged to the same people! We loved it, but were hardly able to say why. Until

---

From *Nazi Culture* edited by George L. Mosse.

that time we had never lost many words over it. But now it was written large, in blazing letters in the sky. And Hitler, as we heard everywhere, Hitler wanted to bring greatness, happiness, and well-being to this Fatherland; he wanted to see to it that everyone had work and bread; he would not rest or relax until every single German was an independent, free, and happy man in his Fatherland. We found this good, and in whatever might come to pass we were determined to help to the best of our ability. But there was yet one more thing that attracted us with a mysterious force and pulled us along—namely, the compact columns of marching youths with waving flags, eyes looking straight ahead, and the beat of drums and singing. Was it not overwhelming, this fellowship? Thus it was no wonder that all of us . . . joined the Hitler Youth.

We were in it heart and soul, and could not understand why our father did not happily and proudly say "yes" to it all. On the contrary, he was quite opposed to it and on occasions he would say: "Don't believe them; they are wolves and wild beasts, and they are frightfully misusing the German people." And on occasions he compared Hitler with the Pied Piper of Hamelin, who enticed the children with his pipe to follow him into perdition. But Father's words were lost in the wind and his attempts to hold us back came to naught in the face of our youthful enthusiasm.

We went with our comrades of the Hitler Youth on long hikes . . . We marched long and strenuously, but we did not mind; we were much too enthusiastic to admit fatigue. Wasn't it wonderful suddenly to have something in common, a bond with other young people whom otherwise we might never have come to know? In the evenings we met at the den, and someone would read, or we sang, or played games and did craft work. We heard that we should live for a great cause. . . . We believed ourselves to be members of a great, well-ordered organization which embraced and esteemed everybody from the ten-year-old boy to the adult man. We felt we were part of a process, of a movement that created a people out of a mass. Certain matters that seemed senseless or left us with a bad taste would eventually adjust themselves—or so we believed. One day, after a long bike tour, as we were resting in our tents under an immense starry sky, a fifteen-year-old classmate said to me unexpectedly: "Everything would be fine—but this business about the Jews, I can't swallow that." The girl leader said Hitler must know what he was doing and that for the sake of the greater cause one had to accept what seemed to be difficult and incomprehensible. But the other girl was not entirely satisfied with this answer; others agreed with her and suddenly one could hear in them the voices of their parents. It was a restless night in the tent, but eventually we became too tired to stay awake. . . .

In our groups we held together like close friends. The comradeship was something very beautiful.

61

Hans had assembled a collection of folk songs, and his young charges loved to listen to him singing, accompanying himself on his guitar. He knew not only the songs of the Hitler Youth but also the folk songs of many peoples and many lands. How magically a Russian or Norwegian song sounded with its dark and dragging melancholy. What did it not tell us of the soul of those people and their homeland!

But some time later a peculiar change took place in Hans; he was no longer the same. Something disturbing had entered his life. It could not be the remonstrances of his father—no, because to them he simply played deaf. It was something else. His songs were forbidden, the leader had told him. And when he had laughed at this, they threatened him with disciplinary action. Why should he not be permitted to sing these beautiful songs? Only because they had been created by other peoples? He could not understand it, and this depressed him, and his usual carefree spirit began to wane.

At this particular time he was given a very special assignment. He was to carry the flag of his troop to the party's national rally at Nuremberg. He was overjoyed. But when he returned we hardly dared trust our eyes. He looked tired, and on his face lay a great disappointment. We did not expect an explanation, but gradually we learned that the youth movement which there had been held up to him as an ideal image was in reality something totally different from what he had imagined the Hitler Youth to be. There drill and uniformity had been extended into every sphere of personal life. But he had always believed that every boy should develop his own special talents. . . . But in Nuremberg everything had been done according to the same mold. There had been talk, day and night, about loyalty. But what was the keystone of all loyalty if not to be true to oneself? . . .

One day he came home with another prohibition. One of the leaders had taken away a book by his most beloved writer, *Stellar Hours of Mankind* by Stefan Zweig.[1] It was forbidden, he was told. Why? There had been no answer. He heard something similar about another German writer whom he liked very much. This one had been forced to escape from Germany because he had been engaged in spreading pacifist ideas.

Ultimately it came to an open break.

Some time before, Hans had been promoted to standard-bearer. He and his boys had sewn themselves a magnificent flag with a mythical beast in the center. The flag was something very special: it had been dedicated to the Führer himself. The boys had taken an oath on the flag because it was the symbol of their fellowship. But one evening, as they stood with their flag in formation for inspection by a higher

[1]Stefan Zweig (1881–1942), the popular essayist and novelist, was both a liberal and a Jew. He committed suicide in exile.

leader, something unheard-of happened. The visiting leader suddenly ordered the tiny standard-bearer, a frolicsome twelve-year-old lad, to give up the flag. "You don't need a special flag. Just keep the one that has been prescribed for all." Hans was deeply disturbed. . . . Didn't the troop leader know what this special flag meant to its standard-bearer? . . .

Once more the leader ordered the boy to give up the flag. He stood quiet and motionless. Hans knew what was going on in the little fellow's mind and that he would not obey. When the high leader in a threatening voice ordered the little fellow for the third time, Hans saw the flag waver slightly. He could no longer control himself. He stepped out of line and slapped the visiting leader's face. From then on he was no longer the standard bearer.

# The New Generation

*SS officer Peter Neumann wrote a personal history of his experiences in a book called* The Black March. *Here we are introduced to his family . . .*

Several months ago Lena got to know a young Untersturmführer of the SS. Since then she has never stopped talking about his physical, esthetic and moral qualities, "like a Greek God" and so on . . . Briefly, she went completely crazy about him.

One day . . . she suddenly decided to introduce this paragon to my father . . . Heinrich Griessling, SS of Hitler's regiment and personal bodyguard, seemed very much at home. Smiling and sure of himself, he swaggered in, bowed to Mutti (mother), gave his hand to my father, and deigned to honor Klaus (brother) and me with a nod . . . Without beating about the bush, he explained to my father that during the last three months he had the opportunity of summing up Lena's good and bad qualities, that on the whole he found that the former outnumbered the latter, and that he had the honor, therefore, to ask for her hand in marriage . . . He also added that this union would be a very auspicious one, since it would conform to the marriage ethics of National Socialism. . . .

To conclude this strange interview, he announced that he would return in three days' time to learn of my father's decision. But he remarked that Lena and he could dispense with his approval if need be

From *The Black March, The Personal History of an SS Man* by Peter Neumann.

. . . As soon as he stalked out we all stared at Lena. Lena with a nasty expression and in a bantering tone, said, "Actually, if all men were like him . . . life would be very much simpler. The Fuehrer wouldn't find it such hard work building the new Germany . . . Heinrich knows what he wants. Me, too! I love him; that's fair enough. There's no need for a long discussion or an interminable engagement!"

"But do you know him at all well?" ventured Mutti. "Do you know what sort of a man he is and if he's capable of making you happy? This job of his, for instance—what does he do exactly?"

"His job?" said Lena icily. "His job is to protect the Fuehrer and the great Nazi Reich! Isn't that enough?"

My father muttered something about her being an idiotic child, or else a fallen woman. To put an end to the discussion, he said that before going any further he would make some discreet inquiries about Griessling.

Unfortunately these inquiries did not produce very favorable results for the Untersturmführer . . .

[Papa Neumann learns that Griessling is a drunkard and a murderer.] In a pogrom in East Prussia . . . his specialty was children. He did not miss them. On the pretext . . . that they were trying to escape, he shot them down with prolonged bursts of fire, spraying the Jews' houses with his submachine gun.

When the operation was over, a large part of the Talmud brigade found itself in paradise. Those who remained alive were shipped off to the concentration camp at Schneidemühl.

Next day Griessling was promoted to Hauptscharführer and, a month later to Untersturmführer.

On reflection, I don't know what to think of this type of disciplinary operation.

Alfred Rosenberg proved in the *Myth of the 20th Century* that the Jews have done great harm to Germany and to the whole of Europe.

The Fuehrer was the first man in the world really to react, with force, against the Jewish menace.

I am convinced that it is essential for our future to eliminate the Jews from certain professions and to prevent them from obtaining control in matters vital to our country.

But I have never understood the use or value of such disciplinary operations and executions.

However, the Fuehrer, who has already demonstrated again and again that he is rarely deceived, doubtless has valid reasons for giving such orders.

I read somewhere that it is necessary for the strength and power of a régime that its goal should not be represented by a purely abstract ideal, but should be made concrete by some especially vulnerable element which may be attacked and easily destroyed.

This spurs on the partisans of the régime and neatly canalizes their hatred.

If this is so, this role would suit the Jews admirably.

All this, however, is of little interest to me.

To return to Heinrich Griessling and my father, I think it would be superfluous to state that Papa Neumann was not overflowing with enthusiasm when he learned that his future—and how!—son-in-law was not the innocent, pure young man that he had hoped for.

It was a noncommissioned officer at the Ludendorff Barracks who told him all this about Heinrich. This worthy soldier added that in his opinion Untersturmführer Griessling was a real hero, with a brilliant future ahead of him. . . .

But you should have heard Papa when he returned that evening! As soon as he saw Lena he went for her, bellowing like a madman, "Never, do you hear! I'll never give my daughter to a murderer!"

Lena went white and drew herself up quickly, rocking the chair on which she had been seated.

"Heinrich, a murderer?"

"He's a foul criminal, that's what he is! A disgusting killer! He has a terrible reputation for cruelty, after that Jewish business at Allenstein. . . . Kirnste told me all about it! And you want me to let you marry this—this sadist who enjoys nothing better than massacring children! You'd like an orange-blossom wedding, I expect. . . . And why not get the brothers and sisters of the kids he murdered to carry your train? And then you can lie beside him in bed all night, and he can give you the gory details! Telling you who he's been murdering all day?"

"Shut up, Father, or I'll *make* you keep quiet," snapped Lena.

Father gazed at her incredulously, uncomprehending. Painfully he gasped out the words, "My own daughter's no better than filth! My daughter. My children . . . They're rotten! They're not human beings any longer!"

I remember that I got up, clenching my teeth. There are some things one will not put up with, even from one's own father.

But before I had time to do anything, he had slapped Lena's face, hard.

My sister did not react. She said nothing. She picked up her coat, went out and slammed the door behind her.

I told Father he had done wrong. He stared at me wildly, as though he did not understand, and then suddenly fell against the corner of the table, sobbing.

I believe that I should have despised him less if he had not given way to this stupid outburst of bourgeois sentimentality.

An hour later Lena returned. She was accompanied by Heinrich.

The Untersturmführer did not greet anyone as he came in. He was

65

furious, and there was a strange expression on his face. His jaw was thrust forward as though he longed to kill somebody.

Without a word he crossed the living room, took a chair and sat down upon it astride. He looked around the room; then his gaze rested on Father. He said, "This is a very tedious business, Herr Neumann. Your daughter has just revealed to me that you are a bad German. You have gravely insulted me and our Fuehrer. That is both unwise and dangerous. Especially coming from a man like yourself."

His eyes rested for a moment on Lena before he went on.

"Your daughter, most fortunately, is a good citizen and was at pains to inform me of something which my superiors . . . will be most interested to learn."

He began to smile slightly.

"There was certainly a slight omission on your part when you filled in your paper this year. Actually you were involved in extremist activities in 1932. You were a member of the Red Front, I believe?"

Father turned toward Lena and stared at her as though he were seeing her for the first time. Then his face hardened.

"Let's get to the point," he muttered. "What do you want?"

"Nothing, Herr Neumann. Nothing at all," replied Griessling. "Only I am rather uncertain as to what the consequences of an inquiry by the State Police might be, unless, of course—"

Father interrupted. "Never, do you hear? You'll never get Lena as long as I'm alive. Even if it means my death."

Heinrich got up at once. His expression was now very unpleasant. "It'll mean your death all right, Herr Neumann; you'll die. Yes, you can take my word for that."

He marched off without another word, taking Lena with him.

Father said nothing; he went up to his room, his shoulders hunched.

Mutti murmured in tones of horror, "Betrayed by his own daughter! Oh, my God, it can't be true!"

She also went upstairs a few minutes later.

Personally, I was very surprised. I was quite unaware that my father had ever been involved in extremist activities. Lena must have learned all this in confidence from Mutti.

But how strange it all is. I cannot imagine him fighting on the barricades! With his mean little life as a railway official, it must have been a sort of revolt, a strange reflex action against a pointless and sterile existence. The Reds certainly crossed his path at the right time and pinned him, like so many others, like a ridiculous butterfly on the great chart of their anarchistic struggles to destroy Germany.

But what had they hoped to achieve, the fools!

The Reich at that time had been in a state of complete chaos and total disorganization. The SA represented the only element of stability upon which we, the German people, were able to lean. As for the Reds, they had had their day.

Disorder, injustice, misery, the breakup of individual lives and of the nation, lies and corruption. . . . That is what they had brought us.

In 1923 the Germans were quite ready to trust a régime which would bring them, now that the war was over, not happiness—that would be asking too much—but a simple assurance of peace and security for the future.

Instead, those people, who talked of nothing but equality, who literally choked themselves with the violence of their insane shouting, bellowing slogans about fraternity and socialism, thought of nothing save how best to fill their own pockets at the expense of the community . . .

The mass of the people were even more wretched, debased and despised than they had been under the Hohenzollerns.

Every sensible German knows that the Jews and the Communists can only bring us ruin and decay, and the inevitable death of our German inheritance.

Only decadent peoples, brutalized by idiotic propaganda, could possibly observe our devotion to our Fuehrer open-mouthed, as though it were something horribly abnormal. The Fuehrer has given us back our faith in a Greater Germany and a better future. Only degenerates can be surprised by our love and trust, by our determination to follow him and to help him turn the pages of our history more quickly so that we may see the results in our own lifetime. . . .

No, I certainly cannot believe that my father was right.

He was mistaken, perhaps. But in some very important matters one is not allowed to make mistakes. He must accept the just punishment for his stupidity and errors. It is sometimes hard to have to reason like this about the persons who brought you into the world, but I do consider of all human contingencies the only one which counts is the triumph of National Socialism. It is only logical that everything must bow before its laws.

Father was arrested three days later by the Gestapo.

Heinrich and Lena were married a month after that.

# Readings

*The Order of the Death's Head* by Heinz Hohne (Coward-McCann, 1970), is well researched and comprehensive from the beginning of the formation of the SS to its end.

*Anatomy of the SS State* (Walker Publishing Company, 1968), is an authoritative work written originally in German by four leading German historians. It discusses the persecution of the Jews, the SS, the concentration camps, and mass execution of the Soviet Russian prisoners of war.

*Gestapo, Instrument of Terror* by Edward Crankshaw, (Viking Press, 1956), is a history of this dreaded organization.

*The Gestapo* by Jacques Delarue (Dell, 1965), integrates the story of the organization with the rise and fall of the Third Reich.

*The Waffen SS: 1939–1945* by George H. Stein (Cornell University Press, 1966), is the factual presentation of Hitler's elite guard at war. Founded as an instrument to terrorize, it became a crack armed force that participated vigorously in the war.

*Waffen SS, The Asphalt Soldiers* by John Keegan is one of a series in the Ballantine's Illustrated History of World War II — paperback series.

*Hitler's SS* by Richard Grunberger is one of a series in the illustrated Pageant of History (Dell Publ.).

*Himmler* by Alan Wykes is part of a series in the *War Leaders* (in Ballantine's Illustrated History of the Violent Century).

*Hitler Youth: The Duped Generation* by H. W. Koch (Ballantine's Illustrated History of the Violent Century, 1972). Recommended.

*I Was There* by Hans Peter Richter (Dell Paperback, 1972), is a personal chronicle by a Hitler Youth from the exhilarating beginnings to the nightmarish disillusions.

# 5.

# FORESHADOWING OF DOOM: FROM BOYCOTT DAY TO *KRISTALLNACHT* (1933-38)

When Hitler came to power on January 30, 1933, he unleashed his private army of some four million storm troopers (SA), who took all his promises and threats in dead earnest. To them, Hitlerism was a full-blown ideology, a way of life. They were now eager to share in the spoils and waited to be appointed to positions which had been vacated by the Jews, communists, and opponents of Nazism. They expected to be able to seize the shops and homes owned by Jews. But the newly appointed Chancellor was not as unrestrained as they had anticipated. He had to consider the Reichswehr, with its officer corps and the generals who rejected amalgamation with the SA. He had to consider the supreme authority, President Hindenburg, the industrialists and financiers, the large number of conservative citizens, and the outside world. In short, Hitler knew that if he let the SA loose, a counterrevolution would ensue. On the one hand, terror kept his opponents from organizing against him. On the other hand, the SA had to be controlled and directed or it would undermine his entire government. An understanding of this dilemma explains the position of the Jews in Germany from 1933 to 1938.

The SA, spoiling for blood and booty, had carried out sporadic boycotts and acts of violence against the Jews. Between 1923, when the SA was founded, and 1932, its members had desecrated over 50 synagogues and 128 Jewish cemeteries. It was one thing for Hitler, when chief of the party, to incite his followers to acts of violence; but it was quite another

69

for him as Reich Chancellor openly to condone such barbaric acts. Unwilling to curb the SA completely, he decided to placate the mobsters by calling a nationwide anti-Jewish boycott to be "controlled" by a committee appointed by himself, with Julius Streicher as chairman.

The boycott, beginning on April 1, 1933, was the first open, official, nationwide attack against the Jews by the Reich. It marked the first phase of the Holocaust. Storm troopers were stationed before some tens of thousands of Jewish shops and professional offices, such as those of doctors and lawyers, to terrorize customers and clients and prevent them from entering. They chanted in chorus the texts of notices plastered on the show windows: "Don't Buy from Jews," "Germany Awake," "Death to Judah," "The Jews Are Our Misfortune."

World reaction was hostile to Germany, especially in the United States and England, countries whose opinions Hitler was most sensitive to. Jews everywhere reacted with counter-boycotts. But this only provided the Nazis with visible "proof" of the sinister international Jewish plot against Germany.

The harmful effects of the boycott were no less serious on the Nazis and Germans than on the Jews. Hindenburg and the old guard were opposed to it; generally speaking, the people were apathetic, and some were downright against it. Hitler called off the boycott after three days, although originally it was to have been a continuous effort. Nevertheless, the outrages continued sporadically.

The German Jewish community faced reality squarely and began to organize for resistance and survival by setting up the Representative Council of Jews in Germany. Other agencies for mutual aid were formed, e.g., a Central Committee for Assistance and Rehabilitation—which retrained Jews displaced from their positions for new vocations, made loans, and set up professional bodies, such as the Doctors' Bureau, which helped physicians who were fired. Counteracting the Nazi slogan "Germans, Buy from Germans," Jews publicized to Jews, "Buy Only from Jews."

Jews were very concerned with assisting the small outlying communities, which were most exposed. Particularly noteworthy was the stiffening of their morale; "Say Yes to Judaism" was the theme that ran through many articles. The communities were galvanized into launching a dynamic program of studies, cultural and educational activities, for old and young. And, above all, every effort was made to get Jews out of the country. Between 1933 and 1938, 300,000 Jews emigrated, 40,000 died, and 160,000 were murdered.

The years following 1933, through the early part of 1936, were comparatively "quiet" years. Germany suffered from a bad name abroad and was sensitive to it. The Reich was in an economic depression. Its reserves in foreign currency, needed to buy the materials for rearmament, were dangerously low. Hindenburg and the conservatives remained a group to be reckoned with. The 1936 Olympic Games were scheduled in Germany, and Germany's face had to be cleaned up for the foreign visitors, and the world press and radio. The Nuremberg Laws were soft-pedaled. Jews began to breathe easier and to hope that the worst was over. Some who had fled returned, and many who were on the verge of emigration had second thoughts.

As late as August 1937, Zionist leader Arthur Ruppin noted in his diary,[1] "I had a talk with Rabbi Leo Baeck; he believes that 80 percent of the German people are against the persecution of the Jews, but they do not dare to voice their opinion." And again, in April 1938, Ruppin entered in his diary the observation that "the aged Rabbi Baeck maintains that 80 percent or 90 percent of the Christians are not anti-Semitic. Perhaps he has this impression because he relates mainly to those of his own generation, who remember the former high status of the Jews and can make comparisons. The post-war generation . . . which has been systematically taught to hate the Jews, has no such misgivings."

## THE NUREMBERG LAWS

In 1933, when Hitler assumed power, he began to institute oppression by legislation, and later, when the Reichstag was dissolved, by personal decree. Periodically, laws were passed driving Jews and anti-Nazis out of the civil service, the legal and teaching professions. Jewish doctors were expelled from the National Health Service. Jewish students were severely restricted from attending schools; those who did attend in the early Hitler years suffered from anti-Jewish hatred and were forced to study courses about their own people's baseness and degeneracy. Thousands of Jewish professionals, who had played prominent roles in the world of the cinema, theater, music, and the fine arts, were driven out of their positions, as were the Jews in the military organizations. The anti-Jewish legislation enacted "legally" by the Reichstag culminated in the racial laws of September 15, 1935, which were proclaimed at the annual Nuremberg party congress.

The Nuremberg Laws were the most crushing blow to German Jewry; they marked the beginning of the end. They defined the term "Jew" as one who was a descendant of at least three Jewish grandparents (full Jews and three-quarter Jews), or from two grandparents (half-Jews), if the Jew concerned belonged to the Jewish religious community as of September 15, 1935. A Jew was also one who was married to a Jew as of the above date or later, or the child of a marriage of three-quarter or full Jews after the above date. Jews were deprived of citizenship, dismissed from public

[1] Arthur Ruppin, *Memoirs, Diaries, Letters* (New York: Herzl Press, 1971), pp. 287, 293–94.

71

office and professions, and forbidden to marry or have sexual intercourse with Aryans (non-Jewish Germans).

They were prevented from shopping in food stores except for an hour a day. They were not admitted to hotels for lodging. Signs reading "Jews Forbidden to Enter" were posted in parks, amusement places, villages, museums, theaters, etc. The laws even affected Jewish veterans of World War I. Month by month the screws were tightened, and the policy became more and more comprehensive and systematized, as, for example, the forced sales of Jewish businesses (called "Aryanization"), the imposition of special property and income taxes, the blocking of bank accounts, the lowering of wages and food rations, the abolition of life-pensions, the restrictions in housing and travel, and the frequent renewal of identification cards. No less than four hundred anti-Jewish laws were decreed from 1935 on. On August 17, 1938, a list of 185 male and 91 female first names was published, from which Jews were required to select names for their newborn children. Those already born, and adults whose names were not distinctly Jewish, were required to adopt a middle name: males, Israel; females, Sarah. On the Day of Atonement (September 29, 1939), the holiest day of the Jewish year, Jews were ordered to surrender their radios. On September 1, 1941, all Jews were required to wear a six-pointed star of yellow cloth with black borders, equivalent in size to the palm of the hand, with the inscription *Jude* in block letters. The star was sewn to the left breast of the garment, and had to be worn visibly. Even as late as 1944, a law was decreed forbidding Jews from entering heated rooms during the winter. To cap it all, the Jews were compelled to publish, on their own, a periodical news sheet in which these regulations were printed and distributed.

The torrent of new orders continued almost to the time of Germany's surrender. Eventually, the few remaining Jews (by the Nazi definition) were required to give up all their gold and silver objects (except wedding rings), furs, woolen articles, bicycles, typewriters, and so on. Many were forced to move into "communal housing." Telephone connections were cut; public transport was forbidden without police permits; Jews had to stand in the streetcars, and they could not buy newspapers or books.

In the organized destruction of the Jews, the whole complex of German society was involved. Identifying the Jews, their dismissal from all professions, the cancellation of their pensions and insurance policies, the terrorization, the imprisonment, the slave labor, and the machinery for murder involved all the governmental departments. In the measured words of Robert H. Jackson, the American judge advocate at the Nuremberg Trials, "Germany became a gigantic torture chamber."

When Austria was annexed to the Reich in March 1938, all the laws decreed until then were automatically immediately imposed and brutally enforced on the 200,000 Jews of Austria. The same happened later in Czechoslovakia.

## *KRISTALLNACHT*

The assassination of the third secretary of the German embassy in Paris by Herschel Grynszpan sparked a nationwide pogrom. Grynszpan's action was a violent protest against the situation of his parents, who, with some seventeen thousand other Polish Jewish citizens living in Germany, had been expelled. Poland had refused to take them back, and they were now living in appalling conditions on the border between the two countries. The shooting was given the widest possible coverage by the Propaganda Ministry, headed by Josef Goebbels, and was portrayed in the news media as an act of war by the Jews against Germany. Pogroms broke out all over Germany. To their distress, the Jews found themselves defenseless and isolated; no world government or international agency intervened.

The night of November 10, 1938, went down in infamy as *Kristallnacht* (the Night of Broken Glass). The first report, submitted by Reinhard Heydrich, the SS commander in charge, noted that 191 synagogues were burned, and 76 completely demolished. Many Jewish community centers and cemetery chapels were set on fire. About twenty thousand Jews were arrested, thirty-six were killed, and thirty-six severely injured. Seven thousand Jewish businesses were destroyed. On each destroyed site was affixed a sign that read in part: "Death to International Jewry." All insurance claims paid to Jewish property owners were confiscated by the Reich. Further, the victimized owners were ordered to repair the damage at their own expense and to clear the rubble off the streets. But that was not all. Goering, speaking on the radio on November 10, declared, "For their abominable crimes the Jews must pay a collective fine of one billion marks." This money helped finance the huge rearmament program of the Reich.

The Nazi economy and image were badly hurt. The world press reacted with shock and revulsion at this new barbarism. Boycotts against German exports intensified and spread. The American ambassador in Berlin left in protest. The severe reaction of world opinion had some effects. Anti-Jewish excesses by the "mob" were curbed, and anti-Jewish measures were now planned more carefully, systematically, and surreptitiously. But they did not stop.

During and after the pogroms came arrests by the Gestapo. Between November and December approximately thirty thousand Jews were sent to concentration camps set up for Jews, liberals, and anti-Nazi suspects. These were the first official concentration camps, and they became the laboratories for perfecting torture and slaughter.

How did the average German react to the atrocities going on before his very eyes? What were the reactions of world leaders? William L. Shirer, radio commentator and European correspondent of leading American news media, writes in his outstanding work, *The Rise and Fall of the*

73

*Third Reich* (New York: Simon & Schuster, 1960), that when he came to take up his work in Germany in 1934, he was puzzled by the people, who did not mind being regimented to an extent they had never been before, and who seemed unconcerned that "so much of their culture had been destroyed." They seemed to support the Nazi regime with genuine enthusiasm. They all read the anti-Jewish signs; no one could plead ignorance of what was happening.

However, the new Germany seemed to have impressed some foreign leaders. David Lloyd George, Britain's Prime Minister during World War I, was duped, as were many of his colleagues. After a visit to Germany he wrote in the *London Daily Express* (November 17, 1936) that he was enchanted with Hitler, and described his regime as a miracle of achievement. Despite Hitler's cruel stamping out of all opponents, the Nuremberg Laws, etc., Lloyd George and other world-renowned personalities, such as Charles Lindbergh, the American poet Ezra Pound, and the Norwegian Nobel Prize laureate Knut Hamsun, showed enthusiasm for Hitler.

# "Sell Your Business Immediately Or Else"

*Douglas Miller, American emissary, sent a confidential report on the "aryaniza-tion" of German Jewish business firms through the U.S.A. Diplomatic Pouch which passed through untouched. He quoted the following letter received by a Jewish merchant.*

"Your letter of the 21st of this month to the chief of the Department of Egg Wholesalers, Eugen Fuerst, has been turned over to me with the request to give my opinion and prepare an answer.

"I wish to state, right now, that it is no part of the duties of the German Labor Front to give advice or guidance to non-Aryans. If, however, I do answer your letter, it is only in the interest of your employees, for I wish to prevent German fellow-countrymen from losing work and bread. For this reason I advise you to attempt to sell your business, i.e., to turn it over into Aryan ownership while this still remains possible; it is well known that with the existing shortage of

From *Via the Diplomatic Pouch* by Douglas Miller

supplies Aryan firms are given the preference in having their orders filled. In this way, it would also be made possible for your employees to continue receiving wages. Of course, I must reserve the right to withhold my approval of such a sale in order to make absolutely sure that the business actually becomes Aryan. Also, I must reserve my approval regarding the person of the buyer. It will not have escaped your notice that in recent times with the co-operation of the German Labor Front very many non-Aryan plants have been turned over to Aryan control, among them undertakings with a turnover amounting to millions.

"If today, in the entire country, the Aryan import trade and the Aryan wholesale trade refuse to sell to Jews, this is accounted for by various reasons, and there can be no possibility of raising a claim of interference in the business rights of non-Aryans. The unwillingness to deliver goods is based upon the fact that the present foodstuff trade is well aware that for military and political reasons this trade must be in Aryan hands. Furthermore, the supplies of fresh goods are actually very short and one cannot blame the trade if they think first of their Aryan customers. There is no sense in your pointing to the Nuremberg Laws and the regulations which have been published in connection with them. I refer you to the leading article in the *Voelkischer Beobachter* of November 22nd of this year, entitled 'Unwritten Laws.' In recent times it has been repeatedly stated by the Fuehrer and by other persons that the Party rules the State. If a member of the Party enters into business relations with a Jew, he incurs the danger of coming into conflict with the written and unwritten laws of the Party and accordingly of being called upon to assume the responsibility for his acts. Neither the Ministry of Economics, the Agricultural Ministry, the German Labor Front nor any other Government office can compel an Aryan importer or wholesaler today to sell goods to Jewish firms, particularly, in view of the above-mentioned facts.

"When you refer to the fact that you were a front fighter, let me remind you in this connection that this was the self-understood duty of every able-bodied man. I have become acquainted with your activities on the front and know that these did not continue for four years, even if you did wear a uniform of a front fighter for four years. Your main service was passed in Belgium behind the lines and in Berlin in the hospital service. You even had the opportunity during the war to look after your business in Berlin.

"Your wish to be allowed henceforth to receive goods cannot be granted on account of the reasons which I have just given. In the last paragraph of your letter you refer to the regulations regarding the citizenship laws of November 14th, 1935, as they affect Jewish officials who were front fighters. This law removes from public employment the last remaining Jewish front fighters, but all of them are to retain their pensions. But you were not an official but are in business for yourself, and revolutions have always had their effects upon certain types of business, and, in this particular case, upon non-Aryan firms in the foodstuff industry.

"I can only advise you to sell your business immediately, as long as it has any value at all; for when you have once lost your customers to those Aryan firms which are able to deliver goods, your business will depreciate or become completely valueless."

*"Signed:* Hoffheinz"

# The Yellow Star: Mark of Identification and Humiliation

*To identify, isolate, and expose the Jews, the Nazis especially revived the Yellow Star of the Middle Ages. Made of yellow material on a black background with the word "Jude" (Jew) in black lettering, it was required to be sewn and worn fully visible on the left breast of the outergarment by all Jews six years and over.*

*Inge Deutchkron recalled her experiences on the day the Yellow Star was introduced . . .*

Alice Licht was my friend. She was a very pretty girl of my own age. She had jet black hair with a centre parting, and was slim and dainty with the face of a spoilt doll. Her big, black eyes could bewitch any man who came near her—and did she know it!

On that morning—September 16—she came to call for me. We had decided to travel to work together. We were going to support each other; for on this particular day, for the first time, we were wearing the Magen David on the left side of our coats, above the heart, sewn on with fine stitches, all according to regulations.

'How do you feel?' I asked Alice.

'Just like you do.' She tried to laugh, but her charming child's face was a rigid mask behind which she endeavoured to hide her pain and humiliation.

'It's best for us just to make nothing of it,' I said. 'We'll pretend it's a decoration.'

'A decoration!' Alice laughed, but it was a grim laugh.

---

From *Out of the Night* by Michael Horbach.

## Foreshadowing of Doom

We went arm-in-arm from the Bayerischen Platz towards the underground station. My heart contracted, because I knew that on the train I'd see a young man who, every morning during the journey to work, used to give me appreciative glances. How would this fair-haired young man behave today? How would he react to the Jewish star?

'Better keep a stiff upper lip,' I said, and laughed. But it wasn't a natural laugh.

The train roared into the station and came to a halt; the doors opened with a hiss of compressed air and we got on.

Everyone looked at us; like every morning. Their gaze moved over our faces, our coats. Not an eye fixed itself on the star of David. It was as if we weren't wearing it at all.

There was my young man, too. He stood a couple of paces away from me; and smiled, as always.

I looked around me. I saw dozens of people also wearing the star of David—people one would never have taken for Jews; blond men, red-haired women, a white-haired old gentleman with the boldly etched features of a Viking.

All of them Jews; all wearing the yellow badge of shame which was to stamp them as pariahs.

But we were not pariahs.

Today, more than twenty years later and in the perspective of time, I can swear as I could have sworn then:

A secret, intangible, and yet immediately perceptible wave of sympathy flowed towards us from our non-Jewish fellow-citizens of Berlin.

One of the passengers made no bones about this sympathy. A middle-aged man, who got up from his seat.

'Please, young lady,' he said, pointing to his place.

'I'm not allowed to sit,' I said, and remained standing.

'But I insist,' he said, in the same polite tone.

I was not allowed to sit; Jews were not allowed to sit. But I could not draw attention to myself, either.

'Please,' said the gentleman, who had taken off his hat and now stood before me. 'Please sit down. Nothing will happen to you; I'll guarantee that. I offer you my protection.'

He said that so confidently that I could do nothing but sit down.

The young man who stood a short distance away smiled again. His smile said: All right, don't be afraid. It won't be all that bad. But we deceived ourselves, all of us; we Jews and those sympathetic Berliners in the underground that morning. It was going to be very bad for many millions of my co-religionists in Europe, and for millions of Germans, too.

The great massacre was just beginning.

In the period immediately after September 16 we experienced many instances of humanity on the part of non-Jewish Berliners. Now we realised, for the first time, that there was another Germany, not just that of the brown oppressors. Shopkeepers sneaked us food for free—vegetables, fruit, bread; and sometimes I found in my pocket cigarettes that someone had pushed in there furtively, in the underground crush. For a time I even received meat tokens regularly from some anonymous benefactor by post. I never found out who this friend in need was.

I was very young then, and despite the sympathy many people showed us, wearing the Jewish star got me into such a state of nervous hysteria that I simply couldn't bear it any more. Before we had to wear the yellow star we could still get round the curfew, which prevented Jews going out in the evening, now and again. That was over now. But fourteen days after the star was introduced I decided that I'd disguise myself at every favourable opportunity, no matter how severe the penalty. So from then onwards I always used to carry a second item of clothing in my briefcase, without the yellow star sewn on—a sweater, a blouse or a jacket, which I'd pull quickly over me in some doorway when no one was looking. In this way I could go to the theatre or cinema occasionally, or attend a concert or lecture from time to time. If I had been found out I'd have been deported to a concentration camp at once.

As I said, we lived in the Bayerischen Platz at the time. The journey to and from work took about an hour and a half. Not being able to sit in the tube added a lot to the burden of the hard work—ten hours of it—which I had to perform standing up. As for working conditions, they were particularly bad for Jews. In our factory (A.C.E.T.A.) the yellow star for Jews during working hours had already been introduced in 1940. Our rest-rooms with their rough wooden benches, and the toilets—naturally segregated from the 'Aryan' toilets—were extremely primitive. Any contact with 'Aryan' workers, male or female, was strictly forbidden, of course. For some unknown reason, too, we Jewish girls were subjected to regular gynaecological examinations by the factory doctor. I was just eighteen then!

I was constantly racking my brain for a means of escaping these humiliating surroundings, and the hard work which I just wasn't up to. I turned in my trouble to Mrs. Gertrude Prochownik, a former director of the Jewish Labour Information Bureau. She sent me to a Mr. Weidt, who ran a workshop for the blind in Rosenthaler Strasse. He employed, exclusively, Jewish blind people and deaf mutes.

Otto Weidt was a small man with a creased-up face; he was slim and fragile, but had a lion heart. He employed in his workshop, over the years, 165 physically handicapped Jews; he financed 56 Jews living "underground" and procured food and board and lodging for them.

The Gestapo came to search his house fifty-two times and he was arrested eleven times. Twenty-seven of "his" Jews survived the war. Inge Deutschkron was one of them.

Weidt did everything for "his" Jews. He employed far more of them than his little business could support financially; he negotiated, on behalf of others, with sympathetic firms ready to employ Jews on the quiet. Also, though Inge did not know it at the time, he hid a number of hunted Jews in a place behind the workshop.

The day Inge went to Weidt her right knee was swollen up through being on her feet constantly, and even the Nazi doctor at A.C.E.T.A. had to issue her with a certificate to the effect that she was no longer fit for standing work. Weidt, who was himself half blind, put on his blind armband and went with Inge to the Jewish labour office. He managed to convince the staff there that the young girl, since she was "of no earthly use to anyone else," would be best taken care of at his firm with the other physically handicapped. In the end Weidt got permission to engage her. At the time he didn't have a single vacancy she could fill; but he knew of a way out. He came to an arrangement with a firm in the same line—i.e., brush manufacture—that they should employ Inge, though Weidt would still carry her on his books. This job with the Meyer firm was, of course, illegal.

---

# The Burning of Books

*On May 10, 1933, in a plaza between the University of Berlin and the State Opera, Josef Goebbels and Alfred Rosenberg staged a medieval spectacle—the public burning of books written by Jews, Christian liberals, and humanitarians. The wife of the famous Edgar A. Mowrer, journalist and radio commentator, herself a writer, describes what she saw . . .*

When I revisited Berlin in 1935 a German official I had known for many years came to see me . . . He occupied a very important position, so he came well after midnight in the fashion of independent-minded Germans under the Nazis. My friend and I sat listening to him until nearly six in the morning, unaware of the passage of time, and it seemed as if he could not pour his words out fast enough. "You journalists," he said, turning accusingly to me, "for you

---

From *Journalist's Wife* by Lilian T. Mowrer.

the terror is no longer a 'front-page story.' I tell you that we Germans look back on those first months of Hitler's reign as paradise, compared with what we are going through now. . . ."

It exasperated me sometimes to hear people on a brief visit to the country, with official contacts only, deny the fact that anything unusual was happening. "But you *must* be exaggerating," they always argued, "everything is so calm here, there is no disorder, and the Germans are such pleasant people . . . how could they allow such things to happen?"

Obviously there was no outward change to be seen at that time; and it was hard enough for journalists, trained observers, to find out what was going on. The window-boxes were just as gay, the streets as smoothly polished; *Schupos* [police] controlled traffic with the same admirable precision; at railway stations, trains arrived and left on time; and hikers with packs on their backs walked happily through the countrysides.

Germans are among the most likable people in Europe and surely average no greater number of bullies and sadists than any other nation: the difference was that Hitler's régime was built on sadists and bullies, from the top down. Even had the rest of the population realized what was happening (and many were genuinely ignorant), there was little they could have done about it. Sentimentalists who talked glibly about the German people not wanting war, or anything else unpleasant, failed to understand the essence of the totalitarian state Hitler instituted. In the Third Reich the German People just did not count.

Yet living in the midst of these horrors, depressed by the daily recital of them, I still was not prepared for everything. I never believed there would be a Jewish boycott, until April 1 when I saw the bright yellow notices posted up over Jewish department stores, shops and offices of professional men, and those lines of SA's, with linked arms standing outside, bawling to bystanders to avoid these "places of shame."

Though for fourteen years the Nazis had whined about the humiliation of Versailles, they overlooked no opportunity of humiliating their "enemies."

Armed with my American passport, I pushed past these bullies and entered . . . a Jewish-owned concern, though few of the salespeople were Jews. The place was practically empty—the only customers, foreigners, like myself, protesting against the boycott. The salesfolk stood around, silent and miserable. I wanted to buy up everything in sight. All morning I shopped in Jewish places, and Edgar chose that day to go to his doctor to have the plaster and iron removed from his leg. The doctor looked like a ghost and hardly dared enter the consulting room.

Yet even after this shock, when Edgar came home and told me one day that there were to be public bonfires throughout the country, and that all "un-German" books were to be burnt, I thought that someone had taken him in.

"Oh, you *can't* cable a story like that," I protested, every instinct in me rising to defend these people among whom I had been so happy for so many years. "That must be some vile rumour."

"Sorry," said Edgar, "but I have just been talking to the man who is seizing the books for the Berlin *auto-da-fé*.[1] Want to meet him?"

He was one of those charming, blue-eyed, blond young giants whom tourists are so fond of quoting. He had the mind of a public schoolboy fired by the fanaticism of a Spanish Inquisitor, for I am convinced he really believed that the books he took from public and private libraries (with or without the consent of their owners) were detrimental to the German soul. True, he had not read many of them.

The evening of the bonfire, the Soviet Embassy gave a big party. Though no particular mention was made of the prospective holocaust, there was a prevailing atmosphere of smug superiority on the part of our hosts. "At least *we* did not burn books," they seemed to say.

About eleven o'clock we crowded to the front-room windows as the torchlight procession swept into sight. Thirty thousand university students and schoolboys marched down Unter den Linden brandishing fire and singing patriotic songs. At regular intervals in the parade were huge trucks loaded with books.

"There go the tumbrils [carts]," I said, and with most of the guests, we left the Bolsheviks and walked towards the great square between the Opera House and the new University auditorium. Many people had assembled to watch the ceremony, but not nearly as many as I had expected. Shame kept them indoors.

We cut through the crowd and stood by the great unlighted pyre erected in the middle of the square. Dr. Goebbels limped to the microphone and addressed the spectators. This was his particular show: he had organized it with his customary showman's eye, and was the only important member of the Government taking part in it. How triumphant he must have felt, burning Werfel, Schnitzler, Sternheim— he, the neglected author whose puerile play, *The Wanderer*, had been refused by every theatre in Germany between 1925 and 1930; who had not been able to obtain even a reporter's job on a Berlin daily under the Republic. He talked sarcastically of the "blight of internationally minded authors" and urged his hearers to foster "national culture." I held my breath while he hurled the first volume into the flames: it was like burning something alive. Then students followed with whole armfuls of books, while schoolboys screamed into the microphone their condemnation of this and that author, and as each name was mentioned the crowd booed and hissed. You felt Goebbels's venom behind their denunciations. Children of fourteen mouthing abuse of Heine!

[1] literally "act-of-faith," a public burning or execution in the days of the Inquisition

Erich Remarque's *All Quiet on the Western Front* received the greatest condemnation . . . it would never do for such an unheroic description of war to dishearten soldiers of the Third Reich.

The burning of the books affected me more deeply than anything else. I could not have been more shocked by the sight of martyrs at the stake, for although torturing prisoners was revolting enough, regimentation of the mind was ultimately more sinister, and the Nazis were beginning to apply their racial theories with ruthless efficiency. Every activity and association, even down to local chess clubs, had to be *gleichgeschaltet* (synchronized) and brought into line with the prevailing views.

# Journalist Bella Fromm Notes in Her Diary, Prelude to the November Pogroms

June 28, 1938. Another wave of Jew-baiting. Scenes of ferocity and misery are carved in my mind. My friend Mia, a member of the Diplomatic Corps, had warned me about it in one of our cryptic telephone conversations. We met and covered the town from end to end in my car. Mia had a cleverly camouflaged camera for obtaining evidence to be smuggled out of Germany.

The renowned old linen house of Gruenfeld was the first place we saw surrounded by a howling mob of SA men. Mia took a picture of them "working" on an old gentleman who had insisted on entering the shop.

We proceeded, finding the same thing going on everywhere. Varying only in violence and ignominy. The entire *Kurfuerstendamm* was plastered with scrawls and cartoons. "Jew" was smeared all over the doors, windows, and walls in waterproof colors. It grew worse as we came to the part of town where poor little Jewish retail shops were to be found. The SA had created havoc. Everywhere were revolting and bloodthirsty pictures of Jews beheaded, hanged, tortured, and maimed, accompanied by obscene inscriptions. Windows were

From *Blood and Banquets, A Berlin Social Diary* by Bella Fromm

smashed, and loot from the miserable little shops was strewn over the sidewalk and floating in the gutter.

We were just about to enter a tiny jewelry shop when a gang of ten youngsters in Hitler Youth uniforms smashed the shop window and stormed into the shop, brandishing butcher knives and yelling: "To hell with the Jewish rabble! Room for the Sudeten-Germans!"

The smallest boy of the mob climbed inside the window and started his work of destruction by flinging everything he could grab right into the streets. Inside, the other boys broke glass shelves and counters, hurling alarm clocks, cheap silverware, and trifles to their accomplices outside. A tiny shrimp of a boy crouched in a corner of the window, putting dozens of rings on his fingers and stuffing his pockets with wrist watches and bracelets. His uniform bulging with loot, he turned around, spat squarely into the shopkeeper's face, and dashed off.

The little old Jew kept his poise and tried to reassure *us*. "I am only glad that my wife died ten days ago. God spared her this ordeal. We have been starving for a long time. Business was dead. The law prevents us from getting out of a lease or dismissing an employee as long as a penny can be squeezed out."

I was worried about two old protégés of mine whom I had helped with little sums of money and food during the last two years. They had lost their two sons during the World War. Killed for Germany! We went to find out whether they had suffered.

Their shop was in ruins. Their goods, paper and stationery, trampled into the gutter. Three SA men, roaring with obscene laughter, forced the trembling old man to pick up the broken glass with hands that were covered with blood. We stood there, choking with rage, trembling in horror impotent and helpless.

Next day, when we returned to bring them food and see what else we could do to help them, we found two coffins surrounded by silent neighbors. The faces of the old couple seemed peaceful and serene amid the broken glass and destruction. As we put down our basket and stood there wretchedly, a young woman spoke to me. "It is better for them. They took poison last night."

A big department store near by had also been despoiled. It happened to belong to English Jews. Consequently, the municipal authorities were forced to remove the paint from the huge stone building. The less fortunate Jewish shop owners, of course, were left to scratch the filth off their walls as best they could. Whenever a boycott was "called off" they got just a couple of hours respite "to return their shops to the original state."

I deemed it wiser last week to stay away from home for a while, and went to spend some time with Aryan friends the key to whose house I have carried in my pocket for the last two years. My foreign friends informed me that non-Aryan drivers were dragged from their cars. They were taken to police stations and released after a day or two. Their cars were kept. People who had the slightest driving fine in their records, even years back, were kept under arrest. Some of the trials, I learned, surpassed the most vivid imagination. One of the most dreaded police sergeants opened each inquisition by barking: "Jewish swine, step back five meters from my desk, you stink foully."

# *Kristallnacht:* Pogrom in Emden

*A Youth Aliyah immigrant, aged sixteen, related this story to Norman Bentwich, prominent British Israeli jurist and writer.*

"Dead silence—not a sound to be heard in the town. The lamps in the street, the lights in the shops and in the houses are out. It is 3:30 a.m. Of a sudden noises in the street break into my sleep, a wild medley of shouts and shrieks. I listen, frightened and alarmed, until I distinguish words: 'Get out, Jews! Death to the Jews!' I jump out of bed and call my parents, who do not seem to have heard anything. I stop and listen. 'They' are at our neighbour's house. Suddenly I hear shots. . . . Then again: 'Death to the Jews!' What shall I do? In a second they will be here. Is there still a hope of escape? Perhaps I should try to crawl over the roof into the house of our Christian neighbours? They would not give me away. Or perhaps? . . .

"Fists are hammering at the door. The shutters are broken open. We can hear the heavy cupboards crashing to the floor; the whole house trembles and shudders. Two Storm Troopers rush upstairs, shouting at the top of their voices: 'Out with the Jews!' I run out of my room, and down the stairs. There I meet my parents, and silently we exchange a look. They shot at us from the street. We were forced to descend the steps during the shooting, my eyes looked straight into the guns. Fear left me. I knew there was no escape from the bullets. 'I am hit,' stammers my father, before he breaks down on the stairs. I am forced to go on, but I can see blood on the stairs and a dark stain on my

---

From *Jewish Youth Comes Home* by Norman Bentwich

father's back. My mother takes him back to the bedroom. I have reached the street, and one of the Storm Troopers holds me by the neck. The others rush upstairs and compel my mother, despite her pleading, to leave my father and come with them.

"We are led through the dark streets of Emden. Where are we going? We do not know. We pass the savages at work in all the Jewish houses. The sky reflects a red glare: our synagogue has been set on fire. We reach a big square lit up by searchlights and hemmed in by Storm Troopers. We were the first to arrive, but the square is gradually crowded. All our friends and relatives join us. Some are clad only in a coat, others are barefoot. A young woman whispers into my ear: Had I seen her husband who was separated on the way? I know the answer, but I did not reply. I had seen the Storm Troopers knock him down and torture him to death.

"Then I saw Troopers dragging my father to the square. Now and then he broke down, and every time they beat him until he got up and stumbled on. When he reached the centre of the square, he fell and remained lying on the ground, and they threw a sack over him. We were forced to follow the Troopers. One ordered us to form a circle round him, and shouted: 'Lie down! Get up!' And we had to obey.

"At seven the sun rose. Police appeared in the streets. There was great excitement among the population who went to their work. In front of every Jewish house that had been wrecked crowds were gathering. The police came to our square and called for the Jewish doctor to examine the wounded and bandage them. My father was wounded in the lungs, and the ambulance came to take him to hospital. The police behaved decently and assisted the Jewish doctor in his task. A little later men over sixty-five, women and children, were released. I was not among them, but when I said good-bye to my mother, she said: 'I am sure you will be home before night.' Then she left the square, alone.

"For us who remained a terrible day began, and it was followed by a more dreadful night. A group of men and boys, and I among them, were taken in to a big hall which was normally a gymnasium. During the night we had to lie on the floor and close our eyes. In the darkness Storm troopers sat round a big table. That was the 'Tribunal.' When one of us was called, he had to get up, walk over to the table, and answer every question. The 'Accused' was almost blinded by a powerful searchlight. One of my friends was called and accused of 'Rassen-schande.'[1] Judgment was passed: Death.

"Although we had been ordered to keep our eyes closed, I opened them from time to time to see what was happening. But I did not realise

---

[1] "race-violation"

that one of the Guards stood by my side. He shouted: 'Get up!' I went to the table, and the searchlight was directed on my face. It blinded me. My name was written down; then I was asked: 'Are you a student of the Talmud?' 'No.' 'Do you know the Talmud?' 'I know that there is a book called the Talmud. Its contents are not known to me.' 'Is it true that a sack of stones is put into the graves of your dead so that they may stone Jesus in the other world?' After that, I with others was taken into the yard. Again we were made to run in a circle, again they shouted: 'Get up, Lie down.'

"At seven next morning that was over. One of the Guards ordered us to lie down. He explained that soon some 'Gentlemen' would be arriving, and to their question how we had slept, we should answer: 'Very well.' Gestapo officers arrived. They asked us, and we replied as we had been instructed. Then we were marched to the railway station. During that time I had never lost my self-control, but when we passed the hospital where my father was dying, I could hardly keep going.

"It was Friday morning. All of us had had our last meal on Wednesday evening. We were taken by train to Oldenburg, and led through the streets of the town. The Hitler Youth were lined up and abused us as we marched. At midday we continued the journey to our unknown destination. Where will they take us? Everyone brooded over this question. All we knew was that we were going towards an ill fate.

"At eight in the evening, the train stopped. We could not see where we were. The Guards opened the doors, and ordered us to get out. As soon as some had left the train, we heard screams. Storm Troopers set upon all those who had got out, striking them with the butt-ends of their rifles. I hid in a corner of my compartment and waited. Outside hundreds of Storm Troopers had suddenly appeared out of the darkness. All the carriages were emptied. We were about two thousand Jews from our town, Bremen and Hamburg. A mad hunt began. We were driven to a forest-path, and forced to run as fast as we could. Those who stopped were beaten. We ran and ran, without seeing anything; we stumbled over roots, against the trees—we knew we ran for our lives. If one could not drag himself any further, if the beating was of no avail, he was thrown on a van.

"Suddenly, lights and searchlights in front of us. Crowds of Storm Troopers came towards us. We were driven through big gates, and found ourselves in a huge open space surrounded by high walls. Barbed wire on top of the walls, watch-towers in the four corners, Storm Troopers with machine-guns. We knew where they had taken us: to the concentration camp."

# *Kristallnacht:* Burning of Synagogues

In Dusseldorf, Rabbi Eschelbacher had just returned home at midnight on 9 November when the telephone rang: A voice, trembling with horror, shouted—"Rabbi, they're breaking up the synagogue hall and smashing everything to bits, they're beating the men, we can hear it from here." It was Mrs. Blumenthal who lived next door. . . . I was just about to go there, but almost at that very moment there was a violent banging at my own door. I switched off the light and looked outside. The square in front of the house was black with SA men. The next moment they were upstairs, pushing in the front door of the flat. The staircase swarmed with men, of all ranks. They rushed in on us shouting: "Revenge for Paris! Down with the Jews!" They pulled mallets out of their pouches and in a moment splintered glass flew from window-panes and mirrors, and splintered wood from the furniture. The gang came up to me with clenched fists, one of them got hold of me and ordered me downstairs. I felt certain I would be beaten to death. I went into the bedroom, put down my watch, wallet and keys and took leave of Berta.

Downstairs the street was full of SA men. Counting those in the house there must have been between fifty and sixty altogether. The shout met me: 'Give us a sermon!' I began to speak of the death of Vom Rath, saying that his murder was more of a misfortune for us than for the German people, that we were in no way guilty for his death. . . . On the corner, in the Stromstrasse, the street was covered with books that had been thrown out of the window, together with papers, documents and letters. The ruins of my typewriter were there also. . . . I myself was gripped by an SA man and hurled across the street against the house. . . . The party Kreisleiter [official] said to me: 'You are under arrest.' [Rabbi Eschelbacher was then escorted to Dusseldorf police headquarters by SA men who sang in unison "Revenge for Paris! Down with the Jews!" Passers-by joined in the chorus.]

From *Pogrom, November 10, 1938,* by Lionel Kochan

# Terror in Vienna

*Art critic and historian, Alfred Werner, recounts his experiences of the fall of 1938 in Vienna . . .*

Twenty years is a long time in a man's life, but the events of the fall of 1938 are burned into my memory. . . . On November 10, in the morning, on the way to a friend who lived in the center of the city, I happened to read at a newsstand the headlines of the *Neue Freie Presse,* one-time mouthpiece of liberalism (Theodor Herzl once belonged to its editorial staff). The "aryanized" paper reported the death of Herr vom Rath in inflammatory Jew-baiting language in the vein of Julius Streicher's notorious *Stuermer.*

Cautiously I watched the expressions of my neighbors. Apparently they were little influenced by the Nazi editorials. A Jewish lad had killed a petty official in Paris—so what? By that time, the Austrians were more concerned with the growing food shortage than with Nazi politics. But I found it advisable to postpone my visit and return home. I rushed to the nearest telephone booth to call up my friend.

My friend's wife talked very nervously. Jacob had gone to a grocer two hours ago but had not yet returned! I tried to comfort her as much as I could when a man peremptorily demanded that I leave the booth. "I am sorry," I said to him, "you have to wait until I've finished my call." He waited, hot with anger. "We are not in Paris, mind you!" he muttered threateningly, when I left the booth. He wore the badge of the veteran Party members.

I decided to go home. But after a few minutes I was stopped. "Are you a Jew?" The man who asked me this question had the look of a criminal; he wore no badge. Frequently Jews were robbed in the streets of Nazi Vienna in broad daylight. So intimidated were the Jews that they often did not dare to call for help.

I tried to elude the man by walking faster. He caught up with me. A short struggle ensued. People gathered around me. I found out what I should have known from the start: that not all Austrians were Nazi sympathizers. Although all of these people were wearing swastikas (for self-protection), they rallied to my aid, regarding my assailant as a common gangster. "Let him alone, at once!" they commanded my foe. But the latter scornfully shouted at the crowd: "Off with you—

From *Congress Weekly* (November 10, 1958)

Gestapo!" He took a badge out of his pocket. I had never seen such a stampede before. . . .

The Gestapo-man put handcuffs on me. I was dragged like a common criminal through the crowded streets of my native Vienna on that gloomy November day I shall never forget. We happened to cross the Judenplatz (Jews' Square) . . . Next we came to the Schulhof, so named because it had once been the site of the local synagogue. I glanced at a memorial tablet commemorating in corrupt medieval Latin the expulsion of the "Hebrew dogs" (in Jewish chronicles of the late Middle Ages, Austria is often referred to as *Eretz ha-damim,* the "Land of Blood"). With another glance I ascertained that the statue of Lessing, fighter for tolerance and a close friend of Moses Mendelssohn, was still there. . . .

Eventually I found myself in the cell of a police station along with fifty or sixty other Jewish men arrested in the streets like myself, or dragged from their shops or homes. Our number increased as every five or ten minutes another battered Jew was thrown into our already crowded cell.

It was two o'clock in the afternoon when we got some water but no food. Too exhausted for talk, we sat on the floor, or did whatever walking could be done in the small cell. Now and then a policeman came in. He would not tell us about the looting of the few remaining Jewish-owned shops, or the burning of the synagogues (of all this we were to learn much later). In fact, he tried to reassure us, but with little success. It was clear to us that he was uneasy and that he even felt ashamed.

At eleven P.M. stormtroopers arrived to take charge of us. We were herded into a dark prison van and driven to a Nazi barracks. On our arrival we had to run the gauntlet of a wild mob who beat us with sticks and iron bars. The first to enter the barracks was shot at once. On entering the hall, he had stumbled against a Nazi guard, and another Nazi, interpreting it as a hostile act, had pressed his trigger.

We spent the night in the pitch dark rooms of what had been a school house. No one slept since we could hear the turmoil going on in the street. At about 2 A.M. the noise gradually subsided, but few of us managed to fall asleep. We kept thinking: What will become of us? What has happened to our families?

Three or four persons went mad that night. A boy of eighteen tried to commit suicide by jumping out of the window. As his head smashed through the glass he was seized and pulled back by one of our men, a former police sergeant. The man was too late. The boy had cut one of the arteries of his neck and he died despite the frantic efforts of some doctors in our midst to stop the flood of blood.

During the seven days that followed we got, now and then, a few slices of black bread and some tea. The Nazis (some of them Germans, to

89

judge by their accents, but the majority Austrian riff-raff) played with us as nasty boys would play with their "pets." They did not allow us an hour of rest. Once a grim-faced man, a devil, entered our room, demanding that we should choose one among us who should pay with his life "for the sins of the others." We refused instantaneously and declared that we would rather all die than accept this demand. He was not satisfied with this offer. He chose a man himself, and we did not see the victim again.

Another Nazi singled out the youngest of our group, a boy of seventeen, put his revolver on the youngster's chest and barked: "Say your prayers!" The brave youth replied: "Shoot, you coward!" Whereupon the Nazi beast became so infuriated that he beat the youth with his revolver until his victim collapsed.

One evening—it was the last we were to spend in the barracks—all of us, several hundred people, were called from the classrooms into the big gym where one of the Nazis made a short speech:

"You have murdered Herr vom Rath," he shouted. "Every one of you is a Hershel Grynszpan. But our Fuehrer will destroy Jewry in all parts of the world, and not even your Jehovah will help you!"

Then we had to perform physical exercises under the mocking supervision of the Nazis. From ten in the evening to eight in the morning we were chased through the overheated gymnasium. We had to run, jump, kneel without pause. Not only young strong men, but also the elderly and the sick had to keep up the pace in spite of the exhaustion from a week's dreadful strain and lack of food and sleep. Several men collapsed. The Nazis "took charge" of these "recalcitrant" ones in such a way that in the morning two or three were found dead and a number of others badly injured. I still wonder how I was able to hold out. . . .

In the morning we were told to put on our coats and hats and to go to the offices where we would be informed as to what we could expect. A ray of hope gleamed through our bitterness and despair. . . . Perhaps . . . the mortal foes had abated—or the democratic world powers (especially the U.S.), in whom we still believed, had intervened in our behalf. We would be released soon. We would see our families again. We would shave and wash and go to bed—sleep in our own beds. We would have a substantial meal next morning and again try to get visas from the embassies of some South American or African state (practically all European countries were hermetically sealed to refugees from the Nazi terror).

It was not until we were herded into cattle cars and the train began to move that our hopes of liberty sank. The train, we understood, was carrying us off to that hell on earth—the concentration camp of Dachau. It was there that I learned from Bavarian, Prussian and Silesian Jews that Austria and the whole of Germany had become *Eretz ha-damim* (land of blood)!

Poland was next on the agenda. But the nations of the world that had failed to grasp the importance of the "Black Thursday" also failed to grasp the fact that the invasion of Poland would initiate a global war. I was in America—after a half year in Dachau, and a year in a British internment camp—when a U.S. Senator naively told an interviewer: "I take no stock in the argument that the United States cannot live peaceably in the world—and live comparatively well economically—if Europe is dominated by totalitarianism."

He failed to realize that mankind could never hope to live happily in a world half slave and half free.

---

# The Time Was Midnight

*Rabbi Joachim Prinz (Temple B'nai Abraham, Newark, N.J.) was one of Germany's "controversial" rabbis because he knew that "The Time Was Midnight" and did not hesitate to say so . . .*

The year 1933 was the beginning of the Nazi era. German Jews by and large were not prepared for it, but we Zionists were prepared. Since the assassination of Walther Rathenau, in 1922, there was no doubt in our minds that German developments would be towards an anti-Semitic totalitarian régime. When Hitler began to "awaken" the German nation to racial consciousness and superiority, we had no doubt that he would sooner or later become the leader of the nation. As Zionists, we did not identify with the German people. We were not German patriots. I came from the Blau-Weiss (Blue-White) movement[1] which was particularly aware of the trend. One group went to Palestine in 1923. Things were much simpler for us, but we were a tiny minority, and the vast majority of German Jewry, people of my parents' and grandparents' generation, were totally unprepared. To them, Hitler represented an unpleasant episode which had to be accepted, but which would surely soon pass. It could not last much longer, and soon the German people would turn against their Leader.

My personal reaction to the Hitler revolution, as it related to the pulpit and my work in the synagogue, had something to do with my general concept of the special rabbinical functions in the synagogue and my concept of the sermon. At first, I found a great many people, particularly among the older generation, opposed to my concepts. I

---

[1]Zionist Youth

---

"The Time Was Midnight," *Jewish Spectator Magazine,* by Joachim Prinz

never held that the sermon should serve merely as a means of momentary spiritual elevation. It was always for me a forum of education, not merely religious but national education as well. I was twenty-three years old when I became a rabbi in Berlin, and I had to go my own way which was different from that of my colleagues. I refused to separate Judaism as a religion from the reality of the Jewish people. I believed in the unity of people and faith. This approach was tested most dramatically at the Friday Evening Service preceding April 1, 1933, the day of boycott against the Jews. At that Service it became quite clear to me what it was that we had to do. On that evening the synagogue had to be closed one hour before the Service started because there was not a single seat vacant. This remained the pattern throughout my four years of preaching during the Hitler régime.

In an article in the *Juedische Rundschau* (1935), I formulated the experience of the preceding years and said that the only place in Germany which was not a ghetto was the synagogue. Everything else was ghetto and persecution: streets, parks, theatres, schools, places of work. But the synagogue was a place of security, or at least where the people felt secure. The yearning to be with other Jews was overwhelming. It included all kinds of Jews—converts to Christianity and thousands of marginal Jews who were so assimilated they had never seen the inside of a synagogue.

At that Friday Evening Service every seat was taken. Many stood in the aisles, leaned against the walls and sat on the steps which led to the altar. That night I saw famous Jewish actors, writers and other prominent people who had come for the first time to pray with Jews. The most touching experience was the moment when we all rose to recite the *Shema* together. The choir and the organist were drowned out. The organist was so overwhelmed that he could not continue to play. At that time the organ and every other trapping of the synagogue were proved to be artificial and superfluous. They revealed their Protestant character and seemed no longer to fit into the atmosphere of daily peril.

Outside the synagogue in the ghetto, that is, in the newspapers, on the radio, in the speeches of the government people, wherever Jews listened, on the propaganda placards of the Nazi régime, in the cartoons of the anti-Semitic papers, the Jew was depicted as a non-person—ugly, immoral, uncreative, cowardly, useless and inferior. I told them from the pulpit, in every sermon, that to be a Jew is to be beautiful, great, noble, and that we had every right to feel superior . . . There are times when people who have been degraded and humiliated have to say that in reality they are "beautiful." Sometimes I exaggerated. But it was planned exaggeration. I spoke about the Jewish face, the beauty of the Jew as human being; I spoke about the Jewish contribution to civilization and that the world could not really exist without us, and that Christianity and Islam were indebted to us. All this was designed not merely to reject the Nazi propaganda, but to replace it with a sense of superiority—moral, cultural, religious and human.

The sermon then was also an attempt at collective therapy. Some strange formulations emerged. I spoke about hammer and anvil, and that the hammer had to be rejected and detested. It hurt to be the anvil, but it was morally superior. I often preached about "pity the persecutor," and how superior are the people who are subjected to persecution, how much pride there is in suffering because we believe that in the end hammers and persecutors will be discarded while we shall continue to live. It was not always easy to say this because many of our people did not live. Jews were killed by the Nazis, and I officiated at many of their funerals.

It was most important for me to demonstrate that I was not afraid of anything. It is difficult to imagine now how important it was to Jews sitting in the pews to listen to someone expressing himself freely and often brutally critical of the Nazi régime, in spite of the fact that two Gestapo men always sat in the first row. I especially remember preaching a sermon against *Der Stuermer,* the most violent anti-Semitic paper whose editor Streicher was hanged after the Nuremberg trials. I took a copy of the paper with me to the pulpit. I opened it to a page on which were printed vicious caricatures of Jews, and said: "Is this what we really look like? Look at yourselves and look at each other. Is this the true picture of the Jews?" Amazingly, the Gestapo agents did not arrest me after the Service. Instead, they forbade me to preach for a whole month. I then had to find a substitute for my sermons. I found it in the prayerbook. Instead of the sermon, in the presence of the Gestapo agents and my most faithful worshippers, I read the following prayer:

> *My God, guard my tongue from evil,*
> *And my lips from speaking deceit . . .*
> *Open my heart through Thy Torah,*
> *That my soul may follow Thy*
> *commandments,*
> *And all who rise up against me for evil*
> *May speedily see their design as naught,*
> *Their purposes defeated.*
> *Do so for the glory of Thy name.*
> *Do so for Thy power.*
> *Do so for Thy Torah.*
> *Do so for Thy holiness.*
> *Answer my prayer, and save me through*
> *Thy strength.*

After the Service the two agents approached me saying that the prayer was more dangerous than the sermon. Suddenly the old prayers and biblical verses leaped to a new life. When I read the passage in the prayer: "And all who rise up against me for evil, may speedily see their design as naught, their purpose defeated," I was delivering an anti-Nazi sermon, and everyone knew it.

In those days we read the prayerbook in terms of our daily experiences, and we quickly began to understand why we responded so readily. Many of the prayers had been written in the medieval context of persecution. Even the Psalms spoke about "the table prepared in the presence of mine enemies."

Many Bible stories began to make sense or had a new and different meaning. David and Goliath became a story of hope. If he could slay the giant man, so could we in the end be victorious over the people who called themselves supermen of a super-race.

The Jewish holidays, too, assumed new importance and were subject to new interpretations. No longer were they perfunctory observances. They became part of the context of danger, fear, death and hope in which we lived. Three Jewish holidays stood out. Passover was now the great day of hope for delivery from our own Egypt. The whips which beat the naked bodies of Jewish slaves in Egypt were those that struck our bodies. Slavery was no longer an abstract term, foreign to the world of the twentieth century. We could now identify with the slaves for we, ourselves, were third-class citizens, and therefore slaves. Those who had been taken from their homes and whom we no longer saw, but about whose fate we knew, illustrated the *Haggadah* in colors much more telling than those of the most graphic illustrations we had ever seen. The Passover slogan "From slavery unto freedom" became the song of our lives. If the slaves to Egypt could be delivered from their fate so would we.

All the songs of the Seder were sung with new emphasis, new meaning and great religious fervor. When we read that "in every generation it is one's duty to regard himself as though he personally had come out of Egypt" and "it was not only our fathers whom God set free from slavery," the identification was complete. It was not history. It was not history at all. It was the reality of every day and the hope of everyone. Some day, we said, we shall be free. But the strongest identification came when we read: "Not merely one persecutor has stood up against us, but in every generation they persecuted us to destroy us, and the Holy One saved us from their hands." I did not then know that I was later to sing "We shall overcome some day." But when I did, I remembered the songs of the Seder under Hitler.

The many Community Seders were crowded, and hundreds of people could not be seated. There was a great hunger for Jewish knowledge because there was a necessity to identify with the Jewish people. Passover was only one of the means of identification, a very beautiful one. The old songs were no longer old. For many of our people, they were brand new. The texts did not have to be changed. The old texts sufficed. They had proved their durability. Passover had become relevant.

The second significant holiday was, of course, Purim. People came by the thousands to the synagogue to listen to the story of Haman and Esther. This, too, became the story of our own lives. Haman meant Hitler. The *Megillah,* read in Hebrew and translated, made sense. It was again the story of our life. Haman's plot bore a strange resemblance to Hitler's plot to wipe out the Jewish people. Many came to ask me if Hitler had ever read the story of Haman. It was so similar to his own designs for the Jewish people. Then the turning point came. Haman was unmasked, and exposed to disgrace and death. Never had I heard such applause in a synagogue when the names of the ten sons of Haman were read, describing their hanging from the gallows. Every time we read *Haman,* the people heard *Hitler,* and the noise was deafening. The little noisemakers which have become part of the Purim festival became more than toys. They were the instruments of a demonstration in the midst of frustration. Outside in the streets and in the homes one could not talk against Hitler, but here in the synagogue there was no limit. No one, however sensitive, objected to the passages of revenge which in a climate of peace and tranquility seem to have no place in Jewish life.

But the climax was Hanukkah. German Jews had adjusted Hanukkah to Christmas. It had become little more than the giving of gifts to and the joyous acceptance of them by children. A Christmas tree was found in many German Jewish homes. It had now been replaced by the *Menorah.* Under Hitler, and quite naturally, it was the Hanukkah story which interested us most: the battle of a handful of Jews, the Maccabees, against overwhelming odds. Jews are not cowards, we said. Here is the story of the Maccabees, and it is proof of Jewish courage and stamina, and above all of our ability to be victorious. Never mind that Germany is so powerful. Never mind the uniforms of the SS and the Storm Troopers, and the German Army. Do not overestimate the weapons, for we say in the Hanukkah Haftarah: "Not by might and not by power." The perfunctory holiday, which used to please Jewish children and teach them not to be envious of their Christian neighbors, now returned to its original meaning. When we placed the *Menorah* on the window sills in accordance with Jewish tradition, we proclaimed clearly and visibly that this house was inhabited by Jews, and we were proud of it.

More important than anything else was the hunger for Jewish knowledge. The German Jewish community was extremely small, amounting to less than 1% of the total population. But its roots reached into the Middle Ages, and many of our generation had been living in the same

95

places where, during the fifteenth and sixteenth centuries, our forefathers had resided. But many of them had forgotten. Many generations had passed since the Emancipation. Conversions to Christianity were not rare. Intermarriage was rampant. Now those who no longer wanted to be Jews had no choice. In the eyes of the law they were Jews and treated as such. Even if they could have escaped, their sense of pride and decency drove them to identification with the Jewish fate. In those days I visited the head of the banking house of Mendelssohn, the leading private banking firm in the country. Franz Mendelssohn was the president of the Evangelical Church of Germany. He was a direct descendant of Moses Mendelssohn, the philosopher. The conversion of the family had taken place in the early nineteenth century. Felix Mendelssohn-Bartholdy was the famous first Mendelssohn convert. Even according to the Hitler law, which declared converts to be treated as Jews if the conversion took place three generations ago, Mendelssohn was not a Jew. He had been knighted by the emperor. The family was now part of the German nobility. I visited him to ask him to contribute some money for Palestine. He received me in his beautiful office in an eighteenth-century building, and then took me into a special room which had been kept like a museum. It contained a collection of busts and engravings connected with the life of Moses Mendelssohn, the Jew. We looked at them together, and then he said: "I have resigned from my position as president of the Evangelical Church. I cannot return to Judaism. I am a Christian. But I must return to my people."

It would be good to have an exhibit of the books which were printed by Jewish publishing houses during the Hitler régime. It is not enough to exhibit destruction and murder. It is equally important to show our creative reaction to the Hitler catastrophe. I myself wrote five books under the Hitler régime, and each of them was printed in tens of thousands of copies. Jews were eager to learn. They no longer *read* Jewish books, they *devoured* them. I was invited to give a course in Jewish history. There were 7,000 applicants! There was no hall large enough to hold them. We rented one in north Berlin with a seating capacity of 3,500 and I taught two nights every week for many months. On each night, there were 3,500 students—young, old, converted, assimilated, pious, marginal. There were other courses and lectures. To be a Jew was a discovery, and to emphasize one's Jewishness in the face of danger and disgrace became the thing to do.

I preached many sermons urging Jews to leave the country. I thought of total emigration. This brought me into conflict with the Jewish establishment which was eager to maintain itself and was altogether obsessed with the idea that the Hitler days, bad as they were, would pass, and the German Jewish community would maintain itself and even prosper. I did not share such opinions, and whenever I could

96

I encouraged Jews to leave. To the Jewish establishment, this was a threat to its existence. One Friday night in an overcrowded synagogue when things had become particularly dangerous, and when I foresaw that some day the Jews might be deported by the thousands, I went to my pulpit, and instead of delivering a sermon I told the following story from Alfred Polgar's little essays.

"Once upon a time I decided to visit the town where I was born. It was an old town with medieval houses still standing, with a tower on the square the clock of which used to announce every hour. My first visit when I arrived was to that tower, the remnant of a castle which had burned down during the seventeenth century. I heard no sound. There were no chimes. I looked up at the clock and I saw that its hands were not moving. The clock was dead. It had ceased to be at five o'clock. Sadly I went home to consider the strange phenomenon about the clock which evidently had died. But then I came to this conclusion. A clock is never dead. Now it shows the hour of five, but twice a day the hour is indeed five. What is the moral of the story? Timepieces cannot die. It depends upon you to look at the clock at the right time and be told what it is."

I said to my congregation: "Some people believe time stands still. Many of you really do not know what the time is now. Many of you live as though nothing was happening. But I am telling you the time is midnight. It depends upon you to understand it, to look at the clock and understand what it really means. At midnight people should pack up and go, for it may very well be that they will have no opportunity whatsoever to look at the clock again."

Among the thousands of people who had attended the Service was the president of the Jewish Community of Berlin who disagreed violently with me. He was very eager for the Jewish community to remain. After the Service he said to me angrily: "The tower and the clock are right here in this country. And if I read it well, it is not midnight at all. Tomorrow will be a new day, and some day the hour will strike, and we will be free."

I decided to visit him at his home so as to explain why I thought his policy was wrong and that the Jews had to leave the country.

He was a rich man, independent and highly respected, and he lived in a splendid villa not far from my house. As I entered the living-room I saw that his famous collection of Impressionists had been removed from the walls. I inquired about the paintings. He replied that he had sent them to his son in Belgium because they were no longer safe here. I looked at him with great amazement and said: "Evidently to save the paintings is important; to save Jews is not." I never saw him again. It must be said to his honor that he was a victim of his own convictions. He died in Theresienstadt.

97

# Strawberries and Euthanasia

. . . It was in the strawberry season. That is in June or July [presumably of 1940]. I was part of the staff that accompanied a transport of patients. Usually, we wore civilian clothes. Before the transport started, I was told to put on a physician's white coat, however, so that as far as the patients were concerned, I would appear to be a doctor or a doctor's helper. The members of the transport were told that they were going to be moved. But they were not told where. The transport went to the city of Brandenburg, to the old prison downtown, parts of which had been rebuilt into a crematory, since the prison was empty. During the trip, we had to be careful to see that the busses' white curtains were drawn. On the way, between Berlin and Brandenburg, we stopped in Werder,[1] and everyone got a basket of strawberries, and then we delivered the people in Brandenburg.

We went in with these people. We stayed around, for the SS guards told us, "Why don't you have a look at the show." The people were sorted out, the men in one group, the women in another.

Everyone had to undress completely. The reason they were given was that before being moved to another building, they would have to take a bath and be deloused. All patients had to open their mouths, and an automatic four digit stamp was pressed against their chests. By looking at the numbers, the staff later knew who had gold teeth. In order not to alarm the sick people, physicians gave them a superficial examination. They then were taken into the shower room. When the intended number of people were inside, the door was locked. At the ceiling, there were installations in the shape of showerheads through which the gas was admitted into the room.

I think that 50 people entered for such a gassing. There were a few young girls among them, and we said to ourselves, "Boy, what a shame." There was only a single door to the room, and you could see through the peephole exactly when all were dead.

About 15 to 20 minutes later, the gas was let out of the room, since it was clear from looking through the peephole that no one was alive any more. Next, by use of the stamped numerals, it was ascertained who the people were who, as the examination had shown, had gold teeth. The dead had their gold teeth broken out. . . .

[1] famous for its orchards

From *The Nazi Years, A Documentary History* by Joachim Remak

# Readings

*The Twisted Road to Auschwitz (1933–1939)* by Karl A. Schleuness (University of Illinois, 1970), deals with the first five years of the chaos and the in-fighting to gain control over Nazi policy, and Hitler's maneuverings until he arrived at the formulation of the Final Solution.

*The Nazi Years, A Documentary History* (Prentice-Hall, 1969), edited by Joachim Remak, is a compilation of documents. *The Jews* is one of the eleven sections in the book.

*Pogrom, 10 November 1938* by Lionel Kochan (André Deutsch, 1957), is a factual account of the three days preceding the *Kristallnacht* (also known as the Night of the Broken Crystal Glass), the pogrom itself, and its aftermath.

*Cold Pogrom* by Max L. Berges (Jewish Publication Society, 1939), is a documentary novel on the rise of Hitlerism to the beginnings of the Tragedy.

*The Oppermans* by Lionel Feuchtwanger (Viking Press, 1934), is a celebrated novel about German Jewry during this period by the renowned German-Jewish author.

*The World of Yesterday: An Autobiography* by Stefan Zweig (Viking Press, 1943), is a memorable chronicle of the period (particularly in Austria) by one of the great German-Jewish writers.

# 6. | SILENT, PASSIVE WORLD

Between 1933 and 1939, Hitler repeatedly tested the reactions of the German people, the churches, and world public opinion to his brutal policies. Seeing that the world was passive, Hitler was spurred on to the extreme policy of the Final Solution, i.e., total extermination.

## THE CHURCH

How did the religious communities react to the outrageous acts of the Nazis? German statistics show that, in the thirties, over 90 percent of the population were recorded as churchgoers. In 1939, some 43 percent of Germans were Catholics, who had always been a very substantial segment of the population, as well as comprising the nation's leadership, including Hitler. (In 1938, nearly 25 percent of the SS were Catholics.) The record shows that during the twenties, organized German Catholicism denounced "the destructive influence of Jews in religion, literature, art, and political and social life." Thus, while Catholic leaders deplored "racialism," they justified "self-defense" against the Jew. In 1933, Cardinal Michael Faulhaber of Munich, in defending the "Old Testament of the Children of Israel," took "no position with regard to the Jewish question today." The position of the high Catholic clergy was that Jesus was a Jew but that he had been fundamentally different from the Jews in his lifetime. The Jewish people were guilty of Jesus's murder and have been cursed ever since. In their writings, many of the clergy pointed out that Karl Marx was a Jew (his father had converted to Lutheranism) and that Bolshevism was led by Jews. The Church approved the "patriotic motives behind Nazism." It supported Hitler's policies and invasions.

100

Silent, Passive World

Many Jews sought escape through conversion. An estimated fifty thousand converted after 1933. Despite their efforts, in the end most of them were not saved from joining their brethren in deportation to the death camps. When the deportations began, Catholics who were born Jewish, or whose parents had been Jews, were also affected. At this stage the Church faced "its moment of truth." In 1942, highly placed Catholics in the German Military Intelligence Service and other ministries were keeping the German bishops informed of the atrocities. The bishops appealed especially on behalf of the "non-Aryan" Catholics and also complained about the outrages inflicted generally. But the language of the protests was guarded, and the pleas for the persecuted did not mention the Jews by name. In January 1944, Cardinal Bertram, who was the voice of the Church, warned that "The German Catholics, indeed numerous Christians in Germany, would be deeply hurt if fellow Christians [i.e., non-Aryan Catholics] now had to meet a fate similar to that of the Jews."[1]

This resignation to Nazism must be judged against the background of the Church's success in opposing euthanasia, student dueling, and cremation (instead of burial). It must also be contrasted to the opposition of the French, Belgian, and Dutch churches. Never did the Catholic Church in Germany threaten to excommunicate those participating in the killing of Jews, as it did in other European countries.

In contrast to the passivity of the Church as a whole, there were notable instances of Catholic priests denouncing anti-Jewish excesses. To mention but two: A distinguished Catholic leader in exile, Waldemer Gurian (pseudonym: Stefan Kirschmann) denounced the Nuremberg Laws as violations of the teachings of the Church. He predicted that these measures are "only a stage on the way to the complete destruction of the Jews."[2] Provost Bernhard Lichtenberg of Berlin will also be remembered for his denunciations of Nazi persecutions and his crying out against the *Kristallnacht* pogroms of November 1938. He prayed for the Jews daily. On October 23, 1941, he was arrested, and two years later he was sent to Dachau, where he died.

As with the Catholic Church, so with the Protestant. In 1933 it adopted an "Aryan" clause against accepting baptized clergy of Jewish origin, and in 1939 it demanded proof of non-Jewish origin from students preparing for the ministry. As late as December 17, 1941, Protestant leaders published a statement reading: "The National Socialist leadership of Germany has given irrefutable documentary proof that this world war was instigated by the Jews. . . . As members of the German national community the undersigned . . . stand in the front line of this historic struggle which has made necessary such measures as the official police recogni-

[1]Gunther, Lewy, "Pius XXII, the Jews and the German Catholic Church," *Commentary*, February 1964.
[2]Gunther, Lewy, *The Catholic Church in Nazi Germany*, p. 281.

tion of Jews as the born enemies of the Reich and the world. The undersigned . . . have therefore severed all links with Jewish Christians. We are determined not to tolerate any Jewish influence on German religious life."[3]

Not all Protestant churches acquiesced. A militant minority organized a group which called itself the Dissident Confessing Church. Some seven hundred of its ministers were arrested.

In 1950, five years after the tragedy, a group of German Protestant and Catholic theologians summarized this tragic chapter with the confession that "a few courageously helped the persecuted, but the large majority failed disgracefully in the face of this unheard-of provocation of the merciful God."

In ascertaining the reactions of the religious communities in Europe, we must certainly study the role of the Papacy. On March 2, 1939, Pius XII became Pope. Before this he had served as the nuncio, i.e., the representative of the Vatican, in Munich and Berlin and was known to be friendly to Germany. Soon after he ascended to his exalted office, Pope Pius XII wrote a letter to Hitler (March 6, 1939) saying, "We shall pray for the protection of Heaven and the blessing of the Almighty God for you and all members of your nation." (This was *after* Hitler had invaded Austria and Czechoslovakia and shortly before he overran Poland—all predominantly Catholic countries.) During the war, although he was apprised of the killing of Jews in the camps, he failed to protest publicly. In September 1942, when asked by the American government, the Jewish Agency for Palestine, and other bodies to ascertain the actualities of the Final Solution and if the Vatican could do anything to prevent these atrocities, his reply was diplomatic and ineffectual. Later, when the request was repeated, he answered that everything was being done to help behind the scenes. Several times the Pope declared that he had pleaded for more humane conduct toward the suffering, but that his pleas were met with resistance. The real extent of his efforts is disputed to this day.

When, in the fall of 1943, the Nazis rounded up thousands of Jews in Rome for deportation, the Pope's policy faced a real test. He was silent. It is true that more than four thousand Jews found refuge in Catholic monasteries and churches with his approval, but he did not issue a public statement of outrage and protest against the round-up and deportation.

When the Chief Rabbis of Palestine, Isaac Halevi Herzog and Ben-Zion Meir Uziel, sent a telegram to Pope Pius XII on May 22, 1944, appealing to him to save the Jews of Hungary and the Balkan states, it remained unanswered. When the Chief Rabbis wished to present concrete propos-

---

[3]For detailed and documentary evidence of the role of the Church in Germany, read Friedrich Heer, *God's First Love* (New York: Weybright & Talley, 1967), chaps. 11–12. Dr. Heer is a prominent Austrian Catholic.

als for rescuing Jews, he refused to see them, but instead sent an intermediary, who met with Rabbi Herzog in Cairo. The gist of the Pope's reply was that he feared his "activity might have an effect contrary to the one intended, and cause the death of still more Jews." (In contrast, it should be noted that Msgr. Angelo Giuseppe Roncalli, the apostolic delegate in Turkey, was a tower of light and strength to the Jews and non-Jewish victims in Central Europe and the Balkans. He later succeeded Pope Pius XII as Pope John XXIII and was beloved by all mankind for his humanity and goodness.)

Rolf Hochhuth, non-Jewish editor of a large German publishing house, wrote a stirring play called *The Deputy* (1964), condemning the Pope for not crying out against the Nazi crimes. This play was translated and produced in many capitals of the world and had a shattering effect. Hochhuth documented his play with a section entitled "Sidelights on History," which contained explosive documentary evidence of the Pope's silence.

Saul Friedlander, a young refugee historian whose parents were killed by the Nazis, supplemented Hochhuth's findings and published a documented book, *Pius XII and the Third Reich* (New York: Alfred A. Knopf, 1966). He included letters from the President of the Polish government-in-exile imploring the Vatican "that a voice be raised . . . to condemn those in the service of evil."

The role of the Pope during the catastrophe is still debated. Why did Pius XII sacrifice Catholic Poland to Hitler's SS?[4] Why did he not protest the massacres in Holland, Belgium, and France, where large Catholic populations lived? Could he have saved the lives of Jews and non-Jews had he publicly protested the Nazi atrocities? Could he have been effectual had he excommunicated Hitler and other Nazi leaders of Catholic faith, such as Himmler and Goebbels? Would the threat of excommunication to all participants in the Holocaust have helped the victims by creating dissension and disunion in the Reich? Why didn't he at least reveal to the world the atrocities in the death camps of which he was aware? Or would his public stand have caused harm to the Catholics and damage to the Vatican? Denmark's stand against Hitler, which saved Danish Jewry, is evidence that resistance could be successful. It is possible that the fate of the Jews might not have been improved if the Pope had spoken out, but it could not have been worsened. Lacking evidence to the contrary, we may say that the Pope's failure to protest vigorously at a time when mankind was undergoing torture and spiritual agony is in itself one of the greatest tragedies of our era.

---

[4]Col. Jozef Beck, the former Polish foreign minister, declared after the war, "One of the main sources of responsibility for the tragedy of my country was the Vatican" (*God's First Love*, p. 319).

# THE NATIONS OF THE WORLD

In 1938, President Roosevelt announced plans for a world conference on the refugee crisis. Thirty-two nations were invited to help plan the emigration from Germany and possibly Austria. Germany was not invited; Fascist Italy refused to attend.

On July 6, 1938, the representatives of these nations convened in Evian, France. The conference met for nine days. It was marked by confusion, disharmony, and fear. Many suspected Roosevelt's motives in trying to create a new agency for refugees when the League of Nations already had at least three. Further, they did not believe that the President could persuade the foes of immigration in his own country to relent.

One after another, the nations found excuses for not welcoming the refugees. Fearful of the Arabs, Britain declared that Palestine was out of consideration. France feared increasing her already "heavy" burden. Canada, which had vast territories available for immigration, was reluctant to open its doors. Many had looked to the Latin American countries for succor, because they were underdeveloped and underpopulated. But their refusals, couched in eloquent speeches, were unanimous (with the sole exception of the Dominican Republic). Some of the countries were afraid of German retaliation; many needed farmers and laborers rather than professionals, merchants, and intellectuals.

It must be noted that the Evian Conference was convened after the annexation of Austria and during the period of appeasement typified by Chamberlain's policy. Almost all the participants gingerly avoided the mention of Germany. William Shirer, who attended the conference, entered in his *Berlin Diary* (July 7, 1938), "The British, the French and Americans seem too anxious not to do anything to offend Hitler. It is an absurd situation. They want to appease the man who is responsible for their problem."

And so the Evian Conference turned out to be a cruel disappointment. One delegate called it a "modern wailing wall." It accented the spiritual bankruptcy of the nations of the world and the conspiracy of silence and passivity that prevailed toward the suffering and the persecuted. The indifference of the world's rulers served Hitler well. He found in them "partners" who shared his attitude. It stiffened his resolve not to relax the laws he had enacted against the transfer of Jewish property and capital.

The one outcome of the Evian Conference was the organization of the Intergovernmental Committee on Refugees (IGC) to search for havens of resettlement and to negotiate with Hitler over the emigration of the actual and presumably potential refugees. By and large this committee, like the conference, engaged in mere words and futile gestures.

The promise of the United States to admit a small number of refugees was mere lip service, considering the country's size and its reputation as the Mother of Refugees. Various rescue projects which were championed by some members of the American government, notably Harold Ickes, secretary of the interior, failed because of a lack of support from the Roosevelt administration. Many of the shrewd schemes to block immigration were the work of Breckinridge Long, assistant secretary of state, and are detailed in Henry Feingold's and Saul Friedman's books (see Readings). They leave the reader with a heavy heart.

Beyond passivity, even the muffling of the agonized cries from overseas seems to have been the accepted policy of the Allies and of the United States. Thus, in January 1942, eight governments in exile met in London's St. James' Palace and issued a declaration of accusation branding Germany's atrocities, but did not mention the Jews by name. One of the shameful acts of the U.S. State Department was its deliberate restricting and, when deemed necessary, even halting of the flow of information about the mass killing of Jews. Various U.S. ambassadors and ministers in European countries forwarded the gruesome facts of torture and slaughter. The Roosevelt administration was finally forced to release these reports, which shocked the world and set off large Jewish protest demonstrations—alas, too few and too late.

Washington's silence was broken in May 1943, when Breckinridge Long at long last informed his department, with characteristic restraint, that "it may for present purposes be accepted as more than Jewish propaganda that a large number of Jews have been killed."[5]

Another instance of Allied passivity was the refusal to bomb the German railways, deportation trains, and death camps, despite the pleas of world Jewish organizations. Replying to a request by Dr. Chaim Weizmann, Anthony Eden, the British foreign secretary, stated that the proposal was "put to the Secretary of State for Air . . . but . . . that, in view of the very great technical difficulties involved, we have no option but to refrain from pursuing the proposal in present circumstances."[6]

# The Evian Conference: Exercise in Futility

*Myron C. Taylor, James G. Macdonald, and others who were President Roosevelt's representatives, as well as Dr. Bernard Kahn, Chairman of the J.D.C.'s European Council and the writter, S. Adler-Rudel, traveled together from Paris to the Evian Conference . . .*

[5]*Politics of Rescue*, p. 177.
[6]Raul Hilberg, *The Destruction of the European Jews* (Chicago: Quadrangle Books, 1961), p. 771.

The Conference was inaugurated without much ado at Evian on the 6th July, 1938. For weeks, world attention and in particular the hope of the refugees and of the Jews in Eastern and Central Europe had been focused on the idyllic little spa on the French side of Lake Geneva. In the name of the French Government, Senator Henri Bérenger welcomed close to 200 delegates, journalists and observers ... He assured the various refugee associations who had come of their own free will (i.e. uninvited) that they were nonetheless most welcome; if they had not been asked to participate, it was because this meeting was not meant as a conference of official international character, but rather as a body which the President of the United States wished to see created as a means for collaboration between America and governments from other continents. The Conference, he added ... would give birth to something of value for refugees all over the world ...

The opening took place ... in an atmosphere from which cynicism was not absent. The invitations sent out by the United States Government had indicated that any financing of the emergency emigration would have to be undertaken by private bodies. But the private Jewish organisations had already spent, for the relief and migration purposes of political victims, some 50 million dollars in the first five years of Hitlerism. The assurance that no country would be expected or asked to receive a larger number of emigrants than was foreseen by its existing legislation was rather puzzling as this existing legislation was one of the very obstacles which the prospective immigrant had to face. It furthermore "was not clear from the invitation issued by the United States what the scope of the work of the Committee should be and whether its deliberations should be confined to the situation created by the action of Germany in Germany proper and in Austria, or whether they should extend to the question of refugees generally."

After the formalities ... , the Chairman, Senator Henri Bérenger, invited President Roosevelt's representative to address the Conference.

In a frank and clear statement, Myron Taylor explained the purpose of the Conference and urged the establishment of a permanent intergovernmental committee to deal with refugee problems:

"Some millions of people, as this meeting convenes, are, actually or potentially, without a country. The number is increasing daily. ...

"The American Government prides itself upon the liberality of its existing laws and practices, both as regards the number of immigrants whom the United States receives each year for assimilation with its population and the treatment of those people when they have arrived. I might point out that the American Government has taken steps to consolidate both the German

From *Leo Baeck Yearbook*, 1968 by S. Adler-Rudel

and the former Austrian quota, so that now a total of 27,370 immigrants may enter the United States on the German quota in one year ..."

Mr. Taylor was followed by Lord Winterton, Chief of the British delegation, whose address, although very carefully worded, contained indications as to the differences of opinion between the American and the British Governments, concerning the creation of a new intergovernmental organisation in addition to the existing Nansen Office[1] and the Office of the High Commissioner for Refugees of the League of Nations. . . .

Through its marked silence about immigration into Palestine (which was hinted at only by mentioning overseas territories where "local political conditions" hinder admission), Lord Winterton's speech was a bitter disappointment. Later, the importance of Palestine as a country of refuge was referred to so often at the private meetings and more particularly in the relevant Sub-Committee, that he once more took the rostrum on the last day of the Conference to explain England's position in this matter by stating that . . .

"It has been represented in some quarters that the whole question, at least of the Jewish refugees, could be solved if only the Gates of Palestine were thrown open to Jewish immigrants without restriction of any kind. I should like to say, as emphatically as I can, that I regard any such proposition as wholly untenable. First, Palestine is not a large country, and apart from that there are special considerations arising out of the terms of the mandate and out of the local situation which it is impossible to ignore . . ."

The next speaker was Senator Henri Bérenger, French Governmental representative on the governing body of the High Commission for German Refugees, who had on several occasions defended at Geneva the rights of religious and racial minorities and had, since 1933, been furthermore intimately involved in the work for the relief of refugees from Germany. He welcomed President Roosevelt's initiative and eloquently expounded . . . :

"... France continues to be true to the long-standing tradition of universal hospitality which has characterised her throughout all her history.... Though she has herself reached ... the extreme point of saturation as regards admission of refugees, France understands the new effort proposed by President Roosevelt. ..."

The statements by the representatives of the three great democratic powers . . . provided the keynote for the addresses by the delegates of the smaller countries. Although anxious to please the President of the

[1]an agency for distributing passports to stateless persons

United States, they lacked the courage to deal with the cause itself by naming the country which was creating the refugee problem; instead they merely discussed the consequences which were affecting some of their countries. There were three groups of countries differing in many respects from each other but united by the same negative attitude, and each delegate said "no" while trying to say it in a way not offensive to the President who had issued the call.

The first group consisted of European countries[2] bordering on Germany, all of them densely populated. Their representatives referred repeatedly to the "tens of thousands" of refugees they had already admitted. They even inflated the figures by reverting to refugees of World War I, but failed to remember that Belgium and France, for instance, at that time had had need of foreign labour. Referring to the present situation, they underlined that their countries had reached the point of saturation and that all they were in a position to offer were transit visas for short periods. Such permits, of course, could be issued only to persons in possession of immigration visas to overseas countries.

The second group were the countries of the British Commonwealth and Empire.[3] Their position was rather odd. The Empire embraced most of the globe's rich but sparsely populated land. Canada's population did not exceed ten million for an area larger than that of the United States which counted 130 million souls. Australia, with an area of three million square miles, had approximately seven million inhabitants. The white population of the Union of South Africa was about two million, while that of Rhodesia was insignificant. The governments of all these countries had erected carefully-studied legal barriers to keep out immigrants. Actually, the British Empire could have made a most important contribution towards the solution of the refugee problem. . . .

The third and perhaps most important group was the bloc of the American Republics.[4] Far from Europe and its worries, their representatives had little understanding of the emergency with which they were asked to deal in Evian. Most of them came from agricultural countries which had no need of "intellectuals and traders. . . ." Nearly twenty-five speakers participated, reading one by one the carefully prepared speeches referring to the particular character of their countries, to the existing laws of entry, to the necessity of negotiating with Germany concerning some kind of transfer of capital belonging to the emigrants, and to the fact that they were not in a position to make any commitment with regard to future immigration.—The only exception was the

[2] Belgium, Denmark, Netherlands, Switzerland
[3] Australia, Canada, Ireland, New Zealand, and the United Kingdom
[4] Argentina, Bolivia, Brazil, Chile, Colombia, Costa Rica, Cuba, Dominican Republic, Ecuador, Guatemala, Haiti, Honduras, Mexico, Nicaragua, Panama, Paraguay, Peru, Uruguay, Venezuela

representative of the Dominican Republic who indicated certain possibilities for large-scale agricultural colonisation:

"The Dominican Government, which for many years past has been encouraging and promoting the development of agriculture by appropriate measures and which gives ample immigration facilities to agriculturists who wish to settle in the country as colonists, would be prepared to make its contribution by granting especially advantageous concessions to Austrian and German exiles . . .

The Government . . . would also be prepared to grant special conditions to professional men who, as recognized scientists, would be able through their teaching to render valuable service to their Dominican colleagues."

Another speaker, Mr. M. J. M. Yepes from Colombia, deserves mention here for his courage in pointing to the roots of the problem in the following words:

"The problem of political refugees offers two aspects which I should like to outline briefly. First of all, there is the *question of principle,* which can only be studied and settled by collective effort; and, secondly, there is the *question of fact,* which each country must settle by its own means and in the light of its special circumstances. We cannot . . . ignore the questions of principle which may become its most important aspect, for it is they which determine the matter for the future and for all time: Can a State, without upsetting the basis of civilisation, and, indeed, of all civilisation, arbitrarily withdraw nationality from a whole class of its citizens, thereby making them Stateless Persons whom no country is compelled to receive on its territory? Can a State, acting in this way, flood other countries with the citizens of whom it wishes to get rid, and can it thrust upon others the consequences of an evil internal policy? The whole tragedy of these thousands of unfortunates who are bandied about from country to country, at the caprice of the alien police and exposed to the boorishness of frontier officials, the whole tragedy lies in the fact that this preliminary question was not settled in time. It would be useless for us to-day to find homes for the present political refugees and to hear the grievances . . . of those who have come to voice their complaints before this modern Wailing Wall which the Evian Conference has now become. So long as the central problem is not decided we shall be doing merely ephemeral work, work that will last but a day and which will have to be begun over again tomorrow . . . The worst thing is that the bad example of the Old World may be copied in other continents, and the world will then become uninhabitable.
. . .

Another man who must be remembered here, though for other reasons, is the Swiss delegate, Dr. H. Rothmund, Chief of the Police Division in the Swiss Justice and Police Department, a prime example of the kind of man to whose hands the fate of the refugees was entrusted. He spoke at length about his country's liberal tradition in receiving political refugees, using the most elaborate humanitarian terminology and supporting his remarks with figures which had little relevance to the problem facing the Conference. What he refrained from telling the Conference, however, was that he had just completed a round of negotiations with the Nazi authorities, whom he had advised that his Government intended to stop the immigration of Austrian Jews into Switzerland. He informed the German Legation that "in order to protect Switzerland from the immense influx of Viennese Jews", his Government had ruled that all holders of Austrian passports would henceforth require a visa in order to enter Switzerland. Rothmund complained that the authorities in Vienna were trying to circumvent this regulation. If this is not stopped, he said, "Switzerland, which has as little use for these Jews as has Germany, will herself take measures to protect Switzerland from being swamped by Jews with the connivance of the Viennese police."

After leaving Evian, Dr. Rothmund pursued his negotiations with the German authorities. The result was the introduction of the marking of German passports issued to Jews with a big red "J", thus jeopardizing from the very outset their chances of rescue, as not only Switzerland, but many other countries as well took to looking with disfavour upon bearers of passports stamped in this way. . . .

# Rescuing the Fugitives of the S.S. St. Louis (1939)

*One of the first "phantom" ships (p. 556) was the S.S. St. Louis, which sailed (May 14, 1939) with 907 German Jewish refugees aboard who had obtained visas to settle in Cuba. These documents had been sold to them by impostors or by officials of the Cuban Consulate. But when they docked at Cuba, they were not admitted, nor were they allowed to disembark anywhere else. The ship was ordered back to Hamburg where the German concentration camps awaited them. Many passengers threatened to commit suicide. Jules A. Braunschvig, president of the Alliance Israelite Universelle was one of the leaders in rescuing the fugitives . . .*

It was in the evening, at a meeting of the Central Committee of the Alliance in Paris, that I first learned about the 907 refugees on their way back to German concentration camps. All efforts to obtain admit-

From *The Alliance Review* by Jules A. Braunschvig

tance for them, in almost every country, were of no avail. The same stereotyped reply everywhere: we have too many Jewish refugees already.

I went home heartsick, disgusted. Here were 907 human beings on their way back, probably to death, certainly to insupportable tortures. And nothing could be done to save them. The whole world, the Christian world, was "tired of the Jewish victims."

The whole night I could not sleep. The monotony of the clock's ticking spiralled into unbearable intensity. I could not cease thinking that with every passing hour the ship was coming closer to Europe—to Germany . . .

In the morning, I phoned Baron Robert de Rothschild, head of the Paris Jewish Community and President of the French National Committee for German Jewish Refugees.

"Is there really no hope that the French government will change its mind?"

"Not the slightest hope," he answered with gloomy finality.

I decided to try. I had just come back from the International Zone of Tangier (North Africa) where I had watched the work of the small but efficient *Comite para los Refugiados*. I also remembered that the French Consul there was a friend of mine. Matters pertaining to admission of foreigners into the Zone were under the jurisdiction of the French Consul.

I called him on the phone. He was willing to help, but the final decision had to be made by the French Foreign Office. He made me a very important promise, however: If the Foreign Office asked his opinion, it would be favorable.

I rang up Baron de Rothschild again.

"Can we go to see Bonnet [George Bonnet, then French Foreign Minister]?"

"I will arrange it."

Early in the morning Rothschild and I were in Bonnet's office. The Minister was affable, but "What can we do? France has already accepted so many Jewish refugees. More than 200,000 were granted temporary or permanent asylum. No, we cannot admit the *St. Louis* passengers."

"How about admitting them to Tangier?" I asked.

"Well, we cannot do it without consulting our Consul there."

"Would you wire him?"

"All right, I will do that."

I saw a ray of hope.

It was Saturday. I thought: if the wire does not go out today, Monday may be too late. I told Bonnet that I was going to take up residence at the Ministry until the wire was sent.

At 4 P.M. the wire went out.

111

The answer from Tangier was, as expected, in the affirmative. Tangier would accept a few hundred refugees.

In parallel the Jewish organizations approached the Belgian, British and Dutch Governments. (Mr. Max Gottschalk, who was also a member of the Alliance and a Belgian citizen, took the same initiative in his country as I did in France, but neither of us was, at the time, aware of what the other was doing.) France is taking care of a part of the *St. Louis* refugees. Will you take a share? Great Britain, Belgium and the Netherlands agreed to follow France's example.

Then it was not difficult to persuade Albert Sarrart, the French Minister of the Interior, that, after all, since France was involved anyhow, why admit these people to Tangier; why not to France proper, where the Jewish organizations were better equipped to help them?

This, too, was granted.

\* \* \*

Maurice Tropper, the European Director of the Joint Distribution Committee, who took a leading part in all the endeavors on behalf of the *St. Louis* refugees, sent me a big cigar "in token of his appreciation." I put the cigar in the drawer of my desk and made a vow: I will smoke it the day Hitler is dead.

The day Hitler was buried under the ruins of the Chancellery in Berlin, I was unable to smoke the cigar—I was a prisoner of war in Germany. When, a few weeks later, I returned to Paris I found that my home had been ransacked during the German occupation; everything had disappeared, including the desk with the Joint Distribution Committee cigar.

Postscript: Many of those saved from the *St. Louis* were later deported to the death camps, following Nazi invasion of the countries in which they found refuge.

---

# "Without Mercy, We Were Ordered Back"

---

*In Reverend Dr. Paul Vogt's* Armor Has No Fear, *published in April 1943 [Switzerland] a letter was quoted. This letter was distributed to Swiss newspapers by the National Press Service on February 17, 1943. But its publication was prohibited . . .*

---

From *The Life Boat is Full* by Alfred A. Hasler

With aching feet and an even more aching heart I have just come out of—Switzerland! Yes, you are not mistaken, I was in Switzerland, even if only for six hours. On Sunday, the twenty-second [of November 1942], I made it into Wallis with a fellow from ———. What I went through cannot be put into words. My mountaineering outfit consisted of a pair of rubber overshoes, open at the top; I had no stockings, only wrappings. We climbed up to a pass fifty-five hundred feet high, through snow twenty inches deep, and, after twelve hours of walking through snow and ice, we entered Switzerland in the western part of Wallis. For food each of us had a half loaf of bread, plus melted snow. Our feet and lips were constantly chapped. But it was impossible to stop and rest, because my shoes were always full of water and, if I stopped, there was the danger that the water would freeze. . . . With all this we had snow and wind and police and customs men and soldiers to contend with. So at twelve o'clock, more or less, after exactly twelve hours of traveling, we came into Switzerland through the fifty-five-hundred-foot high pass. Everything went all right in the border area, and we started down into the valley. After we had walked for about a half hour a Swiss border guard caught us. He interrogated us and said we must go back. When we pleaded with him and pointed out how bad my shoes were and how swollen my feet were, he took pity on us and took us with him to Champéry. . . . After a two-hour descent we reached the Champéry customs post, where we could rest for a half hour, and then, in spite of all our entreaties and requests at least to spend the night there and rest, we were compelled to make the four-hour climb back up to the pass through all the snow, which was now three feet deep, even though it meant sixteen hours in the high mountains. Without mercy we were ordered back to where we had crossed the border at nine o'clock. If a good-hearted customs man had not made hot tea for us and given us a little *pâté* to eat, we never would have got through without catching pneumonia. At ten o'clock it was back to France, in a snowstorm. Unable to see the narrow path, we made the dangerous climb down through the snow. In two hours, after a brief stop in a hut, we were in the valley. The rags round my feet were so stiff that they could stand upright in the room. Then, in spite of cold and hunger, I fell asleep out of sheer exhaustion.

This experience was so powerful and overwhelming that I am still not completely able to grasp it and I would think I had been dreaming, if it were not for the huge blood blisters on my feet and the prospect of the punishment camp. This was how it was in Switzerland on November 23 at Champéry in Wallis. In spite of the very different stories in the newspapers and all the rest. Believe me, I would never in my life have thought this possible. Even to me it all seems like a novel. . . .

# Readings

*Pius XII and the Third Reich, A Documentation* by Saul Friedlander (Knopf, 1966), offers primary historical evidence on the "silence" of the Vatican about the Nazi atrocities.

*While Six Million Died* by Arthur D. Morse (Random House, 1968), is as the subtitle indicates, *a Chronicle of American Apathy.* The author points his finger to the callousness and obstructions of the State Department and the initial indifference of the Roosevelt administration, which could have rescued untold numbers of trapped victims.

*The Politics of Rescue* by Henry L. Feingold (Rutgers University, 1970), discloses a factual account of the Roosevelt administration's lack of action, 1939–45.

*No Haven for the Oppressed* by Saul S. Friedman (Wayne University, 1973), complements the above book by offering a comprehensive statement on U.S. policy toward Jewish refugees, 1938–45.

*The Silence of Pius XII* by Carlo Falconi (Little Brown, 1970), is based on documentary evidence and reveals the personality of the Pope and why he was silent. The author is an Italian historian.

*The Catholic Church and Nazi Germany* by Guenter Lewy (McGraw-Hill Book Co.), is an outstanding study on the subject.

*The Mission* by Hans Habe (Coward-McCann, 1966), is a gripping semi-documentary novel about the Evian Conference.

# 7. | EXODUS AND FLIGHT

Jews had lived in Germany for over sixteen hundred years. About 525,000 Jews lived in Germany in 1933 (not including the Saar region); they comprised only 0.8 percent of the total population. What happened to them in the years that followed is summarized in Table 1.

As the peril grew, an exodus of Jews began which accelerated in 1933. The young (under twenty-five years of age), who comprised the majority of those who fled Germany, were 27 percent of the Jewish population in

TABLE 1
The Disappearance of German Jewry

| Date | Jewish Population |
|---|---|
| 1925 (census) | 564,370 |
| January 1933 (estimate) | 525,000 |
| June 1933 (census, not including the Saar region) | 499,682 |
| September 15, 1935 (estimate) | 450,000 |
| September 1937 (estimate) | 350,000 |
| May 17, 1939 (unpublished census) | 235,000 |
| September 1, 1939 (estimate) | 215,000 |
| November 1, 1940 " | 160,000 |
| November 1, 1941 " | 120,000 |
| May 1, 1942 " | 80,000 |
| October 1, 1942 " | 40,000–50,000 |
| September 1, 1943 " | 5,000 |

Source: *Hitler's Ten Years' War on the Jews* (New York: Institute of Jewish Affairs of the World Jewish Congress, 1943).

1933; in 1939 they were 14 percent. (This was the period when the Youth Aliyah to Palestine began.) Those who remained were older and less intent on seeking a new life elsewhere.

Polish Jews had been evacuating their homeland at the rate of about 100,000 a year. Massive numbers were leaving Lithuania, Latvia, Estonia, Rumania, and Hungary. They were even more poverty-stricken than their German brothers.

German Jews, however, were deeply rooted in their *Vaterland.* They hoped against hope that their fellow citizens, among whom they had lived for so many centuries, would not throw them to the wolves. Every time there was a pause in persecution, they would breathe easier. Some, who had fled in 1933 and 1934, began to trickle back home. And there were even a few who naively hoped to win Hitler's protection by becoming Jewish Nazis.

Until Boycott Day (in April 1933), Jewish emigration was unorganized and on an individual basis. The far-sighted realized the danger and fled. Leaving their birthplace, where they had thrived, was indeed tragic, but each one was able to take along a goodly part of his possessions and the equivalent of about fifty dollars in foreign currency. The number of these refugees was not large (about eighty thousand), and countries of refuge were still open to them; some two-thirds settled in Palestine. When the Nuremberg Laws were passed in 1935, emigration began to be "organized" and channeled through the German Jewish community, international Jewish organizations (such as the American Joint Distribution Committee), and non-Jewish agencies. The Gestapo, which was charged with emigration matters in 1938, even encouraged Zionist efforts to foster and further the exodus. Jewish "patriots" who proposed to remain were viewed by the Nazis as imposters, "who deny their race and plot to overthrow the Nazi principles." Some thirty-seven thousand Jews left in 1937, but by this time the emigrés had to leave behind most of their capital and property. They were permitted to take only the equivalent of four dollars to countries bordering on Germany and eight dollars to other countries. The limited export of their belongings was subject to the whim of local authorities.

Conditions worsened after November 1938. This was the year that marked the transition from more or less orderly flight to panic. In 1938, between 120,000 and 140,000 left Germany. Expelled without any means of support, they found the doors of the world closed to them. The Gestapo and the SS, coordinated by Adolf Eichmann, drove them like beasts across the borders or dumped them on ships, sending them abroad with no visas. The office of the High Commission for Refugees of the League of Nations, and other agencies, were overwhelmed. Refugee camps were set up in neighboring lands as a temporary respite. But the suffering of the refugees was intense, and they became dependent on charity and relief organizations. When, during 1938–39, Austria and Czechoslovakia were occupied, 400,000 more Jews were expelled.

116

Like beasts fleeing from a forest fire, the refugees sought escape wherever there was a possible opening, temporary or precarious though it might be. Never in their two thousand years of wanderings did the Jewish people face such a widespread and wild dispersion. In their headlong rush for deliverance, the refugees were ready to grasp at any straw and many thousands were cheated, robbed, and led astray.

The countries which accepted Jews between 1933 and 1943 are listed in Table 2.

## YOUTH ALIYAH

Out of the chaos and anguish of this period arose one of the most magnificent chapters of Jewish defiance and survival: Youth Aliyah, founded by Recha Freier. Recognized as a most effective and potent instrument for saving and redeeming blighted orphaned lives, it gave the uprooted, destitute, and culturally deprived children new homes in which they became productive, happy citizens. In spite of grave difficul-

TABLE 2
Absorption of Jewish Refugees, 1933–43

| Country | Number Admitted | Percentage |
|---|---|---|
| Total | 811,000 | 100.0 |
| United States | 190,000 | 23.5 |
| Palestine | 120,000 | 14.8 |
| England | 65,000 | 8.1 |
| France | 55,000 | 6.8 |
| Holland | 35,000 | 4.3 |
| Belgium | 30,000 | 3.7 |
| Switzerland | 16,000 | 1.9 |
| Spain | 12,000 | 1.4 |
| Other European Countries | 70,000 | 8.8 |
| Argentina | 50,000 | 6.2 |
| Brazil | 25,000 | 3.1 |
| Bolivia | 12,000 | 1.4 |
| Chile | 14,000 | 1.7 |
| Uruguay | 7,000 | 0.8 |
| Other Latin American Countries | 20,000 | 2.4 |
| China | 25,000 | 3.1 |
| Australia | 9,000 | 1.1 |
| South Africa | 8,000 | 1.0 |
| Canada | 8,000 | 1.0 |
| Other Countries | 40,000 | 4.9 |
| TOTAL | 811,000 | 100.0 |

Source: Aryeh Tartakower and Kurt R. Grossman, *The Jewish Refugee* (New York: Institute of Jewish Affairs, 1944), p. 343.

ties, the organization brought over ten thousand children to Palestine during the war. When the Jewish tragedy engulfed other parts of the world, Youth Aliyah was extended to Jewish children in other countries of Europe, as well as Islamic countries of Asia and Africa. When the Jewish Brigade was formed, some two thousand Youth Aliyah graduates joined its ranks; they, in turn, helped rescue Jewish children wherever possible.

---

# The First Youth Aliyah Group, 1932

*The beginnings and the early history of the epic Youth Aliyah movement is recorded by Recha Freier in her book,* Let the Children Come. *Wife of a Berlin Rabbi, she was the first to conceive of, and launch, the organization which Hadassah later took under its wing and to which the immortal Henrietta Szold gave her best years of inspiring leadership. . . .*

At the beginning of 1932, a year before the Hitler regime . . . several youths came to my home in Berlin. There they stood, thin, excited, gloomy, despair on their pale faces. They told me that they had been sacked from their jobs for no other reason than that they were Jews. They were looking for a way out. Could I help them to get to Western Germany? They had heard that there were chances of finding employment in the coal-mines. Perhaps I had other advice for them?

. . . I do not remember why the boys came to me particularly. However, that visit disturbed my peace of mind. The right to work, that is the right to exist, had been taken from these boys and this—because they were Jews. Yet they possessed the full right to live. The utter senselessness of Jewish life in the Diaspora stood palpably before my eyes.

The following day I went to the Jewish Labour Exchange in Berlin, the director of which was a member of Poalei Zion (Socialist-Zionist). He, too, knew of boys being sacked because they were Jews. He shrugged his shoulders. "This state of affairs is undoubtedly due to the general unemployment in the country," he said. "As soon as this comes to an end, the Jewish boys will get work again." He advised me to let matters take their course. . . .

---

From *Let the Children Come* by Recha Freier

118

# Exodus and Flight

In the evenings unemployed people used to assemble . . . in North Berlin, to hail Communism as their solution. There I saw the boys who had come to me. If Zionism found no answer to their problem, then they would have to get it from other sources.

One night a very simple and clear idea came to my mind, a solution to the problem. The boys should go to Palestine, to the workers' settlements, where they would receive a training for life on the land of Palestine. Should Jewish youth, ready for work and for life, go to ruin somewhere or other, when their people needed them for its own work of rebuilding? Just as the rebuilding of the nation needs its youth, so the youth, albeit unconsciously as yet, desires to be rooted in their nation. I was sure that this idea could be realized, for it was absolutely true and it was timely.

Enzo Sereni[1] was then in Berlin and I explained my plan to him. He was the emissary of the kibbutz movement, and his opinion would certainly be identical with that of the kibbutz leaders in Palestine. He jumped up: "Do it," he said, "and revolutionize the entire German Zionist Movement!" He advised me to get in touch with the Workers' Federation in Palestine.

Thus in the spring of 1932, I asked the Federation if it were possible for groups of youths, aged between fifteen and sixteen years, to be educated and trained in the kibbutzim with a view to their settling in the country. The reply I got . . . was positive and encouraging enough to make a start.

When the boys came for further advice and help, I revealed my plans to them. I had kindled a spark which at once became a flame.

I turned to the Zionist leaders in Germany, explaining the problem of Jewish youth and placing my solution before them. They laughed at me. "Fantastic! Impossible!" they cried. "Send the lads to German farmers where they will really learn something and where the money will be properly spent. In a Palestinian kibbutz they will be spoilt," said the leader of the Zionists in Germany . . .

The apathy of the official Zionist leaders towards the problem of Jewish youth, which was the first sacrifice in the oncoming flood of anti-Semitism, their blindness to the signs of impending disaster and their disregard of the kibbutzim in Palestine encouraged my desire for action, and I perceived more and more the rightness and necessity of my plan: the formation of a great and permanent movement for the transfer of Jewish youth from the Diaspora to the Palestinian colonies, to enable them to live and to take root in the soil of their fatherland. . . .

The Workers' Federation [of Palestine] sent me the first details of importance, i.e. the names of those colonies that were prepared to accept youth groups, and an estimate of the expenses involved. Among the colonies were Ein Harod, Geva and Nahalal. . . .

[1] Italian-Jewish Zionist youth leader (p. 560)

In order to appeal for wider support, I prepared a memorandum entitled "Productive Activity of German-Jewish Boys in Palestine." It pointed out the serious position of unemployed Jewish youths in Germany, the dark future in store for them in the Diaspora and the way out by their becoming rooted in the soil of Palestine. It also described the agricultural settlements in which the Jewish youths were to be trained. . . . However, neither the *Juedische Rundschau*[2] nor any other Jewish newspaper in Germany would publish it. . . .

[Hearing] the news of my plan, the Jewish youth of Berlin became so excited that the communal bodies were worried and concerned. I was again asked to appear before the executive of the Zionist Organization in Germany. I reported on the preparatory steps I had taken. After some days, Dr Georg Landauer, member of the Executive, informed me that the Zionist Organization in Germany was prepared to accept my plan, provided that the Vaad Leumi[3] (National Council) in Palestine established a satisfactory body to supervise arrangements for settling the children and their education and provided they accepted responsibility for financial matters. Dr Landauer suggested I should get in touch with Miss Szold,[4] director of the Social Department of the Vaad Leumi in Jerusalem.

I wrote to Miss Szold about the problem that had arisen in Germany and my plan for its solution. After some delay I received her reply—a negative one. Miss Szold pointed out the existing difficulties with children already in Palestine. There were neglected, retarded and mentally defective cases which could not be dealt with because of lack of funds. . . .

Here also the idea of a great Youth Aliyah found no response. . . .

Meanwhile, pressure from the young people was becoming stronger and stronger. They were yearning for life and they felt with their healthy senses what the adults did not wish to see. My faith in the ultimate success of my mission was likewise becoming stronger and stronger. I was convinced that the task I had taken upon myself was a vital necessity and that it was up to me to fulfil it. Fascinated by the goal, I did not see the obstacles to it in all their magnitude. . . .

I got in touch with the Kibbutz Ein Harod which I hoped would be the home of the first group. This kibbutz had agreed to take the children. The emissaries of the kibbutz who were then in Berlin contacted me in order to arrange the aliyah of this first group. However, on receipt of Miss Szold's negative reply, every hope of obtaining entry permits was gone, since she was the head of the Youth depart-

[2]German-Jewish Zionist weekly
[3]National Council representing the Jews of Palestine
[4]Henrietta S. Szold, founder of Hadassah, Women's Zionist Organization (1912) and outstanding Zionist leader. She soon became the leader of the Youth Aliyah movement

ment of the Vaad Leumi and it was she who would have to apply to the British Government for immigration certificates and give the required guarantees.

At that moment of despair in June 1932, I got a telegram from Dr Siegfried Lehman, the founder and director of the Ben Shemen children's village. He informed me of his impending visit to Berlin and asked me not to come to a final decision about the group till he had seen it. The meeting with the group took place at my home. About forty youths were present, standing round him in a circle, listening with excitement and expectation to what he said. Finally he told me that he could offer me twelve immigration certificates and twelve places in Ben Shemen.

I was in a dilemma. Our goal had been the Kibbutz Ein Harod and not a children's village. Dr Lehman's certificates were valid only for Ben Shemen. Without the help of the Vaad Leumi no certificate could be had for Ein Harod. It would mean a long and bitter struggle to get them. In the meantime twelve boys would be in Palestine, would announce my plan and justify its execution. The unbearable tension which had been pressing upon us would lessen. Moreover, delay was fraught with danger. The difficulties on all sides could only be overcome by quick action. Facts would speak for themselves and bring the necessary help. Above all considerations stood the imperative: start working and provide convincing facts. . . .

The preparations were made with the knowledge of the parents but not with their full consent. Now they had to sign their agreement. They realized the importance of that solemn moment. They all signed. The date of leaving was fixed for Wednesday, 12th October 1932. . . .

The eve of the departure of the group had come. . . . This little group was leaving Germany in order to pave the way for the liberation of others. All the youth movements and many other children crowded the platforms singing Hebrew songs. Many adults were there as well. All were excited. Wilfried Israel [the guide] whispered to me: "This is an historic moment!" The platform seemed to tremble under my feet. The work had begun; no one could interfere with it any more; it would progress and develop and all those children standing there around me, full of hope, excitement and enthusiasm, would reach their goal. Cheering broke out as the train left.

The parents wept.

# The Children Flee

*Karen Gershon was a child refugee who came to England and established a reputation as poet and writer. She has excelled in skillfully compiling collective accounts into "group autobiographies" as in her book,* We Came As Children, *from which the following were selected. She now lives in Israel.*

The World Movement for the Care of Children from Germany was the response of the British people to the pogrom of 10th November 1938. . . . When the war broke out 9,354 children had come, of whom 7,482 were Jewish. Those who had relations or friends and were therefore individually sponsored were classified as 'guaranteed'. The 'non-guaranteed' were those whose maintenance was undertaken by the organisation itself or by local committees. Jewish children who had no friends or relations in Britain were selected in Germany by the Central Jewish Organisation, and in Austria by the Jewish community. The Christian, "non-Aryan" children were selected in Berlin by the Christian body, Paulusbund, and in Vienna by the Society of Friends.

Lists with particulars and photographs of the children were sent to the Movement in London, and travel arrangements were made on the continent after permits had been issued by the British Home Office and passed by the German police. Priority was given to those whose emigration was specially urgent because their fathers were in concentration camps . . . or because they were homeless, or orphaned, or old enough to be in danger themselves. During the first few months several large transports of these children, Jewish and non-Jewish together, reached England. . . . The rate at which children could be brought to England . . . decreased [after April 1939].

## Trevor Chadwick Rescues Children

In 1938 I was teaching at our family prep school. Rumours of the many distressed children in Central Europe reached us, and it was decided to adopt two, according to Home Office regulations, which required a full guarantee of care and maintenance until the age of 18; strict personal references covering the guarantor's character and solvency were also demanded.

Another master at the school and I set off for Prague to select our pair. We did not know where to begin, and had interviews with various

From *We Came As Children* by Karen Gershon

people. . . . Within a few days we had found a couple of small boys of about eight and ten.

We got a clear impression of the enormity of the task. We so often saw halls full of confused refugees and batches of lost children, mostly Jewish, and we saw only the fringe of it all.

Soon after our return I felt that I had to do more about it. I went to Friends House, and later to the Movement for the Care of Children from Germany. They were busy finding guarantors, and I flew back to Prague to find children who would fit in with the guarantors' wishes.

I took my first air transport rather proudly, on a twenty-seater plane. They were all cheerfully sick, enticed by the little paper bags, except a baby of one who slept peacefully in my lap the whole time. . . . Then [came] the meeting with the guarantors—my baby was cooed over and hustled off, and the other nineteen were shyly summing up their new parents, faces alive with hope for the love they were obviously going to be given. I felt depressed as I returned to Prague. Only twenty! This was late that winter, early in 1939.

But on March 15 the air transports came to an end when the Nazis came in. By then I had a hundred or so children waiting to be sent to England . . . On March 13 I had a telegram from home—'advise return immediately'—and thinking one of my sons was ill flew back at once. It appeared that war was feared, but it was only the *Einmarsch*.[1] I made all haste to fly back. . . .

On the morning of the 15th I got no further than Rotterdam. No flights to Prague. Thwarted and angry I flew to Berlin and began to hammer on tables, except at the British Embassy, where I asked politely for help and was politely refused. Goebbels' office coldly explained that no foreigners could travel to Prague that day (except Germans!). But early the next morning, at the Alexander Platz police station, I was given a special pass enabling me to travel to Prague by train.

A member of the Czech cabinet lent me an office, and I had two young helpers. The whole days, from 7 until 7, with twenty minutes for lunch, were taken up with interviewing, filing and writing letters to the guarantors, which perforce could not be scrappy. I can't say how many children were on my books, but it must have been in the thousands, but only hundreds, alas, got away.

Attention had primarily to be paid to the wishes of the guarantors. The majority stipulated girls seven–ten and if possible fair. Boys of twelve and upwards were hard to place. Girls were in the majority on the transports.

I tried to find the most urgent, helpless cases. This was not easy. Many were already refugees from Germany and Austria; many parents had "disappeared".

I had contacted a Prague travel agency, because special trains were

[1] invasion into Czechoslovakia

needed. Now money was getting difficult, and my only hope of financing the thing seemed to be to allow the Movement to pay the travel agency in London, and to ask the connections of the little travellers to pay cash in Prague, or as much as they could afford. Many, of course, were penniless.

The Nazis had arrived. But Kriminalrat [lawyer] Boemmelburg was an elderly, smiling gentleman, far from sinister, who eventually proved to be a great help . . . He was really interested in my project, and his only Nazi-ish remark was a polite query why England wanted so many Jewish children.

He happily gave his stamp to the first train transport, even though I had included half a dozen adult "leaders" on it. I went to the station accompanied by a Gestapo clerk, and all the children were there, with labels prepared by my helpers tied round their necks. The train took them off, cheering, through Germany to the Hook of Holland, a hundred or more.

Soon Boemmelburg sent for me. (He insisted that we speak in French, not German or English . . . We were both appalling at it.) He said people were throwing dust in my eyes. It was now absolutely forbidden for any adult to leave the country without a special permit and the "leaders" of my transport had really escaped illegally. I expressed my deepest sorrow and grovelled. I was a blue-eyed boy again, and thereafter he agreed to stamp my lists of children for transport without delay. A kindly Jewess with an American passport was good enough to go with them. I sealed my friendship with Boemmelburg by "confessing" after the second transport that I had discovered later that one child was not Jewish. (There were several "Aryans" in all transports.) He praised my honesty and begged me to be careful, because of course the Nazis would look after "Aryan" children.

The second train transport was illegal—from the British point of view. Each child on the transport had to be accompanied by a Home Office document . . . These took a long time to arrive. They just didn't realise. If only the Home Secretary could have spent a few days with me, seeing brutality, listening to, not arguing with, young Nazis, as I often did, he would doubtlessly have pushed the whole thing along fast. If he had realised that the regulations were for so many children the first nudge along the wretched road to Auschwitz, he would, of course, have immediately imported the lot. But that is too much wisdom after the event.

I could wait no longer. Letters explaining urgency bore no fruit. I had my guarantors lined up and the children waiting. The next transport was taking shape. There had to be documents, so I had some made, as near as possible like the Home Office ones, and away the train went. I informed everybody and awaited the Home Office telegram in reply. I betted myself that it would contain the word "irregular" and I won. It also contained a threat to send them back, but I figured the mob of legally accepted guarantors would stop that one. . . .

It became obvious to me as summer developed that certain of my movements were at least suspect, and that B. and his boys might turn sour. This would jeopardize the children, so I explained these things to London and they arranged a replacement. I shall always have a feeling of shame that I didn't get more out.

## The Children Recall . . .

My mother took me to Berlin; when I left home my father was lying in bed ill, the concentration camp had damaged his health. He held me close and bade me look after my mother when she got to England in case he did not make it. I was then just ten years old. We got to Berlin to learn that I was too late for the first transport, but would be able to go on the second. There was of course no money for me to go back home, so my mother took me to friends in Berlin, who kindly put me up for a fortnight or so. My mother had to leave me there, and the last I ever saw of her was in the Berlin Street, outside the friends' house, walking backward along the pavement to get a last look at me, until she rounded the corner and we were parted.

\* \* \*

We were allowed one suitcase each containing only clothes. I remember my main worry being that I might not be allowed to take my love tokens—a collection of small cloth animals. My mother, with the insight of selfless love, knew that these objects must be packed in the suitcase at all cost, and reassured me. I was twelve years old.

\* \* \*

I left home late in the evening with the whole family to see me off. At the station we were ushered into an enormous waiting room which was packed with children and parents weeping, crying and shouting. It occurred to me there for the first time that our grief was no longer a personal one. We all belonged to a group, but not a group that was determined through social, economic or intellectual dividing lines; we were all refugees. We were ordered to take leave of our relatives quickly and go straight to the train, which had sealed windows and once we were all inside it the doors were sealed as well. Shortly before the train was due to leave our relatives appeared again on the platform. From behind the sealed windows I saw my parents again, rigid and unsmiling like two statues, for the last time ever. I was sixteen years old.

\* \* \*

All the children from the different towns met at the Hauptbahnhof

125

[main station] in Berlin, each with a small suitcase, ten shillings in German money and a label round our necks giving our names. I was put into a compartment with several other children of my own age—I was eleven, my sister into the adjoining one because she was older. I recall vividly our arrival at the German-Dutch frontier, when the Nazis boarded the train for a last inspection, before it crossed into another country. One Nazi per compartment. . . . The one in our compartment pulled down the blind, made us stand in the gangway, pulled down all the suitcases from the racks, opening them and throwing everything on to the floor. He took one or two small items, really of no value, except a sentimental one. He also asked us for our money, taking the equivalent of nine shillings from each child, and so we left the fatherland with a shilling in our pockets. . . . Fear was in all of us, until the moment the whistle blew, the Nazis left and the train passed over the frontier. At this moment we opened the windows, shouting abuse and spitting at them. . . . It was terrible that we children should have learned such hatred. At the first stop in Holland, we were met by some wonderfully kind ladies who stood waiting for us on the platform with big carts, filled with hot drinks, chocolate, sandwiches, etc. . . .

\* \* \*

I left home two weeks after my sixteenth birthday. Two compartments were reserved for us—a small number of girls and boys, all of whom I knew well. As we had been told to limit our luggage to one piece, we each had one enormous suitcase, so heavy we could hardly lift it. Leave-taking was restrained and brief. My mother kissed me and the train moved out. It was a final good-bye; I was never to see her again. The trip to Cologne was uneventful. The railway officials were not merely courteous, they were even helpful. I cannot remember what we talked about or even what I felt. My only fear was that we might all be turned back at the frontier, but there was really little likelihood of that since the Nazis were only too glad to be rid of us. Cologne station was the point where we joined other transports and the station was full of many hundreds of children from all parts of Germany from toddlers up to the age of seventeen. When we moved on we were all looking out of the windows for the first sign that we were in Holland. At the first Dutch station a large number of people were on the platform and as our train drew in they waved and cheered—they actually cheered. We were momentarily stunned and then returned the cheers and waved frantically. We were not only free, we were welcomed back to humanity by humanity. There followed a distribution of milk, lemonade, fruit, chocolate, sweets and sandwiches. I doubt if any of us were really hungry, most of us were stuffed with whatever our parents had provided. But this first meal on foreign soil, on free soil, I ate with genuine feeling of gratitude and thanksgiving. This touching reception intoxicated us. The milk might as well have been brandy. Up to then we had been subdued children—understandable in view of our recent experiences and the even more recent separation from our parents. But from this point onwards we were a noisy, boisterous bunch of boys and girls; being our age in fact. Whenever in subsequent years I dreamed about Germany there was always a fog. In these dreams when I was questioned I was unable to answer in English when I was trying to deny my German origin.

\* \* \*

Not only had I never been on a large ocean-going ship but I had never even seen the sea. Alas, it was a night-crossing and I saw very little. The ship had been specially chartered for us. The only adults on board were the crew and those in charge of us. While they were busy I explored the ship, top to bottom, bow to stern. I stumbled into the crew's quarters, engine room and all kinds of places I had no business to be. The only place I was denied was the bridge. Everything I saw was new to me, it was fascinating. My cabin had been allocated to someone more in need of comfort and I spent the night in one of the saloons which had been improvised into a dormitory. Not much sleeping was done there that night. There were about forty or fifty boys, all about fifteen or sixteen years old, in that room. We did not know each other yet. We were all a little over-excited and for the next hours we exchanged, in the dark, all the political jokes which we had picked up. They were mostly variations of "Hitler, Goebbels and Goering. . . ." The jokes, as such, were not memorable, but the occasion was. We did not need to look over our shoulders or lower our voices and the realisation that we could say what we liked with impunity engendered an atmosphere of enormous gaiety.

# Gestapo Emigration Office

*Vojta Beneš, brother of Dr. Eduard Beneš, President of Czechoslovakia, writes about the experiences of Jews seeking to emigrate . . .*

Every Jew leaving the "protectorate" [Czechoslovakia] regardless of his nationality, has to pass through the Gestapo offices in Prague . . . I have spoken recently to a young American Jewess, wife of

From *Ten Million Prisoners* by Vojta Beneš

an Aryan Czech physician. She had just arrived from Prague and gave me horrifying details which she, an American citizen, had undergone. She spoke calmly, factually, saying:

"At this Zentralstelle [office] the Jews were treated miserably. As you approached the building, you would see a long line of Jews standing, awaiting their turn, the men with bared heads. They are not permitted to keep their hands in their pockets, and if caught doing so, would be brutally assaulted. The Nazis are always afraid of concealed weapons.

"Just before the war, many more Jews passed through here. When I finally reached the building, I was not allowed to lean against the wall, tired as I was. Anyone caught leaning would be mistreated. The whole house resounded with the brutal shouting and yelling of men in command who handled their victims worse than dogs.

"Inside the office, a young man at a table opposite me shouted at each Jew as he passed by, 'You stinking Jew, say: Please, may I pass by?' I could not believe my eyes or ears. To me, the man seemed completely insane.

"Finally, I reached the table where my papers should have been settled. The officer in charge looked at me and shouted: 'Why are you laughing?' to which I barely whispered, 'I am not laughing, if you please.'

"Another Nazi jumped up and shouted still louder: 'How dare you talk to us that way, you stinking Jewess,' and added, 'Where is your husband?'

" 'My husband is a physician,' I replied. 'He is an Aryan and will stay here.'

" 'Oh, so he's sorry he married you, you stinking Jewess.'

" 'What's your nationality?' another one barked at me.

" 'I am an American citizen,' I replied, having regained my composure.

The Gestapo stopped shouting. They gave me my documents without further questioning and I dashed out of that house as though haunted."

# Readings

*The Jewish Refugee* by Aryeh Tartakower and Kurt R. Grossman (World Jewish Congress, 1944), deals with the diverse aspects of the refugee and migration problems.

*Visas to Freedom: The History of Hias* by Mark Wischnitzer (World Pub. Co., 1956), presents the work of the Hebrew Immigrant Aid Sheltering Society.

See also readings on the chapters on *The Children* and *Rescue Efforts.*

*Island Refuge: Britain and Refugees from the Third Reich 1933–1939,* by A. J. Sherman (University of California Press, 1973).

# 8. | WAR

## WAR AND THE FINAL SOLUTION

On November 12, 1938, at a gathering of the Council of Ministers called to assess the results of *Kristallnacht,* Hermann Goering ended the meeting on an ominous note. "If in the future," he said, "the German Reich should come into conflict with foreign powers, it goes without saying that we in Germany should first come to a showdown with the Jews. . . ."

That showdown began on September 1, 1939, when Germany invaded Poland. Two days later, England and France declared war on Germany.

Hitler's cataclysmic advance brought in its wake destruction, terror, murder, and terrible suffering. His barbaric hordes were let loose in the very heartland of world Jewry: Poland, and later Lithuania, the Ukraine, and Russia. The Germans were freer now to perpetrate their crimes because they were at war, fighting the "enemy." Moreover, they were not deterred by the fear of being exposed to world opinion as they had been in Western Europe.

The route of Hitler's armies lay through the largest Jewish population centers, the Pale of Settlement, those provinces of Czarist Russia where Jews had been permitted residence and which they had populated densely. The invasion was a bloody field day, with the victims set up as if in a shooting gallery. The barbarities which the Nazis had initiated in Berlin and Vienna now became more highly developed. They invented acts of terror the like of which had never been imagined or practiced before. This invasion marked the second phase of the Holocaust. A 1931 census had recorded 3,130,581 Jews living in Poland. Allowing for a normal population growth of 10 percent, it is estimated that on the eve of World War II there were 3,400,000 Jews, or 9.5 percent of the total Polish population of 35,000,000. Over three-quarters of the Jews lived in cities, and their concentration made them convenient prey for their killers.

130

For centuries, Polish Jewry had been the fountainhead of Jewish learning and spirit. Its rabbis, scholars, and talmudical academies were world-renowned. It had given rise to Hasidism and to Zionism. It was the center of Hebraic and Yiddish literary creativity. Before the war, 130 Hebrew and Yiddish periodicals, 11 scientific, and 94 literary magazines were published in Poland. In 1937, 443 Hebrew and Yiddish books were printed there, which sold over 675,000 copies. Its schools, academies, libraries, and synagogues were outstanding. In a couple of months, this great cultural, spiritual, and religious center, which had taken centuries to develop, was reduced to ashes and rubble.

## THE NAZI GHETTO

To expedite the Nazi plan, the far-sighted Reinhard Heydrich, to whom Goering had assigned the task of implementing the Final Solution, forced all Jews living in Polish villages and hamlets to move into ghettos in urban centers. No Jewish community was permitted to have fewer than five hundred souls, except in areas located near a railroad, so that loading and transportation to the death camps would be convenient and economical. For similar reasons, concentration camps were built as close to evacuation centers as possible: Treblinka near Warsaw, Ponar near Vilna, Majdanek near Lublin, Auschwitz near Cracow, and so on. Most of the camps were established amidst populations that were anti-Jewish so as to minimize "difficulties."

Jewish property and Jews themselves, above ten years of age, were immediately marked with the yellow star (this medieval stigma was introduced in Poland two years before it was forced on German Jewry). The movement of individuals was prohibited except within very restricted areas or by special permits. Groups were allowed to congregate only with official permission. Jewish property was "registered"; assets beyond minimal existence were seized and bank accounts frozen; life insurance and pensions were wiped out. Systematically, Jews were stripped of wealth, life savings, holdings, resources, hope, and future.

The ghettos became vast workshops manufacturing brushes, mattresses, blankets, even cigarettes. At first the Germans integrated the ghettos as a productive enterprise in the war machinery, and the mobilization for work helped allay fears of deportation. Prominent German businesses established branches nearby for the manufacture of clothing, chemicals, shoes, etc., all to aid in the war effort. In return for the materials produced, the slave laborers received food rations according to their output. The rations were not fixed but fluctuated, depending on a predetermined schedule of annihilation through starvation, and were subject to the whims of the ghetto commandant. In 1942 a month's ration consisted of two pounds of bread, nine ounces of sugar, three and one-half ounces of jam, and one and one-half ounces of fats.

131

The ghettos were set up in the worst slum areas, selected with an eye to isolation, maximum confinement, and complete control. Following the Nazi policy of deception, the ghettos were called "Jewish quarters." Walls were built, surmounted with jagged glass and surrounded with barbed wire. Construction costs were borne by the Jews.

Here again, Nazi cunning was exercised: the ghetto walls, they said, were to quarantine the inmates from epidemics. Indeed, some of the imprisoned victims welcomed living amidst their brethren. They were spared the humiliations and sufferings in the open towns, where Jews were tortured and abused, and were forced to perform "gymnastics" for public amusement. The ghetto population changed frequently as new hordes of wretched deportees were sent to fill the places vacated by the dead and those taken away to be killed.

The overcrowding was incredible. The density of population inside the Warsaw Ghetto in 1940 was reported to be 5.5 per room, and the situation worsened with time. (General Jurgen Stroop, who crushed the Warsaw Ghetto uprising, reported that in 1943 there were as many as thirteen in a room prior to the mass deportation.) The working day was unlimited. Coal mines, agricultural enterprises, fish and poultry breeders, iron foundries, munitions factories, textile factories, and other industrial enterprises all waxed rich on the free labor. (The Krupp family, who manufactured munitions, alone ruled 138 privately owned concentration camps.) Provision contracts to provide food for the workers were not met, but production quotas were more than exacted; those who dropped at their work were shot. But for two deterrents, the starved, caged-in people would have been decimated more rapidly: the fear of epidemics (which would also infect the Germans), and the widespread practices of food smuggling and of bribery, to which the Nazis were prone.

Smuggling was accomplished through sewers, holes in the walls, via funeral carts, and by means of other subterfuges. Children were particularly suited to smuggling because they were small, thin, and more sprightly than adults. They often worked in gangs, wriggling through tight holes in the ghetto walls and sewers to get to the "Aryan" side and bring back food for the very few who could pay the high prices. Since a quick death was preferred to dying slowly by starvation, the fear of being caught was somewhat mitigated.

In the early years, 1939–40, the American Jewish Joint Distribution Committee provided soup kitchens and other forms of relief. Packages of food and medicines were allowed through. When Nazis thwarted this program, the JDC arranged for the British Royal Air Force to drop money into the ghetto. But by 1941 more than 100,000 people in Warsaw were subsisting on a ration of one daily meal of soup, sometimes made of hay, which was provided by the efforts of the Jewish Council for Self-Help, an amalgamation of Jewish welfare societies. All bread was black and tasted like sawdust; jelly was made of horse bones; horse meat was a delicacy.

No food scraps were thrown away; everything was eaten. Nevertheless, starvation took its toll, and epidemics spread. The dead lay in the streets covered with papers. They died nameless so that their ration cards might not be taken away from their families. And nameless they were buried in common graves.

The SS used the famine as a fiendish trap to ensnare more Jews for extermination. Thus in Warsaw, in July 1942, they posted a notice that those "who will present themselves for selection for resettlement will receive three kilograms of bread and one kilogram of marmalade." Hungry and desperate Jews flocked to the railroad station, where they were packed into deportation trains without food. Why feed people who were soon to die?

## THE JUDENRAT

To relieve themselves of the responsibility of executing their own directives, the Germans swiftly set up a control instrument for the administration of the ghetto: the *Judenrat,* or Jewish Community Council. In this way, they unloaded the burden of management and control onto the victims so as to save German manpower and absolve themselves from guilt. Many council members were individuals who had been prominent in social and communal affairs, and who were conscripted and forced to serve. The councils' functions were many, and included taking care of welfare, sanitary, health, and medical facilities, administering a Jewish police force, distributing food and ration cards, providing work battalions and skilled workers to the SS, sheltering the new arrivals, and keeping records of births and deaths. In short, they served as the governing mechanism of the SS in almost all areas of ghetto life. Following Nazi principles, a headman was appointed. Thereafter, he and his councilmen had to keep the ghetto in line. In addition, they had to cater to the whims and insatiable appetites of their SS captors.

Although the council members enjoyed certain privileges, their lot was unbearable. The job was an impossible one and worsened with every passing day. On the one hand, they were feared and sometimes despised by their fellow Jews; on the other hand, they were treated like mongrel dogs by their masters and were faced with death if they disobeyed. Life became intolerable for them in the final phases of ghetto life, when they had to deliver ever increasing quotas of Jews for deportation. Gathering the doomed and delivering them to the death-train or vehicles was the responsibility of the council's special Jewish police. Many could not bear up to this act of collective homicide and broke down mentally and physically. Some committed suicide; others were dispatched, or went voluntarily, to face death with their fellow victims. And there were some who became callous and unfeeling themselves and inflicted suffering on their fellow men no less than their "masters."

133

# INNER LIFE

Despite these indescribably horrible conditions, the will to live persisted on an amazingly broad front. Surrounded by death, the people nevertheless did their best to survive, both physically and morally, with dignity. Dr. Hillel Seidman, a surviving chronicler of the Warsaw Ghetto, records the astounding fact that, during the tragedy, there were fewer suicides than before the war. Suicide was viewed as desertion. "Nobody wanted to desert, so strong was the faith in life . . . the will to live. . . . In all minds there is only one thought: to endure, to hold out and to survive!"

Deeply stirring is the story of the Warsaw Archives organized and conducted by Dr. Emanuel Ringelblum, who brought together the scholars of all the groups in the Warsaw Ghetto to prepare, collect, and edit its history. They met regularly on Saturdays in the guise of an *Oneg Shabbat* (festive Sabbath gathering). Toward the end of 1942, when the "action" marking the end of the ghetto took place, the archives were buried underground. Some of them were dug up after the war. One collection was published in *Notes from the Warsaw Ghetto* (see bibliography). It is a rich mine of information for the history of the day-to-day happenings in Warsaw. More was found later and published by Yad Vashem under the title *Polish-Jewish Relations During the Second World War* (1974).

Another remarkable chapter was a project headed by Dr. Israel Milejkowsky, chief of the Warsaw Judenrat's Health Department. It produced a study on the effects of starvation on the human body, which is considered by medical scientists to be of basic and lasting value. The research team had at its disposal an abundance of laboratory subjects—walking skeletons, wasted bodies, and they themselves, who were slowly dying. Unable to cure their "clients" (food, which was unobtainable, would have rehabilitated them), they endowed meaning and nobility to their lives by using their plight to increase scientific knowledge.

Whenever deportations struck, their work was interrupted but not abandoned. According to experts, the statistical material was gathered in a manner "that could not be bettered in the best universities in Europe." Before the liquidation of the ghetto, the findings were smuggled out to the "Aryan" side and deposited with a professor of the University of Warsaw. (The names and qualifications of twenty-eight of the medical researchers, as well as the facts of the research and its conclusions, are reported in *The Uses of Adversity* by Leonard Tushnet [Thomas Yoseloff, 1966].)

When, at the end of 1942, the mass deportations to the death factories began, active physical resistance replaced the passivity that characterized the first two years. Underground self-defense and resistance began. The life-and-death struggles united all groups as one.

# Flight to Soviet Russia

After two scant weeks of war with the Germans, when the beaten Polish armies were still facing the west, the Soviet army pulled in behind them from the east. The forward units crossed the border in light tanks. Towards evening appeared lines of shiny black cars with lamps for eyes. Following them, at a snail's pace, came heavy tanks with their cannons jutting forward. They crept like antediluvian creatures with upturned snouts full of glittering saw teeth. The next morning masses of infantry in grey cloaks as hard as tin marched through the streets. The soldiers' faces were dimmed and weary after the long march, but above each cap burned a red star. And over the tens of thousands of heads there floated as though in a fog a face with the smile of a tiger and a long black moustache . . .[1]

The working class areas, the markets, and even the merchants' streets took on a festive appearance. People ran toward the soldiers with outspread arms; others even wept for joy: if not for the Soviet incursion we would have fallen into the hands of the Germans. Now we were saved! . . .

A much larger crowd gathered around the tanks. Youths stroked the cold steel as a rider strokes the velvety flanks of the horse that had just saved his life. The tank crew, wearing plaited black caps, stood by the cannons and sang Soviet songs.

"We know these songs," shouted a girl with a flaming face. "We heard them secretly on the radio, behind the backs of the Polish *pans*. We knew that a land with such joyous songs must be very happy."

"How long did the march from the Soviet border to Vilna take?" asked a youth in a black shirt and even blacker hair. "I mean how long did it take to get to us?"

"We've been on our way to you for twenty years, ever since the October Revolution," a blond pug-nosed Russian answered sharply. . . .

The reply spread through town: they've been on their way to us for twenty years. They've been working day and night for two decades, preparing to liberate us. "But here we didn't sleep either. We prepared the groundwork," the young men and women said elatedly, strolling arm in arm in the streets. Whenever a shiny black car passed, the girls stopped and smiled into the curtained windows. They had no idea who sat there, but they knew that the cars contained officers and commissars.

[1]Stalin.

From *The Seven Little Lanes* by Chaim Grade.

Once one of these cars stopped and a tall man with a leather coat emerged. Behind him came a shorter man in uniform, evidently of lesser rank. The commissar in the leather coat smiled and loudly asked his chauffeur so that the others would hear:

"Do we have enough gas for Bialystok?"

The chauffeur nodded indifferently, but the Army man said with a smile full of meaning:

"We even have enough gas for Warsaw."

"And perhaps for Berlin, too," the commissar added, laughing. . . .

Just as the Russians left Vilna unexpectedly, so they suddenly returned almost a year later. Henceforth, they declared Vilna would be the capital of Soviet Lithuania. The Russians remained part of the summer and through autumn and winter. In the spring, in honor of May Day, the streets were filled with red flags that fluttered day and night. The Russian soldiers marched and sang, and the youths marched along and cheered them: "Long live the Red Army! The enemy won't dare to take an inch of Soviet soil."

But in town everyone whispered the report heard on the B.B.C. that the Germans were massing troops and armor on the Soviet border. An attack was expected any day.

One Sunday morning, the 22nd of June, the first day of summer, I was alone in my house. My wife, Frume Libtche, was at work in the hospital. . . .

That day the airplanes flew higher than usual. I wondered why. My lips became dry. Maneuvers, I consoled myself. Russian maneuvers. I wanted to open the radio, but my hands shook and I shouted to myself: I don't want to hear any news! I was hungry and wanted to go down to buy bread. Once more I shouted that I was not hungry, and I turned from the window, no longer wanting to look at the street.

Suddenly, I heard a metallic whistling. My ears were pierced by a shrill noise; a dull thud sounded somewhere, and the windows shook. The explosion paralyzed me and made me speechless. A moment later the factory sirens began to scream. There was another explosion; the windows shook even more severely, and I snapped out of my paralysis.

War.

"I won't run away. The Russians won't retreat, and even if they do, I still won't run away and abandon my mother. I won't become a refugee and, like the Polish refugees, curse the day I left home. The Russians won't let anyone flee. They'll shoot all those who create panic and disturb the movement of military convoys on the roads. It's better that way. I'll shave. Today is a day like any other."

In the street, I saw large trucks standing in front of many of the houses. Soviet women, wearing shaggy berets, were hastily carrying bundles of clothing out of their apartments. Together with the chauffeurs they lugged benches, tables and dressers and stacked them on the trucks. The owners of the apartments where the Red Army officers and their wives were quartered suddenly felt the suspicion, the strangeness and the indifference that the Soviet citizens displayed toward them, the veteran residents of Vilna. The Jews then gathered in little groups and spoke excitedly, absolutely without any fear:

"Why are they running off? They said that the Red Army soldiers never retreat," someone shouted.

"They consider a broken bench more valuable than living human beings. They have enough people, but not enough furniture!" someone else called out.

"It's impossible that the Germans will kill all the Jews," a third stammered. "During the First World War the Germans dealt with Jews."

And a fourth wept, "On the roads the Germans kill with small arms and the peasants slay with axes."

"I'm not afraid of bombs and I'm not afraid of peasants with axes. It's the Germans I'm afraid of," I said.

The next day, when the Russian Army began retreating from Lithuania, I left, accompanied by Frume Libtche, with a knapsack on my back and a little Bible in my pocket.

We both ran to my mother and bid her farewell. The streets were packed with people rushing on all sides; they were leaving the city singly and in couples, carrying children in their hands and bundles on their backs.

A gloomy silence pervaded the streets; everyone, it seemed, had been changed into nighttime shadows.

All the neighbors had gathered in my mother's and stepfather's apartment. The walls there were thick, the windows were covered with wire mesh, the ceiling was low and vaulted; hence, the neighbors had chosen it as a shelter from the bombs. They sat on chairs, on the sofa, on empty fruit crates; they sat in despondent silence, like members of a family that gather at the cemetery, in the purification room, where the shroud is sewn for the corpse. My mother, wrapped in her shawl, sat at the table like a stranger, and when Frume Libtche and I entered, her wandering eyes did not recognize us. Her husband, Reb Rafael,[2] constantly stared out the window as though there were no war going on at all. I could not say a word. "We are fleeing," Frume Libtche told my mother. "There are no more trains leaving from the station. We'll have to go by foot."

My mother rose slowly. Her lips trembled at great length like a mute; then suddenly, she fell on my neck with the cry:

"I'm coming too."

[2]The author's stepfather.

137

At once Reb Rafael appeared beside us. He took his hands out of his sleeves and groaned a bit, as though laughing and crying at the same time:

"On foot!"—were the only words he uttered, addressing my mother.

My mother immediately sat down on her chair, her fate sealed. I clung to her, to bid farewell, but she tore herself away and pointed to her husband. . . .

"First say goodbye to Reb Rafael," she said, her face stern, just as it had been when I was a child and she taught me the proper way for a Jew to behave.

I bade goodbye to Reb Rafael; to my mother I said farewell in haste, and dashed out to the courtyard. My mother ran after me through the courtyard, and by the gate held my head in her hands.

"My child, don't forget Yiddishkeit.[3] Keep the Sabbath."

And she pushed me through the wicket of the gate, and Frume Libtche followed me.

At the outskirts of the city, Frume Libtche began to slow down. The Soviet trucks, packed with furniture and officers, sped by like demons. The host of foot travelers tried in vain to halt the vehicles. They wept, screamed and fell on their knees. The trucks swerved and weaved and flew by. The refugees feared that the motorized German divisions would catch up to us and shoot us. Remaining on the roadside was sure death, but in Vilna we might stay alive. The tall golden corn waved silently, the surrounding forest roared, and the twigs in full leaf shook piously. It seemed as if they were asking: "What's the rush? A needless panic!" And so, the refugees turned back to Vilna. One person encouraged another; everyone was happy that the next man was returning home, too.

"We'll even arrive in town before the Germans."

But I strove forward, dragging Frume Libtche, despite her cries that her feet were swollen. We finally arrived at the village of Rekvin, where a few years back we had spent a summer honeymoon in a cottage. . . . We went there for a while—just a little while—to get some water and let Frume Libtche rest her legs.

Our old peasant-landlord stood next to the cottage, barefoot and calm, as though he had just arisen from sleep, and gazed at us in open-mouthed astonishment. He took us into the house, gave us milk, and persuaded us to stay with him. His wife, sympathizing, wiped the tears from her eyes, and asserted that no matter how bad off a person was at home, he was worse off when he took up a wanderer's staff. Frume Libtche and I went outside to think the matter over. But the outdoors misled us, deceived us again . . . My eyes swept over the surrounding

[3]Judaism.

138

fields and forests, and I dreamed of a forest hut where we could wait out the war. What joy it would be to find such an abandoned hut. We would live on chestnuts, leaves, roots—so long as no one would find our hidden cabin. It could even be in the hollow trunk of a tree, or even in a pit bedded down with leaves—anything so as to remain alive.

Frume Libtche snapped me out of my daydream. She decided to spend the night at the peasant's, and return the next morning to my mother.

"The Germans won't touch women and children," she said. "But it's dangerous for you. You go! Go!"

And I went. As soon as I left night fell, as though I had entered a subterranean cave. I walked along the forest path and thought: soon I'll be attacked by a robber or a beast; a German will catch me—it wasn't important who, but I would not arrive, I would surely not arrive.

"Who goes there?" someone shouted. I did not know who had spoken: someone to me, or I to myself.

Red Army soldiers stood by a truck, holding flashlights and rifles. They were waiting for some Soviet trucks to come and give them gasoline. They asked me who I was and where I was going. When I told them I was fleeing the Germans, one of them sang out jubilantly:

"The Soviet Union is huge and there's room enough for everyone."

They paid no further attention to me. They remained silent and dejected, and breathed heavily, covered from head to toe with mud. A thought flashed: they've run off from their defeated units without an order for retreat. I gave them cigarettes and they promised to take me along. Finally a long overdue truck speeding from Vilna arrived. The soldiers stretched themselves across the road and in unison raised their rifles toward the driver. The truck stopped.

"We want gas."

The driver jumped down, gave them a few gallons of gasoline, and departed. Soon another truck passed, and a third, until finally our tank was full. One of the soldiers told me: "Climb up on top."

I faced the direction from which I had come. If it were not so dark, I thought I could have seen Frume Libtche standing in the village—no more than a mile away—where I had left her. About an hour had passed since we had separated. I'll tell the soldiers and ask them to have pity and wait. . . .

But the soldiers were already standing on the truck. Two soldiers holding machine guns sat next to the driver. He started the motor. I realized that they would not even wait a second. The Germans might catch us any moment. I just managed to jump on at the last minute, as the truck tore itself from its place and slid into the darkness. . . .

Parched with thirst, our group spied a well and ran up to it. Screaming and fights ensued, which resounded in the still, clear morning. The

139

water hoist creaked on its way down and up. Peoples' heads pressed into the pail; they drank thirstily; others scooped water in their hands until they were thrust aside by others behind them. In line ahead of me was the peasant who had walked behind me and pushed me in the back. He contemplated me by the light of day and evidently decided that he had nothing to fear from me. He took his drink, but when my turn came, he held onto the pail with both hands. The hair on his withered, wrinkled face stood up like needles.

"I'm a citizen of the Soviet Union, a bookkeeper in a *kolkhoz*.[4] Who are you?"

I pushed him away with my left elbow and seized the waterpail with my right. Suddenly I heard a severed cry:

"Run. A German plane!"

An airplane swooped down at us. Its wheels and fuselage suddenly became enormous. In another second he would cast a bomb into our group and cut us up with his wings. But we had already scattered, and jumped into the surrounding trenches. The soldiers with us shouted: "Get his motor! The motor!"

Our machine guns opened up with a heavy crossfire. The bullets flew over our heads. The sky seemed to be torn open and falling in fiery chunks. The plane that had dived down over the well suddenly reversed course and ascended, like an activated spring. Caught in the hail of bullets, the plane turned toward the forest, its tail smoking. Dazed, it spun and emitted awful metallic grating sounds, and came down behind the trees with one wing lowered.

In my trench also lay the peasant with the prickly-haired face. He looked on, pleased, with a twisted, angry smile as I huddled close to the ground, wanting to dig in deeper.

"You afraid?" he bared his teeth.

"No more than you," I replied.

To my left lay the tall broad-bearded Russian. He watched the plane disappearing beyond the tree line, and attempted to calm me as he had done the other day.

"It will pass," he said sleepily.

We crawled out of the trenches, our faces filthy, disheveled and covered with dust. I sprang to the well, pushed my face into the pail and choked over the water that the peasant, my enemy, had left over. Behind me other people gathered. But the soldiers drove the crowd away from the well. They did not permit us to stay together, lest an enemy plane attack us again. Our crowd broke up into smaller groups, and in a crouch, we crawled through the fields to the nearby forest.

In the forest we were surrounded by soldiers in green uniforms— the border guards. They did not let us pass, until they had inspected

[4]Collective farm.

140

our documents and questioned us. This was the Soviet front. In the thicket stood a large tank camouflaged with leafed branches. The crew milled around it. Deeper in the wood stood a cannon with a long, upraised nozzle. On a nearby hill the crashed plane burned like a pile of hay. No one paid any attention to it.

"Is that the one that attacked us?" I turned to a soldier from our group.

"That's the one," he said indifferently, looking gloomy and dejected. After the investigation we civilians were permitted to continue. But the Red Army soldiers who had wandered along with us were kept back so that a new unit would be formed which would perhaps soon go into battle.

I was waiting my turn to be questioned. I removed the knapsack from my back, unbound it, and tapped my passport in my chest pocket. "I'm Jewish," I whispered, the incantation that had conducted me through all Soviet guards, and which I would soon have to repeat.

As I approached the investigating officer my breathing became increasingly uneven. I saw the crowd dispersing, making way for me, as though afraid to show there had been a bond between us. The peasant from the *kolkhoz* whispered something into the commanding officer's ear and pointed at me. I felt my limbs turning to stone; I was over-whelmed by fatigue and a strange heat, the sort of warmth a frozen man feels before he expires. Hitherto I had been detained by civilian Soviet militia. But these men were frontier guards who had orders to shoot every suspicious person. I saw that the commander was no longer looking at the others in our group, but only screwed his gloomy eyes into me. Two soldiers, bedecked with rows of hand grenades, pushed me closer to the investigating officer.

"I'm Jewish," I told him in Russian, and showed him my passport. He turned the stamped pages, compared the little picture in the booklet with my face, and then asked:

"Why did you keep looking around on all sides during your journey? Did you want to hide in the woods?"

"I thought . . . It was hard for me to walk," I stammered. I wanted to say that I thought my mother and my wife were calling me back. But I caught myself in time, for such a reply would have prompted a gale of laughter and intensified the suspicion against me.

"We know," the officer nodded, as though expecting the excuse. He poked through my knapsack and ordered another soldier to search my pockets. The soldier tapped me and felt a hard object in my coat pocket.

"Found it," he said, pulling out my little Bible.

"And what's this?" the commander asked, leafing through the pages.

"That's a Bible."

"Are you a German? A German pastor?" he asked, pushing the visor

141

of his cap further up; his narrow hairy forehead wrinkled and became even smaller.

The soldiers and the civilians—the ones who had accompanied me—surrounded us, and, with eyes lowered, smiled crookedly. I didn't know if they were smiling because the commander was having some fun with me, or if they were wondering why I didn't realize that I was a lost man.

"Me a German? A German pastor?" I tapped my face. A thought flashed through my mind: Yes, perhaps I do look like a German pastor. My thinning clumps of hair, my unshaven blond beard, the Bible, my accent . . . A pastor! I knew that I should say something, scream out, but instead of justifying myself, I burst out in uncontrollable laughter. I knew that this could be my death sentence. Even if the commander had not been serious until now, he might now become enraged by my laughter and order me to be finished off. But my innards twisted within me, and I had to laugh. One of the officers in blue uniform leaped toward me in a rage, pulled out his pistol and pressed the cold muzzle to my temple.

"You'll really be laughing in a minute! You saboteur, you spy!"

The investigating officer remained calm and still. He gave both my passport and my Bible to one of the soldiers and said curtly:

"The passport is forged. Take him to headquarters." . . .

"Where are you taking me?" I shouted to the guard.

"Move on!" cried the guard behind me.

"What do you need your shoes for? Give them to me," laughed the soldier at my right.

"And the things in your knapsack you give to me and I'll send them home," said the soldier on my left.

They wanted me to take off my shoes. Barefoot men are not led to staff headquarters. Barefoot men are taken to be shot. It must be awful to die in one's shoes. They'll shoot me and not one Jew would witness my death. My mother and Frume Libtche would never find out. They would assume that I was alive, that I'd return—but I would be rotting somewhere in a field. Mother! Frume Libtche! Now I could think of both at once, something that I could not do previously.

We emerged from the tall corn into a meadow ringed by a wood. A rider on a horse galloped full speed toward us. When he reached us, he stopped his steaming, panting horse, which stamped its feet and would not stand still. The horseman, who had a red band around his cap, and red stripes on his trousers as though he were surrounded by flames, bent over the saddle and measured me with a glance.

"Who is he?" the officer asked.

"A suspect!" said one of the soldiers.

One of the guards gave the horseman my passport and my Bible. But before he glanced at my passport, he inspected my Hebrew Bible, a thick, small, square edition, bound in black covers and with gold letters on the binding. Then with a sad and gloomy countenance, he carefully turned the pages. He gave me a sidelong glance and immediately looked at my passport. Sensing that he would save me, I rushed toward him.

"I'm a Jew. I'm fleeing the Germans, and they take me for a German. The book that the comrade officer is holding is the Old Testament in Hebrew. I took it from home."

"Why are you playing the fools?" the officer berated the guards. "Let him go!"

"They ordered us to bring him to headquarters," the guard behind me stepped forward.

"Go back. Run to your positions," the officer shouted, pulling his horse at them, as though about to trample them; and with his head down over the horse's mane he galloped towards the forest whence we had come. The soldiers left me and began to run toward their positions, as though they had gathered from the officer's voice that the enemy was approaching.

I remained alone on the meadow, my passport in my left hand, and the open Bible in my right, astonished, as though I had just noticed the world about me. In the thick branches birds chirped, flies buzzed in the tall green grass. Silence all around, a singing silence. The air shimmered with gold and blue. My glance fell upon a verse and I read it as though in a dream:

> For I am with you, says the Lord,
>  to save you.
> For I will make a full end of all the
>  nations whither I have scattered you,
> But I will not make a full end of you;
> For I will correct you in measure,
> And I will not utterly destroy you.

I replaced the Bible in my coat pocket, and the passport in my chest pocket, and hurried away. I did not know where I was going, I only knew that I had to leave this place. I dared not meet up with any of my previous company. The peasant might betray me to yet another military post. I moved across the meadow to the forest. My mind was a jumble of haphazard thoughts which had torn themselves from their frozen state:

The horseman was a Jew. Surely a Jew. He had Jewish eyes. His fingers trembled as he slowly leafed through the pages of the Bible. He purposely avoided my eyes so that the soldiers would not notice that he regarded me as kin and with compassion . . . I hoped that I would not lose my passport or my Bible, and that I would not forget that verse. "I will correct you in measure . . ." Was it a miracle? I had abandoned my mother, abandoned Frume Libtche, and had fled alone, fled with my Bible in my pocket.

The next morning I found myself on the Minsk-Moscow highway, where I met a group of Jews from Minsk. . .

Suddenly we heard quiet, secretive footsteps. At once we saw a host of people in the forest. From somewhere nearby an entire *kolkhoz* had uprooted itself. Peasants and young women were running without any bundles. Everyone wanted to be the first to catch up to us and tell us what had happened. One blonde girl with full rosy cheeks whispered to us quickly as though fearing that the trees might overhear:

"The Germans are coming! Advance scouts!"

I sprang up and took to my heels. The dying sun, flaming between the branches, kept dancing in front of me from all sides, seeking to make me dizzy and enwrap me in its fire. Torn up roots entangled under my feet. I slid down a hill, fell over a fallen tree, jumped up and continued running. But I could not suppress the thought that the Germans had succeeded in penetrating the Red Army's front in the forest. The green-uniformed soldiers who had led me to be executed were perhaps dead now. And the Jewish officer on horseback, the one who had saved me—was he dead, too?

People were running in front of me, behind me, until we reached meadows that were overgrown with tall vegetation. Then the peasants scattered left and right, and I followed them. I knew that I dared not let them out of my sight—they were native to this region and knew the way. Ahead of me ran an old woman I had met the day before. She shouted something, but I passed her, caught up to her son and was almost up to his wife, who was first, holding a child in her arms. I heard the cries of the old woman.

"My children! Why are you leaving me behind?"

"I don't want my child to be an orphan," the young woman screamed, not even turning so as not to lose a moment.

"My son, why are you leaving me behind?" I heard the old woman's wail, like the echo of someone lamenting in an empty cemetery. "My son!"

"Goodbye, mother. If we're destined to live, we'll meet again," the young woman shouted to the wind blowing at her.

I remained riveted to my place. I could not move hand or foot. The young man who ran behind his wife and ahead of his mother caught up to me again. Seeing me standing, he stopped too, tearing the hair from his head and scratching his face with his fingernails.

"What should I do? What should I do?" he cast his glance about, looking once toward his wife and once toward his mother. "What should I do? What should I do?"

"Come, I say!" his wife turned to him, holding the child in her hands. "My baby hasn't yet lived in this world. Neither have I."

144

The son no longer looked back to his mother but sprang forward to catch up to his wife. I felt the veins in my temples enlarging, bursting. I leaped after him and seized his throat with both my hands.

"You're going to abandon an old mother?" I gagged on the words, as though his hands were on my throat, choking me.

For a moment he stopped and let me shake him. Suddenly his rolled back eyes glittered in a rage and he forcibly wrenched himself away from me:

"And you?" he sprayed the words into my face, teeth grating. "Where's your family? You ran away without them."

Seeing my confusion, his eyes flashed angrily, content with his revenge. He strode ahead, and I ran after him, not sure whether I just wanted to catch up to him, or seize him by the throat again.

"Run away, children, save yourselves," the old woman shouted.

I turned my head, unable to believe that this was the same woman who had previously pleaded not to be abandoned. But it was she, the same old woman. She was already far behind me, becoming smaller, shrunken, but I still saw the white skeins of her hair fluttering about her head. Her voice resounded over the meadow:

"I'm a broken pot. It's a sin before God for me to compare myself to you. Run quicker, my children. Quicker . . . Qui . . ." . . .

And I continued to flee, deep into the heart of the Soviet Union, where I spent the war years wandering, until my return home to Vilna at the end of the war.

# Walled In: Rise of the Ghetto of Warsaw

*Alexander Donat, now residing in New York City, describes the construction of the ghetto walls and its effects on Warsaw Jewry. We shall meet him again later in this book . . .*

For a year walls had been under construction in various places, but it was still impossible to be sure just where the boundaries of the putative ghetto would fall. Everyone was kept guessing, on edge, and everyone had a different version of which streets would be

From *The Holocaust Kingdom* by Alexander Donat.

included in the ghetto, which excluded. Then, finally, there was general apathy on the subject. Characteristically, the Nazi tactics began with a careful alternation of solemn promises which inspired hope and terror which provoked despair. Their agents constantly planted contradictory rumors. There would be, there would not be, a ghetto. A definite date has been set; but no, by enormous bribes the project has been postponed indefinitely. The Nazis want a ghetto, but the *Wehrmacht* and the health authorities are opposed. This demoralizing uncertainty was kept up right down to the last minute before the Ghetto was actually established.

Rosh Hashanah of 1940 fell on October 3. On that date the Germans proclaimed the establishment of a ghetto in which all Jews would in the future be quartered. The same day ... the Nazis appeared in large numbers in various Jewish neighborhoods to recruit forced labor. Prayers were being said in many private homes and some Jews had put up Yiddish signs reading "House of Prayer." Those houses were raided and the worshipers, many still in prayer shawls, were driven into the streets, abused, and then loaded onto trucks to be taken away for forced labor. Older, bearded men were particularly singled out.

By the terms of the Nazi decree all Jews in predominantly Gentile neighborhoods were to move to the Ghetto, all non-Jews living in the quarter where the Ghetto was to be located had to leave. The transfer was to be accomplished within four weeks, by October 31, and though it was what had been anticipated for months, the panic was indescribable. More than 100,000 Jews and even more non-Jews were affected. Jewish property "outside" included many stores, workshops, and factories: all these had to be abandoned. Jews moving to the Ghetto were permitted only their bedding and what was called a refugee bundle. Jews who lived in Aryan sections and who attempted to circumvent the decree about what could be taken with them were frequently caught by the police, by janitors of the buildings where they lived, and often by "friendly neighbors." Moving vans were stopped in broad daylight and hijacked as soon as the hoodlums involved ascertained that the property belonged to Jews. Many Jews forced to move to the Ghetto left their finest possessions to Gentile acquaintances either to be returned to them later, or not at all.

Those who lived on the border of the future Ghetto suffered most. They were left guessing to the last minute about whether they would be inside or outside the walls. ... Cousins of mine who lived on Sienna Street moved seven times, an extremely unnerving experience. ... Of the half-million people who eventually were penned inside the Ghetto walls, half had come either from the Aryan sections of Warsaw or from the provinces. The moves involved the loss of the bulk of their belongings and a severe comedown in the world. And with the shifting of domiciles, men also lost most of their means of making a living.

The streets of Warsaw looked as if the genius of chaos ruled.

146

Wagons, carts, wheelbarrows, baby carriages, frequently pushed by women and children while the men toted the heavy bundles, jammed the streets. The two-way shift of populations, Poles and Jews, was macabre and explosive with panic and hatred. Thousands, half-crazed because they no longer had roofs over their heads, stormed the housing bureaus of the *Judenrat* and the Warsaw municipal authorities. As in the days of the bombing of Warsaw, signs blossomed on the fronts of houses advertising "exchanges." The *Judenrat* sent inspectors out to list empty living quarters and apartments that could hold more people. Some families willingly invited others to share their apartments to avoid having to accept unknown tenants later on. Unscrupulous individuals, some of whom worked in the housing bureaus, did a lively business in bribes. . . .

When . . . the Ghetto was finally closed off, thousands of new problems were created. Some 1,700 dwellings of all types made up the Ghetto, 27,000 apartments and an area of 750 acres, with six or seven persons to a room. Because Jews had not previously been permitted to exercise the exalted profession of janitor, some 1,700 Polish janitors and their families had to be moved out and 1,700 Jewish janitors chosen to replace them. Similar replacements were required in business, industry, and municipal administration. A Jewish police force (the Ghetto police) of about 2,000 was created. There was a wild scramble for these new jobs and an obscure *Judenrat* councilman named Kupczykier suddenly became the most prominent man in the Ghetto because he made appointments to the Jewish police. The *Judenrat* took over management of all Ghetto real estate. It also was empowered to appoint janitors, superintendents, and managers for the larger buildings. Bribery flourished. People paid as much as 3,000 zlotys to get a manager's job. Jews in the pay of the Gestapo, of whom Abraham Ganzweich was the most notorious, could also be bribed to obtain jobs. He founded the infamous organization subsequently known as "The Thirteen," because it was housed at 13 Leszno Street, which early took over managing a large number of the Ghetto apartment houses. The Tenants' Committees fought stubbornly to have their own men appointed to the now-important position of janitor. Often, two or three candidates for a job—all of whom had bribed some *Judenrat* employee—discovered that two or three other candidates—all of whom had bribed members of The Thirteen—had simultaneously been "appointed" to the position.

As though by concerted agreement, members of the Jewish intelligentsia, with lawyers predominating, made a mass assault on the new police jobs. The war had ravaged the ranks of lawyers perhaps more than any other single group. All justified themselves in the same way— "Better us than the Germans!"—but once it became known that the police would not be paid salaries, the rest of us realized something of what we might expect from their ministrations.

**147**

A special problem was created by the Jewish converts to Christianity. The Germans treated them as Jews and the Jews looked on them as renegades. They were by no means a negligible number altogether and some had been baptized as long as fifty years. In the case of mixed marriages, where there were children born as Catholics, the establishment of the Ghetto broke up many families. Some converts still thought of themselves as Jews and Prodigal Sons; others had become completely estranged and hated their origins. For these last, confinement in the Ghetto was torment. Still other converts continued even in the Ghetto to think of themselves as Gentiles and remained aloof.

Rudolf Langer, the elderly lawyer who lived with us on Orla Street, had years before converted to Christianity. For some reason he lived in terror of blackmailers and informers. Gray-haired, highly cultured and distinguished-looking, he did his best to calm his wife, also a convert, when she loudly lamented that the Nazis had forced her to share the fate of the Jews. "They haven't got the right," she repeated over and over again, "I'm not a Jew." As fate would have it their only child, a daughter they worshiped, had fallen in love with a most self-conscious Jew. Not only had she gone back to the Judaism her parents had renounced; she had become an ardent Zionist to boot.

To the Jewish community's credit it must be said that, throughout this period, these converts were never discriminated against, though it must also be admitted that they were never very popular. Several Christian churches with priests remained in the Ghetto. Among the converts were a number of prominent scientists and people from the stage. For a while the Catholic organization *Caritas* took care of them and they had the illusion of being in a privileged position in the Ghetto. So potent an illusion was it that after the Ghetto was established several hundred Jews converted to Christianity. . . .

When the Ghetto was officially sealed off, a sociological "experiment" without parallel began. Half a million people, locked behind walls in the heart of a great city, were increasingly isolated from that city and from the rest of the world. Had the Ghetto been only one phase of Nazi "Jewish policy," intended to segregate Jew from Gentile because of the "noxious cultural and economic influences of Jews," or had it been intended only as a prelude to eventual "resettlement" in Madagascar or elsewhere, it still would have caused enormous damage and suffering. But the real purpose of the Warsaw Ghetto was to exterminate its inhabitants after robbing them of all their worldly goods. . . .

At each gate of the Ghetto three guards were posted: one German, one Polish, and one Jewish, a member of the newly created Ghetto police force. These last had no uniforms but wore blue caps with *Jüdische Ordnungsdienst* (Jewish Civil Service) inscribed on them, and either stars or metal insignia. Belts and jack boots enhanced their authority; later they were issued rubber truncheons. Crowds of Poles and Jews gathered on both sides of the gates, trying to get in or out. At first, passes were easy to get; the price was 5 zlotys at the *Judenrat* office. Or you could bribe the guards.

A number of Aryan factories remained open in the Ghetto and their owners received special police passes. The plan was gradually to replace Polish workers with Jews. The big Czyste Street Jewish hospital was outside the Ghetto walls and nearly a thousand doctors, nurses, and other hospital personnel daily had to get to work there. The Germans gave no more than a few dozen individual passes a day, and every morning at seven the rest had to line up at one gate to be marched in columns to the hospital. Polish pharmacies stayed open, too, and special police passes were issued for managers and clerks. Every day the people in the pharmacy where Lena [the writer's wife] worked brought in food at the low prices which existed outside the walls.

Once the gates were closed, looting fell off rapidly, and manhunts and beatings in the streets seemed to be over. But as I soon discovered, that was an illusion. Walking in Leszno Street one day, I stopped to talk to an acquaintance. Suddenly people around us began to run in all directions. Before we could grasp what was happening, three men in SS uniforms—with the skulls on their caps that gave them, in Ghetto slang, the name of "corpses"—fell upon us. As German regulations required, we bared our heads at once, came to attention, and stood rooted to the spot. They ran past us, brandishing their clubs, in pursuit of the Jews who had fled at the sight of them. In a few moments bloodcurdling screams and the sound of falling bodies told us that the SS men had found those they were chasing. . . .

A patrol car manned by "corpses" cruised along Leszno and Karmelicka streets every afternoon between one and four o'clock on its way to Pawiak Prison. Never did it make a trip without pausing to shed its ration of Jewish blood. . . .

All day long Karmelicka Street was full of people, crowded together from wall to wall across its entire width. The "corpses" enjoyed driving down the street full speed, without warning. Not content with running down their victims they would get out of their cars wielding their clubs at random, felling men, women and children indiscriminately, or singling out one victim, stopping a few paces from him and beckoning, "*Komm, komm . . .*" Once you were caught in Karmelicka Street, there was no dodging or evading. A more perfect arena for the Nazi sadists could scarcely have been devised. Their favorite targets were the "rickshas," two-seat, man-propelled tricycles which were the Ghetto's primary means of transportation. They collided with them head-on and full speed, turning them over together with the passengers and the driver. . . .

In addition to the normal Nazi beatings and commands to do arduous gymnastics or to lie in the mud, selected victims were ordered to pick up a heavy brick in one hand and a hollow one in the other. When they'd done so, they were ordered to bend forward and because of the imbalance of weights, they invariably fell down, which provided another pretext for beating them. Chlodna Street was haunted by the notoriously brutal guard, "Frankenstein," who required at least one sacrificial victim daily.

To handle all Ghetto exports and imports a special organization called *Transferstelle* was set up in Krolewska Street; it charged exorbitant fees. Goods shipped in by train were unloaded at a siding on the corner of Dzika and Stawki streets at the so-called *Umschlagplatz*[1] (reloading point), later to become a tragic landmark. By controlling the flow of goods going out and coming in the Germans hoped to starve the Ghetto to death. But a city of half a million takes a lot of plugging up.

Never was so unique or elaborate a smuggling system put into operation as that devised by the Ghetto Jews in their struggle to survive. The official food ration barely sustained life for two or three days a month, and smugglers consequently became the Ghetto's most important citizens, its heroes, for though there were a thousand ruses, a smuggler risked his life in employing any one of them.

Tycoons among the smugglers organized huge rings which employed dozens and even hundreds of people on both sides of the wall. One of the biggest rings was located at 7 Kozla Street. . . . where two houses joined; passages connecting Jewish and Gentile apartments were cut through on every floor. These passages were artfully concealed by cupboards, stoves, bookcases, armoires, and so on. During the day goods were collected in the Gentile flats and at night transferred to the Jewish flats and immediately distributed. Men who carried the merchandise away and parceled it out also shared in the profits and both Polish and Jewish "teams" were kept busy twenty-four hours a day. Even milk got through—piped. The tenants in both buildings, the janitors, and on the Jewish side the members of the Ghetto police who served as lookouts were all in on the smuggling.

Such smuggling lasted only until the Germans eliminated all adjacent buildings. Once that was done, the Ghetto was enclosed by walls that ran through the middle of the street and the nature of smuggling changed. Goods either had to be thrown over the walls or passed through openings in the walls made for that purpose. Smuggling became riskier and daily more people lost their lives attempting it. But the Biblical saying in Lamentations (4:9), "They that are slain by the sword are better off than those stricken by hunger," remained appropriate and executing smugglers never stopped their trade.

The thousands of Jewish workers who marched out of the Ghetto every morning for forced labor also were constantly engaged in bringing back food, paid for by money or valuables they smuggled out with them. The Jewish police at the gates played an important role in this

[1]Later the deportation depot.

activity . . . They bribed German and Polish guards so that whole cartloads of goods could be brought in at one time. Wagons entered the Ghetto drawn by a team of horses, and left empty and drawn by a single horse. The other horse was slaughtered for food. The "fiddlers," as such Jewish policemen were called, earned enormous sums of money. . . .

Gentile members of smuggling rings tossed parcels to their Jewish confederates from streetcars which crossed portions of the Ghetto without stopping. Hearses served to transport foodstuffs. Garbage collectors and Poles employed by the public utilities—such as gas, light, water—also played important roles in smuggling. . . .

Perhaps the most dramatic part in keeping the Ghetto supplied with contraband was played by hundreds of poor children between the ages of four and fourteen, who would cluster at the gates looking for a chance to slip out. Many of them wore loose-fitting windbreakers, which they kept tightly belted so that they could slip contraband under their jackets and keep their hands free. Sometimes the lining of their clothes served the same purpose. On their small legs, and with their bulging middles, they looked like sparrows. Occasionally a guard would look the other way when a covey of those sparrows slipped out of the Ghetto in search of food. Often, however, they opened fire on them; children, too, were enemies of the Third Reich. Henryka Lazowert wrote a touching little song called "The Little Smuggler," which was popular for some time. Its refrain was:

*Around walls, through holes, past guards,*
*Over the rubble, fences, and barbed wire,*
*Hungry, determined, and bold, I sneak . . .*

# A Fateful Decision: Collective Suicide or Collaboration?

*Leib Garfunkel, a survivor of the Kovno ghetto, reported at a Yad Vashem symposium . . .*

When the ghetto was being set up, the Germans brought us 5,000 white certificates with orders to distribute them only

From *Jewish Resistance during the Holocaust* (Proceedings of the Conference on Manifestations of Jewish Resistance, Jerusalem, April 7–11, 1968.

among labourers and artisans. At that time there were 29,000 Jews in the Kovno Ghetto and we were well aware of the Germans' purpose in having us distribute those grim white certificates. So we were faced with the tragic question of how to distribute them. Were we to accept the fact that death transports awaited all the intellectuals, the women and the little children in the Ghetto? A terrible dilemma confronted us. Suddenly an idea was presented—I do not know by whom—to burn all the certificates and tell the Germans that we refused to distribute them. In other words, "Do what you will." We knew well enough what they would do. But as soon as the idea became known in the Ghetto, dozens of people came to us speaking on behalf of hundreds of the common folk, common folk in the best sense of the term, and said to us, "You want to send us to death. What right have you to do that?" They did not speak about the generations to come. They spoke a very prosaic language, but it was the language of their instinct to live. There were only two alternatives in the Kovno Ghetto. One was to delay matters as long as possible. Almost any price would be paid to gain time. The other alternative was to go out against the Germans with bare hands, in other words to do something that in realistic language meant collective suicide. And I ask you, has anyone the right to decide that a community must, even for considerations of honour or any other lofty motive, commit suicide? There are situations in life when the suicide of an individual or even a community is rational. But to go and ask somebody why he did not commit suicide, to go to somebody with the accusation that he did not demand of somebody else that he commit suicide or persuade him to do so—that is very hard to comprehend.

# The Agony of the Judenrat of Shavel: Murder of the Yet Unborn

*The Minute Book of the Shavel Judenrat was found by the Army of the Soviet Union. The minutes were written in Yiddish and Hebrew by Eliezer Yerushalmi.*

*The selection below, translated into English, is quoted from* The Black Book: The Nazi Crime Against the Jewish People, *which was prepared by the Jewish Black Book Committee representing the World Jewish Congress, Vaad Leumi (Jewish National Council in Palestine) and other bodies; it was published in 1946 and submitted as evidence to the U.N. War Crime Commission.*

# War

*On March 24, 1943, the Shavel Judenrat met to discuss the problem that was, in the most literal sense of the words, one of life and death. On the order of business was: How to avoid childbirth in the ghetto.*

*The following account is taken from the minutes of that meeting. . .*

M. Leibovich, in opening the meeting said:

"We turn again to the question of childbirth. The law forbidding childbirth is strictly enforced in all the ghettos. Recently, in Kovno, there was a case of childbirth, and the whole family was shot. Yet, in our ghetto, we take this matter too lightly. Several cases of pregnancy have already occurred against which no preventive methods have been employed."

Dr. Blecher asked whether it was possible to force a pregnant woman to submit to an abortion. He also asked for statistics on the number of pregnant women in the ghetto.

Dr. L. answered:

"Since the 15th of August last year there have been three births; at present there are about twenty pregnant women, most of whom are in the early months. One is in the eighth month. Only two of these women have agreed to undergo an abortion: one is having her third abortion and may well become sterile."

Dr. F. said that all the women must be convinced of the necessity of an abortion.

It was proposed by Dr. Burshstein that all physicians and midwives be forbidden to assist during childbirth.

M. L. said, "We must not permit this propaganda against childbirth to come out into the open." He suggested that all the pregnant women be called into the clinic and be warned of the danger which threatened them, in the presence of doctors and representatives of the *Judenrat*.

Dr. L. asked how it would be possible to perform an abortion on a woman in her eighth month. "We must take the feelings of mother-hood into account. We certainly won't be able to influence this woman. And if we can induce a premature birth, what will we do with the child? Such an operation cannot be performed at home; and if it were done in a clinic, the child could not possibly remain there. So if the child is born alive, shall we then put it to death? I could not undertake such a thing with a clear conscience."

Dr. Blecher admitted that such a thing would be impossible; that no doctor could take upon himself the responsibility of putting a child to death, since such an act is murder.

Dr. F. suggested, "Perhaps we can let the child be born and then turn it over to a Gentile," to which Dr. L. replied, "We dare not let the child be born, since we shall have to report it. We have been asked three times already, whether there have been any births in the ghetto. We have answered each time that there have not been any." B. K. added: "If it were up to the family alone, we would leave it to them to face the

153

responsibility of bringing their child into the world. But as it is, the entire ghetto is exposed to danger. It might result in the most horrible consequences! We must use every means to prevent these births."

A. K. said: "The abortions must be performed only by doctors, who must convince the women to go through with it. If words won't convince them, then the matter will have to be turned over to an administrator, who, if necessary, will employ sanctions against the pregnant woman's family: deprive them of food cards, transfer their working members to worse jobs, deprive them of medical assistance, of fire-wood. If that doesn't work, then the woman must be called in and given an ultimatum—either an abortion or the committee will have to inform the security police. As to the woman in the eighth month, her child must not be born, for if the child is born and is alive, it will merely encourage the others.

"During all of these dealings, not a single member of the committee should be present, but only the parties concerned. No one must know that any member of the committee knows of any pregnancy cases in the ghetto."

"At first, only the doctors will know of the cases," said Dr. B. "Later, however, when sanctions will be employed, it will become obvious that the committee knows about it. As to the woman in the eighth month, it should be treated as a case in which the mother's life is endangered, in which event it is imperative that the child be put to death."

Dr. L. said, "I cannot do it!"

Dr. F: "A premature birth can be induced at the clinic, and another doctor could assist in it. Putting the child to death can be done by a nurse with an injection, but the nurse herself need not know what is in the needle."

A. K., summing up, said, "A premature birth must be induced at once, because every day brings the danger closer. In every case we will employ all means to influence the mothers to go through with an abortion—through talks, sanctions, ultimatums and even threats to inform the security police."

The methods were approved, and it was decided to inform the entire medical staff of these decisions. As to the woman in the eighth month, it was decided to induce a premature birth immediately.

We now know that all these tragic arguments were futile.

154

# Epidemics in the Ghetto

*The historian of the Nazi ghetto was Emanuel Ringelblum. His chronicle* Notes from the Warsaw Ghetto *is the source for historians and novelists. He organized a group which met every Saturday night under his direction for recording the events from September 1939 to 1943 when he was martyred with his brethren.*

All the disinfection techniques are of no avail. Instead of combatting typhus, the "sanitation columns" spread it, because they blackmail the homes where the rich live, where there really is no need for any disinfection, with the threat of ruining their linen, clothes, and the like. On the other hand, the filthy houses that really require disinfection are let off if the residents pay them. So the lice move freely all through the Ghetto. The overwhelming majority of typhus cases . . . are concealed. The German health department speaks in terms of some 14,000 cases. The houses [where the typhus cases are concealed] are not disinfected; the lice carry the typhus from there all over Warsaw. The doctors are making a fortune out of treating people secretly, taking 50 and 100 zlotys for a visit. At the same time they decide in advance how many visits they will make each day. It is worth mentioning at this point that the "sanitation columns" are so busy blackmailing the rich that they haven't the time to board up properly the windows of houses where typhus is discovered, to make them something like gas chambers; the result is that the lice survive and even increase. The populace resorts to all kinds of measures to avoid the lice, but if one has to go through Karmelicka Street, which is crowded whichever way one turns, or through the bazaar . . . or if one has to take the streetcar, or visit the public kitchen, one is bound to become infected sooner or later. The employees at the community institutions, such as the Joint Distribution Committee, or CENTOS children's aid, and particularly at TOZ medical aid, are particularly subject to infection. These officials have no money to have themselves inoculated (nor have the common people), and the serum is very expensive—one injection costs 400–500, and even as high as 600 zlotys. It is typical that all the serum comes from the hospitals of the Other Side or is imported . . . The cost is high, because in the first place the labor involved in making the serum is difficult (the internal parts of at least 150 lice have to be extracted by hand). In the second place, the serum has to pass through a number of

From *Notes from the Warsaw Ghetto: The Journal of Emanuel Ringelblum* edited by Jacob Sloan.

hands, being contraband, and the price increases with each agent. People carry around all kinds of camphor and other noisome chemicals which are supposed to repel lice. Some people smear their bodies with lysol and other disinfectants. The poor people are not permitted to enter the houses of those who are better off, because they are carriers of lice . . .

# Janusz Korczak's Last Walk

*Janusz Korczak, born Henryk Goldshmidt of an intellectual assimilated Jewish family in Warsaw, was graduated as medical doctor but singlemindedly devoted his life to pedagogic writings and the direction of a prominent Jewish orphanage in Warsaw. His philosophy of child and youth education, written in Polish, has been translated in many languages. His martyrdom made him a living legend of our time.*

The day was Wednesday, 5th August, 1942, in the morning.

The gendarmes close off the streets. The Ukrainian police surround the house. The Jewish policemen enter the courtyard.

Horrible screams: "All Jews—out!" (in German); and then in Yiddish: "Quickly! Quickly!" The efficient organisation for which the Orphanage—thanks to Steffa Wilczenska—is well known can now be seen in operation. The children who, surprised in the middle of their breakfast . . . descend quietly and line up in fives below.

Miss Steffa and the Doctor go down with the children without forgetting to take the green flag with them—the flag of the Orphanage. . . .

According to eye-witnesses, the children were dressed in their holiday clothes, as though they were going for a trip or for a holiday in the country. . . . Somehow or other, Korczak's children were always distinguished from the general poverty around them. Even on ordinary days their clothing was clean and neat. That was why the impression made by the small, quiet and well-behaved group, which was following the Doctor with complete confidence, was so pleasant and aesthetic.

Janusz Korczak walked at their head. We know that at the time he

---

From *The Massacre of European Jewry.*

was weak and that he had been ill. His feet were swollen and his heart was giving him trouble. I doubt whether he had the strength to carry two of his charges in his arms—even the tiniest ones . . .

They were pulled, stopped, crowded together and pulled along again in the burning heat of August, accompanied by cruel cries and rifle-blows. If Korczak really took some child with painful feet into his arms, it was probably the five-year-old Romacia Sztockman, daughter of two of his pupils, Rosa and Yosef, who had returned to work with him in the Orphanage. It is possible that Korczak held the feverish, tired, sweating hands of two children, as they drummed with their little feet to his right and his left . . .

Did Korczak tell them they were going for a picnic, to the country? We cannot know . . . but the terror, the fear of death and of deportation, must have affected all of them, and it is very doubtful whether it was possible to delude them—at least the older children—with a fiction of this sort. It is, however, almost certain that to the very last moment he assured the children of something which he himself no longer believed—that they were going to work in agriculture, in the forest, felling trees. . . .

At the assembly place near the waiting carriages, Dr. Korczak was called aside. In that world of bestial cruelty, tempered with a few European conventions, a physician's position and person still commanded some respect, because he was needed. Korczak was well known and respected in the ghetto. He could be of some use in the future. He could serve as a disguise and a decoy.

We may therefore have full confidence in the story of the offer to release him at the last moment. We do not know whether the matter took a long time or not, nor in what manner they wanted to pardon Korczak.

Neither do we know Korczak's words: but we know their content. He refused, without any hesitation. Can it be considered as bravery? Undoubtedly. Many people, motivated by their animal instincts, often forgot all moral obligations in the face of death—and saved their own lives at the expense of loved ones or parents. On the other hand, there is a very old rule, which says that a captain goes to the bottom of the sea together with the passengers on his boat.

As though in a dream . . . the children's procession marches forth with song and flag. The tired old man, in the officer's uniform, whose heart is breaking from unbearable pain, slowly leads it. The nightmarish ghetto street is dusty, parched and burning . . . The children are suffering and sweating. They want to drink. They are overcome by heat and terror. Now and again they raise their voices and we can hear the weak, childish choir. Then they lose the tune and the choir ceases. The Doctor moves his legs with great difficulty, bending beneath his

157

load and his troubles—but then straightens himself in a mighty effort to hold out to the end. Above him flutters the green flag of the Orphanage.

Steffa, who is accompanying the older children, is at the end of the procession. She is so large, with her broad shoulders. She is so good hearted—a shield against trouble in bad times. This time, though, her aid is ineffectual.

They continue walking. They cross the border between life and death, cross the bridge between now and eternity. They shall never return.

Of all the deeds and creations of Janusz Korczak, the artist and reformer; of all Steffa Wilczenska's efforts[1]; of all the games, smiles and hopes of two hundred boys and girls—this one last walk will be remembered for ever . . . This small group, under the leadership of Janusz Korczak, has received eternal glory. . . .

Our eyes still see them walking slowly and quietly—the Doctor's companions in spirit, his travelling companions in their fateful ghetto journey: Stephana Wilczenska, Mr. Henryk Osterblum, the veteran bookkeeper of the Home, Felix and Balbina Gzieb, Natzia Boz, Rosza Stockman, Sabina Leiserowicz, Dorka Solnicka, the four Moniushes, little Hanka with the lung trouble. Yolek who was ill, Abrasha of the burning eyes, who only a short time ago so successfully played a child about to die. . . .

To the accompaniment of the green waving flag they will go on to eternity in all time and in all countries of the world. From the scaffold of the ghetto and from the smoking crematoria of Treblinka—they travel on their way to eternity.

# Jewish Self-Aid

*Chaim A. Kaplan of Warsaw, a Hebrew teacher, kept a full diary in which h. described the heroism and the corruption of Warsaw Jewry.*

*November 29, 1940*

Polish Jewry has become a self-contained organism. It is forced to rely on its own powers. Despite all its poverty it must support its own destitute. . . . Willing or not, the misers of Poland are forced to give.

[1]His life-long associate.

From *The Warsaw Diary of Chaim A. Kaplan* edited by Abraham I. Katsh.

The Jewish Self-Aid, which no one believed would succeed at the time of its establishment, has become a far-reaching charitable organization which brings in more than 100,000 zloty a month. Self-Aid is a kingdom in its own right, and from the administrative standpoint it has no connection with its sister, the Joint,[1] which is still alive and functioning . . .

The lowest rung in its broad organization is the courtyard committee. This is a successful organizational invention, of a kind that was never attained in times of peace when a raucous press existed. At that time no public project percolated down to the masses. This time every Jewish home from great to small has been affected. At the head of the courtyard committees stand men of the people who awaken the drowsy public to give.

Their words, which emanate from simple hearts, penetrate into simple hearts. They find expressions which their listeners can understand, and so are successful. Social action is thus diffused through all levels of the broad public, and there is no boy over ten who does not have some public duty in his courtyard. There is not a tenant who is not among the members of some committee, or in charge of some courtyard duty. Every courtyard committee is divided into reporting subcommittees (financial, sanitary, educational affairs, political affairs, apartments, dress, food supplies, etc.), and each of these is further divided and subdivided, and in this way everyone is kept busy. Self-Aid is a legal organization and it thus gives the legal right to all its branches to call meetings and conferences, and to put their decisions into practice. At every meeting there is a broad field for politics, rumors, and all manner of gossip and slander. Everyone says whatever enters his mind without fear that his words will be carried to those in power. The hatred of the conquerors is so deep that everyone is sure no one will carry anything he says beyond the room.

The Self-Aid is supported by regular monthly payments which the courtyard committees impose upon their "subjects" by the income derived from special projects and drives. Nearly every month it raises a hue and cry about a different rescue project. Once it was a drive to save the children, and the "children's month" became a watchword; then came the "holiday month"; third, there was the "immigration month"; the fourth, which we are presently involved in carrying out, is the "soul ransom" project to raise money for "social improvements." The organization of these projects is not always successful, because it is a time of crisis and everything must be done in haste, without the technical and organizational tools required. But even if they are not a hundred percent successful, the people are satisfied with a sixty percent success. Compulsory giving has served to educate us. The recognition of collec-

[1]Joint Distribution Committee.

tive responsibility which was so lacking in our brethren has penetrated to everyone. Everyone has come to realize that he is an organic part of a whole body. Anything good for the whole body is good for him too, and the reverse. This concept was brought to us by the conquerors. That which is good must be accepted from whatever source it may come.

The concept that "all Jews are responsible for one another" has stopped being merely a slogan or a metaphor. It is realized in us.

The courtyard committees operate on the principle that the affairs of their own courtyard come first. And so they impose a double monthly payment upon their "subjects"; one for the benefit of the Self-Aid, which supports the soup kitchens in the ghetto, the other for courtyard needs. This payment need not necessarily be in cash. It may be made in foodstuffs, prepared meals, or used clothing.

When the ghetto was about to be set up and people were concerned about the hoarding, the courtyard committees began taking care of all the residents of the courtyard without exception, including even the middle-class and wealthy ones. It was deemed entirely possible that a day would come when all the private hoards would be eaten up and it would be necessary to set up a common soup kitchen for all the residents of the courtyard. So the courtyard committees hastily created a "permanent fund" for the establishment of soup kitchens. At once the necessary (relatively speaking) sums were collected to enable them to buy in advance a certain quantity of foodstuffs, to be stored in a special cellar belonging to the courtyard committee. It will thus remain, ready for whatever trouble may come.

When historians come to write the history of the courtyard committees during the days of the Nazi war against the Jews, let them end their chapter with a blessing of consolation: "May the Lord remember them with favor!"

## Sukkot in the Ghetto

*October 25, 1940*
*End of Sukkot, 5701*

In the midst of sorrow, the holiday of joy. This is not a secular joy, but a "rejoicing of the Torah," the same Torah for which we are murdered all day, for which we have become like lambs to be slaughtered, for which we have gone through fire and water. . . . After a year of physical and mental tortures, never equaled in history, darkness reigns in our souls as well. The holiday was spent under the impress of the ghetto, with all the sights which accompany its creation and appearance. It is clear to us that the ghetto will be a closed one. They will push us into a Jewish section, fenced in and separated from the world outside, like sinners and criminals.

But we have not shamed our eternal Torah. This was not a raucous

160

celebration, but an inner one, a heartfelt joy, and for that reason it was all the more warm and emotional. Everywhere holiday celebrations were organized, and every prayer group said the wine blessing. The Hasidim were even dancing, as is their pious custom. Someone told me that on the night of the holiday he met a large group of zealous Hasidim on Mila Street, and they sang holiday songs in chorus out in public, followed by a large crowd of curious people and sightseers. Joy and revelry in poverty-stricken Mila Street! When they sang, they reached such a state of ecstasy that they couldn't stop, until some heretic approached them shouting, "Jews! Safeguarding your life is a positive Biblical commandment; it is a time of danger for us. Stop this." Only then did they become quiet. Some of them replied in their ecstasy: "We are not afraid of the murderer! The devil with him . . ."

## Hanukkah in the Ghetto

*December 26, 1940*

Hanukkah in the ghetto. Never before in Jewish Warsaw were there as many Hanukkah celebrations as in this year of the wall. But because of the sword that hovers over our heads, they are not conducted among festive crowds, publicly displaying their joy. Polish Jews are stubborn: the enemy makes laws but they don't obey them. That is the secret of our survival. We behaved in this manner even in the days when we were not imprisoned within the ghetto walls, when the cursed Nazis filled our streets and watched our every move. Since the ghetto was created we have had some respite from overt and covert spies, and so Hanukkah parties were held in nearly every courtyard, even in rooms which face the street; the blinds were drawn, and that was sufficient.

How much joy, how much of a feeling of national kinship there was in these Hanukkah parties! After sixteen months of Nazi occupation, we came to life again.

This time we even deceived the *Judenrat* itself. It tried to ban the holding of Hanukkah parties without a permit from a special office set up for this purpose. But this too took effect only on paper; the *Judenrat* was fooled. Hundreds of celebrations were arranged and the stupid *Judenrat* did not get a single penny. . . .

This year's Hanukkah celebration was very well attended. . . . Dr. Lajfuner gave a speech full of jokes and we all laughed heartily. There was one truth in his speech which should be stressed: "In all the countries where they want to bury us alive, we pull the gravediggers in with us." Witness Czarist Russia, Poland, and Rumania. Nazi Germany will have the same fate—and in our own time.

There were also historical and scientific speeches, sermons, and all kinds of talks. . . . Everyone used Yiddish except me: I "ruined" the evening by speaking in Hebrew.

# Libraries in the Ghetto

## By Rachel Auerbach

*When Jewish community workers were wracking their brains where and how to find bread and shelter for the homeless and hungry masses of Jews, two librarians, Leib Schur and Bassia Berman, labored to find spiritual sustenance for the children. They were the first to appreciate the value of a book as a weapon against despair.*

People had never shown such a ravenous appetite for books as in those days. This hunger derived, in the first instance, from an attempt to forget the constant peril that hung over people's heads, to bolster our sagging self-esteem.

And if this was so among the adults, all the more so among the children. The child in the Ghetto was deprived of everything: the river, green trees, and freedom of movement. All these he found again in the magic world of books.

It was the winter and summer of 1940. Bassia Berman worked in the clothing store. Others collected only old clothing to distribute to the destitute, but Bassia mainly collected books for children. And in order to "legalize" her activities she called her collection "Toys and Booklets." She discovered that many of the children still retained their pre-war books and toys, and that they were exchanging them with their neighbors. Thus the "rich" had their own circulating libraries. There were even house committees that had organized clubs, and children's centers. But the most deprived were the unfortunate inmates of the refugee centers, the orphans, the homeless ones—they had nothing. . . .

It is November 1940, and the decree announcing the formation of the Ghetto is at hand. At Lishna Street there is the Old Polish public library, where Bassia used to work. But that institution was ordered to move to the "Aryan" side. Bassia, nevertheless, procured a permit to open the library of the Ghetto in another place.

Yet the place must be camouflaged with children's paper-cut-outs, with little dolls and toys on the shelves, with colored leaflets and books, to give the impression more of a playroom than a place for reading and study. . . . Underneath this facade there was hidden a veritable treasure of books in Polish and Yiddish. These books came mainly from Schur's[1]

[1]Leib Schur was founder of the Vilna publishing house, Tamar.

---

From *Flame and Fury* compiled by Yaakov Shilhav, edited by Sara Feinstein.

private library; he had simply donated all his books which were suitable for children. . . .

Thus, the library prospered. In a very short while it acquired over 700 youthful subscribers. Many of the children could not read Yiddish, or knew no Yiddish at all. But Bassia had a method to attract those children as well. She would lend them two books simultaneously—one Polish and one Yiddish. Many times the Yiddish books opened a new world to the children; they gave them a key to their inner selves. And many of the children developed a passionate attachment to the Jewish books.

From time to time the library would arrange readings from Jewish books. . . . The children themselves sometimes read aloud to each other. For the assimilated teachers lectures in Jewish literature were given. Here also met the Jewish cultural leaders in quiet and intimate discussions. There was a warm atmosphere in this house of the Jewish Child and the Jewish Book. . . .

But Bassia's best helpers were the children themselves, whom she trained for this work. . . .

The most urgent and the most difficult task of the library was to supply special books to the unfortunate children in the quarantines, in the hospitals, in the jails, many of whom were infected with contagious diseases. The books they used could not be returned to the common pool, for sanitary reasons. Thus, for instance, there were special books for children afflicted with sores . . .

In the shelters the children lived in horrible conditions, in spite of all efforts to ameliorate them. They had no shoes and clothing, and there was no fuel to heat those places in the winter. Yet these children also borrowed and read books. They would send representatives, dressed in whatever warm clothes they possessed in common. In the library these "delegates" were immediately recognized by their bald head, a souvenir of the sweatbaths they were forced to go through for sanitary control. Their eyes were often decorated with baggy swellings, the result of starvation, sleeplessness and tears. They would perform the act of exchanging the books with uncommon earnestness and skill. They would reach for the precious gift of books, the magic balm for their afflictions, with their outstretched, emaciated arms . . . In some of the shelters where there was no heat at all, we organized public readings . . . The children would huddle under one blanket and listen rapturously to an adventure story that took place somewhere under blue skies in the sunny lands of Asia or Africa . . .

Among Bassia's clients there was one who was known as a "book swallower." This boy, Merrel, once returned a book infested with lice. But, in the library, they did not scold him for that. It was not his fault that lice inhabited his body as well as his books . . . Books also played a pathetic part later, during the period of the "actions." For even in the first days of the "actions" most children did not forsake their books, if they could help it. Bassia remembered one little girl by the name of Simcha, who was very courageous. She was not afraid to walk in the street; her father worked in a protected factory, she said, and the Nazis would not take her. To prove it she showed her special pass. But we knew the worthlessness of these passes; the books borrowed that day were never returned. Some of them were, no doubt, packed into the little bundle which the deported ones were allowed to take with them on their trip eastward. They surely were scattered, together with the prayerbooks and adult books in the yards of Treblinka . . .

I can see now one boy whose mother had decided to join him, of her own free will, on his fateful journey to the "Umschlagsplatz."[1] She collected a little food from her neighbors in the midst of the terrible confusion of a city suddenly besieged by a merciless foe . . . But the twelve year old boy is absorbed in his own private world. He stands in a corner of the yard, hearing and seeing nothing of what is happening all around him. His head is immersed in a torn and tattered book with a shabby red binding . . .

---

# Report on Underground Cultural Activities in the Ghetto

## By Emanuel Ringelblum

*Through the offices of the Ministry of Interior of the Polish Government in London, the Yiddish Scientific Institute received a report on the underground Jewish cultural activities in the Polish ghettos, dated March 1, 1944. The report, written in Polish Government code, was deciphered in London and forwarded to the Yiddish Scientific Institute of New York.*

Dear Friends:
    We write to you at a time when 95% of the Polish Jews have already

[1]Deportation depot.

---

Letter to the Yiddish Scientific Institute, the Yiddish Pen Club, Sholem Asch, H. Leivick, J. Opatoshu, and R. Mahler. All names were omitted from the letter for reasons of security. It was signed by Dr. Ringelblum and another person. It was this second person who probably attached the postscript on p. 168.

died in the throes of horrible tortures in the gas chambers of the annihilation centers of Treblinka, Sobibor, Chelmno, Oswiecim, or were slaughtered during the numberless "liquidation campaigns" in the ghettos and camps. The fate of the small number of Jews who still vegetate and suffer in the few concentration camps has also already been determined. Perhaps there will survive a small group of Jews who are hidden in the "Aryan districts" in constant fear of death or who wander through the woods like hunted animals. That any of us, the community workers, who carry on under conditions of twofold secrecy, will outlive the war, we greatly doubt. We, therefore, want to take this means to tell you in brief about those activities which link us most closely to you.

At the moment when the Polish Jews fell under the horrible Hitlerite yoke, the more active elements of the Jewish population began conducting a program of broad scope with the rallying call of self-help and struggle. Through the active and generous aid of the American Joint Distribution Committee, a network of institutions for communal welfare was spread throughout Warsaw and in the country, conducted by the Jewish Society for Social Welfare (ZTOS), the Central Organization for the Protection of Children and Orphans (CENTOS) and the Society for the Protection of the Health of the Jewish Population (TOZ). The ORT, too, carried on considerable work. Tens of thousands of adults and children were able to survive for a longer period because of the help of these institutions and of the ramified network of house committees which cooperated with them. These organizations conducted their self-sacrificing work up to the last minute, as long as even the slightest spark of life still burned in the Jewish group. Under their cloak all the political parties and ideological trends conducted their clandestine activities. Under their cover practically all the cultural activities were organized.

The watchword of the organized groups of the Jewish community was "To live with honor and die with honor!" We made every effort to carry out this watchword in the ghettos and concentration camps. An expression thereof was the wide scope of the cultural work which was undertaken notwithstanding the horrible terror, hunger and poverty, which grew and spread until the martyred death of Polish Jewry.

At the time when the Warsaw Ghetto was hermetically sealed, a clandestine cultural organization was formed with the name Jewish Cultural Organization (YIKOR). It conducted broad educational work, organized series of lectures, literary anniversaries (in honor of I. L. Peretz, Sholem Aleikhem, Mendele, Borokhov, *et al.*) and literary and dramatic programs. The spirit of YIKOR was the young scholar Menakhem Linder, an economist, murdered by the Germans as early as April 1942.

Under the cloak of CENTOS' children's kitchens and homes, a network of underground schools of various ideological trends was

165

spread (CISHO, Tarbut, Shul-Kult, Yavne, Horeb, Beth Jacob, etc.).[1] The secular schools using Yiddish as the language of instruction were particularly active. They were organized by the unforgettable leaders Shakhne Zagan and Sonia Nowogrudzki, both of whom were led to death in Treblinka.

Clandestine central Jewish archives were formed under the innocent name of a Society for the Pleasures of the Sabbath. Under the direction of Dr. Emanuel Ringelblum, the founder of the archives, and with the active cooperation of . . . the archives amassed materials and documents relating to the martyrology of the Jews in Poland. Thanks to the intensive work of a large staff, tens of crates were collected with extraordinarily valuable documents, diaries, memoirs, reportages, photographs, etc. All of the materials were buried in . . .; we have no access to them. Most of the material sent abroad originates from our archives. We raised a cry to the world with exact information about the greatest crime in history. We are still continuing the archival work. Notwithstanding the terrible conditions we are still collecting memoirs and documents about the martyrdom of the Jews, their struggle, and the present living conditions of the remnants of the Polish Jews. In 1941 and 1942 we were in contact with . . . in Vilna, who, under German control, classified the materials of the Yiddish Scientific Institute—Yivo and secretly hid a good deal of them. Now there are no more Jews left in Vilna. The great center of Jewish culture and of modern research work has been completely destroyed.

Lively underground educational activities were conducted by almost all parties and ideological groups, particularly youth organizations. During almost the entire time in which the Ghetto existed, an underground press issued newspapers, journals and miscellaneous volumes. An especially stimulating press was maintained by the following organizations: Jewish Workers Alliance—Bund *(Buletin, Tsayt-Fragn, Yugnt-Shtime, Za Nasza i Wasza Wolnosc, Nowa Mlodziez)*, Left-Wing Poale-Zion *(Proletarisher Gedank, Yugnt-Ruf, Avangard, Nasze Hasla)*, Hashomer Hatzair *(Przedwiosnie, Jutrznia, Oifbroiz* and a number of miscellanies), Dror *(Dror-Yedies, Hamadrikh, Gvure un Payn)*, Right-Wing Poale-Zion *(Bafrayung)*, Anti-Fascist Bloc *(Der Ruf)*, Communists *(Morgn Frayhayt)* and others. Some of these publications which were issued in Warsaw were, despite the exceptional difficulties of communication and contact, disseminated in all the ghettos.

Extensive educational activity among children and youth was conducted by the Central Organization for the Protection of Children and Orphans (CENTOS) under the leadership of . . . and of the unforgettable Rosa Symchowitz (who died of typhoid contracted in her work

[1] In September 1940 Ringelblum reported that 600 minyan groups conducted daily religious services.

166

with homeless children). With the aid of teachers, educators and artists, hundreds of children's programs were presented in dormitories, homes and clubs.

A central library for children was organized by . . ., a theater under the direction of . . . and . . ., and there were courses in Yiddish language and literature. In connection with the activities of the "Children's Month" especially impressive programs were presented to which thousands of persons came to free themselves for a few hours from the pressure of reality and to pass the time, free of care, with the children. Several hundred children from the CENTOS institutions and schools participated in these highly artistic productions. Today there are no more Jewish children left in Poland. The Hitler criminals murdered ninety-nine percent of the children.

A symphony orchestra under the able leadership of Szymon Pullman was active in the Ghetto. Whenever the occasion presented itself, concerts of beautiful orchestral and chamber music provided moments of rest and escape. Pullman and almost all the members of the orchestra, including the violinist Ludwik Holcman, were killed in Treblinka. The young concertmaster Marian Neuteich was murdered in the Trawniki camp. New talents appeared in the ghetto. The phenomenal young singer Marysia Ajzensztat, "the nightingale of the ghetto," daughter of the choir director of the Warsaw synagogue, shone like a meteor. She was murdered by the SS during the "liquidation campaign." Choirs, too, were organized. Of especial high quality was the children's chorus under the direction of J. Fajwiszys. He was killed in the Poniatow camp. Other choir leaders like W. Gladstein, Zaks and others were murdered in Treblinka. The Jewish artists and sculptors, living in extreme poverty, occasionally prepared exhibitions. Particularly active in this field was Feliks Frydman. All Jewish artists were put to death in Treblinka.

Even in the SS concentration camps to which some of the Jews from Warsaw and other cities were taken, the organized elements of the Jewish group did not cease working; they were not broken, and continued at their task of serving the community. In Poniatow and Trawniki and in other camps a clandestine society for self-help was organized. From time to time even cultural programs and commemoration meetings were secretly held. As long as life still fluttered in the Jewish group, so long did the stream of cultural activities continue to flow. Know then that the last surviving educational workers remained true to the ideals of our culture. Until their death, they held aloft the banner of culture in the struggle against barbarism.

When the period of murderous deportations began, the idea of self-help gave way to the idea of active resistance. In the forefront were our heroic youth of all groupings and the active corps of the workingmen, primarily of the pro-Palestine organizations. The superb epic of the

Jewish armed struggle in Poland began: the heroic defense of the Warsaw Ghetto, the magnificent struggle in Bialystok, the destruction of the annihilation centers in Treblinka and Sobibor, the battles in Tarnow, Bedzin, Czestochowa and other points. The Jews showed the world that they could fight with arms, that they knew how to die with honor in the struggle with the arch-enemy of the Jewish people and of all humanity.

This is all that we wanted to tell you, dear friends. Not many of us are still alive. The names of the writers who write and work with us are . . . We do not know if they are still alive. Help them through the International Red Cross. We are enclosing a list of murdered persons who were among the most active in our educational organization.

We doubt whether we shall ever see you again. Give our warmest greetings to all Jewish cultural leaders, writers, journalists, musicians, artists, all builders of modern Jewish culture and fighters for the salvation of the Jews and of all humanity.

Dr. E. Ringelblum

NOTE: This letter was written on March 1. A week later, March 7, 1944, the underground shelter in the "Aryan district," where Dr. Ringelblum was hidden, was uncovered by the Gestapo. Dr. Ringelblum, his wife and son, and thirty-five other persons, most of them intellectuals, were brutally tormented by the Germans and shot on the ruins of the Ghetto. This was the manner in which this excellent historian and zealous communal leader, the enthusiast of modern Jewish culture, met a martyr's death.

# A Pole Visits the Warsaw Ghetto and Reports to Szmul Zygelbojm

*Jan Karski was the penname of Jan Kozielewski, an official of the Polish pre-war Ministry of Foreign Affairs, who during the war served as liaison officer of the underground Polish Home Army and the Polish Government-in-Exile in London. He stole into the beleaguered Warsaw ghetto to see conditions with his*

From *The Story of a Secret State* by Jan Karski.

*own eyes before leaving to report to his superiors in London. (Since his book was written before the end of the war, he did not mention the names of his interviewers in the ghetto.)*

Is it still necessary to describe the Warsaw ghetto? So much has already been written about it, there have been so many accounts by unimpeachable witnesses. A cemetery? No, for these bodies were still moving, were indeed often violently agitated. These were still living people, if you could call them such. For apart from their skin, eyes, and voice there was nothing human left in these palpitating figures. Everywhere there was hunger, misery, the atrocious stench of decomposing bodies, the pitiful moans of dying children, the desperate cries and gasps of a people struggling for life against impossible odds.

To pass that wall was to enter into a new world utterly unlike anything that had ever been imagined. The entire population of the ghetto seemed to be living in the street. There was hardly a square yard of empty space. As we picked our way across the mud and rubble, the shadows of what had once been men or women flitted by us in pursuit of someone or something, their eyes blazing with some insane hunger or greed.

Everyone and everything seemed to vibrate with unnatural intensity, to be in constant motion, enveloped in a haze of disease and death through which their bodies appeared to be throbbing in disintegration. We passed an old man standing against a wall staring lugubriously and with glassy eyes into space, and although he barely moved from his spot, he, too, seemed to be strangely animated, his body tormented by a force that made his skin twitch in little areas.

As we walked everything became increasingly unreal. The names of streets, shops, and buildings had been printed in the old Hebrew characters. My guides informed me that an edict had been issued forbidding the use of German or Polish for any inscriptions in the ghetto. As a result many of the inhabitants could not read the names at all. From time to time we passed a well-fed German policeman who looked abnormally bloated by contrast with the meagerness of those who surrounded him. Each time one approached we hastened our steps or crossed to the other side as though we had been contaminated.

We passed a miserable replica of a park—a little square of comparatively clear ground in which a half-dozen nearly leafless trees and a patch of grass had somehow managed to survive. It was fearfully crowded. Mothers huddled close together on benches nursing withered infants. Children, every bone in their skeletons showing through their taut skins, played in heaps and swarms.

"They play before they die," I heard my companion on the left say, his voice breaking with emotion.

Without thinking—the words escaping even before the thought had crystallized—I said:

"But these children are not playing—they only make-believe it is play."

We heard the sound of a large number of footsteps rising and falling in unison. A group of about a hundred young men were approaching us. They marched in formation in the middle of the street and were accompanied by policemen. Their clothes were torn and dirty like the rest but they were obviously stronger, better-nourished. The reason was apparent. As they passed us I noticed that each carried a ragged bundle from which protruded the end of a loaf of bread and some green vegetable tips.

Their physical condition was indubitably better than that of their neighbors. But there was something uncanny, robotlike, about their appearance. They walked stiffly. The muscles on their faces seemed to have set rigidly into a mold of habitual, unbroken fatigue. Their eyes were glazed and blank and focused straight ahead as though nothing could distract their attention.

"Those are fortunate," the Bund leader informed me. "The Germans still find them useful. They can work repairing roads and tracks. They are protected as long as their hands last and their muscles move. Everyone in the ghetto envies them. We supply as many people as we can with forged documents proving that they hold similar jobs. Otherwise they would be murdered. We have saved thousands of lives this way. But this cannot work much longer."

Frequently we passed by corpses lying naked in the streets.

"What does it mean?" I asked my guide. "Why are they lying there naked?"

"When a Jew dies," he answered, "his family removes his clothing and throws his body in the street. If not, they have to pay the Germans to have the body buried. They have instituted a burial tax which practically no one here can afford. Besides, this saves clothing. Here, every rag counts. . . ."

I saw an old, feeble man staggering along, lurching against the walls of the houses to keep from falling.

"I don't see many old people," I said. "Do they stay inside all day?"

The answer came in a voice that seemed to issue from the grave.

"No. Don't you understand the German system yet? Those whose muscles are still capable of any effort are used for forced labor. The others are murdered by quota. First come the sick and aged, then the unemployed, then those whose work is not directly connected with the German war needs, finally those who work on roads, in trains, in factories. Ultimately, they intend to kill us all."

Suddenly my companions seized my arms. I saw nothing, did not know what was happening. I became frightened, thought I had been recognized. They rushed me through the nearest entrance.

"Hurry, hurry, you must see this. This is something for you to tell the world about. Hurry!"

We reached the top floor. I heard the sound of a shot from somewhere. They knocked at a door. It opened half-way to disclose a white, emaciated face.

"Do your windows face the street?" the leader asked.

"No, the courtyard. What do you want?"

The Bund leader slammed the door shut furiously. He rushed to the opposite door and battered upon it. It opened. He pushed aside a young boy, who ran back into the room with frightened cries. They urged me to the window, pulled down the shade and told me to look through the slit at the side.

"Now you'll see something. The hunt. You would never believe it if you did not see it for yourself."

I looked through the opening. In the middle of the street two boys, dressed in the uniform of the Hitlerjugend,[1] were standing. They wore no caps and their blond hair shone in the sun. With their round, rosy-cheeked faces and their blue eyes they were like images of health and life. They chattered, laughed, pushed each other in spasms of merriment. At that moment, the younger one pulled a gun out of his hip pocket and then I first realized what I was witnessing. His eyes roamed about, seeking something. A target. He was looking for a target with the casual, gay absorption of a boy at a carnival.

I followed his glance. For the first time I noticed that all the pavements about them were absolutely deserted. Nowhere within the scope of those blue eyes, in no place from which those cheerful, healthy faces could be seen was there a single human being. The gaze of the boy with the gun came to rest on a spot out of my line of vision. He raised his arm and took careful aim. The shot rang out, followed by the noise of breaking glass and then the terrible cry of a man in agony.

The boy who had fired the shot shouted with joy. The other clapped him on the shoulder and said something to him, obviously complimentary. They smiled at each other and stood there for a moment, gay and insolent, as though aware of their invisible audience. Then they linked their arms and walked off gracefully toward the exit of the ghetto, chatting cheerfully as if they were returning from a sporting event.

I stood there, my face glued to the window. In the room behind me there was a complete silence. No one even stirred. I remained where I was, afraid to change the position of my body, to move my hand or relax my cramped legs. I was seized with such panic that I could not make the effort of will to take a single step or force a word out of my throat. It seemed to me that if I made the slightest movement, if a single muscle in my body so much as trembled, I might precipitate another scene such as I had just witnessed.

I do not know how long I remained there. Any interval could have passed, I was so completely unconscious of time. At length I felt

[1] Hitler Youth organization.

171

someone's hand on my shoulder. Repressing a nervous start, I turned around. A woman, the tenant of the apartment, was standing there, her gaunt face the color of chalk in the dim light. She gestured at me.

"You came to see us? It won't do any good. Go back, run away. Don't torture yourself any more."

My two guides were sitting motionlessly on a dilapidated couch, their heads between their hands. I approached them.

"Let's go," I said, stammering. "Take me out of here . . . I am very tired. I must go immediately. I will come back some other time . . ."

They rose quickly and silently and placed themselves at my sides. We clattered hurriedly down the broken staircase without saying a word. In the streets I almost broke into a run while they kept up with me as best they could. I kept going this way, at a half-run, through the door and cellars of the secret building until we reached the door that led to the other side.

It is hard to explain why I ran. There was no occasion for speed and, if anything, our haste could have aroused suspicion. But I ran, I think, simply to get a breath of clean air and a drink of water. Everything there seemed polluted by death, the stench of rotting corpses, filth and decay. I was careful to avoid touching a wall or a human being. I would have refused a drink of water in that city of death if I had been dying of thirst. I believe I even held my breath as much as I could in order to breathe in less of the contaminated air.

Two days later I repeated my visit to the ghetto, to memorize more vividly my visual impressions. With my two guides I walked again for three hours through the streets of this inferno, the better to testify the truth before the leading men and women of the free countries of the world. I reported my experiences to outstanding members of the British and American governments, and to the Jewish leaders of both continents. I told what I had seen in the ghetto to some of the world's great writers—to H. G. Wells, Arthur Koestler, members of the P.E.N. Club[2]—as they could describe it with greater force and talent than I. I told it to others, too, less well-known and to one, in particular, who will never be heard from again.

## . . . And Reports to Zygelbojm

*Zygelbojm (1895–1943), to whom he reported, among others, was the leader of the Jewish Socialist Bund. At the end of 1939 he was sent to London to represent the Bund[3] in the Polish Council. There he presented Karski's report . . .*

In London, five weeks later, a meeting was arranged for me. To me,

[2]Writers club.
[3]Jewish Socialist party.

172

it was one of innumerable such meetings and not the most important. . . . I expected one of the leaders of the Jewish Bund. His name was Szmul Zygelbojm. He had been in Poland until 1940, had worked in the Jewish Underground, had been a member of the Council of the Warsaw ghetto and had, I believe, even been held for a time as a hostage by the Nazis.

We were to meet in the Stratton House, near Piccadilly . . . the seat of the Polish Ministry of the Interior. When I entered one of the small rooms Zygelbojm was already there, sitting in an office chair and waiting quietly. I was tired and studied him casually while we introduced ourselves. Since the war I have had to deal, without exaggeration, with thousands of people and always with an insufficient amount of time. Consequently, I have had to learn to size up character at a glance. . . .

To me, Zygelbojm looked like a type I had often encountered among Jewish leaders. He had the hard, suspicious glance of the proletarian, the self-made man who could not be cajoled, and was constantly on the alert for falsehood. . . . I shall have to be careful and exact, I thought.

"What do you want to hear about?" I asked.

"About Jews, my dear man. I am a Jew. Tell me what you know about the Jews in Poland."

"Are you entitled to see the material I received at the joint conferences with the leaders of the Jewish Bund and the Zionists?"

"Yes, I am. I represent the Jewish Bund in the Polish National Council and I was one of the leaders of the Bund in Poland."

I began my story in a cut-and-dried fashion. I had finally, after much experience, mastered a kind of formula for these situations. I had found that, on the whole, the most effective way of getting my material across was not to soften or interpret it, but to convey it as directly as possible, reproducing not merely ideas and instructions but the language, gestures and nuances of those from whom the material came. That has been my job—faithful, concrete reproduction.

Zygelbojm listened intently, thirstily, with an avid desire for information it was impossible to satisfy. . . . His dark, wide-open eyes were staring fixedly at a point on the ceiling far behind me. They never blinked. The expression on his face hardly varied, not a muscle of it moving, except for the occasional contortion of his cheek in a nervous tic.

"Conditions are horrible. The people in the ghetto live in constant agony, a lingering, tormenting death," I was reciting almost by rote. "The instructions their leaders gave me cannot be carried out for political and tactical reasons. I spoke to the British authorities. The answer was the one your leaders in Poland told me to expect—'No, it is impossible, it can't be done.'"

Zygelbojm rose abruptly and advanced a step or two toward me. His eyes snapped with anger and contempt. He dismissed what I had just told him with a sharp wave of his hand that made me feel as though I had been slapped in rebuke.

"Listen," he almost shouted. "I didn't come here to talk to you about what is happening here. Don't tell me what is said and done here. I know that myself. I came to you to hear about what is happening *there*, what *they* want *there*, what they say *there!*"

I answered with brutal simplicity and directness.

"Very well, then. This is what *they* want from their leaders in the free countries of the world, this is what *they* told me to say: 'Let them go to all the important English and American offices and agencies. Tell them not to leave until they have obtained guarantees that a way has been decided upon to save the Jews. Let them accept no food or drink, let them die a slow death while the world looks on. Let them die. This may shake the conscience of the world.'"

Zygelbojm started as though he had been bitten and began to pace around the room agitatedly, almost breaking into a run. Worried lines formed between his contracted eyebrows and he held one hand to his head as though it ached.

"It is impossible," he finally said, "utterly impossible. You know what would happen. They would simply bring in two policemen and have me dragged away to an institution. Do you think they will let me die a slow, lingering death? Never . . . they would never let me."

We talked at great length. I gave him all the details of my instructions. I told him all I knew about the Jews in Poland and all I had seen. He asked innumerable questions, wanted more and more concrete and even trivial details. Possibly he felt that if the picture I gave him was clear and minute enough, he could suffer together with them, be united with them. He asked me what the houses looked like, what the children looked like, what were the exact words of the woman who put her hands on my shoulder while I was watching the "hunt." What was my impression of the Bund leader, what did he wear, how did he talk, was he nervous? He asked me what the corpses of the dead Jews on the ghetto street looked like and did I remember the words of the child dying in the street.

He shrugged his shoulders.

"Ah, I forget. You can't talk Yiddish, you are not a Jew."

I did my best to satisfy his thirst for facts and details, emptying my memory of everything that it had stored up for just such an occasion. At the end of the interview I was utterly fatigued, my powers of response completely sapped. He looked even more tired, his eyes nearly starting out of their sockets, and the tic occurring with increasing frequency. We shook hands, Zygelbojm gazing directly into my eyes, intent and questioning.

174

"Mr. Karski, I'll do everything I can to help them. Everything! I'll do everything they demand—if only I am given a chance. You believe me, don't you?"

My answer was rather cold and impatient. I felt tired, frustrated, strained. So many interviews, so many meetings . . .

"Of course I believe you. I feel certain you will do all you can and all they demand. My God, every single one of us tries to do his best."

At the bottom, I think, I felt that Zygelbojm was boasting or, at least, thoughtlessly promising more than he could perform. I felt nettled, harassed. He asked so many needless questions which had no place in the interview. "Do I believe?" What difference did it make if I did or did not? I no longer knew what I believed and what I did not believe. He had no right to perplex me further. I had enough of my own troubles. . . .

Some weeks later I had all but forgotten Zygelbojm in the endless grind of interviews and meetings. I was sitting in my room in Dolphin Square during a brief respite, resting, when the telephone rang. I deliberately let it ring three or four times and then picked up the receiver reluctantly. It was an employee of the Stratton House.

"Mr. Karski, I was told to inform you that Szmul Zygelbojm, a member of the Polish National Council and Representative of the Bund in London committed suicide yesterday. He left some notes, saying that he did all he could to help the Jews in Poland but failed, that all his brothers will perish, and that he is joining them. He turned on the gas in his apartment."

I hung up.

At first I felt nothing at all, then a wave of mingled shock, grief, and guilt. I felt as though I had personally handed Zygelbojm his death warrant, even though I had been only the instrument. Painfully, it occurred to me that he might have found my answer to his last question cold and unsympathetic. I had become, I thought to myself, so cynical, so quick and harsh in my judgment, that I could no longer estimate the degree of self-sacrifice possible to a man like Zygelbojm. For days afterwards I felt all my confidence in myself and in my work vanishing and I deliberately forced myself to work twice as hard in order to avoid these intolerable reflections. . . .

## Postscript: Below are excerpts of Zygelbojm's suicide letter . . .

"I cannot be silent—I cannot live—while remnants of the Jewish people of Poland, of whom I am a representative, are perishing. My comrades in the Warsaw ghetto took weapons in their hands on that last heroic impulse. It was not my destiny to die there together with them, but I belong to them, and in their mass graves. By

175

my death I wish to express my strongest protest against the inactivity with which the world is looking on and permitting the extermination of my people.

"I know how little human life is worth today; but as I was unable to do anything during my life, perhaps by my death I shall contribute to breaking down the indifference of those who may now—at the last moment—rescue from certain annihilation the few Polish Jews who are still alive. My life belongs to the Jewish people of Poland and I therefore give it to them. I wish that this remaining handful of the original several millions of Polish Jews could live to see the liberation of a new world of freedom, and the justice of true socialism. I believe that such a Poland will arise and that such a world will come. . . ."

# Readings

*Notes from the Warsaw Ghetto*, edited and translated by Jacob Sloan (McGraw-Hill, 1958), is "must" reading to learn about, understand, and appreciate the Nazi Ghetto. It was painstakingly compiled and preserved by Emanuel Ringelblum, *the* Ghetto archivist and historian. The records, dug up in 1946 and later in 1950, are a product of research by a special group which he founded and directed. They constituted the raw material for novels like John Hersey's *The Wall* and Leon Uris' *Mila 18*.

*Polish-Jewish Relations during the Second World War* by Emanuel Ringelblum (Yad Vashem, 1974), was edited by Joseph Kermish and Shmuel Krakowski, from the manuscript discovered hidden underground on the other side of the wall, in the "Aryan" sector. A first-hand account on the subject.

*Scroll of Agony*, edited and translated by Abraham I. Katsch (Macmillan, 1965), is a personal diary of the martyred Chaim A. Kaplan, a leading Warsaw Hebrew educator, who kept his diary from September 1, 1939 to August 4, 1942; it was stolen out and preserved.

*The Holocaust Kingdom: A Memoir* by Alexander Donat (Holt, Rinehart and Winston, 1965), is one of the best personal accounts on the ghetto and other subjects, e.g., deportation, labor camps, resistance, and liberation. An impressive chronicle.

*The Stars Bear Witness* by Bernard Goldstein (Viking, 1949), is an outstanding personal account of a leader of the Jewish Socialist Bund. Records of the role of the Bund in the resistance and rebellion are included in this book.

*Judenrat* by Isaiah Trunk (Macmillan, 1972), is the first thorough, objective analysis of the Jewish Community Councils. It is a definitive, comprehensive study of the so-called Jewish "self-government" in its various phases.

*Studies of the Epoch of the Jewish Catastrophe 1933–1945*, YIVO Annual of Jewish Social Science (Vol. VIII), edited by Koppel S. Pinson, 1953. This is a valuable collection including a diary of the Vilna ghetto, scientific studies of aspects of life in the ghetto, and historical episodes relevant to the subject.

# 9. THE DESTRUCTION AND RESCUE OF JEWISH BOOKS AND RELIGIOUS TREASURES

Jewish cultural institutions suffered unparalleled destruction in the Nazi era. Historian Philip Friedman reported that in 1939 there were over 3,300,000 Jewish books housed in 469 libraries of 1,000 volumés or more in twenty European countries. With the many smaller libraries in synagogues and other centers added to these, the total number of books in these countries must have reached well over 5,000,-000. Between 1933 and 1938 book burnings were common in ceremonial bonfires; Torah scrolls, sacred objects, and religious libraries were burned, defiled, and scattered.

When the Nazis invaded Poland and other European countries, this policy of brutal destruction intensified. With German efficiency and thoroughness, the Nazis even appointed special army squads to burn and destroy Jewish books. The robbing of Jewish literary treasures was carried out in all European Jewish communities and affected such famous institutions as the Bibliotheca Rosenthaliana in Holland, the Yivo treasure house of Jewish history and literature and the Strashun Library in Vilna, and the yeshivot of Poland, Lithuania, and other countries. The Nazis intended to destroy all evidence of Jewish contributions to civilization, and to distort the Judaic cultural heritage so as to convince the conquered

178

nations that Hitler had to rid the world of every aspect of the Jewish Problem.

This new ideology was adopted by Nazi academicians in the world of the social sciences, theology, biology, genetics, etc. In 1936, a Department for Research on the Jewish Question was established in the University of Munich with great fanfare, and was attended by the Nazi elite. After the November 1938 pogroms, all the books remaining from the bonfires and the destruction of the synagogues and other Jewish cultural institutions were transfered to the Munich Institute. Scholarships and grants were offered to initiate research projects on the Jewish question. Courses, seminars, and forums were arranged so that the Nazi doctrines were covered by a scholarly facade of technical language and subtle pseudoscientific terminology. With each period of the Nazi onslaught— from its very establishment in January 1933 to the end of the war—the Nazis supplied the theoretical and academic bases for rationalizing their barbaric acts. Some of the academicians were noteworthy scholars who worked out of Nazi institutes which subsidized their research and published their works. They were integrated into the German military, propaganda, and political apparatus to spread their "science" globally.

To feed the new science of Judaeology,[1] Alfred Rosenberg, Hitler's "intellectual" minister, established offices in some twenty-five European centers to loot Jewish libraries, museums, archives, synagogues, publishing houses, yeshivot, seminaries, and institutes of Jewish learning. From Copenhagen to Salonica, and from the Black Sea to the Atlantic, books and manuscripts were catalogued by librarians and scholars. Those books selected for shipping to Rosenberg's bureau were kept, the others were sent to paper mills to be recycled. Torah scrolls were used to bind books and for manufacturing shoes, pocketbooks, and other leather products. Some ancient scrolls were preserved as antiques for exhibit or for future sale.

## RESCUE OF JEWISH BOOKS

A heroic chapter was written by the Jewish employees of Rosenberg's task force, who, at the risk of their lives, frequently smuggled out valuable manuscripts and books, burying them in safe places. Some of these precious items were later recovered and returned to Jewish institutions.

In fact, after Germany's defeat in 1945, a feverish search began. The work was entrusted to the Jewish Cultural Reconstruction Committee, headed by the eminent professor of Jewish history, Salo W. Baron of Columbia University, and staffed by Dr. Joshua Starr of New York City, Dr. Shlomo Shunami of the Hebrew University, Mordecai W. Bernstein of Poland, and others.

The searchers systematically examined every place that offered clues.

[1]The term was coined by Professor Bernard D. Weinryb of Dropsie University, Philadelphia.

Soon discoveries were made by the American and Allied Military Occupation Forces in Frankfurt, who had assigned special details to recover, sort out, and return the books to their origin. Many thrilling incidents abounded in the rescuing of books, even as in the rescue of prisoners.

The full story of the recovery of the Jewish books has yet to be told. Mordecai W. Bernstein's personal account is given in two illustrated volumes in Yiddish that were published in Buenos Aires, Argentina—*In the Labyrinth of Ages: A Millennium of German Jewry* (Yivo, 1955) and *Brands Plucked Out of the Fire* (Yivo, 1956).

# In the "Kingdom" of Alfred Rosenberg

The Rosenberg Staff in Vilna was appointed to round out the physical job of extermination by destroying the Jewish religion and culture. In a short period of time they planned to obliterate five centuries of the Jewish spiritual heritage.

On August 1, 1940, Noah Prilutzki (Yiddish linguist and grammarian) was arrested. He was sitting in his home writing his work on *Yiddish Phonics,* when he was apprehended and transported to the cellars of the Gestapo. There he was met by Dr. Gotthart, the German "specialist" on Judaica, who had arrived in Vilna to collect all rare Jewish cultural objects. He received Prilutzki with an outward politeness and chatted with him on cultural matters. He requested of his prisoner that he draw up a list of Jewish incunabula[1] that were housed in the world famous Shtrashun Library[2] (the director, who was a grandson of the founder, could not bear the vandalizing by the Gestapo and hanged himself by the thongs of his phylacteries).

And so Prilutzki settled down in the Gestapo cellar room with a friend, the Yiddish writer, A. I. Goldschmidt. Every morning they were taken to the library where they listed the incunabula. When the "Judaic Scholar" left for Berlin, they were forgotten and were confined in the cellar. Sometime later the librarian Haikel Lunsky, who was imprisoned with them, told me that before they were removed from their cell

[1]Books printed from movable type before 1500.
[2]A famous library established by Matythiahu Shtrashun (1817–85).

From *Vilner Ghetto* by Avraham Sutzkever.

they were discussing the teachings of Maimonides. About a month later Prilutzki was seen lying on the floor almost naked, his shirt wrapped around his head soaked with blood, and near him lay Goldschmidt; both were killed.

Dr. Pohl, director of the Frankfurt Institute for the Study of the East European Nations, who also served on the staff of "Der Stuermer,"[3] arrived in Vilna, January 1942, to carry on the work of the Rosenberg Department. With him came a full staff of "scholars" headed by Drs. Miller and Wolfe. They were joined later by Messrs. Sporket and Gimpel. Immediately on arrival, they requisitioned twenty workers from the ghetto who were appointed to gather all Jewish cultural articles in Vilna and sort them out to be forwarded to Germany.

"We're at war," Dr. Miller declared, "and there is a grave danger that these valuable objects may be destroyed. We must prevent their loss; that is why we shall send them for safekeeping in Germany to be returned after the war."

Among the twenty were to be included five specialists in Yiddish and Hebrew literature who would help orient the German "scholars" in the search for valuable manuscripts and printed works. I was selected as one of the specialists. I set for myself the goal to rescue whatever I can. I was housed in the Rosenberg Staff quarters. The first assignment which Dr. Miller gave me was to burn the rich medical library of the University Hospital. Soon Dr. Pohl issued a general order to create a "ghetto" of Jewish books. The forty thousand books of the Shtrashun Library and the collections of Biblical, Talmudic and scholarly volumes of the three hundred houses of worship and study in Vilna were "deported" to a building located at 3 University Street.

In 1933, the same Dr. Pohl had been sent to Jerusalem by the Nazi party where for three years he studied at the Hebrew University. He returned "knowledgeable" in Jewish literature and became the advisor of the Rosenberg Staff in this field. Soon it became evident that, like his colleague the SS Vilna mass-murderer Schweinenberg, he, too, was engaged in making "selections" for survival or liquidation. He gave us orders to sort out the mass of books and manuscripts according to the years of publication. He himself went over the selections and, depending on his "judgment," consigned them to be sold for reprocessing in the newly-erected paper manufacture factory or to be transported to Frankfurt. Out of more than 100,000 volumes he shipped to Frankfurt, 74 crates containing some 20,000 books. The rest, many of which were valuable publications, were sold as pulp at 19 marks per ton. A similar fate (for survival or oblivion) was meted out to manuscripts, works of art and sculpture.

As soon as Vilna was occupied, the Yiddish Scientific Institute

[3]An extreme anti-Jewish and pornographic newspaper.

(YIVO) was transformed into a kind of garrison. All the archival materials and publications were thrown down into the cellar like a heap of garbage. Himmler's advisor, Dr. Gotthart, burst into YIVO in search of . . . gold. When he saw the vaults in the cellar he summoned a locksmith who broke open the locks and found manuscripts written by Sholem Aleichem and Yehuda Leib Peretz[4] neatly arranged, which greeted him sardonically. In a rage he threw them on the floor and ground them into the dust.

The YIVO building was converted into a depository for all the works gathered from the public institutions and private homes, except the Shtrashun Library which had already been liquidated. When the sculpture of Mark Antokolsky (1843–1902) was delivered from the Ansky Museum,[5] Dr. Pohl shattered many of the precious pieces. The leaden matrices of the Romm Edition of the Talmud which took some twenty years to set in print (and from which at least 50 editions were published) were sold at 39 marks per ton to be melted down for munitions. He sent off five cartons containing rare editions to Berlin but at the railroad depot, his co-worker Sportek exchanged them stealthily for pigs which he smuggled into the Vaterland.

Herr Sportek sold some five hundred Torah scrolls to a leather factory to be converted into innerlining for knee high boots. The marble tombstones of the Zarecher cemetery he ordered to be transported to Germany where they were cut up and used to pave roads. Just as the Gestapo murdered numberless non-Jews together with Jews, so did the Rosenberg Staff loot and destroy Polish libraries and museums. They were no less conscientious in ferreting out Jewish publications than they were in looking for Jews in hiding. The director of the University of Vilna told me that after the Rosenberg task force removed all Jewish books and books written by Jews, they ripped open the floors and for several days searched to make sure that no volumes had been hidden away.

During the year and a half we worked for Alfred Rosenberg, a number of us managed to save many precious volumes. We bricked them up in walls, buried them in cellars, bunkers and caves, hopeful and prayerful that the day will come when they will be recovered. The most important manuscripts and smaller books we hid under our clothing and stole them into the ghetto. Once I begged Herr Sportek to permit me to take along some "scrap" to use as kindling for warming my room. He consented and wrote out a pass for the guards at the ghetto gate. In the package of scrap were letters of Tolstoy and Gorky,[6] C. N. Bialik (Hebrew poet-laureate), Romain Rolland (French novelist),

---

[4]Distinguished Yiddish classic writers.
[5]Named after Sh. Ansky, author and dramatist (1863–1920).
[6]Famous Russian authors.

manuscripts of Sholem Aleichem (Yiddish classicist, 1859–1916), rare editions published in the 15th and 16th centuries, Theodor Herzl's diary, the only manuscript extant written by the Gaon of Vilna (1720–1790, the greatest Talmudic scholar of the modern era), sketches by the renowned artist Marc Chagall, and tens of other precious items. Once the precedent was established my colleagues and I succeeded in smuggling out many precious things. But since our efforts were perforce limited, we skillfully built a bunker nearby where we hid about five thousand rare volumes. Especially dangerous was the rescuing of statues and sculpture. We coped with this difficulty and accomplished limited success. First we hid the pieces in the courtyard, then we somehow transported them stealthily into the ghetto.

In one of the museums of Vilna whose exhibition pieces were brought to us for sorting, I found a document signed by the Polish-American freedom fighter in the American Revolution, Thaddeus Kosciusko (1746–1817). I gave this document to a Polish woman who had saved a score of Jews from slaughter by hiding them. When she saw Kosciusko's name she fell on her knees and kissed the signature. The next day she appeared at my desk at YIVO and told me that when she showed the document to the members of her underground group, it kindled sparks of courage in their breasts and they vowed to resist and overcome. They asked her to transmit to me that not only they, but their children and children's children will remember me with deep gratitude. (A list of those who helped in all the above efforts follows.)

The most valuable manuscripts of the Jewish classical writer Yehuda Leib Peretz (1852–1915) I gave to the Lithuanian journalist Ona Simaite[7] to hide and preserve. Simaite did not survive. For helping Jews she was tortured to death. In the Vilna ghetto archives I found a letter she sent to a Jewish teacher, Nina Nerstein, the morning after she attended a play in the ghetto. I cite a portion of her letter in reverent memory of this extraordinary human being:

"Dear Nina,

Forgive me for writing to you even though we are not personally acquainted. Your dramatic presentation in the ghetto youth club, Bialik's "Merry Time" and Raisin's "The Wall," colorful scenic designs and the captivating Jewish folk melodies enraptured and warmed my heart. Yes! Only a people of genius can create such artistic productions amidst the nightmares we experience around us. Together with the members of your superior Jewish youth club I believe and hope that ultimately the walls will crumble and the brotherhood of all peoples will reign supreme."

---

[7] Ona Simaite was eternized by Yad Vashem as one of the noble Christians, Righteous among the Gentiles.

# My Work in YIVO

## Rachel Pupko-Krinsky

*The author, a teacher in Vilna, lost her husband in a concentration camp. She, too, spent several years in Nazi camps. After the war she was reunited with her daughter—who had been hidden with a Christian friend—and settled in the United States where she remarried. Here she describes her fourteen months working in YIVO . . .*

My only memories of the occupation that arouse neither fear nor horror are those of the fourteen months I worked in the Vilna Yiddish Scientific Institute—YIVO. What we called the "YIVO" was actually the Rosenberg Confiscatory Squad, which the Germans had installed in the former YIVO building, at Number 18 Wiwulskiego.[1] Fourteen months was a very long time. One time ghetto dwellers will recall that a month had days without end. It was hard to believe that dimensions of time had not changed, and an hour still consisted of a mere sixty minutes.

The YIVO was my fourth assignment. My first job had been cleaning sidewalks (at the Uhlan barracks, on Calvary Street). The second was working as a chamber maid at the student house (on Buffalo Street, converted into an officers' billet). I particularly fancied washing the windows, for while so engaged, I could see not only the street and people below, but also a certain Gentile woman, who would pass by several times a week, wheeling a baby carriage. Lying in the carriage was my own little daughter.

My third post was in a tailoring establishment, in the courtyard of the Anski Museum, on Cszeszko Street. Sentries kept watch at the front door and a German sat in the shop all day, even though torn uniforms was all we ever saw. The only pedagogue in this stronghold of tailors, I found my surroundings both novel and interesting. For comic relief, there was a one-eyed tailor, "Shmulinke" by name. While fitting a uniform, Shmulinke would tug at it from behind, and fixing his good eye on the German's face exclaim: "May the healthy bear you well, Herr Lieutenant." For this pious wish he was rewarded with a cigarette, while the rest of us, understanding where Shmulinke wished to see him

[1] The street of the YIVO.

---

From *The Root and the Bough* edited by Leo W. Schwarz.

184

borne, could hardly restrain our laughter. However, we were cut off from all contacts with the outside world here; consequently, I was glad when I was ultimately released.

It was our ghetto neighbor, Herman Kruk, that first suggested I might go to work in the YIVO. The Rosenberg organization had just called upon the ghetto labor office for the services of several Jews. Kruk, who had been working there himself, knew all about conditions within the Rosenberg staff. The suggestion did not immediately appeal to me, as I felt it would be appalling to stand by and watch the Germans destroy what had been built up with so much love and care. Kruk promised, however, that he would help me obtain a release when I wanted to leave and try to place me where I would be in touch with Gentiles. Kruk had contacts in all the work sections, and knew pretty well what was going on. . . .

The way to the YIVO led past my former home. I could still see the nameplates, "Bramson" and "Krinsky," at the front door. It was like reading the inscription on my own tombstone; months passed before I was able to shake off this feeling and go calmly on my way. (At 18 Wiwulskiego, too, the gate, the trees and the roof were the same as before. Only a few panes were missing from the attic windows; a single windowpane had been smashed in the lecture hall. The blue paint on the front door had been rubbed off in spots; crates of books stood in the vestibule.) The map of Jewish populations the world over still hung over the turn of the staircase, surmounted by an electric clock; but the clock had stopped; and over all was the sign of the swastika.

Soon after our arrival, we were summoned to appear in the office of one of the supervisors, Willy Schaefer. He looked us over from head to toe, and questioned us about our education, background and occupation, just as if we were candidates for constructive research jobs. Apparently our qualifications satisfied him, for he gave each of us an assignment.

Our second supervisor, Sporket, was an elderly German with the face of a brute. In private life he had been a fodder dealer (his driver told us). A Baltic German, he spoke Russian, and was in charge of the Soviet division. His bellowing used to shake the walls, and threw everyone into panic. We trembled at the mere sight of him, and tried to make ourselves scarce whenever he was about. Sporket would strut from room to room and stop suddenly next to one of us, with the result that our fingers turned to butter, and we would drop whatever we held. He did not even pretend to be a judge of culture, as Schaefer did. Pointing to a certain object, he once asked a worker what it was. When she began to explain its historical significance, however, he only hissed "Scheisse!" [shit] and walked out. Fortunately, he preferred riding around town to being closeted in the YIVO.

Sporket had warned us that we were required to rise when a supervi-

185

sor entered the room. Sutzkever thereupon proposed that we stand as soon as we saw the Germans drive up, so they would find us at work, on our feet.

In addition to the Germans, we also had a Polish supervisor, Wirblis, by name. His job was to keep an eye on us, when the Germans were away. Having been wounded in the war, however, he was a little deaf. Whenever the Germans left, therefore, each of us promptly took up his "real" work. Most of the time, Sutzkever would read to us from his beloved poets: Leivick, Leyeles, Yehoash, Glatstein, and many others. This brought us solace and forgetfulness for a time. At other times, Sutzkever would write. Practically all his ghetto poetry, in fact, was written in our little workroom in the YIVO. I loved the room, with its view of the laurel trees, the tall, unfinished church on the corner, and the shadowy outlines of a forest, far away on the horizon. Katcherginski wrote many of his poems in what had been the reading room; while in another room, once the lecture hall, Uma drew designs for the ghetto theater stage sets. Here, too, she designed the ghetto emblem, as well as furniture for the ghetto cafe. Zunser, a young mathematician and violinist who had been put to work on the music collection, would "hear" music. By reading the notes, he told us, he could hear each selection, just as if he were at a concert.

There was a deluge of books in the YIVO just then—Yiddish, Polish, Russian, German, English and French—rounded up from the city libraries and the surrounding countryside. We would each hide a book in some secret nook, and wait for the Germans to leave; for all we knew, these might be the last books we would ever read. The books, too, were in great danger: we were their last readers. Many had been sold by the Germans, as scrap, to paper mills.

At three in the afternoon, we began to pack. Real ingenuity was required to conceal whatever we hoped to smuggle into the ghetto, without arousing the suspicions of our Polish guard, Wirblis. Our coats were kept not in the YIVO itself, but in the garden cottage occupied by the former concierge of the YIVO. The woman spied on us regularly, and informed Wirblis of our doings. Fortunately, she could not make herself understood by the Germans.

Nevertheless, we seldom left the YIVO empty-handed. Even the transport workers, assigned to unload the books and deliver them to the various floors, managed to smuggle some scrap into the ghetto, thus supplying shops with paper, and earning a bit of bread.

Once out of the YIVO courtyard, we had but a single thought: What was going on at the ghetto gate on Rudnicka Street, and how we might soonest slip into the ghetto. On a number of occasions, we were stopped on our way home and warned that the Germans were at the gate. We would then turn down a side street, and tarry until the enemy was gone. At times when we were heavily laden, we would go back to

Szepticki Street, where the workers of the Kajlis leather factory were housed, and leave our books with friends. If, upon reaching the corner at Zawalna, we saw no Germans at the gate, we fairly flew, lest the police or SS Murer himself appear out of nowhere. The ghetto police did not search us long. We were the "paper commando"; they knew they'd find no food on us. Sometimes a Jewish policeman would ask for a good novel to read, but that was all. With the gate thus behind us, we would joke and laugh, as if we had really succeeded in thwarting Rosenberg's plans. The objects we brought in were handed over to Kruk, who hid them temporarily in the ghetto library, to be transferred elsewhere, for safekeeping, later on.

Naturally at one time or another we ran into situations that made our blood curdle. I myself once met up with Murer, while carrying a silver beaker Sutzkever had "lifted" from a special exhibit. The exhibit had been prepared by the Germans, to convince their superiors that the work in Vilna was no trifling matter, and their own merits were not to be discounted. Silver ritual objects, Torah scrolls and valuable books made up the bulk of the exhibits. On one wall, too, hung a painting of the Vilna Gaon, directly opposite some pictures of Chekists,[2] with drawn revolvers. Just how they proposed to prove that the Chekists, with their degenerate faces, were the spiritual brethren of this saintly preeminent scholar, we could not imagine.

We had turned the corner of Zawalna, when we noticed Murer. There was no going back. Someone ahead of me turned and shouted: "Go into the Order Office, and give the beaker to a Jewish policeman." The Order Office was the place where the Germans left their orders for the ghetto workshops. Surrendering the beaker there would have been a good idea, except that we had already passed the office, and I would have had to turn back. Before I could make up my mind, we were at the gate, and the Jewish police lined us up for inspection, as usual. This time, Murer did not search us himself. Instead, he would point out the victim to be searched by the police. They were coming closer to me. Murer fixed his cold eyes on me.

"Have you got any money?" he asked.

"No," I answered, as if in a trance.

My answer rang true. He had taken my mortal dread for calm, and waved me past the gate. Once inside the ghetto, however, my legs refused to budge.

It was soon evident that, whatever of the YIVO treasures we managed to remove, we could smuggle into the ghetto only a small part of what we hoped to hide and preserve. At the same time, we supplied the cultural needs of the ghetto: textbooks for schools, books for the library, study material for clubs, scripts for the ghetto theater. Sutz-

[2]Soviet secret police.

kever then proposed concealing valuable material within the YIVO building itself. Having studied the attic carefully, he decided to pry some boards loose beneath the beams; much could be stowed away there.

To reach the attic stairs, we would have to go through Schaefer's office. It was accessible only when Schaefer left for lunch, provided that we could distract Wirblis. Dr. Feinstein, who was quite friendly with him, learned that the Pole was far from entranced with his position. For one thing, he had not been able to complete his schooling because of the war. We convinced him that it was not too late to study, and undertook to prepare him for his examinations. Dr. Feinstein taught him mathematics; Dr. Gordon, German; I coached him in Latin. The lessons took place during lunchtime. Rachel Prener remained on guard in our room, while Sutzkever and Katcherginski worked undisturbed in the attic.

We also took advantage of the lunch period to meet our Gentile friends. Victoria, the wife of a Polish captain who had hidden dozens of Jews, came to see us frequently, as did a number of other Poles and Lithuanians. Meanwhile the concierge continued to threaten and harass us. Once, when a Gentile visitor came, she locked the gate and announced she wouldn't give the key to anyone but Schaefer. He'd find out about these goings on, she muttered darkly, as soon as he came back from lunch. I don't know what would have happened, if Katcherginski hadn't taken things in hand just then. Seizing the witch by the arm, he ordered her to return the key immediately; if she didn't, he would beat her up, regardless of the consequences. Apparently malevolence is not coupled with bravery, for she grew frightened and returned the key.

Katcherginski's good friend, the Lithuanian Jankauscas, also came frequently during lunch time. On many of these visits he would bring arms, which were concealed in the YIVO, and later smuggled into the ghetto by members of the United Partisan Organization. A special providence seemed to protect us from detection. Once a cache of weapons was actually waiting to be smuggled into the ghetto, when Schaefer had chosen to show some visitors around. Coming to our room, he began to pull out books at random, and show them to his guests. I saw Sutzkever's face turn a chalk-white, and understood that the arms were close at hand. Sutzkever left the room; the attention of the visitors would have to be drawn to something else, at any cost. In desperation, I picked up a manuscript dating back to the Kingdom of Poland in 1830, and said to the Germans: "I've found an interesting document, about the Polish uprising." Schaefer glanced at it, then hastily herded his guests out.

The Gentile woman who had been taking care of my little daughter had to flee in December, 1941, after someone had informed on her.

188

She left Vilna and took up quarters in a village near by. I wrote her to come to town for a day, and we met in the YIVO garden. Terrified of the concierge, I thought a Gestapo man was lurking behind every bush. Our interview lasted ten minutes. I remember I gave my little girl a blossom, and asked if she liked flowers. By way of reply, she turned to the Gentile woman: "You know, mummy," she said, "this lady is nice, and I'm not afraid of her."

Each day we said farewell to the YIVO. We tried to leave everything tidy, so if we did not return, the Germans would not suspect what we had done. One day, while checking if we had forgotten something, Sutzkever found the leather-bound visitor's book. As we turned its pages, memories of what the YIVO had once been flocked back to us. Selig Kalmanowitch came in and took a look at the book. We used to consult him frequently about where to hide things, and how best to save them. He would answer with unwavering faith: "Don't worry. It will not be lost. The Germans will not succeed in destroying everything. They're on the run themselves, right now. Whatever they have stolen will be found after the war and taken from them." (Now I know that this prophecy has been at least partially fulfilled.) We decided to inscribe our names in the book and hide it in the attic. We never doubted that the Germans would lose the war, but we did not foresee the political complexion of Europe. I solemnly believed that Dr. Weinreich, one of the YIVO directors, or my brother would return from America to look for our remains and traces of the YIVO; one of them would then find our last message. Sutzkever inscribed the final stanza of his poem, *A Prayer to a Miracle*, beloved in the ghetto. Being a pessimist, I only wrote: "Morituri vos salutant." ("Death I Salute You") . . .

Some weeks later, the ghetto was sealed off; it was nearing liquidation. We had been prepared for the end, yet being completely imprisoned was a heavy blow. Looking back, the YIVO seemed like a lost paradise. Its loss meant forfeiting the last shred of humanity left us in the ghetto. For us the YIVO had been the boundless blue sky, the sun, the fragrant laurels of Wiwulskiego, from which we used to snap off twigs to take home to the ghetto, where no trees grew. The YIVO meant the fragrant balsam in its garden and the rose bushes about to bloom—too late for us.

# Books Return Home: The Search for and Recovery of Jewish Books and Religious Treasures

In 1945 when the German armies began their retreat, scarcely a Jewish book, Torah scroll or religious object could be found on the continent. The World Jewish Community set up a mission, called the Jewish Cultural Reconstruction Committee (headed by Dr. Salo W. Baron, eminent Jewish historian) whose aim it was to find, if possible, what happened to the renowned Jewish libraries of Europe and where, if anywhere, they could be traced and recovered. They knew that the Nazis had established an Institute for researching the "Jewish Question." They planned to lull the conscience of mankind by justifying the destruction of European Jewry and to further their program of genocide to embrace world Jewry.

The Cultural Commission set up a task force who questioned survivors, German officials, librarians and whosoever could offer a clue to the whereabouts of the plunder. Early in their search they were rewarded when the American Military Occupation Forces found 100,-000 books in Frankfurt. After negotiations with the AMOT (who were instructed to return all loot to their countries of origin), the books were finally sent to the Hebrew University in Jerusalem. Encouraged, the task force relentlessly continued to ferret out every lead that came to their attention. They found collections of books numbering tens of thousands. But these finds were insignificant compared to the vast lootings which the Germans had carried out.

Dr. Shlomo Shunami of the Hebrew University, a member of the task force, narrated the following incident[1] which illustrated the persistence of the searchers.

It happened in the summer of 1953. He was making his rounds when he stepped into a government office somewhere in Austria and asked the usual questions of the official who received him: Did he know

---

[1] From *Hadassah Magazine,* May 1962, by Gloria Goldreich.

of any Jewish books, documents, Torah scrolls, religious and ceremonial objects that may have been hidden away somewhere, etc.? The official listened silently and without a word drew forth a single sheet from a file and said, "I know nothing of what you are asking . . . And now I must leave you." He left the room swiftly, but he turned the document around so that it faced Dr. Shunami. Almost in a trance, the latter read its contents telling about a shipment order for several hundred thousand books specifying their destinations. Dr. Shunami, still stunned, copied the information and left before the official returned. Why had this man made the information available? Dr. Shunami can attribute it either to a passion for justice—or to an uneasy conscience.

After some difficult negotiations with the Austrian government, who viewed the searchers as "dreamers" and "fanatics," the Commission recovered hundreds of thousands of valuable books and ceremonial and religious objects.

As the work proceeded, books were found in the most out-of-the way places in small towns. (When the large cities were bombed by the Allies, the Germans evacuated all they could hastily and dumped the books wherever they could.)

The Commission established depots where more or less trained staffs, guided by Jewish scholars, collected and catalogued the books, photographs and documents. Soon consignments were being shipped to the Netherlands, France, Italy where the shelves of famous existing Jewish libraries were refilled by the recovered treasures; and Israel, the United States, Great Britain and other countries where the survivors were rebuilding their lives anew. Captain Isaac Berkowitz, who was in charge of the largest depot at Offenbach, Germany, poured forth his deepfelt sorrowful emotions on his experiences:

"I would walk into the loose document room to take a look at the things there and find it impossible to tear myself away from the fascinating piles of letters, folders, and little personal bundles. Not that what you held in your hand was so engrossing, but rather what the next intriguing item might be. Or, in the sorting room, I would come to a box of books which the sorters had brought together, like scattered sheep into one fold—books from a library which once had been in some distant town in Poland, or an extinct Yeshiva.[2] There was something sad and mournful about these volumes . . . as if they were whispering a tale of yearning and hope long since obliterated.

"I would pick up a badly worn Talmud with hundreds of names of many generations of students and scholars. Where were they now? Or, rather, where were their ashes? In what incinerator were they

[2]Talmudical academy.

destroyed? I would find myself straightening out these books and arranging them in the boxes with a personal sense of tenderness as if they had belonged to someone dear to me, someone recently deceased.

"There were thousands of loose family photographs without any identification. How dear all these tokens of love and gentle care must have been to someone and now they were so useless, destined to be burned, buried, or thrown away. All these things made my blood boil ... How difficult it is to look at the contents of the depot with the detachment of someone evaluating property or with the impersonal viewpoint of scholarly evaluation."[3]

Space does not permit further elaboration of this project. It is sufficient to note that if not for the Commission's dedicated work, the volumes and objects would have rotted away. Some two thousand collections of Jewish cultural, religious and ceremonial treasures numbering many hundreds of thousands of items were sorted out and restored to the European Jewish communities which survived and to world Jewish centers where the survivors established new homes. In addition, it was estimated that more than 2,000,000 volumes of non-Jewish content, which had also been looted by the German occupation forces, were returned to their countries of origin.

[3]From "Books Go Home From the Wars," by Leslie I. Poste, in *The Library Journal,* December 1, 1948.

# 10. DEPORTATION

In their cunningly masked vocabulary, "resettlement" was the name the Germans gave to the deportation of millions of victims to their deaths. Skilled in psychological warfare, the Germans used every possible ruse and camouflage in order to dupe their prey into going without much resistance, as well as to allay the fears of those who remained behind.

The deportees were told they were going to work, and instructions were generally issued that each person could take along enough food to last for two days, a bowl, a spoon (no knife), two blankets, warm clothing, a pair of heavy shoes, a suitcase marked with the owner's name—fifty-five pounds in all (the baggage was later added to the Nazi loot). They were generally taken by truck to a train of some twenty cattle cars which usually held a thousand persons. So that other people should not witness the miseries of the deportees, the trains were kept away from stations; instead, they stopped at sidings which were at a distance from passenger depots.

Requisitions of equipment for trains, maintenance of the rolling stock, the huge amounts of fuel required, setting up of schedules to avoid delays and collisions, providing personnel and provisions (even on a starvation level)—all this severely taxed the German war economy, which was already dangerously strained. Supplies were short; personnel unavailable. But the "total solution" to the Jewish Problem received top priority even in the face of imminent German defeat. It is estimated that about three million Jews were transported to their death in this fashion.

To expedite the deportations, an organized chain of authority was set up. The German Foreign Ministry made the diplomatic arrangements in the occupied territories to provide "labor for the war effort." The local police or the Gestapo rounded up the "laborers," the Ministry of Transport took care of the logistics and mechanics of deportation, and the SS gave the "finishing touches." The amount of assistance by the local authorities in the conquered countries was regarded as a measure of their loyalty to Germany. Moreover, Himmler hesitated at gassing Reich Jews on Reich territory. It was safer and more fitting to do so on foreign territory, e.g., at Auschwitz in Poland. In October 1939, transports in large numbers began to arrive in western Poland. The haste was such that no places had been prepared to receive them. The deportees were dumped in old barracks and stables, and, when no walled structures were available, in the open fields. Most deportees had traveled in freight cars or trucks which were completely jammed; many had to stand for days. The cars were windowless. Bread and a sorry-looking gruel that passed for soup were doled out once daily during the long trip. There were no provisions for drinking water, no sanitary facilities, no heating. Much of the human cargo suffocated, especially infants, children, women, the aged, and the sick. Because the captors had to account for the total number that checked in at the point of departure, nobody, dead or alive, was removed until the destination was reached and the numbers tallied. In fact, in December 1939, the commander of the German army in Poland, Field Marshal Johannes Blaskowitz, complained about finding in the freight cars children frozen to death and people dead from starvation. The death rate of deportees to Lublin was nearly one-third, and those who remained alive arrived close to death.

Evil-starred names of new geographical sites sprang up: Buchenwald, Mauthausen, Ravensbruck, Sachsenhausen, Bergen-Belsen, Ponar, Westerbork, Chelmo, Sobibor, Treblinka, Majdanek, Auschwitz, Birkenau— some were combined slave-labor camps; some were out-and-out slaughterhouses. A few, such as Theresienstadt, passed as "showplaces" for the visiting Red Cross teams, but in fact were transfer camps where the victims marked time until the ovens were ready for them.

# First Deportation From Cracow, Poland

*There are many eyewitness accounts of the deportations. The one quoted here was written by Tadeusz Pankiewicz, the only known non-Jew who by accident (his*

From *And the Crooked Shall Be Made Straight* by Jacob Robinson.

*pharmacy happened to lie within the perimeter of the ghetto in Cracow) witnessed it. From his pharmacy he had a view of Harmony Square, the place where the deportees were assembled. He told his story in a remarkable book published in Cracow in 1947. Below are excerpts of his account of the first deportation, the least horrible of the five he witnessed and reported . . .*

## Preparations

... The commissions, consisting of members of the Gestapo and officials of the Labor Office, have been working in the building of the Jewish Social Self-Help on May 29, 30, and 31, 1942. Small tables have been put up in the large hall in the building . . . In front of each table long lines of people are waiting with trembling hearts to see what their fate will be. Crowds are standing in front of the building for long hours in lines that extend for hundreds of meters. The Gestapo men arbitrarily decide on the spot who is to remain and who is to leave the ghetto. Those who do not receive permission to remain in the ghetto are too frightened to ask: Where will we be deported? What will happen to us? Will we be permitted to take some of our belongings with us? They are trying to reassure each other. Nobody believes in total annihilation. Nobody thinks of crematoria, gas-poisoning, or death by burning. Rumors spread for the first time that the Germans had disclosed secretly that the deportees will be taken to the Ukraine, where they will work on farms.

German railroad workers tell about large barracks that are awaiting the deportees. People believe these rumors, but new worries arise: where to get food, and whether they will be allowed to take along large amounts of provisions. In the meantime, the struggle for life goes on with all vigor. People try with all the means at their command to get their identification cards stamped by the *SS und Polizeiführer* (police chief), since only these stamps give the right to remain. Nobody realized at the time that the stamps determined life and death, and that their dispensation depended entirely on the whims of the Germans . . . Paradoxical events take place: One person is denied the stamp, but gets the stamp without difficulty at the same table an hour later. Another person is refused the stamp at one table, but gets it at another. Coincidence, luck, the mood of the Gestapo man, his caprice, the extent of one's connections, the amount of bribe money, the sparkle and the size of the diamond—these are the chance occurrences which decide whether one remains or has to leave. The two-day registration is finished. People without stamps await their fate.

On June 1, 1942, the Jewish police are ordered to remove all persons without stamps from their homes to Harmony Square. At night the Jewish police inspect the apartment houses and check identification cards. Persons destined for deportation are seized. This procedure goes on all through the night. Like a nightmare, like a dark vision of

195

ghosts, the column of people, men and women, march at the dawn of June 2nd. Like shadows they move at a slow pace, carrying on their shoulders all their possessions, which bear down on them as does the tragic destiny of their wandering. Harmony Square is slowly getting crowded with people and with heaps of bundles . . . and other imaginable pieces of luggage. The sun burns mercilessly. . . . Thirst parches the throats. Peoples' nerves are strained to the extreme. Two cars enter the Square through the gate and stop about 50 meters from my pharmacy. From the first car two Gestapo men get out. One of them walks over to the second car and exchanges a few words with its occupants. The second car then starts in the direction of the Jewish police. My pharmacy is open as usual, as on any other day. I am looking out, watching what will happen. What is going on? After a short while I notice that the two Gestapo men who remained at the Square take their guns out of their holsters, release the safety catches, and walk slowly toward the pharmacy. . . . We go through weird moments of waiting until the door opens and both of them enter, tall, handsome-looking men in excellently tailored SD uniforms, with opaque skull emblems on their caps. Without a word of greeting they approach the counter. "What would you like?" I ask, but get no reply. Their steely, penetrating eyes wander over our faces, over the pharmaceutical equipment and the medicines; glide over each thing, move over the walls, contemplate for a second the lighted holy icon, and look back at me and my staff. It is as quiet as a grave. . . . Without even exchanging a word between themselves, they put their guns on the marble counter, take out the ammunition clips and load their guns. We hear the crackling noise of guns being loaded and once more they release the safety catches. A faint smile appears on their lips, and they leave the pharmacy without saying goodbye.

The streets leading to Harmony Square became deserted. People are hiding in the halls of the buildings. Spiro [the chief of the Jewish police], accompanied by his entire staff, runs around like mad. The Gestapo men have already left the pharmacy, closing the door behind them. We look out and see one of them aiming his gun in the direction of Józefińska street. The Jewish policemen shout at the people. Suddenly we hear a shot fired—one shot, a second, and a third, and we see the gun being slowly lowered in the hand of the shooter. No voices are heard anymore; only the quick steps of running Jewish constables interrupt the deadly stillness. Whom did he aim at? Did he hit? Why did he shoot? Perhaps only to frighten people? Did he aim at anybody? These thoughts rush through our minds. It turns out, after all, that the shot found its mark. . . .

New cars arrive all the time and new Gestapo men appear in the ghetto. . . . They came to gloat over the unusual spectacle. New clusters of people approach the Square. The crowd becomes thick and fills every open space. At first, people stand, but after a while they find places to sit, either on the ground or on their bundles. The scorching sun is merciless, the heat makes for unbearable thirst, dries out the throats. People come to the pharmacy continually; physicians, hospital nurses . . . to get medicines for those destined for deportation. Valerian drops, bromides, sedatives, heart medicine are the last purchases for those who are leaving. The crowd is standing or sitting—all wait, frozen with fright and uncertainty. Vans and trucks appear. People run toward them. They push each other, anxious to find a seat or room for their bundles. First place goes to those able to push forward or to make room for themselves with their elbows, force, and youth. It takes only a few minutes for the vehicles to be overcrowded with people and bundles. The Gestapo men watch, malicious smiles on their faces. For the second time today the door of the pharmacy is opened by Gestapo men. Two young ones, about 26 years old, come in. This time they greet us *"Guten Tag"* and ask whose pharmacy this is and how to get to the balcony above. I give the directions, they thank me and leave. Above, on the balcony, they take pictures so as to be able to demonstrate to the world how humane the German people are during the "resettlement," as they call it (because it was forbidden to use the term "deportation," just as the term "Jewish quarters" was used for the forbidden word "ghetto").

The cameras click, the pictures are taken, the film is turned in the professional Leica cameras. The propaganda fake is finished. Now it can go out into the world and become a document to testify some day to the innocence of the Germans. And people are still waiting. The heat torments without mercy, people fall off their feet from fatigue. Suddenly, a short order is heard: . . . All out, hurry out. It sounds repulsive. In a split second the vehicles are emptied. The Germans with the Jewish police at their command throw the suitcases and the bundles out, yank out old people, shove the younger ones, hurry, hurry. Frightened, people look at each other, as if to ask: What does all this mean? Was the show with the trucks staged only to take propaganda pictures?

The crowd of sitting people rises when the Germans start shouting, moves closer to each other. At first slowly, then more and more quickly people leave the Square chased and shoved, punched and set upon by the howling Germans. Their luggage bearing them down, some throw away the heavier pieces, while the SS men grab the belongings of others. Pushed, pressed and beaten, the crowd of scampering deportees, like a big snake, moves on alongside the street-car tracks . . . Presently, the Square becomes empty. However, trucks full of bread continue to arrive, the last gift for the deportees from the remaining population (the *Judenrat* gave the order to all bakeries to bake bread the night before). The Square is empty and quiet. It was teeming with people just a short while ago, but now there are only the bundles they

197

left behind. Those who remain cannot believe that all that has happened only a moment ago really took place. The impact is devastating. Shock has made it impossible to comprehend the events.

The ghetto is deserted. Right after the departure of the deportees the high-ranking Germans, the SS and Gestapo men, left in their cars. Only the Jewish police and the Specialists for Jewish affairs remained. Two hours later, they too left the ghetto. The walls of the ghetto are still surrounded by closely spaced guards: a sign that the action is not finished for today.

A terrifying, agonizing night approaches, a night during which nobody would close an eye. . . . The ghetto makes telephone calls in all directions. Conversations with the chiefs of the various places where Jews are employed are going on incessantly. In many cases these interventions were successful. Either the employers came over personally or they settled the matter by talking to the Labor Office in the ghetto or to the Gestapo people by phone.

The Germans, however, are not satisfied with the number of the deportees. According to their estimate, not all people without stamps have reported for deportation.

An order is given to check the documents of all inhabitants of the ghetto and seize everyone without a permit. During the night of June 3–4, the Gestapo, the German Special Service, and the Jewish police checked the documents of people in the streets, hospitals, homes for the aged, in the apartment houses and homes. Beating, kicking, humiliation took place all the time. It lasted until morning. Early in the morning strong detachments of the German Special Service enter the ghetto fully armed. Alongside the Germans appear for the first time detachments of Polish police, the "blue ones," and groups of the Polish boys forcibly recruited for the so-called *Baudienst* [Construction Service]. German police take up positions at the Square. They stack their rifles before them. . . . Across [the way] is the "blue" police and next to it, in a small side street, there are assembled Jewish physicians, men and women, and hospital nurses and stretcher-bearers, altogether a small group of ten people. According to a German order, their alleged task is to assist people who may faint. The white uniforms and aprons of the hospital personnel look uncanny against the blue uniforms of the police and the green ones of the German Special Service.

The march of the deportees has started. The first rows appear at the Square; people are pushed, stamped on, hit; like ghosts, they keep moving on at a slow pace, quietly, gravely, but with dignity. A few run in clusters, some run singly, others look as if they had lost their minds. They are all surrounded by German police, each one with his rifle in his hands, the finger on the trigger ready to shoot. . . . All this is taking place amid constant screaming of the Germans, merciless beating, kicking, and shooting. Many are killed, many wounded during these very first moments of the deportation.

198

# Deportation

Before my eyes, as in a fiendish kaleidoscope, pictures appear simply not of this world; sounds of firing are heard in the ghetto; the Germans shoot at random into the crowd, at the wounded carried on stretchers, even at the dead; smoke pours out of their rifles. German officers carry revolvers, pokers, heavy staffs, or walking sticks. The hospital attendants take care of the wounded and the dead, picking their way through the dense crowd under constant shooting. The Germans shoot like mad, aim at random, at whim and fancy. . . .

According to the official German order, it was still permitted during this first transport to take along luggage, and this was not searched at the Square. This time the Germans thoroughly search many people either in the open at the Square or in halls and stores. As a rule, they take away the luggage and hit and maim people regardless of age or sex.

Physicians, nurses, and Jewish policemen constantly rush into the pharmacy to get medicines and bandages for the beaten, wounded, and those who fainted. The seriously wounded are taken to the hospital . . . New groups of people hauled out of their homes arrive at the Square. Old people, women, and children pass by the pharmacy windows like ghosts. I see an old woman of around seventy years, her hair loose, walking alone, a few steps away from a larger group of deportees. Her eyes have a glazed look; immobile, wide open, filled with horror, they stare straight ahead. She walks slowly, quietly, only in her dress and slippers, without even a bundle, or handbag. She holds in her hands something small, something black, which she caresses fondly and keeps close to her old breast. It is a small puppy—her most precious possession, all that she saved and would not leave behind.

Laughing, inarticulately gesturing with her hands, walks a young deranged girl of about fourteen, so familiar to all inhabitants of the ghetto. She walks barefoot, in a crumpled nightgown. One shuddered watching the girl laughing, having a good time . . . Old and young pass by, some dressed, some only in their underwear, hauled out of their beds and driven out. People after major operations and people with chronic diseases went by . . .

Across the street from the pharmacy, out of the building at No. 2, Harmony Square, walks a blind old man, well known to the inhabitants of the ghetto; he is about seventy years old, wears dark goggles over his blind eyes, which he lost in the battles on the Italian front in 1915 fighting side by side with the Germans. He wears a yellow armband with three black circles on his left arm to signify his blindness. His head high, he walks erect, guided by his son on one side, by his wife on the other. "He should be happy that he cannot see, it will be easier for him to die," says a hospital nurse to us. Pinned on his chest is the medal he won during the war. It may, perhaps, have some significance for the Germans. Such were the illusions in the beginning.

Immediately after him, another elderly person appears, a cripple

199

with one leg, on crutches. The Germans close in on them; slowly, in dance step, one of them runs toward the blind man and yells with all his power: *"Schnell!"* [Hurry!] This encourages the other Germans to start a peculiar game. Two of the SS men approach the old man without the leg and shout the order for him to run. Another one comes from behind and with the butt of his rifle hits the crutch. The old man falls down. The German screams savagely, threatens to shoot. All this takes place right in the back of the blind man who is unable to see, but hears the beastly voices of the Germans, interspersed with cascades of their laughter. A German soldier approaches the cripple who is lying on the ground and helps him to rise. This help will show on the snapshot of a German officer who is eagerly taking pictures of all scenes that will prove "German help in the humane resettlement of the Jews." For a moment we think that perhaps there will be at least one human being among them unable to stand torturing people one hour before their death. Alas, there was no such person in the annals of the Cracow ghetto. No sooner were they saturated with torturing the cripple than they decided to try the same with the blind war invalid. They chased away his son and wife, tripped him, and rejoiced at his falling to the ground. This time they even did not pretend to help him and he had to rise by himself, rushed on by the horrifying screaming of the SS men hovering over him. They repeated this game several times, a truly shattering experience of cruelty. One could not tell from what they derived more pleasure, the physical pain of the fallen invalid or the despair of his wife and son standing aside watching helplessly. . . .

The shots are echoing all over the ghetto. There are dead bodies; wounded people are carried on stretchers; blood leaves marks of German crimes on the sidewalks and streets. More people assemble in the Square. As on preceding days, the heat is unusual. Fire literally pours down from the sky. It is impossible to get water. People faint from heat and thirst. A small military car is parked in front of the pharmacy. The SS men are continuously loading valises filled with valuables they took from the deportees during the searches. Everything they see is taken; rings, wedding bands, watches, cigarette cases, even cigarette lighters. Some deportees look at each other; others wait for their turn; indifference and apathy show on their faces. . . .

When will all this end? This disturbing question is on everybody's mind. I look out of the pharmacy window, standing far back so as not to be seen from the outside. The Germans don't like witnesses to their crimes. Each time during such actions the streetcar traffic was discontinued and even German cars were stopped.

I look out and see a group of high SS dignitaries approaching the pharmacy. They stop right at my door. I hear their voices, I can understand each word, particularly since, as is their custom, they don't talk, they yell. I walk over close to the door and hide in a nook in the wall. It appears that they find the number of deportees to be unsatisfactory and assistance of the *Judenrat* to be at fault. They blame the chairman, whose name they constantly mention. A moment later I hear one of them yelling and whistling in the direction of the Jewish policemen . . . I hear the running of the Jewish policemen and see among them Spiro who stops not far from the SS men. He stands at attention, salutes, gets a sharp order to immediately bring over the chairman of the *Judenrat*, Dr. [Artur] Rosenzweig.

A man of 40, slim, his long face haggard, with nervous gestures, approaches the Germans. He talks to them quite unafraid, he speaks excellent German; his name is David Guter. A few minutes later, Rosenzweig appears; he walks slowly, hatless, his gray hair is blown by the wind, a middle-aged gentleman. He stops in front of the Gestapo and SS men and bows his head slightly. A moment of stillness, and then the dreadful words are snapped out by one of the SS men, who is using the abusive second person singular form: "Rosenzweig, you are dismissed from your position as of this moment. The action has not produced the desired results: neither the number of people delivered to the Square nor the method of their delivery was satisfactory." Dr. Rosenzweig does not answer, again he bows slightly and departs. The Germans turn to Guter and tell him that as of now, he will be responsible for everything. *"Jawohl!"* ["Yes, Sir!"], Guter replies, jumping at attention. . . .

Immediately after his removal from the office of chairman, Dr. Rosenzweig was arrested with his entire family, and was included in a group destined for deportation on that very day. Undoubtedly, it was not convenient for the Germans to have him around. Dr. Rosenzweig was an extremely fine and intelligent person, whose hands were clean. He had a university education and knew how to think and to reason critically. He was not impressed by the honor the Germans bestowed on him; it undoubtedly was a burden to him . . .

## Deportation

The deportation has started. The Square slowly becomes empty of people. Some are transported in cars, others walk on foot, rushed on by the shouting Germans, pushed around, trampled on, beaten. They run along the . . . streets in the direction of Płaszow. On the way, guards of the German Special Service fire at those who cannot catch up with the others. The road of the deportees is marked by dead bodies.

At the railroad station . . . they were loaded into cattle cars with quicklime sprinkled over the floors and small grilled windows up on the ceilings. They packed 120 persons to a car. The doors tightly closed, a German guard was posted at each car. No water or bread was allowed, and the scorching heat was unbearable. Some people had brought along their locksmith tools and manged to escape by breaking loose the window grill and jumping out of the train. They endangered their lives by hitting themselves against the railroad poles or by falling under the wheels of the moving train; but mostly death awaited them from the bullets of the escorting policemen.

There were some who broke the boards of the car floors while the train was moving and escaped through the hole when the train stopped at a station. After the train started again and passed over the bodies of the escapees, their further fate depended entirely on individual luck. A youngster whom I knew told me later that he had jumped off the moving train but was seen by the German guards. They fired at him several times. While jumping out, he hit a signal pole and, in addition, was wounded by the Germans; he lost consciousness and rolled down the railroad bed. He did not know how long he had been lying there. When he woke up it was night and dark. He crawled for a few hours until he reached the first house. It was the house of a peasant. Later he continued crawling from house to house during daytime. Not always were doors opened to him, not always did he get a friendly word of sympathy, but neither did anybody betray him. For weeks he aimlessly kept on going. His wounds had healed by the time he returned to the ghetto and there he stayed until it was completely liquidated on March 13, 1943. . . .

All people in the ghetto talk about the fate of the deportees. Members of families left behind are trying to get some concrete news by all possible means. All kinds of speculations come up, the most unthinkable rumors are spread, each of them from the "very best source." Germans were always the authors of all this news, the so-called honest ones, those who allegedly betrayed the secrets of the German authorities. Such was the method the Germans used: to reassure by all means, to deceive and give hope that those deported are alive, so that people won't despair, and the aim of it all was to avoid any attempt at revolt. . . .

Rumors are spread that the deportees were taken to the Ukraine, that they will work on the farms there. Certain German railroad workers tell that they have seen with their own eyes a great number of barracks in which dwell Jews from all over Europe. They have a good life, work hard, but have everything they need, food and clothes. Naturally, they are heavily guarded, barbed wire encircles the barracks, nobody is allowed to come near; they are not allowed to write letters and this is the reason why no news is forthcoming from them. These story-tellers are flooded with requests that they visit the deportees, take messages from their loved ones, bring back replies. At first, the Germans pretend to refuse, say that they cannot do it now, that perhaps they will accommodate at a later time. To increase the price of the favor they make it look very difficult. People don't think of money now, pay as much as is requested, eager to cling to the little spark of hope. No consolation, nothing definite comes into the ghetto. The German disappears into thin air as soon as he gets the money, and people wait and hope . . .

When we try to think now how the June deportations were organized, we can clearly perceive the deliberate perfidy the Germans applied to deceive the people, in order to rob their valuables together with their lives. The Germans, to make their job easier, issued glibly worded ordinances. The first order about the resettlement sounded very innocent, saying that because the ghetto is overcrowded, and in order to improve the living conditions of the inhabitants and to avoid the danger of infectious diseases, the authorities will have to resettle part of the Jewish population. Everybody is, however, entitled to take along as much as one can carry. In fact, people took large amounts of luggage, primarily, of course, their most valuable possessions, assuming that their fate would be the same as that of their predecessors whom the Germans transported to the Lublin area, and set free there. Others thought that they might perhaps be sent to another ghetto. The people of the first transport actually took along all the luggage they were able to carry, but on their arrival at the station, the things were taken from them, though nobody was searched. The search was probably made after they arrived at their destination. This tactic had the purpose of convincing the people in the next transport to take along only small things and refrain from the heavier luggage. The Germans knew well that everybody would be eager to take along small valuables, jewelry, money, gold. When the time came for the second deportation, the Germans applied another method: they searched all people on the spot, thoroughly robbing them of everything they could lay their hands on. What they could not find was left to their colleagues at the places of destination. Larger bundles and bulky luggage were, as a rule, robbed at Harmony Square. What was left in the homes was taken by the laborers of the [Polish] Construction Service, who were specially brought in for this purpose.

---

# The Journey to Eretz Yisrael

*The writer was born in Opoczno, Poland (1921). In his youth he became a member of the Hehalutz movement. In 1942 he, his family, and other Jews were deported. They were promised that their destination was Eretz Yisrael . . . He jumped off the train, reached the Warsaw Ghetto where he joined the Revolt and*

From *Extermination and Resistance: Historical Records and Source Materials.*

One day at the end of December 1942 the gendarmerie came to the *Judenrat* of Opoczno very cheerfully, as it seemed, and announced that orders had been received to prepare a list of Jews who had relations in Eretz Yisrael. The purpose was to arrange for an exchange of prisoners of war. For every German prisoner of war who was released they would permit ten Jews to proceed to Eretz Yisrael. The Jews would be taken by passenger train to a neutral country, where the exchange would take place.

At first we viewed this rumor suspiciously, regarding it as a trick to deceive us. But judging from the preparations and the efforts which the Germans devoted to the lists and to their inquiries, we began to believe that there must be something to it . . . Special officials checked every detail. And this exactness was what misled us.

Once again the light of hope began to shine in people's eyes. Everybody began searching for letters and envelopes, in order to remind themselves of forgotten addresses. People who had no real relations "tricked" the Germans. They gave the addresses of acquaintances, they attached themselves as kinsfolk to those who did really have relations, and all in order to be among the happy ones . . . They began to treat us better. Jews hiding in the villages were allowed to return to the Ghetto without punishment or guards. The German policing was almost withdrawn, and the task was left to the Jewish Police only. Faith encompassed us all—a madness of belief. Each list of relations was handed over to the gendarmerie; and in order to show that the matter was too urgent to allow delay, each list was sent on by teleprinter to the Gestapo at Tomaszow.

Even Jews with false Polish papers returned to the Ghetto and straightened themselves out, and were all included in the list of those going to Eretz Yisrael. According to the information we received, the exchanges were to take place on the German-Swiss frontier. Hence it followed that our journey was to be westward to Germany, and afterwards to the Swiss frontier. Nobody even imagined that in order to liquidate a few hundred families the Germans had to make use of such tactics and deceit. We were entirely in their hands, after all . . .

The Poles joked and said: "We always used to shout—Jews, go back to Palestine! And now it's coming true!" On the 4th of January we were informed that we were leaving the next day . . . The official order declared that each person was entitled to take with him both money and belongings, not exceeding a weight of 15 kilos [about 33 lbs.].

Early in the morning of January 5th, 1943, we were all dressed and ready . . . Horses and carts had been brought in order to take us off . . . We were ordered to climb onto the carts. Unnecessary bundles were taken from their owners and placed on the ground. We felt that there was something not quite in order if they were treating us like that when we were leaving. But we consoled ourselves with the thought that the real reason was insufficient room in the carts. Then all of a sudden they began to pull good coats off a number of the Jews. "You're going to a hot country and you won't need overcoats."

The convoy was ready to start. It was headed by an SS man with all the various documents and papers. At the end came a number of Polish policemen . . . The official reason for their presence was to defend us against robbers and highwaymen. There were a great many of us, and we could have liquidated them with ease on the way but we never even dreamed of any such thing.

Local Polish residents stood on either side of the road and parted from us with farewell cries and gazes. Some of them shouted to their acquaintances to throw them a keepsake, and a few of us did so . . . Children came out into the street, stared and pointed their fingers. Poles stopped along the road. Passers-by stared at us in astonishment and asked: "Whither?" It was hard to answer that we were going to Eretz Yisrael. We felt that there was something ridiculous in such an answer. Maybe we knew deep within ourselves that we were not being sent there. And how about running away? The idea occurred to someone, flickered there for a moment or so and promptly went out. For it is so good to be at ease, in the bosom of belief . . . We faced a riddle which we solved too late; and that delay was going to cost us our lives. At that moment everyone felt concerned with the riddle . . . "Let's see where they'll take us, east or west. If they take us off to the west, it's a sign that they were telling the truth . . ."

We reached the railway junction as day turned to evening, but here all our belief was undermined. All of a sudden we realized that there were disguised and hidden guards all round us. The sense of freedom which we had felt on the way vanished as at a wave of the hand. Our hearts began to thud in fear, and our knees trembled. On either side of the road appeared Germans who began to urge the carters on with shouts and curses . . . The SS man with the papers handed us over to the local commandant.

Here we found many Jews from all the small towns of the neighbourhood. They told us the same story: They were being taken to Eretz Yisrael, to be exchanged against prisoners of war. We of Opoczno were the last, and with our arrival the concentration of those to be exchanged was finished . . .

Next morning we heard the yells: "Juden raus!" (Jews, out!) Standing behind us we saw the Ukrainians and the "Blackies"—Germans in black uniforms. One of us cried: "They're the extermination squads!"

They began to line us up in fives. Family members crowded together not to be separated. From here we were led to the railway station. One

205

of the officers counted the groups of five. Somebody plucked up courage and asked where we were going, and the answer was, "Nach Deutschland!" (to Germany).

When we left the town it was already bright day. The Germans were lined up to the right and the left of us. Ahead marched the officers with the documents, and on either side were the SS men. After we had all passed through the exit gate it was closed behind us . . .

Each one tried to keep with his family and friends. Our family concentrated in two groups, one next to the other; my brother Moshe and I in the center and my sisters on either side. We could see all of them. Mother entreated Moshe to ask one of the Germans where we were being taken. Moshe refused. There was nothing to ask, said he, the question wouldn't help and wouldn't change anything.

Mother was upset and impatient and she herself asked, "Mein Herr, wohin fahren wir?" At first the German did not answer, but afterwards he doubtless felt sorry for her and answered in a Yiddishised German, "Don't cry, don't cry Mamma, we are going to Germany."

Every report of this kind spread as on wings and was passed in a whisper from row to row . . . We were going to Germany, westward . . . The people of Opoczno walked together, including the Rabbi and a woman belonging to his family, a very old pair. We remembered the Rabbi with the long white beard, but now he was without the beard. It had been cut off. One of the SS men shouted at us to keep in fives and not to loiter. He paced along the earth banks beyond the ditch, and shouted, "Anyone who hangs behind will be killed on the spot!"

People began to crowd together. The police in the rear began to lay into them with their whips. The crush grew worse. But many could not continue at the pace required, and broke up the fives. An SS officer wearing spectacles jumped across the ditch, dashed among the rows, caught the Rabbi by the hand and shouted, "You're messing up the row!" The Rabbi fell in fear and exhaustion. The other pushed him with his foot into the ditch and emptied a round of bullets into him. That was the second victim from the time we had left Opoczno. The woman began to weep and wail and he killed her as well . . . It was dreadful to see a man lying dead on the snow. The white and the blood were startling and terrifying. Now all our faith was lost, but belief and trust began to steal in from some other dark corner . . . Would they be afraid to tell us the truth if it were really something different? After all, we were in their hands. So it followed that they must be taking us to Eretz Yisrael. Yet at the same time a shiver ran down the back in case, in just a little while, they should hit you.

Here we were formed up in fives, with our faces to the rails, and we were given an opportunity of looking at the faces of the Germans properly. The officers and all the non-commissioned officers stood in front of us, and the privates behind. There they were, standing joking together, smoking cigarettes and pointing at us with their fingers.

# Deportation

Meanwhile it grew colder and colder, and we began to stamp our feet in order to warm up. Many members of the Jewish police came with their official caps. They believed in the power of the cap and hoped that it would help them. Somebody moved over to one of the policemen and said: "Well, big shot that you are, well, show what you can do! You drank together with them! Ask them, maybe they'll tell you where we're really going."

All of a sudden a prolonged whistling was heard, but it came from the east . . . As the train approached the whistle began for a third time. It was so prolonged and piercing that we felt the world must be coming to an end. Out of the trains came Ukrainians and Mongolians, and opened the carriage doors. Then came the order:

"Put down any parcels you are holding, at your feet." We all put down our bundles and parcels. Then came a second order, short and sharp:

"Up with all this crap."

They divided those who were standing there according to carriages; and then we began the climb into them. At first it was possible to help the women and tired ones, but within a few moments the overcrowding and pushing began. The carriages were already full to overflowing. The Ukrainians began to shoot into the people in the carriage. We pushed and tried to shrink together in dread and fear of death, and lo and behold, there was room for more. As each carriage filled up, it was closed and barred from the outside.

All our family did their best to be together, and we helped one another to climb up. When I got in, the carriage was already half full. The smell of chlorine caught at my nose. The walls and floor were white. This was some disinfecting material. I at once felt a strange dryness in the mouth and throat, and an acidity; thirst began to torment me . . . We crowded into an empty corner and clung together. With us was my sister Bracha, and her family. And now the door of our carriage was closed and we were cut off. Voices from the outside were harder to hear. Those next to the window were a kind of lookout, and gave us information about what was taking place outside. Every trifle became something remarkable and rare. "The engine-driver is filling the tank with water." "A German has gone out." "A German has come in . . ."

Before we entered the train, and when we were ordered to leave our little bundles beside the rails, many who had hidden their money and valuables in the bundles began to claw through them in order to save something. They were beaten mercilessly. These were not encouraging signs of our being taken to Eretz Yisrael. Now those who stood beside the window reported that the officers who had handled the papers had already left, and only the Ukrainians remained. The transport was ready for the journey . . .

At last, the train moved. It grew hotter from moment to moment . . .

We were stupefied, half-crazy. The instinct of survival seemed to operate on its own, without any control. Our consciousness grew clouded. Here and there could be seen clear signs of lunacy. To this day I shiver when I remember the fellow who cried out the Deathbed Confession, and asked the dreadful question: "What did I do all my life long? What did I do all my life long? I stole, I robbed, I hid money away and kept it. I became rich. Curse the money I have with me! What shall I do with the money I have with me! I'm going to my death . . . I'm going to my death . . . To my death, that's where I'm going."

There was black terror all round. The man shrieked and tore his hair and rolled his eyes. Everybody began gazing into his own soul and life. I turned to look at my family. Father was sitting moaning quietly. He sighed more and more; dumb sighs without words. Mother sat weeping bewailing all of us, mourning for us as you mourn for the dead . . . All of a sudden she wailed piercingly, "They are taking us to our deaths, to our deaths!"

We all stood weeping, and in a choking voice I tried to calm her. Father's sighs grew louder. My little sisters held on to mother and also cried. I stood between father and mother, with my brother Moshe beside me. I gazed at his face. There was a heavy cloud on it. There were unshed tears deep within his eyes. But despite all the gloom, I saw that he was thinking all kinds of thoughts, that plans were being woven. Dear Moshe with his inventions! He did not lose this quality even here.

"Can you see where we are?" he asked me quietly.

He repeated the question several times. I casually turned my head towards the window. It was high up, and those who stood beside it barely reached it with their heads. It was a long narrow window with an iron mesh over it . . .

We had already been travelling for hours. Thirst was burning our throats and mouths. All of a sudden the train stopped. A tumult broke out in the carriage.

"Why have we stopped? Why have we stopped?" came the question from every side.

Those beside the window answered that the train had stopped to take on water. The very word made us even thirstier.

"Shout out and ask for a little water. Shout through!" came the suggestion from every side.

Those who stood by the window shouted and asked for a little water. Outside were Poles—workers on the railway line. From time to time one approached the carriage, picked up snow from the ground, rolled it into a ball, and shouted to those at the window: "Give us money and you'll get snow"!

Somebody flung out a coin, and a snowball was flung into the carriage for him. People started up from all parts of the carriage to buy snow. Hands containing coins were held out to the window. From outside came the cries of the railway workers, "Money, give money"!

208

Many of us had money ready and waiting. Others began to search round, to take it from its hiding place. There were some who did not have any money at all. A price of a hundred zloty was promptly fixed for each snowball. At first these reached those who were paying for them, but within a few moments the whole carriage was in a whirl. Hands stretched out to seize a few melting snowflakes, like a drowning man flinging up his arms for aid. Everyone was thirsty, and hands beat against one another. Each person stuck out his tongue and licked the bits wherever they fell.

All this took place at the first stop. Suddenly a shot sounded in the open, and the trade in snow stopped. We were sitting in a distant corner, and therefore were not privileged to receive this "vital" commodity. My hand with the currency note in it stretched out in vain.

Moshe kept on trying to find out where we were. I heard him shouting to one of the fellows standing beside the window, "Mendel, look well and see where we're going!" Mendel calmed him down, and answered that we were travelling westward . . .

The snow story began again. This time prices had increased and they demanded 500 zloty for a snowball. Since the goods had become more expensive, far more care was taken of them. Somebody put out a pot and the snowball was placed in it, so that strangers should not grab any. Those who had no money went wild. Somebody wailed and shouted "Give me a little snow as well. I'm also a human being, I also want to live!" We also paid the price of the snow, and after waiting and shouting our turn arrived at last.

There were some families which looked after one another and divided the snow equally among themselves. But snow which contains no salt or minerals, only increases the thirst. The throat becomes more drier and sorer from moment to moment. The temperature rose. Drops of water began running down from the ceiling. Those who stood by the walls licked the moisture as it dripped down . . .

There came another long whistle like that at our starting point. Now it was even longer—a satanic hooting that was enough to turn one crazy, piercing like a drill through the ears, through the brain and the skull . . .

After the whistling there came a deep strange silence. Everybody was still listening to the echoes, which were barely dying away. It was the quiet before the storm. All of us kept still in order to hear how the train was moving and in which direction. I looked at Moshe and saw that he was thinking hard. The train stopped. The watchers by the window reported that they could see many Germans, policemen, trains, and so on.

Suddenly came a bumping, first backwards and then forwards. Moshe had been listening hard all the time, and a sudden cry of alarm burst from him. But he promptly controlled himself, went on listening for a few moments and then whispered to me:

"That's the engine. When it's uncoupled from the carriages, you feel a movement like that. If what I'm afraid of is true, we'll soon feel a jerk like that from behind . . ."

The engine passed the length of the train, closed up from behind and once again we felt a jerk as before, but reversed; first forwards and afterwards backwards. We had learnt that several carriages containing more Jews had been attached to the train. Within a few moments the train began to move off. At first there was a terrifying silence. Everybody waited for a miracle to happen or an abyss to open.

But the miracle did not happen, and within a few moments we knew definitely that the train had changed its direction and we were travelling eastwards. It was as though there was an explosion and a collapse in the carriage. People shrieked to the high heavens. The little children in the carriage could not understand what it all meant, but they also began to cry at the tops of their voices. I looked at my own family members and it seemed to me as though they had all grown old in a single moment. My little sister Malkale, who was nine years old, understood what it all meant and was weeping bitterly, "Mother, but I never did anybody any harm." My sister Rochele, who was twelve years old, clung to me and said, "Aaron, I am terribly afraid. Look after me . . ." and she clung to me with all her strength.

My sister Bracha, who was pregnant, wept in a loud voice. She was about twenty-eight. "But my baby hasn't even been born yet, and never sinned, why is he doomed?" Her husband stood stroking her hair. Looking at them I could no longer restrain myself, and also began weeping; but did my best to weep silently, so that my voice should not be heard.

Moshe began to talk openly and to estimate the situation. He said in so many words that we were lost, that he had not wanted to upset our belief all this time. But now it was plain that we were being taken to Treblinka.

I looked round at the people. They were images of dread and horror. Some tore their hair, some flung themselves about in despair, and some cursed with all their strength. A woman clutched her baby to her breast with all her force. The child began to make strangled noises, while the woman whispered loving words to it and pressed it to her heart all the more.

"Look what she's doing, look what she's doing . . . She's gone mad," came cries from all sides.

"It's my child, mine, and I want him to die a holy death. Let him die a holy death." And by the time people succeeded in getting the child away, he was choked.

One Jew near us went mad. Round his neck was a white scarf. He took it off and tried to tie it to one of the iron hooks in the carriage wall in order to hang himself. People tried to stop him. He punched and kicked with tremendous force and cried: "Let me hang myself!" They succeeded in dragging the scarf out of his hands and he collapsed in the corner . . .

It was evening already. The train was travelling very fast. Moshe was weaving plans. He was weaving them hastily. Our Moshe was blessed with an imagination . . . He calculated that we would reach Treblinka that night. It meant that this was our last night and our last opportunity. Everything was quite open and quite bare in the carriage. There were no longer any secrets or things to be hidden. Everybody still capable of thought was thinking aloud. Many were making their death confessions, but not according to the established formulas and verses. This was a stormy, demented confession of all that the hopeless heart could remember. Father remembered the preparations he had made long ago to proceed to Eretz Yisrael, preparations which had never been followed up. Now he remembered that mother had been against it, and among other and more serious arguments she had said jokingly that she was afraid to travel by boat . . .

Moshe whispered to me that this was our fateful night. We had to try to jump out of the carriage, for otherwise we were doomed. The rest of the family heard him whispering. Mother sat at a loss. "What will happen to us? Don't leave us. Don't let us separate. Don't let us separate. Death is lying in wait everywhere. Let us die together, at least."

Father sat silent, his head hanging down as though he had fainted. I had a little of home-brewed liquor in my pocket. Now I took it out and gave it to father to drink and gain some strength. When he saw the bottle he became very excited, but would not drink.

"My sons, worse moments are ahead of us. Let us leave this for those moments." He had begun talking about the bottle, but went on about something else. "Look, children, I am more than fifty years old already. At that age there are people who die a natural death, so it's easier for me to accept the end ahead of me. But you, children, you are young. If you can do anything to escape from here and save yourselves, don't miss the opportunity. Don't miss it, children."

Mother broke in: "No no no, there's no escape. There's nowhere to run away, and to whom will they leave Rochele and Malkale, and all of us? Only together, to the last breath."

It seemed to me that this was not mother talking, but a stranger whom I had never heard before.

Once again father spoke to us, saying that we must run away if there was any opportunity, and that he was not suggesting this, but ordering us to do it; for every moment was precious, and in an hour's time it might be too late, God forbid.

Moshe unquestionably took heart from father's words, and decided to go. For the moment this was only a bare idea, with nothing real to it. It was night already. The moon was shining in at the carriage-window.

Suddenly the train stopped. Outside could be heard the beating of iron and creaking of bars. Then the door was opened. The half-light of night time and the chill air burst into the carriage and beat down on the exhausted and fainting travellers. What was this? Had we already reached Treblinka, came the thought. Had we already missed our chance?

Into the carriage climbed a group of Mongols and Ukrainians, sub-machineguns in their hands. The carriage was crowded from end to end, but still room was made for them. Everybody crowded and crushed together in fear, while they began to rob and pillage the passengers. Ample experience had taught them where such travellers hid their belongings. First they went to the women, tore off whatever clothes they were still wearing, thrust their hands into their bosoms and their private parts, and found money and jewelry. They pulled rings off fingers. Most of the travellers were exhausted and had no spirit of resistance. The few who refused or resisted were beaten with the rifle butts.

"*Diengi davay!*" (Hand over the money), they kept shouting and cursing and abusing. It had been clear enough that we were being taken to slaughter, but now it was undeniable. Escape . . . But so far nobody had dared to be the first.

And now could be heard the terrifying shouts of Protas, who had commanded the Jewish police under the Germans. He had gone crazy, and shouted and wept and wailed in disjointed, incoherent phrases: "Me they've taken, me . . . *Dem groissen kommandant* (the big police commander) . . . They weren't ashamed to take me . . ."

He was still wearing his police hat.

What had happened in the carriage was being passed on from mouth to mouth . . . Przdlowski, head of the *Judenrat,* said that now the end had come, and anyone who could run away should do so.

We made up our minds, and began to take leave of the family. Father went on encouraging us, and tried to strengthen his words and raise our spirits with quotations from our sages of blessed memory.

"He who saves a single soul is as though he had saved a whole universe. And if you are saved I shall also have been a cause of it, and the merit of your deliverance will be part of my own merits too."

Mother took the money which she had hidden with her and with Malkale and Rochele, and divided it equally between Moshe, myself and our kinsman Joseph Lewkowicz. We began to kiss one another. When I came to my sister Bracha I almost changed my mind and wanted to go back on my resolution.

"What has my unborn baby done? Why is he doomed never to see the light of the world?" she went on whispering in a tremulous voice.

My hands seemed to weaken and my heart was lost. But I heard Moshe saying that this was the opportunity. In a little while it would be too late. What was happening with our family was happening with others too. It was like a signal passing through the carriage, and starting the young men and the healthy folk on their way: "To the window." Those standing at the window were ruffians, but they seemed to lose their strength in face of those who were daring enough to break out and try to run away.

We saw people climbing over heads. Moshe took hold of someone's shoulders and climbed over the heads of those standing, moving towards the window. I was stupefied. I didn't want to let go of Moshe, who was an experienced soldier. So I also quickly climbed up and began to crawl to the window.

And now quite a number of young fellows who were next to the window had resolved to jump out of the coach. We all took hold of the grating and began to tug at it, this way and that. The grating was fixed in a frame which was firmly set in the carriage wall, but as we dragged and tugged and pulled it began to creak and shift until it was pulled right out. We set the frame by the wall. It served as a kind of little step by which to mount and reach the aperture. Shooting could be heard outside all the time. You could feel the strange awe at the daring ones within the carriage.

But nobody wanted to be the first, nobody knew how to jump out of a noisy carriage; and we were all afraid of the jump itself. And now, as though automatically, Moshe became the central figure. He began to give explanations and instructions in a quiet voice, and everybody listened.

"Can you hear the fusillade?" he asked. "At the end of the carriages is a German guard. He shoots along the line of the windows to keep people from trying to escape. Each burst has ten bullets in it; then another burst and then another. Three bursts like that make one load for a machine gun. Now there's a pause and you don't hear any shots. He's changing the magazine and then the shots start again. We've got to use the intervals."

And having given the explanations, he told us how to jump. The first who jumped was a lad from a small hamlet, wearing a longish robe which caused him difficulties. His skirts caught on something and he had to get back inside and start again. Then it was my turn. I felt dead afraid. It was Moshe's idea that I should be first, so that he should tell me what to do before I jumped. We had arranged that I would wait for him where I was, and he would join me there.

I raised my hands and did all he had told me, waiting until the end of the three bursts. Before I jumped Moshe flung my overcoat out. And again I heard him: "Don't move from the spot, I'll come and join you!"

I pushed myself out of the window. For a moment I flew through the air, then I landed in a ditch filled with snow and sank right in. It was a strange feeling; as though I had been born again and were alive . . . Night, sky and moonlight. I had known them ever since I could remember. How new they were! New and terrifying. I was in an alien and hostile world, frosty and cruel . . .

213

# Readings

*Betrayal at the Vel d'Hiv* by Claude Levy and Paul Tillard (Hill and Wang, 1969). Round-up and deportation in Paris.

*Year of Fear* by Phillip Mechanicus (Hawthorn Books, 1964), is a stirring description of the author's deportation (May 28, 1943) with fellow Dutch Jews to Westerbork, Holland, a transit camp, life at the camp and the final deportation to Auschwitz (October 9, 1944), where he was killed.

*Black Sabbath* by Robert Katz (Macmillan, 1969), is a minutely reconstructed story of the grim Sabbath day in Rome (1943) when hundreds of Jews were seized by the Germans and deported to Auschwitz; only 15 came back. This happened in the Eternal City under the very nose of the Pope and Vatican authorities. The book was filmed under the title *Massacre in Rome*.

# 11. THE DEATH CAMPS: AUSCHWITZ

Arrival day at a camp was a grim test; for most, it was a day of crushing despair and surrender. For a few hardy individuals, it was a day of resolve to hold on to life with tenacity, come what may. There were other such critical turning points in the camp experience: the intermittent "selections" for the gas chamber, witnessing the killing of those near and dear, the fear of breaking down, the fear of torture, which was greater even than the fear of death.

On arrival, Jews from Western Europe were greeted with a false politeness; the others with brutality. A movement of the thumb to the left, usually by an SS doctor, meant selection for instant death; to the right, a short life of slave labor. For the latter, the next onslaught was the denial of the victim's human identity by the painful tattooing of numbers on his left forearm. Survivors, without exception, attest to the traumatic shock of this action. With the stroke of a needle, each body became a number among countless numbers. The "number" was then stripped and shaved in public by brutal "barbers" with dirty and blunt razors. Next came the "disinfection," which consisted of washing and drying the shaved portion of the body with biting corrosive chemicals which generally brought on rashes and skin infections. Sometimes trained dogs corraled the victims to take hot baths, then cold showers, and they then were given lice-infected clothing, thrown to them at random.

No one will ever know the exact numbers exterminated in the death camps, but it is estimated that some ten to eleven million, of whom six million were Jews, were murdered there. This mass production of death added a new word to the international vocabulary—"genocide," from the Greek *genos,* meaning "race," and *cide,* "to kill." Dr. Mark Dworjetski, chronicler of the Holocaust, estimates that of all the camp inmates, only 500,000 survived.

215

The pride of the German death camps was Auschwitz (in Polish, Oświeçim), which has become a symbol of the Holocaust as a whole. Auschwitz really consisted of three camps: the main camp; Birkenau (named for its birch trees), which was the place of murder; and Monowice, which housed industrial plants.

Built in 1940, Auschwitz was located over fifty miles west of Cracow, in an unhealthy, malaria-infested swamp area. It covered some 1,150 acres and contained hundreds of barracks, blockhouses, and assorted buildings. Around Auschwitz were some thirty smaller labor camps for farming, coal mining, gardening, fish breeding, and the manufacturing of synthetic rubber, munitions, and other products, as well as camps for prisoners of war. Two rows of electric fences encircled the complex. The prisoners were confined in various units which were separated by trenches, and were kept in ignorance of what was going on about them. Camp guards had to sign documents swearing that they would not reveal the happenings in the camps.

To the outside world, Auschwitz was allegedly a labor camp whose inmates were presumed to be working for the war industry. The main entrance carried the now infamous sign reading: *Arbeit Macht Frei* (Work Makes Free).

When transports arrived, an estimated 60–90 percent of the deportees were driven from the train directly to the gas chambers. They were told that they were to be disinfected. Women and children were the first to die; the strong and fit were used for slave labor until the "normal conditions" of camp life destroyed them.

It is estimated that the ovens "processed" as many as seven million people. This number does not include those who were killed by other means—starvation, disease, and other afflictions. Those who wasted away from starvation and filth, called *mussulmen*, were shut up to die without food or drink; malaria patients were disposed of with injections of phenol or gasoline. Tuberculosis was rampant, as were diseases of the skin, inflammations of the glands, and other fatal infections. The authorities did everything to increase the "normal causes" of liquidation by making inmates eat, drink, sleep, and defecate in filth and disease. At the same time, they surrounded them with signs which read, "Your health depends on cleanliness," "Be honest," "Don't forget your soap and towel," "Respect your leaders," and other such mocking slogans.

There were about 200,000 prisoners and 4,500 SS in Auschwitz at any one time. In addition to its being the greatest slaughterhouse in history, it was a source of "raw materials." Everything was used: even the ashes of the bodies were taken for fertilizing the beautiful lawns and flower beds of the SS homes and offices. Everything useful was removed from the corpses: hair for making mattresses, slippers, and caulking; gold and silver fillings from teeth for the Reichsbank; bones were crushed for phosphates; for a while human fat was used to make soap.

The treatment of those put to work was much worse than the actual

216

labor itself. When they returned to the camp after a day's work, the SS men would often make them drill for hours on end, particularly in rainy weather, on muddy ground.

The prisoners were entitled to receive 350 grams[1] of bread and a liter[2] of soup daily, and 150 grams of margarine, 50 grams of sausage, 40 grams of marmalade, and 30 grams of cheese weekly. But in fact they received little more than half this ration. The nutritional value of the bread and soup was almost nil. The bread was mixed with parsnips and sawdust, and contained a lot of bacteria, while the soup was watery, with some turnips and grass, and very rarely a bit of potato. In the morning each prisoner received half a liter of black, bitter "ersatz" (substitute) coffee.

Generally, there would be about two hundred dishes and thirty spoons for the eight hundred people in a barracks. Since time was limited, everyone tried to grab a dish, with no pause to wash it after the preceding user. The result was the spread of disease and epidemics, of which many thousands died.

Under these horrible conditions, few prisoners could live more than two or three months. The commandant of the men's camp of Auschwitz II once asked a prisoner how long he had been there. "Seven months," answered the prisoner. "Then you must have cheated us, because you could not live on the camp food for more than three months."

In summer and winter the prisoners were clothed in tattered, thin, striped cotton suits. In winter they would occasionally be given an overcoat of the same material. They wore small caps, pieces of cloth for socks, and boots or crude wooden clogs, which bruised their feet. Sometimes a strip of hair, running from front to back, was shaved off their heads, to identify them as inmates.

The prisoners were classified in various categories. Above their tattooed number, they had to wear an inverted triangle of one or another color; a letter above the number showed their nationality. This system distinguished between political prisoners, criminal offenders, deserters, homosexuals, Gypsies, Jews, and others.

## MEDICAL EXPERIMENTS AND RESEARCH

In addition to serving as a reservoir of slave labor for industry, Auschwitz and the other camps served as "laboratories" for all sorts of barbaric "experiments," and for the testing of new drugs on human guinea pigs. Nazi doctors and scientists tortured prisoners to death by subjecting them to "experiments" of the most inhuman kind. Some two hundred physicians took part, and several hundred more had intimate knowledge of the "experiments." Not one rose up to denounce these medical crimes.

[1]100 grams is approximately three and one-half ounces.
[2]A liter is approximately one quart.

A summation of these atrocities is found in the book *Doctors of Infamy* (New York: Schuman, 1949). Collaborating in this report were prominent American medical men, several of whom took part in the U.S. Military Tribunal (No. 1) in Nuremberg, which opened on December 8, 1946, and lasted through August 1947.

In the opening statement, among other charges demonstrating the degradation of medicine and science, the prosecution stated, "The Nazis have, to a certain extent, succeeded in convincing the peoples of the world that the Nazi system, although ruthless, was absolutely efficient, that although savage, was completely scientific. . . . The evidence which this Tribunal will hear will explode this myth. The Nazi methods of investigation were inefficient and unscientific, and their techniques of research were unsystematic. . . . The experiments were not only criminal but a scientific failure."

Among the experiments were:

1. High-altitude rescue experiments conducted in decompression chambers on ground level. Unfailingly, as the pressure dropped and a vacuum was created, the prisoner's lungs ruptured after intense pain and suffering.
2. Rewarming persons after subjecting them to extreme cold in icy water or exposing them completely naked in zero or subzero weather. No one survived.
3. Testing the effectiveness of poisoned bullets.
4. Testing the effects of drinking different solutions of sea water.
5. Injecting typhus and other viruses into the body, and gasoline into the veins, to study the resistance of individuals and racial or ethnic groups.
6. Performing surgical experiments involving bone, muscle, and nerve grafting; measuring the effects of electric shocks.
7. Testing the effects of inhaling mustard gas and being inflicted with phosphorus burns.
8. Performing castrations, sterilizations, and abortions to determine the most economical and effective methods of eliminating "inferior" races.
9. Making an intensive study of the characteristics of twins and the effects of bodily damage on them (presumably to increase the Aryan birth rate and produce the "superior" race).
10. Performing complicated operations on sensitive parts of the body, and diverse experiments, equally lurid.

# The Song of the Slaughtered Jewish People

*Yitzhak Katzenelson, the great poet of mourning, wrote for the underground magazines published by the Halutz youth groups. After many wanderings he came to his end in Auschwitz (1944). His literary work was buried in many places. That which was found is now in the Yitzhak Katzenelson House in the Ghetto Fighters Kibbutz in Israel. We quote below four stanzas of his stirring poem . . .*

*Alas, I knew it, and my neighbors too;*
*All of us, big and small, we knew the truth.*
*But not a word was said—hush, not a word*
*Before each other, nor in our inmost thoughts.*
*We kept the secret buried in our breasts.*

*Before they penned us within ghetto walls,*
*Before Chelmno or Belzetz, long before Ponar,*
*If we met any friend upon the street,*
*We'd quickly look away and only press*
*Each other tightly, tightly by the hand.*

*Not lips, not eyes, not words: we even feared*
*To look directly in each other's faces.*
*For glances may reveal what the heart dreads:*
*But our hands spoke; our silent hands spoke loud.*

. . .

*The birds and fishes knew—all of us knew:*
*The Gentiles all around us—they knew too.*
*We would be murdered: each of us was doomed.*
*No reason given; nothing to be done.*
*The order had been issued, stark and plain:*
*"Slaughter the Jewish people!"—child and man.*

From *The Massacre of European Jewry.*

# Reception at Dachau Camp

*Moshe Sandberg (now Sanbar) is sole survivor of a Hungarian Jewish family. He went through the ordeals of the camps, the B'riha (p. 557), the War of Independence, and the heroic period of the rise of the State of Israel. He has served as the Governor of the Bank of Israel. When Hungary was occupied he was 18. At first he was mobilized for labor service in the Hungarian army; then he was handed over to the Germans on the pretext that he would rejoin his exiled family . . .*

After a short march we reached the gates of a large camp and entered. We looked all around and were surprised to see people in strange garments occupied in work of various kinds. They looked at us, but without saying a word. They waved their hands to us, but stopped the moment they saw any of the Germans looking in their direction. We understood that these were prisoners and that the strange clothing was prisoner's uniform. We were taken out to a big open space where there were already several hundred like us. There then appeared a man in prisoner garb, carrying a chair, which he mounted. He told us that he was the "Camp Elder" in that part of the camp and that therefore everything had to be done as he required. Whoever did not obey his orders exactly and strictly would be punished with death. Having become used to threats we did not take him seriously, though the death punishment seemed strange. Could one prisoner threaten another with death? Where were the Germans? What had they to say to such arrogance? We looked to the right, the left, but saw no Germans anywhere. They had disappeared, and in their stead stood prisoners in uniform all round the place. From this we understood that the Germans had given the Camp Elder wide powers and that we would have to take his words seriously. After uttering his threats he told us that we would have to wait where we were until our turn came to be registered in the camp records and given prisoners' uniform. At the same time we would have to hand in all our valuables, which would of course be returned to us when we were released against the receipt we would now receive. When we said that we were hungry he asked us to be patient; we would be given food after the registration. He warned us not to drink water from the place where we were standing as it was typhoid-infected.

He then left us and we scattered about discussing the situation. Time

From *My Longest Year* by Moshe Sandberg.

passed and nobody approached. The prisoners on guard, standing like dumb creatures, would not answer our questions. More time passed and we became hungrier. When we saw people from other work groups beginning to eat food that they had brought with them we asked them for some, which they gave us, satisfying our hunger. It appeared that they, too, had been in the Hungarian Labour Service and had just then come straight from the Russian front. There they had belonged to various units which had been decimated. The few survivors had been assembled together and brought here. After the good meal we felt our thirst. Some of us wanted to drink the contaminated water but were prevented by the prisoner-guards. Meanwhile other prisoners came with brooms to clear the area. Approaching us they asked in a whisper for bread and cigarettes, which they quickly hid in their garments and then moved away. They must have been in a state of deathly fear, for in spite of what we gave them they wouldn't speak at all and made off as fast as possible.

Gradually fewer people remained. From time to time the same prisoners came and took off groups of about thirty. My group was taken to a building which, before entering, we were again warned that we must hand over all our valuables. We could see how the men of the preceding group left through the further door with their heads completely shaved and wearing all sorts of old clothes only some of which had the stripes of prisoners' clothing. I tried to get near them and find out what was happening with them, but was stopped by a veteran prisoner who told me it was forbidden to talk to others. However, he could answer my questions. I asked what they would do to us in the building. He said they would strip us naked and take away everything we had. Then we would be disinfected and shaved and finally given prisoner's clothes. Before I could ask him anything else he suggested that I should give him my watch, which he would return as I left through the other door. After some hesitation I agreed on condition that he fill my bottle with good water. I could no longer endure my thirst, not having had a drop of water for 36 hours. Within a few moments he returned with the bottle. While he was away I was able to exchange a few words with one of the earlier group, who confirmed what the veteran had told me. I decided to give the latter my watch in spite of my suspicions about its return. If the worst came to the worst I preferred some other Jew to have it rather than the Germans. All this lasted only two or three minutes, all the time with fear that we would be seen talking. Naturally, I didn't get the watch back, but I still consider the exchange of the valuable watch for a litre of water the best bargain in my life. . . .

I had barely time to drink the water when I had to enter the hall, which was full of clothing and all sorts of other things. We had to undress and hand over our clothes and knapsacks to one of the

221

prisoners. We were allowed to keep only our shoes and a pair of socks. So, with the shoes in one hand and in the other our money, valuables and identity documents, we moved to a long table where about ten men were sitting. We handed over the money, valuables and documents "for safe keeping," receiving in exchange a number, which was to serve as our identity instead of our name. From that moment we ceased to be human beings with family name and personal name and became a number. In my new metamorphosis I was No. 124753.

From the table we proceeded to a large hall full of showers. A prisoner with a large brush smeared some kind of ointment over our bodies while another quickly shaved off our body hair.

The ointment burnt our skins and the shaving without soap was most painful. Our protestations that we had no lice did not help. On the contrary, those who continued complaining only got a further dose of the ointment or a more brutal shaving. From the shaver's hands we passed to the barber's, who with large clippers rapidly and roughly took the hair off our heads and then again with smaller clippers in such a way as to leave a parting in the middle about four centimetres wide as a further mark to distinguish us as prisoners. After these preparations we again went under the showers, where our cries of pain were to be heard from the hot water forcibly spraying on skin already inflamed and injured by the ointment and the shaving. From there we passed to a smaller room where several men each threw to us an article of clothing: pants, a shirt, pullover, prisoner's suit and cap, and overcoat. There was no selection as to size, big men getting small-size garments and small men big ones. They said they had no time for changing these and we might do this among ourselves afterwards. We dressed ourselves somehow, formed up outside, and left the place. Outside I looked for the man to whom I had given the watch, but he had disappeared.

From there we went to our new quarters. The prisoners were lodged in long huts ("blocks") which adjoined but did not communicate with one another. The only door opened on to a road lined on both sides with huts. We were put into hut No. 16 . . . where we were received by the "Block Elder" with a speech similar to that of the Camp Elder. He, too, announced his complete control over his block and said he required exemplary order and the most exact discipline, failure of which would earn us beating till we died. He and his assistants assigned each of us to his place. For beds we had a kind of shelves two metres[1] wide and extending the length of the hut from wall to wall. The shelves one above another gave no more than one metre of room. On them were thin straw mattresses and one blanket per man. Shortly afterwards we were given a piece of bread and a slice of so-called sausage.

[1]One metre is 39.37 inches.

222

We had five minutes to eat this and then the lights were put out and we were ordered to sleep.

We were awakened next day while it was still dark. With shouts and blows we were ordered to dress quickly and fall in near the block. Among the shouts were the repeated words *"Appel"* (roll-call) and *"Appellplatz"* (parade ground), from which we understood that it was to ensure that we were all present. . . . We could not understand why the orders were given in a tone at once threatening and respectful. The parade seemed to make the Block Elder and his assistants apprehensive. But why? We did learn during the four days we were at Dachau that the Germans appeared at the parade, received a report from the Block Elder and carried out inspection before they left. Roll-call took place twice a day, but always with this apprehension. . . . We learned the reason only a few days later.

Nothing special happened on the first day. . . . We had no contact with the people in the other blocks. We talked with the few veterans among us, who explained various basic conceptions. The big building to be seen at the other end of the camp was the "crematorium."[2] Life in the concentration camp—as this and many other camps was called— was no life, but a slow road to death. . . . Food was not even minimally sufficient, and whoever had to rely on that alone did not last longer than a few months even without sickness or being beaten to death. Thus it was necessary to procure additional food . . . But how to get more food? When we asked that question we were told we would soon learn. And, indeed, they did get food as the Block Elder's assistants, while he himself had so managed things that he had already been in Dachau for five years and was not dead. He was one of the very few who managed it, but he was alive because perhaps others died a little before their time. And if he died with the others would that have been better? The veterans felt they had said somewhat too much and they finished briefly; only he who looks after himself alone and is not softhearted, only he will manage to keep going in this struggle for existence in which each is against the others.

Why should each fight the others and not all together fight for life? The answer was a smile, the smile of the teacher who doesn't know whether to be angry or to smile at the foolish question of a child. To fight? Against whom? The Germans? That is the height of folly! Through all the day's hours Germans surround us who would enjoy any opportunity of killing us. They have guns, many guns trained on us from the watch towers always ready for use. To escape? That also is folly. Round the camp is a wire fence, which electrocutes whoever touches it. And should someone somehow succeed in crossing the first fence he would find more fences between which German guards

[2]Used for burning the bodies of prisoners who died from hunger, epidemics or torture.

patrolled, besides those in the watch towers. And even if all this is overcome, what awaits you outside the camp? Other Germans only too glad to kill the Jew, certainly not help him to hide and survive. So revolt is collective suicide and flight individual suicide. Only one way remained: to remain and fight the battle for survival inside the camp. From the Germans it was impossible to obtain food, nor was there any possibility of stealing it. It was therefore necessary to ensure that the total quantity distributed should be divided out in such a way as to increase the portion of the successful ones, the strongest, those with the greatest initiative. That is the secret of success! There is no other! And what will happen to the others? They will die anyway and it is stupid to worry about them. Now we began to understand the first threats of the Camp Elder and the Block Elder. Now we realized that the threats were real, that that was the situation, that not only the Germans controlled life and death but also—perhaps more so—did the superior ones, the successful ones, the strongest, those with the greatest initiative.

When will they take us to our parents, our family? Again, instead of an answer came laughter, but this time laughter from the heart, the laughter of a father to the innocent question of his little child that amuses him. And they continued like the father calming his child: "Tomorrow, or the next day. Who knows?" And we, like innocent children, believed it. They, too, believed it, but according to their own understanding. For they knew that we also would go the way of our families with whom sooner or later we would be reunited, yes, reunited in another world, in the world of the dead.

We asked them why they were so apprehensive about the parades, and this time they answered without laughing: "As we have already told you, the Germans can do with us whatever they like, and whenever we meet them we have to fear some change. And in this place we are afraid of any change. At the parades we meet the Germans, and those are the occasions when they decide our fate for the next twelve hours. Here nobody plans for the future, for the future is in the hands of the Germans and it is during the parades that they reveal our future for a further twelve hours. They can send us to hard work or easier work or relieve us from work. They can also send us for no special reason to the crematorium, or they can make a game of us in which not only the ordinary prisoners must take part but also the superior ones like the Block Elders. There were instances when they found the block not in order and then they made up a game confined to the superiors, among them the Block Elder. They decide whether the parade is to last five minutes or five hours, and it is not the greatest of pleasures to stand at attention for long hours in the cold and frost, especially when those hours are deducted from our rest time."

That is clear, but what is this game? For this the Germans devise ways of punishment that amuse them. It can be "fencing," with cudgels given to two prisoners ordered to hit one another and to keep on at it until one of them cannot get up, and then they give the cudgel to a third in his place, and so on. The game can be a "race." The prisoners are lined up in two long rows facing each other at a distance of not more than a metre or a metre and a half. Every prisoner has a cudgel with which he must beat the prisoners chosen to compete in the race that is run between the two rows. These wretches run as fast as they can while their fellow-prisoners beat them over their bodies without ceasing. Should anyone out of pity not strike with all his force then he himself is made to do the running in which death is almost certain since few succeed in reaching the end of the line, and even these are so weakened that they have little strength left to keep up in the struggle for existence in the camp. At this point one of the veteran prisoners told us that he had seen another game in which the participants did not have to beat one another but took part in a contest with trained dogs. . . . This spectacle no doubt resembled the Roman games in which early Christians had to fight lions. Here, however, the games were more modern. A group of completely naked prisoners were put into a fenced-in tennis court, followed by half the number of great dogs. The dogs were trained not to kill, but to bite arms, legs or private parts. The prisoners ran about from one end of the small enclosure to the other, with the dogs hunting and savaging them. Some tried to jump over the fence, but there stood Germans who beat them back. Such was the sport in a modern form.

But all that is terrible! Better to die than go on living in the camp! Why don't you kill yourselves! Why don't you run on to the electrified fence?! It is not easy to answer such questions, they said. We, too, thought them, especially at the beginning. But we always overcame such ideas. Man wants to keep alive, to believe that his fate will be different from others'. Man is always hopeful and refuses to believe that these dreadful things will happen just to him. Those who did not hold on to such hopes were the first to succumb. The important thing here is the will to live! Without the will to live the struggle for existence is hopeless. Even animals wish to live and it is only the Muselmann[3] who is apathetic about life and death. And the Muselmann is in fact already without life. He can still move his limbs, he has not yet given up the ghost, but he is on the way to death. Without the will to live one dies anyway, without having to commit suicide.

This lesson in the basic concepts of life in the camp completely confused us and crushed our spirit. We tried to find contradictions in the logic of the veterans, and we saw some. At the same time we felt that

---

[3]The name *"Muselmann"* seems to have been devised by the Germans from the supposed resemblance of the shaking of Moslems at prayer to the tremors of the "skin and bones" of the prisoner in his last physical stage before death.

here logic had no value. We sensed that there was a grain of truth, even more than a grain, in their terrible description of the situation. Perhaps they exaggerated, but it was impossible to believe that they made it up merely to frighten us. Why should they want to frighten us? Only now did we realize what a great mistake we had made in not escaping while still in Hungary and had let the Hungarians transport us to Germany.

. . .

In all my time in the concentration camp I found no further opportunity for such candid discussion with people of standing in the camp. On the first day we were equals, but as time went on the distance between us increased. We still did not know this for we could not possibly imagine that there was truth in what we heard about the crematorium, the unlimited authority of the prisoners with special duties, the games, the Muselmanns. But was it possible to lie about such things? The Germans devised such terrible treatment for us that no exaggeration was possible.

In the days that followed we did not have much time to think about what we had heard. Moreover, we began to experience them ourselves. Hunger began to have its effects on us, filled our mind and dominated all our other thoughts. Apart from the constant hunger, which did not cease even after a meal and perhaps was aggravated by it, the Germans saw to it that our day was filled. Next day, at the morning parade, the Block Elder announced that he had to take us for medical inspection that morning. It was the strangest medical inspection I have ever seen. We were ordered to appear on the parade ground, which was covered with snow, completely naked. The roll call was gone through hurriedly. Nobody was misssing. But for some reason we were not given the order to proceed to the doctor. We waited and waited, almost frozen. Suddenly came the saving order. We moved forward in one long line and the first men entered one of the huts. When my turn came to enter I wanted to look round, but was not able to. As soon as I was inside I received a blow on the right shoulder, which made me turn. Before I could find out what happened I was pushed forward and received another blow, this time on the other shoulder, and was then again pushed forward. I had not recovered when I found myself in a different room where I was asked my occupation. I was then sent to join one of the three separate groups in the room. That ended the "medical inspection." But where were the doctors? Apparently they were the Germans sitting in the first room at two tables who between them had pushed us forward. The purpose of the blows on the shoulders apparently was to turn us rapidly to each side so that the doctors on each side could look over all our body. It was an "assembly line" inspection like that in an up-to-date factory. What the diagnosis was, who made it, and when, I did not know. Only after my release did I learn that indeed it was a diagnosis, a fateful one: to send the Jew to

226

the gas chamber or to send him to work. Of the three groups in the second room one probably went straight to the gas chambers, for not one of them was ever seen again. The second group consisted of people with training in various occupations, who were sent to factories, as was learned after the liberation. The third group, mine, went to a labour camp.

---

## 2  The Blue Pen

*Concentration camp prisoners were classified in various categories which were identified by an inverted triangle sewn on the left side of the breast of their tattered, striped suits in various colors: green for Germans, red for political opponents, purple for religious objectors like Jehovah's Witnesses, black for criminals, yellow for Jews. On the yellow triangle was superimposed another, generally in red or black, to form a Star of David.*
*On the right side of the trousers was sewn a ribbon bearing the prisoner's number. In Auschwitz, the number was tattooed on the skin of the left forearm.*

    The days follow each other, always the same. The feeling of loss, always there, and it is only that, the feeling of loss, over and over again. Wanting to stop time and start it all over. Wanting to be myself in somebody else in some other place. All the things I did not do . . . too late for any of them now. So many questions inside my head, but nobody to answer them. Never to know. (And Ivan? Why didn't I? It is not a loss I feel. It is that I did not give when I could give. When I think about him, I see him somewhere on a mountain. They took him away, where I cannot get to him. I don't think of him as being dead. I *know* he is, but I never think about it. With Karel it is different. I would like to know. How did he feel? I picture him getting up and getting dressed. Why do you have to get dressed? What did he think about?) I remember the men, a long, long time ago, walking to that small door, to be hanged. To think I will finally know how they felt. I don't want to know. Suddenly the French verbs come to me: *Je suis, tu es, il est.* I did learn many things. I am, you are, he is. I know it even in Latin. I know the start of Caesar's speech on the tomb of somebody. Maybe one day, when everything is over, they will make poetry about us. How we died here. Yes, I think they will make poetry. That's nice. What year is this? I can't remember the year of my death. I must ask somebody. October, it

---

From *Tell Me Another Morning* by Zdena Berger.

227

will be. We wrote many compositions about October. I think it was because of the leaves that fall, and their color on the sidewalks, orange and yellow. . . . We would go into the park and pick up the big chestnut leaves and make a bouquet out of them. On the way home we would throw them away and maybe next day we would go again. It was important to have dry chestnut leaves then. But I never liked October. A neutral month that does not belong anywhere . . . So this year will have only ten months for me. . . . Who started to divide the year in twelve? I think the Romans. They started everything.

, Ilse comes running through the barracks. She rarely comes here. She climbs the ladder to me and says, "Listen. They prepare something."

"What . . . They can't. . . . It's too soon."

"I know. But I didn't see him the whole day and that means they are preparing something. I saw a green one walking with long sheets of paper."

My mouth is dry. "Maybe they are just counting us. Or something like that."

"Maybe. Anyway, don't say anything to anybody."

"I won't."

"If I find out more, I will come and tell you."

"Yes. All right."

After she leaves I feel very much alone. The place is changed. The corners of the room are closer. The edges sharper. I reach in the wall, into that crack of wood, where I keep a piece of soap. It is green and rough to touch. I pick up the piece of cloth that is my towel and climb down. I should wash my hair . . .

I walk along the road. The men are working there as always. The camp is as always. I feel light-headed and I wonder why it is important that I should wash my hair. The washroom is empty. I bend my head down under the faucet and let the cold water run on my head. The soap does not make suds. This is a poor soap. I rinse my hair and feel the burning of my scalp. I undress completely then and wash my whole body. I look down at myself. The skin is smooth over my bones and white. I feel very clean and cold now.

Walking back, I hear a whistle. The shapes along the road start to run, disappearing in barracks. I run too, the wet cloth swinging on my arm. The soap slides out of my palm and I stop to pick it up. The air is cool on my head. I enter the barracks and find the women in a large group in front of the Elder. I press my nails into the gritty soap.

"Walk out by twos, toward the last barracks. And no talking on the way." The Elder goes away.

Mother's face is bleached. She looks at me as if I had the answer. "It's nothing, Mama. They are going to distribute something. I saw Ilse."

"Yes. That's what I thought."

We walk out and I see the green ones at the last barracks. We are put in a line and I cannot see what they are doing there, but the line shortens. I can see some girls now, with pens in their hands, the green ones telling them something. Ilse is among them. She too has a pen. It has a blue handle.

It is in front of Ilse that I finally stand. She smiles at me and whispers, under her falling hair, "It won't hurt, Baby."

She takes my arm and slowly the blue pen's point sinks into my skin. It burns a little. I watch. A number starts to show from under my skin. It was not there before. I have a number in my skin now. I walk away holding my arm with the other hand, and read again: B-4828. I am glad Ilse has such a nice handwriting. It is very small and neat. Between the B and the number there is a little dash, very straight.

Mother is walking beside me now. "Show me yours, Mama." It is not Ilse's handwriting and the number is big.

"I think this is very good, Tania."

"What? That they gave us numbers?"

"Yes. Maybe they want to . . . keep us. Why would they otherwise?"

"Maybe, Mama."

Mother stops in front of Father's barracks, to wait for him. I continue walking alone. And entering the smell of the barracks, I whisper to myself: *"Je ne suis pas, tu n'es pas, il n'est pas . . ."*

"I am not, you are not, he is not . . ."

---

# Daily Routine

*One of the first to reveal to his fellow Germans the full story of the Horror was Eugene Kogon, who clung to life for six years in Buchenwald. In his orderly and precise study,* The Theory and Practice of Hell, *he details the background, nature, organization, and statistics of the camps, the psychology of the SS and the prisoners, and an abundance of relevant data.*

The camp was awakened by whistles, in the summer between four and five o'clock, in the winter between six and seven o'clock. Half an hour was allotted to washing, dressing, breakfasting and bed-making . . .

A number of camps insisted on morning calisthenics, performed winter and summer at break-neck pace for half an hour before the regular rising time. They consisted mostly of everlasting push-ups in

From *The Theory and Practice of Hell* by Eugene Kogon.

the snow and muck. Because of numerous fatal cases of pneumonia, this practice never persisted for very long.

Breakfast consisted of a piece of bread . . . and a pint of thin soup or so-called "coffee," without either milk or sugar. The bread ration was issued at different times to different barracks. Those who had got it at night and had immediately eaten it up had no bread for breakfast.

Next came morning roll call. On a signal the prisoners from each barracks fell in on the camp street and marched eight abreast to the roll-call area. Thousands of zebra-striped figures of misery, marching under the glare of the floodlights in the haze of dawn, column after column—no one who has ever witnessed it is likely to forget the sight.

Each barracks had its own assigned place in the roll-call area. The entire strength of the camp was counted, and this roll call usually took an hour, until it was light enough to start work. Morning roll call was not as important as its evening counterpart . . . for little change was likely to take place overnight—deaths during the night were reported ahead of time from the prisoner hospital. After roll call came a thunderous command from the Roll Call Officer over the public-address system, addressed to the army of shorn men: "Caps off!" and "Caps on!" This was the morning salute for the Officer-in-Charge. If it was not executed smartly enough, it had to be repeated again and again . . .

Now came the dreaded call: "Prisoners under orders to the gatehouse!" It affected all those who had received a slip from the Orderly Room the night before. In Buchenwald six numbered signs were mounted at the wall of the left wing of the gatehouse. There the prisoners had to await the nameless terror about to engulf them. . . . The prisoners often had to wait for hours, haunted by uncertainty. If their families had only known the fear they could engender by routine inquiries and business matters! It was impossible to evade such a summons, and the waiting prisoners were at the mercy of the SS men who always loitered near the gatehouse.

Often prisoners so summoned were not given notice the night before at all. Their numbers were simply called out at the end of morning roll call and they were ordered to report to such-and-such a sign. I can state from personal experience that such an unexpected announcement of one's number was like a stab in the heart, regardless of what was involved.

The next command was "Labor details—fall in!" There was a wild milling about, as the prisoners moved to their assigned assembly points with all possible speed. The camp band, in the winter-time scarcely able to move its fingers, played merry tunes as the columns moved out five abreast. At the gatehouse caps had to be snatched off again, hands placed at the trouser seams. The details then marched off in double time, the prisoners compelled to sing.

Work continued until late afternoon, with half an hour for lunch, out in the open. For a long time the prisoners were not permitted to carry bread with them. . . . The work schedule differed from camp to camp, but by and large it followed the schemes here described.

In the winter work ended around five o'clock, in the summer, around eight . . . At the conclusion of the work day the prisoners were marched back to camp, past the band, again ordered to play sprightly tunes. Then came evening roll call.

In every camp this head count was the terror of the prisoners. After a hard day's work, when ordinary men look forward to well-deserved rest, they had to stand in ranks for hours on end, regardless of rain or storm or icy cold, until the SS had tallied its slaves and established that none had escaped during the day. The preliminary work for these roll calls often had to be done by prisoner clerks, since few SS men were capable of making an accurate tabulation. The prisoners always endeavored to avoid the slightest error, especially in counting the numerous inmates on "permanent detail," whose work brooked no interruption and who therefore never appeared in line, though they were, of course, counted. Any slip, even though not a man was missing, was likely to result in hours of checking and delay, depriving the exhausted prisoners of the last shreds of leisure. So long as the number of prisoners to be accounted for did not exceed 5,000 to 7,000, any absence was quickly noted. It was a different matter when the number swelled to 20,000, to say nothing of 50,000. A great many non-German inmates looked on this roll call as just another form of Prussian drill, to be evaded whenever possible. On many occasions a shirker would simply sleep away roll call in some hiding place, while tens of thousands of his fellows stood in stupor and agony until the culprit was found. (His would be an unenviable lot—no one took pity on him!) If a single prisoner was absent, hundreds of names and numbers from various barracks had to be called out—Polish names, Russian names, French names that could be pronounced only with the aid of interpreters. The SS men would lose their tempers, bellow, and let their fists and boots fly. Few roll calls took less than an hour and a half.

Whenever a prisoner actually escaped, the whole camp was kept on its feet until he was recaptured, often a matter of many hours. Guards were kept posted around the entire camp area during roll call, to insure that no prisoner could lurk about the headquarters area . . . Successful escapes drew such savage punishment upon the entire camp, especially in the early years, that the political prisoners renounced even the attempt until the final months. Then a few escapes, undertaken with the approval of the underground leadership, proved necessary in order to establish contact with the approaching Allies.

During evening roll call on December 14, 1938, two convicts turned up missing at Buchenwald. The temperature was 5° above zero and the prisoners were thinly clad—but they had to stand in the roll-call area for nineteen hours. Twenty-five had frozen to death by morning; by noon the number had risen to more than seventy.

During the fall of 1939 there was another occasion when the entire camp was kept standing for eighteen hours on end, because two convicts had hidden in the pigsty. Oh, it is easy enough to write about now—standing like that, after a full day's work, throughout the night and until next noon, without food! The cold death figures can be set down—but not the permanent damage suffered by hundreds who later perished of the after effects. What a relief when the war in the air forced even the SS to black out, when the floodlights could no longer be turned on! From that time onward, roll call simply had to be called off after a certain period, whether there were any absences or not. In the complete blackout the SS would have lost control of the camp, would have had good reason for fear in its own ranks.

From time to time the Block Leaders were ordered to "frisk" the inmates during roll call. Pockets had to be emptied and the contents were examined by the SS, a process during which as a rule much money and tobacco simply disappeared. One Sunday in February 1938, the prisoners were compelled to stand stripped to the skin for three hours on such an occasion. The wife of Commandant Koch, in company with the wives of four other SS officers, came to the wire fence to gloat at the sight of the naked figures.

Roll call was a time for many special tortures. Often, following the head count, the command would be heard, "All Jews, remain behind"—to sing over and over again deep into the night the vile jingles known as the "Jew song":

> For years we wreaked deceit upon the nation,
> No fraud too great for us, no scheme too dark.
> All that we did was cheat and lie and swindle,
> Whether with dollar or with pound or mark.

It ended with the following verses:

> But now at last the Germans know our nature
> And barbed wire hides us safely out of sight.
> Traducers of the people, we were fearful
> To face the truth that felled us overnight.

> And now, with mournful crooked Jewish noses,
> We find that hate and discord were in vain.
> An end to thievery, to food aplenty.
> Too late, we say, again and yet again.

This choice product of Nazi culture was the work of one of the "asocials" who sought to insinuate himself into the favor of the SS. . . .

An especially popular procedure for entertaining visitors to the camps was to have the Jews line up in the roll-call area to the left of the tower and sing the vile tune.

Everyone had to appear for roll call, whether alive or dead, whether shaken by fever or beaten to a bloody pulp. The only exceptions were inmates on permanent detail, and those in the prisoner hospital. The bodies of men who had died during the day, either in the barracks or at work, had to be dragged to the roll-call area. During particularly virulent sieges, there were always dozens of dying and dead laid in neat "rank and file" beyond the block formations, to answer the final roll call. For the SS exacted order and discipline down to the last breath. Not until after the roll call could the dying be taken to the hospital, the dead to the morgue.

Once evening roll call was over, with the commands of "Caps off!" and "Caps on!" there usually followed another command: "Left face!"—and the public punishments were meted out. Or one of the Officers-in-Charge might call for a song. It might be raining or storming. The prisoners might scarcely be able to keep to their feet. All the more reason for exacting a song, as much as possible at odds with the situation—once three times, five times in succession—"I saw a little bird flying," or "Something stirs in the forest." Most of the camps had songs of their own, written and composed by prisoners, on command. Some of these have become widely known, notably "The Peat-Bog Soldiers" and "The Buchenwald Song."

It might have been thought that once the final "Fallout" had sounded the day's torments were over and the prisoners could sit down to eat and rest at leisure. But often they returned to the barracks, only to be confronted by the results of the inspections conducted during the day by the Block Leaders—lockers overturned, their contents scattered in every direction. The search for one's mess kit often led to savage clashes among the prisoners, driven beyond the limits of human endurance.

When the prisoners worked through the day, the main meal was issued at night. Of course it was cold by the time a protracted roll call was completed. The remaining ration, when issued at night, consisted of bread, a dab of margarine, and a bit of sausage or possibly a spoonful of cottage cheese. At any moment during "dinner" the Barracks Orderly might suddenly sing out: "Attention! B-wing of Barrack X reporting! One hundred and thirty-five prisoners at mess!" Some SS sergeant had conceived the notion to pay a visit. Not yet through the door, he would bellow: "Get under the tables, you swine!" Benches would be overturned, mess gear clatter to the floor. Still, there were always a few left over who, try as they might, could not find room under the tables and became the particular whipping boys. There were many variations on this tune. A Block Leader might simply order a

233

barracks cleared during the meal, having the prisoners execute some senseless command, such as standing on their heads in the snow. To execute a headstand is not the easiest thing, even for a youngster. But even the aged and decrepit had to do it as a matter of course, just as they might have to double-time endlessly around the barracks. Any hesitation drew kicks and beatings. Even when nothing whatever happened in the barracks after roll call, the prisoners were obsessed by the fear that lightning might strike at any moment.

If roll call had been concluded with reasonable dispatch, work had to be continued for several hours deep into the night by certain prisoner groups. The rest might stroll about the camp streets, in front of the barracks, in the washrooms or toilets—unless they preferred to retire immediately. When taps sounded—between eight and ten o'clock, according to season—everyone except those on detail had to be indoors, half an hour later in bed.

Prisoners were permitted to wear only their shirts while sleeping, even in the deep of winter, when the barracks grew bitter cold and the damp stone walls often coated with ice at the windows and corners. Block Leaders frequently conducted night inspections, ordering all the inmates in a barracks to line up beside the beds or even outdoors, in order to catch those who might be wearing an additional garment. Whoever was found in socks or underwear could expect merciless punishment. On occasion an entire barracks was chased around the block for as much as an hour, barefoot and dressed only in shirts.

These nocturnal invasions did not occur regularly. They came from time to time, at irregular intervals, unexpectedly, generally when the Block Leaders were drunk. But they *could* happen at any moment. The threat was ever-present. Mercifully, the prisoners were far too exhausted to brood on the danger. For a few short hours each night sleep spread its balm over the misery. Only the aged, the fretful, the sick, the sleepless, lay awake in a torment of worry, awaiting the ordeal of another day.

# Yom Kippur in Auschwitz and the Selection

*Elie Wiesel, outstanding writer on the* Shoah, *survived Auschwitz and Buchenwald, where he lost his parents and sisters. (Two sisters survived.) In his first*

# The Death Camps: Auschwitz

book, Night, *the young prisoner bares his soul and his feelings on the holy day of Yom Kippur—the Day of Atonement. It was followed by a "New Year's Gift," the* Selection . . .

The summer was coming to an end. The Jewish year was nearly over.

On the eve of Rosh Hashanah, the last day of that accursed year, the whole camp was electric with the tension which was in all our hearts. In spite of everything, this day was different from any other. The last day of the year. The word "last" rang very strangely. What if it were indeed the last day?

They gave us our evening meal, a very thick soup, but no one touched it. We wanted to wait until after prayers. At the place of assembly, surrounded by the electrified barbed wire, thousands of silent Jews gathered, their faces stricken.

Night was falling. Other prisoners continued to crowd in, from every block, able suddenly to conquer time and space and submit both to their will.

"What are You, my God," I thought angrily, "compared to this afflicted crowd, proclaiming to You their faith, their anger, their revolt? What does Your greatness mean, Lord of the Universe, in the face of all this weakness, this decomposition, and this decay? Why do You still trouble their sick minds, their crippled bodies?"

Ten thousand men had come to attend the solemn service, heads of the blocks, Kapos, functionaries of death.

"Bless the Eternal. . . ."

The voice of the officiant had just made itself heard. I thought at first it was the wind.

"Blessed be the Name of the Eternal!"

Thousands of voices repeated the benediction; thousands of men prostrated themselves like trees before a tempest.

"Blessed be the Name of the Eternal!"

Why, but why should I bless Him? In every fiber I rebelled. Because He had had thousands of children burned in His pits? Because He kept six crematories working night and day, on Sundays and feast days? Because in His great might He had created Auschwitz, Birkenau, Buna, and so many factories of death? How could I say to Him: "Blessed art Thou, Eternal, Master of the Universe, Who chose us from among the races to be tortured day and night, to see our fathers, our mothers, our brothers, end in the crematory? Praised be Thy Holy Name, Thou Who hast chosen us to be butchered on Thine altar?"

From *Night* by Elie Wiesel.

I heard the voice of the officiant rising up, powerful yet at the same time broken, amid the tears, the sobs, the sighs of the whole congregation:

"All the earth and the Universe are God's!"

He kept stopping every moment, as though he did not have the strength to find the meaning beneath the words. The melody choked in his throat.

And I, mystic that I had been, I thought:

"Yes, man is very strong, greater than God. When You were deceived by Adam and Eve, You drove them out of Paradise. When Noah's generation displeased You, You brought down the Flood. When Sodom no longer found favor in Your eyes, You made the sky rain down fire and sulphur. But these men here, whom You have betrayed, whom You have allowed to be tortured, butchered, gassed, and burned, what do they do? They pray before You! They praise Your name!"

"All creation bears witness to the Greatness of God!"

Once, New Year's Day had dominated my life. I knew that my sins grieved the Eternal; I implored his forgiveness. Once, I had believed profoundly that upon one solitary deed of mine, one solitary prayer, depended the salvation of the world.

This day I had ceased to plead. I was no longer capable of lamentation. On the contrary, I felt very strong. I was the accuser, God the accused. My eyes were open and I was alone—terribly alone in a world without God and without man. Without love or mercy. I had ceased to be anything but ashes, yet I felt myself to be stronger than the Almighty, to whom my life had been tied for so long. I stood amid that praying congregation, observing it like a stranger.

The service ended with the Kaddish. Everyone recited the Kaddish over his parents, over his children, over his brothers, and over himself.

We stayed for a long time at the assembly place. No one dared to drag himself away from this mirage. Then it was time to go to bed and slowly the prisoners made their way over to their blocks. I heard people wishing one another a Happy New Year!

I ran off to look for my father. And at the same time I was afraid of having to wish him a Happy New Year when I no longer believed in it.

He was standing near the wall, bowed down, his shoulders sagging as though beneath a heavy burden. I went up to him, took his hand and kissed it. A tear fell upon it. Whose was that tear? Mine? His? I said nothing. Nor did he. We had never understood one another so clearly.

The sound of the bell jolted us back to reality. We must go to bed. We came back from far away. I raised my eyes to look at my father's face leaning over mine, to try to discover a smile or something resembling one upon the aged, dried-up countenance. Nothing. Not the shadow of an expression. Beaten.

Should we fast? The question was hotly debated. To fast would mean a surer, swifter death. We fasted here the whole year round. The whole year was Yom Kippur. But others said that we should fast simply because it was dangerous to do so. We should show God that even here, in this enclosed hell, we were capable of singing His praises.

I did not fast, mainly to please my father, who had forbidden me to do so. But further, there was no longer any reason why I should fast. I no longer accepted God's silence. As I swallowed my bowl of soup, I saw in the gesture an act of rebellion and protest against Him.

And I nibbled my crust of bread.

In the depths of my heart, I felt a great void.

## The Selection

The SS gave us a fine New Year's gift.

We had just come back from work. As soon as we had passed through the door of the camp, we sensed something different in the air. Roll call did not take so long as usual. The evening soup was given out with great speed and swallowed down at once in anguish.

I was no longer in the same block as my father. I had been transferred to another unit, the building one, where, twelve hours a day, I had to drag heavy blocks of stone about. The head of my new block was a German Jew, small of stature, with piercing eyes. He told us that evening that no one would be allowed to go out after the evening soup. And soon a terrible word was circulating—selection.

We knew what that meant. An SS man would examine us. Whenever he found a weak one, a *musulman* as we called them, he would write his number down: good for the crematory.

After soup, we gathered together between the beds. The veterans said:

"You're lucky to have been brought here so late. This camp is paradise today, compared with what it was like two years ago. Buna was a real hell then. There was no water, no blankets, less soup and bread. At night we slept almost naked, and it was below thirty degrees. The corpses were collected in hundreds every day. The work was hard. Today, this is a little paradise. The Kapos had orders to kill a certain number of prisoners every day. And every week—selection. A merciless selection . . . Yes, you're lucky."

"Stop it! Be quiet!" I begged. "You can tell your stories tomorrow or on some other day."

They burst out laughing. They were not veterans for nothing.

"Are you scared? So were we scared. And there was plenty to be scared of in those days."

The old men stayed in their corner, dumb, motionless, hunted. Some were praying.

237

An hour's delay. In an hour, we should know the verdict—death or a reprieve.

And my father? Suddenly I remembered him. How would he pass the selection? He had aged so much. . . .

The head of our block had never been outside concentration camps since 1933. He had already been through all the slaughterhouses, all the factories of death. At about nine o'clock, he took up his position in our midst:

"Achtung!"

There was instant silence.

"Listen carefully to what I am going to say." (For the first time, I heard his voice quiver.) "In a few moments the selection will begin. You must get completely undressed. Then one by one you go before the SS doctors. I hope you will all succeed in getting through. But you must help your own chances. Before you go into the next room, move about in some way so that you give yourselves a little color. Don't walk slowly, run! Run as if the devil were after you! Don't look at the SS. Run, straight in front of you!"

He broke off for a moment, then added:

"And, the essential thing, don't be afraid!"

Here was a piece of advice we should have liked very much to be able to follow.

I got undressed, leaving my clothes on the bed. There was no danger of anyone stealing them this evening.

Tibi and Yossi, who had changed their unit at the same time as I had, came up to me and said:

"Let's keep together. We shall be stronger."

Yossi was murmuring something between his teeth. He must have been praying. I had never realized that Yossi was a believer. I had even always thought the reverse. Tibi was silent, very pale. All the prisoners in the block stood naked between the beds. This must be how one stands at the last judgment.

"They're coming!"

There were three SS officers standing round the notorious Dr. Mengele, who had received us at Birkenau. The head of the block, with an attempt at a smile, asked us:

"Ready?"

Yes, we were ready. So were the SS doctors. Dr. Mengele was holding a list in his hand: our numbers. He made a sign to the head of the block: "We can begin!" As if this were a game!

The first to go by were the "officials" of the block: *Stubenaelteste*, Kapos, foremen, all in perfect physical condition of course! Then came the ordinary prisoners' turn. Dr. Mengele took stock of them from

238

head to foot. Every now and then, he wrote a number down. One single thought filled my mind: not to let my number be taken; not to show my left arm.

There were only Tibi and Yossi in front of me. They passed. I had time to notice that Mengele had not written their numbers down. Someone pushed me. It was my turn. I ran without looking back. My head was spinning: you're too thin, you're weak, you're too thin, you're good for the furnace. . . . The race seemed interminable. I thought I had been running for years . . . You're too thin, you're too weak . . . At last I had arrived exhausted. When I regained my breath, I questioned Yossi and Tibi:

"Was I written down?"

"No," said Yossi. He added, smiling: "In any case, he couldn't have written you down, you were running too fast. . . ."

I began to laugh. I was glad. I would have liked to kiss him. At that moment, what did the others matter! I hadn't been written down.

Those whose numbers had been noted stood apart, abandoned by the whole world. Some were weeping in silence. The SS officers went away. The head of the block appeared, his face reflecting the general weariness.

"Everything went off all right. Don't worry. Nothing is going to happen to anyone. To anyone."

Again he tried to smile. A poor, emaciated, dried-up Jew questioned him avidly in a trembling voice:

"But . . . but, *Blockaelteste,* they did write me down!"

The head of the block let his anger break out. What! Did someone refuse to believe him!

"What's the matter now? Am I telling lies then? I tell you once and for all, nothing's going to happen to you! To anyone! You're wallowing in your own despair, you fool!"

The bell rang, a signal that the selection had been completed throughout the camp.

With all my might I began to run to Block 36. I met my father on the way. He came up to me:

"Well? So you passed?"

"Yes. And you?"

"Me too."

How we breathed again, now! My father had brought me a present— half a ration of bread obtained in exchange for a piece of rubber, found at the warehouse, which would do to sole a shoe.

The bell. Already we must separate, go to bed. Everything was regulated by the bell. It gave me orders, and I automatically obeyed them. I hated it. Whenever I dreamed of a better world, I could only imagine a universe with no bells.

Several days had elapsed. We no longer thought about the selection. We went to work as usual, loading heavy stones into railway wagons. Rations had become more meager: this was the only change.

We had risen before dawn, as on every day. We had received the black coffee, the ration of bread. We were about to set out for the yard as usual. The head of the block arrived, running.

"Silence for a moment. I have a list of numbers here. I'm going to read them to you. Those whose numbers I call won't be going to work this morning; they'll stay behind in the camp."

And, in a soft voice, he read out about ten numbers. We had understood. These were numbers chosen at the selection. Dr. Mengele had not forgotten.

The head of the block went toward his room. Ten prisoners surrounded him, hanging onto his clothes:

"Save us! You promised . . . ! We want to go to the yard. We're strong enough to work. We're good workers. We can . . . we will. . . ."

He tried to calm them, to reassure them about their fate, to explain to them that the fact that they were staying behind in the camp did not mean much, had no tragic significance.

"After all, I stay here myself every day," he added.

It was a somewhat feeble argument. He realized it, and without another word went and shut himself up in his room.

The bell had just rung.

"Form up!"

It scarcely mattered now that the work was hard. The essential thing was to be as far away as possible from the block, from the crucible of death, from the center of hell.

I saw my father running toward me. I became frightened all of a sudden.

"What's the matter?"

Out of breath, he could hardly open his mouth.

"Me, too . . . me, too . . . ! They told me to stay behind in the camp."

They had written down his number without his being aware of it.

"What will happen?" I asked in anguish.

But it was he who tried to reassure me.

"It isn't certain yet. There's still a chance of escape. They're going to do another selection today . . . a decisive selection."

I was silent.

He felt that his time was short. He spoke quickly. He would have liked to say so many things. His speech grew confused; his voice choked. He knew that I would have to go in a few moments. He would have to stay behind alone, so very alone.

"Look, take this knife," he said to me. "I don't need it any longer. It might be useful to you. And take this spoon as well. Don't sell them. Quickly! Go on. Take what I'm giving you!"

240

The inheritance.

"Don't talk like that, father." (I felt that I would break into sobs.) "I don't want you to say that. Keep the spoon and knife. You need them as much as I do. We shall see each other again this evening, after work."

He looked at me with his tired eyes, veiled with despair. He went on:

"I'm asking this of you. . . . Take them. Do as I ask, my son. We have no time. . . . Do as your father asks."

Our Kapo yelled that we should start.

The unit set out toward the camp gate. Left, right! I bit my lips. My father had stayed by the block, leaning against the wall. Then he began to run, to catch up with us. Perhaps he had forgotten something he wanted to say to me. . . . But we were marching too quickly. . . . Left, right!

We were already at the gate. They counted us, to the din of military music. We were outside.

The whole day, I wandered about as if sleepwalking. Now and then Tibi and Yossi would throw me a brotherly word. The Kapo, too, tried to reassure me. He had given me easier work today. I felt sick at heart. How well they were treating me! Like an orphan! I thought: even now, my father is still helping me.

I did not know myself what I wanted—for the day to pass quickly or not. I was afraid of finding myself alone that night. How good it would be to die here!

At last we began the return journey. How I longed for orders to run!

The military march. The gate. The camp.

I ran to Block 36.

Were there still miracles on this earth? He was alive. He had escaped the second selection. He had been able to prove that he was still useful. . . . I gave him back his knife and spoon. . . .

# "Organizing" to Celebrate Passover

*Son of a rabbi in Bratislava, Czechoslovakia, the writer and his family began their harrowing journeys in 1944 from camp to camp. He was the only one saved at Camp Nieder-Orschel, sustained by a profound religious faith. He described his suffering and endurance in a deeply moving book, from which we quote . . .*

The knowledge of the early approach of the *Purim* and Passover festivals infused us with some hope and courage.

I approached Schiff again, asking him to "organize" some more paper from the office so that in addition to the Jewish calendar I would be able to write the *Haggadah* and finish it in time for Passover. Schiff obliged with some discarded odd pieces of paper, most of which bore on the back architectural drawings of fighter aircraft.

Each day, upon returning from an almost workless night shift, I spent an hour on my *Haggadah*. Writing from memory the story of the Exodus of the Jews from Egypt was a worthwhile task. It helped to keep my mind off our terrible tragedy and worries about the future. Even during working hours I tried to direct my attention to passages of the *Haggadah* that required writing. Happy memories were brought back to my mind of my childhood, and of the *Seder Nights* at home, when I sat at our table listening excitedly and attentively to Father's recital of the *Haggadah* which he always did so beautifully and inspiringly.

Indeed, this work served as a source of great courage and hope for me. It was a reminder that our people have gone through many difficult and tragic experiences in our long history, and have been freed each time, by the will of God, from bondage and slavery. How wise, I thought, of our great rabbis of the past to command that the stories of *Purim* and *Pesach* be repeated every year and thus remain alive among the Jewish people. Where would we have gained the courage and strength to survive all our experiences of bestial cruelty, were it not for our great and historic past?

Yes, I felt that Passover ought to be celebrated in the camp, and not just by reciting the *Haggadah,* but also by eating the traditional matzos.

I went to a foreman who worked on the tool bench, a quiet and kindly little man who occasionally dropped a small sandwich near my machine for me to pick up.

"*Herr Vorarbeiter,*" I said, "I want to ask you a very great favor."

"What is it?" he said, looking surprised.

"Oh, nothing incriminating," I assured him hastily. "I want to beg you to bring me half a pound of plain flour which I require most urgently."

"Flour? What the devil do you want that for? Birthday cake?" he added facetiously.

"I require it for a purely religious purpose," I explained, "and nobody will ever find out that it came from you. You know there is no one else I can turn to."

He looked cautious. "Things are hard nowadays, the guards are strict in their inspections, and the atmosphere is tense. I can't promise."

From *The Yellow Star* by S. B. Unsdorfer.

He spoke no more than the truth. On top of the lack of raw material and transportation difficulties, ever-increasing air raid alarms reduced our working time to a few hours per shift. When work did resume, frequent power cuts would stop us again. It was obvious that within a matter of weeks, or possibly days, great changes would overtake us. The factory would have to close, and we might either be liberated in the nick of time or transported elsewhere. At the back of our minds we hoped that we would still be at Nieder-Orschel when the first American tank bulldozed its way into the village.

There were joy and laughter throughout the camp when one bright Sunday morning, during an air raid, an Allied fighter came down in a whistling dive from a cloudless sky and shot one of the guards out of his watchtower.

Within minutes of the incident, as was to be expected, we were summoned out for a special *Appell*.[1] They were all there: "The Dog," and his Alsatian, *Schaarfuehrer* Adams, who we heard had ordered the camp tailor to make him a civilian suit, and the Commandant, the red-faced *Oberschaarfuehrer*.

"Wipe those grins off your faces," the Commandant yelled as he ordered us to attention. "Even if your friends the Russians have made some little headway on the front, and even if they have managed to pierce our lines temporarily, I want you to know something . . . We are still here. We have managed to deal with millions of Jews. We shall deal with you, too. You might as well know right here and now that your hour will never come. DISMISSED!"

How well the *Oberschaarfuehrer* managed to wipe the grin off our faces. We returned into the barracks on that Sunday afternoon sunken, devastated, and completely demoralized. Prisoners sat in groups of three or four at the table, or on their lice-ridden bunks, carefully digesting the Commandant's words.

"It can only mean one thing," I said to Benzi, as we sat on our bunks. "They have plans to finish us all, should they have to evacuate."

Benzi looked worried as he advised: "We must surely keep our heads if we want to see liberation."

"Well, what do you suggest?" Grunwald cut in bitterly. "Do we sit here and wait for the machine guns to mow us down?"

Benzi raised his voice. "What do *you* suggest—that we storm the electric wire? Or go out and buy guns and revolvers?"

Others joined us in the conversation. "We can 'organize' tools, and arm ourselves with knives, daggers, hammers, and spanners," Fischhof declared. "We can even make long spears from the waste metal. All we need is the proper team, working together."

"It is quite possible," Benzi speculated, "that the Commandant

[1]roll call.

envied our pleasure at seeing an S.S. man shot down and decided to frighten the life out of us. It is highly improbable that he would warn us in advance that we are to be shot. If such a plan really existed, it must have been top secret."

"Yes," agreed Grunwald, "but it is equally possible that the Commandant, in his fury, lost control of his tongue and let the cat out of the bag. We would be fools to treat his warning as an empty threat."

Others thought likewise, and Benzi decided to contact some of the other room elders and discuss the provision of homemade arms. But we had little hope in the venture. As Benzi said wisely: "Nothing short of a miracle could help us succeed in overpowering these bastards."

While we were talking much and doing little about the provision of arms, others took more drastic steps. Only a few days after the Commandant's warning, there was panic at *Appell*. Two prisoners were missing. "The Dog," who took the *Appell,* hastily summoned the *Oberschaarfuehrer.*

Raving like a madman, the Commandant cleared everybody from the camp. Even the cook, doctors, patients, and stokers were ordered out for *Appell.* He counted and recounted us in fury.

"Idiots!" he burst out madly. "How far do they think they will get?"

The Commandant obviously feared the reaction of his own superiors. "We will catch them," he yelled frantically. "We will have them within a few hours."

He left us standing on the *Appell* ground well into the early hours of the morning, while he and his men searched every inch of the entire camp. After a very brief rest, we were out at *Appell* again and then off to work.

In the middle of the afternoon, the buzzer sounded unexpectedly and we all ceased work. The two huge doors of Halle One were opened wide and the two escaped prisoners, both Russians, were marched in handcuffed, surrounded by a dozen S.S. men bearing guns.

It was a pathetic sight. The *Oberschaarfuehrer* halted his men in the center of the Halle to make a statement:

"These two fools have exactly three more hours to live! Nothing can save them! Anyone here thinking of making a break will meet precisely the same fate. There is no escape for any of you. Not now, and not ever."

The escorting S.S. dug their rifles into the prisoners' backs, motioning them forward. They were yet to be paraded before the men in Halle Two and in the barracks. The Commandant ordered us to "carry on" with our jobs.

But no one moved. These two poor prisoners were as good as dead. As they filed out of the Halle, we pulled off our caps and stood in respectful silence.

# The Death Camps: Auschwitz

There was no longer any doubt in our minds as to the earnestness of the Commandant's threats. That night, Benzi and the other room elders got down to some serious work on a program of opposition.

Meanwhile, work ceased completely. Not only was there no more raw material, but even the tool shop ran out of drills and spare parts.

On Saturday morning the civilians collected their personal belongings. . . . In the rush the friendly *Vorarbeiter* sidled up to me as I did the final cleaning of my machine.

He pushed a small bag of flour into my pocket and whispered: "We shan't be coming here any more. I brought you the flour and good luck to you."

"If we are to get any matzos," I said hastily to Benzi, "it must be done this evening immediately after the termination of the *Sabbath,* otherwise we shall have no fire to bake it on."

And indeed, at the end of the *Sabbath,* Grunwald, Fischhof, and I sneaked out of the barrack and into the smithy's workshop. Fischhof worked desperately at the bellows to liven the dying embers, Grunwald worked hastily on the dough, while I cleaned up a dirty tin plate to serve as a platter.

Within half an hour three tiny little round matzos were taking shape and color, accompanied by our happy murmur that these matzos were being prepared for the sake of God and His Commandments.

Nothing as soothing and as satisfying as the knowledge that even in this Godforsaken death camp—in this dirty little backyard of humanity, where the value of a cigarette was greater than that of a life—that even here, three little matzos had been baked in preparation for the forthcoming Passover Festival.

There were tears in the eyes of every one of the eighty inmates in Room Ten, when, after nightfall on Wednesday, March 28, 1945, I opened my little handwritten *Haggadah,* lifted up the three little matzos, and recited the first chapter, beginning with the familiar opening words: "This is the bread of affliction which our forefathers ate in the land of Egypt! Let all who are hungry come and eat, let all needy come and feast with us! This year we are here, next year may we be in Jerusalem. This year we are slaves, next year we shall be free men!"

There was no longer a "religious table" and a "free table" in Room Ten. Everyone was at our table. Rabbi Domany, a little old man from Hungary who lived in the next room, was asked to sit at the head of the table and conduct the *Seder.* I read the passages from the *Haggadah* as loud as I dared, and the rest followed in a whisper.

Then, raising up a rusty cup of black coffee which he had saved from the morning in place of the traditional glass of red wine, Rabbi Domany called out in a tear-choked voice the words of the *Haggadah*: "And it is this promise which has stood by our ancestors and by us. For it was not just one person who rose up against us to destroy, but in every generation men rise against us to destroy us. But the Holy One, blessed be He, delivers us from their hand."

How true were these words on that evening: how apt and how meaningful were they, as we sat on that quiet and very solemn evening, eating crumbs of matzos in an atmosphere of true Jewish faith and devotion.

Never before have so many men at one and the same time been so overawed in their trust of Almighty God as on that evening in Room Ten at Nieder-Orschel; never before was there such a truly solemn *Seder* service; never before was there such longing for God and His protective arm.

The verses of the *Haggadah* were apt, but in a different way the very words "Jewish Exodus" became alive again on that Passover week; for on the night of Sunday, April 1, 1945—Easter Sunday—a detachment of S.S. stormed into the barracks, driving us out of our bunks and onto the dark *Appell* ground.

Panic overtook us as screaming S.S. men with wild Alsatians [dogs] cleared the barracks in a matter of minutes. Before I left, I managed to grab hold of my little *Haggadah* which I had faithfully promised to treasure until the end of my days.

Once outside, I ran to Benzi, and clasped his hand tightly. "This is the end," I cried. "I may as well meet it with my hand gripped in yours."

Benzi, always optimistic, remained silent. His plan, and that of his colleagues, had failed miserably as everyone was beaten out of the barracks, leaving the few "arms" behind in the bunks and under the straw.

Nobody expected the "call" to be so sudden and so quick. None of the S.S. men was familiar to us. When and from where had they all come?

Some prisoners wept in their terror, some prayed, and others fainted from shock and panic, as the entire S.S. population of the camp encircled us, their machine guns mounted on both sides of the *Appell* ground.

There was no need for the *Oberschaarfuehrer* to order us to be silent. No one spoke on that moonlit night. The tension was unbearable.

"We are leaving this camp tonight for another destination," the Commandant announced. "Before leaving, you will each receive a loaf of bread and whatever other food we have in store. From the moment we pass the gates, strictest order will prevail. Anyone leaving the column will be shot without warning. There can be no escape! Never ...!"

A deep sigh came forth from the hushed crowd, as the *Oberschaar-fuehrer* concluded his words.

But not for long. Some argued that they would not kill us here, in the center of a populated village: they would take us out into the fields and finish us off there.

"But why the bread and rations?" the ever-present ray of hope made itself heard.

"Camouflage . . . deception," answered the fear within us. Within an hour Camp Nieder-Orschel was quiet and deserted.

# "Human Life Never Ceases to Have Meaning"

*World renowned psychiatrist Viktor E. Frankl of Vienna recalls his experiences as a concentration camp prisoner . . .*

The opportunities for collective psychotherapy were naturally limited in camp. The right example was more effective than words could ever be. A senior block warden who did not side with the authorities had, by his just and encouraging behavior, a thousand opportunities to exert a far-reaching moral influence on those under his jurisdiction. The immediate influence of behavior is always more effective than that of words. But at times a word was effective too, when mental receptiveness had been intensified by some outer circumstances. I remember an incident when there was occasion for psychotherapeutic work on the inmates of a whole hut, due to an intensification of their receptiveness because of a certain external situation.

It had been a bad day. On parade, an announcement had been made about the many actions that would, from then on, be regarded as sabotage and therefore punishable by immediate death by hanging. Among these were crimes such as cutting small strips from our old blankets (in order to improvise ankle supports) and very minor "thefts." A few days previously a semi-starved prisoner had broken into the potato store to steal a few pounds of potatoes. The theft had been discovered and some prisoners had recognized the "burglar." When the camp authorities heard about it they ordered that the guilty man be given up to them or the whole camp would starve for a day. Naturally the 2,500 men preferred to fast.

On the evening of this day of fasting we lay in our earthen huts—in a

From *Man's Search for Meaning* by Viktor E. Frankl.

247

very low mood. Very little was said and every word sounded irritable. Then, to make matters even worse, the light went out. Tempers reached their lowest ebb. But our senior block warden was a wise man. He improvised a little talk about all that was on our minds at that moment. He talked about the many comrades who had died in the last few days, either of sickness or of suicide. But he also mentioned what may have been the real reason for their deaths: giving up hope. He maintained that there should be some way of preventing possible future victims from reaching this extreme state. And it was to me that the warden pointed to give this advice.

God knows, I was not in the mood to give psychological explanations or to preach any sermons—to offer my comrades a kind of medical care of their souls. I was cold and hungry, irritable and tired, but I had to make the effort and use this unique opportunity. Encouragement was now more necessary than ever.

So I began by mentioning the most trivial of comforts first. I said that even in this Europe in the sixth winter of the Second World War, our situation was not the most terrible we could think of. I said that each of us had to ask himself what irreplaceable losses he had suffered up to then. I speculated that for most of them these losses had really been few. Whoever was still alive had reason for hope. Health, family, happiness, professional abilities, fortune, position in society—all these were things that could be achieved again or restored. After all, we still had all our bones intact. Whatever we had gone through could still be an asset to us in the future. And I quoted from Nietzsche: *"Was mich nicht umbringt, macht mich stärker."* (That which does not kill me, makes me stronger.)

Then I spoke about the future. I said that to the impartial the future must seem hopeless. I agreed that each of us could guess for himself how small were his chances of survival. I told them that although there was still no typhus epidemic in the camp, I estimated my own chances at about one in twenty. But I also told them that, in spite of this, I had no intention of losing hope and giving up. For no man knew what the future would bring, much less the next hour. Even if we could not expect any sensational military events in the next few days, who knew better than we, with our experience of camps, how great chances sometimes opened up, quite suddenly, at least for the individual. For instance, one might be attached unexpectedly to a special group with exceptionally good working conditions—for this was the kind of thing which constituted the "luck" of the prisoner.

But I did not only talk of the future and the veil which was drawn over it. I also mentioned the past; all its joys, and how its light shone even in the present darkness. Again I quoted a poet—to avoid sounding like a preacher myself—who had written, *"Was Du erlebt, kann keine Macht der Welt Dir rauben."* (What you have experienced, no power on

248

earth can take from you.) Not only our experiences, but all we have done, whatever great thoughts we may have had, and all we have suffered, all this is not lost, though it is past; we have brought it into being. Having been is also a kind of being, and perhaps the surest kind.

Then I spoke of the many opportunities of giving life a meaning. I told my comrades (who lay motionless, although occasionally a sigh could be heard) that human life, under any circumstances, never ceases to have a meaning, and that this infinite meaning of life includes suffering and dying, privation and death. I asked the poor creatures who listened to me attentively in the darkness of the hut to face up to the seriousness of our position. They must not lose hope but should keep their courage in the certainty that the hopelessness of our struggle did not detract from its dignity and its meaning. I said that someone looks down on each of us in difficult hours—a friend, a wife, somebody alive or dead, or a God—and he would not expect us to disappoint him. He would hope to find us suffering proudly—not miserably—knowing how to die.

And finally I spoke of our sacrifice, which had meaning in every case. It was in the nature of this sacrifice that it should appear to be pointless in the normal world, the world of material success. But in reality our sacrifice did have a meaning. Those of us who had any religious faith, I said frankly, could understand without difficulty. I told them of a comrade who on his arrival in camp had tried to make a pact with Heaven that his suffering and death should save the human being he loved from a painful end. For this man, suffering and death were meaningful; his was a sacrifice of the deepest significance. He did not want to die for nothing. None of us wanted that.

The purpose of my words was to find a full meaning in our life, then and there, in that hut and in that practically hopeless situation. I saw that my efforts had been successful. When the electric bulb flared up again, I saw the miserable figures of my friends limping toward me to thank me with tears in their eyes. But I have to confess here that only too rarely had I the inner strength to make contact with my companions in suffering and that I must have missed many opportunities for doing so.

# SS Captain Kurt Gerstein
# Sees a Gassing

*SS Captain Kurt Gerstein's sister-in-law was a victim of the euthanasia pro-*
*gram. Perhaps because he was so shocked by her death, he joined the concentra-*
*tion camp service where he provided the death gas. He compiled a report of what*
*he saw and first took it to the Papal Nuncio in Berlin who refused to see him.*
*Later he approached a Swedish diplomat who took it to Stockholm. When the war*
*ended the existence of this report was confirmed. It was also revealed that its*
*contents had been forwarded to the authorities in London in August 1945* after
*the war. Did Sweden keep it secret because it wanted to maintain neutrality?*
*What would the Allies have done had they learned of Hitler's* Final Solution of
the Jewish Question?

*Gerstein gave himself up to the Allied troops at the end of the war and while in*
*prison committed suicide. Was he a saint? A coward? The controversy about him*
*is still unsettled.*

*Following is his eyewitness report of what he saw at Belzec . . .*

"Then the march began. To the right and left, barbed
wire; behind, two dozen Ukrainians with guns. Led by a young girl of
striking beauty, they approached. With Police Captain Wirth, I stood
right in front of the death chambers. Completely naked, they march by,
men, women, girls, children, babies, even a one-legged person, all of
them naked. In one corner, a strong S.S. man told the poor devils in a
strong voice: 'Nothing whatever will happen to you. All you have to do
is to breathe deeply; it strengthens the lungs. This inhalation is a
necessary measure against contagious disease; it is a very good
disinfectant.'

"Asked what was to become of them, he answered: 'Well, of course,
the men will have to work, building streets and houses. But the women
do not have to. If they wish, they can help in the house or the kitchen.'

"Once more, a little bit of hope for some of these poor people,
enough to make them march on without resistance to the death chambers. Most of them, though, knew everything, the smell had given them
a clear indication of their fate. And then they walked up the little
staircase—and behold the picture:

"Mothers with babies at their breasts, naked; lots of children of all

---

From *Harvest of Hate* by Leon Poliakov

ages, naked, too; they hesitate, but they enter the gas chambers, most of them without a word, pushed by the others behind them, chased by the whips of the S.S. men.

"A Jewess of about forty years of age, with eyes like torches, calls down the blood of her children on the heads of their murderers. Five lashes in her face, dealt by the whip of Police Captain Wirth himself, drive her into the gas chamber. Many of them said their prayers; others ask: 'Who will give us water before our death?!'

"Within the chambers, the S.S. press the people closely together; Captain Wirth has ordered: 'Fill them up full.' Naked men stand on the feet of the others. Seven hundred to eight hundred crushed together on twenty-five square metres, in forty-five cubic metres! The doors are closed!

"Meanwhile the rest of the transport, all naked, waited. Somebody said to me: 'Naked in winter! Enough to kill them!' The answer was: 'Well, that's just what they are here for!' And at that moment I understood why it was called the Heckenholt Foundation. Heckenholt was the man in charge of the diesel engine, the exhaust gases of which were to kill these poor devils.

"S.S. Unterschaarführer Heckenholt tried to set the diesel engine going, but it would not start. Captain Wirth came along. It was obvious that he was afraid because I was a witness of this breakdown. Yes, indeed, I saw everything and waited. Everything was registered by my stop watch. Fifty minutes . . . seventy minutes . . . the diesel engine did not start!

"The people waited in their gas chambers—in vain. One could hear them cry. 'Just as in a synagogue,' says S.S. Sturmbannführer Professor Doctor Pfannenstiel, Professor for Public Health at the University of Marburg/Lahn, holding his ear close to the wooden door.

"Captain Wirth, furious, dealt the Ukrainian who was helping Heckenholt eleven or twelve lashes in the face with his whip. After two hours and forty-nine minutes—as registered by my stop watch—the diesel engine started. Up to that moment, the people in the four chambers already filled were still alive—four times seven hundred and fifty persons in four times forty-five cubic metres! Another twenty-five minutes went by. Many of the people, it is true, were dead by that time. One could see that through the little window as the electric lamp revealed for a moment the inside of the chamber. After twenty-eight minutes only a few were alive. After thirty-two minutes, all were dead.

"From the other side, Jewish workers opened the wooden doors. In return for their terrible job, they had been promised their freedom and a small percentage of the valuables and the money found. The dead were still standing like stone statues, there having been no room for them to fall or bend over. Though dead, the families could still be recognized, their hands still clasped.

251

"It was difficult to separate them in order to clear the chamber for the next load. The bodies were thrown out blue, wet with sweat and urine, the legs covered with excrement and menstrual blood. Everywhere among the others were the bodies of babies and children.

"But there is no time!—two dozen workers were busy checking the mouths, opening them with iron hooks—'Gold on the left, no gold on the right!' Others checked anus and genitals to look for money, diamonds, gold, etc. Dentists with chisels tore out gold teeth, bridges, or caps. In the centre of everything was Captain Wirth. He was on familiar ground here. He handed me a large tin full of teeth and said: 'Estimate for yourself the weight of gold! This is only from yesterday and the day before! And you would not believe what we find here every day! Dollars, diamonds, gold! But look for yourself!'

"Then he led me to a jeweller who was in charge of all these valuables. After that they took me to one of the managers of the big stores, Kaufhaus des Westens, in Berlin, and to a little man whom they made play the violin. Both were chiefs of the Jewish worker units. 'He is a captain of the Royal and Imperial Austrian Army, and has the German Iron Cross, First Class,' I was told by Haupsturmbannführer Obermeyer.

"The bodies were then thrown into large ditches about one hundred by twenty by twelve metres located near the gas chambers. After a few days the bodies would swell up and the whole contents of the ditch would rise two to three metres high because of the gases which developed inside the bodies. After a few more days the swelling would stop and the bodies would collapse. The next day the ditches were filled again, and covered with ten centimetres of sand. A little later, I heard, they constructed grills out of rails and burned the bodies on them with diesel oil and gasoline in order to make them disappear.

"At Belzec and Treblinka nobody bothered to take anything approaching an exact count of the persons killed. Actually, not only Jews, but many Poles and Czechs, who, in the opinion of the Nazis, were of bad stock, were killed. Most of them died anonymously. Commissions of so-called doctors, who were actually nothing but young S.S. men in white coats, rode in limousines through the towns and villages of Poland and Czechoslovakia to select the old, tubercular, and sick people and have them done away with shortly afterwards in the gas chambers. They were the Poles and Czechs of category No. III, who did not deserve to live because they were unable to work."

252

# Dr. Mengele's Criminal Laboratory (Auschwitz)

*Dr. Miklos Nyiszli (see p. 6) introduces us to Dr. Mengele, notorious medical doctor who performed criminal experiments . . .*

The Laboratory of Pathology was set up at the instigation of my superior, Dr. Mengele, and was destined to satisfy his ambitions in the area of medical research. . . . The confines of the KZ[1] offered vast possibilities for research, first in the field of forensic medicine, because of the high suicide rate, and also in the field of pathology, because of the relatively high percentage of dwarfs, giants and other abnormal types of human beings. The abundance—unequaled elsewhere in the world—of corpses, and the fact that one could dispose of them freely for purposes of research, opened even wider horizons.

When the convoys arrived, soldiers scouted the ranks lined up before the box cars, hunting for twins and dwarfs. Mothers, hoping for special treatment for their twin children, readily gave them up to the scouts. Adult twins, knowing that they were of interest from a scientific point of view, voluntarily presented themselves, in the hope of better treatment. The same for dwarfs.

They were separated from the rest and herded to the right. They were allowed to keep their civilian clothes; guards accompanied them to specially designed barracks, where they were treated with a certain regard. Their food was good, their bunks were comfortable, and possibilities for hygiene were provided.

They were housed in Barracks 14 of Camp F. From there they were taken by their guards to the experimentation barracks of the Gypsy Camp, and exposed to every medical examination that can be performed on human beings: blood tests, lumbar punctures, exchanges of blood between twin brothers, as well as numerous other examinations, all fatiguing and depressing. Dina, the painter from Prague, made the comparative studies of the structure of the twins' skulls, ears, noses, mouths, hands and feet. Each drawing was classified in a file set up for

[1]Concentration camp.

From *Auschwitz: A Doctor's Eyewitness Account* by Miklos Nyiszli.

that express purpose, complete with all individual characteristics; into this file would also go the final results of this research. The procedure was the same for the dwarfs.

The experiments, in medical language called *in vivo*, i.e., experiments performed on live human beings, were far from exhausting the research possibilities in the study of twins. Full of lacunae, they offered no better than partial results. The *in vivo* experiments were succeeded by the most important phase of twin-study: the comparative examination from the viewpoints of anatomy and pathology. Here it was a question of comparing the twins' healthy organs with those functioning abnormally, or of comparing their illnesses. For that study, as for all studies of a pathological nature, corpses were needed. Since it was necessary to perform a dissection for the simultaneous evaluation of anomalies, the twins had to die at the same time. So it was that they met their death in the B section of one of Auschwitz's KZ barracks, at the hand of Dr. Mengele.

This phenomenon was unique in world medical science history. Twin brothers died together, and it was possible to perform autopsies on both. Where, under normal circumstances, can one find twin brothers who die at the same place and at the same time? For twins, like everyone else, are separated by life's varying circumstances. They live far from each other and almost never die simultaneously. One may die at the age of ten, the other at fifty. Under such conditions comparative dissection is impossible. In the Auschwitz camp, however, there were several hundred sets of twins, and therefore as many possibilities of dissection. That was why, on the arrival platform, Dr. Mengele separated twins and dwarfs from the other prisoners. That was why both special groups were directed to the right-hand column, and thence to the barracks of the spared. That was why they had good food and hygienic living conditions, so that they didn't contaminate each other and die one before the other. They had to die together, and in good health.

The Sonderkommando chief came hunting for me and announced that an SS soldier was waiting for me at the door of the crematorium with a crew of corpse-transporting kommandos. I went in search of them, for they were forbidden to enter the courtyard. I took the documents concerning the corpses from the hands of the SS. They contained files on two little twin brothers. The kommando crew, made up entirely of women, set the covered coffin down in front of me. I lifted the lid. Inside lay a set of two-year-old twins. I ordered two of my men to take the corpses and place them on the dissecting table.

I opened the file and glanced through it. Very detailed clinical examinations, accompanied by X-rays, descriptions, and artists' drawings, indicating from the scientific viewpoint the different aspects of these two little beings' "twinhood." Only the pathological report was missing. It was my job to supply it. The twins had died at the same time and were now lying beside each other on the big dissecting table. It was they who had to—or whose tiny bodies had to—resolve the secret of the reproduction of the race. To advance one step in the search to unlock the secret of multiplying the race of superior beings destined to rule was a "noble goal." If only it were possible, in the future, to have each German mother bear as many twins as possible! The project, conceived by the demented theorists of the Third Reich, was utterly mad. And it was to Dr. Mengele, chief physician of the Auschwitz KZ, the notorious "criminal doctor," that these experiments had been entrusted.

Among malefactors and criminals, the most dangerous type is the "criminal doctor," especially when he is armed with powers such as those granted to Dr. Mengele. He sent millions of people to death merely because, according to a racial theory, they were inferior beings and therefore detrimental to mankind. This same criminal doctor spent long hours beside me, either at his microscopes, his disinfecting ovens and his test tubes or, standing with equal patience near the dissecting table, his smock befouled with blood, his bloody hands examining and experimenting like one possessed. The immediate objective was the increased reproduction of the German race. The final objective was the production of pure Germans in numbers sufficient to replace the Czechs, Hungarians, Poles, all of whom were condemned to be destroyed, but who for the moment were living on those territories declared vital to the Third Reich.

I finished the dissection of the little twins and wrote out a regulation report of the dissection. I did my job well and my chief appeared to be satisfied with me. But he had some trouble reading my handwriting . . . And so I told him that if he wanted clear clean copy, he would have to supply me with a typewriter, since I was accustomed to work with one in my own practice.

"What make typewriter are you used to?" he asked.

"Olympia Elite," I said.

"Very well, I'll send you one. You'll have it tomorrow. I want clean copy, because these reports will be forwarded to the Institute of Biological, Racial and Evolutionary Research at Berlin-Dahlem."

Thus I learned that the experiments performed here were checked by the highest medical authorities at one of the most famous scientific institutes in the world.

The following day an SS soldier brought me an "Olympia" typewriter. Still more corpses of twins were sent to me. They delivered me four pairs from the Gypsy Camp; all four were under ten years old.

I began the dissection of one set of twins and recorded each phase of my work. . . . I washed the organs in order to examine them more thoroughly. The tiniest spot or the slightest difference in color could furnish valuable information . . .

In the exterior coat of the left ventricle [of the heart] was a small pale

255

red spot caused by a hypodermic injection, which scarcely differed from the color of the tissue around it. There could be no mistake. The injection had been given with a very small needle. Without a doubt a hypodermic needle. For what purpose had he received the injection? Injections into the heart can be administered in extremely serious cases, when the heart begins to fail. I would soon know. . . . I extracted the coagulum of blood with the forceps and brought it to my nose. I was struck by the characteristic odor of chloroform. The victim had received an injection of chloroform in the heart, so that the blood of the ventricle, in coagulating, would deposit on the valves and cause instantaneous death by heart failure.

My discovery of the most monstrous secret of the Third Reich's medical science made my knees tremble. Not only did they kill with gas, but also with injections of chloroform into the heart. A cold sweat broke out on my forehead. Luckily I was alone. If others had been present it would have been difficult for me to conceal my excitement. I finished the dissection, noted the differences found, and recorded them. But the chloroform, the blood coagulated in the left ventricle, the puncture visible in the external coat of the heart, did not figure among my findings. It was a useful precaution on my part. Dr. Mengele's records on the subject of twins were in my hands. They contained the exact examinations, X-rays, the artist's sketches already mentioned, but neither the circumstances nor causes of death. Nor did I fill out that column of the dissection report. It was not a good idea to exceed the authorized bounds of knowledge or to relate all one had witnessed. And here still less than anywhere else. I was not timorous by nature and my nerves were good. During my medical practice I had often brought to light the causes of death. I had seen the bodies of people assassinated for motives of revenge, jealousy, or material gain, as well those of suicides and natural deaths. I was used to the study of well-hidden causes of death. On several occasions I had been shocked by my discoveries, but now a shudder of fear ran through me. If Dr. Mengele had any idea that I had discovered the secret of his injections he would send ten doctors, in the name of the political SS, to attest to my death.

In accordance with orders received I returned the corpses to the prisoners whose duty it was to burn them. They performed their job without delay. I had to keep any organs of possible scientific interest, so that Dr. Mengele could examine them. Those which might interest the Anthropological Institute at Berlin-Dahlem were preserved in alcohol. These parts were specially packed to be sent through the mails. Stamped "War Material—Urgent," they were given top priority in transit. In the course of my work at the crematorium I dispatched an impressive number of such packages. I received, in reply, either precise scientific observations or instructions. In order to classify this correspondence I had to set up special files. The directors of the Berlin-

256

Dahlem Institute always warmly thanked Dr. Mengele for this rare and precious material.

I finished dissecting the three other pairs of twins and duly recorded the anomalies found. In all three instances the cause of death was the same: an injection of chloroform into the heart.

Of the four sets of twins, three had ocular globes of different colors. One eye was brown, the other blue. This is a phenomenon found fairly frequently in non-twins. But in the present case I noticed that it had occurred in six out of the eight twins. An extremely interesting collection of anomalies. . . . I cut out the eyes and put them in a solution of formaldehyde, noting their characteristics exactly, in order not to mix them up. During my examination of the four sets of twins, I discovered still another curious phenomenon: while removing the skin from the neck I noticed . . . a tumor about the size of a small nut. Pressing on it with my forceps I found it to be filled with a thick pus. This rare manifestation, well known to medical science, indicates the presence of hereditary syphilis . . . Looking farther, I found that it existed in all eight twins. I cut out the tumor, leaving it surrounded by healthy tissue, and placed it in another jar of formaldehyde. In two sets of twins I also discovered evidence of active, cavernous tuberculosis. I recorded my findings on the dissection report, but left the heading "Cause of Death" blank.

During the afternoon Dr. Mengele paid me a visit. I gave him a detailed account of my morning's work and handed him my report. He sat down and began to read each case carefully. . . . He gave me instructions to have the organs mailed and told me to include my report in the package. He also instructed me to fill out the "Cause of Death" column hitherto left blank. The choice of causes was left to my own judgment and discretion; the only stipulation was that each cause be different. Almost apologetically he remarked that, as I could see for myself, these children were syphilitic and tubercular, and consequently would not have lived in any case . . . He said no more about it. With that he had said enough. He had explained the reason for these children's death. I had refrained from making any comment. But I had learned that here tuberculosis and syphilis were not treated with medicines and drugs, but with chloroform injections.

I shuddered to think of all I had learned during my short stay here, and of all I should yet have to witness without protesting, until my own appointed hour arrived. The minute I entered this place I had the feeling I was already one of the living-dead. But now, in possession of all these fantastic secrets, I was certain I would never get out alive. Was it conceivable that Dr. Mengele, or the Berlin-Dahlem Institute, would ever allow me to leave this place alive?

# The Commercial Side of the Auschwitz Death Industry

*Dr. Philip Friedman, an outstanding historian of the Holocaust, reported on Auschwitz from firsthand experiences . . .*

The Red Army found big store chambers full of shaving brushes, tooth brushes, spectacles, etc. These were only the remains. According to the railway notes two trucks of spectacles were carried away to Germany and 240 trucks of clothing. These garments were distributed among the population in the bombed German towns.

The Germans are a sentimental people. They made a special selection of the best clothing and underwear, and sent it to Germany as wedding gifts for the brides of SS men. These "racially pure" Aryan maidens thus received for their trousseau clothing and underwear which came from murdered Jewish women and children.

There were thirty-five special storehouses in Oswiecim camp for sorting and packing clothing and other articles. Twenty-nine of these were burned down by the Germans with everything in them before they fled. In the six that remained, the following articles were found: 348,820 men's suits, 836,255 women's outfits, 38,000 men's shoes, 5,525 women's shoes, 13,694 lots of bedding. In addition, the Soviet Investigating Commission found in the camp seven truck loads of bedding, packed ready for sending to Germany.

The report by SS Oberschaarfuehrer Reichenbach, found in the camp, shows that in the course of forty-five days, from December 1, 1944, to January 15, 1945, 99,992 articles of children's clothing, 192,-625 articles of women's underwear, and 222,269 articles of men's underwear were packed in the camp for sending to Germany.

Evidence that the civilian population in Germany knew that these gifts came from the murder camps was found in Oswiecim in the shape of orders for goods sent in by private persons in Germany, and by German institutions asking the SS to send various articles like perambulators, suit-cases, clothing, etc. It is clear that the people knew quite well where the articles came from . . . A woman wrote to her husband not to be afraid of sending her articles of clothing which were blood-stained—she would wash out the blood. The Germans were particularly anxious to obtain gold and jewels. The dentists who worked in the camp were severely controlled by the SS and the Gestapo, and they

From *This Was Oswiecim: The Story of a Murder Camp* by Philip Friedman were not to be envied if they left a gold tooth in a jaw. They were sent into the crematorium alive. . . .

Officially the Germans transported six wagon loads of gold to Germany from Oswiecim. It is impossible to say how much remained in the possession of the Camp Command and the important officials and their friends.

The hair, which was packed in sacks of twenty kilogrammes[1] was sent to Germany. The Red Army still found many of these sacks in Oswiecim. In Germany the hair was used for upholstery and for making mattresses. On March 7, 1945, the Soviet Commission found in the Oswiecim tannery 293 sacks of women's hair weighing 700 kilo. The experts established that the hair came from 14,000 women.

In the early period the Germans ground the bones of the victims, and threw them into the river; but later they put the bones to use. From 1943 the Germans broke up the bones and sold them to the German firm "Strem" for conversion into super-phosphates. Documents have been found showing that the "Strem" firm received 112,600 kilo of human bones. They were probably used for soap manufacture. That was the story that went about among the people in Poland, where many people refused, for that reason, to use the German soap which was distributed there. We have no evidence, however, that human bones and fat were taken out of Oswiecim, and used for making soap. But we have evidence that there was such a soap factory in Poland. Terrible evidence about this was given by the Danzig City President, Kotus-Jankowski, at the Session of the National Council held on May 5, 1945.

"In the Danzig Institute of Hygiene we discovered a soap factory in which human bodies from the Stutthof Camp near Danzig were used. We found 350 bodies there, Poles and Soviet prisoners. We found a cauldron with the remains of boiled human flesh, a box of prepared human bones, and baskets of hands and feet and human skin, with the fat removed."

After the installation of the crematoriums the Germans also exploited the vast quantities of ashes there. They established an ashes trading department. The families of victims were sent polite letters saying, "Your relative xx has died in Oswiecim, of xx disease. We shall send you an urn containing the ashes, on receipt of your payment of x marks."

Many people bought these urns of ashes, and kept them, or had them buried in a cemetery, without suspecting that the Hitlerists had played another trick on them. For the bodies were not burned singly. A lot of people were all put together in a retort, and their ashes were mingled. Quantities of ashes were used as fertiliser in the Oswiecim farms and gardens. The rest was sent to the chemical factories as raw material.

[1] 2.2046 lbs. per kilogram.

# Postscript: The Patent

Postscript: A copy of the first pages of the patent lodged by a German Company for an incinerator originally developed for the concentration camps. The patent is still pending.

---

Erteilt auf Grund des Ersten Überleitungsgesetzes vom 8. Juli 1949
(WiGBL S. 175)

## BUNDESREPUBLIK DEUTSCHLAND

AUSGEGEBEN AM
5. JANUAR 1953

23 MAR 53

### DEUTSCHES PATENTAMT

# PATENTSCHRIFT

№ 861 731

KLASSE 24 d GRUPPE 1

*T 1562 V/24 d*

---

Martin Klettner, Recklinghausen
ist als Erfinder genannt worden

---

J. A. Topf & Söhne, Wiesbaden

---

Verfahren und Vorrichtung zur Verbrennung von Leichen,
Kadavern und Teilen davon

Patentiert im Gebiet der Bundesrepublik Deutschland vom 24. Juni 1950 an
Patentanmeldung bekanntgemacht am 31. Oktober 1951
Patenterteilung bekanntgemacht am 13. November 1952

---

Die Erfindung betrifft ein Verfahren zur Verbrennung von Leichen, Kadavern und Teilen davon durch ...uperativ erhitzte Verbrennungsluft und eine Vor...htung zur Durchführung des Verfahrens.

...st alle bisher bekanntgewordenen Einäscherungs- ...hren verwenden im Rekuperativverfahren er...te Luft als Verbrennungsluft für die Verbrennung ... Leichen. In der gleichen Weise wie bei allen ...rbrennungsvorgängen in der Wärmetechnik soll der ...brennungsprozeß durch die Vorwärmung der Luft ...misch auf eine höhere Stufe gehoben und damit ... Verbrennungstemperatur gesteigert werden.

...r Heizwert einer Leiche bzw. ihr Brennwert ...de grundsätzlich nach dem Fettgehalt der ...he beurteilt. Die im Fettkörper der menschlichen ...che enthaltenen CH (Kohlenwasserstoff)-Verbin-

dungen (Fette) weisen zum Teil eine sehr niedrige Zündtemperatur auf und verbrennen bei höchsten Temperaturen. Dagegen ist es bisher nicht gelungen, die im Eiweißkörper in Verbindung mit N (Stickstoff) enthaltenen CH-Verbindungen bei Fehlen von reinen Fettkörpern und damit reinen CH-Verbindungen exotherm zu verbrennen. Der Eiweißkörper setzt mit seinem relativ hohen N-Gehalt (etwa 25 %) seiner Verbrennung heftigsten Widerstand entgegen. Seine Zündtemperatur liegt bei etwa 800° C.

Bei bisher erreichten Lufttemperaturen von 400 bis 500° C konnte somit die im Eiweißkörper enthaltene Stickstofikomponente in ihrer die Verbrennung hemmenden Wirkung nicht aufgehoben werden.

Erfahrungsgemäß vermag erst die Einwirkung von Luft von 800 bis 900° die Trennung des N von den

---

From *The Incomparable Crime* by Roger Manvell and Heinrich Fraenkel.

260

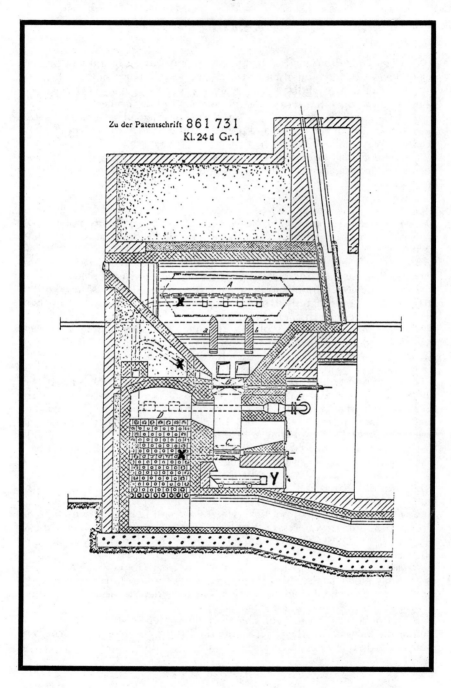

# Readings

*The Theory and Practice of Hell* by Eugene Kogon (Farrar, Straus and Cudahy, 1950), gives a full account of life at Buchenwald and other camps in which the author, a German, lived through six years. Published originally in German, the book began to open the eyes of his countrymen to their crimes.

*Kurt Gerstein: The Ambiguity of Good* by Saul Friedlander (Knopf, 1969), reveals the story of the drama and tragedy of the SS officer (p. 250) in a full, scholarly presentation.

*The Death Factory* by Ota Kraus and Ericha Kilka (Pergamon Press, 1966), is recommended for the most precise and graphic picture of the many horrendous aspects of Auschwitz.

*Human Behavior in the Concentration Camp* by Eli A. Cohen (W. W. Norton, 1953), is a dissertation on the basis of which the author received the degree of Doctor of Medical Science in the Netherlands. It is a superb study based on Dr. Cohen's personal experiences. (The above books and the two books that follow deal with the psychological effects on the prisoners.)

*Man's Search for Meaning* by Victor E. Frankl (Beacon Press, 1963), records the experiences of a world-famous psychiatrist who survived the death camps.

*The Informed Heart* by Bruno Bettelheim (Free Press, 1960), is the record of experience of a distinguished American psychiatrist in Dachau and Buchenwald. Read especially chapters 4 and 5.

*The Terezin Requiem* by Joseph Bor (Knopf, 1963), is a powerful novelette revolving about the fate of the orchestra composed of Jewish artists in Terezin (Theresienstadt). The plot builds up to the stirring climax as they play before Eichmann and his associates.

*Auschwitz* by Bernard Naumann (Frederick A. Praeger, 1966), is a report of the proceedings against Robert Karl, Ludwig Mulka, and other criminals at the Frankfurt Court which began on December 20, 1963, and ended August 20, 1965. The author was a reporter of a prominent Frankfurt newspaper.

*The Janowska Road* by Leon Wells (Macmillan, 1973), is an account of the special command unit engaged in burning dead bodies. The narrative is mitigated by the matter-of-fact presentation.

*Witness to the Truth* by Nathan Shappel (David McKay, 1974), is of particular interest in the second half of the book which deals with the D.P.'s and how the author and his wife helped rebuild the broken lives of the survivors.

*One Who Came Back* by Josef Katz (Herzl Press and Bergen-Belsen Memorial Press, 1973), stirs the interest of the reader with a description of the nightmarish journey on the Vistula River of the Jews who were shipped back to Germany after its defeat.

*In the Hell of Auschwitz* by Judith Sternberg Newman (Exposition Press, 1963), is a deeply moving memoir of the experiences of a nurse in Auschwitz. The remainder of her family did not survive. The book depicts the suffering of the Jewish girls and women in the death camp.

*Belsen,* published by the Irgun Sheerit Hapleita Mehaezor Habriti (Organization of the Survivors of the Camps from the British Zone, 1957), is a compilation of nearly thirty documentaries, with photographs.

262

# 12. EXTERMINATION OF RUSSIAN AND POLISH JEWRY

As Germany conquered country after country, Stalin repeatedly expressed his congratulations and best wishes to Germany for "complete success in her defensive measures." Stalin even told Hitler about Britain's warnings that the German armies would invade Russia. Ignoring Churchill's predictions, and information from his own sources, he continued to praise his Nazi colleague on each victory; little did he suspect that Hitler intended to deal him a knockout blow.

In cunning and brutality Stalin was a match for Hitler. He had the Red Army occupy Russia's terrorized Baltic neighbors, Lithuania, Latvia, and Estonia, and then had them incorporated into the Soviet Union by the unanimous vote of their "newly elected" parliaments. While Germany was tied down by the war in the West, Stalin was having his own bloodless field day in the East.

Flushed with victory in Western Europe, Hitler unleashed Operation Barbarossa, his plan to crush Soviet Russia in a lightning campaign. On Sunday morning, June 22, 1941, Germany's troops poured across the Soviet frontier in a move that recalled the successful assaults against Poland and France. Caught by surprise, the Red Army seemed to be in a hopeless position. For the Jews, thus began the last phase of the Final Solution.

Simultaneously with the advance of the armies, four SS *Einsatzgruppen,* or action groups, were unleashed. Mobile, mechanized units, of 500–800 men, the action groups were well equipped for the job assigned them. Operating independently of the armies, though connected closely with the military forces, the *Einsatzgruppen* were cool, highly efficient, fast-moving bands of killers directed by officers who were university-trained; indeed, some of them were lawyers, physicians, or professors.

Officially subordinated to the field commanders, actually they were on their own. Extermination was a mere day's work to them. Directed by Heydrich, they put to death, with dispatch, over a million remaining Jews, as well as Russian prisoners and civilians of the newly overrun lands. Some of the Jews escaped by fleeing further east into the heartland of Russia, but many old people, women, and children could not flee.

The world will never forget the help given to the SS by Russian and other Eastern European auxiliary forces. Since they had lived together with the Jews for many years, they were able to identify the communal leaders and the intelligentsia and to deliver them to death among the list of victims. Then, since it was the expressed policy of the killers to blot out all possibilities of a Jewish future, they killed the women (the childbearers) and the children.

Heydrich's *Einsatzgruppen* worked in small units moving with great speed behind the advancing army, and "mopping up" the rear. In less than two months, from October 15 to December 12, 1941, the four groups reported killing 300,000 Jews.[1]

The liquidation procedure was standardized. Shooting took place outside the town at a mass grave, either a conveniently available ditch or a trench specially dug by the victims. All valuables and clothing were handed over to the killers. The victims were shot in the back with small arms, mowed down by machine guns, or forced to lie down, layer upon layer, in the grave as they were murdered.

When the news of these atrocities began to be revealed to the world, some army officers tried to remove themselves from blame, fixing it squarely on the Heydrich organization. Others tried to persuade the killers to do their "job" at night. Taking photographs (which many had sent home) was prohibited. Eyewitnesses were highly restricted and other measures were taken to maintain secrecy, but the murders did not abate.

## BABI YAR: A FOURFOLD HORROR

The most appalling Nazi massacre on Soviet soil was at Babi Yar, a ravine outside Kiev, the capital of the Ukraine. It took place on September 29 and 30, 1941. The killers of *Einsatzgruppe* C wiped out 33,771 Jews in barely thirty-six hours, a bloodbath that surpassed even the highest records set by the gas chambers at Auschwitz. The bodies were left in the ravine, which served as a mass grave. This was the first phase of the fourfold horror of Babi Yar.

The second phase took place in 1943. The Germans were on the retreat now, and before pulling out of Kiev, they tried to destroy all evidence of the massacre. The mass grave was opened; the thousands of decomposing bodies were drenched with gasoline and set afire. They continued

[1]Raul Hilberg, *The Destruction of the European Jews,* p. 192.

smoldering for six weeks. Afterwards, the remaining bones were crushed by bulldozers and scattered about. The ashes from the thousands of burnt bodies turned the sand of Babi Yar gray.

The third gross indignity suffered by the victims of Babi Yar was the Soviet refusal to honor their memory. In 1946 a monument commemorating the martyrs was planned, but Stalin, in an outburst of Jew-hatred, forced the cancellation of the project. Khrushchev, Stalin's successor, continued this policy. The book, *Babi Yar*,[2] by the distinguished Russian author Anatoly Kuznetsov, in which he recounted his boyhood memories of the atrocities committed during the Nazi occupation of Kiev, was condemned. So was the poem "Babi Yar" by Yevgeni Yevtushenko.

The final outrage occurred on July 2, 1976, when a memorial was finally unveiled at Babi Yar. Rising from the edge of the ravine, a fifty-foot-high bronze statue, similar to many other monuments in the USSR, was erected. But no word was spoken, no gesture was made to record the Jewish aspect of the tragedy at Babi Yar.

Yet while the Stalinists and their successors have strived to erase the memory of Babi Yar, it lives on in the consciousness of humanity, through the writings of poets, novelists, composers, and others who dared raise their voices for justice, freedom, and decency. And despite the opposition of the Soviet authorities, thousands of Russian Jews gather at Babi Yar every September 29 to remember those who were martyred there.

---

# Liquidation and Defiance: Destruction of Tarnow Ghetto (July 28, 1942)

My brain is bursting, my heart is bleeding and my hand is trembling as I describe what I lived through and what I have seen this past month. One could suspect that this is an account of some nightmarish dream, that it is a phantom apparition; alas, this is reality.

---

[2]English versions have been published by Dial Press (1966) and Farrar, Straus & Giroux (1970).

---

From *The Wrecked Life* by Jacob Herzig.

There are no words in the human language to describe what I witnessed. Our language is too weak . . . to describe the blood-curdling scenes that I saw . . .

The sketching of even a part of my experiences and observations of that day requires an almost superhuman effort; but this is the only way in which I can honor the memory of my dear ones, my faithful mate of a quarter of a century, and my dearest little daughter.

On that day the population of the Tarnow ghetto was murdered. "Liquidation of the ghetto" is the term with which the German beasts defined their slaughter. The mass murders were turned into a great public spectacle in the Tarnow marketplace by the *Herrenvolk* [master-race]. The Jews dwelling in the ghetto were ordered to remove their shoes, and barefooted, were driven with rifle-butts and whips to the large paved square of the Market. There everybody was ordered to kneel, with heads bowed to the ground. Among us bustled the SS . . . as well as Polish policemen in uniforms, . . . secret agents in mufti, and finally, the German police.

In the middle of the market, there was an elevated wooden shed . . . Before it stood two carts with high walls built of rough boards.

Gestapo men walked among the kneeling people and dragged out the children from the crowd, and led them to this shed. From it came continuous revolver shots, and dull blows and stomping; every now and then the Gestapo men, the policemen, the boys from the [Polish] *Baudienst* [construction gang] and those without uniforms flung the bodies of the freshly killed children into the carts, without even bothering to come down the steps.

Blood flowed ceaselessly from the carts to the ground. The Gestapo men ran among the rows of people and killed the Jews with revolver shots, as if playing a game, mostly picking old men, leaving their victims on the spot among the living.

Indescribable lamentation, sobbing and weeping filled the market. One could go mad.

I was kneeling on the right side of the market. My wife and my little daughter were kneeling beside me. Behind me was our co-dweller from the barracks, the master of philosophy.

Several steps behind the master passed one of the more important Gestapo men, whom the man on his knees could not see. Speaking in a very low voice, but so that I could hear his words, the philosophy master said:

"Today there will be a terrible massacre since so many top men have gathered here . . ."

The Gestapo man stopped, asking who dared speak and ordered the man to stand up.

The philosophy master stood up and confessed that he had spoken. The Gestapo man ordered him to come closer, savagely hit him over the head, shouting he would kill him like a dog. The beaten man bled profusely and said:

"If you kill me I'll have the good fortune not to see the cowardly German bandits any more."

The German's face flushed; his whole body trembled, and a moment later, foaming with rage, he asked the master to turn around, stood behind him and shot him in the back of his head. The master fell. He died instantly. The Gestapo man went on.

In the corner of the square a thin, white-haired man was kneeling, and at his side his daughter, a slim brunette . . . A fat Gestapo man stopped near them, drew his revolver and killed the Jew. His daughter then leaped to her feet and cried to the Gestapo man in German: "You scoundrel! What did my father do to you that you shot him?"

The Gestapo man flew at her, hit her and threatened to kill her, too. The girl looked at him with a penetrating gaze. When he turned away, avoiding her eyes, she insulted him again, called him a mean coward who shot defenseless people, and shouted that he dared not look into her eyes.

"Look straight into my eyes, you coward," she cried, "and shoot! These eyes will pursue you and haunt you all your life!"

The Gestapo man winced, turned away from the girl—as if to muster his courage, and after a moment aimed his revolver at her and shot her.

Three large trucks drove into the market. At the command of one Gestapo man they parked along the rows of the kneeling men. Ukrainian SS men stood before the trucks. The Gestapo men still bustled in the square, selecting new victims, mostly old men, women and children.

Polish policemen led those selected to the trucks, and the Ukrainians forced them with blows and kicks to get into them. Two trucks had already been filled so densely that the people standing on them formed one thick, huddled mass. The Ukrainian SS men walked about the trucks and constantly showered blows on those who were mounting the trucks and on those who stood in them. A louder and more plaintive sound of weeping resounded in the square.

Not far from the trucks stood quite a few "Aryans," watching the scene. Some were sympathetic, some expressed revulsion and compassion; others laughed and sneered. Several tattered boys of 8 to 9 ran about the market, laughing.

And then the great calamity came upon me. One of the Gestapo men approached my wife and daughter and ordered them to march quickly to the third truck. I rose to my feet, but the Gestapo man caught me by the waist and threw me to the ground, ordering me to remain lying. My wife and daughter went in the direction of the truck pointed out to them, and I attempted to get up, wanting to run after them. The Gestapo man put his revolver against my chest, threatening to shoot me, which I told him to do.

He would have killed me, but at this moment another Gestapo man approached, who knew me from the ghetto. With a grin on his obese, oily face, he said ironically:

"Take it easy, Jew! You'll follow your family, and you'll meet your Sarah in the lap of Abraham even before the war ends, but now you're going to stay here. Your time hasn't come yet. We can still use you as a physician. You must serve us for some time yet."

"I cannot and I don't want to," I shouted, but a powerful kick in my abdomen threw me back and knocked me out. Meanwhile, the trucks with the poor victims, among them my dear ones, drove away. Several minutes later, when I came to, we heard the salvos of machine-gun fire from the distance. They lasted for a long time.

I am in despair. Today I was torn from my wife and my little daughter; I had lost poor Jozek a long time ago, and Marek had been deported even before I got into the ghetto—somewhere into the crazed world, ostensibly to do forced labor.

Why do I wander over the earth with my great anguish and the nightmare of my memories?

Alas, no one will answer my question.

# From the Ghetto to the Death Pit: Submission or Struggle?

*The testimony of the German engineer H. F. Graebe on the German massacre of the Jews of Dubno in Volhynia, was often quoted by the prosecution at the International Military Tribunal at Nuremberg (2992-PS). Graebe was manager of a German construction firm who did all he could to save his own Jewish employees.*

On 5th October 1942, when I visited the building office at Dubno, my foreman told me that in the vicinity of the site Jews from Dubno had been shot in three large pits, each about 30 meters long and 3 meters deep. About 1500 persons had been killed daily. All of the 5000 Jews who had still been living in Dubno before the pogrom were to be liquidated. As the shooting had taken place in his presence he was still very upset.

Moennikes and I went straight to the pits. Nobody prevented us. I heard a quick succession of shots from behind one of the mounds of earth. The people who had got off the lorries—men, women and children of all ages—had to undress upon the order of an SS man, who carried a riding or dog whip. They had to put their clothes on separate piles of shoes, top clothing and underclothing. I saw a heap of shoes that must have contained 800 to 1000 pairs, great piles of clothes and undergarments. Without screaming or weeping these people undressed, stood in family groups, kissed each other, said their farewells, and waited for a sign from another SS man, who stood near the pit, also with a whip in his hand. During the fifteen minutes that I stood near the pit, I did not hear anyone complain or beg for mercy.

I watched a family of about eight, a man and a woman, both about 50, with their children, aged about one, eight and ten, and two grown-up daughters of about 20 to 24. An old woman with snow-white hair was holding the one-year-old child in her arms, singing something to it and tickling it. The child was crowing with delight. The man and wife were looking on with tears in their eyes. The father was holding the hand of a boy of about ten, speaking to him softly. The boy was fighting back his tears. The father pointed to the sky, stroked the boy's head and seemed to explain something to him. At that moment the SS man at the pit shouted something to his comrade, who separated off about 20 persons and ordered them to go behind the mound of earth. Among them was the family that I have mentioned. I still clearly remember a dark-haired, slim girl who pointed to herself as she passed close to me and said "Twenty-three."

I walked to the other side of the mound and found myself standing before an enormous grave. The people lay so closely packed, one on top of the other, that only their heads were visible. Nearly all had blood running over their shoulders from their heads. Some of them were still moving. Some lifted an arm and turned a head to show that they were still alive. The pit was already two-thirds full. I estimated that it already contained about 1000 people. I looked round for the man who had shot them. He was an SS man, who was sitting on the edge of the narrow end of the pit, his legs dangling into it. He had a sub-machine gun across his knees and was smoking a cigarette. The people, completely naked, went down some steps which had been cut in the clay wall of the pit and climbed over the heads of those already lying there, to the place indicated by the SS man. They laid down in front of the dead or injured people. Some of them caressed those who were still alive and spoke to them softly. Then I heard a series of shots. I looked into the pit and saw that the bodies were twitching or that the heads lay motionless on top of the bodies which lay before them. Blood was pouring from their necks. I was surprised that I was not ordered away, but saw that there were also two or three uniformed postmen standing

269

nearby. The next batch was already approaching. They climbed into the pit, lined up against the previous victims and were shot. When I walked back round the mound I noticed another lorry-load of people which had just arrived. This time it included sick and infirm people. A very thin old woman, with terribly thin legs, was undressed by others who were already naked, while two people supported her. The woman appeared to be paralysed. The naked people carried the woman around the mound. I left with Moennikes and drove back to Dubno in the car.[1]

\* \* \*

This account describes what is regarded as the typical Jewish reaction. This was the picture: The passive Jew, led like a sheep to the slaughter, accepting his fate without resistance. This, it was widely held, . . . characterized the conduct of the victims. . . .

But, nevertheless, the question remains . . . Was this the only fashion in which the Jews reacted? Did they not show any opposition?

It is astonishing that another passage from Graebe's testimony, throwing light on a different aspect, has not been given the same publicity. The account in question deals with the massacre of the Jews in Ghetto Rovno, a town near Dubno. It reads as follows:

. . . Towards evening I went to Rovno and posted myself . . . in front of the house in which the Jewish employees of my firm slept. [Graebe had been given a written confirmation by the Deputy Commanding Officer of the District that no harm would befall his workmen, but to make certain he came to defend them in person.] Shortly after 8:00 p.m. the ghetto was surrounded by a large SS detachment and about three times as many of the Ukrainian militia. Then the electric arclights within and around the ghetto were switched on.

Squads of four to six soldiers began to or tried to enter the houses. Wherever the doors and windows were shut and the inhabitants refused to open the SS and the militiamen broke the windows, forced the doors with beams and crowbars, and forced an entry. The people were driven out as they were, regardless of whether they were dressed or already in bed. Since the majority refused to leave their houses and even defended themselves. . . , the SS men were compelled to use force. Finally, with strokes of whips, kicks and blows with rifle butts they succeeded in clearing the apartments. Since a number of families or groups had barricaded themselves . . . in buildings that were particularly strong, and the doors could not be opened with the aid of crowbars . . . the Germans blew them open with hand grenades. As the ghetto was near to the Rovno railroad, the younger people made an attempt to cross the tracks, to swim across a small river and to flee from the ghetto. This area was beyond the range of the electric lights and for that reason was lit by rockets. Throughout the night these beaten,

[1] From *Trials of War criminals*, Vol. 1 Case 1.

hounded and wounded people were moved along the streets. Women carried their children in their arms, children dragged their dead parents by their arms and legs down the road towards the railway. And without interruption the cries echoed and re-echoed: "Open the door! Open the door!"[2]

This picture is basically different! It describes, it is true, the situation in a single ghetto, but it may be assumed with reasonable certainty that there was little intrinsic difference between the Jews of these two, ghettoes, which were close to one another. But the first account describes the *closing phase* of an "action," when all hope was dead, when the Jews were beyond despair, when they had submitted to their fate with a greatness of spirit that can only evoke admiration—the second account is of the *opening* of an "action." And if the evidence regarding the close of an "action" is accepted, there is no reason to doubt the veracity of the evidence regarding the beginning of an "action." In the latter case, indeed, there is no complete despair, but active resistance, not fatalism, but initiative, not submission, but struggle.

# Human Vultures: Pillaging by the Natives

*Survivor Oscar Pinkus describes what happened after the evacuation of the ghetto of Losice, Poland. The Germans looted Jewish homes and stores, then disposed of the goods that remained through auction or by giving them away to their minions. The auctions, which drew many peasant families from the area around, were obscene . . .*

Days and weeks passed while the liquidation of all traces of Jewish existence in Losice went on. For two months thousands of carts were lugging out Jewish possessions, but despite all this work the homes were not yet completely cleaned out. The job had to be finished, and the Germans solved the problem in a radical way; for a nominal price they sold out all Jewish properties to the Poles.

Under new management the liquidation of the ghetto proceeded with fresh zeal and efficiency. The buyers would appear one day with carts in front of the houses they had bought and empty it to the last rag,

[2]From Yad Vashem Bulletin, March, 1961.

From *The House of Ashes* by Oscar Pinkus.

nail, and board. Since most of the buyers were farmers who had no intention of living in the houses, they took along everything that could be ripped apart. They removed the tiles from the ovens, took out the window frames, and pulled the boards off the ceilings. After this operation, there remained only bare, mutilated walls. The crippled houses filled with water, the roofs sagged—Losice was a complete ruin.

After this, the ghetto was opened to everybody. Whoever cared to, could enter and live in it. A few grocers picked homes nearer their stores; spinsters who had quarrelled with their families, all kinds of thieves, tramps, and prostitutes took advantage of it and moved in. Grotesque situations arose when a single person occupied an eight-room apartment or when one family lived in a three-story house. Still, most of the buildings remained empty. The Germans then sold the houses for scrap. After such a purchase the new owners appeared with axes and shovels and tore the building down. In a few weeks all that was left were the foundations, raw and jagged and filled with rain. The town was disappearing from the map.

There still remained the warehouses with the clothing of the dead Jews. The better clothes were shipped to Germany and the rest were disposed of in public auctions. They heaped the "rags" in the middle of the square and sold them. On days when these auctions took place the farmers piled into town as on a religious holiday. Then Losice was full again. First place was given to German informers, then to the prostitutes that served the Schupo [police], then to collaborating officials, and finally to whoever had stronger arms. Often the Germans just threw the clothes into the crowd, watching the mob tear the things from each other's hands. Sometimes they threw the "rags" in a heap, and on a given command let the Poles run for it.

At work we watched the procession of farmers to these auctions. It was like the holiday of Corpus Christi[1] when over all roads and highways the pious pilgrimaged to the holy rites. The farmers walked on, heatedly talking and arguing among themselves, considering what to get, how to divide the purchased property, and where it was best to go. They came with their entire families, each carrying a sack and a rope around the waist. With evening they walked back loaded with tables, beds, pots, and rags. Since success at these auctions was a matter of luck, some returned loaded to the brim, while others came back empty-handed, full of bitterness and disappointment. When they passed us I always had the impression that they were angry at us for their failure. One heard curses and threats directed against fellow Poles, against the Germans and against the dead Jews. Quarrels resulted on the highway, and the women tore each other's hair fighting over the acquired loot.

[1]A Roman Catholic festival commemorating the "last supper."

At these fights, often vicious ones, tables would be broken, dishes shattered. Most often fights occurred when it came to dividing the spoils, and then not only fists, but clubs and knives were used.

Then the auctions, too, came to an end and a vast silence descended on the ruined town. We were now the sole reminder of the destroyed life here, and events indicated that we, too, would not last much longer. We went on drinking with ever growing abandon and we now also began to drink at work. There was, not far from where we worked, a lonely Polish inn and as the days turned cold and rainy we would sit there for hours watching the leaves fall from the huge elm trees along the highway, and the crows as they hung in flocks over the treetops, crowing their jagged saw-like cry. We would turn our heads away only to stare through the half-open door at the owner's private quarters: clean beds, holy pictures on the walls, and, of course, Jewish furniture. We would see there the owner's daughter, a young handsome girl, studying Latin from a book in her lap. With every visit of ours she inexorably advanced with her studies. One day when we had been told that tomorrow was "the day" (of death), we sat there drinking and waiting while the girl practiced diligently: *habeo, habes, habet.* I thought, as I listened to her occasional errors, that when they buried us she would be studying the third conjugation, and when we started to disintegrate, she would have mastered the *accusativus cum infinitivo.* I smiled at her. She smiled back, blushed. Then I smiled to myself, to the man behind the counter. He came over, offered us some recently arrived halvah. I told him we spent all our money on drinks. "That's nothing," he said, "I will give it to you on credit." We all burst out in violent laughter. The man, thinking that we were drunk, smiled uncomfortably and returned behind the counter.

# At the Janowska "Sands": Death and Cremation

*Dr. Leon Weliczker Wells, an engineer, now living in New Jersey, was sixteen when, in 1941, the Germans invaded the Polish Metropolis of Lvov (Lemberg). He was imprisoned in the Janowska concentration camp, near Lvov. He tried to escape, but was caught and assigned to the Death Brigade, whose task it was to burn bodies, crush the bones and obliterate the vestiges of the millions of corpses.*

*Dr. Wells narrates his experiences with great restraint and in a matter of fact presentation. He testified at the Nuremberg and Eichmann Trials.*

Day breaks and slowly everyone gets up. We move around the cell very slowly. We stop as the sound of music, the "Death Tango," reaches us. Surely, today they are playing for us. Today will be the third day, and from all previous experience of other groups which had worked with the corpses on the "sands" we know that it will be our last one.

The door opens. We hear, "Out!" We all step out and sit down as we had yesterday morning. We are counted, and the number checks. Now they release the people from the other cell. They sit down behind us. We have our breakfast, and after we finish, under heavy guard, march out to the "sands." At the "sands" forty-eight inmates are waiting for us; they have been added to our group. These people previously worked at H.K.P. (*Hepres Kraftfahrt Park*—Military Car Depot).

And so our brigade is enlarged to 129 inmates. The day passes as usual, and in the evening we return to the "Death Cells." This night one of the inmates hangs himself from a rafter with his belt. Now our brigade numbers 128. In the morning, when we leave for work, four inmates, following the command of the SS man, carry this man out and throw him behind the toilet. An hour later he is brought to the ravine with the other corpses from the concentration camp.

Thursday and Friday pass with hard work. Today our brigade is opening a mass grave that contains 1,450 bodies. Many of today's corpses don't have bullet holes in them. They have open mouths with projecting tongues. This would indicate that they had been buried alive.

In the evening my younger neighbor, Roth, tells me his story of the last days of the Jews in Lvov. Roth was caught on the "Aryan" side. He had been able to pass as an Aryan for the preceding ten months. Then one day he met an old school friend. The man immediately reported him to the Gestapo. They arrested him and his younger sister, who had also been passing herself off as an Aryan. Roth himself had tossed her body into the fire two days ago.

So passes the night. We talk, then sleep, and resume talking again. The topic of escape crops up. In order to clarify our situation and to describe how little chance we had for escape, I should like to describe the exact conditions and location of our working place.

In the western section of Lvov is Janowska Street. At the end of this street, as I've said, is a huge sandy area, called the Janowska "sands." These "sands" have high hills, deep ravines, and cover an area of approximately two and a half square miles. There are signs in Polish, German, and Ukrainian around the "sands": "To enter this place is

From *Janowska Road* by Leon W. Wells

strictly forbidden. Anyone nearing this site at a distance of less than 150 feet of the sign will be shot."

Every few hundred feet a Schupo stands guard in this area. On top of the highest sandhill stands the observation point. Here is a tent where the Schupos stay and where ammunition is kept. Here, too, is a telephone with a direct line to the concentration camp and the Gestapo's city headquarters. The houses in the "sands" area had been emptied and taken over by the Schupos. The Schupos, who number over one hundred, are divided into two groups. Each group has twenty-four hours on duty and twenty-four hours off. In addition to the Schupos there are quite a few SD[1] men.

After a long discussion with Roth on how to escape, we fall asleep.

At six in the morning we are awakened. A new day of torture begins—perhaps our last one. Once again this day seems the most critical to us because it is the last day of the week.

It starts as usual. Everybody is at his job. From our brigade the carpenter and one of his assistants have been taken to one of the Schupos' houses to repair something. It is twelve o'clock—lunchtime. Our brigade as usual goes down to the ravine for lunch, but instead of twenty, we number only eighteen today because the two have not returned from the Schupo's house yet.

We are standing in formation waiting to be counted. We stand and wait. Why are they keeping us waiting? Probably to kill us. What else? We all know that today is the last working day in the week. We look straight into the fire—our destiny. Let's get it over with!

But nothing happens. Perhaps we are waiting for the others to join us. At last we see the Schupo and the carpenter arriving on top of the hill, but the carpenter's assistant is not with them. We see the two men are now approached by the second lieutenant, corporal, first lieutenant, and the private. They encircle the carpenter. The second lieutenant has a few words with the Schupo and afterward with the carpenter; he then reaches for his pistol and shoots the carpenter. We all surmise that the assistant must have escaped.

In a minute we hear the command, "Two men up!" Two of us run up the hill, carry the corpse down, and throw him into the fire. Now the second lieutenant himself comes down to the ravine. In silence, beckoning to us, he selects four inmates, most, but not all, of them elderly men, over fifty years of age, and he gestures to them to stand in one line. After that he asks, "Which of you complains?"

One man about thirty-five years old steps forward. "I do," he says. And then he adds, quietly, "Maybe at last I will rid myself of more tortures."

The Untersturmführer motions him to join the line, and picks out

[1]Security Service.

one more inmate. They now number six. They stand in front of the fire, looking at it; they are turned away from us.

Now the Untersturmführer begins his speech, directing it at us. "One of you escaped. Because of him these people will be shot. From now on, for everyone who tries to do the same, I will shoot twenty of you. If I find out that you are planning an escape, all of you will be shot."

After this speech he turns to the chosen six, and shoots one after another. Each is shot in the back of his head, and kicked so that the body won't fall toward the Untersturmführer. When he finishes, he calls for four of us to pick up the corpses and toss them into the fire.

While the bodies are being thrown into the fire, the Untersturmführer walks around us as if looking for someone else. Suddenly he points at Marek and says, *"Komm."*

Marek asks, *"Ich?"*

*"Ja, du, du."*

Tears appear in the boy's eyes. Walking toward the point where the other six stood a few minutes ago, Marek asks again, with a tearful voice, "Why me?"

"Don't babble so—turn around." Marek turns around, and a moment later he, too, is lying dead.

"Two men!" Two men toss him into the fire. Before he is tossed in, the Untersturmführer tells the two men to take off Marek's boots. "Let's not waste such a good pair of boots!"

Now we are counted—122 men. We have lunch. After lunch we march back to the barrack.

Today we work only half a day.

---

# Digging Up the Dead at Babi Yar

*A vivid account of the exhumation operations was given in an affidavit sworn by Shloma Gol of Vilna in Nuremberg on 9 August 1946. Since all such operations were conducted on a similar basis, this description can fit any of the perhaps 200 mass burial places destroyed in this way in the occupied regions in the East . . .*

From the Affidavit submitted by Shloma Gol at International Military Tribunal (Nuremberg, August 9, 1946).

276

# Extermination

I, Shloma Gol, declare as follows:

1. I am a Jew and lived in Vilna, Lithuania. During the German occupation I was in Vilna ghetto.
2. The administration of Vilna ghetto was managed by the SA. The town commissioner of Vilna was an SA officer called Hinkst. The regional commissioner was an SA officer called Wolff. The Adviser on Jewish questions was an SA officer called Muerer. [He was the chief.]
3. In December 1943, 80 Jews from the ghetto including 4 women and myself were ordered by [an] SA officer whose name I forgot, to live in a large pit some distance from the town. This pit had originally been dug for an underground petrol tank. It was circular, 60 metres in diameter and 4 metres deep. When we lived in it the top was partially covered with boarding and there were two wooden rooms partitioned off, also a kitchen and a lavatory. We lived there six months altogether before we escaped. The pit was guarded by SA guards.
4. In the morning the officer standing on the edge of the pit accompanied by 14 or 15 SA men, said to us: "Your brothers and sisters and friends are all near here. Treat them properly and if you complete your work we will send you to Germany where each man can practice his own profession." We did not know what this meant.
5. Thereupon the SA men threw chains into the pit, and the officer ordered the Jewish foreman (for we were a working party) to fasten the chains on us. The chains were fastened round both ankles and round the waist. They weighed 2 kilos each, and we could take only small steps wearing them. We wore them permanently for six months. The four women (who worked in the kitchen) were not chained.
6. After that we were taken to work.
7. Our work consisted of digging up mass graves and piling the bodies on the funeral pyres and burning them. I was engaged in digging the bodies. My friend Belic was engaged in sawing up and arranging the wood.
8. We dug up altogether 86,000 bodies. I know this because two of the Jews in the pit were ordered by the Germans to keep count of the bodies: that was their sole job. The bodies were mixed, Jews, Polish priests, Russian POW's. Among those that I dug up I found my own brother. I found his identification papers on him. He had been dead for two years when I dug him up, because I know that he was in a batch of 10,000 Jews from Vilna ghetto who were shot in September 1941.

277

9. The procedure of burning the bodies was quite methodical. Parallel ditches seven metres long were dug. Over these a square platform of boards was laid. A layer of bodies was put on top, the bodies had oil poured on them and then branches were put on top and over the branches, logs of wood. Altogether 14 such layers of bodies and fuel were put on each pyre. Each pyre was shaped like a pyramid with a wooden funnel sticking up through the top. Petrol and oil were poured down the funnel, and incendiary bombs put around the edge of the pyre. All this work was done by the Jews. When the pyre was ready, the officer himself or his assistant (also in the SA) personally lit the pyre with a burning rag on the end of a pole.

10. The work of digging up the graves and building the pyres was supervised and guarded by about 80 guards. Of these over 50 were SA men, in brown uniforms, armed with pistols and daggers and automatic guns (the guns were always cocked and pointed at us). The other 30 guards consisted partly of Lithuanians and partly of SD and SS. In the course of the work the Lithuanian guards themselves were shot presumably so that they should not say what had been done. The commander of the whole place was Muerer (the expert on Jewish questions), but he only inspected the work from time to time. The SA (assistant) officer actually commanded on the spot. At night our pit was guarded by 10 to 12 of these guards.

11. The guards (principally the SA guards) hit us and stabbed us. I still have scars on both legs and on my neck. I was once knocked senseless onto the pile of bodies, and could not get up, but my companions took me off the pile. Then I went sick. We were allowed to go sick for two days: the third day we were taken out of the pit "to hospital"—this meant to be shot.

12. Of 76 men in the pit 11 were shot at work. 43 of us eventually dug a tunnel from the pit with our bare hands, and broke our chains and escaped into the woods. We had been warned by a Czech SS man who said: "They are going to shoot you soon, and they are going to shoot me too, and put us all on the pyre. Get out if you can, but not while I am on duty."

# Readings

The readings for this chapter are covered in the histories and anthologies listed at the beginning of the book.

*Babi Yar* by Anatoli Kuznetsov, is the novel on the extermination of the Jews of Kiev based on eyewitness accounts and documentation by the celebrated Russian author. There is more than one translation in English—one was published by Farrar, Straus and Giroux; the other by Dial Press.

# 13. KIDDUSH HA-SHEM AND KIDDUSH HA-HAYYIM

Throughout Jewish history, martyrdom to sanctify and glorify the Name of God *(Kiddush Ha-Shem)* has been considered the highest form of religious devotion. Countless thousands of Jews have willingly gone to their deaths rather than forsake Judaism—in ancient times during the Syrian and Roman persecutions, more recently during the Crusades, the Spanish Inquisition, and the Chmielnicki pogroms.

Rabbinical law states that Jews are required to martyr themselves only if forced to commit murder or incest or to engage in idol worship. The concept of sanctifying God's Name has a wider meaning than martyrdom, however; it includes all acts of humanity, goodness, and integrity done in behalf of a fellow human being, whether Jew or non-Jew. The *Shoah* witnessed many such acts of *Kiddush Ha-Shem,* some of which are recounted in the selections that follow.

The agonies of the Holocaust also led to the development of the concept of *Kiddush Ha-Hayyim,* the sanctification of life. This idea was best expressed by Rabbi Yitzhak Nissenbaum of Warsaw, who said, "In the past the enemy sought the Jew's soul, and the Jew gave up his body to save his soul; now the enemy demands his life, and the Jew must defend it to preserve his soul."

As shown by Leviticus 18:5 ("Keep my rules and *live by them* . . .") and Deuteronomy 4:15 ("Be on guard; take care of yourselves"), the preservation of life is not only an expression of the survival instinct but a religious precept. Life is precious, and it is our duty to preserve it, to outwit the murderous enemy, to "hold on" and outlive him. The hunted

Jews of the Holocaust came to know that the preservation of life was the
ultimate sanctification of the Name.

# Two Faces of Kiddush Ha–Shem

The bitter Silesian winter vented its fury on us—the
three hundred Jewish prisoners working in the coal mines, named after
Hermann Goering—as we started the march after work to go back
"home" to *Arbeitslager* (work camp), Jawischowitz. On clear days we
could see the smoke rising from the chimneys at the crematorium in
Auschwitz, the dreaded extermination camp. On that day in early
December 1944 the sun couldn't break through the leaden sky, so the
smoke was hidden. In addition, the wind-driven snow blinded us, even
as it penetrated the thin fabric of our pajama uniforms.

My thoughts returned for the hundredth time to the event which
took place nearly two weeks back when my dearest friend and bunkmate, eighteen-year-old Israel Katz, accomplished something nobody
had ever done before. We knew that there had been two previous
attempts to escape from our camp, and that in each case the "culprits"
were dead before they could get outside the high-voltage fence. One
was shot a mere few steps from it, the other was electrocuted. But Israel
was not deterred by the two fatal failures. And I was the only person to
whom he confided his fantastic plan of escape. Under cover of darkness, he explained, he would shove an empty wooden barrel between
the electrically charged wires and squeeze through it. (Near every
block, there was such a barrel filled with sand which was to be used to
extinguish possible fires. He had only to empty it, push out its bottom,
and he had an insulated shaft.) My repeated efforts to dissuade him
from escaping were totally wasted—his mind was made up. Israel Katz
had set himself the goal to be the first to escape from slavery to
freedom. There were rumors that the Russian army was near Kattowitz, some fifty kilometers from our camp, and he was sure he could
make it through the German-occupied territory.

"Don't worry," he said. "I speak Polish perfectly. I am sure I'll
manage to get some civilian clothes and a bit of food, even if I have to
steal to get them. Here I am a helpless prisoner, but outside I am not

---

From an unpublished manuscript by Mordecai Hauer, a survivor.

afraid of anybody, not even the Nazi beasts! And then, you'll see, I will lead the Russians to this camp. You have heard the SS telling us over and over that no matter who wins the war they'll always have enough time to massacre us before it's over. Well, that's what I want to prevent. I want to make sure that the camp is liberated before the SS can make good their threat. Now you understand?"

The wind and the heavy snow made the march terribly difficult. But even more painful was the memory of the morning *Appell* (roll call) after the night of Israel's escape. The SS *Lagerfuehrer* (Camp Commander) kept the entire inmate-population at the *Appellplatz* for hours, until the SS guards combed every inch of the camp and reported that Israel was not to be found. By then scores of prisoners had frozen to death. My spine felt like glass, about to snap, and my eyes were swelling, pushing against my brains. Then the *Lagerfuehrer* announced in an angry but confident voice that "the criminal *Saujude* (pig-Jew) will be captured within twenty-four hours! And he will hang right here on the *Appellplatz* for all of you dogs to see!" I had no doubt that this would be so, and the only thing I could do was hope for a miracle. I prayed almost constantly for my friend.

The deadline set by the *Lagerfuehrer* passed without Israel's being caught, and I noticed a faint glimmer of hope in the eyes of my fellow prisoners. And as the days went by without Israel's being returned, we began to hope more and more. I felt a secret pride; I think we all did. Israel Katz's accomplishment became the symbol for our own eventual freedom. The omnipotence of German might had been successfully challenged. It appeared that the tight grip of Hitler on the outside world was in the process of loosening after all. Perhaps the Allied victory, which we used to believe in long ago, was to come after all. Possibly the Russians at Kattowitz were really getting ready for an offensive, and my friend Israel may yet help them to liberate us—as he had vowed he would.

But an icy hand seemed to compress my heart as our group reached the gate of the camp. The nearly three thousand inmates of Jawischowitz darkened the snow-covered *Appellplatz*, at the center of which stood a makeshift gallows. We too were led to join the *Appell*. A place was reserved for us right in front of the gallows, near which stood the *Lagerfuehrer* amidst some other SS officers. He was gesturing with his gloved hands, and he wore a cynically triumphant smile. Only, my friend Israel was still not there. My lips started an involuntary prayer . . .

Suddenly I heard the noise of a motor. I turned around and saw a German military vehicle coming through the gate. It rolled to a halt just a little way behind us, and out of it emerged Israel with two SS officers at his sides. The normally animated face of my dear friend was calm, without the slightest trace of fear, and his eyes—those quick, fiery eyes that I knew—had now a strange sadness in them. He was barefoot, and

282

his hands were tied behind his back. His striped jacket was torn and unbuttoned, exposing his bare ribcage to the fierce wind and snow. His steps were steady as he was led to the gallows. The two officers wanted to assist him up the four wooden stairs, but Israel shrugged them off and went up alone. Then one of the officers, obviously in charge of the hanging, took a piece of paper from his breast pocket, and he began to read from it the verdict of the *Waffen* SS tribunal: " . . . for escaping from *Arbeitslager* Jawischowitz, injuring a farmer with a knife, for attempted stealing of food and clothes from the farmer, for seriously injuring with a knife two of the arresting SS men—death by hanging!"

My eyes were fixed on Israel Katz. If he heard the verdict, his face didn't show it. He was looking straight ahead and up over our heads into the snowy-gray far away. I was crying bitterly. "Why, God, why?"

"Israel Katz! Did you understand the verdict?!" It was the raspy voice of the man who read the verdict.

*"Chob farshtanen,"* came Israel's Yiddish reply in the affirmative.

The officer produced a short, very white rope and handed it to the *Lagerfuehrer.* The latter appeared to be surprised, almost hesitant, but not for long. "I want a volunteer to perform the execution!" he shouted at us. Then, as he saw that no one volunteered, he turned to his superior. The two exchanged words in a whisper, and then the *Lagerfuehrer* spoke again. "The volunteer will receive an extra ration of bread for a month!" Still no response. The SS went into an agitated huddle. I was scared. What if they picked one of us? What if they picked me?

I looked again at Israel and was horrified because he reminded me of Jesus on the cross. The thought was even more absurd, almost abominable, because I came from an Orthodox Jewish home. Yet I couldn't help it. When I was a child I often saw images of Jesus, whose pictures and small statues had been sold in my parents' store. I often wondered in those days why the gentle-faced, emaciated and bloodied figure was killed. Now the physical similarity between Jesus and my friend Israel was overwhelming. Like Jesus, Israel had a slight beard. Like Jesus, Israel was mere skin and bones. And like Jesus, Israel showed no anger, only a sad resignation. I tried vainly to banish the terrible thought from my mind. The impasse over the executioner was suddenly resolved when *Blockaltester* (elder) Hans—a convicted German murderer who had been pardoned by Hitler when he offered to serve Germany as Block Elder in a concentration camp—stepped forward. The rope with a steel ring at one end and a noose at the other was handed to him. Hans walked up to the small platform on which my friend stood. He quickly attached the ring to the hook over Israel's head, but then he ran into a snag. The rope was too short, and the noose wouldn't slip below Israel's eyes. Hans was red with embarrassment, not knowing how to complete his task. The SS officer in charge came to his aid. *"Kopf hoch!"* came the command for Israel to raise his head.

I watched with awe and amazement as Israel raised himself on his toes and stretched his head as high as he could. Hans was thus able to slip the noose under my poor friend's chin. He jumped off the platform into the snow and waited for new instructions.

"Pull away the plank, *Dumkopf!*"—came the command.

Hans reached for the wooden platform, and then . . . then I heard Israel Katz speak his last words in a clear, strong voice: "Am Yisrael chai!" (The People of Israel lives and is Everlasting). All along I was thinking that in the last moments I would close my eyes because I didn't think I could witness my dear friend's struggle with death. But now my eyes were wide open. I wanted to see everything—to remember everything. Israel Katz took a chance with his life so that I may live, so that his people may live. And if he had the strength and courage to do that, then I had to have the courage to see him die.

I saw his head tilt down and to the right. I saw him holding his feet together, as if he were a soldier standing at attention. I had never seen a hanging before, but I expected my friend to fight for breath. But the seconds were ticking away and nothing of the sort happened. Israel's body remained motionless—except for a slight pendulous swaying in the strong wind. I understood it then, and I understand it even better now. It was the hero's way to show the cowards what they were. But beyond that, and this I believe with perfect faith, Israel Katz wanted to demonstrate his pride—his undying pride as a Jew. Having failed in his mission, he meant his death to be the supreme sacrifice, a last protest against inhumanity, and a legacy. His last words, "The People of Israel lives," were as much an expression of defiance as of deep and eternal faith. In his last moment on this earth he had chosen to bless, rather than to curse.

Israel Katz, my sweet friend, these past twenty-seven years I have grown older. I don't understand why I live and you don't. But you are still eighteen, and you'll remain so forever. And I haven't forgotten you—not even for one day. I told my wife about you, my three children, all my friends, and to anyone who was ready to listen to *your story.* And I shall keep telling your story, in word and in script, as long as I have the gift of life and memory.

The *Lagerfuehrer* addressed us, inmates of the concentration camp in Jawischowitz, after the hanging of Israel. My ears strained to hear his words, spoken in an almost conciliatory tone. He said something about how it was too bad that a young man like Israel had to die because he foolishly disregarded the facts of life in the camp.

"There is simply no escape from Jawischowitz," he said, "and you would all do well to remember this. If you try to run away, you will have to pay an even worse price than the person you see hanging before you. I say "worse" because I have orders to execute fifty prisoners in addition to the escapee. Thus you won't only commit suicide when you try to escape, you will also commit murder on a large scale. I challenge

284

you to do that!" He looked us over for some time, as if he wanted to make sure that everybody heard him, and then continued: "The body will hang till sundown. I was told that according to Jewish religious practice ten people form a quorum in order to conduct a memorial prayer for the dead. I have specific orders to prevent this from happening. You will be watched by the guards all day, and those caught in the act of holding a prayer service will be shot. I caution you to remember this. *Appell* dismissed!"

## Kaddish and Death

The Chasid Reb Yankele hailed from northeastern Hungary. He was my bunkmate to the right, even as Israel used to sleep to my left. He was in his late twenties. His gentle brown eyes were like precious gems set against white velvet. Miraculously, he had a tiny *Siddur,* despite the thorough and repeated searches in Auschwitz. He and Israel were perpetual antagonists in a philosophical sense. Many a time—too often, I thought—I listened to their carefully whispered arguments over my head, always just prior to falling asleep. The three of us also belonged to the same work-detail down in the coal mine. Israel was the type who would sabotage work every time the Polish foreman, Pan Kovalsky, had his back turned to us. This worried us no end, since sabotage was punishable by death.

Israel used to defame God, to curse and swear at Him, and Reb Yankele used to beg him not to do it. Israel blamed God for the death of his parents and sisters. He insisted that the Jewish people's faith in God—Jewish religion itself—made them docile weaklings. To him Reb Yankele represented the arch-type of those docile Jews who were praying and studying Torah day and night, always relying on God, and he said so without mincing words. "God must hate your kind," he yelled at the young Chasid, "or else he wouldn't allow the butchering of the Jews again and again through history! Or are you going to tell me that there is any virtue in suffering hunger and starvation, in slavery, and in dying like dogs?"

"Don't speak like that, child. You don't mean what you say," replied Reb Yankele. "You are being sacrilegious, God forbid."

"I am not a child, and I mean every word. All your scholarly and religious benchwarming is idiotic and criminal. Our people should have learned how to fight, how to defend themselves." Israel was shaking.

"Have respect for the memory of your parents, God rest their holy souls," said the gentle rabbi.

"My parents, God rest their souls! What a laugh. And where was God when the Nazis shot them and my two little sisters as if they had been stray dogs? Tell me that! A lot of good it did my father to die with the

*Shema Yisrael* on his stuttering lips. And what pleasure did God get from it? The memory of my parents! Oh, I have a memory! I remember that on his last evening on earth, when he knew we would be shot the next morning, his long beard was still black as the night. And I remember that as he faced the machine gun in the morning it was white. Now he is dead. Don't you think he would sooner be alive?"

Reb Yankele was visibly hard pressed for an acceptable answer—acceptable even to himself. Finally he spoke, "How do you know, how do I know, how would anybody know, except God Almighty, that life is better than death? We must have trust that God knows what is best for us. We dare not argue with His judgment."

Such were the arguments between Israel Katz and Reb Yankele, and I was always unhappy about the constant friction between these two whom I so admired—different as they were.

No sooner did we return to our block than Reb Yankele turned to a few of us, insisting that we conduct prayers for the hanged Israel. "Having been his best friend," Reb Yankele pointed at me, "you will recite the *Kaddish*."

I dared not contradict him, but I was frightened. I was almost relieved that he couldn't recruit a *minyan*—eight more men besides us two. Reb Yankele left the block in anger, and I was suddenly ashamed. Apparently others felt similarly, for now there were enough people who wanted to follow the young rabbi, including me. But then I changed my mind. I had an idea. I told the men to wait, and ran after Reb Yankele, who was struggling against the wind and the deep snow as he approached the gallows. I caught up with him.

"Reb Yankele," I said, "we have time to pray *minchah* till sundown. By then visibility will be poor, and the SS won't be able to see us from the guardhouse. Besides, by then they will have been convinced that we are afraid to perform services after the threat of the *Lagerfuehrer*. Why risk lives? Please, Reb Yankele, let's wait. I promise we will have a *minyan*."

The rabbi agreed and returned to the block with me. I tried to sleep, but my thoughts wouldn't let me. I couldn't forget my poor friend, dead out there in the terrible cold. Then the time came to go out, and we were ready. We approached the gallows without trouble, and Reb Yankele started *minchah*. Since the rabbi was facing Israel, with his back to the guardhouse, everybody followed suit. But I had turned my head toward the gate so that I could see whether any SS men were coming. We were in the midst of the *Shmoneh Esrei* (Silent Prayer) when through the thickly falling snow I saw two SS men heading toward us. "Run everybody," I hissed. "They are coming!"

We scattered in an instant. Eight people ran to our block, but I alone ran into the nearby latrine. Safely inside, I looked out through the window and saw—to my horror—that Reb Yankele still stood under the gallows, his feet together, his eyes closed, in deep prayer. The two

286

SS men reached the gallows, and to my amazement disregarded Reb Yankele. They proceeded to cut the rope, and the lifeless body dropped into the snow at the feet of the praying rabbi. Having finished the job for which the SS men had apparently come, the Germans turned to the gently swaying Chasid. My heart nearly stopped beating as I heard one of them shout: "What in hell's name are you doing here?" The tone wasn't very angry; it was more like a mixture of astonishment and surprise. And it only became threatening when Reb Yankele did not reply. "Get away from here, *Dumkopf*, before I make you regret it!" Only, the words were lost on Reb Yankele. If anything, he appeared to pray with even more fervor, and his body moved faster back and forth.

"Stubborn sonafabitch this Jew," one SS man said to the other.

"That he is," came the reply. "But watch me move him. Hey, dog! See this gun?" He nearly hit Reb Yankele in the face as he thrust the automatic forward. "You want a hole in your head?"

I kept praying that Reb Yankele would stop his stubborn disregard of the terrible danger to his life; there was nothing else I dared do. I was frozen with fear. The SS man placed the barrel of his gun to the rabbi's forehead—head and gun were swaying together in a macabre rhythm. "I will count to three," he said, "and then I shoot. I am going to pull the trigger. You hear?" He got no response.

"*Eins, Zwei, drei!*" The shot rang out and I closed my eyes. Suddenly my feet grew weak, my head dizzy, and my tears came in a flood. If I live a thousand years, if I had the power of speech of a hundred orators or poets, I could not express the emotions in my heart as I lay on the cement floor of the latrine. But I know what I did after the river of my eyes dried up to the last drop. I got up somehow and walked to the gallows in the now dark *Appellplatz.*

I dropped to my knees when I reached the two bodies. In the faint shine of the snow I saw my friend Israel, on his back, with eyes wide open, as if he were trying to pry out the secrets of heaven. And I saw dear Reb Yankele, on his side, with his right arm hugging the chest of Israel. The two antagonists were now one, united in death.

I rose, washed my hands with pure snow, and I started: *"Yisgadel, veyiskadash shmei rabboh . . ."*

How do I know that life is better than death? I don't. I don't know why I am here, and why Reb Yankele and Israel are not. But as long as God gives me life and the ability to speak, I must make sure that they are not forgotten. For otherwise my survival has no meaning.

# "Farewell to Life"

*Every three months the Sonderkommando, who burned the bodies which had been gassed, was killed and a new kommando replaced it. Miklos Nyiszli narrates an episode of* Kiddush Ha–Shem . . .

It was 2 p.m. I had just finished lunch and was seated by the window of my room . . . when a strident yell from the oven-room passageway broke the silence:

*"Alle antreten, alle antreten!"*

This was an order we were accustomed to hearing twice a day, in the morning and evening, for muster. Coming at this hour, however, it augured no good.

*"Antreten, alle antreten!"* the order rang out again, this time more peremptory and impatient than before . . .

With sinking hearts we headed for the crematorium courtyard, where a group of well-armed SS already encircled a group of kommando men as we walked up to join them. There was neither surprise nor the faintest sign of protest from anyone. The SS, their machine guns leveled, waited patiently till the last stragglers had joined the group. I glanced around for the last time . . . All was quiet and very peaceful . . .

Our guards had us walk towards number two crematorium, directly opposite. We crossed the courtyard of number two, knowing that this would be the last walk we would ever take. They led us into the crematorium furnace room, but none of the SS guards remained inside with us. Instead, they spread out in a circle around the building, stationed at intervals near the doors and windows, their guns poised, ready to fire. The doors were shut and the windows covered with heavy iron bars, completely thwarting any possibility of escape. Our comrades from number two were also present, and a few minutes later they unlocked the door and sent in the kommando from number four. Four hundred and sixty men in all, waiting to die. The only thing we did not know for sure was the method that would be used to exterminate us. We were specialists in the matter, having seen all methods in operation. Would it be in the gas chamber? I hardly thought so, not with the Sonderkommando. Machine guns? Not at all convenient in a room like this. Most likely they intended killing two birds with one stone, that is, blow up the building and us along with it. A plan worthy of the SS. Or

From *Auschwitz: A Doctor's Eyewitness Account* by Miklos Nyiszli.

perhaps they would toss a phosphorous bomb through one of the windows. That would be an equally effective method, one that had already been tried before, on the deportees from the Milo ghetto. What they had done then was load the deportees into box cars that were so dilapidated as to be of no further use, then toss a bomb inside.

The men of the Sonderkommando were sitting on the concrete floor of the furnace room wherever they could find room, waiting anxiously but silently for the next move.

Suddenly the silence was broken. One of the kommando crew, a thin, sickly, black-haired man about thirty years old whose eyes were magnified by a pair of thick glasses, jumped to his feet and began to speak in a voice loud enough for everyone to hear. It was the "Dayan," the rabbi of a small synagogue community in Poland. A self-taught man, whose knowledge was vast both in the spiritual and temporal realms, he was the ascetic member of the Sonderkommando. In conformance with the tenets of his religion, he ate sparingly, accepting only bread, margarine and onions from the well-stocked kommando larder. He had been assigned to the cremation kommando, but because of his religious fanaticism I had talked the *Ober* into excusing him from this frightful work. The argument I had used with the *Ober* had simply been that this man could not be of much use for the heavy work involved in cremation, since he was weak from his self-imposed, ascetic diet. "Besides," I had argued, "he only slows up the work by pausing over each body to murmur prayers for its salvation. And there are often several thousand souls a day to pray for."

These had been my arguments, but they had sufficed, strangely enough, and the *Ober* had assigned him to burn the pile of refuse which was forever accumulating in the courtyard of number two. This refuse, called "Canada" by the SS, was composed of objects that had once belonged to the deportees, objects of such little material value that they were considered not worth being salvaged: various foodstuffs, documents, diplomas, military decorations, passports, marriage certificates, prayer books, holy objects and Bibles that the deportees had brought with them into captivity.

This little hill called Canada daily consumed hundreds of thousands of photographs—pictures of young married couples, elderly groups, charming children and pretty girls—together with innumerable prayer books, in many of which I found carefully inked notations recording the dates of important events—births, marriages, deaths—in the lives of the various families. Sometimes there were flowers, culled from the graves of beloved parents in all the Jewish cemeteries of Europe, pressed between the pages and piously preserved . . .

This was where the "Dayan" worked, or rather, where he did not work, for all he did was watch the fires burn. Even so he was dissatisfied, for his religious belief forbade him from participating in the

289

burning of prayer books or holy objects. I felt sorry for him, but could do nothing further to help him. It was impossible to obtain an easier job, for we were, after all, only members of the kommando of the living dead.

This then was the man who began to speak:

"Fellow Jews . . . An inscrutable Will has sent our people to its death; fate has allotted us the cruelest of tasks, that of participating in our own destruction, of witnessing our own disappearance, down to the very ashes to which we are reduced. In no instance have the heavens opened to send showers and put out the funeral pyre flames.

"We must accept, resignedly, as Sons of Israel should, that this is the way things must be. God has so ordained it. Why? It is not for us, miserable humans, to seek the answer.

"This is the fate that has befallen us. Do not be afraid of death. What is life worth, even if, by some strange miracle, we should manage to remain alive? We would return to our cities and towns to find cold and pillaged homes. In every room, in every corner, the memory of those who have disappeared would lurk, haunting our tear-filled eyes. Stripped of family and relatives, we would wander like the restless, shuffling shadows of our former selves, of our completed pasts, finding nowhere any peace or rest." . . .

The heavy doors swung open. Oberscharführer Steinberg entered the room, accompanied by two guards, machine guns in hand.

"*Arzte heraus.* All doctors outside!" he shouted impatiently.

My two colleagues and I, and the lab assistant, left the room. Steinberg and the two SS soldiers halted halfway between the two crematoriums. The *Ober* gave me a sheaf of papers he had been holding in his hand on which there was a list of numbers and told me to find mine and strike it out. The papers contained the tattoo numbers of every man in the Sonderkommando. I took out my pen and, after hunting for a while, found my number and drew a line through it. He then told me to do the same for my comrades. This done, he accompanied us to number one gate and told us to return to our room, and not to leave it. We did as ordered.

The following morning a five-truck convoy arrived in the crematorium courtyard and dumped out its cargo of bodies, those of the old Sonderkommando. A new group of thirty men carried them to the incineration room, where they were laid out in front of the ovens. Terrible burn scars covered their bodies. Their faces and clothing were so charred that it was all but impossible to identify them, especially since their tattoo numbers had disappeared.

After death by gas, on the pyre, by chloroform injections, by a bullet in the back of the neck, by phosphorous bomb, here was a sixth way of killing which I had not previously discovered.

During the night our comrades had been taken into a nearby forest and killed by flame throwers. That we four were still alive did not by any means signify that they wanted to spare us, but simply that we were still indispensable to them. In allowing us to remain alive, Dr. Mengele had merely granted us another reprieve. Once again, the thought gave us neither comfort nor joy.

# Nazis Celebrate Purim (5702) 1942

*Rabbi Shimon Huberband was a member of Dr. Ringelblum's Oneg Shabbat Group. He was the acknowledged and respected representative of Polish Orthodox Jewry. He was also awarded a prize for his literary-historical work as member of the Jewish Yikor Cultural Organization of the Warsaw Ghetto. The selection that follows is excerpted from his work* Kiddush Ha–Shem *which was his unique contribution to the chronicles of the Shoah. These were rescued from the ghetto and published by Simha Holzberg, who survived and brought his writings to light.*

*The theme of the account that follows centers around the satanic celebration of Purim, in 5702 (1942), by the descendants of Haman whose ten sons were hanged (Esther, ch. 9) . . .*

In the town of Zdunska Wola, during the winter of 1941–42, the Germans arrested Jews right and left. Heading the list of prisoners were those who had been guilty of offense during the Polish regime. Among them was Nahum Eliyahu Zilberberg, son of a distinguished scholar, who got into bad company and committed felonies of forgery and embezzlement. Nevertheless, he was looked on favorably by his brethren because of his love and selfless devotion for fellow Jews. Nothing deterred him from helping a Jew in trouble. His home was open to those in need; he gave charity freely, sheltered and fed the homeless and paupers. His two boys studied at the small yeshivah, conducted by the celebrated Rabbi of Ger, and were celebrated for their learning and piety.

Nahum had been given a prison sentence of ten years by the Polish government. He was rearrested by the Germans together with those

From *Kiddush Ha–Shem* by Shimon Huberband (translated from the Hebrew by A.E.).

who disobeyed the "new" laws laid down by the Gestapo, e.g., keeping open the stores after hours and on Sundays, not wearing the Jewish Star armband, not removing the hat when passing a German, suspected of smuggling and the like.

In February 1942, rumors spread that all those imprisoned were in danger of their lives. Nahum's children sent letters to Warsaw to the *hasidim* (devotees of the Rabbi of Ger) to intercede for their father. They raised a fund of 50,000 marks to ransom their father—a bribe which generally brought results—but not this time. The situation looked very grave indeed.

In the middle of February the Gestapo turned to the head of the Judenrat (Jewish Council), Dr. Lemberg, the prominent and respected medical doctor of the Kehillah (community), to select ten Jewish prisoners to be hanged publicly on Purim day (March 3, 1942). The Jews were aghast at the order. They joined in fasting and prayers. They invoked the Almighty by heartrending recitation of psalms, dispatched messengers to Warsaw to avert the sentence, but to no avail.

Even more bitter and tragic was the lot of Dr. Lemberg and the members of the Judenrat for, in effect, they were charged with the choosing of the ten to be sacrificed. They debated the options but they were helpless. Were they motivated to save their own skins? This suspicion seemed unlikely, for Dr. Lemberg (and his colleagues) were known as men of integrity. Most likely they were impelled to prevent a blood bath for it was known that if the order was not followed, all will be killed. The Judenrat cast lots and ten men drew death sentences. Among them was Nahum Eliyahu Zilberberg.

When Nahum learned that he would be sacrificed to save his fellow Jews, he was seized with unearthly joy. He began to sing and urged his nine colleagues to join in song, and they were inspired to do so. (When news of this incident reached the Warsaw Ghetto, it inspired the poet Itzhak Katzenelson to write a famous poem based on this event which is a part of his stirring elegy, The Song of the Slaughtered Jewish People, see above, p. 219.)

On Tuesday, the Fast of Esther (March 2, 1942), ten gallows were constructed in the marketplace. Consistent with their fiendish plan, the Gestapo ordered the auxiliary Jewish police to set them up. The next day, Purim 5702, at nine in the morning, the SS, *Volksdeutsche* (natives of German origin), and Polish police invaded the ghetto and drove all the Jews therein, old, young and infants, to witness the public hanging. At eleven, the auxiliary Jewish police brought the ten martyrs to the gallows. The victims arrived singing and crying out aloud intermittently that they were favored and happy because their death will save the life of the townspeople.

All the Jews wept, their heads bowed with grief. The murderers ran about in a fury whipping and flogging all who wept, bowed their heads or turned away from looking. All were forced to look on with open eyes to the execution.

The Jewish police were compelled to serve as the hangmen. The gruesome act lasted forty minutes. Dr. Lemberg had to confirm publicly that each man had breathed his last breath. When the macabre performance was over, Dr. Lemberg was propelled to the platform of one of the gallows and commanded to explain why the death decree was justified. Twice he fainted but he was resuscitated and driven to speak on until the finish.

The martyrs were left hanging until the evening. During the day all the inhabitants of the town, Jewish and non-Jewish, school pupils and teachers, were made to march around the square while the gallows creaked under the weight of the martyred dead. It was as if they joined in the groans of pain and grief of all who mourned the murder of their holy brethren whose innocent lives were snuffed out by the descendants of Haman.

# The Fateful Decision: Life or Death

*The last three spiritual leaders of Warsaw: the revered Rabbi Menahem Zemba, Rabbi Samson Stockhammer, and the youngest, Rabbi David Shapiro, met in the home of Mr. Stolzman, a member of the Jewish Council. The latter informed the Rabbis the "good news" that the highest Roman Catholic Authority in Poland had obtained permission to rescue them from the certain death that awaited the Jews. Some time later K. Shabbatai visited Rabbi David Shapiro, the only one who survived . . .*

I can see sitting here in front of me Rabbi David Shapiro, a brand plucked from the conflagration, a living memorial to the mighty struggles of those three great souls. He sits in his study, surrounded by his books, as he had in the early days in his father-in-law's home. Yet his soul is still in that room in Warsaw, together with those of his two friends, and perhaps not with theirs alone. I had the feeling all the time that he was with those souls whose lives depended upon that decision; with the souls of his wife and four children.

His face became inflamed. The words poured from his mouth.

From *As Sheep to Slaughter* by K. Shabbatai.

Clearly, he still sat in the Warsaw room. He remembered every detail of what was said, although, in fact, very little was said. For the most part, they sat in silence. The silence had something in it of the silence of the three friends of Job who came to comfort him and sat for seven days without speaking. Then, Rabbi Shapiro spoke to me, or rather, he cried aloud and his cry did not seem to be directed at me, but to come out of the void and be swallowed up by it again. It was as though the man were casting up his soul's account for the thousandth time. And in the middle of his description of that silent consultation, and what was said in that mysterious room, he literally returned to Stolzman's room. In his words, I could recognize overtones of longing and pain, remorse and exultation, and above all, joy, the joy of anguish and the joy of mighty deeds. He said, "The (Rabbinic) Court had considered the matter with due seriousness. For anyone who does not believe in God, it was a very simple matter. Yet for those who had made their account with Heaven, it was quite a different matter."

As he spoke, he returned to that mysterious room and the other two. "At that time, I forgot my wife and children," the voice cried out again . . . "I forgot them, quite simply and literally forgot." I knew these words were addressed to those who were lost because of that "forgetfulness"; and who had come here to demand a reckoning. "As surely as your eyes can see me," the voice pleaded, "I forgot . . ."

But he had not yet finished. "Actually, those moments were far more important and grave than the matter itself. Whether we should save ourselves or not was less significant than what happened to us then, during those brief hours." For he did not know how long the meeting had lasted. "Maybe it was a moment, maybe three hours. It seemed to us all like a year." He confessed that very often he returns to those moments and that room. When he does so, he returns from a different world where other winds are blowing, winds that are entirely different from those that were blowing in that doomed city in the Germany of 1945.

The silence (of the three Rabbis in the room) was broken. He was the one who broke it, for from his books he had learned to understand the soul and spirit of man. He knew that light and darkness are always at war in the human soul; that under such conditions there could not be any firm and absolute "yes" or strong, unflinching "no." He confessed to me that he was afraid there might be, God forbid, some other thought in the hearts of his comrades, or, more exactly, fragments of thoughts. And so he broke the silence. He did not wish any such fragment of thought to take on reality. And he was absolutely justified in being the first to speak, for he was the youngest of the group. His family were all still with him. All of them knew how much this young rabbi loved his home and children. It was fitting for him to speak first.

He began, "I am the youngest one present. My words are not binding

294

on you. We all of us know perfectly well that we cannot help these folk in any concrete way whatsoever. Yet by the very fact that we stay with them, and do not forsake them, there is a kind of support, perhaps a bit of the only real encouragement that exists. I don't have the strength to abandon these people."

They were plain, straightforward words, to suit the situation. And then came the end. Simple words, also, which had already been said, and will be spoken, times without number, by honest people whose faith supports them. "There is no place empty of Him, so shall we be hidden from God? The same God Who is there, is here."

As the man uttered the words, an intolerable weight fell from the hearts of all three. Not another word was spoken. They only wept, a great torrent of tears that came from their hearts; a weeping for misfortune and a weeping for joy. They wept because they had been punished by seeing themselves brought to this pass, and because they had been given the strength to make this decision. In that hour, their souls were elevated among those of the pure and holy martyrs of our people; in that hour, when the only words they uttered were, "There cannot be any negotiations on this matter . . ."

# Emanuel Ringelblum's Martyrdom

*J. Hirszhaut, a Jewish journalist, records a memoir . . .*
I remember well the spring days of the year 1944. The air, on the eve of Passover, was filled with a sun-warmed serenity which might indeed instill hope in the hearts of the people who had languished under the bloody yoke of the Nazi occupant for many years . . .

But this spring air had no effect on Dr. Emanuel Ringelblum and his wife and son, who had just landed in the Pawiak prison. By the morning of their second day we had already learned of Ringelblum's presence in the death cell. Ringelblum's name was widely known and honored among the Jewish prisoners in the Pawiak, not only because among them were many Jewish intellectuals thoroughly familiar with Ringelblum's scientific work, but also because Ringelblum had become famous for the leading part he had taken in the social and welfare work in the Warsaw ghetto.

From *Martyrs and Fighters*, edited by Philip Friedman.

In spite of the fact that the Pawiak was completely cut off from the outside world, the news . . . circulated among us that Ringelblum had been hidden, together with thirty-two other Jews, in a bunker under a Polish gardener's house on Grojecka Street. For sheer vengeance the gardener's mistress, who had had some sort of quarrel with her lover, had informed the German police . . . It was even reported that the gardener himself was hanged by the Germans on the spot, right after the Jews were found.

The Jews in the Pawiak were determined to save these new victims from death. But, alas, what possibilities did we have left? Our only hope was Gutman.[1] He was to go to the commander and beg him to assign Ringelblum to some work. Well, it was easy to settle the matter with Gutman. He had known Ringelblum, and when he learned that Ringelblum was in the Pawiak, he was overcome with grief.

"Something," he exclaimed, "must be done," and he started right away to try to think of a way to get through to the commander, Pietsch.

And indeed, Gutman began to search feverishly for an opportunity, and our hopes soared high that Ringelblum might soon rally us. In the meantime we decided to send Ringelblum a comforting message, but it was almost impossible to penetrate through the doors of the death cell. As disinfecting clerk, I was sometimes able to find plausible reasons for entering the various sections of the prison. But I was at a loss to invent a scheme to approach the doors of the death cell. Anyway, I resolved to overcome all obstacles and to break through to Ringelblum in order to convey to him the message of the last Jewish community in Warsaw.

The task was not an easy one, but I finally managed, that same evening, to enter Ringelblum's death cell. My stay there was a very brief one, it lasted hardly a few minutes, but these few minutes have engraved themselves on my memory forever.

The chamber was jammed with people, apparently these were the Jews whom the Germans had seized with Ringelblum in his bunker. Ringelblum himself was sitting on a straw mattress close to the wall, on which hundreds of names had been scratched out by nails. These were the names of the persons who had made their final journey through this cell. On his lap Ringelblum was holding a handsome boy. This was his son Uri. When I approached Ringelblum, I told him, without losing any time, whose messenger I was. I remember how astonished Ringelblum was to learn that there were still Jews left in the Pawiak.

Then I told him that we were making attempts to take him in with us.

"And what will happen to him?" he asked, pointing his finger at his son. "And what will happen to my wife who is in the women's section?"

What could I answer him? We all knew well that even if we succeeded in taking Ringelblum out of there and bringing him to us as a shoe-

[1]of the *Judenrat*.

maker or tailor, his family would still be doomed. My silence conveyed the truth to him, and he added right away:

"Then I prefer to go the way of *Kidush ha-Shem* ["Hallowing His Name"] together with them."

Later he told me how he had been tortured by the Gestapo. The bandits wanted to extort from him the addresses of the persons with whom he was in contact on the "Aryan" side. They inquired about his recent activities. Ringelblum remained silent and did not reveal anything; therefore, they had beaten him murderously for three days. He showed me black and blue spots all over his body, the results of the savage beatings.

In the middle of our conversation he suddenly asked: "Is death so hard to bear?" And then, a little later, he went on with a voice broken from despair:

"What is this little boy guilty of?"—and he again pointed his finger at his son—"It breaks my heart to think of him."

I stood helpless before Ringelblum, I did not know what to answer, and a wave of sorrow swept over my heart.

# Jewish Law and the Holocaust

The responsa literature[1] dealing with Holocaust problems has yet to receive the treatment it deserves. And it is precisely through this literature that we are able to begin to understand the problem of Kiddush Hashem during the Holocaust, in all its manifestations and ramifications.

For example, Rabbi Zvi Meislish tells of a problem involving life and death on which he was called upon to rule at Auschwitz:

"On Rosh Hashana Eve in 1944, 1,400 boys were taken to an isolation block. The following day, the first day of Rosh Hashana, a rumor spread throughout the camp that that evening the boys were to be taken to the gas chamber and crematorium. There were many adults in the camp whose last surviving son was among these boys, and all day they hovered desperately around the isolation block hoping for some miracle.

"A simple Jew came up to me and said: 'Rabbi! My only son is in

[1]Questions and answers pertaining to the Halakha (Law).

From *Jewish Resistance During the Holocaust*, Proceedings of the Conference on Manifestations of Jewish Resistance, Yad Vashem. Article by Joseph Gottfarstein.

there, and I have a chance to save him. But I know that if I do so, another boy will be sent in his place. So tell me, according to Torah Law, am I permitted to save him? I will do whatever you say.'

"Fright took hold of me on hearing this question, which involved a matter of life and death. I said to him: 'My dear, how can I rule on such a matter? When the Temple stood, only the Sanhedrin had the power to rule on life-and-death matters; while here I am in Auschwitz, without a single book of law to check, and without other rabbis to consult, and without even a clear mind . . .'

"But the man wept and pleaded with me to give him an unequivocal ruling, while I begged him to stop insisting, for I could not do so. At last he said: 'Does this mean that you do not permit me to ransom my son? If that is the case, then I gladly accept the verdict.'

"I strenuously objected, but he continued to insist that I give him an unequivocal answer. Finally, seeing that it was no use, he said almost ecstatically:

"'Rabbi, I have done what the Torah has commanded me to do: I have asked the rabbi; and there is no other rabbi here to ask. If your honor is unable to tell me that I am permitted to ransom my son, that is a sign that he cannot find firm ground in the law for doing so. For if the law were clear on the matter, your honor would certainly tell me that I am permitted. In other words, then, the law forbids me to do so. That is enough for me, and my son will be burnt according to the Torah and the law, and I accept this lovingly and joyfully, and I am not doing a thing to save him—all as the Torah commands.'

"I begged him in every way not to put the responsibility for his decision on me. But he went on talking in the same vein, finally erupting into heart-rending weeping, and he kept his word and did not ransom his son. And all that Rosh Hashana day he went around talking happily to himself about how he had been given the privilege of offering up his only son to God, and how, although he had an opportunity to ransom the boy, he was not doing so because he saw that the Torah did not permit him to do so, and God would reckon this like Abraham's readiness to sacrifice Isaac and Isaac's readiness to be sacrificed, which had also happened on Rosh Hashana."

Rabbi Ephraim Oshry, author of *She'elot Uteshuvot Mima'amakim*,[2] was asked in the Kovno Ghetto (among other questions), concerning people who had been compelled by the Nazis to destroy and otherwise desecrate Torah Scrolls, whether they were required to observe a fast on this account. He was also asked whether, in ghetto conditions, it was forbidden to cook on the Sabbath; whether one who commits suicide in the ghetto is entitled to a full Jewish burial; whether it is permitted to make *Tzitzit* (ritual fringed garment) from wool stolen from the Nazis;

---

[2] *From the Depths: Questions and Answers on Jewish Law* (pertaining to the Shoah).

whether those living in ghetto hovels and holes were required to put *Mezuzot* at the entrances to their places; whether it was permitted, under duress, to teach Nazis Jewish sacred literature; whether it was permitted to save one's life by accepting "Aryan papers"; whether the *Kaddish* mourning prayer had to be recited over infants who had died; whether it was permitted to eat *hametz* (bread and other food containing leavening) during Passover in the ghetto; whether it was permitted to perform an abortion in order to save the pregnant woman from deportation or summary shooting.

The Jews of the Kovno Ghetto who asked these questions were, obviously, of the stricter sort, those who did not lightly waive the obligation to observe the different precepts and tenets of Jewish Law. May they not be thought of as having needlessly sought the difficult way or piled up restrictions, for Jewish Law not only does not require this where life itself is involved, but expressly forbids it!

The ordinary observant Jews also showed, at various opportunities, their readiness—unqualified and unreserved—to die for the Sanctification of the Name. And large numbers of them did so unobtrusively, almost casually . . .

There is a variety of reasons for not condemning here those who did not stand the test, reasons which add up to what the Talmudic Sages warned us in Pirkei Avot (The Ethics of the Fathers): "Do not judge your fellow unless you have been in his shoes" (2:44).

When the Rabbi of Grodzisk was being led to the death chamber in one of the German death camps together with thousands of other Jewish men, women and children, he asked and was given permission to speak to the doomed throng. He said:

"Brothers and sisters! One of the Talmudic Sages already said: 'May the Messiah come, but I do not want to be there when it happens.' That wise man did not wish to see all the terrible suffering which the Jewish People would have to endure before the coming of the Redeemer. But he could allow himself such a request: in his time, the Redemption was still far off. Today, however, as we stand on the very threshold of the Redemption; today, as we cleanse without blood the path on which the Redeemer will come; as with our ashes we purify the People of Israel so that it will be fit and worthy to welcome our True Messiah—we are forbidden to say this. On the contrary—we must rejoice at having been given the privilege of paving the way for the approaching Redeemer, and accept this opportunity to sanctify God's Name. So, Jews, let us joyously recite 'Hear, O Israel' and sing 'Ani maamin' ('I believe with perfect faith in the coming of the Messiah . . .')."

And with this song on their lips they moved toward the gas chambers.

# Kiddush Ha-Hayim
# (Sanctification of Life)

## The Indestructible Dignity of Man

The Lithuanian Yiddish writer, Pesah Marcus, tells of the last *Musar*[1] talk delivered in the Slabodka Musar-Yeshiva on the outskirts of Kovno. It was there, moments before the German invasion, that the *Rosh Metivta* (Headmaster) Rabbi Nahum Yanchiker, spoke at length about the dignity of man created in the image of God and the significance which this had for Lithuanian Jewry.

His students posed many objections:

—Let our Master now teach us; does he not see that man is little lower than a wild beast? How can you, Rabbi Nahum Yanchiker, speak at this very moment about the dignity and nobility of man? The Nazi murderers slaughter Jewish babes without mercy. Yet, you continue to upbraid us with words of chastisement—we, who are careful with regard to even the least important property of others? You continually demand that we behave in the best possible way and that we work unceasingly to amend our moral flaws, for we have not yet reached the level of true humanity. Will you not realize that in but a few moments it will be shameful to be called a "man"? Lift up your voice, therefore, and hurl this challenge against Heaven: why are we punished so much and so exactingly?

Rabbi Nahum Yanchiker thought it wrong even to mention the vile name "Nazi" in the holy Yeshiva. Yet, he alluded to the questions as he continued his discourse.

—Were the world to behave in a fit and proper manner, we here in Slabodka might allow ourselves to ignore the task of moral improvement and withdraw from continual combat against the obstinate arrogance of the evil impulse; but, at this moment when wickedness is so universal, who will preserve humanity if not Slabodka? . . .

—Yet, despite the dignity of man which you, Rabbi Nahum, our guide and leader, have built and maintained as a beacon tower and despite much righteousness which should have defended us at this time

---

[1]Exercise of moral discipline.

---

From *Judaism*, Summer 1970, by Joseph Gottfarstein.

of trial, Slabodka is now ringed and besieged and cannot resist the forays of these evil beasts.

The Germans stormed and murdered their way into Lithuania, and the windows of the Yeshiva rattled to the omnipresent roar of their artillery-pieces. The Yeshiva students observed in astonishment that their Rabbi remained serenely calm. He immersed himself in the *Mikveh*,[2] put on his Sabbath clothes, inspected the *Mezuzot* on the Yeshiva door-posts and the fringes of his private prayer shawl. But they discerned also that beneath his outer clothing he wore his burial shroud . . .

Rabbi Nahum took a deep breath and continued his last *Musar*-talk with his students:

—A man must be especially wary lest the evil ones besmirch his soul. He must not, therefore, abjure (renounce) his own body and despair of life. No! It is just now—at this moment—that you should regard your body as precious and preserve it even more carefully than before. At the very same time, you must elevate the level of your love and concern for your souls. It is through this elevation, by your increased love of the body and love of the soul, that you will be readied for the highest rank of spirituality. But, if you do not attend to your body, how then will you attend to the welfare of your soul?

Rabbi Nahum, master of the most profound *Musar,* then spoke of the sanctification of God's name. The door of the Yeshiva opened suddenly and a frightened voice was heard: The Germans are coming!

Rabbi Nahum Yanchiker stretched himself up to his full height and proclaimed in a commanding voice:

—With the full weight of the authority granted to me as your Rabbi, I command you to leave me here. You must flee and save yourselves! Take heed of your bodies and your souls. Do not place your lives in danger unnecessarily because of the lightning bolt that strikes from without, but do not think for one fleeting instant that you must sacrifice your lives for inner spiritual matters. I beseech and adjure you to remember always those of our people who fell at the hands of the murderers. It is not for man to judge which one of them shall be a saint and which not. Everyone slaughtered by the wicked ones is to be judged a saint. My dear students, always remember the Nehardea[3] of Lithuania, the Yeshiva of Slabodka. And when the world returns again to stability and quiet, never become weary of teaching the glories, the wisdom, the Torah and the Musar of Lithuania, the beautiful and ethical life which Jews lived here. Do not become embittered by wailing and tears. Speak of these matters with calmness and serenity, as did our holy Sages in the *Midrash,* "Lamentations Rabbati." And do as our holy

---

[2] ritual bath.
[3] Babylonian center of learning in the early centuries of the Christian Era.

Sages had done—pour forth your words and cast them into letters. This will be the greatest retribution which you can wreak upon these wicked ones. Despite the raging wrath of our foes the holy souls of your brothers and sisters will remain alive. These evil ones schemed to blot out their names from the face of the earth; but a man cannot destroy letters. For words have wings; they mount up to the heavenly heights and they endure for eternity.

# Readings

*The Last of the Just* by André Schwartz-Bart (Atheneum, 1960), is one of the world acclaimed novels which was translated in a score of languages. Based on the mystic legend of the Thirty-Six anonymous immortal just men, on whom the world rests, it traces Jewish suffering, defiance, and *Kiddush Ha-Shem* from the early middle ages to the gas chambers of Poland.

*Sparks of Glory* by Moshe Prager (Shengold Publishers, 1974), is a collection of stories on Jews who clung to their faith and survived the Tragedy.

# 14. | CHILDREN IN THE HOLOCAUST

About two million Jewish children perished in the Final Solution: half were deliberately murdered, the rest died from starvation and disease.

The Nazis subjected children and adults to the same treatment. Many parents, knowing that certain death awaited them in the camps, helped their children to flee, reasoning that they might have a chance to survive even if left entirely on their own.

As a result, all over Europe Jewish children wandered in search of hiding places—terrified, helpless, hunted like animals. Some found refuge with friendly Christian families or in convents and monasteries. Some wandered alone, still others joined together in small groups. They foraged for food and clothing; many were orphans, all were destitute. Most of them had no idea whether any members of their families were still alive.

Emaciated, dressed in rags, living in an emotional void, they were sustained by one hope: the Promised Land. At the end of the war, Jewish organizations devoted themselves to locating, identifying, and aiding the children who had survived. Thousands were brought to Israel by Youth Aliyah. Because of the horrors they had experienced, many of them were in a state of shock—listless, disoriented, neurotic, sometimes even half-savage—and much loving effort was necessary before they could again lead normal lives.

The children who had found refuge with Christians posed another kind of problem. In some cases they had been baptized, and the Church refused to give them up. In other instances, the children and their foster families had developed warm ties with each other, and the children refused to rejoin their real families. Some of these heart-rending cases

304

became world-famous, most notably the case of the Finaly brothers, brought up as Catholics and kidnapped by their Jewish relatives in 1953.[1]

# The First Ones

*They, the children of Israel, were the first in doom and disaster;*
*most of them without father and mother*
*were consumed by frost, starvation and lice;*
*holy messiahs sanctified in pain . . .*
*Say then, how have these lambs sinned?*
*Why in days of doom are they the first victims of wickedness,*
*the first in the trap of evil are they!*

*The first were they detained for death,*
*the first into the wagons of slaughter;*
*they were thrown into the wagons, the huge wagons,*
*like heaps of refuse, like the ashes of the earth—*
*and they transported them,*
*killed them,*
*exterminated them*
*without remnant or remembrance . . .*
*The best of my children were all wiped out!*
*Oh woe unto me—*
*Doom and Desolation!*

*An Extract From "Lament of the Martyred*
*Jewish People"*
*by Yitzhak Katzenelson*

[1] Read Nicholas Bavdy, "The Affair of the Finaly Children," *Commentary*, June 1953. The story was fictionalized in a best-selling novel entitled *Michel, Michel* by Robert Lewis (New York: Simon & Schuster, 1967). Another novel, *The Children of Mapu Street* by Sarah Neshamit (Philadelphia: Jewish Publication Society, 1970), dramatizes the story of the "convent children."

From *The Massacre of European Jewry.*

# Children in the Ghetto

*A survivor and witness at Eichmann's trial, Dr. David Wdowinsky was a practicing psychiatrist in a hospital of Warsaw. "Of all the gruesome scenes and sounds of the ghetto that remained with (him), the saddest and most haunting of all were the sights of the children." . . .*

A common sight on the streets of the Ghetto as I walked from my home to the hospital was children in doorways, leaning against walls, or standing stark still with arms outstretched begging for a piece of bread. Emaciated from hunger, too weak to move, they would stare at me with glazed eyes, their faces like stone. Their blown up bellies were often too heavy for their spindly bony legs, and their little backs would curve in unnatural, graceless positions. Many of them developed pedatrophy, a rare children's disease in civilized countries, which aged infants into senility with hair sprouting from their wizened old faces. Only in primitive societies, hundreds of years ago, do we have any record of this malady. It became prevalent in the Ghetto.

Children were smugglers. Their thin little bodies could be pushed through a crack in the Ghetto wall, or through a sewer, to the other side to beg for bread or some flour amongst the Poles. Sometimes children were sent by their mothers over the wall. The mother talking to the child all the way, gauging his descent from his voice, was often the witness of his death, as a German sniper aimed a gun at the easy mark climbing down the wall. So went a provider of many a Jewish family. Sometimes the child was successful in his mission and in one way or another obtained a loaf of bread from a kindly Pole, only to be attacked by another hungry child or even an adult upon his return into the Ghetto. Such fights were frequent in the Ghetto streets, and often nearly to death. Wasn't this the battle for survival?

One who has not heard the crying of hungry children at night outside the windows of apartment houses, has not heard the piercing anguish of an animal in peril. These were not human cries, nor human weeping. It was the hunted baying of creatures facing death, clinging to life with the only physical effort still left to them—the whistling howl that ripped out of their empty bellies and contracted entrails to fill the troubled night with frightful tremor.

From *And We Were Not Saved* by David Wdowinsky.

## Children in the Holocaust

Ghetto children grew wise before their time. They knew so much of what was not meant for them to know, not yet. A little girl of four cuddled in the arms of her father in a packed train whispers into his ear: "Is this the train to Treblinka, daddy?" And indeed it was the train to Treblinka, the train that brought an end to her fears.

During my one day stay at Auschwitz on the way from one concentration camp to another, I had the opportunity to see the infamous Dr. Mengele at his macabre game, doling out life or death with his forefinger. Like a metronome, this finger swayed from side to side as each victim appeared before him. With a face molded in ice, without a flicker of an eyelash, only the finger was alive like an organism in itself, possessed of a strange power, it spelled out its ghastly message.

How quickly the children sensed the sinister purpose of this game. There were a group of them with us from the Radom Concentration Camp who miraculously somehow survived. They watched the movement of this finger with transfixed fascination, and when it came their turn to stand before this automaton, they stretched out their pitiful arms and pleaded and beseeched: "Please, Herr General, look how strong I am . . . I can work . . . I want to live . . . see how strong . . ." But the calculating machine in human guise swayed the finger to the left and they all went to the gas chamber. German economy had no use for the fruitless efforts of a twelve year old.

There were children who were so sensitive and proud that even starvation could not make them bend their spirit. A son of a friend of ours, who was my godson, was left daily alone to shift for himself. His father was on the Russian side and his mother was working. We suggested that he share our midday meal. The first time his mother brought him to us, and it was understood that thereafter he was to come alone. Several days passed, and when the boy did not come, I went to find out what had occurred. He faced me with tears in his eyes. "I don't want to come like a beggar . . . like the other children, with their arms outstretched all the time." It took a little persuasion to make him realize that he would be a welcome guest.

One cannot mention the children in the Ghetto without touching on the singular situation of the orphanages and the people who headed them. It did not take very long to realize that the children of the orphanages would become one of the first victims of German efficiency. They were just mouths that had to be fed and no value to anyone. The adults who took care of these children kept up a desperate struggle to make their lives as normal as possible, with no hint of the impending doom that was their fate . . .

# Left Among the Dead

*Hadassah Rosen (Age 15; 8 when the war began) . . .*

        I was born in 1931 in the town of Chechanowicz to Mordechai and Nechama . . . Our family consisted of four: my parents, a sister three years younger and I. My father was a teacher. When I was six I started to go to the Tarbut[1] school and did very well. In 1939 we moved to a town called Podborodz, in the district of Vilna. I continued my studies in the school there. I had very few worries; I studied and played with other children my age.

But our happiness vanished quickly. The year 1941 brought the opening of the most frightful chapter in the history of humanity, especially of the Jews. On June 22 the German barbarians crossed the Russian border and at once German planes darkened the sky over our heads and rained fire on our town. My father said: "Well, children, the Germans are approaching; who knows what the future holds for us!"

The very next day the Germans occupied the town. Profound fear seized all the Jewish residents; they went around terribly frightened and depressed. One morning my little sister and I went and took our places in the bread line. We were among the first in line. We were happy at the thought that soon we would return to Mother with a loaf of bread. But suddenly a German officer came over to us and asked: "Are you Jewish?" "Yes," I replied in despair. "Then go to the end of the line. Whatever bread remains will be distributed to Jews!" My sister burst out crying . . .

One day a group of us girls went to the river to bathe. A German approached us and scolded us sharply: "You Jews cannot allow yourselves such luxuries. You ought to be locked up in a ghetto. At home, in Germany, no Jew dares show himself in the street. Get away from here, go on!" We pulled our clothes on and hurried home. When I got home my mother told me that the Germans were establishing a ghetto in two of the filthiest side streets of the town. The Germans actually jammed thirty people into one wretched room. Day in day out they led groups of Jews out to do forced labor. Germans stood over them with clubs in their hands. Each overseer tried to outdo the others in cruelty . . .

[1]a Hebrew Zionist Day-School System.

From *Ehad Ba'eer U'shnayim Ba'mishpacha* ("One in a City and Two in a Family") by Benjamin Tennenbaum (Translated).

308

The minutes turned to hours and the hours to days and weeks. Every moment seemed like a whole year. Time went on as usual and soon the raids began. First they gathered forty men and ordered them to dig pits in the forest. The Lithuanians said that these were ditches for defense purposes. As soon as the Jews finished their job they were sent home. At midnight, however, the very same men together with their wives and children were taken to the pits in the forest and shot . . .

It was very dark that night. Grief settled over the whole town; weeping could be heard on all sides. Outdoors the wind wailed sadly. No one heard the wolves devour the bodies.

In the morning a neighbor's daughter, Reichka Lazarovich, burst into our house and announced that Velvel Abramowitz was in their house; he had escaped from certain death. He had told them, she said, that a great many Germans and Lithuanians had encircled them, ordered them to stand with their backs to the pits they had dug, and shot them down. It was very dark all around and only he alone had managed to escape. This incident affected everyone in the ghetto of Podborodz terribly; we were horrified but completely helpless.

Life in the ghetto continued. The Germans forced all of us to wear white ribbons with a yellow star of David. But those Fascists soon noticed that this was too attractive. They then changed the order and forced us to sew a large patch on our chests and on our backs with the letter *J* in the center, for *Jude* (Jew).

One day my friend Basha Liubitch and I arranged to meet at 9 o'clock in the morning and go outside the ghetto to obtain some books to read. How should we go? With the patches on? But Jews were strictly forbidden to venture outside the ghetto limits and anyone caught breaking this rule was shot on the spot. Take the patches off? That, too, meant risking our lives. Nevertheless we took the chance and crossed over without the patches. Even though the Germans had issued stringent orders that Jews and dogs were not allowed to walk on the sidewalk, we strolled along and no one paid any attention to two girls walking together. Each of us brought back five books which meant weeks of reading in the ghetto. That was how the days passed for us at that time. We were not permitted to attend school. All we had was our books for reading.

But our sojourn in the ghetto did not last long. It was Friday evening, three days before the Day of Atonement, *Yom Kippur*. Suddenly there was a great commotion in the ghetto. The Germans employed lies and deceits to trick the Jews into going to their deaths. In every ghetto they used a different set of lies. In ours they declared they were taking us to a camp called "Paligan" which was near Podborodz.

Some of the Jews caught on and began escaping wherever they could. The murderers then split up into groups and made the rounds of our homes. They herded all the victims into the *bet midrash* (synagogue). Father, Mother, my sister and I hid in the attic of the *bet midrash.* We took some food and water with us and father disguised the trap door so that it would not be noticeable. All night we sat there shaking with fright, listening to the wails of the crowd below. To our sorrow we could do nothing to help.

In the morning we heard the sound of someone creeping softly up to our door. At first we were terrified but then we saw that it was some Jews searching for a place to hide. So we helped them in . . . We squinted through the cracks in the boards and saw them shoving the Jews into wagons. Whoever was slow getting into the wagon was clubbed to death with the butt of the gun. The sight I saw that morning through the chinks in that attic will remain etched in my memory as long as I live. It was very early in the morning; soon afterward we heard volleys of shots. That was how they killed the Jews they took in wagons out of the ghetto of Podborodz.

It upset me terribly to be sitting there in my hiding place while they were killing off people with whom I'd been living in the ghetto, children with whom I had studied, played, walked. Now they were gone, gone forever . . . They would never return. How I longed to get up and go to them! To avenge their innocent blood! . . .

We stayed throughout the Sabbath and Sunday, and now it was Monday morning. The baby (in our midst) was miserable and cried bitterly. Every day the murderers made a tour of the neighborhood. Those beasts of prey had not yet had their fill of Jewish blood. They were still sniffing around; perhaps someone was hiding in this place or that. I think they heard the baby crying and that brought them as far as our hiding place. They asked whether we were armed. Then one decided to have the ladder removed. "Sure, let them jump!" his companion mocked.

Father went down first and took me too. Everyone else came then; some jumped, some crawled, some were tossed down by others. They stood waiting for orders. Three wagons were brought. The baby's mother went up to one of the fiends and implored him: "Let the child go. He hasn't done anything; he's only a baby!" But the murderer's heart of stone was not moved. He replied: "He's a baby now but he'll grow up to be a Jewish man. That's why we have to kill him!"

Desperate and without hope we got into the wagons. Some wept; I sat listless. The final parting from my beloved parents and sister left an empty void within me. Mummy, Papa, little sister! how can we say good-bye? Where are they taking us?

Was this really the end for us all? I could not bring myself to believe it. We are riding . . . riding . . . and will soon arrive . . . Mummy, don't cry, we'll soon be together again . . . No, no, this is not the end . . .

These were the moments between life and death.

As the wagons rolled down the streets I looked at the passersby and thought to myself: In what way are we different from other human beings? All of them are alive, walking around free as air. Why are we sentenced to death?

Finally we reached Malinowa Street which bordered on the forest. This is where they are going to bury us, I thought. We were ordered to stand in a line. I sat so as not to see them shooting at us. The moment came. The shots thundered in my ears. After a while I realized I was still alive and I started to run. I rolled into a small ditch and lay still, listening to the moans of those who had only been wounded.

Not far from where I lay a German was going down the line shooting the wounded. Then the shots ceased. The murderers went away and I remained alone with twenty dead. How my heart ached to know that among the dead were my own mother, father and little sister. I had always thought (as all children do) that my mother would never die. Mother meant eternity. Yet here was an end I had never thought possible . . . Gone, gone forever. I had lost forever all that was dear to me. Where could I turn? I had no one left . . .

It seemed that the only thing I could do was go and give myself up to the Germans. I had no other alternative. Contradictory feelings of life and death were warring within me. One voice seemed to whisper: See, everything is alive, birds are singing, all of nature is gaily attired. It is good to be alive. Liberty will yet come some day and all will be well again! But another voice denied this: Death is all around, corpses everywhere. Wherever you turn you will tread on a body. Death has taken your own parents and sister . . .

Haunted by these feelings I got up and moved away from that spot. I got as far as the station beside the forest when I saw a villager. He gave me a piece of his bread and I bit into it at once. But he realized I was Jewish and told me to move on. I ran.

In the field I saw some peasants digging up potatoes. I went over to them and started digging potatoes too. The woman was glad to have an extra worker for nothing but she was also afraid too. Anyone who had anything to do with even one single Jew faced certain death. I begged her to let me go as far as her house; from there I would continue alone. She demanded money. I had none. But then I remembered that before we left, Mother had put two dresses on me, one on top of the other. Taking one off, I gave it to her.

She walked through the town and across the bridge with me several paces behind her, so that in the event the Germans recognized me and shot at me, she would not be hurt. And so I left the town. I had one last glimpse of our house where I had spent my happy childhood years. The sound of my footsteps was like sobs. Everything was gone. Grief overwhelmed me. I could not utter a sound.

# What Happened to Me in My Childhood

*The Hon. Edwin H. Samuel writes: "I found this document by chance during a visit in December of 1949 to the children's village of Hadassim . . . about an hour's run from Tel Aviv . . . The village was established by the Canadian Hadassah Federation of the Women's International Zionist Organization. . . .*

*"While being shown around the school, I was told by the headmistress of a boy now at the school who had had an extraordinary escape in Poland. He had remained alive only through having been hidden in a cupboard for five years by a Polish Gentile woman. This seemed to be something to write about; but the headmistress said that the boy himself—Ephraim—had already written about his "childhood." He is only eleven years old now. I asked to see the record and, after looking through some old papers, she found a copybook on the outside of which, in straggling Hebrew letters, was written 'What Happened to me in my Childhood—Ephraim Shtenkler.' Inside was the diary . . . After I heard it read aloud, it seemed to me such an extraordinary document that I decided nothing I would write myself could possibly be as important.*

*"So I sat down and translated it into English, trying as far as possible to preserve the archaic Biblical Hebrew in which the diary is written . . ."*

In Bialisk my family was rich and we also had a shop and life was pleasant. But when the Germans came, they took away the shop and drove us from town to town, as they did the other Jews of the Diaspora, until we came to Zvirdje. And in Zvirdje, they took a part for slaughter and a part they kept alive. Although my father, my mother, and I were in the part that was kept alive, my aunt was in the part that was due to be taken to slaughter. But she was saved, as we had a German acquaintance and my father asked him to arrange for my aunt to be transferred to our part and he spoke with the officer and they transferred my aunt to the part where we ourselves were. And the part that was taken for slaughter died and the part that they kept alive was given places in which to live and my father began to work again and we earned our bread. After some months the Germans came and made a ghetto: then my mother fell ill with a serious illness.

One day we heard that the Germans were coming and we broke

From *Commentary Magazine*, May 1950.

through the walls of the ghetto and some escaped. And my father heard that they had broken through the walls of the ghetto and he took me and gave me to a certain Polish woman and said to her, "After the war I'll come back and fetch my son." And the Germans came to our house and my mother lay in bed and they said to her, "Get up!" And she said "How can I get up? I haven't any strength left." And they killed her in her bed and the neighbors heard of this and told my father and my father told it to the Polish woman, and the Polish woman, when she sent me away, told it to me.

And, meanwhile, when my father went with me to the Polish woman, he was delayed among our neighbors and I went by myself to the Polish woman. I don't know what was said between my father and his friends, but the next day my father came and told me that they had killed my mother and murdered women and babies and that now the Germans were seizing those children that remained and were putting them into tarpaulin bags and putting them on the train in a closed wagon and there they were stifled. And my father said "It's good that my only son doesn't suffer as the other children suffer; but it's bad that all the Jews suffer; for why are the Jews to blame?" The Polish woman kept silent, but nevertheless she didn't like Jews and when my father had left she said "Damned Jew! When will you get out of here?" and she knelt before the Virgin Mary.

On the day after I was hidden in the cupboard my father came again. He didn't talk much. He only said "I'll come every day at noon," but those were the nicest words he spoke. And he really did come. Once he brought me a pocket knife and once he brought me a ball. And the Polish woman used to take all these things away from me and give them to her two daughters, one of whom was twelve and the other about sixteen. And my father used to come in silence every day.

One day my father didn't come and on that day the Polish woman wanted to send me away, for she said "The child's father doesn't give me any money, so I'll take him and hide him until he gets sick of it." And she put me under the bed. Suddenly we heard a voice, steps, and a ring at the door. The Polish woman was pleased and opened the door and saw there a friend of my father's and when she asked him, "Have you brought any news?" he said "I have," and she said "Speak," and he began to talk and said "That child of Shtenkler's, I don't know where he is." And when I heard my family name, I peeped out and saw the Polish woman's face was pale. So I understood that she was frightened, for she said "Is there anything else the matter?" as she wanted to change the subject. And he said, "There is," and her face paled and she said "Speak," and he said "Another damned Jew is dead." So she asked "Who?" And he said "Mr. Shtenkler." The Polish woman gaped. She didn't close her mouth: She only closed the door in the man's face and took me and flogged me with her husband's belt, saying "I'll drown you in the well this very day."

In the end she saw that the Germans weren't clearing out, so she was afraid that they might catch me and ask me where I'd been. She knew that then I'd say that it was she herself who had kept me and then they'd hang her and me. So she wanted me to break my heart so that I'd die and she could then tell the Germans that she had found me dead. But, to my luck, she didn't succeed, for I was then a mere child and couldn't understand what death was, so I wasn't afraid of it.

Weeks and months and years passed and nothing happened. And I lay either in the cupboard or under the bed. One day, the elder daughter of the Polish woman came in in a panic and entered with a rush and threw open the door and said "Mother!" And the Polish woman, who was cooking, asked "What's the matter?" "Mother! Mother!" shouted her daughter, "I saw a Hebrew mother and child who were walking hand in hand and a German told the child to let go of his mother's hand and get into the bag. The mother began to plead with him and the fine German shot at the two interlocked hands and took the child and put him in the bag and put him in a wagon and the mother . . ." And the girl stopped speaking. And the mother said "Why don't you go on?" And she said, "I'm afraid that's what'll happen to you, Mother. In the name of the Virgin Mary and Jesus her son, won't they punish us?" And she continued by saying, "And the mother he stabbed." I was terrified. I was then already six years old and understood a good many things and thought that perhaps that's what they did to my mother and I became as white as chalk. After the elder daughter had gone to play outside I wanted to cry, for I envied her. It was already three to four years that I hadn't gone out of doors.

And so the years passed and nothing happened and I was already seven years old, but I didn't know how to walk. And one day, when the war was nearly over, the Polish woman invited in a certain Jew who used to make woolen things—stockings, trousers, sweaters and so on. She thought that he would make her many sweaters, so she invited him in. And when I heard that someone had come I peeped out and in so doing shifted the bottles in the cupboard. He asked "What's that?" I was terrified: I thought it was some German. And the Polish woman, who by this time really wanted to drown me in the well, said, "It's a mouse!" Then he heard the noise again and asked again and she replied "A mouse" until eventually I peered out and he saw me. Then he got furious with her and said, "Why, that's the son of my friend Mr. Shtenkler!" The Polish woman grew pale. And he took me to his house in the next street and asked me what I wanted to wear and I said "Clothes." He laughed and said "Good!" He took out some stockings and a few sweaters and went to the market. I waited for him in his

314

house. Eventually he came with a parcel in his hand. He took off my rags and dressed me in the sort of clothes one wears in this world.

After a day the acquaintance decided to look for a doctor who would treat me so that I could walk. So we got on the train and went to Katowitz. But all of a sudden a man came and spoke to him. In accordance with what he said, I was taken in another train and, like an arrow from a bow, the train flew along, straight to a children's home. There they told him to wait a little. He waited patiently and in the end went into the office and telephoned and after a brief hour a doctor appeared, the one who actually did treat me.

Month after month passed until I learned to walk. It was hard for the doctor to treat me and for me to walk. After I knew how to walk not so badly, they took me to a place in the high mountains and taught me and some other children how to walk. The other children taunted me because I didn't know how to walk properly. I used to walk with crooked legs: my feet were twisted backwards . . .

So passed a whole month. One day they heard a ring on the telephone. This was a woman who had known my father. She wanted to take me away to her house; but this was not allowed as they were afraid that something might happen to my legs. Only after some time did they send me there. She was already waiting for me. She was pleased at my arrival—hale and well—and she took me to her house. There I spent some time. And on one occasion my father's best friend came and took me to *his* house and, later, he took me to a children's home. There I had a good time. Once, three acquaintances of my father's came and told me things and gave candy to the children who were in the room. They told me that I was already a big boy and that I couldn't stay any longer in this [children's] home. And the three men took me and put me in the [youth] movement[1] and I was there for a number of months. And the friend who was in the Polish Army thought of taking me away from there and took me for a day. And when he saw that there wasn't any other place, he went with me to one of the nearby places and said to me, "Go and tell the headmistress that I'll come back in the afternoon and talk with her." And I went and told her that, and the headmistress said "Get out of here!" and chased me away with insolence. So I went to the market. There I met my acquaintance and told him about it. And he said, "Well then, come now," and we went.

When we came she didn't want to receive him and didn't open the gate. So he told her that he'd put me into a rival [youth] movement. She screamed and shouted but nothing was of any use. For we had already got into a train; so we traveled along and came to the railway

[1]The reference here, and subsequently, is to the Jewish youth groups that are affiliated with various Jewish political parties.

315

station. There we found a certain woman who was travelling to one of the places from which it was possible to go where I had to go. This was a children's village in Poland. The place was lovely. There were woods and hills nearby: on one hill was a cemetery. And the time passed pleasantly.

I was there a long time. There the children didn't tease me as they used to in the previous children's home. Now I already knew how to walk. One day they asked which were the orphan children. I was among those children. Everyone wanted to know why they asked us this. Eventually we learned that we were going to be the first to go to Palestine. We were extremely glad. The children danced and sang. The next day all us orphan children got into a car and we rode to the railway station . . . We traveled for many hours; and meanwhile I slept. Eventually we arrived. I heard shouts. There a small ship awaited us—I should rather say a large boat—and they put us all into it and we started off. And the boat rocked on the surface of the quiet waves. All of a sudden the boat heeled over to one side. All the things on the top fell off but by a miracle we were saved. There was a certain soldier there from the Russian Army. He knew what to do in moments like this. And the day passed and it grew darker, until night fell. We were sleeping and the soldier couldn't sleep and went up on top and suddenly he saw something shining in the water. He pulled out his revolver and took his torch and looked and saw and behold there were mines in an enormous line! In that instant he let out a yell. At the sound of that shout we all woke up . . .

It was clear that each youth movement hated the other. Occasionally a fight broke out with knives and sticks. They used to hand out terrible punishments there: for example, spending the whole night out on the balcony. After days of punishments and beatings for every little thing we left Berlin and came to a terrible place where every blow ended in a battle with knives and sticks as if they were gloves. In the end, when they saw that our movement was the quietest of the lot, they gave us a place that really took the prize for beauty . . . There each group was in its own house and they used to beat us for every stupid little attack on the other groups. The names of the groups were Trumpeldor . . . Bar Kochba . . . I was in the Trumpeldor group.

One fine day all us orphans set out for Palestine. They told us many tales then—endlessly. They woke us up at midnight and the car came in the morning . . . Eventually we arrived at one of the camps. The next day we traveled and went on and on without end. But I remember that finally we came by train to France. I don't remember the journey. It was for three days and three nights. And from France we went on board a ship and on the ship no one suffered from seasickness. And when we came to Palestine we were obliged every one of us to hold on to all the bits of paper, even to the numbers of our rooms . . .

How excited we were when at last we were assembled on parade and disembarked from the ship! And we came to Ahuza—the children's village on Mount Carmel and from there to the children's village at Hadassim. And after some time more children arrived.

At that time, I was given a piece of paper and this was written on it . . .

To the Director General of the American
   Jewish Joint Distribution Committee
P.O.B. 640, Jerusalem
Subject: The Child Ephraim Shtenkler
Sir,

In reply to your letter . . . we have to give you particulars of the above-mentioned child and of his family. The child's name is Ephraim Shtenkler, born in Bialisk. Father's name Jacob: mother's name Bilha. Only child. The child is ten and a half years old. He was in the hands of Poles in Zvirdje from the age of two to the age of seven. After the Russian occupation, a certain Jew came and took him and put him in a children's home. The name of his father and mother he learned from a friend of his father's in the Polish Army. These are the details known to the child. We shall be very grateful if you will be good enough to inform us if nevertheless any of the child's relatives are traced.

Yours faithfully
The Secretariat
The Children's Village.

About a month after that letter came, I found my uncle.[2] How delighted the whole village was!

But everyone tells the story differently. One says that my uncle came to me and inquired.

Once I told several of the children all this and it was they who suggested that I should write all this down.

---

[2] The uncle mentioned here was a skilled building worker who had gone to many of the immigrant camps looking for Ephraim. By sheer coincidence, he had been engaged to do some repair work in the school and asked his usual question "Is there any boy here called Ephraim?" and the two were rejoined.—E.S.

# Death and Deception at Theresienstadt

. . . Old people's transport. Ten thousand sick, crippled, dying, all of them over 65 years old.

It's horrible everywhere. The rays of sun fall exactly on my bunk and reach on farther, I try in vain to get away from them into the shade. Today I shan't go and report for "Hilfsdienst". I haven't left out a day yet, but I am too exhausted to stand the sight of misery and suffering again. The old people's transport, the young people cannot volunteer. Children have to let their old parents go off and can't help them. Why do they want to send these defenceless people away? If they want to get rid of us young people, I can understand that, maybe they are afraid of us, don't want us to give birth to any more Jewish children. But how can these old people be dangerous? If they had to come here to Terezin, isn't that enough, can't they let them die in peace here? After all, these old people can't hope for anything else. Half of them will die in the . . . train.

Under the window the Gestapo are shouting and beating people, closing the street. Another group is going. There they are, carrying stretchers, two-wheeled carts with corpses, baggage and the "corpse cart." The street that had blossomed in the August heat was wrapped in heavy, filthy dust. Baggage, stretchers, corpses. That's the way it's been going on for a week. The dead on two-wheeled carts and the living in hearses. Everything is transported in hearses here: dirty linen, bread— we have one, ourselves, in the Home, standing in the courtyard. It has a sign on it, "Youth Care." What's the difference, one cart is like another, and so far no one seems to wonder at it, but to transport people in them, that's a little too much. Again a cart is rattling under the window. In front there are two transport leaders, then the load, and behind are some "Sick people's bearers," and the "Hilfsdienst." And what among the baggage, is that corpses? No, one is moving, through the cloud of dust whirling around the cart a yellow armband shines through. Who could forget that! We met them daily in the kitchen, on crutches, blind, with a little bowl in hand, begging a little coffee, soup, scraping out the unwashed troughs and kettles that had food, or else raking through piles of rotting potatoes, peelings and garbage. Yes, that's who it is,

---

From *Terezin Diary* by Helga Weissova-Hoskova.

skinny, hungry, miserable, there they are, alive in hearses. How many of them will arrive at their destination, how many will return? All the hearses are in operation. For the first time they have a load of the living, and yet this is more fitting than anything else. Where will these human wrecks land, where will their bodies be laid down? No one will weep over them, no one pities them. Some day perhaps there will be a mention of them in readers, and then the only title that would do them justice would be: Buried Alive.

. . . The barracks by the physical culture hall must be cleared out, a special dinner is being cooked, and the reception centre is getting ready. They say some Polish children are coming. This is all incomprehensible. Why, and how does it happen that they are brought here from Poland?

They came yesterday at 5:00 o'clock. No one is allowed near them. In the night they called some nurses, house representatives and doctors. Besides these no one is allowed near their barracks. We managed to get some news from the barracks. None of the children can speak Czech, we don't even know if they are Jewish children or Polish or what. You can see them a little from the fortress wall, and then they went in the morning to the reception centre. They look awful. You can't guess how old they are, they all have old, strained faces and tiny bodies. They are all barelegged and only a very few have shoes. They returned from the reception centre with their heads shaved, they have lice. They all have such frightened eyes.

. . . Yesterday they were taken off, doctors, nurses and house representatives with them. All during quarantine their food was cooked separately and clothes and shoes were collected for them. The only one who came in contact with them was Fredi Hirsch, who is now sitting in a bunker in the camp command for it.

Where they came from we never found out, nor where they were taken either. Rumours were circulating about deportation to Palestine, but no one believes this. They have gone. All that is left is a few lines scribbled on the wall of the barracks, that hardly anyone can figure out.

. . . The commission, because of which a transport left and the three-layer bunks were torn down, has departed, and I believe they were satisfied. They didn't see through very much, stayed scarcely a half day, but that seems to have been only a rehearsal. The camp command issued new orders about the "beautifying campaign" that must be finished in two months.[1]

It's ridiculous, but it seems that Terezín is to be changed into a sort of spa. I don't know why I was reminded of the fairy tale, "Table, set yourself!" But that is how everything seems to me. The orders are

---

[1]Theresienstadt served as a showplace for visitors. These preparations were made for the visit of a commission of the Swiss Red Cross.

received in the evening, and in the morning everyone's eyes are staring with wonder, where did this or that thing come from? For three years it never occurred to anyone that streets might be named anything but Q and L. Where the Magdeburg barracks or the Jäger or any other barracks was, every little child knew. But all of a sudden the Germans had an idea and over night signs had to be put on every corner house with the name of the street, and at crossroads arrows pointed.: Zum Park, Zum Bad, etc. We don't say Magdeburg barracks any more, but BV; I don't live at L410, but Hauptstrasse 10. The school by the construction headquarters that had served as hospital up to today, was cleared out over night and the patients put elsewhere while the whole building was repainted, scrubbed up, school benches brought in, and in the morning a sign could be seen afar: "Knaben und Mädchenschule." It really looks fine, like a real school, only the pupils and teachers are missing. That shortcoming is adjusted by a small note on the door: "Holidays". On the square the newly sown grass is coming up, the centre is adorned by a big rose plot and the paths, covered with clean, yellow sand, are lined with two rows of newly painted benches. The boards we wondered about for so many days, trying to puzzle out what they were for, turned into a music pavilion. We even have a café with the fine sign "Kaffeehaus." And all the shops got new names of firms. The houses will also be painted, they have already started in Lange-strasse. The barracks behind "Magdeburg," where they had had pro-duction and processing of mica, have become a "dining hall." The girls that are specially employed there to heat up the food must wear white caps and aprons. The physical culture hall was turned into a restaurant with carved furniture, plush chairs in the foyer, and big vases with bouquets. On the second floor there is a library and reading room and little tables on the terrace with coloured sunflowers. They have already got quite far in painting the houses. Some of the Danish inmates' rooms got equipment. In two of the barracks some bunks and shelves were painted yellow and they got blue curtains. In the park in front of the Infants' Home they put up a luxury pavilion with cribs and light blue, quilted covers. In one room there are toys, a carved rocking chair, and so on. Then there is a pool, a merry-go-round and see-saws. None of us can explain why they are doing all this. Are they so concerned about that commission? Perhaps we don't even know how good the situa-tion is.

# An Extraordinary Diary by a Boy, in Four Languages (Ghetto Lodz)

*Avraham Benkel, a survivor of Lodz, returned to his old home to find his neighborhood vandalized and plundered by the Poles. He found a boy's diary now in the possession of Yad Vashem.*

The unknown diarist wrote in the margins of a French novel because no other paper was available. The first entry, in English, was dated May 5, 1944. It was written in a remarkably good English for one whose mother tongue was clearly not English. Why did he start the diary? Why in English? It is obvious that the first entry was written as an act of confession for what, in the ghetto, was an unspeakable crime, and that it was written deliberately in a language his sister (who also kept a diary) could not read.

"I committed this week an act which is best able to illustrate to what degree of dehumanization we have been reduced—namely, I finished up my loaf of bread in three days, that is to say on Sunday, so I had to wait till the next Saturday for a new one [the ration was about 33 ounces of bread a week]. I was terribly hungry. I had a prospect of living only from the soup ladled out to forced laborers which consist of three little potato pieces and two decagrams [three-quarters of an ounce] of flour. I way lying on Monday morning quite dejectedly in my bed and there was the half loaf of bread of my darling sister . . . I could not resist the temptation and ate it up totally . . . I was overcome by a terrible remorse of conscience and by a still greater care for what my little one would eat for the next five days. I felt a miserably helpless criminal . . . I have told people that it was stolen by a supposed reckless and pitiless thief and, for keeping up appearance, I have to utter curses and condemnations on the imaginary thief: 'I would hang him with my own hands had I come across him.'"

Days later the unknown diarist started writing also in Yiddish:

"After my fantasy of writing in various languages, I return to my own tongue, to Yiddish, to *mammelushen* (mother tongue) because only in

From *Yad Vashem News*.

Yiddish am I able to give clear expression, directly and without artificiality, to my innermost thoughts. I am ashamed that I have for so long not valued Yiddish properly ... Yet even if I could rob Homer, Shakespeare, Goethe and Dante of their muses, would I be capable of describing what we suffer, what we sense, what we experience, what we are living through? Is it humanly possible? ... It is as possible to describe our suffering as to drink up the ocean or to embrace the earth. I don't know if we will ever be believed ..."

At the end of May he turned his hand to Hebrew, a highly literary Hebrew ...

"Despair increases steadily as does the terrible hunger, the like of which mankind has never yet suffered. With complete assurance we may say that they have not left us even a jot of that which is called body or soul."

The land of Israel and the Hebrew language had gradually drawn him despite his confessed earlier posture as a "socialist cosmopolite." "Dear old Hebrew and ancient Palestine has an irresistible fascination for me," he had written in English, attributing his change of attitude to his conviction that the Poles would not "overnight forget their age-long hate towards the group of people named Jews."

As English was the language in which he confessed the thoughts that he wanted to keep from his sister and in which he wrote his accusations against the "civilized" world and as Yiddish was used to express the depth of his suffering and anguish, so Hebrew was used for philosophical musings, for dialogues with God.

"In truth, the world deserves only that we spit in its face and do as Arthur Zygelbojm did (p. 172) ... Sudden death, hunger, deportation, interrogations, labor, queues, etc., etc., wreak havoc in the ruined vineyard of Israel, among the poor remnant. Will you, o God, keep silent? How can you, having seen it? Send your wrath against these savages, against this scum of humanity, and wipe them out from under your heavens! Let their mothers be bereaved as they have caused Jewish mothers to be bereaved for no cause at all ... Let the verse come to pass: "Blessed is he who seizes and smashes your infants on the rocks" (Psalms 137:9).

He put the same sentiments into Hebrew verse:

> Eli, my God, why do you allow it?
> Why let them say
> You were neutral?
> In the heat of your anger
> The same that makes
> A harvest of us,
> Are we the sinners
> And they the righteous?

# Children in the Holocaust

*Can it be?*
*Is that the truth?*
*After all, you have enough*
*Intelligence to understand*
*That it is not thus:*
*That we are the sinned against*
*And they are the guilty.*

The Russians were advancing all along the eastern front, the Allies were pressing up the Italian peninsula. News of the invasion of Normandy reached the ghetto the same day. "It is true," the diarist wrote on June 1, answering the question with which he had ended the previous day's entry. "The fact has been accomplished. But shall we survive? Is it possible to come out of such unimaginable depths, of such unfathomable abysses?"

Hope and despair alternated. Germany's collapse seemed assured. Why were they hanging on so insanely? The Russians were approaching, their artillery could be heard in the distance. But death and danger continued to stalk the ghetto . . .

His English entry reads:

"We are so tired of 'life.' I was talking with my little sister of twelve and she told me: 'I am very tired of this life. A quick death would be a relief for us.' O world! world! what have those innocent children done that they are treated in such a manner? Truly, humanity has not progressed very far from the cave of the wild beast."

And again, two days later: "I write, and I don't know if tomorrow I shall be able to read it." His doubts had a solid basis: another thousand ghetto inmates were to be taken away to "work." "How one need understand 'work' in the Teutonic interpretation we already know. O heaven! For how long yet will this senseless cruelty be continued? Oh, if it is to turn out this way, why didn't we die five years ago?" . . .

Now, as the Russians came ever closer, the last days of the ghetto approached. Thousands of Jews were being "resettled" daily—to forced labor deep inside the Reich, the Germans claimed. But the majority of Jews had begun to fear, and correctly, that the "resettled" Jews were being sent to be exterminated. It was hard to accept this ultimate cruel reality. We read in the diary:

"Thank heavens that I'm no realist, for to be a realist is to realize, and realizing the whole horror of our situation would have been more than any human being could endure. I go on dreaming, dreaming about survival and about getting free in order to be able to 'tell' the world, to yell and 'rebuke,' to tell and to protest" . . .

The diarist writes of watching a woman arguing in a store about a buckle she wanted for the rucksack she would take with her for deportation, and of his anger at the shopkeeper who commented

323

callously after she had left without buying it that she would not have to carry her rucksack for long, "because those who go to heaven have no need of the like."

Even at the height of his own problems, the diarist could spare an agonizing thought for the thousands of Hungarian Jews who, it was rumored, were being shipped into Poland by the trainload for extermination.

The "resettling" in Lodz was stopped, then resumed again. "My heart is cut to pieces when I perceive how terrible my little sister is tormented. She lost literally everything—no stockings, no clothes . . . no tenderness. O you poor orphan, and what you have to suffer by my unjust treatment, because of my destroyed nerves. You, poor being, must help yourself with substitutes: instead of stockings some rags; instead of boots, some wooden contrivance . . . God seems to have abandoned us totally and left us entirely to the mercy of the heartless fiends. Almighty God, how can you do this?"

The deportations continued. Hans Biebow, the German officer in charge of the ghetto, solemnly told the Jews that this time they would all be "resettled," not as the others had been (which Jews knew all too well meant to death camps) but to work for German war industry. He gave them his solemn promise that this would be so. He asked the assembled Jews whether they were willing to work for the Reich, and they replied, "Jawohl."

"I thought about the abjectness of such a situation. The Germans . . . managed to transform us into such low grovelling creatures as to say 'Jawohl.' Is it not better *not* to live in a world where there are 80 millions of Germans? O shabby miserable human! . . .

"When I look on my little sister my heart is melting. Hasn't the child suffered its part? She has fought so heroically the last five years. When I look on our cozy little room tidied up by the young intelligent poor being I am getting saddened by the thought that soon she and I will have to leave our last particle of home."

That, the last dated entry in the diary, written on August 3, 1944, ended with a cry of anguish: "Oh God in heaven, why didst thou create Germans to destroy humanity? I don't even know if I shall be allowed to be together with my sister. I cannot write more. I am resigned terribly and black spirited."

The last entry in Hebrew had been dated July 31: "Although I write a broken and hesitant Hebrew, I cannot but write Hebrew, for Hebrew is the language of the future, because I shall use Hebrew as a Jew standing proudly upright in the Land of Israel! . . ."

# Workshop in Vilna: The Will to Live

*Yitzhak Rudashevski of Vilna was fourteen when he began his diary, in Yiddish, in June 1941. He wrote it in a small notebook and covers approximately two years through April 1943. It was translated into Hebrew and into English from which the following entry is reprinted . . .*

*Wednesday the 27th, 1943 . . .*

Today our class visited the ghetto workshops on Rudnitski 6. Here the ghetto industry is concentrated. Here our professionals work. This is the foundation of our existence . . . Everything bears the stamp of serious work. Here they are repairing parts of machines. And here they are producing iron badges with numbers which every Jew like a cow will put on around his neck. Here is a forge with two fires . . . The Jewish smith stands and makes horseshoes for the German army. One of the engineers is showing us around. He is angry, strict, shouts at the workers like a boss. Murer's[1] command here extends over everything . . . Here is the department for wood turning, for the clog (wooden shoes) industry. How beautiful, how enticing is the work, the carving, how things are being created before my very eyes! But for whom?

Here are the rooms for the manufacture of furniture. They have their own ghetto history. Murer and the district commissars of Vilna order furniture here. The most beautiful furniture sets are manufactured here. Women stand and polish the beautiful pieces of furniture. Children unintentionally throw down a strip of molding. "Children," says a worker, "dear Murer will come and make a fuss." Murer comes to the workshops very often. And a cold fear engulfs the workshops. You can hear a pin drop. Only the tools speak nervously: "Murer is coming." And he appears in the workshops like a misfortune, like a storm, like a mad, wild beast. He commands the workers to do physical exercise and the workers with good reason practice every day and crawl under the table and above the table . . . Here everything is carried out silently, sullenly . . . People do not sing at their work.

Now a new department is being built where the only specialist, a Vilna Jew, will make artificial hands and feet. "Let's hope that the department will have large orders," people joke.

[1] The Nazi commandant.

From *The Diary of Yitzhak Rudashevski* (Vilna Ghetto).

As I left the workshops I carried away the impression of the power of the will to live which emanates from everything here. It seems that everything I have seen here was created solely by will . . . I think about the fate of our work. Wolves and dogs benefit from the products of our work. But our will to live that I have discerned today proclaims distinctly that the dark game will cease, that finally a specter such as the one named Murer will disappear . . .

# "God Truly Protects Us"

*Anne Frank, age 13, was one of eight hidden in a "hole" in a loft of an Amsterdam dwelling. Her spirits were buoyed up by her friend, Peter, her parents and by writing her diary which began June 14, 1942 and ended August 1, 1944. She addressed her entries to an imaginary "Kitty." Her diary, which was found on the floor in a pile of papers is a moving document depicting her adolescence and maturation. It became a classic and was translated in many languages and read by millions. It was dramatized and filmed. The house in which she lived has become a monument to her memory and is visited by the Dutch people and tourists from all over the world.*

*Tuesday, 11 April, 1944*

Dear Kitty,

My head throbs, I honestly don't know where to begin.

On Friday (Good Friday) we played Monopoly, Saturday afternoon too. These days passed quickly and uneventfully. On Sunday afternoon, on my invitation, Peter came to my room at half past four . . . There was a beautiful Mozart concert on the radio from six o'clock until a quarter past seven. I enjoyed it all very much . . .

On Sunday evening Peter and I went to the front attic together and, in order to sit comfortably, we took with us a few divan cushions . . . We seated ourselves on one packing case. Both the case and the cushions were very narrow, so we sat absolutely squashed together . . .

At half past nine Peter knocked softly on the door and asked Daddy if he would just help him upstairs over a difficult English sentence. "That's a blind," I said to Margot, "anyone could see through that one!" I was right. They (burglars) were in the act of breaking into the warehouse. Daddy, Van Daan, Dussel, and Peter were downstairs in a

---

From *The Diary of a Young Girl* by Anne Frank

flash. Margot, Mummy, Mrs. Van Daan, and I stayed upstairs and waited.

Four frightened women just have to talk, so talk we did, until we heard a bang downstairs. After that all was quiet, the clock struck a quarter to ten. The color had vanished from our faces, we were still quiet, although we were afraid. Where could the men be? What was that bang? Would they be fighting the burglars? Ten o'clock, footsteps on the stairs: Daddy, white and nervous, entered, followed by Mr. Van Daan. "Lights out, creep upstairs, we expect the police in the house!"

There was no time to be frightened: the lights went out, I quickly grabbed a jacket, and we were upstairs. "What has happened? Tell us quickly!" There was no one to tell us, the men having disappeared downstairs again. Only at ten past ten did they reappear; two kept watch at Peter's open window, the door to the landing was closed, the swinging cupboard shut.[1] We hung a jersey round the night light, and after that they told us:

Peter heard two loud bangs on the landing, ran downstairs, and saw there was a large plank out of the left half of the door. He dashed upstairs, warned the "Home Guard"[2] of the family, and the four of them proceeded downstairs. When they entered the warehouse, the burglars were in the act of enlarging the hole. Without further thought Van Daan shouted: "Police." A few hurried steps outside, and the burglars had fled. . . .

The married couple . . . would probably have warned the police: it was Sunday evening, Easter Sunday, no one at the office on Easter Monday, so none of us could budge until Tuesday morning. Think of it, waiting in such fear for two nights and a day! No one had anything to suggest, so we simply sat there in pitch-darkness, because Mrs. Van Daan in her fright unintentionally turned the lamp right out; talked in whispers, and at every creak one heard "Sh! sh!"

It turned half past ten, eleven, but not a sound; Daddy and Van Daan joined us in turns. Then a quarter past eleven, a bustle and noise downstairs. Everyone's breath was audible, otherwise no one moved. Footsteps in the house, in the private office, kitchen, then . . . on our staircase. No one breathed audibly now, footsteps on our staircase, then a rattling of the swinging cupboard. This moment is indescribable. "Now we are lost!" I said, and could see us all being taken away by the Gestapo that very night. Twice they rattled at the cupboard, then there was nothing, the footsteps withdrew, we were saved so far. A shiver seemed to pass from one to another, I heard someone's teeth chattering, no one said a word.

There was not another sound in the house, but a light was burning

[1]The hide-out was behind it.
[2]Those appointed to guard the hide-out.

on our landing, right in front of the cupboard. Could that be because it was a secret cupboard? Perhaps the police had forgotten the light? Would someone come back to put it out? Tongues loosened, there was no one in the house any longer, perhaps there was someone on guard outside.

Next we did three things: we went over again what we supposed had happened, we trembled with fear, and we had to go to the lavatory. The buckets were in the attic, so all we had was Peter's tin wastepaper basket. (Van Daan went first, then Daddy, but Mummy was too shy to face it. Daddy brought the wastepaper basket into the room, where Margot, Mrs. Van Daan, and I gladly made use of it. Finally Mummy decided to do so too.) People kept on asking for paper—fortunately I had some in my pocket!

The tin smelled ghastly, everything went on in a whisper, we were tired, it was twelve o'clock. "Lie down on the floor then and sleep." Margot and I were each given a pillow and one blanket . . . (The smell wasn't quite so bad when one was on the floor, but still Mrs. Van Daan quietly brought some chlorine, a tea towel over the pot serving as a second expedient.)

Talk, whispers, fear, stink, flatulation, and always someone on the pot; then try to go to sleep! . . . I awoke when Mrs. Van Daan laid her head on my foot . . . Then Mrs. Van Daan sat in the chair and her husband came and lay on my feet. I lay thinking till half past three, shivering the whole time . . . I prepared myself for the return of the police, then we'd have to say that we were in hiding; they would either be good Dutch people, then we'd be saved, or N.S.B.-ers,[3] then we'd have to bribe them!

"In that case, destroy the radio," sighed Mrs. Van Daan. "Yes, in the stove!" replied her husband. "If they find us, then let them find the radio as well!"

"Then they will find Anne's diary," added Daddy. "Burn it then," suggested the most terrified member of the party. This, and when the police rattled the cupboard door, were my worst moments. "Not my diary; if my diary goes, I go with it! . . ."

There is no object in recounting all the conversations that I can still remember; so much was said. I comforted Mrs. Van Daan, who was very scared. We talked about escaping and being questioned by the Gestapo, about ringing up, and being brave.

"We must behave like soldiers, Mrs. Van Daan. If all is up now, then let's go for Queen and Country, for freedom, truth, and the right, as they always say on the Dutch News from England. The only thing that is really rotten is that we get a lot of other people into trouble too. . . ."

Four o'clock, five o'clock, half past five. Then I went and sat with

[3]The Dutch National Socialist Movement.

Peter by his window and listened, so close together that we could feel each other's bodies quivering; we spoke a word or two now and then, and listened attentively. In the room next door they took down the blackout. They wanted to call up Koophuis at seven o'clock and get him to send someone around. Then they wrote down everything they wanted to tell Koophuis over the phone. The risk that the police on guard at the door, or in the warehouse, might hear the telephone was very great, but the danger of the police returning was even greater . . .

The points were these:

Burglars broken in: police have been in the house, as far as the swinging cupboard, but no further.

Burglars apparently disturbed, forced open the door in the warehouse and escaped through the garden . . .

Everything went according to plan. Koophuis was phoned . . . Then we sat around the table again and waited for Henk or the police.

Peter had fallen asleep and Van Daan and I were lying on the floor, when we heard loud footsteps downstairs. I got up quietly: "That's Henk."

"No, no, it's the police," some of the others said.

Someone knocked at the door, Miep whistled. This was too much for Mrs. Van Daan, she turned as white as a sheet and sank limply into a chair; had the tension lasted one minute longer she would have fainted. . . .

Henk and Miep were greeted with shouts and tears. Henk mended the hole in the door with some planks, and soon went off again to inform the police of the burglary. . . .

At eleven o'clock we sat round the table with Henk, who was back by that time, and slowly things began to be more normal and cozy again. . . .

Now there are debates going on all the time in the "Secret Annexe." Kraler reproached us for our carelessness. Henk, too, said that in a case like that we must never go downstairs. We have been pointedly reminded that we are in hiding, that we are Jews in chains, chained to one spot, without any rights, but with a thousand duties. We Jews mustn't show our feelings, must be brave and strong, must accept all inconveniences and not grumble, must do what is within our power and trust in God. Sometime this terrible war will be over. Surely the time will come when we are people again, and not just Jews.

Who has inflicted this upon us? Who has made us Jews different from all other people? Who has allowed us to suffer so terribly up till now? It is God that has made us as we are, but it will be God, too, who will raise us up again. If we bear all this suffering and if there are still Jews left, when it is over, then Jews, instead of being doomed, will be held up as an example. Who knows, it might even be our religion from which the world and all peoples learn good, and for that reason and that reason only do we have to suffer now. We can never become just Netherlanders, or just English, or representatives of any country for that matter, we will always remain Jews, but we want to, too.

Be brave! Let us remain aware of our task and not grumble, a solution will come, God has never deserted our people. Right through the ages there have been Jews, through all the ages they have had to suffer, but it has made them strong too; the weak fall, but the strong will remain and never go under!

During that night I really felt that I had to die, I waited for the police, I was prepared, as the soldier is on the battlefield. I was eager to lay down my life for the country, but now, now I've been saved again, now my first wish after the war is that I may become Dutch! I love the Dutch, I love this country, I love the language and want to work here. And even if I have to write to the Queen myself, I will not give up until I have reached my goal.

I am becoming still more independent of my parents, young as I am, I face life with more courage than Mummy; my feeling for justice is immovable, and truer than hers. I know what I want. I have a goal, an opinion, I have a religion and love. Let me be myself and then I am satisfied. I know that I'm a woman, a woman with inward strength and plenty of courage.

If God lets me live, I shall attain more than Mummy ever has done, I shall not remain insignificant, I shall work in the world and for mankind!

And now I know that first and foremost I shall require courage and cheerfulness!

Yours, Anne

# "Kill Me"

*The event described in this story took place in a village near Lublin, where the author of the account was in hiding. . .*

One afternoon I was sitting on a wall by the 'blue'[1] police station talking with one of the policemen, a pleasant elderly man, when a chit of a boy, not more than seven, walked up to us. He stopped in front of the policeman and said in an almost arrogant manner: "I've

[1]Polish auxiliary police.

From *Righteous Among Nations*, edited by Wladislaw Bartoszewski and Zofia Lewin.

come to report." I looked into the eyes of this child and knew every-thing. But the policeman was not so perceptive ...

"What do you want?" he asked.

"I've come to the police," repeated the boy and added after a while: "that you kill me."

I did not look at the boy or the policeman. I was watching the tops of the trees by the roadside ... It was a fine day. There was peace all around us with no trace of the war. The road was completely empty, all people busily attending to their everyday tasks. Children were either doing their school exercises at home or playing somewhere. And here was this boy, God knows where from. The policeman asked him where he had come from. "From Łęczna ..." The policeman inquired about the boy's parents, brothers and sisters, relatives.

"The Germans have killed them ... mummy was killed by a gen-darme in Piaski. He didn't want to kill me, he laughed and said that he would do it another time. So I went to the Polish police, but the man didn't want to shoot me, he said he didn't shoot chits of a boy ... perhaps you? ..."

The policeman coughed with embarrassment: "Hm ... here, too, we don't shoot snots either," he said finally. He looked around, then glanced at me and read from my eyes that he could trust me.

"You'll go with me," he said in a lowered voice, not looking at the boy.

"Will you shoot me?" the boy asked with hope in his voice.

"No ... be quiet ... You must live, become a grown-up man ... Come on."

Then he turned to me as if he wanted to ask me not to tell anybody. "You needn't worry!"

I sat for a long while on that wall and watched the slightly comic figure of the old policeman in a navy blue topcoat and the child trotting at his side, as if unwillingly. The goodness of that man was no acci-dent—it was deep inside him, just like the vileness of the overwhelming majority of his fellows. I know that he took that poor child under his wing and cared for him without recompense.

# "An Accounting of the Soul"

*This is taken from the diary of a young Dutch orthodox boy, Moshe Flinker (originally written in Hebrew). It gives insights into the spiritual torment and*

331

*hopes, before his death in Auschwitz, and grapples boldly with the eternal problems of suffering and divine justice.*

### December 12, Saturday Evening

Thursday was the last night of *Hanukkah*. My father, young brother, and I lit the candles which we had obtained, though not without difficulty. While I was singing the last stanza of the *Hanukkah* hymn *"Maoz Tzur"* I was deeply struck by the relevance of the words:

> *Reveal Thy sacred mighty arm*
> *And draw redemption near*
> *Take Thy revenge upon that*
> *Wicked people (!) that has shed the blood*
> *Of those who worship Thee*
> *Our deliverance has been long overdue,*
> *Evil days are endless,*
> *Banish the foe, destroy the shadow of his image*
> *Provide us with a guiding light.*

All our troubles, from the first to this most terrible one, are multiple and endless, and from all of them rises one gigantic scream. From wherever it emanates, the cry that rises is identical to the cries in other places or at other times. When I sang *Maoz Tzur* for the last time on *Hanukkah*, I sang with emphasis—especially the last verse. But later when I was on my own I asked myself: "What was the point of that emphasis? What good are all the prayers I offer up with so much sincerity? Please, Lord:

> *"Our deliverance is long overdue;*
> *Evil days are endless;*
> *Redeem us for Thy name's sake," I beseech Thee.*

## On Seeing a Nazi Movie

### December 14, Midnight

Yesterday I went to the movies with my sister. When I was still in The Hague, before it was occupied by the Germans, I didn't go to the cinema much. After the Germans had been in Holland for some time, they forbade the Jews to go to the cinema. Then they began showing anti-Semitic films. I wanted very much to see these movies, but I didn't dare, because my identity card was stamped "J" for Jew, and I could have been asked to show my papers at any time, and for such an offense I could have been sentenced to six months' imprisonment. But

---

From *Young Moshe's Diary* by Moshe Flinker.

here, in Belgium, where I am not registered as a Jew, I can go to the movies. In any case, there is not the same strictness here. When we arrived, only the anti-Semitic cinema proprietors had notices posted in front denying entrance to Jews. Now, however, in front of every theater is posted: "By order of the Germans, entrance to Jews is forbidden."

Even so I went to see the film "Jew Süss." What I saw there made my blood boil. I was red in the face when I came out. I realized there the wicked objectives of these evil people—how they want to inject the poison of anti-Semitism into the blood of the gentiles. While I was watching the film I suddenly remembered what the evil one (Hitler) had said in one of his speeches: "Whichever side wins the war, anti-Semitism will spread and spread until the Jews are no more." In that film I saw the means he is using to achieve his aim. And if nothing happens to counteract his work, then surely the poison will spread in people's blood. The way in which jealousy, hatred and loathing are aroused is simply indescribable. One thing I know if we are not saved now by some miracle from heaven, then our end is as sure as I am sitting here. For not only the body of Israel is being attacked, but also its spirit. The Jews are being made so hateful to the world that nothing that anyone can do will be able to undo his work. When I left the cinema, I realized the nature of the fiend and I knew what I had to do, if—God willing—I can attain my objective.

In the film, Jew Süss says to a young girl: "We too have a God, but this God is the Lord of Vengeance." This is a lie, pure and simple. Our Lord is the same Lord who said: "Love thy neighbor as thyself," but now I pray He may appear as a "Lord of vengeance."

# A Pupil's Complaint

*More than in any other sphere, the attempt to retain normalcy and pretend "as if . . ." marked the Jewish schools until the very end . . . In retrospect, this educational policy appears to the educators themselves to have been a mistake. "Today I know," writes Anneliese Ora Borinska, "how wrong this policy of pretending 'as if' was. However, one must understand that we had to try to impart some sense of security to the children in a world which was collapsing around them . . ." Any attempt to evaluate this educational approach, however, must take into consideration the fact that its proponents did not pursue it out of naive irresponsibility or refusal to face reality—they chose it consciously and deliberately.*

As long as it was possible to maintain regular educational activities, these were directed towards emigration purposes. In the words of the last set of directives issued by the National Union of Jews in Germany, the goal was "to educate the pupils as human beings possessing work skills as well as Jewish knowledge, so that they will be able to contend with the difficult life which lies ahead of them." Could the Jewish educator—or should he—have prepared his pupils also for their encounter with death?

A pupil of the Jewish high school in Cracow accused her former instructors in a poem entitled, "To the Teachers."

*You taught us to strive for a life of ideals,*
*You exhorted through verses and poems*
*To soar on the wings of enthusiasm,*
*To unravel life's innermost secrets.*

*You taught us to love the magic of words,*
*To go into raptures, weeping with awe,*
*To press ever onward and search unrelentingly*
*For the truth and the cosmos unrevealed.*

*You enchanted our spirits with "humanist" phrases,*
*You taught us to worship the glory of genius.*
*For this I am now bowed with suffering,*
*I face the cruel world all helpless and lost.*

*We should have been taught to spring from a crouch.*
*To seize hold of a neck with an iron-strong grip,*
*To strike at the forehead with merciless fist*
*Until lifeless he crumples and falls!*

*You should have taught us to shriek till we're heard,*
*How to crash through a gate that is cracked,*
*How to kill to avoid getting killed*
*And get used to the glitter of blood.*

*O, erudite teachers, men of vast knowledge!*
*Did you really and truly not know*
*That the earth has no place for a humanist?*
*Why did you plant yearning in our hearts?*

*(Hela Blumengraber—to Professor Julius Feldhorn)*

From *Jewish Resistance During the Holocaust,* Yad Vashem Conference Proceedings, April 17-11, 1968. Article by Joseph Walk.

Hela Blumengraber's sentiments are almost the only ones of their kind on record. Most people had quite a different view. Survivors of the Holocaust speak with affection and admiration of their teachers who created for them "an island in a sea of suffering." Parents, too, were grateful to the teachers who stood by their side "during one of our most crucially difficult hours," as one father expressed himself to the headmaster of a school. The truth of one of Buber's[1] sayings was reaffirmed in the tragic context of the Holocaust: "It is not instruction which educates: it is the teacher who educates." Even if the pupils did not always follow their precepts, they did not abandon the teachers who taught them—as the latter refused to part with their pupils, in life or in death.

[1]Martin Buber, (1878-1965), world renowned Jewish philosopher.

# Readings

*Diary of Anne Frank* (Doubleday, 1952), is the most renowned book of its kind. It has been translated into many languages, dramatized, memorialized, and immortalized. The diary is a testimony of a young girl who was permeated with faith in humanity and a better world.

*Young Moshe's Diary* by Moshe Flinker (Yad Vashem-Jewish Education Committee Press, 1970), is the record of a religious teenager who was at home in the Bible and the Jewish heritage and wrote his notebook in Hebrew.

*I Never Saw Another Butterfly: Children's Drawings and Poems from Terezin Concentration Camp 1942–1944* (McGraw-Hill), is a moving document, artistically produced; it affords us insights into the inner world of the imprisoned children. The artistic expressions of the doomed children in art and poetry were selected from the collections of the State Jewish Museum in Prague.

*The Children of Mapu Street* by Sarah Neshamit ( Jew. Pub. Soc., 1970), while fictionalized, is based on authentic experiences, movingly narrated, about a group of children in Kovno, the capital of Lithuania, who are caught up in the blood bath that ensued when the Germans invaded Russia.

*We Want to Live* by Allon Schoener (Worldwide Books, 1969), is a short documentary picture-book stressing Youth Aliyah.

*The Diary of the Vilna Ghetto* by Yitzhak Rudashevski (Ghetto Fighters' House and Hakibbutz Hameuchad Pub. 1973), who was a product of the Yiddish culturalist milieu and was more wordly than his peers. His diary began in June 1941 and ended April 7, 1943.

*One Hundred Children* by Lena Kuchler Silberman (Doubleday, 1961).

# 15. HIDING, "PASSING," ESCAPING, AND RESCUE EFFORTS

Along with all the horror and brutality, the Holocaust also witnessed acts of great humanity, self-sacrifice, and decency. Some non-Jews risked their own lives to help Jewish friends or neighbors. Since failing to report a hidden Jew, or even giving him a drink of water or a crust of bread, was punishable by death, this required great courage.

There were many instances of Gentiles hiding and sustaining Jewish families, often for several years. Hiding places of all kinds were used, including attics, cellars, narrow spaces between two interior walls, barns, haystacks, underground bunkers, etc. Providing food to the hidden Jews was a risky operation, since it might be observed by the Nazi authorities or by local informers. When illness or death struck one of the hidden Jews, or a birth occurred, tensions and ingenuity were strained to the breaking point.

Life in these improvised hide-outs was at best difficult and hard to endure. In many instances, small children could be kept quiet only through the constant use of sedatives. Some hiding places were so cramped and crowded that the inmates had to stand almost immobile for long periods, and took turns lying down. Their leg muscles atrophied from disuse.

"Passing" provided a means of escape for those Jews whose physical appearance and linguistic ability enabled them to mix with the general population as non-Jews. This was often easier for women, since Jewish men, having been circumcised, could easily be identified.

Like trapped animals, the victims of the Nazis sought to escape through

337

any available opening. For a while it was possible to utilize escape routes through Italy and the Baltic countries. These were closed off when Italy entered the war and Germany invaded her neighbors and Russia. Some fortunate escapees were able to make their way across Siberia to Japan and then to Shanghai, where they were interned for the duration. Others were able to escape through Vichy France into Spain, but eventually this frontier was also closed. Lisbon, in Portugal, remained an avenue of escape throughout the Holocaust, but only for those able to acquire the proper documents as well as passage across the Atlantic. Many of these refugees were exploited by swindlers who sold fake documents at high prices.

## RESCUE EFFORTS

Two days after Germany invaded Poland, the Jewish Agency opened an office in Geneva, Switzerland, for rescue operations, directed by Dr. Chaim Pasner. (The overall director of the rescue effort was Chaim Barlas, who worked out of Istanbul.) Pasner was the first to learn about the death camps, and he immediately alerted the office at Istanbul, which in turn informed London and New York. On November 16, 1942, thanks to Dr. Pasner, a group of Polish Jews were exchanged for German prisoners-of-war and were shipped to Palestine. This idea of rescue of Jewish victims through exchange with German prisoners-of-war originated in Geneva and saved hundreds of Jews from Holland, Germany, and Poland. But the rescue of some 4,000 French Jewish children was obstructed by the government bureaucracies in Washington and Switzerland and they were doomed to death.

Dr. Joseph Schwartz, European director of the Joint Distribution Committee, set up an office in Lisbon to help in these escape efforts. He did all he could to alleviate the suffering of the refugees and expedite their departure. Later in the war he went to Budapest to help Jews escape by way of the Black Sea. He also found means of assisting Jewish refugees in Switzerland, the Far East, and Poland, but some of his plans, such as an effort to transport five thousand French Jewish children to the United States, met with only partial success, and others failed completely.[1]

Ira Hirschmann, President Roosevelt's courageous confidential emissary in Turkey, saved forty-eight thousand Rumanian Jews from the internment camp at Transnistria[2] as well as several thousand Hungarian Jews. He was helped by Angelo Roncalli, who later became Pope John XXIII.

Among those active in these efforts were Joel Brand, most famous for

[1]Read Herbert Agar, The Saving Remnant (New York: Viking Press, 1960), chaps. 4–6.
[2]Read Julius S. Fisher, Transnistria: The Forgotten Cemetery (Thomas Yoseloff, 1969).

his fantastic negotiations with Adolf Eichmann, and Rezso Kastner[3] One successful JDC effort involved the exchange of Germans stranded in Allied countries for Polish Jews who possessed "foreign papers," i.e., passports or official letters permitting them to emigrate to Palestine or some Latin American country. In the spring of 1945, the Swiss Red Cross aided the JDC in securing the admission of some twelve hundred Jews from Theresienstadt to Switzerland, while the Swedish section of the World Jewish Congress obtained the release of a few thousand prisoners from Ravensbruck, who were then transported to Sweden by the Swedish Red Cross.

Perhaps the strangest rescue effort involved Felix Kerstin, Himmler's personal masseur and physician, who used his influence over the Gestapo chief to secure the release of many thousands of Jewish and non-Jewish prisoners.[4]

Successes were few, however, and the rescue attempts, though tenacious and widespread, were tragically inadequate. Nonetheless, many who are alive today are living testimonies of the dauntless, stout-hearted men and women who saw them through.

# 14 Months in a Sewer

My father found out that the ghetto in Lvov was to be liquidated at midnight. We went to hide in the basement of a nearby barrack. We usually went down there in the afternoon when mother returned from work and that is where we hid, for we were expecting the big 'operation.' I was seven years old at that time and my brother, Pawel, was three. From that basement we went out to the Peltew River, walked straight ahead until we came to the sewer. It was terribly wet and dark in the sewer when I entered it; I was so terribly afraid and I was shivering from sheer terror. I behaved very quietly all the time but constantly asked my father if it was still far away. There were some stones in the sewer, and yellow worms crawling over them. We put all our things on these stones and sat on them. We felt very bad, water was leaking from the walls, and there was a terrible stench which was impossible to bear. I saw some big rats like chickens which ran near us. At first I was horrified but later I got used to it. Pawel was not afraid at

---

[3]The Stories of Brand and Kastner may be found in Alex Weissberg, *Desperate Mission* (Criterion Books, 1958), and Nora Levin, *The Holocaust* (New York: Crowell, 1968).
[4]See "The Strange Case of Himmler's Doctor," *Commentary*, April 1957.

From *Righteous Among Nations*, edited by Wladislaw Bartoszewski and Zofia Lewin.

all. I was lying in mother's lap and Pawel was on father's knees. This went on day and night for five weeks. We could not move about or stand up. There were twenty other people. Every day, from the first day, some Polish sewer-cleaners brought us food: black bread and margarine. They were very good to us. Since they were afraid that someone might notice them, they used to come into the sewer via different entrances through manholes they opened . . . A carbide lamp constantly burned in the sewer; it was hanging on a hook driven in between the stones. The Poles brought us carbide for this lamp. Daddy brought water in a jug which he carried in his teeth as he had to walk doubled right over. I felt so very bad there; I was not allowed to speak out loud, I could only whisper into mummy's ear . . .

This was in the summer, and when it rained the rain would leak into the sewer and when someone flushed a toilet the sewer would fill with water. Then we had to lean low on the stones near the wall so that the water would not run over us. Pawel was very small at the time and he cried often. Mummy became very worried for she was afraid someone would hear and we would be caught. One time a man who had been hiding out with us became so angry with Pawel that he even threatened him with a revolver. But that did not help for Pawel started crying even louder . . . (Discovered, they fled with the help of their saviors to hide in another sewer.)

In this new sewer we felt much better, had more room, and slept on bunks made of planks which daddy built from boards he found in the sewer. There were four such bunks. I slept with daddy and another man. It was very crowded and uncomfortable; I was cramped like a herring in a barrel. My mummy slept with Pawel and some other woman. We had one carbide lamp which burned day and night. The rats used to eat our bread and when daddy frightened them away with a stick they would run away. And Pawel fed the rats like chickens, throwing them bread crumbs and boiled potatoes. The rats would come very close and squeak. But Pawel was not afraid of them in the least. We had a few plates and a primus stove. All this had been brought by our good sewer-cleaners. One woman cooked soup and coffee and mummy divided it among us so that I was not hungry. Pawel got used to everything and he no longer cried. One grey-haired, bent, old woman fell ill and died. And another woman gave birth to a baby. But it died and it was thrown into the Peltew River. Two girls took turns at "duty" and kept the place clean. The lamp was on all the time so I never knew if it was daytime or nighttime. But I guessed that it must be daytime when the sewer-cleaners came. Whenever it rained, the rain leaked into our shelter by way of a pipe through which we could barely make out some bars and a faint light. Sometimes I saw a ray of sunshine, but it was very pale. Once I went into that pipe to look out at the world but I saw nothing; I only felt a little bit of fresh air. I craved

340

so much for the sun and fresh air that I cannot describe it. I could hear cars drive past right on top of us, I heard people's voices and the gay laughter of children playing. I often thought how happy I would be if only I could play like they did . . .

I became ill with measles, at least that is what mummy said, and Pawel caught it from me, and then he developed a hoarseness. One of the sewer-cleaners brought him eggs; the man had to carry them in his teeth because he had a satchel of food in his hands and he had to crawl on all fours to reach us.

One time the primus stove burst into flame and a fire started. Everyone was very frightened; at the first moment some rags were thrown on the primus, but they caught fire too. Then the primus stove was covered with some burnt-out carbide and the fire was put out. I was very frightened, and Pawel, who was even more frightened than I was, ran up on the highest board and hid there. When the fire had been put out everybody was all smeared with soot and we all looked like scarecrows. On another occasion, the next summer, there was a flood. After a bad storm, driving rain started and it flooded our hiding place. Our friends started to throw the water back into the pipes with the help of shovels, so that the water started to go down.

We spent fourteen months this way, and our sewer-cleaners helped us out throughout the entire period. When we became short of money they brought us food for free.

At the end of our stay I heard the wail of sirens and the shooting of guns; I was terrified even though I knew that our liberators, the Russians, were approaching. Then one day we heard some loud banging at the bars of the sewer. It was our sewer-cleaners letting us know that we were free.

We went along the pipe for several minutes, then we pulled away the manhole cover and the sewer-cleaners pulled us out. We looked so bad that we did not even look like children.

People felt sorry for us and one lady bought us some gooseberries. I was very happy to see the sun, the flowers and people. I was very happy, but Pawel started crying and wanted to return to the sewer as he was not used to the light and was afraid of people.

# Descent into Hell: Life Under Manure

*How one family hid for five years is described by Oscar Pinkus. The last two years were spent in a pit dug in a stable and covered with manure. The unbearable monotony, the everpresent fear of being discovered, the worsening living conditions, the danger of asphyxiation from lack of oxygen, made life a veritable hell . . .*

Our shelter was tight and low. The square opening above us was just large enough to let a man through. There was no question of standing up, and in a sitting position the roof was just above our heads. The pit was five feet wide and seven feet long leaving about the width of a foot per person for sleeping. Only the children could stretch their legs. The ceiling consisted of two heavy doors laid atop two logs. Two of the walls were lined with loose boards, but the other two were bare earth. Along one boarded wall was a bunk leaving a narrow corridor along the other parallel wall. At night this passageway was covered with boards so that the entire shelter became one large bed. During the day four could sit on the bunk while the rest squatted in the corridor.

The packs, filled with indispensable items like bedding, underwear, and pots, occupied much of the space in the pit. All these things were to have gone under the bunk, but we discovered that the farmer had not removed the soil there. It was an unbearable situation, but our host ignored our complaints. He did only those things that were an absolute necessity . . . The women were busy all day digging with tablespoons the earth from underneath the bunk, and collecting the dirt in a sack. We hoped that eventually the farmer would dispose of the sack and we would gain some space.

Soon difficulties arose warning us that life could not go on under these circumstances. Trifles turned into insoluble problems. When the kettle with hot soup was delivered we had no place to put it . . .

We mentioned the situation to the farmer again but he pretended not to hear us. When we insisted, he refused, arguing that it was a miracle that he had managed to camouflage the construction of the

---

From *The House of Ashes* by Oscar Pinkus.

shelter and that he had better not take any new chances. In a way we agreed with him, for we too felt that this shelter had come about by some unusual stroke of good luck, and that this would never repeat itself . . . We continued our attempts to get the farmer to extend the pit. He used all kinds of arguments to show that this was impossible; he could not dig too close to the foundations because the walls would collapse; he had no more boards, and so on. It then occurred to us to pay him for the job. At the sound of money all his arguments vanished. When we promised, in addition, to buy him two bottles of vodka as a present, he immediately got down to work.

Yankel and I helped him. We took the manure off the place where the pit was dug and first of all extended its top projection. As soon as the earth had been removed from the top we immediately covered it with boards, so that at least from above nothing could be seen. Then the farmer went inside the shelter and began to dig. I pulled the dirt out in pails and Yankel loaded it into sacks. The farmer's wife stood guard outside. She would run in from time to time yelling: "God, somebody is coming." Then we all scrambled down and the farmer quickly got out. But soon he would be back and the work continued. By evening the job was completed . . .

At the beginning we had a watch with us. It needed repairing and we gave it to the farmer to take to Biala. We never saw it again. We lost many other things in a similar manner, and the farmer always had the most ingenious excuses for such losses. Our intuition took the place of the watch. We woke with dawn, though in the shelter, of course, we never saw daylight. An indication that a new day had started was the squeak of the door in the farmer's house, when he paid his first visit to the livestock. We then heard him fill the troughs and caress the pigs, and this was time for us to get up. The lamp was lit and Belcia made the bed. After converting one half of the pit into a bed and the other half into two benches and a table we more or less dressed and sat down . . . We kept some water and this had to suffice for all our various needs. For washing we used one of the pots in which we ate. We had one comb which we all used and which was rapidly losing its teeth. With this, the morning toilette was over and a "normal" day began.

We waited for coffee. The farmer brought it rather early. He would open the cover with one hand and with the other lower the soot-black pot. At first he made soup for breakfast, but then he said it was too much to cook twice a day and he replaced it with coffee. This coffee made of roasted rye had one virtue: it was always hot. We sweetened it with saccharine, and since there were not enough cups we drank in shifts.

Dinner was the greatest event of the day although it was not a feast for the stomach. There was never enough of it, and all our pleas for more were of no avail . . .

We had to be content with whatever the farmer gave us, which was not much. Still, dinner was a great event, for the satisfaction of physical hunger was associated with a spiritual excitement. We developed sharp senses and could tell how much lard the farmer had used, or whether there was a spoonful less soup today than yesterday. Despite this shortage of cooked food there was no starvation at that time. We had enough dry provisions and fats and the farmer sold us as much bread as we wished.

After dinner we waited for dark. From the outset the most longed for time was night. Night was our ally, the only friend in times when everything was our mortal enemy. We knew about the approach of evening by the sound of livestock being watered; and when we heard the women milk the cow we knew that it was already dark. The farmer would than spread straw in the stall, give the cow some hay, and lock the door.

At night we shaded the lamp to prevent any light from leaking into the shed and we talked in whispers. Then we ventured out, cautioning each other to maintain absolute silence. Upon getting out of the pit one had the sensation of leaving a hot bath. The sty was pitch dark, and from outside we heard the howling of the wind, and the crunch of the falling snow. We always felt an urge to run back down. Everything was frightening: the breathing of the animals, the phosphorous eyes of the sheep, the distant howling of dogs. Fright sucked at our bones when we realized that we were separated from the outside world only by the thin walls of the shed, a distance which seemed infinite down below.

Then we aired the shelter. The ventilation consisted of exchanging the hot air of the pit for the smelly air of the shed. We opened the cover and sat silent and motionless feeling the waves of cold air descend into the pit. Then we went to sleep. . .

The farmer's wife continued to demand that we leave . . . She was angry at her husband and more than resentful of us. Karbicki[1] would come over, bring the food, tell us what was going on in his home, in the village, quipping that in the warm cozy cave, we had it like "in America." Oftentimes he genuinely envied us for not having to do any work . . . The woman, however, never came near us. After he had dug the shelter the farmer brought his wife and showed her how it looked. She ran away, and never again came to look . . . They had frequent brawls at home on our, or some other, account and the farmer often beat her. She then went on strike, ran away from home and the farmer had to do all the chores himself. Scenes also arose when she demanded money from him. And Karbicki would rather have parted with an arm or an eye than with money . . .

Despite our fears that we would suffer from cold it was actually too

[1]The farmer.

344

hot in the shelter. The earth insulated us and seven human bodies converted the warmth into oppressing heat. The worst was the humidity. Three times a day we got hot pots; the steam condensed on the walls, dripped down, and having no escape, evaporated anew. Hot kerosene vapors, the breath of the people, the sweat and body odors, made the air foul and nauseous. The only time we could ventilate the place was at night. During the day we had to keep the lid closed as the farmer often brought people to the shed to show them his livestock, and we had to prevent the steam from freezing above the shelter which would have been an easy clue to our presence.

Cleanliness was a major problem. First of all we lacked water. The farmer gave us one jug daily and this had to suffice for drinking, washing dishes and our toilette . . . In order to wash to the waist we collected water for a week and adding half of the daily hot coffee one of us could take a "bath." We washed in the largest pot that was used also for eating. The matter of laundry was also complicated as the Karbicki woman was unwilling to wash our clothes. Besides, even with all the washing, it was almost impossible to stay clean as the dirt from the walls and the seeping manure made our attempts quite futile.

The most important problem was to find some occupation. The question of mental endurance was no less important than our physical resistance. It was impossible to sit all day and gaze into the dim light of the kerosene lamp and the four walls of the pit which we already knew down to each single crack. The most interesting occupation at the beginning was reading. The books were not too select but whatever we had was a priceless possession. The first few weeks we read Sholom Aleichem . . . and it helped us endure our new existence. The second occupation was chess. We played almost all day long creating interest not only for the players but also for the kibbitzers. To make the games more challenging, we played for stakes, for a potato or a spoonful of soup, food being the most precious of things to us. The losing side had to yield part of dinner, and we fought with bitter determination . . .

Mother mended clothes and also read a little. Father, who knew most of the Yiddish books by heart, watched us play chess and specialized in stealing or rearranging pieces. This in turn brought about arguments and debates which killed time—a priceless gain . . .

And so, through difficulties, dangers, and discomforts, there started and flowed the life of the shelter. Each movement crystallized, each function settled, the tracks of our existence were cut with microscopic precision. We endured everything at the beginning with stoic patience. Nobody complained, no one sagged . . . We were in a daze that eliminated memories and dulled reactions, two powerful elements which later began to rip the shelter apart. We rejoiced at passing time, confident that we were being brought closer to the final day which was surely waiting for us somewhere on this nightmarish road. We rejoiced

345

at the security of the shelter, and the success of our undertaking . . . We prayed every day for patience and endurance to carry on. We grew roots; we became a part of the pit. It was all we had left.

It did not take long for the first complications to arise. Some collected in an undercurrent until they rose to the surface; others appeared suddenly, erupting like little earthquakes. Being in a hurry to construct the shelter, the farmer had not bothered to build a new bunk, but gave us an old one from his house. One day we noticed a bedbug on the wall. Next day we noticed two more dive into the wallcracks. At first singly, eventually they came in swarms. As soon as we went to sleep they crawled out from the straw, fell from the ceiling, invaded us from the walls, so that we no longer knew from which side they were attacking. In the middle of the night, when we lit the lamp suddenly, we saw them run for cover by the thousands. As soon as the lamp was doused they returned. Odious, bloody, and smelly, they filled the shelter to the brim.

The second calamity was rats. The food attracted them. At first they just scratched gently at the corners and we even had some sympathy for them. Later however, they became obnoxious; they staged frivolous performances, catapulted over our heads, squeaked, did not let us sleep. There was one large family of them, a mother with many young . . . Their preferred sport was to stage races around the pit. Then they began to cause damage; they spoiled the food, chewed open the flour bags, and spilled the cans with fat. It reached a point where we could not keep any food in the cave. And here too, the problem was similar to the bedbugs. It would not end with this single group; this was the nucleus of an army.

Seepage was another plague. As manure kept accumulating overhead, the pressure caused the liquid excretion to run down the walls of the pit and collect at the bottom in smelly nauseating puddles. The scum stained sheets, soiled the linen, dripped on our faces. It caused an unbearable stench. The smell was often so strong that it woke us from our sleep and caused splitting headaches . . .

Several weeks after our arrival the Karbicki woman burst into the shed yelling that police were heading in our direction. I told her to stop crying and get out of the shed. I lowered the cover of the pit so that it would not yield in case they stepped on it, dimmed the lamp and we froze in silence, ready for whatever was to come. Yankel, who had a cold, began to cough. We put him under the bunk stuffing his mouth with a pillow. Then the rats came out. With the sudden silence and the dimmed light they thought it was night and began their maneuvers. They scratched for a while at the logs; then they came up the edges of the ceiling, ignoring us completely. We watched the rusty glare of the lamp, and surrendered to that peculiar tension in the spine and the

346

collapse of the muscles that usually accompanied these moments. Each minute contained the patience of unlimited time, and the whole world was reduced to the contemplation of a single familiar image. We stayed that way until evening when the woman finally came and told us that the police were gone . . .

Whenever police came into the village, whenever Germans arrived for levies, we had our "bath" . . . The farmer would pile almost a carload of manure on it, sealing the shelter like a tomb. It got hot, and we undressed almost to the skin. The lamp was turned down to a flicker and we sat contemplating how it would look when they came for us. We kept our clothing and shoes ready for that moment from some peculiar wish not to be led to the execution naked. The heat became intense and we sagged to the floor of the shelter where the air seemed a little cooler, pressing our faces to the cool earth. We soon lost all sense of time and fell into a daze.

A moment came when the lamp light began to flicker, to jump convulsively and finally it went out. Surprised, we lit the lamp again. Then we watched the flicker repeat the same convulsions and die again. Finally we could not even light a match and we realized that there was not enough oxygen in the cave. In the evening when the farmer opened the shelter we all lay on its floor half unconscious and it took a few minutes before the cool, fresh stream of air from above returned us to life. These experiences we called "baths" . . .

All kinds of nausea, itches, pains, and cramps began to plague us. We had to find some relief and we thought about the loft of the shed, where, when it was filled with straw, one could stay without being seen from below. We mentioned it to the farmer when we were giving him money for some new transaction and this had a decided influence on his agreeing to this scheme.

The trip to the loft was the major attraction of the day, each of us being given half an hour of it. In the bright winter days the loft was full of sunshine and high blue skies, and in the vast quiet of the countryside the sounds of the village in the distance were haunted melodies of longing and peace . . . Another great moment for us was a sprint to the farmer's house. In the shelter where the slightest innovation—a fuller pot of soup, an extra loaf of bread, a new wick in the lamp—was news, a visit to the farmer's house was a historic event . . . Karbicki came with nightfall, and when he opened the shed a blast of fresh cold air hit my face and stopped my breath . . . The farmer motioned us to move on and we followed him amid the snow, the milky sky, the space. I slowed down to prolong the short walk, but the farmer urged me on and I ran across the yard and into the house . . .

Christmas Eve. The night was clear and over the blue landscape flickered the sparks of farms and villages. The stars, high above the torn thatch roof of the shed, were cold and pensive; snow drifted off the edges of the roof . . . The night listened to the lovely song. A cosmic Hallelujah rang in the stillness and floated into the shed with associations as sad as the face of Christ.

For the first time memories flooded the heart. In times past we, too, had celebrated holidays. In times past our children, too, had sung songs. There had been a time when over our thresholds, too, had stepped the brightness of these ancient rites, and we all sat together at festive tables: grandparents, children, and our mothers. There were, in those days, white tablecloths and lit candles. Listening to the quiet flow of the carols we sang all the Jewish songs we knew, songs which had floated once upon a time, over this land together with the songs of Christmas.

The next day the farmer treated us to cake he had baked for the holidays, for the first time doing something that was not dictated by monetary considerations. In return, we treated him to a bottle of vodka and we all sat in the pit and raised toasts . . . He became almost tender, and I watched him with surprise never believing that in those narrow slit eyes and hardened face could glow any abstract feeling. He sat there, this time not against, but with us, and told us about his poverty. How he had gone about barefoot all winter and had toiled for the rich farmers who made fun of him. He now had the satisfaction of having overtaken all others in wealth and he felt regret that he could not show it to them. For the first time he expressed pity for us and, looking at Belcia and Berko, shook his head. "Such young children . . ." For the first time we felt and shared the commonness of our fate, the commonness of danger, the possibility of a common grave. He finished almost half a liter of vodka, and sipping the last glass, mused: "Maybe I drink on my last holiday. Next Christmas I will be dead."

# In the Sewers of Warsaw

*A year after the Warsaw uprising (pp. 393) six Jewish men and a woman hid in an underground bunker (September 1944–January 1945). They had participated in the Polish underground army. Among them was Charles Goldstein from whose book,* The Bunker, *we quote some of their experiences . . .*

## The Plague of Flies

Many dangers threaten us here: discovery by the Germans; death from shells or bombs; hunger; disease as a result of the filth around us,

From *The Bunker* by Charles Goldstein.

the ground we lie on, the smells coming from the sewers, the corpses strewn throughout the debris. To all this, there is now added yet another torment: the flies.

It is summer; we wallow in filth; we are near the sewers—and so dense swarms of flies buzz around the bunker. During the "day," when we remain lying in the darkness, we hear such buzzing that terror takes hold of us. And as soon as the fire is lit they descend on us. They get inside our ears, our nostrils, our mouths. Our lives are one great struggle against them.

The greatest difficulty arises when we are having our meal. With one hand we have to protect our food so the flies will not get to it and with the other, our faces. Each of us has adopted his own particular method of combatting this scourge. Sometimes these methods are so peculiar and give us such a comical appearance that we cannot help laughing. For us to be able to laugh is an infinitely precious thing. We need laughter almost as much as we need food and drink.

Ignace wraps his face and head in a duster, in which he has made two little holes for the eyes and another for the nose and mouth. Masked in this fashion, he walks among us. The sight of him arouses laughter. And we can't help laughing when we see how Haskel, armed with a rag, chases the flies toward the canal. For to judge from his expression he seems to be imploring them: "Haven't we enough misfortune without you? Must you add to our misery?" When he sees that neither the rag nor his supplications are effective, he gets angry, and addresses the most murderous insults to the flies.

It is at these moments that Hannah, smilingly, has to say to him: "Mr. Haskel, flies do *not* understand Yiddish!"

And everyone, including Haskel, starts laughing heartily.

And yet most of the time we could weep. When it comes to the flies, we have no defense; and we have no means of fighting them. One day we try a concerted attack; we start chasing them toward the canal. Having succeeded in getting rid of them, we cover the entrance to the canal with a piece of cloth so they will not be able to return. But we cannot stay shut in like this for long. Soon we are short of air, and we are forced to remove the cloth. Immediately the flies swarm back into the bunker. More than once we are forced to put out the fire and remain in darkness in order to be able to breathe a little.

Only much later, when the first cold spell starts, will the flies finally disappear.

## Prescription for Life: To Struggle for Existence

I am a prey to the deepest despondency. I try in vain to take myself in imagination to pleasanter places. But the bunker pervades my thoughts.

I tell myself that it is the very difficulties of our life underground that help us to go on living, to overcome all sorts of obstacles and keep alive our instinct for survival. One day it is food we are short of, another day we have no water; now danger threatens us from the canal, now the menace seems to come from outside in the yard. One day we struggle against rats, another day against flies; we fear bombardments, stray bullets, patrols. But this daily struggle for existence is good in that it keeps us from becoming apathetic, it forces us to employ all our efforts, all our ingenuity, in order to survive. Without these difficulties we might go mad in this dark, stinking, suffocating hole.

Later, this fact is to appear as clear as daylight to me. But for the moment, lying on the ground in our bunker, I am in such a state that the slightest movement represents an almost superhuman effort for me; it is more by instinct that I struggle against apathy and anguish. I try to take myself back to Paris . . . where I lived before I was deported and where I left my wife and two children . . . I toss and turn on the hard ground. There is a loud hammering in my head. Pictures of my life in France suddenly disappear, giving way to visions that I am unable to drive away.

June 1942—the road to Auschwitz—jammed into cattle trucks. Three days without air, without food, squashed together in an atmosphere made foul by the fetid smell of human excrement. But even then not one of us imagined that we were all being taken to our deaths . . .

I feel as though I cannot breathe. I cry out. Hannah and Daniel rush over to me. Hannah feels my forehead. "He's burning!" she says to Daniel.

She covers me with some old clothes and I fall asleep again. This time, I sleep more peacefully. I am very fortunate. After a day's rest, I am once more on my feet.

# "I am smiling for my life . . ."

*Catherine Klein, wife of a Jewish doctor, while working as a slave laborer managed to obtain a forged passport in the name of "Francesca Borelli." Leaving her identification papers and a suicide note by the river Spree, "Signora Borelli" boarded a train for Switzerland to join her husband in England . . .*

"Where is the luggage to go?" inquires the customs official.

From *Darkness Over Europe, First Person Accounts of Life in Europe, 1939–1945,* edited by Tony March.

"First to Zurich," I tell him.

"Ticket and passport, please."

My escort [the Italian travel agent who was paid to get her passport] eagerly produces both from his pocket and hands them to the official, pretending to be quite calm. But I can see that his hand is shaking.

Two pairs of eyes are firmly glued to the official at his desk, following his every movement. With the stiff self-importance typical of his class he opens a huge book, then closely scrutinizes the first page of my passport. I hold my breath.

The Italian, in his anxiety, keeps a perpetual sugary smile on his face.

The official spells out in a loud voice, "F-R-A-N-C-E-S-C-A B-O-R-E-L-L-I," entering my name into his book.

"Where are you living? I mean, are you residing in Berlin?"

I begin to stammer. In my excitement I have completely forgotten where I am supposed to be living . . .

I look to the Italian for assistance. He is gasping for breath. Evidently he has not the faintest idea.

"Don't you understand German? I am asking you, where in Berlin are you living?"

An awkward silence follows.

After what seems ages, the voice of the Italian suddenly breaks in: "Madame lives—lives at—Seven Viktoria Luise Platz."

This seems to satisfy the official's curiosity. He merely notes it down.

"Open your luggage."

My fingers are quite numb while I fumble in my handbag for the keys.

The Italian firmly takes the bag from me, extracting the bunch of keys with miraculous swiftness and unlocking my suitcases for me.

Every article is carefully examined.

I may now close my suitcases.

They each get a pink label fixed across the locks: "Passed by the Customs," and are taken to the luggage van by the porters.

Longingly I follow them with my eyes until they disappear. How I envy them! They have passed their final test and are now on the road to liberty. Whereas I—shall I ever see them again?

Thinking of my passport, I have serious doubts. Only this morning did I realize the passport was finally in order. Uncle Ruggero [who altered and forged passports] had done his best.

Glancing at the document on which my life depended, I have to admit that two superfluous die-stamps have actually disappeared from the photograph. But on closer examination I find that the paper where they had been has lost its color completely and has also become considerably thinner. The overlay on a spot just on the back of my photograph shows the paper so badly damaged that only childish trust or criminal negligence could keep an official from realizing that the passport has been tampered with.

351

To divert attention from the damaged area, Uncle Ruggero had hit on one of the oldest forgery tricks. He had sprinkled a blob of water on the opposite page, thus blotting the writing. Quickly closing the passport, he had transferred the ink to the damaged page, and it had certainly made it look a mess, which might fool an unsuspecting official.

The Italian was quite beside himself in his exultation over this masterstroke, and I had to remind him repeatedly of the fact that it was not only the Gestapo who were guarding the frontiers. They were reinforced by picked SS troops, well versed in every branch of trickery. Nothing would escape their attention. "You must realize what this means: Gestapo and SS. Do you believe in miracles? I don't . . ."

Languidly I walk along the platform. While producing my ticket for inspection, I make a lot of fuss—rearranging my handbag, looking at myself in my mirror, bringing the powder puff into action. The Italian urges me to come along.

I take no notice and calmly walk across to the bookstall, looking at the titles which are barely visible in the blacked-out station hall. Finally I decided on a magazine, the front page of which shows a German U-boat crew that has achieved a record number of sinkings, proudly displaying their brand new decoration and singing the popular little song: *"Denn wir fahren gegen Engeland."* ["Because We Sail on England"].

I think to myself, Don't you show off. Now it is *my* turn to go to England.

The train is rather full. Mostly men in uniform.

I find myself a corner seat in a first-class compartment. Putting my small suitcase on the luggage rack, I spread a traveling rug on my seat. The Italian warms to the part of helpful escort and gives a splendid performance. Somehow I manage to whisper to him that I would prefer to be left alone in the compartment. So he takes up his post outside the open window of the train and, partly in Italian and partly in German, he gives me some last-minute instructions—not so much intended for my own benefit as for the ears of my fellow passengers and anyone else who might care to listen.

I can see the stationmaster's right arm raised slowly, pompously, with Prussian exactitude. I hear the engines beginning to fume, and for the last time I look at the city I once loved so much; all I can see of it is the sooty gray station wall.

Good-bye, Berlin. Never will I see you again. The train is beginning to move. The last thing I notice is a nervous twitch on the Italian's face.

I sink into my soft seat and close my eyes, trying to relax. There is nothing further to be done. Fate will have to run its course. All I can do now is sit and try to remain inconspicuous.

It is bitingly cold in the unheated compartment. I bury myself in my rug . . . I keep looking at my watch. Oh, only twenty minutes have

352

passed and the journey to Basel, on the German border, takes thirteen hours. Silent and reserved, we all sit in our respective corners, mostly with our eyes shut.

I go to sleep, apparently for quite a while, for when I wake up there are two new faces in my compartment.

" . . . and I just went and tackled that school master. 'Sir,' I said—and when I say 'sir' everyone knows what to expect—'Sir,' I said, 'do you think that I put my children into the world that they should be taught when Homer wrote the *Iliad*? Sir, you cannot stop the march of time,' I said. 'We Germans have to concentrate on more important subjects these days. The whole world is waiting to be ruled by us and our children. Sir, you had better impress on these young minds the only theory worth knowing, the only theory we acknowledge today—the racial theory,' I said to him."

This avalanche of words comes from a little fat man now sitting opposite me who, decorated with countless swastika badges, continues to provide samples of his general outlook on life and is applauded vigorously by two officers.

The train stops at a station. Looking out, I discover in the first gray light of dawn that we have reached Frankfurt am Main . . .

In another six hours' journey we will reach the frontier; I am frightened of these six hours.

Again the faces of my companions change. This time I have two quiet, reserved civilians in my compartment. They take no notice of me.

Each turn of the wheels brings us nearer the frontier. I am getting restless, my arms and legs begin to feel heavy like lead, breathing becomes difficult, I cannot sit still any longer. So I go into the corridor where the temperature is below zero. But the extreme cold eases my aching head.

There is no one about except an elderly gentleman smoking a cigarette. I seem to represent the answer to his silent prayer; he wants to have a morning chat. And before I can take any precautionary measures he has asked me where I come from, where I am going.

"Oh, you're going to Switzerland, too? Are you as nervous about it as I am?" he asks me. What did he say?

"Yes, I am terrified of the frontier," he confesses. "It is such an uncanny feeling. Here we are in the midst of war and suddenly you come to a country where it might quite easily happen that you find yourself sitting next to an American or an Englishman without even knowing it. My wife at home is trembling for my safety; she knows what I am like. I cannot keep my mouth shut. For two pins I would get up and tell these foreigners exactly what I think of them. But I must remember that I only got my exit permit as manager of a dancing troupe, trying to arrange for an extensive tour through Switzerland, to

353

bring back foreign currency. So I suppose I will have to keep my mouth shut, in the national interest."

The train stops at Mannheim.

It is getting much emptier now.

Returning to my compartment, I find it occupied by the Duke of Windsor.

In speechless surprise I stare at him.

The gentleman laughs, "Now, young lady, don't you start telling me that I look like the Duke of Windsor—I just could not bear it. In peacetime it used to be a magnificent joke; but now I would not mind wearing a placard round my neck: 'No, I am not what you think I am. I happen to be a good German.'"

"That wouldn't be a bad idea at all," says a bony hooknosed civilian who has also just come into the train. "The state should force everyone to display a badge clearly indicating the nationality of the wearer. If you make a study of racial history as I have, you will soon find how easy it is to be fooled by members of inferior races. Just look at the Jews, for instance. Some of these Jew-women have managed to acclimatize themselves so well, through being permitted to live among us Aryans, that even nature has come to their help. It amounts to mimicry. Only the other day in Prague I had a most distressing experience. I must add that it was in the evening; I ran into a girl near the Wentzelplatz and spoke to her. I can tell you she was blue-eyed, blonde, tall, slim, straight little nose, small well-made mouth. I looked closer and suddenly discovered a yellow Jew star. That was a lesson to me. I won't be taken in again so easily."

I feel how he fixes his glance on me while talking, how he takes stock of the red of my hair, the blue of my eyes.

"Soon there will be no Jews left anywhere," our delightful fellow traveler continues to air his views. "The Jewish question will solve itself automatically. We have seen to that. But what we Germans should take into serious consideration is the introduction of badges for all non-Germans. If you once make it clear to yourself how many Poles, Russians, French, Dutch, Czechs, Danes, Americans, English, and other conquered nationals will be working for us here after the war, you will realize that it will require some means of differentiation between the masters of this country and the vanquished."

Feverish scarlet spots appear on his cheeks . . . All the time his eyes do not leave my face for a moment. Although I am listening intently, I have so far not shown by a single gesture whether I agree or disagree.

"My superiors knew what they were doing when they put me into my present post," he continues. "I am so thoroughly versed in these matters that nothing escapes me now, nothing at all."

Again I feel his searching glance and I need all of my self-control to present a picture of equanimity which I am far from feeling.

I should like to go to the washroom and take a sedative. Cautiously I remove the passport from beneath me—I hope my weight has pressed it to open at the desired page—and put it in my handbag. But I dare not get up; my knees are trembling too much.

All the while the express is racing toward the frontier.

The fear, bordering on certainty, that this devil knows exactly who I am, that he is sent here by the Gestapo to catch me, and that he is now playing a cat-and-mouse game with me—that fear drives me nearly crazy.

The way that creature is talking. The way he keeps staring at me all the time. The way each one of his words seems to be meant for me, and me alone. There is no doubt in my mind, he is a Gestapo official.

And again I feel his eyes on me. I feel how he enjoys watching my fear, the pleasure he finds in keeping me guessing. I suppose he will only snatch me at the last moment, just when I am reaching out for freedom.

No! The cry comes from within me. No, you won't get me. Not alive, anyway! And as if haunted by a thousand ghosts, I rush in sheer terror from the compartment into the corridor. I could scream aloud in torment. The torment of miserable helplessness, being a victim once more, waiting in a kind of hypnotized stupor until it pleases the enemy to fell the final blow.

Outside, the dancing-troupe agent has apparently been waiting for me. He refuses to let me pass.

"Well, young lady," he says, and his voice comes to me as if out of a mist, "now we'll soon be over the worst. My mother, who used to be a devilishly clever woman, dead these twenty-five years—no, let me see, it must be twenty-seven years this March—my mother used to say . . ."

Murmuring an excuse, I hurry swiftly past him and lock myself into the washroom.

Catching hold of the basin, I try to steady myself. My legs are shaking so much that I am hardly able to stand upright. Tears are rolling down my face.

So near the goal, within the very reach of life itself, and now it will have to be death after all!

The train is steaming toward the frontier.

I shall have to act quickly if I am to escape the Gestapo. In a few minutes' time we will reach Weil, the last German station before Basel. That is where German customs and passport officials will board the train; it will be too late for me then. .

I open the window.

A gust of icy-cold fresh air blows in. The country is covered with snow, and the bare branches of the trees are weighed down by it.

Now the sun is breaking through the clouds. What a picture of perfect peace. It looks like an enchanted garden.

I breathe in deeply.

Gradually hysteria and fear leave me, and sanity seems to return.

I look at the embankment. To have to end up among the rubble down there! What a ghastly thought.

No, I don't want to die! Not now, when I have got this far. I want to start life again, join my husband, return to normalcy.

Catching sight of myself in the mirror, I discover that I look absolutely wild, with strands of hair falling over my face.

While repairing the damage with combs and hairpins, I begin to wonder if I have not been imagining things. Surely if this man were really a Gestapo official, he would not have talked so much. And just as only three minutes ago I was fully convinced that this man was my deadly enemy, I am now quite certain that he is nothing but a pretentious ass.

My head feels clear and calm now, but my limbs are still trembling.

From the confusion of my fears and obsessions there suddenly comes the thought of my good old standby . . . my sedative. Yes, I shall take two of the Luminal tablets.

On and on races the express, soon we will reach the frontier.

Upon trying the water taps, I find that there is no water. The pipes are frozen. How am I to swallow my tablets? With endless trouble and by sheer determination I manage to get them down at last, even without water.

The mere fact that I have swallowed them makes me feel calmer at once. But then the drug really begins to take effect. Soon I have regained complete self-control.

I rearrange my hair, renew my makeup, use lipstick and lots of perfume, and, without blinking an eyelid, Francesca Borelli, the Italian glamour girl, sweeps back to her compartment.

My fellow passengers seem to have been discussing me, for they stop talking the moment I reenter the compartment. Their gossip must have been of a harmless nature, as the friendly smiling faces are eager to testify. Even the pseudo Gestapo-man has interrupted his recital of revolutionary schemes and measures and is concentrating on a few interesting-looking sandwiches, which he consumes with a repellent mixture of relish and noise.

The train comes to a standstill.

Outside our window a station poster appears: "Weil" . . .

Outside, a railway guard calls out . . . "Last station before the frontier."

For months I have been afraid of this very moment, day and night. In my waking and sleeping hours I have imagined how I will feel, wondering how I can possibly stand the strain, expecting to find myself trembling with excitement, neither being able to see, to hear, or to take in what is being said. And now I find that I am in complete control of all

356

my faculties. I feel not a vestige of fear; I am best compared to a robot who neither thinks nor feels any emotions.

Rising from my seat, I let the window down, and with absorbed interest I watch the greater part of the train being disconnected . . . The engine starts to move again.

I feel as if I were watching a play being enacted. The tension takes hold of me and I share in the general excitement but the idea that I am personally involved in this, that in a few seconds' time the final curtain may fall on my own life—that idea does not even occur to me . . .

Being now thoroughly under the influence of the peace-giving drug, I am not even worried by excited voices coming from the next compartment. The passport control officials are in there now.

Something seems to be wrong.

I discover that my three fellow travelers are much more nervous than I am. The "Gestapo-man" is furiously biting his nails while the "Duke of Windsor" suddenly has the urgent wish to go to the restroom. Hardly has he opened the door when it is pushed back from the outside by a sergeant major, who shouts at him, "Stay where you are."

Next door the babble of voices rises to a concert pitch. Although we are all listening intently, we unfortunately cannot hear one word clearly. Then suddenly all is still.

In the corridor outside our compartment window the white face of the ballet manager, followed by a huge soldier, passes. Our eyes are still following this ill-matched couple when our door slides open.

"Heil Hitler, passport control."

Even the Luminal tablets fail me now. No dose would be large enough to counteract the sudden spasm of fear running through my body. My instinct for self-preservation revolts at the idea of giving myself up without a final struggle. My lips are beginning to quiver, my teeth are chattering, and I am trembling all over.

"Heil Hitler," replies the fellow on the seat opposite mine. His face has become hard and repulsive again, now that he is no longer munching sandwiches or biting his nails. He just smiles at the official without attempting to produce his identity papers.

"What happened just now with that ballet chap next door?" I heard him whisper. "The man seemed harmless enough to me."

"You never heard such impudence," one of the officials answers still breathing with fury.

"Impudence indeed," chimes in the other official. "I have had plenty to deal with on this train, but that was the crowning glory. You will get your report in Basel."

I stare at my compartment-mate. So my first instinct was right. He belongs to the Gestapo. Apparently his job is to watch us for a few hundred miles before we even reach the frontier. Or is he only investigating particularly suspicious cases, such as mine, for instance?

357

Now the official holds my passport in his hands. As intended, he opens it on the photograph page and, hardly glancing at it, turns a few pages until he comes to my transit visa to Switzerland. Undoubtedly of greatest interest from his point of view is the German exit and reentrance visa, which he examines minutely. In my trembling fear, I feel that he is taking hours over it. But, at last, even this comes to an end. Apparently satisfied, he turns a few pages back, now looking at each one separately.

I am only fearful of the damaged back of my photograph. Miraculously, he seems not to notice it at all. Meanwhile, I feel the searching glances of the other official and his colleague opposite me, watching my every move. I smile in splendid unconcern. I am smiling for my life. I cannot stand the oppressive silence any longer. Someone must speak.

"Will I have to change at Basel?" I ask.

No reply.

The inquisitor has come back to the photograph, examining it much more closely now than before, comparing it with my face over and over again.

Suddenly he starts.

Lifting the book quite close up to his eyes, he exclaims, "What's this? Something exceedingly queer." Each one of his words strikes me like a whip.

Nevertheless, I keep smiling. There is no change in my expression, none at all.

He waves to the other official to follow him and they both leave the compartment, posting themselves in the corridor with their backs to me, consulting.

My face behaves splendidly. It is still smiling all by itself.

The horrible gentleman opposite me watches my every move.

I can hear quite distinctly one of the men saying to the other, "There is something fishy here." And clearly I hear the other one reply, "Try to tear off the photograph. Let us see if the stamp runs on underneath it."

All the while the train is hurrying toward the frontier.

My thinking apparatus has stopped functioning. I am possessed of fear—naked, wild fear. I feel as if I were being slowly strangled to death.

A voice comes from outside: "We had better investigate the whole thing at Basel."

The game is lost.

The rope around my throat is tightening. There is no way out for me now. I am not even free to choose my own death. Jumping out of the window is out of the question, and the only other possible way is barred by the officials.

Again comes the voice: "I believe the die-stamp must have slipped here."

"Yes," replies the other. "Underneath it seems to be quite all right."
And they continue their whispering.

In a minute they will be back in the compartment, they will take me between them, and we shall start on a road from which there is no return.

Farewell, liberty; farewell, life.

How long does it take—days, hours, minutes? Suddenly I hold my passport in my hands again.

"Do you understand German, madame?" one of the officials asks me.

"I was born in Berlin," I tell him.

"On your return there, you will have to go to your consulate at once and ask for a new passport. You will have nothing but trouble with this one. Never have I seen anything like it. The die-stamps are in the wrong place, and the mess behind the photograph! We wouldn't permit a German to travel about with a passport in a condition like that. Heil Hitler!"

And they are gone. The nightmare is over.

My lips are positively aching from the petrified smile I have kept on my face during the ordeal. And yet, I must not drop the mask yet. The unwavering stare of the gentleman opposite me warns me that I am still in the power of the Third Reich.

Here is the official back again, too.

"Have you any newspapers, magazines, books? You are not allowed to take anything across the frontier." I hand him the magazine I bought at the bookstall last night. It is confiscated for the benefit of the Red Cross.

"How much money have you with you?"

I hold out handbag and wallet.

"I want to know how much money you have?"

"Sixty-five marks."

He neither checks up nor comments on it. And he is gone.

I gradually awake to the certainty that this is no dream. These are no phantoms of my ever active imagination. I have passed the final test, I have graduated with honors. It is all over now. I have won. Liberty is mine now!

The train is slowing down, and we are passing houses, streets; we draw into a station.

Basel, Badisher Bahnhof, still part of Germany.

We all have to leave the train.

There are not many people left who climb out of the two carriages.

The three frontier officials, with the ballet manager in their midst, disappear quickly into one of the station buildings. A door slams behind them. I stare after them for quite a while. And then a huge wave of gratefulness engulfs me, flowing through my veins, making my pulses beat faster. How easily I might have become the fifth of that party! Thanks to a kindly fate, I have been saved from defeat by what now seems a miracle to me. And for the first time in years, a simple little prayer of thanksgiving rises to my lips, such as I was taught when a child.

As from another world, a friendly voice sounds in my ears in unmistakable Swiss dialect. It comes from a Swiss porter offering his services to me.

"No, thank you, I can manage my two little suitcases by myself. It's only to the next platform."

"To the next platform! That's what you think. That's how it used to be in peacetime. All that is changed now. You have to walk on foot into Switzerland. Quite a long way through no-man's-land. There will be a few formalities to go through; you had better let me help you."

I agree to everything. Only quickly away from German soil. No time is to be lost.

"Have you changed your ten marks into Swiss francs yet?" The porter remains quite unperturbed. "You get a much better rate of exchange here."

I am burning to get away but show no signs of impatience. Playing my part to the end, I change my ten marks and deposit a sum of money for the return journey. This is the last time that the Nazis grab money from me, I reflect with joy in my heart.

My porter and I start off on our way. It is a walk between two worlds, but for me it means much more: the road from death into new life.

Slowly, slowly, we wander through a long covered tunnel. There is no one about. Our steps resound in a sepulchral silence.

Suddenly the corridor widens into a glass-roofed hall and much to my horror we are again confronted by German uniforms, five of them. German luggage and foreign currency control.

All five descend on me like a storm, snatching my cases and handbag, searching every corner.

Is there no end to these Nazis at all? I sigh to myself, as I pass on with my good old porter.

"How much longer until we get into Switzerland?" I ask him a few moments later.

"Switzerland? We have been walking through Switzerland these last three minutes," he replies.

# Passing: Agonies and Fears of Being Discovered as Circumcised

*Yankel Kuperblum (Jack Kuper) returned to his village home in Poland, to find his family gone. This shattering discovery set him off on a harrowing four years of constantly fleeing for his life. To survive he had to pass as a Christian, forget his religion, language, and Jewishness. Gradually he comes to believe himself as Christian but for one physical evidence on his body . . .*

I drove the cows to pasture. In the fields I met other boys, some about my own age, but most of them older. They inquired little about me except my name and whom I was working for. We chased rabbits, we cut branches from trees and made whistles out of them, and when it rained we'd drive our cows into the forest, congregate under a tree, and talk.

On one such day, I found myself sitting on the wet grass with a potato sack covering my head, listening to stories about all the girls in the village . . . We laughed as each one told of witnessing some interesting sexual contact between his father and mother, sister and boyfriend, or even strangers. One outdid the other, and each succeeding story was more interesting and revealing than the last one.

"What about you?" a voice directed the question at me. "Haven't you ever seen or done anything?" I blushed, smiled, shook my head, then turned to look for my cows.

"He's too young," I now heard someone else say.

"How old are you?"

"Twelve," I answered.

"I bet he doesn't even have hair yet," a husky voice laughed. "Do you have hair, Jan? Does it tickle you? Show us if you have hair." There was laughter all around me. "Perhaps only little hairs, just coming out!" the laughing voice said. I saw a tall boy with small, half-closed eyes coming towards me. At that moment he looked like a monster.

"Let's see if he has hair." The others jumped to their feet, and the forest suddenly echoed with a loud, "Yeah, let's see!"

"No!" I yelled. A pair of firm, strong hands were attempting to undo

From *Child of the Holocaust* by Jack Kuper.

361

my belt. Another pair of hands were holding my shoulders pinned to the ground. I turned and twisted. I screamed, "No! Let me go, let me go!" They were all laughing. I held onto my belt with all the strength in me, but not for long. The more I fought, the funnier they found the game. Soon my belt was gone. Someone was holding my feet, another was holding my hands, and still another was now unbuttoning my fly. I tried to shake loose, but without success.

"We won't hurt you, Jan." The laughter was now deafening. One button, two buttons, another button, laughter . . . hysterical laughter. Someone was pulling at my pants. I now saw the rabbi at my brother's circumcision: the knife cuts the skin, my brother Josel cries, the rabbi smiles.

"Mazel tov," someone said. I see a bottle of wine and a large basin full of beans.

I scream and now cry. I've finally met death. In a few minutes they'll know I'm a Jew. Why, dear God, did I have to be circumcised?

Faces all around me looking down.

"Let's see it," someone shouted. "Take off his pants."

With all the strength within me, I somehow managed to free myself and hold on to my pants.

"Leave me alone," I said, and began to weep. "May Christ curse you for this," I shouted at them.

There was a deathly silence around me. I buttoned my fly, someone threw me my belt, I stood up, walked a short distance, then stopped under a tree, panting and still crying.

"We just wanted to see your hair," said one of them. "No reason to cry, it's just for laughs."

"Yes," said another, "we meant no harm. Just wanted to see your penis, that's all, Jan." Soon they dispersed.

"Something very peculiar about that one," I heard one of them say, and then the words echoed through the forest . . .

For several days I ignored them, but soon we made up and now during the long summer evenings we ran around playing games.

At first we played ball, then hide-and-seek. Later, as the summer progressed, we tired of that and changed to "spy." One of us, chosen to play the spy, would hide and the rest had to find him. When this too became boring, someone suggested we play "Jew."

"What kind of a game is that?" asked one boy.

The one who had suggested it then explained, "We choose a Jew. He hides, we count till ten, then we search for him. When we find him we take everything away from him and then we turn him over to the Germans."

"What if he runs away?" asked another boy.

"Then we shoot him," came the reply.

In the days and nights that followed, my friends and I hunted for

362

our made-up Jew . . . The game had a real appeal to everyone, including myself. For after all it was only a game and it did offer a lot of suspense. Whenever the Jew was discovered, he immediately raised his arms. We'd surround him, remove his valuables from his pockets, and then shoot him by pointing a wooden revolver at him and yelling:

"We've got you!" a voice shouted from behind me. "Hands up, you dirty Jew!" I turned quickly and saw two of my companions behind me. One of them ran out and yelled, "We've got him! We caught the Jew!" The other approached me and began to search my pockets with one hand, while with the other he pointed his wooden pistol at my head.

When he turned his attention away from me, I lowered my arms, turned, and ran away.

"Bang! Bang!" I heard him shout after me, but I paid no attention. "Bang! Bang!" came the sound. My feet carried me towards the back fields. "You're dead!" he shouted after me. "I've shot you, Jan!"

I ran as fast as I could. Deep in the fields I stopped and listened. All was quiet except the crickets and the frogs in a nearby pond . . . When I stopped panting, I slowly got up and leisurely walked back towards the village.

Upon seeing me, my companions were extremely annoyed, especially the one with the wooden pistol. "I shot you three times, Jan!" he shouted. "You're dead; I shot you and you're supposed to fali dead."

"I ran away," I defended myself.

"How could you run away if I shot you three times?"

"You shot at me," I answered, "but you missed every time."

"You're crazy!" he shot back with anger. "You don't know how to play a Jew."

He turned in disgust, and pocketing his wooden revolver, he went home to sleep.

One wet, rainy day, a German soldier appeared at the small, narrow, winding river which passed through the village. He had a number of grenades around his belt. We followed him along the river's edge until finally he motioned to us to move away and lie down on the ground. He then released the pin of a grenade and threw it into the river and ducked for cover.

A small explosion followed, sending a spray of water into the air. We all stood up and ran down to the water, and there we saw fish after fish coming to the surface, floating as if dead. Several boys took off their clothes, jumped in, and threw the fish towards the soldier. A little further down the river, he threw another grenade and the same operation was repeated. When his knapsack was full of fish, he threw the rest towards us and then left . . .

We fell on the remaining fish, each grabbing as many as he could, and then ran through the village yelling, "We've got fish! We've got fish!"

This happened in the early spring, but by the time summer arrived . . . the boys thought very much about swimming.

On any hot summer midday, a passer-by making his way through the village would have noticed a group of boys completely naked, diving into the river's cold water, coming out, and diving in again.

"Why don't you come swimming with us today, Janek?" my friends would ask.

"Perhaps tomorrow; I have to help Mr. Kozak," I would answer, or, "I'll meet you there later," or, "I have a cold," or, "The water is too cold today."

As the days passed, my excuses became weaker and I began to fear the consequences. My companions grew suspicious.

"What's the matter with you? Perhaps you only have one ball, eh?" they laughed. "Or no balls at all!" added another.

I lay awake at night worrying about the next day and hoping it would rain or be cold so I wouldn't be invited to go swimming. I thought of adding a piece of chicken skin to my penis, but how to go about it, I didn't know. I have to find a way. I must go swimming, but how? Perhaps in my underwear! No, this is not the answer, it will make me stand out.

It was an extremely hot day when two boys came looking for me.

"Today you're coming with us, Janek," they stated, grabbing me by my arms.

"No!" I protested.

"Why not?"

"I have work to do."

"Go, Jan, go swimming," I heard Mr. Kozak say. I turned and saw him standing behind me. "Go, boy, go. It's too hot to work. I'm going to sleep and you go swimming. Enjoy yourself." I turned to my friends who were now smiling. I turned back to Mr. Kozak, but he only smiled and motioned with his hand for me to go.

On the way to the river my two friends talked without stop, but I couldn't hear them; my mind was elsewhere. "Isn't that right, Jan?" I seemed to hear them ask.

"Yes, yes," I answered, but everything was turning in front of me.

Again I saw the rabbi with his knife; he was cutting . . . It fell to the ground and now I realized he wasn't a rabbi, but the ritual slaughterer, the Shochet, and the object on the ground was a bleeding chicken's head . . .

"What are you waiting for?" someone was shouting. "Come on!"

I now stood on the edge of the river. Around me my friends, all nude, were diving into the water, splashing each other, coming out, and diving in again.

I began to undress. Slowly I pulled the cotton shirt over my head and

364

threw it to the ground. I looked about me; no one was looking. I sat down on the grass, I undid my belt, then one button, then another, and another.

"Come on, Janek!"

"What's taking you so long, Jan?" screamed another.

Still sitting, I began to remove my pants with one hand, while with the other I covered my genitals. I now stood up, still holding my private parts, and with my free hand outstretched, I dived into the water.

I'm safe, I thought, and swam from one edge of the river to the other. Someone splashed me, someone else laughed, another boy pushed my head under, and still another wanted to know if I could swim under water. My companions dived continuously, not noticing that once in the water I remained there.

An hour or so later when it was time to go, I managed to come out of the river in the same manner in which I had entered, with one hand covering my penis.

In the following days I went swimming, and each time I gained more confidence in dressing and undressing in such a way as not to reveal my complete nakedness. I sometimes marveled at my own manipulations and at the fact that none of the others seemed to notice my rather unusual habits.

Then it happened! "Why do you cover your penis, Janek?" a boy asked curiously one day. The others immediately turned their eyes towards me, waiting for a reply. "Why, Janek, why?" I heard the boy say again. I had just removed my pants and was about to dive. A terrible fear gripped me. They may forcefully remove my hand and disclose my secret. "Why, Janek?"

"Perhaps he's a girl," and a gale of laughter echoed through the fields.

I covered my penis with both hands and held on tightly. The boys now surrounded me, their eyes focused on my hands.

"Why, Janek, why?"

I wanted to run, but was afraid.

"You see," I began, "I come from a village near Pulawy, and there we have a large river, the Vistula. People come to bathe there from Warsaw and Lublin and all over, and no one goes swimming in the nude; they wear bathing suits." I looked up and noticed that my friends were listening attentively. "My father taught me that only animals walk around in the nude, not civilized people. So if you want to be like animals, go on displaying yourselves to everyone who passes by here. I, lacking a bathing suit, intend to keep my dignity by at least covering myself with my hands."

A long silence followed during which I stood up, walked to the river's edge, and in my usual manner, dived into the water.

From then on, anyone who passed along the back road of the village on the way to Piaski would have noticed a group of noisy boys diving into the water, their right arms outstretched and their left hands covering their uncircumcised penises.

# Escape to the Aryan Side

*Feyige Pelteh-Miedzyrecki became known as Vladka Meed. Soon after she was seventeen, she became an underground worker on the Aryan side of Warsaw. Her appearance met all the criteria for "passing" as an Aryan. She was both eyewitness and participant in the battle for life and death in the Ghetto. Her book deals with the period from July 22, 1942, to the liberation . . .*

One evening, I heard a knock on the door. In the dim light of the corridor, I failed to recognize the tall man asking for me . . . It was none other than Michal Klepfisz, an engineer active for many years in the Bund[1] and in *Morgenstern,* a Jewish sports organization. "Michal, what a pleasant surprise!" I exclaimed. "What brings you here? You've been out of the ghetto for quite a while . . ."

"I've come to take you away, Feigel," he answered. "Get ready; you'll be leaving the ghetto within two days, and meanwhile I'll prepare documents for you, and try to notify people in the Polish sector."

I felt my heart would leap into my mouth. I could hardly believe my ears.

"Well, get ready," he continued. "I'll wait for you at the ghetto gate at eight in the morning. You'll have to walk out with a labor battalion; that's the best way."

"In case we should miss each other, leave me an address I can find you at," I suggested.

A moment's silence, then he answered, "I have no such address yet. I'm still living in someone's cellar. But don't worry. I'll give you a temporary address . . .—just memorize it—no written notes of any sort . . ."

The thought of escaping the ghetto was gathering momentum among the workers (in my shop). It seemed the only way to survive. But escape was easier said than done. For one thing, to slip across the wall, one had to pay an exorbitant sum to the Gentile smugglers. Moreover, while one might bribe the German sentinel, one could never be certain

[1]Jewish socialist organization.

From *On Both Sides of the Wall* by Vladka Meed.

that he might not decide to shoot his victim. To walk out with a Jewish labor brigade was the only available alternative—but a most dangerous one.

Quite a few Jews with Aryan features—and a well-lined purse—had already attempted to leave the ghetto. Some of them had been apprehended, and either killed on the spot or deported. Such dangers did not deter others from the wall, symbol of a dream that very few could realize.

Outside the ghetto lay an alien world where one had to seek refuge, contact Gentile friends who might help one to get forged documents, prepare living quarters, find a job. Above all, there had to be a great deal of money to pay for every little service. Desperate Jews endeavored to contact Gentile acquaintances on the "other side of the wall," but most of the appeals fell on deaf ears.

Some of those who had succeeded in crossing into the Aryan sector had returned after a few weeks. They had not been able to cope with the blackmail rampant there.

I searched the ghetto for a means of escape, but in vain. The German sentries had been increased. The only way was with a labor brigade. The foremen of the labor gangs employed outside the ghetto were occasionally able to make a substitution for an absentee. Such opportunities were rare indeed, and cost a great deal. Nonetheless, I paid my way. I had to take along the last issue of the underground bulletin, which carried a detailed description and map of the Treblinka extermination camp. My roommates, aware of my preparations, advised me to conceal the bulletin in my shoes. Tearfully, we took leave of one another. A few words, a sad, reassuring smile, the promise that we wouldn't forget each other, the last handshake, and I was ready. Who knew if I would see them again?

December 5, 1942, 7:00 a.m. The street was astir with people streaming to work. A brisk business of barter went on as Jews traded their last pitiful belongings—a coat, a skirt, an old pair of shoes—to those working on the Aryan side for chunks of black bread. Later, the commodities would be smuggled out of the ghetto and sold to Gentile vendors.

After some searching, I found a Jewish leader of a forty-man labor battalion who permitted me to join his group for five hundred zloty. I was the only female in the group. We marched in column formation to the ghetto gate, where we joined thousands of other laborers, men and women.

The morning guard, heavily reinforced, was busy inspecting the throng. Jews pushed and jostled wherever they could, hoping to elude the Gestapo scrutiny—to escape to the Aryan side, to smuggle a few belongings out of the ghetto. The inspection had just started. We waited apprehensively, shivering in the morning frost. The actions of the Germans were unpredictable!

Some Jews who had just been inspected were retreating, clutching their bruised faces—each having been found to possess an extra item. Another Jew hopped barefoot in the snow; the German had taken a liking to his shoes. Several Jews, half-undressed, stood trembling in the biting cold, as a warmly dressed German took his time examining them. An old Jew argued with a German trooper that he did not want to be separated from his thirteen-year-old daughter. "She's a regular worker, just like me; here is her factory card!" he argued heatedly. The soldier rebuffed him brutally. In his despair, the old man looked about with pleading eyes. No one dared help him. His daughter was shunted aside to a wooden shack from which she gazed forlornly at her father. My detachment was next to be inspected. Everything was going smoothly.

"How did a woman get in here?" the German barked . . .

"She's employed in the factory kitchen," the group leader explained.

The trooper eyed me with disdain and snapped, "I don't like your face. Get in there!" pointing in the direction of the wooden shack.

"I don't envy her," someone remarked. My blood ran cold at the thought of the underground bulletin being found on me. In that event the entire labor battalion—not just me—would be detained. I saw consternation and helplessness in the faces of those around me. A Jewish policeman appeared. The place was swarming with troopers and police; there was no chance of escape.

"Please let me slip away while the German is away," I whispered to the policeman.

"Do you expect me to lay down my life for you?" he snapped back, aghast. "The German will be right back!"

A bruised and bleeding Jew lay at the entrance to the wooden shack. Off to a side, the young girl. I stood a moment, stunned. The policeman shoved me inside. I found myself in a dimly lit room, blood-spattered walls papered with maps, charts, and photographs of half-naked women. Tattered clothing and shoes lay strewn about the floor. A knout dangled from the little window. I stood by the wall and waited. A guard entered and began the interrogation.

"Full name."

I answered.

"Place of work."

I named the place to which the battalion was headed.

"Oho! Now, show me what you are carrying on your person." He pulled off my coat and dress, and examined them closely, under a light, searching the hem and pockets. He should only not ask for my shoes! If he does, I am lost!

"All right, now the shoes!" he demanded.

A chill passed through me. My mind was racing. I started stalling for time, unlacing my shoes slowly. Staring angrily, my interrogator barked impatiently: "Hurry up—stop fiddling around! Let's have those shoes! Do you see this knout?" As I continued to stall, the Nazi grabbed the knout and started to advance on me. At that moment, miraculously, the door flew open, and someone shouted, *"Herr Lieutenant,* please come out at once! A Jew has just escaped!"

The officer dashed out, banging the door shut. I was left alone. Dressing hurriedly, I tried to sneak out.

"Where to?" a guard stopped me.

"To the labor battalion," I replied casually. "I have already been inspected."

The guard eyed me suspiciously for a moment, then let me go. I was soon swallowed up by the throng on the Aryan side, about to march out . . . Before long, all of us piled into a wagon, and were rolling through the Polish streets. Our white armbands testified to our being Jews . . . We were nearing the work project. I racked my brains for a way to break away quickly. The others were aware that I had to attend to matters on some Polish street. They urged me to discard my armband and jump off the vehicle. I followed their instructions, and started to walk briskly away. Then I turned off into another street and slackened my pace . . . I was a stranger on the streets of my own city . . . The contrast with the ghetto was startling. Here there were trolleys, automobiles, bicycles racing along. Businessess open; children headed for school; women carried fresh bread and other provisions. It was another world, a world teeming with life . . .

At last I arrived at the address Michal had given me. I made my way to the cellar, and banged on the door. A blonde Gentile woman opened it. Upon entering, Michal welcomed me warmly, "You're here at last! I waited at the gate for hours for you" . . . We greeted each other warmly. I breathed a sigh of relief; here was a friend in an alien world.

"I didn't expect you to venture out today; the guards were extremely strict," Michal observed, pouring some tea for me. I glanced around the living quarters. Two small, low-ceilinged rooms inhabited by a family of four. Stephan Machai, a Gentile, looked amiably at Michal. Before the war they had worked together . . . Now a "ricksha" pusher, the stocky Gentile considered it an honor to have the one-time engineer as his guest here . . . Sensing that Michal was a bit despondent, I asked him what had happened.

"My sister Gina died in the hospital," he informed me quietly: "and is being buried today. If you wish you can accompany me to the cemetery."

I refrained from telling him of the ordeal I had undergone while leaving the ghetto. My experience paled in the presence of death. I had known Gina Klepfisz before the war, having worked with her in the *Zukunft* at Praga (a Warsaw suburb), where she had organized a

369

children's group. She had been both serious and kindhearted; children adored her. Recently, she had worked as a nurse . . . Now, I had hardly stepped into the Aryan sector, only to be confronted with news of her death. Michal and I walked silently to the hospital where Michal was to meet his wife.

Within a few moments, his wife appeared, trying to hold back her tears. A nurse motioned to us to follow her into the morgue, where we found Gina's corpse, clothed in white. My eyes were riveted upon this lifeless body—all that remained of the woman whom I remembered as vivacious and energetic, and who, as a hospital employee, had been instrumental in smuggling Jews out of the *Umschlagplatz*.[2] Under cover of darkness, she would steer doomed men and women across the barbed wire, at the risk of her own life. Once she had been caught by a Jewish policeman. Her courageous stand had dampened his ire somewhat, but he had dismissed her from her job, then and there. Whereupon, together with her brother, sister-in-law, and year-old child, she had crossed over to the Aryan side.

At a signal from the nurse that someone was approaching, we crossed ourselves; that a Jewess had died while undergoing surgery in a Christian hospital must not be known . . . On her deathbed, Gina had confided to the Polish priest that she was Jewish, and the father had pledged secrecy. She was to be interred as a Christian . . .

A strange funeral indeed: of the ten mourners following the hearse, only two were Christians. The funeral was carried out in accordance with Roman Catholic tradition and the grave was marked with a cross.

We took our leave of Gina Klepfisz—one of the few Warsaw Jews to be buried in a cemetery at a time when tens of thousands of Jews were being gassed and cremated.

# "What Strength Was Needed!"

*Gusta Davidson, the writer of this memoir, came from Cracow, where she and her husband were members of the underground. Both were executed in 1943. She wrote the "Diary of Justina," which is available in Polish and Hebrew but has not yet been published in English . . .*

[2]deportation center for the death camp.

# Hiding, "Passing," Escaping . . .

One had to go back to the Middle Ages to appreciate the mutilation of personality involved in being kept out of every area of life, isolated from world culture, to understand what it meant to a human being to be imprisoned in a cage and told: "Sit here and wait. We are getting your death ready" . . .

For passing outside the ghetto walls—the sentence was death. For appearing in the street without a blue and white armband on your right arm—death. For trying to conceal your Jewish origin—death. Entering a street car, wagon, train, automobile—all punishable by death. There was no need to be a revolutionary—it was enough simply to be what you were, to take one false step, to fall into the trap laid for you—because you were a Jew.

If you stayed in the ghetto it was impossible to do anything except sit with folded hands waiting for deportation and the gas chamber. Anyone who wanted to act had first of all to leave the ghetto—and that was a step which already constituted warfare.

It's so easy to say, "Run away!" But how do you get through a barbed wire fence guarded by police? How, for that matter, do you take one step across the street to the free side? They'd see the armband—and here's a bullet in your head! Stand and remove the essential gewgaw—someone is sure to notice, and hand you straight over to the police. Take it off surreptitiously and even in the darkest doorway there will always be an eye to observe that you went into the doorway a Jew and came out—what? Yes, what?

For you could remove the armband a thousand times, but you could not jump out of your skin and become someone else. Become, simply, a Jew without an armband. Every unquiet movement, every uncertain step, the slave's stoop, the scared look of the quarry, everything about you—your entire stance, face, eyes, all bear the print of the ghetto, testify that you're a Jew. You are a Jew, simply, not so much because of the color of your eyes, hair, skin, the shape of your nose, et cetera, but because of your insecurity, your lack of dignity, your intonation, language, behavior, and the devil knows what other signs. And you have betrayed your Jewishness ultimately because everyone was looking for it in you; they were all looking for a chance to attack you, they couldn't bear the thought of your escaping death. At every step they'd stare into your eyes, brazenly, suspiciously, provocatively, to unnerve you, send the blood rising to your cheeks, make you lower your eyes. You would have lost—you could not conceal the fact that you were a Jew.

And so, even before you gained the nearby railroad station you had behind you many eye battles, dumb struggles with the enemy hidden in every passerby. Frequently, you had adventures with extortionists that left you with just enough money to take you to the next town. Then,

---

From *Commentary Magazine*, July 1958 ("Diary of Justina") by Gusta Davidson.

after eventually reaching the station, you came within firing range of the men in uniform. For there were many policemen specially trained to uncover disguised Jews—secret Polish, German, Ukrainian agents. There were also detectives, many of them of your own faith. How much coolness was needed to pass erect through the waiting room, shrugging off confidently the probing looks of secret agents . . .

Once on the train you were at the mercy of the lowest class of human being. There was no way of escaping their eyes; they had no sense of delicacy, they shot glances like bullets into the most private parts of your heart, smelling the Jew everywhere, eager to hand him over to the police, or, in any case, torment him, blackmail him, threaten him . . .

At times—through a powerful tensing of muscle—you were able to wipe out your footsteps. But it was impossible to escape the most painful situation—the conversations on the train that froze the blood in your veins. For what did people talk about? About the Jews, of course. "Good for them. They finally got what they deserve. They tried to run away, but, our luck, they got caught. They planned to take their gold with them—it was confiscated in time." Slander, rumors, disgusting lies—and worst of all, the animal joy at the murder of hundreds of thousands of old men, women, and children. They hung around waiting to grab up Jewish property, like hyenas waiting for a man to die . . . While here, in a corner of the train, sat a human being whose heart was twisted with pain over the loss of those dearest to him. But he dared not show his agitation with the tremor of a muscle—for that would betray him as a Jew . . .

Anyone who's been through a single experience of that kind and come out alive is entitled to write an epic. If you're not a Jew you can travel anywhere in relative comfort. But if you're a Jew every movement outside the barbed wire fence is an incursion into enemy territory, under cross fire. Here only accident can protect you. Accident, and inner strength—the most desired weapon . . .

But first you had to purge yourself in a powerful mental crucible. You came out of the inner fire psychologically either refined or debased. The distinction between the two is narrow and slippery; the abyss threatened. It was the easiest thing in the world to succumb to self-disgust. For he who begins by denying himself ends by despising himself. He who imitates others is bound to resemble them in time. He who conceals his true personality degrades it. He who degrades himself outwardly is degraded inwardly.

Who would ever have believed that *they* would sink to the level of concealing their Jewishness—they, who had been proud of it for years and had maintained their dignity in the face of insult? *They,* who had dedicated their carefree youth to Jewishness, in which they saw their personal renascence, the meaning of their lives? How could they deny themselves even for an instant, concealing their origin like cowards?

But this was necessity, compulsion, an ineluctable act, without which they could not move a step. So, having suppressed their inner rebellion, the voice that commanded them to fling a cry for battle into the face of the inert masses—they decided to put on a mask. No, there wasn't a thing they wouldn't do to reach their goal. Every means to their end became holy. It did not matter if on the surface they seemed to be denying themselves. That very denial strengthened their essential feeling of self a hundred times—their personalities expanded. As the debasement forced on them from the outside grew, their inner pride in being Jewish increased. Compelled to hide their Jewishness, they delighted in it, resolved to stand by it to their last breath. Never, not for a fleeting instant, did the thought flash across their minds that if they were not Jews they would not be standing on the brink of this abyss. They would not have given up their identification with their people for all the money in the world. They were full of bitterness because they could not make an open fight, as Jews. That was the only thing that could have contented them. They believed their hour would strike, soon; meanwhile, they worked in the underground with that consoling expectation.

Could anyone ever understand them—this group of madmen who had long been deprived of the right to live, because they were Jews, yet who insisted not merely on living, but on taking arms, as well? Could their fear be understood—the revolutionary's fear of failing before he had accomplished what he had set out to do? Could anyone possibly understand their fear of dying before they had done anything for the cause? Not a man of them feared death; they all feared to fall into the enemy's hands, prematurely, being picked up by the authorities for some inconsequential matter . . .

Hence, their first efforts were concentrated on the problem of disguising themselves. Characterization, costume, posture—these were their daily concerns. Facial makeup, outward appearance, became matters so serious that every other criterion for judging people became relatively unimportant. Courage could have no decisive meaning if it was not accompanied by the prerequisite of a successful outward appearance. Eventually, they learned to overcome that obstacle. Youth and self-esteem came to their aid. The ghetto was unable to stamp their fresh faces with the mark of slavery. They left the ghetto with heads raised, proudly, striding with an assurance that made others give way for them. No one sensed that they were persons in flight, no one dared to insult them. And yet their personal security hung by a hair. It was enough for one terrible memory, one tragic thought, to hang a cloud of anxiety across their forehead, their eyes to darken—and they betrayed their Jewishness. At such a moment nothing could save you—neither blond hair, nor blue eyes, nor a straight nose . . .

Nor was there any lack of occasion for such betrayals. How many wonderful girls attracted attention simply because of their beauty! In vain they dyed their hair blonde—their black eyes never lost their native charm. At every street corner, in every street car, danger lurked! Here an old friend, there an extortionist, there a secret agent, an over-observant policeman, a body search—the path to freedom was beset with obstacles that made it as impenetrable as a dense forest.

And then, this was all new to them. Never in their lives had they played any role but themselves; they had always, everywhere, been completely natural. Now, before engaging in the activist operation, they had to wage an inner battle with themselves, where defeat meant death. They had to play their role to the bitter end. How often, even after you had fallen into the hands of the police, you had to deny you were a Jew—and to the last. What strength was needed!

Very often, your nerves couldn't hold out, and at the decisive moment they snapped like a string. In such moments of despair the thought would seize you: "I have lived as a Jew, I will die as one!" The confession rises to your lips; but suddenly, your mind clears and commands you to save yourself, to look for another way out, for the sake of the cause. The nerves tense again, finally under control. But mostly, it's a matter of luck, so it's really hard to talk about a personal victory . . .

---

# Forty-Eight Thousand Lives in Exchange for Four U.S.A. Visas

*Prominent in the world of merchandising, industry, music, and diplomacy, Ira A. Hirschmann went on a secret mission to Turkey for President Franklin D. Roosevelt to rescue Jews, especially children. He wrote about his extraordinary experiences in three books,* Lifeline to a Promised Land, Caution to the Winds, *and* The Embers Still Burn.

On a barren stretch of scorched earth laid waste by retreating Russians in what had been the Ukraine, the Rumanian government had set up a vast concentration camp where they imprisoned 175,000 Jews and anti-Fascists. This was the infamous camp of Transnistria . . .

From *Caution to the Winds* by Ira A. Hirschmann.

374

Since Rumania was close to my post in Turkey, I received direct reports on the horrors of Transnistria. Thousands were perishing daily because of cold and hunger. Roads were littered with the sick, the dying and the dead. By the time of my arrival in Turkey the camp's population had been reduced to approximately 100,000; the death rate was estimated at 1,000 a day.

To be so close to this death trap and not to be able to do anything about it was an unbearable frustration and weighed heavily on those of us who were charged with the task of rescue. But the stubborn reality was that these men, women and children were prisoners in enemy territory . . . Against a background of Allied bombardment of the Ploesti oilfields and the city of Bucharest, I decided that my only recourse was to find some way to meet with the enemy and to offer some sort of deal . . . The situation was desperate, and I could find no alternative to the extreme measures it called for.

Again I was fortified by preparations made in New York before coming to Ankara. In the last days before my departure, I had met Carol Davila, the pre-war Rumanian Minister to the United States, where he was living in exile resulting from his opposition to the deal made with the Nazis by the Rumanian dictator, Antonescu, leader of the Fascist Iron Guard. Without knowing whether it would ever be of any use, I asked for and obtained a letter from Davila to Alexandre Cretzianu, Rumania's Minister to Turkey. Now, having decided to risk an approach to the enemy, I gave this letter to Gilbert Simond, the representative of the International Red Cross in Ankara, and asked him to act as my intermediary to arrange a clandestine meeting with the Rumanian Minister if he could . . .

To make this overture I used a special government sanction which had been given me by the Secretary of the Treasury, Henry Morgenthau. He alone was authorized to waive the restrictions of the Trading with the Enemy Act which made it a crime for any American citizen to consult or negotiate with the enemy in time of war . . . Morgenthau had foreseen the possibility of a situation such as the one that confronted me and our embassy in Turkey was advised of his decision while I was en route.

It was an unprecedented vote of confidence and the very first thing Ambassador Steinhardt had mentioned to me on my arrival in Turkey. "They have given you the broadest powers of any envoy that I have known—broader than an ambassador's," he told me, adding, "You are even permitted to deal directly with the enemy."

Still, a meeting with the enemy involved many risks. I knew that I was under the surveillance of German and Japanese agents in Turkey. I learned later that I was even being shadowed by the British. I had been warned in Washington that any revelation of my negotiating with the enemy would destroy my usefulness and force my recall. The State

Department would have to disavow any actions that would embarrass our government.

Nor was I by any means incognito or unrecognized. I can still recall with something of a shudder the evening I heard startling proof of this. I was in my hotel room turning the dials on my radio in quest of some good music when I accidentally caught a propaganda broadcast from Berlin which startlingly demanded, "What is Jew Hirschmann doing in Ankara? Certainly, he can be up to no good."

I was plagued by the news of what was happening in Transnistria. While the flow of refugees across the Black Sea was encouraging, it was heartbreakingly slow. I was impatient for a major break-through.

Simond was almost as excited as I was when he brought me the news that Cretzianu had agreed to a rendezvous. It was set for Saturday evening at Simond's house on the outskirts of Ankara.

By agreement, I arrived an hour before the time for our meeting. I paced the floor of Simond's modest living room which was almost hermetically sealed by blinds. As the time grew near, I succumbed to the temptation of the piano standing there in open invitation for the release of my tension . . . Simond, who had come into the room during my impromptu recital, was now pacing the floor. Then the doorbell rang. Cretzianu had arrived.

He turned out to be an attractive and urbane man in his early forties. Despite his years as a diplomat, Cretzianu couldn't hide the same nervousness that had attacked me.

I cited the Emergency Order of the President of the United States that authorized my discussion with him, and we sat down to talk. "Do you mind if I take notes?" were his first words. For an hour we spoke in generalities. Our pencils were poised over our blank pads, but neither of us wrote a word. Nothing worth reporting had transpired.

As best I could, I steered the conversation from one subject to another, searching his face for an indication of interest or any emotional reaction. My clue came after a casual mention of the Russians. I could sense almost as much, as I could see a shadow pass over his face. Suddenly he said:

"It's the Russians we fear, not the Americans."

This was what I had been looking for. Dropping all caution and with it all formality, I looked straight into Cretzianu's eyes and coldly, almost brutally, said: "Mr. Minister, you, Antonescu and your families are going to be killed." He winced, but I continued in the same vein: "The Russians will do it."

After a pause during which neither of us said a word, I resumed: "I will offer you a visa for every member of your family in exchange for one simple act which will cost you nothing."

"And what is that?" he queried.

"Open the door of the camp in Transnistria. These are your citizens, but if you don't want them, we will take them."

He seemed genuinely shocked. "And why does the President of the United States send a personal representative to negotiate for some Jews?"

"That is why the United States is what it is," I countered, "and why Rumania is where it is today" . . .

I told Cretzianu that I knew of his father's fine record as a diplomat in Washington in the 1920's and I expressed the hope that in better times he might continue in the tradition of his family. He might even serve in the United States. This brought a bemused smile, but I could see that he was preoccupied with our previous conversation.

Encouraged by the rift in his armor resulting from this personal conversation, I ventured far beyond my terms of reference and as a tentative gambit said, "Why not get out of the war? We will offer you an honorable peace and you will have the distinction of being the first Balkan country to break away from Hitler."

Of course I had no authority to do this, but Cretzianu responded directly. "If we could only have some assurance that American influence would remain in the Balkans," he said.

After two and a half hours, he asked, "Precisely what do you want and what do you offer?" I was ready for this. "We request first," I replied, "that you disband the camp at Transnistria and that those remaining be permitted to return to their homes immediately. Second, that you release five thousand children, facilitate their passage to Constantsa, provide exit permits for them, and expedite the debarkation of ships which we will provide to take these children to Istanbul and from there to Haifa in Palestine. Third, we ask that Antonescu put an end to all persecution and repressive acts against minorities in Rumania."

Cretzianu finished writing his notes on my demands before he said: "It is not impossible. I promise to recommend it. But what will you offer in return?"

"It should not be necessary to offer anything to a government to have it stop killing its own citizens," I said. "But I promise you visas for entrance to the United States for you and the three members of your family. In addition, I will offer you the good will of the Government of the United States of America to serve as an indication of an open door for you to break with the Nazis."

We parted cordially after Cretzianu promised that he would immediately fly to Bucharest where he would "recommend warmly" his government's acceptance of my proposal. He would get an answer through to me by way of Gilbert Simond . . .

A week later there was a call from Simond to hurry to his home. I was about to leave for Istanbul, but the apparent breath of urgency in his voice made me change my plans. I hastened to the little house on the side street.

In less than five minutes the dapper Rumanian envoy, who must have been waiting near-by, rushed into the room. The slick, urbane manner had disappeared. Catching his breath with difficulty he read snatches from a telegram from Antonescu. General Gheorghe Potopeanu had already been instructed to break up the camp in Transnistria. The prisoners were already leaving for Bucharest. The 5,000 children would soon reach Constantsa for embarkation. All persecutions were stopped. Coincidentally, the telegram ended in the middle of a sentence. The decoding device had broken down. "I must get the rest of the telegram," he said, and was soon out of the room.

The next day while I was sitting in Ambassador Steinhardt's office, the telephone rang. It was Simond. He said: "I have just had a report from our representative in Bucharest. It reads: 'Due to reasons unknown to me, the camp in Transnistria has been disbanded.'"

I stared straight ahead of me; instead of reacting with excitement, I was stunned. The feeling of relief that gradually came over me was indescribable. A huge weight seemed to fall off my shoulders, followed by an awareness that it was now my turn to deliver. I couldn't duck my commitments to Cretzianu.

Before he left, Cretzianu had said something which, while it caused a twinge of conscience, strongly reinforced my belief in unhesitant, affirmative action. He said: "If this means so much to you in the United States, why didn't you come sooner? You could have saved more lives."

Then and there, I resolved never again to indulge in hesitant mercy. All those in my own family, friends, businessmen who had tried to discourage me from undertaking what seemed to them in New York to be a hopeless mission, were wrong, pessimistically and unimaginatively wrong. And I blamed myself for not having acted sooner.

I wrote a report of my negotiations and sent it off to Washington. Not trusting the cables or intervening desks at the State Department, I held back my promise of visas for Cretzianu's family but requested permission to return to the States for consultation. I wanted to discuss that delicate matter in person.

Luck was with me in Washington. Adolph Berle, a former professor at Columbia University and an old colleague in the La Guardia administration, had, in my absence, been appointed Assistant Secretary of State in charge of refugee matters. I told him the entire story and explained the promise I had made as a price for the release of the people in Transnistria. To his credit, he agreed with alacrity and recommended to Secretary Hull that the visas be issued and made available at the American Embassy in Ankara.

Many of those released from the camp at Transnistria have survived. I meet them all over the country and in Canada on my speaking trips. Only recently I met a man who had left the camp as a boy and made his way to Palestine in one of the little boats. He is now the manager of the King David Hotel in Jerusalem.

The broader implications in my talks with Cretzianu tragically were not realized. For, in spite of my lack of authorization to suggest peace talks, I had made an opening for negotiations with Rumania. This was contained in my report to Washington. Great Britain, the allied power controlling that theater of operations, had been fully advised. They made contact with the Rumanians but while they shifted their negotiations to British Headquarters in Cairo, the Russians moved into Rumania which became firmly established behind the Iron Curtain.

As was to be expected, Antonescu and his henchmen as well as their families were all executed by the Russians: Their Minister to Ankara, Alexandre Cretzianu, escaped with his family. In fact, some months later, he visited me in my office in New York.

Most of the former inmates of Transnistria are still trapped in the vise of Communist Russia. Some of them have made their way to freedom in Israel. At the risk of seeming to be facetious about a matter of the utmost seriousness, I must say that this was the best merchandising deal I ever made in a lifetime of dealing. We saved 100,000 lives[1] in exchange for four visas given as bribes.

# "Operation Baptism": The Future Pope John XXIII Saves Hungarian Jews

The deportation of Hungarian Jews had been stepped up to a rate that indicated the frantic efforts of Eichmann and his murdering crew to finish their genocide before the end of the war . . . From April 10 to May 21, twenty-nine transports had gone from Hungary to Auschwitz, carrying 94,667 Jews to their death. The next seven days saw fifty-eight transports take away 184,049 Jews, and from May 28 to June 7, another 175,415 were slaughtered. Finally, between June 6 and June 28, 61,944 more of these defenseless people were rounded up and shipped to the gas chambers, leaving all of Hungary

---

[1]Dr. Jacob Robinson in his article on the Holocaust in *Encyclopedia Judaica* states that the actual number saved was 48,000.

---

From *Caution to the Winds* by Ira A. Hirschmann

outside of Budapest "*judenrein* (free of Jews)"—the most devastating mass annihilation of human lives in the history of mankind.

We didn't know all the facts in Turkey, but enough were available to us to realize that time was racing against death. Something had to be done to save the Jewish population of Budapest—approximately a quarter of a million men, women and children.

I turned once again to Gilbert Simond. I pleaded with him to prevail upon his friends in the Catholic Church to help us in the name of humanity . . . After a short spell during which I assume Simond made an effort along the lines I had requested, he made a sounder suggestion that we go directly to the Apostolic Delegate of the Church who was then in residence on . . . an island in the Marmora Sea, forty minutes by boat from Istanbul. I jumped at the suggestion and Simond arranged a meeting with the delegate, Angelo Roncalli . . .

The house of the Pope's highest emissary in the Middle East was a spacious, old-fashioned home sitting high atop a hill . . . We were ushered into a well-appointed room where we waited for Roncalli. After a few minutes, a short, rotund man . . . entered the room. Good humor was immediately evident in his eyes, twinkling under his black skullcap. Warmly and graciously he welcomed us in Italian, bidding us be seated. As I did, I offered a silent prayer of thanks for the Italian I had learned some years back: it established an easy contact between us.

Once Simond and I were comfortably settled, our host turned to a small cupboard from which he took a bottle of red wine. After admiring its color, he poured out three glasses and insisted on drinking to our health. Anxious about my mission, I discreetly tried to introduce the reason for my visit. But Roncalli brushed me aside, saying, "That will come later. First we must enjoy the view, the conversation and the wine."

His personality was so radiant and his conviviality so genuine that for the moment I let the purpose of my presence escape me. In fact, it wasn't until a second bottle had been downed that he would permit any thought of practical discussion. Then, suddenly, he announced, "*Dunque, cominciamo* . . . Now, let us begin."

Roncalli listened intently as I outlined the desperate plight of the Jews in Hungary. I cited the meager statistics available to me and the many eyewitness accounts of underground operatives. As I emphasized each salient point, he nodded sympathetically. Then he pulled his chair up closer and quietly asked, "Do you have any contact with people in Hungary who will co-operate?" After my affirmative reply, he hesitated a few moments before asking, "Do you think the Jews there would be willing to undergo baptism ceremonies?"

Not prepared for this suggestion, I equivocated a bit and said that I could only guess or assume that if it meant saving their lives they would be ready to do so gratefully. I added, "I know what I would do."

He went on to say that he had reason to believe that some baptismal

380

certificates had already been issued by nuns to Hungarian Jews. The Nazis had recognized these as credentials and had permitted their holders to leave the country.

We agreed that we would communicate with his representatives in Hungary and that I would get in touch with our underground connections to arrange for either large-scale baptism of Jews, or at least certificates to be issued to women and children. It would be up to them to decide later whether they would wish to remain in the Church or "go their way."

The proposal and agreement had been accomplished in what seemed like a few minutes. It was clear to me that Roncalli had considered this plan before my arrival, and that he had created an atmosphere in which to test my credentials, my discretion and my ability to help put the operation into practical effect. I had no doubt that the wheels would soon be set in motion in Hungary for Operation Baptism under the auspices and with the mercy of the Catholic Church.

Simond and I were silent as we sailed back to Istanbul in the little ferryboat. Somehow, we were awed by the scope and direction of the events of the afternoon, arrived at so simply and without inhibition, but so fraught with possibilities. In our silence we were attempting to take stock of their implications.

My mind flashed back to the first moment when I had heard the name Roncalli. It dated back to the first days after my arrival at the Ankara Palas Hotel in Ankara. I was informed that the Chief Rabbi of Palestine, Isaac Halevi Herzog, was in the hotel, confined to his room by illness. Fortunately, his brilliant young son, Yaacov, was with him to attend him. Herzog had come on his own initiative to try to use his persuasion to help rescue the persecuted Jews. The Rabbi told me that chief among the men whom he planned to see was the Catholic Apostolic Delegate—Angelo Roncalli.

I had spent several rewarding hours at the bedside of this venerable rabbi. Originally from Dublin, Ireland, he spoke with a beautiful English-Irish brogue. To me, an American, this seemed charmingly incongruous coming from the lips of an Old-Testament sage with a white beard. His words of wisdom and faith could not have been better timed for me—about to set out on an uncharted sea of human rescue.

On the way back to the mainland I recalled my bedside visits to the Chief Rabbi. Might it even have been possible that this means of rescue of Hungarian Jews had been broached by Roncalli in his fateful visit in February, 1944?

We were approaching twilight and as our little steamer skimmed through the water, the lengthening shadows of the fading day stretched ahead of us like moving phantoms across the sea. Could this be a portent, I mused, of the lifting of a curtain to reveal a new freedom for those who waited for our help?

For some unaccountable reason, historians have glossed over this instance of warmth and compassion in a period of violence and hate. In my report to Washington I stated, "For the record, it should be stated that the Catholic hierarchy, which enjoys a large influence in Hungary, took unusual spontaneous measures to rescue Hungarian Jewish citizens wherever possible. This was reported to you in my No. 131, August 12, and related to the baptism of thousands of Hungarian Jews in air-raid shelters, in spite of energetic Nazi protests."

Some years later at a Thanksgiving Day dinner in New York, I was seated next to a woman who spoke with a European accent. When our conversation revealed that she had come from Hungary, I asked casually if she had known any Jews who had been baptized in Budapest in the last days of the war. Quickly and nervously, with obviously controlled emotion, she said: "I was baptized and saved at the last hour in a bomb-cellar." She went on to describe how the underground in Budapest had given her a certificate of baptism from the Catholic Church which served as her passport for escape from the Nazis to Switzerland and eventually to the United States. Hearing similar stories from many others in the course of the ensuing years has never failed to move me deeply . . .

Try as I may, I have not been able to ascertain exactly how many Hungarian Jews were saved or had their lives made easier with these baptismal certificates. They must number in the thousands. And all this was due to the kindly intervention of the benevolent Apostolic Delegate to the Middle East. Is it any wonder that I was moved to tears when in 1958 I read the headlines which announced to the world that Angelo Roncalli had been elected Pope, the ruler of the Catholic Church? . . .

# 16. HASIDEI UMOT HAOLAM: THE RIGHTEOUS GENTILES

According to Holocaust survivor K. Shabbatai[1] the Nazis and many of the peoples they conquered were united by a common desire to wipe out the Jews. Many Europeans were active or passive anti-Semites, others were "neutral" so far as the Final Solution was concerned, but some were devoted, courageous friends who did all they could to help the Jews.

These noble friends, whose deeds have engraved their memories in the hearts of a grateful Jewish people, are known as the *Hasidei Umot HaOlam*—the Righteous Among the Nations of the World. Brave, compassionate souls, they were motivated by ideals of humanity and justice.

Father Marie-Benoit, a French priest, Bible scholar, and theologian, was an outstanding hero. Working first in France and then out of the Capuchin college in Rome, he was active in the French and Italian resistance movements and built up an organization for smuggling Jews and anti-Nazis to safety. His "passport factory" in Rome provided forged passports, ration cards, and other documents. With funds provided by the JDC and other interested parties, he helped thousands to escape.[2]

Plain folk in all the countries of Nazi-occupied Europe risked their lives

[1] See his *As Sheep to the Slaughter? The Myth of Cowardice* (World Federation of Bergen-Belsen Survivors, 1963).
[2] Read Father Benoit's full story in (Fernand), *The Incredible Mission* (Garden City: Doubleday, 1969).

to perform deeds of rescue. In Vilna, for instance, Ona Simaite was a tower of strength to the ghetto, a savior of Jewish lives and cultural treasures. She survived despite inhuman tortures by the Nazis and in 1946 visited her "children" in Israel. In Radom, Poland, Wladislaw Misuina hid scores of deportees on the rabbit farm he operated to provide fur for winter clothing worn by German soldiers in Russia. Martyred Jop Westerweel of Holland is remembered ardently by many Jews whom he smuggled into Spain. Eduardo Focherini, of Bologna, Italy, was also martyred, leaving a widow and seven children, for helping Italian Jews to escape to Switzerland. And there were many other such Righteous Gentiles, some of them anonymous. All exemplified the golden rule: "And thou shalt love thy neighbor as thyself" (Leviticus 19:18), in many cases sacrificing their own lives to save others.[3]

Gloriously outstanding among the righteous are the Danes. The whole Danish people rose as one on Rosh Hashanah, October 1, 1943, to rescue the Jews of their country. Using fishing boats and pleasure craft, they conveyed almost the entire Jewry of Denmark to neutral Sweden; in addition they hid a hundred Torah scrolls and many other valuable ceremonial objects and historical documents belonging to the Jewish community. After the war most of Denmark's Jews returned home, receiving a rousing welcome from their Gentile neighbors.

What is most extraordinary is that the Danes were truly unaware that they had done anything remarkable. They could not quite grasp why the world reacted with such great admiration and praise. They could not imagine that it was possible to have done anything else: how could they have surrendered their Jewish fellow citizens to a certain death at the hands of the Nazis? The very idea was unthinkable.[4]

Bulgaria also acted to protect its forty-eight thousand Jewish citizens. Although the Bulgarian Jews were subjected to persecution, the nation's political and religious leaders intervened to prevent the Nazis from deporting them to concentration camps.[5]

There were even a few brave Germans who resisted the Hitler tyranny and went to martyrdom unflinching. The stories of some of them are recounted in *Dying We Live* (New York: Pantheon Books, 1956), a unique collection of letters and stirring personal testaments. Some of these opponents of Nazism were communists or socialists, others were

---

[3]Many episodes of heroism and self-sacrifice by Christians who saved Jews are recounted in Philip Friedman, *Their Brother's Keepers* (New York: Praeger, 1954). The brave efforts of righteous Poles to save Jews are covered in Wladyslaw Bartoszewski and Zofia Lewin, *The Samaritans* (New York: Twayne Publishers, 1972).

[4]For further information on the rescue of Danish Jewry, read Harold Flender, *Rescue in Denmark* (New York: Simon & Schuster, 1963), Aage Bertelsen, *October '43* (New York: American Jewish Committee, 1973), and Leni Yahil, *The Rescue of Danish Jewry* (Philadelphia: Jewish Publication Society, 1969).

[5]Frederick B. Chary, *The Bulgarian Jews and the Final Solution* (Pittsburgh: University of Pittsburgh Press, 1972).

nonpolitical, but they were all people of integrity who would not compromise with evil. Among them was the noted Protestant theologian Pastor Dietrich Bonhoeffer, who in 1941 wrote, "I pray for the defeat of my country. Only in defeat can we atone for the terrible crimes we have committed."[6]

When the catastrophe came to an end, the Jewish people remembered their saviors with feelings of intense awe and gratitude. Yad Vashem in Israel has eternalized their names, and long rows of trees have been planted in their memory along the Avenue of the Hasidei Umot HaOlam in Jerusalem. The heroes, or their heirs, have been awarded impressive medals bearing the inscription, "He who saves one soul is considered as if he preserved the whole world" (Talmud, *Sanhedrin* 37), and many of the survivors have invited their brave benefactors to visit Israel.

# "Money Poured in from All Quarters": The Spirit of the Danes

*Dr. Aage Bertelsen headed the second largest college in Denmark and achieved prominence as a writer. He became a leader of the Underground, with a price on his head . . .*

One morning on my way back after a nightly transport had been sent off, I was standing in the aisle of the subway train . . . We were talking about what was on our minds, and we did it quietly . . . It was inconceivable that anyone could overhear our conversation. Yet suddenly a woman in the car got up from her seat and went straight up to me and said, "Would you like some money?" "Yes, thank you, very much," I said immediately. She took her purse out of her bag and emptied its entire contents in bills into my hand, and then went back again to her seat without further comment. I do not remember having seen her before or after that.

That minor incident is one of many which proves that . . . the will to

[6]For further information on Germans who helped the Jews and opposed the Nazis, read H. D. Leuner, *When Compassion Was a Crime: Germany's Silent Heroes (1938–45)* (London: Oswald Wolff, 1966), and Michael Horback, *Out of the Night* (New York: Frederick Fell, 1969).

From *October '43* by Aage Bertelsen.

help the persecuted, penetrated the entire atmosphere of our country. Money poured in from all quarters, for instance, from schools where the pupils made their contributions toward the transports . . .

My first thought when the registration with us of destitute Jews began to increase was that I would go direct to the government . . . (which then existed under the Germans only in the shape of a management by the heads of individual departments) to Mr. Dige of the Ministry for Finance. I did so quite confidently, feeling convinced that if it was humanly possible he would help. As I had expected, I met the most complete understanding . . . but I soon realized that direct help from the Treasury was inconceivable. If the Germans got the slightest suspicion that the state was granting funds for purposes directly contrary to German interests, it might bring about the most serious consequences for the entire Danish people. At that time the German control of our finances was so thorough that it would have been extremely difficult to camouflage any payments to assist the Jews. On the other hand, we both considered it an absolutely intolerable thought that the Danish state had had to pay a fine of 1,000,000 kroner for a German who had been killed during some disturbances not long ago, while now many persecuted Jews were in danger—if the necessary means were not provided—of being handed over to a fate which everybody considered worse than death.

Without any definite promise from Mr. Dige—except that he would do his best to find a way out—I left him with a hope amounting almost to certainty that the economic problem of the help to the Jews would eventually be solved. And I was not disappointed! Not only did private individuals devote great sums to the relief work, but other sources as well soon supplied us with ample means to carry it on . . .

The answer with which our collecters of funds were sometimes dismissed—"Let the Jews themselves pay, let them help their own people, they have money enough"—might seem convincing. However, it was based on ignorance of the facts, as well as less pardonable lack of sympathy. The few times I heard that remark I saw before me a picture of people drowning, the old, the young women and children, while at a suitable distance—so they were not annoyed by cries for help from the drowning people—a crowd of passive, though interested, onlookers said: Let them take care of themselves. What business is it of ours? They should have provided themselves with life preservers in time! . . .

The whole of this question must be viewed in connection with the special character of the persecutions of the Jews in Denmark. In contrast to those in the homeland of Nazism and several other countries . . . where true autos-da-fé marked the culmination of a slow development of the continuous restriction of human and civil rights of the Jewish community, diabolic suddenness was employed in this country. Nobody could have foreseen with any degree of certainty what was

386

going to take place in Hitler's "model protectorate," and the unfortunates were not given any chance whatsoever to take any joint precautions to prevent a situation which they knew—as in other countries—would occur almost as a historical necessity. Up to a few days before the raid, the highest Danish authorities advised the Jews not to attempt to arrange a general evacuation, in order not to risk rousing German suspicions and in that way provoking a persecution. The very thought of an organized flight had to be given up in advance as hopeless. The only country of refuge was Sweden, and all ships and smaller boats which were not being used for commercial purposes had been removed from the Danish coasts . . . And it was not until the persecutions had become an accomplished fact that the Swedish ambassador to Denmark, Gustaf von Dardel, persuaded his government to promise a sanctuary for all Danish Jews in Sweden . . .

We tried to carry out the idea of letting the refugees themselves pay for one another during those first days of chaos and money shortage . . . The Jews who wanted to pay for themselves as well as for their fellow sufferers gave us a power of attorney to dispose of their furniture and other property, and at the same time they handed over the keys to their homes and shops. One such power of attorney was sent to a Copenhagen lawyer, who had taken upon himself to arrange that sort of business for the Jews who feared that, as in Germany, their property might be confiscated by the Nazis when they left the country. In other cases we administered them ourselves . . . We collected the goods . . . and one of my co-workers, who runs a second-hand shop himself, undertook the sorting and selling of the varied stock. Only things which we thought were of personal value were kept against the return of the Jews concerned. The money brought in by these sales was deposited temporarily in a secret account . . . so that each individual owner had a certain number known only to the bank manager and me. But as it happened we very soon began to get money in other ways, and we left the amounts untouched, so that they would be at the disposal of the Jews when they returned . . .

In the end we got the money we needed from the refugees themselves, as well as through subscriptions and funds, private or official. We even got more than we needed . . .

The extreme relationship of trust existing among the helpers of the Jews (is illustrated by this episode). One day . . . when it was announced at the Rockefeller Institute, where the entire staff headed by Professor Ege and his wife participated in the relief work, that a raid could be expected, all those who were involved left the laboratories and scattered all over the nearby park and along adjacent roads. The professor's wife, who was walking up and down Juliane Mary Road, was suddenly stopped by a man she did not know, who asked if she was

Mrs. Ege. When she answered yes, he pulled 10,000 kroner out of his pocket, gave it to her, and disappeared. A few minutes afterwards another unknown man appeared, and the whole incident was repeated.

Mrs. Ege went in behind a bicycle shed and hid the money in her stocking and resumed her very profitable walk. A little later a third man appeared. When he asked if she was Professor Ege's wife she looked forward to receiving more money. However, this man did not want to give her money—on the contrary. He was going to help some Jews to get out of the country himself and needed 10,000 kroner. He was told to turn round, and a moment later Mrs. Ege had conjured up the money he needed—much to his surprise . . .

---

# The Merciful Danes

*Thousands of Jews were hidden in the hospitals. They were sheltered by diverse ingenious ways. The entire medical profession, nurses and aides were involved. One night, relates Dr. Lund . . .*

. . . we received information that Bispebjerg Hospital was surrounded by Germans. We therefore drove there to examine the situation from close quarters and found that the Germans had indeed stationed police guards and members of the Schalburg Corps, who examined all the ambulances entering and leaving the hospital. Moreover, there were also German guards on all the staircases. Since there were two hundred refugees in the hospital that night, it cannot be said that the situation was particularly encouraging. Because of the guards we could not remove the Jews from the hospital but we took them all to the nurses' quarters, since we thought that this was the safest place should the Germans carry out a search during the night. We thought it likely that such a search would be carried out in view of the stationing of guards around the hospital over a period of several hours. After this watch had continued for some time without anything happening, we came to the conclusion that no search order had been given by a higher authority. Only such a higher authority had the power to order a large-scale action such as searching the hospital. We knew that the authorities in *Dagmarhus* (the Gestapo headquarters) would only come to their offices in the morning and that we had to move the people quickly, before anything happened. Thus it was that at nine o'clock in the

---

From *The Rescue of Danish Jewry* by Leni Yahil.

morning a funeral cortege left the chapel. The procession consisted of twenty to thirty taxis all filled with refugees. The operation succeeded and the refugees, who knew nothing of the danger they were in, had all slept well in the nurses' apartments placed at their disposal. But the nurses themselves did not sleep much that night.

# Operation Rescue

*In his memoirs, published after the war, Leni Yahil who took part in the rescue action divides the operation into four phases: establishing contact with the Jews; finding hiding places near the coast; obtaining the necessary money; and acquiring boats . . . .*

The first phase may be said to have begun with the warnings. A woman who worked in a government office relates:

I had made no plans for possible flight. On September 15, 1943, I returned to Copenhagen after having spent some time in the country and a few days later a very good friend of mine, now head of a government department, rang me up . . . She asked me if I could not pay a short visit to her office and, she added, bring a reasonable amount of money with me. I had at the time heard certain rumors, and therefore could imagine what she wanted of me.

[At her office] she suggested two alternatives: I could either move into her apartment in Copenhagen, which she was not using at the time since she was living with her mother in Holte (outside the capital), or I could come and live with her there. On the basis of what she had heard she did not think that I would any longer be safe in my own home. She then gave me the key to her apartment in Copenhagen—and with cordial thanks and a promise to make a decision, I left her . . .

A few days later I visited her again, this time to thank her and return her key, and to inform her that I had it from the best sources that the danger had passed and that I would therefore remain at home. She had, she told me, also received similar information; but she added that her offer was of course still valid if I wished to avail myself of it at a later date.

About a week later . . . I came home late in the afternoon and at

From *The Rescue of Danish Jewry* by Leni Yahil.

about five o'clock the telephone rang. A voice I did not recognize said that he was ringing from *Politiken* (one of the large newspapers) and asked me to come to the newspaper office as soon as possible . . . I asked to whom I should go and was told that I would find out when I came. As I occasionally did a little typing work for *Politiken,* I asked whether I should bring my shorthand notebook. The reply was negative, and I then realized what it was all about. I went up to *Politiken* and was at once received by—whom I had known for many years, and who asked me, "Would you like to go to Sweden?"

"No, certainly not," I replied, "I too have heard certain rumors—"

"They are no longer rumors, but extremely grave facts," he broke in, "and in any case you must promise me not to be at home on the night of October 1."

"I am not accustomed to giving promises of that sort," I replied.

"Well," he said, "you will not leave here until you have promised me."

Only then did I think that I understood. "But if things are like that," I continued, "then there are lots of people I must warn."

"You should only think about your nearest relatives," was his reply, "since measures will be taken to have everybody informed."

I promised to leave my house and, shaken to the core, I left my acquaintance, whom I was not to meet again until May 1945.

I had only just returned from the newspaper office when one of my colleagues (also a Jewess) who lived nearby, came to warn me. *Folketing* [Parliament] member Alsing Andersen [the head of the trade union movement] had visited her personally to inform her of the danger and had requested that she also inform me; otherwise he would do it himself—but there were so many he had to go round to.

The work of delivering warnings was not always easy. However, most of the Jews left their homes within a few hours and also passed on the news to one another. From the moment that people were convinced that there was no choice but to run and go into hiding, they generally adapted themselves rapidly to the situation, also helped by acquaintances, friends, and even strangers. Many recall that they managed in the space of a few hours to make arrangements for their property . . .

# A "Lamed-Vovnik"—One of the "Thirty-Six"

*Jewish chaplains played colorful and often even crucial roles in the rescue of DP's. The history of the American Jewish Chaplaincy, and the record of its exploits, especially during World War II, are presented by Chaplain Harold Superstein . . .*

There is an old Jewish legend of the *lamed-vovniks*, thirty-six saintly men upon whom the existence of the world depends. They are found in unexpected places; they are totally unaware of their spiritual stature; they are often unrecognized by those around them. In God's eyes, however, it is their merit which justifies humanity's survival. If I were asked to make nominations for the "Thirty-Six", I would not hesitate to place among them le Vicaire Andre, a man who wears the collar of a Catholic priest and who, to me, comes as close to being a saint as any man I have ever known.

My first contact with le Vicaire Andre came after VE Day when we arrived at my final station in Europe, in Namur, Belgium. I had not been in Namur an hour when I heard of the local Catholic priest, credited with saving the lives of many Jews. I immediately sought him out and found with him more than 20 Jews, some of them Belgians, most of them East European survivors from concentration camps. They were living in his home and were being maintained through his personal efforts.

I learned the details of his story only gradually.

An accidental meeting with Jewish refugees who had fled from Germany to Belgium made him aware of the fate of the Jews under the Nazis. When the War came and Belgium fell, word spread that the Nazis would soon be in Namur. The priest took his Jewish friends into hiding in his home, giving them his own bed and sleeping on the floor for years. For others he found hiding places in the homes of his parishioners. He carried on his secret labors under the very nose of the Gestapo, bringing messages from one refugee to another, carrying food and hope to those in hiding. Eventually the Nazis learned of his deeds and came for him, but he had found out their plan in advance and was able to flee just before they arrived.

After the War, le Vicair Andre returned. Through some mysterious underground, refugees learned of him and came from concentration camps in distant lands. He welcomed them and sheltered them. This was the situation I found when I came to Namur. I did what I could to lighten his burden. I had a regular agreement with our mess sergeant who gave me quantities of left-over food after each meal to bring to the refugees. The priest encouraged them to maintain their religious loyalties and we celebrated the cycle of autumn festivals together.

We also took over a little store as temporary headquarters for the Jewish community, and I visited there every day to see how things were going. One morning I received from Rabbi Abraham Klausner, then stationed at Dachau, a mimeographed list of that camp's survivors. I

---

From *Rabbis in Uniform*, edited by Louis Barish.

hastened down to the DP's headquarters with it and everyone crowded around to go through the long list of names, hoping to discover some loved ones still alive. Other duties called me away and several hours passed before I could return. As my jeep rounded the corner, one of the young men came dashing into the street, his eyes shining, his hands waving hysterically. Unable to wait till I reached him, he kept shouting, "Captain, I found my brother!" I couldn't help thinking how much better the world would be if no man were without a brother—if all of us were brothers to each other.

Finally, I made arrangements for the young people in the group to be turned over to Jewish children's homes in Brussels (most of them eventually went on to Palestine). The evening before they were to leave Namur, we had a dinner party honoring the priest and I formally presented him a program we had printed which all of us signed. He received it with great emotion.

I shall never forget the parting scene the next morning as the youngsters prepared to leave for Brussels. Each in turn kissed and embraced the priest, who had been a real father to them, before receiving his blessing. As we pulled away I looked back. Le Vicaire Andre was standing in the middle of the road, tears streaming down his cheeks. The youngsters, meanwhile, began singing such Hebrew and Yiddish songs as *Am Yisroel Chai* and *Vos mir zeinen zeinen mir, uber Yiden zeinen mir* . . .

# 17. | WARSAW GHETTO REBELLION

The Warsaw Ghetto uprising, in 1943, epitomized the agony and heroism of the *Shoah*. The day on which it began, April 19, is now observed by Jews everywhere as a time for mourning and solemn pride.

Hitler's birthday was on April 20, and Himmler, wanting to present his master with a "burnt offering" as a gift, chose April 19 as the date for making the Warsaw Ghetto *judenrein,* free of Jews. Thousands of well-equipped SS and other German troops, reinforced by Ukrainian, Polish, and Latvian paramilitary police, moved in to liquidate the ghetto. They were met by the ghetto's fighting units, who countered the Nazi tanks, artillery, and flamethrowers with a pitiful assortment of knives, pistols, and rifles, and some homemade grenades and fire bombs. To quote Ringelblum, "The battle was between a fly and an elephant."

Before long the entire ghetto had become a battlefield, "enveloped in a thick smoke cloud, increasing in intensity from hour to hour. . . . the Germans had decided simply to smoke out the ghetto, having in the meantime realized that they could not break their resistance in open fight. Thousands of women and children were burnt to death in the houses . . ."

From the outset the ghetto fighters knew they were doomed, especially when their appeal for aid to the Polish underground went unanswered,[1] but they fought on bravely from house to house, making the Nazis pay in blood for every inch of ground they gained. Finally, on May 16, when the last Jewish bullet was expended, the Wehrmacht managed to overwhelm the few surviving defenders. According to Nazi records, not a single Jew

---

[1] See Reuben Aizenstein, "The Warsaw Ghetto Uprising and the Poles," *Midstream,* June 1963.

gave up voluntarily throughout the battle. On May 8, when the Jewish headquarters bunker at 18 Mila Street was surrounded, Mordecai Anie-lewicz and the other Jewish leaders committed suicide rather than surrender.

At the conclusion of the battle, SS General Juergen Stroop, who was later executed as a war criminal, announced triumphantly: "There is no more any inhabited Jewish quarter in Warsaw." He reported 56,065 Jews killed and 631 bunkers destroyed. To celebrate the "historical victory," Stroop dynamited and destroyed Warsaw's Great Synagogue, a magnificent edifice that had been one of Poland's architectural landmarks.

The example set by the Warsaw uprising led to many other Jewish uprisings—in the death camps of Treblinka (August 2, 1943) and Sobibor (October 14, 1943), and in the ghettos of Bialystock (August 16–23, 1943), Vilna, Cracow, and other towns. Jews everywhere were profoundly moved and inspired by the heroic struggle, and it also had a great impact on the non-Jewish world. On the first anniversary of the uprising, the official newspaper of the Polish Workers' Party said, "The unequal struggle which took place a year ago in Warsaw has proved to our people that to fight the blood-stained invader is not only necessary, but possible." Even Goebbels noted in his diary, "It shows what the Jews are capable of when they have arms in their hands."

# Seder Night Amidst Death and Destruction

On the night of April 19 I entered the house at 4 Kurza Street to get flashlights for our men. Wandering about there, I unexpectedly came upon Rabbi Maisel. When I entered the room, I suddenly realized that this was the night of the first Seder.

The room looked as if it had been hit by a hurricane. Bedding was everywhere, chairs lay overturned, the floor was strewn with household objects, the window panes were all gone. It had all happened during the day, before the inhabitants of the room returned from the bunker.

Amidst this destruction, the table in the centre of the room looked incongruous with glasses filled with wine, with the family seated around, the rabbi reading the Haggadah. His reading was punctuated by explosions and the rattling of machine-guns; the faces of the family

From *Between Tumbling Walls* by Tuvia Borzykowski

around the table were lit by the red light from the burning buildings nearby.

I could not stay long. As I was leaving, the Rabbi cordially bade me farewell and wished me success. He was old and broken, he told me, but we, the young people, must not give up, and God would help us.

He also gave me several packages of matzos for my comrades. Should we all survive until morning, he said, I should come again and bring with me Zivia.[1] I fulfilled his wish, and next evening I paid the rabbi another visit, this time in the company of Zivia.

Coming back to my unit was like entering a different world; it felt warm to be back again with comrades, to be in an environment where no one shed tears. I appreciated anew the indomitable spirit of our fighting organization.

The night was coming to an end, and members of our group who had been sent on various errands started coming back. We also received couriers from the Central Command . . . The arrival of couriers brought us information on the events of the first day of the uprising in all parts of the ghetto, and on the situation in all posts. We no longer felt lonely as we had all day.

As the day dawned, we fortified our base at 4 Kurza Street. We waited all day for the Germans to arrive, but they did not appear in our vicinity. We knew of the fighting in other parts of the ghetto from the sounds of shooting and explosions which reached us.

# A Survivor's Report from One Shelter

*This is not a history of the Warsaw Ghetto revolt, that explosion of despair, martyrdom, and heroism which marked the death of a people. It is only a survivor's report of one shelter in one Warsaw Ghetto apartment whose fate was typical; Jewish Warsaw was consumed by fire and flame, the traditional accessories of Kiddush Hashem . . .*

Late on Sunday night, April 18, 1943, Polish police began to surround the Ghetto. Within an hour, the underground had learned of it and declared a state of emergency. Fighters were assigned

[1]Zivia Lubetkin, "Mother of the Ghetto" (p. 402).

From *The Holocaust Kingdom* by Alexander Donat.

to their posts. Weapons, ammunition, and food were distributed; so were supplies of potassium cyanide (poison for suicide). By 2 A.M. next morning (April 19) the Polish police were reinforced by Ukrainian, Latvian, and SS units, ringing the Ghetto walls with patrols stationed about thirty yards apart. What we had so often expected and dreaded was about to take place: the final liquidation of the Ghetto was at hand. Small groups of Jewish fighters went from house to house, informing everyone of developments, ordering people to take arms or to go to shelters.

I had just come on guard duty at our apartment house when two Z.O.B.[1] boys arrived. They were . . . between eighteen and twenty. One was tall and fair-haired, with the thin features and dreamy eyes of a poet. He wore long trousers and an unbuttoned shirt under his jacket. The other was short, chubby, with pink cheeks, dimples, and merry eyes. He wore high boots and a windbreaker. Both were bareheaded, carried rifles in their hands and grenades in their belts. They spoke softly, but their voices carried. These were our children, the doomed defenders of the Ghetto.

It did not take long to alert everyone. I awakened (my wife) Lena and the others in our apartment. We put on our best clothes and took the linen bag we had prepared with lump sugar and biscuits cut into small squares.

About thirty of us gathered in our shelter. In addition to Lena and me, blond Izak, Adek and Bronka, and the carpenter's family, there were other neighbors I scarcely knew. We had only a single weapon among us: Izak's revolver. Izak crouched at a peephole near the entrance to the shelter, from which he could see part of the courtyard. By dawn the Ghetto was a ghost town . . .

Hundreds of people living in the Ghetto had been preparing for this moment, and had documents and lodgings on the Aryan side, but as always, the long-expected operation came upon them suddenly enough to upset all plans. They had expected to slip over quickly "at the last minutes," but all their elaborate preparations were now useless. The grandiose plans Kapko and I had made were also useless. The back streets of the Ghetto and the tunnels and shelters would be our guerrilla woods. There we would make our stand and there we would die.

We sat in the shelter, but nothing happened. Everyone was silent, caught up in his own bleak thoughts, drawing up the balance sheet of his life. We had to prepare to meet our deaths. One important thing, at least, we were thankful for: that two weeks before we had been able to smuggle Wlodek (my son) out of the Ghetto with Mrs. Maginski.

A few hours later, at eight o'clock on Monday morning, the shooting came close to us. The Germans marched through the gate at the corner

[1]Jewish Fighting Organization also known as J.F.O.

of Gesia and Zamenhof streets and took up positions in the little square in front of the *Judenrat* offices. They put rows of Ghetto police in the front ranks, convinced that the defenders would not fire on fellow Jews and that the Germans could thus get through to Zamenhof Street behind a human screen. Our fighters let the Jewish police go by, but when the German troops passed, they loosed a barrage of bullets, grenades, and Molotov cocktails. The battlefield now became the corner of Zamenhof and Mila streets where resistance fighters occupied all four corner buildings and fired on the Germans from all sides. One homemade incendiary bomb set a tank afire, burning the crew alive, and spreading panic and disorder among the Germans. But the German officers rallied their troops. Another tank appeared and before long it too met the same fate. Germans, Ukrainians, and Latvians scattered in disorder: one German, his leg smashed by a grenade, limped to a doorway using his rifle as a crutch; another, his helmet on fire, ran screaming around the square, a human torch. Scores of dead and wounded lay scattered on the pavement.

We watched the battle from our attic and more than once Izak's finger was on the trigger of his revolver, but his orders were to cover the withdrawal of "our unarmed people should it be necessary to leave the shelter . . ." Guns and riding crops in hand, German officers urged on their disorganized *Judenhelden:* the men who had shown so much combativeness with defenseless women, children, and old men, now broke before the fire of our resistance. Then field artillery . . . opened fire on the Ghetto from no-man's land, and the shelling continued intermittently throughout the day.

When we returned to the shelter, we told the others what had happened, and although we were all doomed to a terrible death, we were gripped by a strange ecstasy. We embraced and congratulated one another; women cried and laughed; people began to sing psalms in a low voice; and one gray-haired man spoke the blessings aloud: How wonderful it was to have lived to see such times!

Suddenly I felt beyond life and death. I felt sure we were going to die; but I felt a part of the stream of Jewish history. We were part of an ancient and unending stream of immortal tradition that went back to Titus and his Roman legions ravishing Jerusalem, to persecution in Spain under Isabella and Ferdinand, to Khmelnitsky massacres, and to more recent pogroms and massacres at Kishinev and under Petlyura.

Later we learned from some of the fighters that the first battle had taken place at the corner of Nalewski and Gesia streets. A German unit, singing lustily, had marched into the Ghetto to be met by bullets, hand grenades, and homemade incendiaries when it reached that corner. The Germans scattered, leaving their dead and wounded, and pursued by harassing fire; then came a battle of several hours' duration before the Germans finally withdrew.

Fighting continued intermittently at that corner all during Monday.

Ghetto fighters kept moving from building to building, springing up in the enemies' rear to strike unexpectedly and effectively. By nightfall, however, the meager supply of grenades and Molotov cocktails had given out, and they had to retreat . . . Before pulling back they set fire to the big warehouse where the SS stored looted Jewish property.

The shooting stopped when it grew dark, but flames and billows of smoke shot up from around Nalewski Street. When it was quite dark, we went down to the courtyard of our apartment house to wait for word from our fighters. It was about 10 P.M. when the gate opened slightly and two men in SS uniforms silently entered. They wore battle helmets and carried automatic rifles slung over their shoulders. Their high boots were wrapped in rags to silence their movements, and they called out to us in Yiddish, "Don't be alarmed, Jews, it's us." They were our boys and they gave us an account of the day's events . . . At one stage in the battle, a German unit which had fought in the skirmishes on the corner of Gesia and Nalewski streets had retreated . . . and the resistance fighters had attacked them from the rear and destroyed the entire unit, capturing their weapons and uniforms. After that, our blue and white flag was raised on the roof of their building.

Later in the afternoon, a second German unit equipped with howitzers and flame throwers and bolstered by tanks had made its way to the square . . . The square was defended by . . . the best-armed, best-trained unit of the Ghetto resistance. Equipped with rifles and plenty of hand grenades, they occupied the houses along the eastern and southern sides of Muranow Square, and from that favorable position, they opened fire on the attackers. They inflicted especially heavy losses on the Germans with a machine gun in the attic of an apartment house . . . which overlooked the entire plaza. By using the passageways between apartment buildings, the defenders were able to keep changing the direction of their fire and inflicted even more casualties on the Germans, who finally withdrew at sunset taking their dead and wounded with them . . .

The Germans then showed their heroic qualities in dealing with the defenseless inhabitants of the Ghetto hospital . . . The building had been shelled and set on fire after the SS had gone through the wards shooting and killing without mercy. Those patients and staff members who had made it to the shelters died in the fire.

As one fighter concluded his grim report, he observed that that was what we could all expect if we fell into their hands. He inhaled deeply on his cigarette and in its glow we realized that this was not the chubby, cheerful boy of yesterday.

Someone blurted, "Where's your comrade?" The young soldier's voice went suddenly shrill. "You won't see him again. He fell on Gesia Street." "Killed," "perished," or "died" would have seemed almost normal at the moment when Jewish life in the Ghetto was so cheap, but

398

with his quiet, dignified choice of the word "fell" the young soldier made a lump rise in our throats. A woman next to me began to sob.

"Don't cry," one of the neighbors admonished her. "He's better off than we are. He sold his life dearly. What do we have to look forward to: being burned alive, like the people in the hospital?" He turned to the boys in uniform. "Give us weapons. We want to go down fighting, too, at least die like men."

The young man drew himself up, his voice slightly raised, and his manner showed he had thought about the issue often. "When we mourned the victims of the July massacre, we swore we would never again be led to slaughter without fighting back. You are soldiers without weapons. If you had weapons you would fight, too; fight with us to the last. Only we don't have the guns." He told us that their way of fighting was easy, the usual way, with guns. They were fighting because they were young and defending our dignity. But our way of resisting was unique; we were choosing a martyr's death. We could have surrendered; died the swift, clean, scientific death of the gas chamber. Instead, we had chosen flaming crucifixion: torment.

We felt that we were resisting Nazi military force barehanded, that our refusal to surrender was no less heroic than the armed resistance of those who fought them with guns. We were co-fighters, not just fodder, excrement, meaningless sacrifices.

Hand in hand, Lena and I slowly climbed the stairs to our attic fortress. Bound together by an evil fate no less than by our vows, my beloved wife, companion of my bad days as well as my good, was now closer to me than ever.

---

# View from the Outside

*Renia Kulkielko was fifteen when the Catastrophe began in Poland. She joined Kibbutz Bendzyn (her home town). While engaged in preparing for Aliyah to Palestine the group also carried on an intensive resistance program. Disguised as a native, she witnessed the battle of the Warsaw Ghetto from the outside . . .*

All streets leading to the Ghetto were crowded with soldiers in tanks, buses, and motorcycles. They wore helmets and were equipped for assault. The heavens were red with the flames of buildings afire. The cries were deafening. The nearer I came to the place,

---

From *Escape from the Pit* by Renia Kulkielko.

the more horrifying and distinct did the shrieks and groans become. Shots were heard. The Ghetto was surrounded on every side by the Germans of the "Annihilation Squad." Behind ramparts hastily erected by the Germans lay soldiers and police, manning machine-guns.

Tanks appeared from every direction, firing. Planes were over the Ghetto, dropping bombs and incendiaries. The streets adjoining the Ghetto were also in flames . . .

Poles and Germans stood about, contemplating the sight from some distance—a sight that human imagination could scarcely conceive.

Young mothers were dropping their babies from fifth or sixth story windows; husbands were pushing their wives off the roofs, sons—their aged parents, then leaping to death themselves. Elsewhere lay men with gouged out eyes, screaming, begging the Germans to shoot them. The Germans laughed derisively. After some moments, the men disappeared in the flames.

Others were in no position to commit suicide. They were situated on an upper story. The floors below were already enveloped in flames and the fire broke through, extending higher and higher. Suddenly the brick walls tottered and fell. A roar arose from among the mounds of ruins. Mothers saved from the flames, babies in their arms, wailed with inhuman voices, entreating the Germans to spare the little ones. But the Germans were doing what they had set themselves to do. They tore the children out of their mothers' arms, dropped them to the ground, trampled upon them with heavy boots, split them with their bayonets. The little bodies squirmed with pain, as if they were worms split apart, crawling on the ground. Afterward the Germans threw the corpses into the fire. They then stabbed the mothers with their bayonets. A tank finally crushed the mothers to death.

The Jews defended themselves valiantly. On the roofs of houses not as yet enveloped by flames, boys manning machine guns could be seen through the smoke, as through a heavy fog. Girls fought heroically, armed with pistols and bottles of explosives. Small boys and girls attacked the Germans with stones, sticks, and iron bars. People in the street, seeing the developing battle, seized whatever weapon they could find and joined the fighters, for, to them at any rate, nothing was left but death. The Ghetto was full of corpses. Many Jews died, but Germans, too, were falling.

Every onlooker reacted in his own way. There were Germans who spat at the sight and turned away. They could no longer endure the horror. A Polish woman stood at the window, stripping the garments off her body and shouting that there was no God in Heaven, if he could see all this and remain silent. She had become crazed at the awful spectacle. I felt that my legs would no longer support me and was therefore compelled to move away. I was crushed to earth with sorrow at what I had seen; yet I was somehow glad that there still were Jews alive who could fight back.

Broken in spirit, I returned to the inn. The sights I had witnessed pursued me and distressed me. At times I could not believe that my eyes actually saw all this. Hadn't I somehow been deceived by my senses? How could Jews, crushed as they were and weak with hunger, battle so heroically? Was it true indeed that millions had fallen quietly without resisting, without revolting, yet now others had arisen who wished to die like self-respecting human beings?

It was rumored that proclamations from the Ghetto were circulated daily in the city. Listed in detail were the number of Germans killed, the weapons taken from them, and the number of tanks disabled. It was also stated that the Jews would fight on to their last breath. The din of planes was heard throughout the night and the ground trembled with the bombs they dropped.

Early the next morning, I went to the station. I went from car to car, and all the people were marvelling at the heroism and bravery of the Jews. There were others who said that many Poles were probably fighting with them; it is inconceivable that mere Jews were capable of such a valiant struggle.

The battle of Warsaw lasted approximately six weeks. Zivia (Lubetkin) and Isaac Zuckerman miraculously arrived safe in the Aryan section. They reported that scores of fighters still lived in the tunnel beneath the houses. Comrades living in the Aryan pale . . . decided to save these people. One day, disguised in police uniforms, they drove a bus to the site of the tunnel serving as an exit to the Aryan side. The uniforms had been removed from the bodies of Germans killed during the battle in the Ghetto. With great effort they succeeded in removing to safety approximately eighty persons.

This is how it was done: German guards still continued to rove about the Ghetto. It was necessary, therefore, to be very careful. The young men dressed as policemen sat armed on top of the bus, surrounding their counterfeit prisoners. When halted in the street, the "policemen" showed their false papers. The Gestapo examiners saluted and went on their way. The bus ran out of town, towards the forest.

Our people got off the bus, entered the forest, and the bus driver returned to town in order to fetch other "prisoners." Some of those saved continued moving ahead in any direction they could. Some lived in the woods, heedless of the Germans into whose grasp they might fall at any time. As luck would have it, a decent watchman was living in the forest, and he brought them some food daily.

The Germans were still kept occupied in the Ghetto. They dynamited houses, to make certain that there were no more Jews left in the bunkers; they sprayed gas into every sewer. Occasionally at night, one of the watches failed to return from its beat. The guards were found dead, killed by Jews wearing police uniforms.

Not many persons succeeded in making good their escape. Once one of the young men, dressed as a policeman, was standing at the gate of the Ghetto with a group of *bona-fide* policemen. No one recognized him, for the gendarmes did not know one another. They had been brought from the environs of the city. He started calling upon the Jews to come out. He then approached, dragging a couple of "prisoners" by their hands along with him. Other Jews, noticing that this gendarme did not shoot, quickly followed. The Germans paid no attention. They probably assumed that a new system was being tried—the gendarme was merely taking away the Jews before killing them.

Scores of Jews were thus saved. The persons rescued fled without knowing where they would be safe. Many fell into the Germans' grasp while wandering about the streets, not knowing where to go. However, many did save themselves. To this day no one knows who this kind-hearted gendarme really was.

# Escape Through the Sewers

*Zivia Lubetkin, wife of Itzhak Zukerman, was a prominent leader of the resistance and the Warsaw rebellion. She was one of the few who escaped from the burning ghetto. She now lives in Israel with her husband . . .*

Out of our desperation, a new plan arose. A small group, about twenty chaverim in all would be sent into the sewers. Leaving at night, they would hide in the ruins of deserted houses on the Aryan side. There, they would contact some of our comrades who were of Gentile appearance, and together with the Polish underground work out an escape.

We made our final preparations for departure. Dressed and armed, we parted from our friends. Would we ever see each other again? Outwardly we were calm; we smiled and even joked, pressed the hands of our comrades and left.

One by one, on all fours, we crawled out of the bunker, through the narrow, stone-covered passage. Outside it was a shock to realize that it was night. Somehow, we had always visualized the outside as light and sunny in comparison to the damp darkness of the bunker. After weeks of continuous night we yearned for a little light. Above ground, we drank in the fresh air with open mouths. We moved ahead quietly, our footsteps deadened by the rags bound round our shoes. "There is firing on the left; keep to the right and you will be able to pass," the guard posted near the bunker whispered as we passed.

From *Unsung Heroes* by Hakibbutz Hameuchad.

The Ghetto was strange to us, more difficult to recognize after each stay in the bunkers. The skeletons of burned buildings, ruins of streets and stores, were all we could see. Occasionally a smoldering house flared up in a spurt of flame. The most terrible of all was the dead silence. In these streets so teeming with colorful life, all was still. From time to time the quiet was broken by a window swinging on its hinges or by a falling brick from a ruined house.

Silently, feeling each step, our fingers on the triggers of our revolvers, we stole through hidden alleys. Occasionally we met survivors, who were encouraged at seeing armed Jews still active. They regarded us with envy, having no idea that we were as helpless as they. After some encouraging words, we left them and crawled across the dark ruins.

We were approaching the entrance to the sewer. It was difficult to leave the Ghetto, with its ruins and its memories of dead comrades. Each of us was thinking of past times, and of chaverim, still alive who were being left behind. Though logic told us that nothing could be done except what we had decided to do, there were some who refused to go and leave those who were still in the Ghetto. Again, our decision was reaffirmed and it was decided that each one in the group would go.

With heavy hearts we descended into the sewer. It was an abyss of darkness. I felt the water splash around me as I jumped, and then resume its flow. I was almost overcome by a dreadful nausea there in the cold, dirty water. Others felt the same. Some fell, and begged to be left lying there. But no one in all that journey was abandoned.

Many hours later we reached a spot which our guides thought would be favorable for an exit. We figured that it must be early morning, so we assigned two of the chaverim to leave the sewer and arrange for the exit of the others. They lifted the manhole cover. For a moment light streamed in, and we breathed deeply the fresh air. It was as if a new lease on life had been given us. Hands were pressed and hasty words of farewell whispered, and the two left.

We sat in the water and waited. That day we had no word from them. We could carry on practically no conversation so we sat quietly busy with our thoughts. The idea of returning to the Ghetto and leading out the others seized us. Many volunteered for the mission. But only two were assigned. One was Shlamek, a youth of about seventeen. Everybody knew there was no one better suited for the daring job. We all remembered how he had saved his unit from a burning house surrounded by Nazis in the earlier days of the Ghetto battle. He had broken through a wall of Germans by flinging hand grenades, and when they recovered from their surprise he had already cut a path for himself and his comrades. He was joined by an older comrade whom we valued for his intelligence and courage. They left us and returned to the Ghetto.

We waited all day for news of the two who had gone out of the sewer to contact the underground. When they had opened the manhole, and disappeared into the street above, we had waited for the sound of shots. We had heard none. Now after so many hours had passed, we began to think that perhaps something had happened to prevent their return and our exit from the sewer. We remembered the trip here, crawling through the narrow sewer, bent almost in half, the filthy water reaching up to our knees. We had half-walked, half-crawled like this for twenty hours, one behind another, without stopping, without food or drink, in that horrible cavern. Now another eighteen hours had passed. We were hungry and thirsty, weakened by the continuous soaking in the dirty water, breathing the stale air with difficulty.

It must have been midnight when we heard sounds on the manhole. With bated breath we waited as the cover was lifted—till the faces of our chaverim appeared. Some food, soup and loaves of bread were handed down to us. We wanted only to drink, and couldly hardly touch the food. They would return the next day to take us. We replied that we would wait for the others.

The night was interminable. Toward morning our messengers Shlamek and his companion returned, their faces distored with suffering. All the sewer passages to the Ghetto had been blocked. There was no possibility of reaching the chaverim who had been left. This new blow almost broke our spirit. Physical and spiritual strength were ebbing.

At ten o'clock, we again heard noises above the sewer. When the tunnel was suddenly flooded with bright light, we hurriedly fled deeper into the depths of the sewer. We were sure that the Germans had discovered our hiding place. But it was our chaverim who had come to release us. With excitement they helped us climb the ladder. Near the exit stood a truck, behind it another. In a few minutes we were on the truck, and on our way.

Now when we saw each other by daylight—dirty, wrapped in rags, smeared with the filth of the sewers, faces thin and drawn, knees shaking with weakness—we were overcome with horror. Only our feverish eyes showed that we were still living human beings. All of us stretched out on the floor of the truck in order to be invisible from the street, each with his weapon beside him.

In this manner the truckload of armed Jewish fighters, among the last survivors of the Warsaw Ghetto, proceeded through the very heart of Nazi-occupied Warsaw. We traveled for only one hour, but the minutes dragged. Several times we were sure we would be stopped by Germans, but by some chance we managed to cross the bridge, and escape from the city. Thus we reached the forest and comparative freedom.

# SS General Stroop Reports: The Uprising and Destruction of the Warsaw Ghetto

*19th April 1943.* Ghetto sealed off from 3:00 hours. At 6:00 hours deployment of the Waffen-SS . . . for the combing of the remainder of the ghetto. Immediately upon entry strong concerted fire by the Jews and bandits . . .

We succeeded in forcing the enemy to withdraw from the roof-tops and strong-points situated in high positions to the cellars or bunkers and sewers . . . Shock patrols were then deployed against known bunkers with the task of clearing out the occupants and destroying the bunkers . . . The presence of Jews in the sewers was established. Total flooding was carried out, rendering presence impossible.

*20th April 1943.* The pockets of resistance located in the uninhabited, not yet opened up part of the ghetto were put out of action by an assault squad of the *Wehrmacht*—sappers and flamethrowers . . .

*21st April 1943.* Setting fire to the buildings had the result that Jews who were, despite all searching operations, concealed under the roofs or in the cellars and other hiding places, appeared during the night on the outside fronts of the blocks of buildings somehow to escape the fire. Large numbers of Jews—entire families—already on fire, jumped from the windows or tried to let themselves down by means of sheets, etc., tied together. We made sure that these, as well as the other Jews, were liquidated immediately.

*22nd April 1943.* It is unfortunately impossible to prevent a proportion of the bandits and Jews from hiding in the sewers under the ghetto where they have evaded capture by preventing the flooding. The city administration is not in a position to remove this inconvenience. Smoke-bombs and mixing creosote with the water have also failed to achieve the desired result . . .

From "Extracts of the Daily Report of SS General Stroop," quoted in *The Yellow Star* by Gerhard Schoenberner.

*23rd April 1943*. The whole *Aktion* is made more difficult by the cunning tricks employed by the Jews and bandits, e.g. it was discovered that live Jews were being taken to the Jewish cemetery in the corpse carts that collect the dead bodies lying around, and were thus escaping from the ghetto. Permanent guard on the corpse carts had blocked this escape route . . .

Today 3500 Jews from the factories were caught for evacuation. So far a total of 19,450 Jews have been caught for evacuation or have already been transported . . .

*24th April 1943*. At 18:15 hours the search party entered the buildings after they had been cordonned off and established the presence of a large number of Jews. As most of these Jews resisted I gave the order to burn them out. Not until the whole street and all the court-yards on both sides were in flames did the Jews, some of them on fire, come out from the blocks of buildings or try to save themselves by jumping from the windows and balconies into the street on to which they had thrown beds, blankets and other things. Time and time again it could be observed that Jews and bandits preferred to return into the flames rather than fall into our hands.

*25th April 1943*. If last night the sky above the former ghetto was filled with the glow from the fire, this evening an immense sea of fire is to be seen. As with the methodical and regular combing operations a large number of Jews continue to be ferreted out . . .

*26th April 1943*. It is becoming increasingly obvious that it is now the turn of the toughest and most resistant Jews and bandits. Several times bunkers have been forcibly opened, the occupants of which had not come up to the surface since the beginning of the *Aktion*. In a number of cases the occupants of the bunker were no longer in a position, after the explosion, to crawl up to the surface. According to statements made by Jews caught, a considerable number of the occupants have been driven mad by the heat and smoke and explosions. . .

*27th April 1943*. It has been established by the SS men who descended the sewers that the bodies of a great many dead Jews are being washed away by the water . . .

*29th April 1943*. Several sewer shafts have been blown up. Two outlets located outside the ghetto have likewise been made unusable by blowing up or walling up.

Statements by various occupants of bunkers confirm that these Jews have not been outside for 10 days and that as a result of the long duration of this *Grossaktion* their food supplies, etc., are giving out . . .

*1st May 1943.* A considerable number of the Jews caught were brought up out of the sewers. The systematic blowing up or blocking up of the sewers was continued . . .

A shock patrol has established an unascertainable number of corpses floating in a main sewer under the ghetto . . .

*3rd May 1943.* In most cases the Jews use weapons in resisting leaving the bunkers. There are therefore two wounded to report. Some of the Jews and bandits fire pistols with both hands.

*4th May 1943.* Countless Jews who appeared on the roof-tops during the fire have perished in the flames. Others did not make an appearance on the top storeys until the last minute and could only save themselves from being burned to death by jumping down . . .

*5th May 1943.* Today also the Jews in various places have put up a resistance before being caught. In several cases the openings/hatches of the bunkers were closed or barred by force from the inside so that a large explosion was the only way to force an opening and destroy the occupants.

*6th May 1943.* Today particularly those blocks of buildings that were destroyed by fire on May 4th were combed. Although it was hardly to be expected that people would be found alive in them, a whole number of bunkers, which were red-hot inside, were discovered . . .

*7th May 1943.* The Jews state that they come out into the fresh air at night as it is becoming intolerable to stay in the bunkers without a break for the long duration of the *Aktion.* An average of 30 to 50 Jews are shot by the shock patrols every night.

From these statements it must be assumed that a considerable number of Jews are still underground in the ghetto.

*8th May 1943.* According to statements made, there must still be about 3000–4000 Jews in the underground cavities, sewers and bunkers. The undersigned is determined not to terminate this *Grossaktion* until the very last Jew is destroyed . . .

*10th May 1943.* The resistance put up by the Jews today was unabated. In contrast to previous days, the members of the Jewish main fighter groups still in existence and not destroyed have apparently retreated to the highest ruins accessible to them in order to inflict casualties on the raiding parties by firing on them . . .

*12th May 1943.* A considerable number of Jews have probably perished in the flames. As the fire had not burnt itself out by the onset of darkness, the exact number could not be ascertained.

*13th May 1943.* For two days the few Jews and criminals still in the ghetto have been making use of the hiding-places still provided by the ruins to return at night to the bunkers known to them, eating there and supplying themselves with food for the next day . . .

*15th May 1943.* The last undamaged block of buildings still in existence in the ghetto was searched through once more and then destroyed by a special raiding-party. In the evening the chapel, mortuary and all the adjoining buildings in the Jewish cemetery were blown up or destroyed by fire.

*16th May 1943.* The former Jewish quarter of Warsaw is no longer in existence. With the blowing up of the Warsaw Synagogue, the *Grossaktion* was terminated at 20:15 hours . . .

Total number of Jews caught or verifiably exterminated: 56,065.

# Warsaw Without Jews

It was summer, 1943. Warsaw, which before the war had the largest Jewish community of some 350,000 and during the war about half a million, had now, after the Ghetto Uprising, officially no Jews at all. It was, as the Germans said, *Judenrein.* The only silent witness to this erstwhile community was—until May, 1943—the large Tlomackie Synagogue. It had remained undamaged because it was not in the ghetto. It stood shuttered, silent and secretive, as if shrouded in deep melancholy.

It was obvious to all that even this solitary symbol would disappear in time—and it did, after the Ghetto Uprising had subsided. I was out in the street and saw what happened to the Tlomackie Synagogue. One sunny morning, two SS vans drove up, sealed off the surrounding streets and blew it up with dynamite. All that was left was a mound of rubble. The detonation caused a great deal of blast damage in the neighbourhood and the pavements were covered with broken glass. Their job done, the SS left happily, hoping that the pile of debris would convince everybody that the Jews of Warsaw were no more. Their next

From *A Warsaw Diary* by Michael Zylberberg.

plan was to clear away the ruins of the ghetto and lay out a park in the area, to be called the Adolf Hitler Park. To this end the Germans brought in hundreds of Jews from other countries to remove the ruins and prepare the site. Work continued for over a year. The detonations required to demolish the empty shells of buildings could be heard all over Warsaw, and people who lived nearby looked with horror at the clearance program inside the ghetto walls. The Polish Uprising of 1944 put a sudden end to the work; the Germans left the ghetto in a hurry, and many Jews doing forced labor were freed by the Polish fighters. There was never a Hitler Park in Warsaw.

It was said that there were no Jews and no symbols of Jewishness in Warsaw. But for those of us who had survived, the streets of the city were filled not only with memories of the past, but with actual objects freely seen, identified and sold. There were Jewish books that had belonged to libraries and private collections. The pages were used for wrapping goods in shops, as there was a great shortage of paper. Former Jewish-occupied flats were now in the possession of Polish tenants, and their specifically Jewish contents used to light fires. Wood and coal were in short supply too, and every day my landlord brought home sacks of Jewish books which he burned in the stove. He pointed out that the Jewish religion was going up in smoke.

In all the market places there was a brisk sale of long woollen prayer shawls—*taleisim*. Wool was scarce and these articles had great value. The large prayer shawls were the right size for a woman's dress, so they were dyed and, when remade, bore no resemblance to the original article. Pious women were seen in the church in these smart new outfits.

A different value was placed on the scrolls of the law. They had multiple uses and were sold by the yard. Shoemakers bought them for inner linings, hat-makers acquired them, and so did other groups of artisans. In the market places the scrolls could be seen lying in the mud with heaps of junk. There were some literary and intelligent connoisseurs who concealed a whole scroll in their homes. They felt that the time would come, after the war, when it would fetch a good price.

In the Old City, I often visited a provision shop whose owner was drunk half the time. He was hardly concerned about his business. One day he called me aside to whisper something to me. He wanted to sell me a scroll which he described as a "Torah"—using the Hebrew word. The proceeds of the sale were, of course, to buy drink. He said his daughter had been given the scroll by a German in return for one kilo of sausages. He had it in his house, he said, winking broadly at me at the same time. His wife, who had heard the conversation, yelled out at this point, "Don't listen to him. He is a fool and a drunkard." I left the shop frightened and never went there again. Obviously they both knew who I really was.

A sad fate also awaited the synagogical silver objects associated with traditional Judaism. Shops in every street were selling them off and they were also on free display in the markets: goblets, candlesticks, scroll decorations, spice boxes and money boxes. They had once been the proud possessions of countless Jewish homes, used and displayed at feasts and festivals. They were now being sold for next to nothing but customers were scarce. In time of war these were luxury items, unlike wool and paper.

Thousands of former Jewish flats still had the mezuzahs nailed up on the doorposts. The new owners did not even bother to remove this sole relic of destruction. There were no more Jews, but the symbols of Judaism were everywhere . . .

Again, Jews were one of the main topics of conversation in the streets, markets, public houses and shops. They were discussed with callousness, often with hate; even as a scourge that had to be wiped out. The Germans were continuing to churn out propaganda inciting the Poles to hatred of the Jews. They exploited the murder of Polish officers at Katyn, saying they were killed by Jews in Russia. Suddenly leaflets were distributed in Warsaw describing the "ritual murders" of the Middle Ages, when Jews were supposed to have killed Christian children for their Passover feast. These tales were lavishly illustrated. It seemed that the Germans were trying to justify their criminal actions. It is not surprising that such propaganda poisoned the minds of many people, even when those against whom it was directed had disappeared.

An incident in the Old City demonstrates this point well. Two German officers were shot by the Polish Underground in broad day-light. I saw the two dead men lying in Freta Street. As if by pre-arranged design, everyone in the vicinity was heard saying that the Jews had done it.

I looked at the relics of what had been, listened to the things which made a mockery of human intelligence, and had to remain silent.

# Readings

*Martyrs and Fighters* by Philip Friedman (Praeger, 1954), the eminent historian of the *Shoah,* consists of a compilation of authentic eyewitness and first-hand documents, as well as diverse selections on the epic story of the rebellion in the Warsaw Ghetto.

*Uprising in the Warsaw Ghetto* by Ber Mark (Schocken Books, 1975), was written in Polish and Yiddish, and was translated into English. It presents a detailed day-to-day account by an eminent Polish Jewish historian who was founder of the Jewish Historical Institute in Warsaw. Includes selected documents, letters, and communiques. Authoritative.

*A Tower From the Enemy* by Albert Nirenstein (Grossman Publishers, 1959), is a comprehensive account of the destruction of the Warsaw Ghetto, and the resistance in the Polish ghettos and extermination camps; it contains documentary and eyewitness accounts.

*The Fighting Ghettos,* edited by Meyer Barkai (Lippincott, 1962), contains eyewitness accounts of the uprising in the ghettos and reports of survivors.

*Muranowska 7* by Chaim Lazar (Massada, 1966), depicts the story of the Warsaw Ghetto uprising from personal and eyewitness accounts.

*To Die with Honor: The Uprising of the Jews in the Warsaw Ghetto* by Leonard Tushnet (Citadel Press, 1965), is a short history of the uprising for young readers.

*On Both Sides of the Wall* by Vladka Meed (Ghetto Fighters' House and Hakibbutz Hameuchad, 1973), who was an underground leader in the Resistance on both sides of the Ghetto wall. The book narrates the exploits from July 1943 until liberation.

*A Warsaw Diary (1939-1945)* by Michael Zylberberg (Vallentine Mitchell, 1969), is basically the stories of the Jews who lived on the Aryan side of the wall.

# 18. RESISTANCE AND REBELLION

Utterly alone, completely isolated, surrounded by hatred or, at best, indifference, forsaken by humanity, the Jews fought back in many different ways. Resistance was waged in all areas and on all fronts: physical, economic, cultural, and psychological.

In general, however, the Jews were late in initiating physical resistance against the Nazis. At the outset they simply could not believe that anyone might sink to such depths as the destruction of an entire people. Moreover, Germany was renowned for its advanced civilization. The cultural and artistic achievements of the German people were notable, and during World War I the German conquerors of Eastern Europe had behaved with decency. When the Jews finally awakened to the horrible truth, they had already paid a grievous toll. They were not the only ones duped; the French and Russians, as well as the other nations overrun by the Nazis, were equally unprepared for the onslaught.

The Nazis utilized deceptions and cunning tricks of all kinds to trap their victims. But even after the bitter truth became evident, there were many deterrents which kept the Jews from fighting back. The Jewish leaders had a deep-felt sense of responsibility, and they feared that resistance might result in costly reprisals against the innocent. They remembered, for instance, how the Nazis, in June 1942, had wiped out the Czech town of Lidice in revenge for the murder of Heydrich.

Those who condemn the lack of Jewish resistance must reckon with the fact that the five million non-Jews in the concentration camps did not resist either. In Bergen-Belsen, for instance, fifty thousand Soviet prisoners of war, all of them trained soldiers, were liquidated by starvation, freezing, shooting, and disease. None of them fought back. In fact,

412

several million Russian prisoners died in this manner without fighting in their own defense.

Moreover, the Jews suffered from fateful handicaps. Unlike the French, Poles, Czechs, Yugoslavs, and others, they did not have a government-in-exile to plan, direct, and coordinate their activities and to supply them with arms. In Western Europe the Jews were scattered among the general population, and therefore found it hard to organize. In Eastern Europe, they were isolated from the generally hostile or indifferent non-Jewish populace. Unlike other guerilla fighters, the Jews could not fall back on friendly local populations for assistance or refuge.

Despite these factors, it soon became evident that the choice was between resistance and extinction. Going it alone, the Jews were the *first* to rebel against the Nazis. The example of the Warsaw Ghetto uprising was soon imitated throughout Nazi-occupied Europe, from France to Yugoslavia. Moreover, Jews led the uprisings at Auschwitz, Sobibor, Treblinka, and other death camps.

It should be mentioned that resistance has many faces. Helpless physically, the Jews resisted heroically on the spiritual and religious planes. Risking their lives to do so, they persisted in observing the Sabbath, Passover, and Hanukkah, and other festivals. Group worship and other activities kept the spark of life burning. No matter how grim the situation, the Jews carried on an effective and morale-strengthening psychological counter-warfare.

There was also resistance on a more dramatic level. In March 1944, Jewish parachutists from Palestine were dropped from British planes into Hungary, Italy, Yugoslavia, and Rumania to join the partisan resistance movements in those countries. Of the 32 parachutists dropped, eight were caught and killed. Among them was the poetess Hannah Senesh (1921–44), the immortal heroine and martyr who is sometimes called the Jewish Joan of Arc. Her thrilling story is found in Marie Syrkin's *Blessed Is the Match* (Jewish Publication Society) and in *Hannah Senesh: Her Life and Diary* (Schocken Books and Herzl Press, 1970).

# I Kill a Nazi Gauleiter

*In February 1936, David Frankfurter, a Jewish student from Germany studying in Switzerland, assassinated the Nazi leader of Switzerland. His soul-searching experiences are described in his autobiography . . .*

413

It was my firm conviction that the disgrace of the Jewish people could only be washed away by blood. And gradually an awareness grew within me that it was *I* who should perform this terrible act of vengeance. It may sound pompous and yet for the sake of truth it must be said: I felt myself to be an insignificant weapon in the hand of God . . .

A Jewish student of philosophy . . . played a critical role in the maturing of my plan. One afternoon we were sitting in a pleasant little café in Berne . . . where we could talk undisturbed. The conversation turned to the terrible situation of the Jews in Germany . . . I made some general remark about the need for taking up arms against the ferocious Nazi beast.

At this, my friend pulled a little revolver out of his pocket and said: "See, I've just bought this gun for a few francs from a gunsmith. . ."

Could it be that simple to procure firearms in this country? Why yes, no license was needed, the name of the purchaser didn't even have to be registered. You could buy a gun as easily as a pack of cigarettes . . .

Several times I sauntered past the door of the gun shop. Once you buy a gun, I said to myself, you must act. The purchase of the gun was a long step forward on the road from conception to deed.

At last I gave myself a jolt and went inside. A woman waited on me . . . The saleswoman showed me the mechanism of the revolver, a six-shooter; she packed it up and threw in a few rounds of tracer shells. My weapon had cost only ten francs, hardly more than a shirt.

No one in the store had noticed how excited I was. But the moment I stepped out on the street, I myself knew that my destiny was sealed. The pledge was in my coat pocket.

And yet many weeks were to pass before my attack on a representative of the new Amalek, Hitler-Germany. The time was not yet ripe for the pistol shots that were to echo through the whole of Europe . . .

The news from Germany made it plain that the Nazi poison was eating deeper and deeper. The summer of 1935 brought the Nuremberg laws . . . The case of the journalist Berthold Jacob, whom Nazi agents had lured back to Germany from Switzerland, showed me that Nazism did not stop at frontiers, but was spinning a web over every country in Europe. My bitterness mounted with every day that passed, but I had not yet found my specific target.

Then in November the name of Wilhelm Gustloff captured my attention. A deputy named Canova had raised certain questions in the Swiss parliament with regard to the activities of the Nazi "Gauleiter" for Switzerland—this was Gustloff.

At the time of the First World War (in which he had not taken part), Gustloff had come to Davos, the famous health resort, to be cured of a

From *Commentary Magazine*, February 1950, by David Frankfurter.

lung ailment . . . He had never acquired Swiss citizenship, but for many years had been employed by the Swiss government, preparing weather maps in the Davos meteorological institute. He had joined the Nazi party in 1923. In the fall of 1934 he entered upon full-time political activity, resigned from his position at the weather station, and became National Socialist Gauleiter for the "Gau" of Switzerland . . .

Under Gustloff's leadership, Davos became a hotbed of Nazism. On the Kurpromenade, arms flew up in the Hitler salute, Nazi emblems marred the beauty of the lovely resort town, meetings and parades were held continually. Gustloff compelled all German citizens to take an oath of loyalty to the Fuehrer, and he had ample means of putting pressure on those who opposed his decrees (denunciation in Germany, withdrawal of passport, boycott).

With the benevolent protection of the Swiss deputies Motta and Baumann, Gustloff founded no less than forty-five local Nazi groups, fifty "bases of operations," and twenty-one party headquarters in Switzerland. He had under him a whole army of informers to report on the activities of every German and every Jew. He disposed of unlimited funds and his organization was growing steadily. On Nazi holidays he brought in Gauleiters and other big party officials from Germany for mass meetings, and Nazi youth groups held military maneuvers under his direction in the border zones.

After Gustloff's name was brought up in the parliament, the press was full of his activities. It soon became clear to me that there could be only one target for the weapon that I really wanted to fire at Hitler— this *accessible* target was Wilhelm Gustloff.

My original motives had been to retrieve the sullied honor of the Jews and to create a beacon for the world. To these was now added a third motive: to save democratic Switzerland, which had favored me with its hospitality and brought me away from the Nazis into contact with truly democratic people.

But I was not yet ready to act. One winter day I drove out to the public rifle range at Ostermundingen. The place was deserted. A young employee went into the pits and worked the target for me in return for a small tip. I fired six shots—two of them were bull's eyes, not bad for a beginner. I held my revolver in a trembling hand. Before me stood the concentric circles on a white disk. But beneath them I could see the detested face, the mustache and the oily forelock combed down over the right eye, the mask behind which an inhuman brain was hatching out plans of mass murder. I saw before me the hideous caricatures of Jews which appeared week after week in Streicher's *Stürmer* (officially banned yet available in Switzerland) marking minds that were often perfectly innocent with a monstrous travesty of the Jewish face, demonic and ridiculous at once, which could only be hated and despised.

415

Pull the trigger, fire! said my inner voice, and I fired upon the gigantic imaginary foe behind the target . . .

I left Berne carrying only a briefcase. But it contained the one thing that I really needed for my journey—the revolver.

What baggage does a man need who has resolved to write "finis" to his own life? Naked we go forth from the womb, and naked we return to the womb of the earth—taking nothing with us but our deeds. And I was determined to take with me into the land of truth a deed whose implications could not be measured. Not for a moment did I ask myself whether I should be able to hold my own before God's judgment seat. My own conscience was my guide. And my conscience proclaimed in a loud voice: This is what you must do!

By way of Zurich my journey led to the clear mountain world of Davos. In the train I had an encounter which would have been entirely irrelevant under normal circumstances. But now it took on meaning. The conductor started a political discussion with me. The subject was of course Nazi Germany. Resolutely and passionately this simple man of the people rejected the violence and injustice of Switzerland's great neighbor country.

Here spoke the true *vox populi*, the voice of the simple man from the mass, and in my present situation it became for me the *vox Dei*, the voice of God, demanding vengeance for the spilled blood of Israel . . .

We arrived in Davos about four in the afternoon; the sky was darkening. It was my first sight of the world-famous health resort. I went to the Hotel Metropol-Löwen, a good middle-class establishment, and registered under my own name. I had after all nothing to hide. What I had to do I meant to do openly. Gustloff should not be killed from ambush, he should not fall by the hand of an unknown—no, I meant to confront him openly: Jew against Nazi.

Only as I entered my room and slowly closed the door behind me, to gather my thoughts in solitude, did it occur to me that the Sabbath was beginning. This was the hour of grace, when Princess Sabbath, the bride of Israel, is greeted in all the synagogues, when the angels of peace are invited to the festive board, when the candles flicker, and bread and wine stand in readiness for the blessing.

And in this hour of peace, in this pause in the work of Creation, I was to go out and—commit murder. My weapon fell from my hand. . . .

A radiant winter day rose over Davos. The mountain world lay before me in its virginal majesty . . .

But what had men made of this divine world, which might have been a paradise? The accursed symbols of the Nazis had penetrated even into the peace of this mountain world. On the Kurpromenade, a sign

416

showed the way to the house of the "National Socialist Party Leader, District Switzerland"—*my* way.

The shadows grew longer and the Sabbath departed from the earth. Many hundreds of miles from here my father would be saying the blessing over wine, herbs, and fire, accomplishing the symbolic division between the consecration of the Sabbath and the week of man's work. The division between life—and death.

My last day of grace had passed. Now, now I must act. And still I could not. Still there was something soft and hesitant within me. It is so easy to conceive an idea and so infinitely hard to realize it—when this realization means nothing less than the destruction of another man's life and one's own.

Sunday passed in inactivity. I watched a skating race, and yet how far outside of this merry activity I already stood. What goal did these people pursue? A bright flag. I can still hear the voice of a Hungarian lady, cheering her lover, encouraging him to race faster and faster over the glistening ice, to summon up his last strength—for what? To be first to reach the little flag.

And where was my goal? The sign on the promenade pointed to it, to the home of Wilhelm Gustloff, "National Socialist Party Leader, District Switzerland."

On Monday I took a long walk up to the Jewish sanitorium, the Ethaniya. I saw the director and, as though I had years of life ahead of me, we discussed the possibilities of an interneship when my studies should be completed. I was like a dead man, attempting to return to the land of the living.

How did I fill in the slowly passing hours of this last period of waiting? Mostly with a long, long inner dialogue.

With the clarity of one who knows himself to be on the brink of the grave, and from this vantage point casts his eyes back over history, I saw before me the destiny of Israel, an unfortunate nation. Bleeding from a million wounds, it dragged on its painful mission as the suffering servant of God among the nations. Why had the Jews to suffer so immoderately? . . .

When I awoke on Tuesday morning, after another restless night, it occurred to me that this day is known in the Jewish popular tradition as "*Ki Tov*," because in speaking of this day the book of Genesis twice used the words "*ki tov*"—that it was good. On this Jewish lucky day, my plan was bound to succeed.

On the afternoon of this Tuesday, February 4, 1936, I sat alone in my hotel room. Before me lay two postcards by which I wished to take my leave of my father, my brothers, and my sisters. I don't remember how long it took me to write these few lines. My hand grew heavy. I had the

remote feeling that I should soon be reunited with my beloved mother
¹who had gone before me to that other world of which we know nothing
and which yet, in the decisive moments of our lives, rejoices us with an
intimation of its presence. I sensed that something more than nothingness awaited us beyond the grave.

"My dearly beloved father: I have always given you much sorrow and
worry, and little joy. I cannot go on. Forgive me; it is not hard for me to
leave this life, knowing that you will never doubt my boundless love for
you and my blessed mother. Be strong and trust in God as you have
always done. You have Alfons and Joe, Ruth and Naomi, who will still
give you much pleasure. I have lost my faith in myself and mankind. I
cannot go on. My last wish is that you say Kaddish for me. I hope soon
to be united with my dear mama before God's judgment seat. Be
strong, you and the children. May God in his mercy give you and all
Israel a better fate. Farewell. Your unhappy son, David."

"My dearly beloved brothers and sisters: For the last time I send you
greetings, with a prayer that God in his mercy may keep our dear
father and you healthy and strong. You alone shall know what moves
me to depart from you and the world. I can no longer bear the
sufferings of the Jewish people, they have destroyed my joy in living.
May God avenge all the wrong that has been inflicted upon us Jews. I
myself hope to be an insignificant tool in His hand. Farewell and
forgive me, I could not do otherwise. Even in death, Your faithful
brother David."

My head sank down on the table. I barely noticed that the chamber-
maid had entered and was glancing down, no doubt with some surprise, at the melancholy guest. In the pocket of my jacket I had a
cigarette box, in the bottom of which I had noted the exact "plan of
action" (in the Yugoslavian language):

"The sentence must be carried out on Monday 3/2, at 9:30 A.M. First
call up and ask if he is home. If he does not come out and cannot be
seen, attempt to escape; otherwise, go through with the suicide. One or
two shots in the chest. Revolver in righthand pocket of jacket, not of
overcoat, ready to fire. As soon as I am in the room, suddenly pull it
out, fire three shots at his head or chest."

But the time had passed for the execution of this plan. I no longer
felt it possible to proceed so systematically. What was the use of
telephoning? I knew the way, and I knew the flat-roofed, blue house at
Kurpark Number 3. Without announcing myself, I must go there and
carry out the mission that had been imposed on me by the hardest of all
taskmasters: my own conscience.

It was now dark in the room. The last night of my life (as I could not
help seeing it then) had fallen. I loaded my revolver. A ghostly calm
had come over me. The hour of decision had struck.

When I left my hotel at about half past seven, it was black night. On the Kurpromenade I met two acquaintances from Berne, whose house I had frequented. They invited me to tea. What an irony of fate: to be asked to tea on the way to execute the blood verdict.

Lord, that all this still existed. Prosperous Jewish ladies who had come up here for the air. Carefree people, spending vacation days between the Promenade and five-o'clock tea. People untouched by the events of the time, that made it impossible for me to breathe even here in the purest air of Europe.

I was through with myself and the world. In the silence of my room I had uttered the prayers with which a Jew takes leave of life. *Viddui,* my confession of sin, and *Shema Yisrael,* the eternal and immutable invocation of God's oneness, that battle-cry of Israel, with which our martyrs entered the fire, that cardinal creed of Judaism, inscribed in every Jewish heart with the blood of our holy men. And softly I added the Kaddish, the prayer for the dead. Was it for my mother or for myself?

But now none of the softness of this hour of leavetaking remained in me. Now my heart was as hard and as cold as the snow that crackled beneath my feet. Like a second I, standing outside myself, I coolly observed every step, every motion that I made in the next half hour.

Now I stood outside the enemy's house. Beside the door there was a sign: Gustloff NSDAP. I rang. A woman called down from the second floor landing and asked me what I wished. I heard my own voice echo in the stairwell: "Is Herr Gustloff at home and can I speak to him?" The woman—in this moment of hyperaesthesia I knew she must be Frau Gustloff—answered in the affirmative. I mounted the stairs. Each step brought me closer to the most terrible moment of my life.

Frau Gustloff showed me in and asked me to wait in her husband's study. I sat in a chair facing Gustloff's desk. In my overcoat pocket my hand convulsively clutched the revolver.

My eyes fell on a large, framed picture of Hitler, with a personal dedication from the Fuehrer to "My dear Gustloff." And under the arch-enemy's picture, Gustloff's "dagger of honor" which as an SS-leader he was entitled to wear. "Blood and Honor" was inscribed upon it, but underneath, in invisible letters, was another motto, the words that the Nazi gangs shouted as they marched through German cities: *"Wenns Judenblut vom Messer spritzt dann gehts nochmal so gut."* ("When Jewish blood spurts from the knife, things will be twice as good.")[1]

Blood and honor . . . so be it. Now I would speak to this representative of the world's biggest gang of murderers in his own language, the only language he understood.

From the corridor I could hear the sound of a man's voice speaking

---

[1] From the Horst Wessel Song.

on the telephone. Gustloff seemed to be speaking with one of his accomplices. I heard something about "dirty dogs" or "Jewish swine" who would soon see something.

An uncontrolled rage rose up in me. If I hesitated for so much as a moment, the picture, the dagger on the wall, and the brutal voice on the telephone, mouthing threats and vilification, restored my determination.

I had not long to wait. In the passage by which I had entered scarcely five minutes before, the man appeared: a giant, filling the whole doorway. Goliath. "Here I am!" That was his greeting.

Aside from that, not a word was spoken between us. And yet in that second everything was said that needed to be said. I pulled my hand from my pocket and aimed the revolver at Gustloff. The hammer clicked, a misfire. A shell fell to the ground. With frantic speed—for Gustloff had already grasped the situation and was rushing toward me—I took a step backward and fired again.

And now a shot rang out and the enemy was hit. Then I fired a second, third, and fourth shot into him, a fifth went into the wall. Gustloff staggered and fell, and lay before me in a pool of blood. Goliath, Goliath!

I ran out through another door, hung with heavy portières, and found myself in a dark room. Yet somehow in my dashing haste I found the way out. Frau Gustloff came running into her husband's room, and I can still hear her cries ringing in my ears.

With the smoking revolver in my hand, I ran through the corridor and down the stairs. Alarmed by the shots and the woman's cries for help, people rushed out of neighboring houses. "Make way or I'll fire," I heard myself shouting. I brandished my weapon in the face of everyone who tried to bar my path. I was like a madman. I fled, and yet I had already pronounced judgment on myself.

And then the coolness of the night surrounded me. A few yards away from the house, I blundered into a snowy field where I zig-zagged for a time. All was silent around me. But there was buzzing in my ears, and my heart pounded as though it would burst. I threw myself down and pressed my burning face into the cold snow. Over me the stars glittered. Cold and calm is creation, I thought, immutable is the course of the stars. And yet, hadn't something just happened that transgressed against their primal meaning? I have killed. Yes, I have killed, because the power that stood behind my victim dared to tamper with the fundament of creation. Did not Kant write that the stars above me and the moral law within me form an eternal harmony together? I have not disturbed this harmony but rather restored it by an act that had to be done and now has been done.

And yet my task was not completed. The hardest part of it was still before me. I had still to carry out the sentence against myself. There must be no escape. My act must not be debased by any cowardly evasion. The sentence against Wilhelm Gustloff has been carried out; the sentence against David Frankfurter remains to be executed.

I must have spent about twenty minutes tramping about in the snow, beneath the eternal stars in that fearful night. I still held the revolver in my hand. In that time I lived through my whole life.

Now I lay feverish in the snow and pointed my pistol first to my heart, then to my temple. The scenes of my past ran before my inner eye like a film strip. Childhood and youth, the loving atmosphere of my home, the fierce, arrogant hatred I had encountered in Germany. What a contrast. But this contrast summed up my whole life.

What have you lived for? asked a soft but insistent voice within me— and my answer had been the shots which had just been fired at Kurpark Number 3. I had not lived in vain. I might have failed in many things, but it had not all been in vain.

I don't remember whether I simply couldn't bring myself to pull the trigger or whether I had used up all my cartridges. My memory fails me and the trial records, which would surely supply the answer, are not available.

I picked myself up. The damp snow clung to my clothes. What was I to do now? I had put my gun back in my pocket. The sentence had not been carried out.

Was I to take flight after all? Betray myself and the purity of my deed? No—there was no turning back. If I could not carry out the judgment myself, there was only one thing to do: I must give myself up to the police.

In the house next door to Gustloff's, I saw a light burning. It was Kurpark Number 2. I mounted the steps and rang. A bent old man opened the door. His wife, who was no less aged, stood behind him. I didn't want to frighten the old people and summoned up all my self-control. Forcing a natural tone of voice, I asked if I might use the phone. They led me to the telephone and showed me the phone book. Today it seems surprising to me that in those moments of mortal agitation I found the number of the police station at once. It was about a quarter after eight when I rang the station house. I felt sure that the old people must be scared to death. Should I say in their hearing that Gustloff's murderer was speaking and they should come to pick him up? No, I had acted alone, and now I must suffer alone. No one should be drawn into my trouble. And least of all these perfectly innocent, unsuspecting old people, into whose tranquil home I had been led by chance.

"This is Kurpark Number 2," I heard my own voice speaking into the mouthpiece. "I suppose you know what has happened at Number 3, next door. You can obtain exact information here. Send someone at once." Then I hung up and left the house, to wait for the policemen downstairs . . .

Trembling with excitement I rang at the wicket of the police station in the town hall. A young policeman looked out and absently asked me what I wanted. "I suppose you've heard what happened at Kurpark Number 3," I stammered. "I'm the murderer." . . .

The reaction of the policeman on duty was completely unexpected. He didn't pounce on me—he didn't handcuff me. He didn't say: "I arrest you in the name of the law," the way they do in novels. Nothing of the sort. He just smiled placatingly. He simply didn't believe me.

It is well known that after almost every crime that attracts any attention a number of people report to the police and confess. A pathological desire for attention impels totally innocent persons to accuse themselves of the most monstrous crimes. The uniformed man behind the desk seemed to take the view that he had to do with a masochist. Accordingly he asked me to prove that I had shot Gustloff . . .

I reached into my coat pocket and laid the revolver on the desk. Now the policeman changed color and recognized that I was speaking in dead earnest. He put the weapon away in his drawer and asked me to identify myself. I handed him my papers, offering the additional explanation that my Yugoslavian pass had been deposited in Berne. I gritted my teeth to preserve my composure while attending to all these formalities, although I sensed that my strength was fast dwindling.

"Do you realize the full meaning of what you've done?" asked the surprised official, who presumably had never heard of a murderer giving himself up to the police with a full confession. "Yes," I said firmly. "And I don't repent of it. What I have done, I have done alone. There is no one behind me. I belong to no political group—but I hate the Nazis because I am a Jew." . . .

I remained about an hour, without handcuffs and treated with perfect politeness. Then the door opened and an elderly man in a dark suit entered. This was Salomon Prader, president of the kreis (township) of Davos. He was followed by several officials, some of them wearing the uniform of the cantonal police, some in civilian clothes. And with them came Frau Gustloff, who dashed up to me and cried out: "That is the murderer!"

Now that she was standing right in front of me, I was able to get a good look at her. She was a woman of about thirty-seven, tending somewhat to plumpness, neither pretty nor homely. At this moment I was strangely impressed by her power of self-control. Her eyes showed that she had been crying, but there was no sign of the horror she must have lived through in that hour. She laid her hand on my forehead, thrust my head far back (there was something almost sorrowful in her

422

gesture), and said: "You look so kind. You have such good eyes. Why did you do it? Did you know Gustloff personally?"

I could not answer. Something choked me. My words stuck in my throat. Good eyes—she had said. That was a good joke. The German racial sense seemed to have abandoned this "noble Aryan" at the moment of confronting me. She apparently regarded me as a democratic-minded Swiss, who had acted in protest against the rape of his country by the Nazi Gauleiter. And this idea no doubt accounted for the moderation she imposed on herself.

"If you had known him," she continued in a soft voice, "you wouldn't have done it. Why did you do it? Did you have personal reasons?"

Now my power of speech returned. I did not leave my seat. I looked at the dead man's wife and flung the truth straight in her face: "No, not for personal reasons."

"Why did you do it then?" she screamed in mounting agitation.

"Because I am a Jew!" I replied coldly. Then the dike burst, her self-control was gone. That was more than she could bear. That a Jew had dared to avenge the disgrace of Israel upon her husband, that Gustloff had fallen by a Jewish hand, that was intolerable. She began to scream hysterically: "Scoundrel!" she shouted, and turning to the twenty-odd people in the room she began to lay bare her heart. She accused not only me but the Jews in general of everything that was vile and criminal in the world. "The Jews, the Jews, the Jews!" her voice filled the council chamber. Her voice broke, she worked herself into a boundless rage, strangely contrasting with her previous calm. Finally they had to lead her out.

Herr Prader remained with me for a few minutes and asked for a brief account of the crime. How often in the next few weeks and months was I to repeat this same story, at bottom so simple and obvious. He was polite and reserved, and indeed none of the officials or policemen present betrayed the slightest brutality or incorrectness. On the contrary. In these little people, I felt a definite sympathy, sometimes concealed, sometimes perfectly open. They all knew that my bullets had struck a *common* enemy.

At about eleven that night Dr. Dedual arrived in Davos. This was the examining magistrate appointed to the case by the state's attorney's office in Chur. Accompanied by a corporal of the criminal police, he had hurried over the snow-covered roads to examine me—for the greatest importance was attached to this case from the outset—

This tall, blond man, with his well-proportioned face, his hard mouth surmounted by a little mustache, now began to fire questions at me with a clear resonant voice. This went on for two hours—until one in the morning. His eyes bored into me as though to illumine the innermost corners of my soul. But throughout the hearing Dr. Dedual was polite and perfectly correct. His duty was to reveal my guilt, but he did not abuse his office to attack me in any way.

Dead tired, I was taken up to the town hall tower, the "Gugi," as it is amiably called in Switzerland; here a tiny, ice-cold cell received me. A bunk with a straw tick, a cracked pitcher, and a battered porcelain basin were its only furnishings. Through the little barred window I could see the stars, the eternal consolers. The walls were scribbled over with all sorts of obscenities and curses (against the police). These were the visiting cards of my predecessors, the thieves and tramps who had been locked up here for the night.

Only those who have been deprived of their freedom, only those who have languished between prison walls, will understand the horror that befell me when the door clanged shut behind me. I was under arrest. I was no longer master of my will. The sufferings of a long imprisonment had begun.

## Postscript:

Frankfurter was imprisoned for nine years in Switzerland. On release he had many attractive offers to go to the United States; Hollywood wanted to make a film about him and so on. He chose to settle in Tel-Aviv, Israel, where he has been employed in a modest government position which is concerned with the rehabilitation of war casualties.

---

# Why? Why? An Agonizing Self-Appraisal

*Alexander Donat, whom we met before and shall meet later, describes the excruciating soul-searching rationalizations for not having "put up a fight." . . .*

After the first sorrow came the soul-searching. How had it all come to pass? How could 300,000 people have let themselves be led to slaughter without putting up a fight? How could young healthy parents hand over their children without bashing in the criminal skulls of guards and executioners alike? Was it not a father's first,

---

From *The Holocaust Kingdom* by Alexander Donat.

most elemental duty to save his child's life even at the cost of his own? Or for a son to die defending his mother? Why had we not lain in wait, axes in our hands, for the assassins? There is a time to live and a time to die, and when the time to die comes, we must stand up and accept death with dignity. Over and over, the Ghetto Jeremiahs asked each other aloud, "Why didn't we go out into the streets with whatever we could lay our hands on—axes, sticks, kitchen knives, stones? Why hadn't we poured boiling water on the murderers or thrown sulphuric acid? Why hadn't we broken out of the Ghetto walls and scattered all over Warsaw, all over Poland? Perhaps 20,000, even 50,000 of us would have been slain, but not 300,000! What a disgrace, what an unspeakable shame!"

It was an agonizing self-appraisal. We were bitter to the point of self-flagellation, profoundly ashamed of ourselves, and of the misfortunes we had endured. And those feelings intensified our sense of being abandoned alike by God and man. Above all we kept asking ourselves the age-old question: *why, why?* What was all that suffering for? What had we done to deserve this hurricane of evil, this avalanche of cruelty? Why had all the gates of Hell opened and spewed forth on us the furies of human vileness? What crimes had we committed for which this might have been calamitous punishment? Where, in what code of morals, human or divine, is there a crime so appalling that innocent women and children must expiate it with their lives in martyrdoms no Torquemada[1] ever dreamed of?

In vain we looked at that cloudless September sky for some sign of God's wrath. The heavens were silent. In vain we waited to hear from the lips of the great ones of the world—the champions of light and justice, the Roosevelts, the Churchills, the Stalins—the words of thunder, the threat of massive retaliation that might have halted the executioner's axe. In vain we implored help from our Polish brothers with whom we had shared good and bad fortune alike for seven centuries, but they were utterly unmoved in our hour of anguish. They did not show even normal human compassion at our ordeal, let alone demonstrate Christian charity. They did not even let political good sense guide them; for after all we *were objectively allies* in a struggle against a common enemy. While we bled and died, their attitude was at best indifference, and all too often "friendly neutrality" to the Germans. "Let the Germans do this dirty work for us." And there were far too many cases of willing, active, enthusiastic Polish assistance to the Nazi murderers.

There was, of course, a handful of noble Poles, but nobody listened to them; their voices never carried over the barbaric yawp of hatred. Heroically they managed to save some individuals, but they could bring

[1]Grand Inquisitor of Spain during 1483–1498.

no mitigation of Nazi ferocity. The very bases of our faith had crumbled: the Polish fatherland whose children we had always considered ourselves; two thousand years of Christianity, silent in the face of Nazism; our own lie-ridden civilization. We were despairingly alone, stripped of all we had held sacred.

We hounded ourselves with our own guilt. Terrible as the pogrom was, had there been at any point a solution we had neglected out of ignorance, weakness, or cowardice? Could we have thought of something which might have saved us? Suppose that Czerniakow, before killing himself, had summoned the Ghetto to resistance. Would the Ghetto at that point have been capable of organized armed resistance? Not even the greatest optimist among us could answer that question affirmatively. We had lost our political and intellectual leaders. The majority of our young men, including the most militant, were in exile in the Soviet Union. Three years of hunger and epidemic had brought a sharp rise in male mortality, so that there were, when the Resettlement Operation began, four women to every three men. The Ghetto had been systematically ground down for three years, by savage Nazi discrimination and repression, by famine and disease, by traitors among us, by the Ghetto police, by the Gestapo, by the misgovernment of the *Judenrat,* and finally by the April and June massacres. No, at the time of Czerniakow's death, the Ghetto would not have been ready to offer mass armed resistance.

Militarily, the uprising of a single quarter in a great modern city—without a trained army or military organization, without arms or a chance of obtaining arms, without natural cover in which to hide, or means of retreat and maneuver—holds no prospect of the slightest success. Such a quarter could be promptly brought to its knees by cutting off food supplies, turning off the water. And it is much easier when the men rebelling are undernourished and heavily burdened with women and children.

There were other factors. Nothing in Jewish history had prepared the Ghetto for armed rising. The Ghetto Jews were not warriors. For more than two thousand years the Word had been more highly respected than the Sword. We were the descendants of that people who had created the image of the lion and wolf lying down with the lamb, of swords being beaten into ploughshares. The history of the Jews in Diaspora was a history of being driven from place to place, too often locked up in Ghettos, subjected to periodic persecution and pogrom, and it was not conducive to development of the military virtues. Heroic armed exploits by Jews in the Diaspora had been the exception, not the rule.

Not that Jews lacked courage. Jewish participation in the underground revolutionary movement in Tsarist Russia and in the political life of interwar Poland supplied abundant examples of bravery and

426

dignity. The Sholom Aleichem *batlanim* and *luftmenschen*,[2] Marc Chagall's surrealistic fiddlers, Franz Kafka's neurotic intelligentsia, and Martin Buber's exotic Hasidim were undergoing revolutionary change in the prewar years. They were becoming disciplined workers organized in trade unions, educated in the revolutionary traditions of the 1905 uprising (against Tsarist Russia), developing armed self-defense groups against pogroms, becoming a people of Zionist pioneers and toilers. But, despite all that, they were not prepared for military action against the Nazis. The unmerciful use of collective responsibility by the Germans kept even the most hotheaded in check. This use of terror had begun immediately after the occupation: on November 22, 1939, the Germans shot 53 Jews from the house at 9 Nalewski Street; in January, 1940, they shot 100 Jewish professionals—physicians, lawyers, and engineers; on April 17, 1942, they shot, in the street in the middle of the night, 52 people suspected of underground activities . . .

The feeling we had for the Germans cannot be oversimplified into hatred. Hatred we felt, but the chief emotion was terror. We couldn't think of the Germans as human beings. They were mad dogs unaccountably loosed from the chains of history and morality. You don't hate a beast of prey, you feel loathing and terror. We feared the Germans with a dreadful, paralyzing panic stronger than the fear of our own deaths. During the final liquidation of the Ghetto, a Jewish woman, on her knees, begged a Polish policeman, "Shoot me! Shoot me. I'm more afraid of the Germans than of dying." One day a German came to take a Jewish child from its mother. When she pleaded for its life, he said, "If you can guess which of my eyes is artificial, I'll give you the child." She looked intently at him and said,"The right one." Astonished, the Nazi replied,"That's so, but how could you tell?" After hesitating for a moment, she told him, "It looks more human than the other one."

The basic factor in the Ghetto's lack of preparation for armed resistance was psychological; we did not at first believe the Resettlement Operation to be what in fact it was, systematic slaughter of the entire Jewish population. For generations East European Jews had looked to Berlin as the symbol of law, order, and culture. We could not now believe that the Third Reich was a government of gangsters embarked on a program of genocide "to solve the Jewish problem in Europe." We fell victim to our faith in mankind, our belief that humanity had set limits to the degradation and persecution of one's fellow man. This mentality underlay the behavior of the Jewish leadership at the very beginning of the Resettlement, when the overwhelming majority voted against armed resistance. Some felt we ought to wait for a joint rising with the Poles. Others were resigned to sacrificing 70,000 Jews rather

---

[2]ne'er-do-wells.

than jeopardizing the entire community of 400,000—the Nazi policy of collective responsibility was very much alive in our memories. Still others were religious Jews, committed to the tradition of *Kiddush Hashem:* that is, a martyr's death in the name of God. They believed that, when the enemy came for us, we should be dressed in our prayer shawls and phylacteries, poring over the holy books, all our thoughts concentrated on God. In that state of religious exaltation, we should simply ignore all Nazi orders with contempt and defiance; resistance, violence, only desecrated the majesty of martyrdom in sanctification of the Lord's name. I heard the following unexpected argument in favor of non-resistance.

"Try to imagine Jesus on the way to Golgotha[3] suddenly stooping to pick up a stone and hurling it at one of the Roman legionnaires. After such an act, could he ever have become the Christ? For two thousand years we have served mankind with the Word, with the Book. Are we now to try to convince mankind that we are warriors? We shall never outdo them at that game."

Lastly, there was the fact that there can be no struggle without some hope. Why does the man unjustly condemned to death fail to turn on his guards as he is led to the gallows? Why did the three thousand Turkish prisoners Napoleon ordered drowned put up no resistance? Why did fifty thousand French Huguenots permit themselves to be slaughtered in a single night by French Catholics?[4] And what of the Armenians?

There is no precedent for the eventual uprising of the Warsaw Ghetto because it was undertaken solely for death with dignity, and without the slightest hope of victory in life.

---

# Two Ghetto Heroines

The heroic girls, Chajke and Frumke—they are a theme that calls for the pen of a great writer. Boldly they travel back and forth through the cities and towns of Poland. They carry "Aryan" papers identifying them as Poles or Ukrainians. One of them even wears a cross, which she never parts with except when in the Ghetto. They are in mortal danger every day. They rely entirely on their "Aryan" faces and on the peasant kerchiefs that cover their heads. Without a murmur, without a

[3]The hill where Jesus was crucified.
[4]St. Bartholomew Day, August 24, 1572.

---

From *Notes from the Warsaw Ghetto: The Journal of Emanuel Ringelblum,* edited by Jacob Sloan.

second's hesitation, they accept and carry out the most dangerous missions. Is someone needed to travel to Vilna, Bialystok, Lemberg, Kowel, Lublin, Czestochowa, or Radom to smuggle in contraband such as illegal publications, goods, money? The girls volunteer as though it were the most natural thing in the world. Are there comrades who have to be rescued from Vilna, Lublin, or some other city?—They undertake the mission. Nothing stands in their way, nothing deters them. Is it necessary to become friendly with engineers of German trains, so as to be able to travel beyond the frontiers of the Government General of Poland, where people can move about with special papers? They are the ones to do it, simply, without fuss, as though it was their profession. They have traveled from city to city, to places no delegate or Jewish institution had ever reached, such as Wolhynia, Lithuania. They were the first to bring back the tidings about the tragedy of Vilna.[1] They were the first to offer words of encouragement and moral support to the surviving remnant of that city. How many times have they looked death in the eyes? How many times have they been arrested and searched? Fortune has smiled on them. They are, in the classic idiom, "emissaries of the community to whom no harm can come." With what simplicity and modesty have they reported what they accomplished on their journeys, on the trains bearing Polish Christians who have been pressed to work in Germany! The story of the Jewish woman will be a glorious page in the history of Jewry during the present war. And the Chajkes and Frumkes will be the leading figures in this story. For these girls are indefatigable. Just back from Czestochowa, where they imported contraband, in a few hours they'll be on the move again. And they're off without a moment's hesitation, without a minute of rest.

# Revolt in Auschwitz

*The revolt in Auschwitz was carried out by 853 prisoners (about half of them Jews), who were members of the "Sonderkommando," the task force which cremated the victims. Each succeeding "Sonderkommando" cremated the preceeding group. The twelfth in the series, knowing full well that they would die, rebelled. All were liquidated after killing 70 SS guards, destroying one crematorium, and inflicting considerable damage. Fifty who escaped from the camp immolated themselves. The eventful day was October 7, 1944 ...*

[1] There were more than 60,000 Jews in the Vilna Ghetto when Germany invaded the Soviet Union in June, 1941. Most of them were massacred at that time.

429

The Sonderkommando was awaiting the final blow. Day after day, week after week, month after month, terror had hovered over our heads, suspended by the thinnest of threads. And now, in a day or two, it would descend bringing with it instantaneous death, leaving in its wake only a pile of silvery ashes. We were ready for it. Hourly we awaited the arrival of our SS executioners . . .

We were not certain of anything, but I felt the imminence of death. Since I was unable to work, I left the dissecting room and went to my room, planning to take a healthy dose of sleeping tablets. I smoked cigarette after cigarette, my nerves completely shot. Unable to stay put, I crossed into the incineration room, where I found the Sonderkommando crew working half-heartedly, despite the fact that several hundred bodies were stacked up in front of the ovens. Small groups had formed and the men were talking in whispers. I went upstairs to the kommando's living quarters and immediately noticed that something was amiss. Normally, after morning muster and breakfast, the night shift turned in. Now, however, at 10 o'clock, everyone was still up. I also noticed that they were dressed in sport clothes, with sweaters and boots, although the room was bright with a warm October sun. Here too, many of the men were huddled, talking in whispers, while others moved about feverishly, arranging and packing their clothes in suitcases. It was obvious that some sort of plot was being hatched. But what? I entered the small room that housed the kommando chief and found the various leaders of the night shift seated around the table: the engineer, the mechanic, the head chauffeur and the chief of the gas kommando. No sooner had I taken my seat when the kommando chief took an almost empty bottle from the table and poured me a large glass of brandy. . . . I downed my glass in one gulp. Now, in the waning hours of the Sonderkommando's fourth month, it might not be a life-prolonging elixir, but it was none the less an excellent remedy for dulling the fear of death. My comrades presented me with a detailed account of our situation. All evidence seemed to indicate that the Sonderkommando's liquidation would not take place before the following day, and perhaps the day after. But careful plans had been made for the 860 members of the kommando to try and force their way out of the camp. The break was scheduled for that night.

Once out, we would head for the loop of the Vistula two kilometers away. At this time of year the river was very low and could easily be forded. Eight kilometers from the Vistula there were vast forests, extending to the Polish border, in which we should be able to live for weeks, even months if necessary, in relative safety. Or perhaps we would run into some partisans along the way. Our supply of weapons was adequate. During the preceding few days a shipment of about a

From *Auschwitz* by Miklos Nyiszli.

hundred boxes of high explosives had reached the camp ... The Germans used it for blowing up railroad lines. Besides this stock, we had five machine guns and twenty hand grenades.

"This should suffice," said one of the group. "With the element of surprise on our side, we can disarm the guards using only our revolvers. Then we'll take the SS by surprise in their dormitories and force them to come with us until we have no further use for them."

The signal to attack would be given by flashlight signals from number one crematorium. Number two would immediately transmit the signal to number three, which would in turn alert number four ...

We adjourned the meeting until the evening, the order being that, until the moment the signal was given, everyone should accomplish his task as usual, scrupulously avoiding any act liable to arouse suspicion ... To know that within a few hours we would be outside these barbed wires and free again lifted a dark cloud from my mind, a cloud that had hovered there since my first day in the KZ.[1] Even if the attempt failed, I would have lost nothing.

I looked at my watch. Half past one. I got up and asked my colleagues to join me for the autopsy (of a Russian officer who was killed) so we could be ready with the report when Dr. Mengele arrived to pick it up. They followed me silently into the dissecting room, and we began the autopsy immediately. Today one of my associates was performing the dissection, while I recorded his findings on my typewriter.

We had been working for about 20 minutes when a tremendous explosion rocked the walls. In the echoing silence, the steady staccato of machine gun fire reached our ears. Peering through the green mosquito netting that covered the main window, I saw the red-tiled roof and supporting beams of number three crematorium blow off, followed by an immense spiral of flame and black smoke. No more than a minute later, machine gun fire broke out just in front of the dissecting room door. We had no idea what had happened. Our plans called for tonight. (Two possibilities occurred to me: either someone had betrayed us, thus enabling the SS to step in and break up the planned escape, or else a considerable force of partisans had attacked the camp.) The dismal wail of sirens began in both Auschwitz I and Auschwitz II. The explosions grew louder and louder, and the rattle of submachine guns more and more persistent. Then we could hear the harsher staccato of field machine guns. I had already made up my mind what to do. Whether it was a question of treason or of a partisan attack, it seemed best for the moment to remain in the dissecting room and see how the situation evolved. From the window I saw 80 to 100 trucks arriving. The first one pulled up in front of our crematorium. Half a

[1]Concentration camp.

company jumped out and formed up in battle formation in front of the barbed wire fences.

I began to see what had happened. The Sonderkommando men had taken possession of number one crematorium and, from every window and door, were spraying the SS troops with bullets and grenades. Their defense seemed effective, for I saw several soldiers drop, either dead or wounded. Seeing this, the besiegers decided to resort to more drastic methods. They brought up 50 well-trained police dogs and unleashed them on the Sonderkommando entrenched behind the walls of number one. But for some strange reason these dogs usually so ferocious and obedient, refused to budge: ears back, tails between their legs, they took shelter behind their SS masters. Perhaps it was because the dogs had been trained to deal with prisoners wearing striped burlap, whereas the Sonderkommando never wore this "uniform." Or perhaps, too long used to dealing with weakened, unarmed prisoners, they were momentarily frightened by the smell of powder and scorched flesh, the noise and confusion of a pitched battle. In any case, the SS soon realized their mistake and, without letting up on their fire, began to haul some howitzers into position.

It was impossible for the Sonderkommando to hold out against such numerical and material odds. Shouting exultantly, they erupted through the back gates of the crematorium. Firing as they went, they poured through the electrified barbed wires that had been cut ahead of time, and headed for the loop of the Vistula.

For about ten minutes the fighting was heavy on both sides. Loud machine gun fire from the watch towers mingled with the lesser blasts of the sub-machine guns, and interspersed could be heard the explosion of hand grenades and dynamite. Then, as suddenly as it had begun, everything became quiet.

Then the SS stationed in front of the crematorium advanced, leaving behind the two howitzers, which they had not used. With fixed bayonets, they attacked the building from all sides, and scattered through the rooms in the basement and ground floor. A group of SS entered the dissecting room. Guns leveled, they surrounded us and drove us, under a rain of blows, into the courtyard. There they made us lie down on our bellies, our faces hard against the ground. The order rang out:"Anyone who makes a move, or raises his head, will get a bullet in the back of the neck!" A few minutes later I could tell from the sound of footsteps that another SS group had rounded up and brought back a considerable number of Sonderkommando men. They too were made to lie down beside us. How many of them could there be? With my head pressed against the ground it was impossible to tell for sure. Three or four minutes later another group arrived and was made to lie down behind us.

While we were lying there inert on the ground, a hail of kicks and blows from the guards' clubs fell on our heads, shoulders and backs. I could feel the warm blood trickling down my face, till its salty taste reached my tongue. But only the first blows really hurt me. My head was spinning, my ears were ringing, my mind was a blank. I could no longer feel anything. I had the impression I was slipping into the indifference that precedes death.

For some twenty or thirty minutes we lay on the ground waiting for the bullet from the SS guards standing behind us. In this position, I knew it was with a bullet in the head that they intended to kill us. The swiftest of deaths at least, and in these circumstances the least horrible. In my mind I imagined my head blown off under the tremendous impact of the bullet fired point-blank, my skull exploding into a thousand pieces.

Suddenly I heard the sound of a car. It must be Dr. Mengele, I thought. The political SS were awaiting his arrival. I didn't dare lift my head to look, but I recognized his voice. An order, from the lips of an SS: "Doctors, on your feet!" All four of us got up and stood at attention, waiting for what would follow. Dr. Mengele made a sign for us to approach. My face and shirt were bloody, my clothes covered with mud as I appeared before him. Three high-ranking SS officers were standing beside him. Dr. Mengele asked us what part we had played in all this.

"No part," I replied, "unless carrying out the orders of the Hauptsturmführer could be construed as guilt. We were dissecting the body of the Russian officer when the incident occurred. It was the explosion that interrupted our dissection. The unfinished autopsy report is still in the typewriter. We did not leave our posts and were there when they found us."

The SS commander confirmed our words. Dr. Mengele looked hard at me and said: "Go wash up and return to your work."

I turned and left, followed by my three companions. We had got no more than twenty steps when a burst of machine guns sounded behind us. The Sonderkommando's life was over . . .

## What Had Happened: An Account of the Day's Events

At 2:00 P.M. a truckload of political SS arrived at number three crematorium. Their commander ordered the Sonderkommando to assemble, but no one moved. He must have had an inkling of what was brewing. In any event, he apparently figured he would get better results if he tried lying to the Sonderkommando, and God knows the SS were past masters in the art of lying. Stopping in the center of the courtyard, he gave a short speech, worthy of the SS:

"Men," he shouted, "you have worked here long enough. By orders of my superiors, you are to be sent in a convoy to a rest camp. There

433

you will be given good clothes, you'll have plenty to eat, and your life will be easier. Those whose tattoo numbers I call out, step forward and line up."

Then he began the roll call. He first called out the numbers of the Hungarian members of number three Sonderkommando, 100 in all. The KZ's "youngest" prisoners, they lined up without further protest. More fear than courage was visible in their expressions. A detachment of SS immediately took charge of them and removed them from the courtyard (then marched them to D Camp and crammed them into Barracks-13).

Meanwhile, in number three crematorium, roll call continued. Now it was the turn of the Greeks, who failed to show a similar alacrity in lining up, but nevertheless obeyed. Next, a group of Poles. Grumbles and muttered protests swelled to a surly roar. The SS called another number. Silence; no one moved. When the officer raised his head and frowned, a bottle fell at his feet and exploded. Seven SS, including the group commander, fell dead or wounded. The bottle had been thrown by one of the Poles. The SS opened a deadly fire on the rioters, who retreated and took up defensive positions inside the crematorium. Thus protected, they began tossing other explosive-filled bottles into the courtyard. A burst of machine-gun fire from some of the SS mowed down the Greeks, who were still lined up in the courtyard. A few tried to escape, but were killed as they reached the gate.

Without letting up on their fire, the SS moved in towards the crematorium entrance. It was no easy job, for the Poles put up a stout defense. Their cascade of bottles succeeded in keeping the SS at a respectful distance. Just then, a tremendous explosion rocked the area, felling those attackers who had moved in close to the building. The crematorium roof blew off, sending a shower of beams and shingles flying in all directions, while smoke and flames billowed skyward. Four drums of gasoline had exploded, reducing the building to rubble and burying the Sonderkommando men inside. A few of those who escaped with their lives tried to carry on the fight, but the SS machine guns made short work of them. Others, wounded but still able to walk, headed towards the door with their hands up, but another burst tumbled them as well. They expected what they got, but fire was gutting the building and they chose the easier death. At the same time, the hundred Hungarians were hastily returned to the courtyard and executed on the spot.

Thus the riot began in number three. In number one, work continued as usual till number three exploded. The sound of the explosion brought the tension, already at a high pitch from the wait, to a paroxysm. No one knew exactly what happened during the first few minutes. The men working at the ovens left their posts and gathered at the far end of the room, where they tried to figure out what was going on and what steps to take.

They did not have long to puzzle, however, for the SS guard came over and asked who had given them permission to stop work and leave the ovens. Apparently the work boss's reply failed to satisfy him, for he dealt the man a withering blow on the head with the curved end of his cane—each of the SS guards carried one, the better to encourage the Sonder men in their work. Rumor had it that a second Sonder man also had his head split open by the same cane. But the work boss, the toughest man in the kommando, was only staggered by the blow. His face was covered with blood, but he was still on his feet. He quickly drew a sharp knife from the top of his boot and thrust it into the guard's chest. As the guard fell two alert members of the kommando grabbed him, opened the door of the nearest oven, and shoved him headfirst into the flames.

The whole incident happened in the space of a few seconds, but another SS guard, drawn by the crowd, apparently arrived just in time to see the booted feet disappear into the oven. He knew it could only have been a Sonder man or an SS guard, but before he had time to learn which, one of the Sonder crew floored him with a sharp upper-cut. With the help of a buddy, he shoved the second SS guard in beside the first.

After that it took only a few seconds to break out the machine guns, hand grenades and boxes of dynamite. Firing broke out, the SS stationed at one end of the room, the Sonderkommando at the other. A hand grenade tossed into the midst of the SS killed seven and wounded a number of others. Several kommando men were also killed or wounded, and the situation of the survivors was becoming increasingly desperate. But when a few more SS dropped, the remainder, about 20 in all, took to their heels and ran for the crematorium door. There they were met by reinforcements, more than enough to turn the tide of battle in their favor.

The rest was history. Seven of us were left in the crematoriums. The twelve fugitives were rounded up during the night. They had succeeded in crossing the Vistula, but were completely worn out and had sought shelter in a house they thought might furnish them with at least a temporary hiding place. But the owner had informed an SS detachment combing the area, and all twelve had been ambushed and recaptured.

I was already in bed, almost asleep, when a new burst of machine-gun fire roused me from my state of semiconsciousness. A few minutes later heavy footsteps echoed in the hallway. My door opened and two SS staggered in, their faces covered with blood.

The twelve prisoners had attacked the patrol that had brought them back to the crematorium courtyard, in a desperate effort to seize their weapons. The twelve had had only their fists to fight with; the result had been swift and sure: all twelve had been quickly killed. But they had succeeded in badly mauling the SS guards, who now asked me to treat their wounds. I mutely carried out their orders.

The loss of these twelve companions was a terrible blow to me. After so much effort and loss of life, still no one had succeeded in escaping to tell the world the full story of this hellish prison.

Later I learned that news of the revolt had nevertheless reached the outside world. Some of the KZ prisoners related the story to the civilians who worked with them. And besides, the tongues of certain SS guards were said to have wagged.

It was indeed an historic event, the first of its kind since the founding of the KZ. Eight hundred and fifty three prisoners, and seventy SS were killed. Included among the latter were an Obersturmführer, seventeen Oberschaarführer and Schaarführer and fifty-two Sturm-männer. Number three crematorium burned to the ground. And number four, as a result of damage to its equipment, was rendered useless.

---

# A People Stands Before God

*Rabbi Leo Baeck was the renowned and venerated spiritual leader of German Jewry. He was a scholar, teacher, head of the National Association of German Jews, B'nai B'rith, and of leading religious and cultural institutions. Although he was offered invitations to occupy important positions outside of Germany, and had many opportunities to leave Germany, he stayed with his people . . .*

By the beginning of 1943 only about ten thousand Jews were left in Berlin. So far I had been spared deportation because of my work as head of the National Association of German Jews.

I had always been in the habit of rising early, but for some reason on January 27 I got up earlier than usual. I was fully dressed when the bell rang at quarter of six. Only the Gestapo would come at that hour. My housekeeper let in two men in civilian clothes. One of them addressed me:

"We have orders to take you to Theresienstadt."

From *We Survived* by Eric Boehm.

436

I had a few last things to attend to, so I said, "Please wait a little while. I must get ready."

"You must come with us at once."

"You are two and can use force to take me. But if you will wait an hour I will go with you as you wish."

One of them went to make a phone call. He returned and said, "We will wait."

I sat down at my desk and wrote a farewell letter to friends in Lisbon. They would send it to my daughter Ruth and her husband in London. Then I made out postal money orders for my gas and electric bills. My housekeeper had packed my bag. I was ready to go . . .

The next morning I was taken to the Anhalter station where hundreds of unfortunate Jews were boarding a train. I was put into a compartment by myself. Before long the train moved out and I was occupied with my thoughts . . .

Theresienstadt meant much to me even before I saw it. Three sisters of mine had died there, and a fourth died shortly after my arrival.

At first I performed all sorts of chores such as pulling garbage wagons, but after my seventieth birthday that year I was free to minister to the living, the sick, and the dying. Sometimes so many people died that I felt as if I existed in a graveyard.

I had heard of the crowded conditions, but not until I saw with my own eyes did I fully understand what it meant. Bunks were often constructed in four and five decks, with so little space between them . . . Often people did not have enough room to stretch out. It was a luxury to have an opportunity to sit on a chair. The inadequacy of latrines was one of the worst trials. Many had dysentery, and it was most humiliating for these good people to defile themselves when they had to wait. When I too was affected I fasted for three days and was blessed with recovery.

A package came for me not long after I arrived in Theresienstadt. Its contents had been removed and it was really only an empty cardboard box. But it gave me joy in the knowledge that someone had thought of me in exile. I recognized the sender—a Christian friend—by the handwriting, although he had used a fictitious name.

Our greatest delicacies were the tins of sardines which the Joint Distribution Committee sent from time to time.

There was always hunger at Theresienstadt—for intellectual and spiritual as well as physical food. Most of our property was stolen by the SS when we arrived. Hence books were rare and people would give a slice of bread for the loan of a book for two weeks.

There were great scholars there from all the countries of Europe. They joined in giving lectures on many subjects—literature, history, economics, mathematics, philosophy, law, and astronomy. We gradually expanded these into an extensive scheduled lecture program, and ended up with a veritable small university.

Sometimes when we went to some barrack dormitory for a lecture people were so eager to hear that they clustered on the bunks like grapes on a vine. The SS tolerated the surreptitious lectures but they had an ironclad rule against the education of children. Not even in the worst periods of persecution in the Middle Ages had the Jews failed to receive at least enough schooling to make them literate. And so, although it had to be done secretly and with great caution, our children in Theresienstadt did receive schooling.

Religious services were held wherever and whenever a group felt the desire for it. In the evening or early hours of the morning we maintained our faith and gave strength to all in prayer. In our services we recalled biblical times—the commandments, the prophets, the Messianic idea—and earlier persecutions of the Jews. Thus a community arose out of a mass and we could forget the misery around us.

One day in August of 1943 a fellow inmate came up to me. He introduced himself as a Czech engineer by the name of Grünberg and asked to talk with me alone. He bound me to silence. Then he spoke.

"I have to tell someone. I was waked last night by my best friend whom I have not seen for a long time. I knew that he had not been sent to Theresienstadt, so I asked how he got here. He cut me short, and told me to listen carefully. He had to tell me. I had to know. But first I must promise not to tell anyone else.

"He was half Jewish and had been sent east. He ended up in the huge camp of Auschwitz. Like everyone there he went through a process of selection and was assigned to do slave labor. The others were led away and gassed to death. He knows that definitely; everyone at Auschwitz knows it. He was sent to a labor camp from which he escaped and made his way back to Prague . . . He was much excited and said he wanted to warn me and save me."

So it was not just a rumor or, as I had hoped, the illusion of a diseased imagination . . . I decided that no one should know it. If the Council of Elders were informed the whole camp would know within a few hours. Living in the expectation of death by gassing would only be the harder. And this death was not certain for all: there was selection for slave labor; perhaps not all transports went to Auschwitz. So I came to the grave decision to tell no one . . .

One November day all of us had to walk out of the camp and stand in a field until evening. We did not know what was to happen to us. I was afraid that they would use gas bombs to kill us on the spot. It turned out that they were checking up on account of irregularities in the list of inmates.

That day had seemed the hardest of all to bear; but its anguish and disappointment were surpassed in the summer of 1944 when a commission of the International Red Cross came to inspect the camp. They appeared to be completely taken in by the false front put up for their benefit. Many of the houses were so overcrowded that a tour through one of them would quickly have revealed the real state of things. But since the ground floor could be seen from the street the SS shrewdly ordered two-thirds of the people living there to move to the upper floors. Flowers were put in the windows. The commission never bothered to climb one flight of stairs. Perhaps they knew the real conditions—but it looked as if they did not want to know the truth. The effect on our morale was devastating. We felt forgotten and forsaken.

Transports were dreaded, but when they did leave people were careful not to give the SS satisfaction by creating scenes. I had already learned in Berlin to admire the self-restraint and inner strength of our people—even when families were torn apart.

The largest transports left Theresienstadt in September and October of 1944. I should judge that about twenty-five thousand people were sent east during those two months, and fifteen to eighteen thousand were left behind. In December and January Jews of mixed marriages, who up to now had been spared deportation, began to arrive. Many families were being torn asunder. The complexion of the ghetto changed, for numbers of the new arrivals had been raised as Protestants and Catholics.

About the middle of January, 1945, I heard of feverish activity in the town fortifications. Deep tunnels were being dug into them, allegedly as storerooms. That did not appear likely; their real purpose could only have been gas chambers. We spread the word that if the SS ordered any groups to go to these tunnels, they should lie down—simply lie down—wherever they were. There were perhaps three hundred SS men attached to Theresienstadt, and it would have taken two of them to carry one of us to a gas chamber. Fortunately nothing happened, no doubt owing to the approach of the American and Russian armies.

But disease threatened to wipe us out. As the winter drew to a close trainloads of people ill with typhus were sent to Theresienstadt. As the cattle cars came in we unloaded those who had died on the way. In March we trudged knee-deep in mud carrying the pitiful victims of the disease. In the first week a dozen doctors and more nurses died. We tried to isolate the sick in separate barracks, but the disease spread through those who took care of them.

One day I was told that a typhus patient wanted to see me. I did not recognize her as I approached, she was so emaciated; but when she spoke I realized that it was Dorothea, my grandniece. She had passed through Auschwitz and been sent to Theresienstadt from a labor camp near Dessau.

Through the connivance of the Czech gendarmes guarding the

439

camp the Czech Jews could often arrange to receive packages from friends. They readily shared their food with the sick; they never turned me down when I asked them for help for the ill.

About this time the Danish Jews were sent back to Denmark. They had always been in a privileged position on account of the packages they received regularly from home.

One day it was announced that anyone who wanted to be in a transport to Switzerland should sign up. Of course we suspected a trap, but many did sign. Some two or three hundred people left one day —and really went to Switzerland. I understand that the International Red Cross paid the SS several hundred Swiss francs for each person.


In the street one day that spring a Prague doctor came up to me and exclaimed in surprise, "I just heard that you were dying!"

"I did not know of it. You see that I am walking around."

In the next few hours a number of people looked at me as if I were an apparition. The answer to the mystery was that a rabbi from Moravia named Beck had just died; and since the death of Jews of professional rank, such as doctors or rabbis or Justizrats, had to be reported to Berlin, Rabbi Beck's had been reported to the Gestapo office. Weeks later some people still thought it was I who was dead, and were surprised to see me.

I did not understand the full significance of my "death" until one day in April when I was talking to Hofrat Klang in one of the offices where we kept valuables for camp inmates. The door opened and an SS officer entered. It was Eichmann. He was visibly taken aback at seeing me. "Herr Baeck, are you still alive?" He looked me over carefully, as if he did not trust his eyes, and added coldly, "I thought you were dead."

"Herr Eichmann, you are apparently announcing a future occurrence."

"I understand now. A man who is claimed dead lives longer!"

Feeling certain that I had little time left to live, I wasted none with him. I walked to the door, he stepped aside, and I went to my quarters. I gave my wife's and my wedding rings to a friend and asked him to hand them on to my daughter in England. Then I wrote farewell letters, and was ready for what might come.

But other events moved more quickly than the SS. In the next days we heard the sound of artillery. The Russians were not far away.

The SS commandant Rehm, published a list of ten more men who were to be sent to Switzerland. My name headed it, followed by . . . other well-known persons. But to have left then would have been tantamount to desertion, so we said we would stay. Rehm told us we had no choice.

Yet we stayed, and the SS left instead. They started packing, loading

440

cars, and moving out. After a few days only the commandant and a few SS men were left. We were beginning to breathe more easily. But typhus still took a heavy toll of the living.

Then one day toward the end of April a representative of the International Red Cross, Paul Dunand, arrived at Theresienstadt. He had just driven through the combat lines, and he informed me that it could only be a matter of days until we were liberated. He appointed me head of the town. It relieved us greatly to be given sound support with which to combat disaster in these last chaotic days.

I asked Mr. Dunand about the transports to Switzerland.

"Transports?" he questioned. "There was only one."

"But had a second one of ten men been planned?"

"No, certainly not."

After I had told him about it he observed,"You would have gotten as far as the Bohemian Forest and been shot while trying to escape." . . .

On May 12 the Red Army liberated Theresienstadt. I was asked to go to the Russian commanding officer . . . When I entered the office a colonel and a dozen officers sitting there rose and each offered me his chair. The colonel said in broken German, "We have come so that we can help you. Help us to help you."

The Russian troops distributed food and aided us in every way possible. The camp was put under quarantine, those sick with typhus were kept strictly isolated, and Red Army doctors and nurses who had been immunized against the disease assisted in medical care . . .

Then began the task of getting the people out of the camp. Some electrical engineers worked together to build a small broadcasting station. When it was finished we broadcast lists of survivors and asked for transportation to take them back to their countries of origin. Before long buses from Luxembourg and Holland started to arrive. When anyone worried about what would happen to them, someone always remembered the Joint Distribution Committee and cheered them with, "Don't worry, the Joint will help us." And indeed they sent us food, starting with a shipment of rice.

In the latter part of May a young American officer arrived and asked for me. He had a letter for me from Eric Warburg, son of Max Warburg, the great Hamburg banker and philanthropist, who had been instrumental in founding the National Association of German Jews. It was my first news from the outside. The young officer brought delicacies that I had not seen in years, and took a letter for my daughter.

In the first days in June I was called to the Russian commandant. An American officer at the Defense Ministry in Prague, he said, wanted to hand medicines for the camp to me personally. A doctor and I were driven to Prague in a Russian truck. At the Defense Ministry we met Major Patrick Dolan, who gave us some wonder drugs which strengthen the heart. As we were about to leave Major Dolan said quietly:

"You have a special permit to go to England. Tomorrow?"

"No, not now. I am responsible for the many unfortunate persons at Theresienstadt." . . .

On Sunday July 1 the Russians took me to Prague, and Major Dolan escorted me to the airfield, where a four-motor Fortress was standing. He and his adjutant and I stepped in. The plane crew all gave me something—one handed me candy, another socks, a third pencils.

In Paris the Joint Distribution Committee took care of me, and I had the opportunity to phone (my daughter) Ruth and on the afternoon of July 5 I landed at a London airport. Ruth had been there for hours, waiting for me as she had waited and hoped all those years.

# Readings

*And The Crooked Shall Be Made Straight* by Jacob Robinson (Jew. Pub. Soc, 1965), distinguished scholar and historian of the *Shoah,* contains the most forceful refutations to the charges of Jewish "complicity" with the Nazi killers which are echoed by Hannah Arendt, Raul Hilberg, Robert Katz, and Jean François Steiner.

*They Fought Back* by Yuri Suhl (Crown Press, 1967), is an impressive collection describing acts of heroism, resistance, and rebellion. It is a companion volume to Philip Friedman's *Their Brothers' Keepers.*

*The Fighting Ghettos* edited by Meyer Barkai (Lippincott, 1962).

*A Tower from the Enemy* by Albert Nirenstein (Orion Press, 1959).

*Jewish Resistance During the Holocaust* (Yad Vashem, 1971), is an authoritative work containing the proceedings of a conference on the subject which was held in Jerusalem 7/11/68.

*Flame and Fury* compiled by Yaacov Shilhav and edited by Sara Feinstein (Jewish Education Committee Press), contains materials for commemorating Yom Hashoah, National Remembrance Day (Nissan 27th).

*The Noble Saboteurs* by Ronald Seth (Hawthorne, 1966), is a book depicting resistance, written for teenagers.

*Secret Press in Nazi Europe* by Isaac Kowalsky (Central Guide Publishers, 1969), is one of the later revelations of resistance. It spreads before us the facts, pictures, and documents of two presses set up by the United Partisan Organization of Vilna, and the U. P. O.'s activities in strengthening the hands of the partisans.

*Forged in Fury* by Michael Elkins (Bantam Books, 1971), is a suspenseful stirring book on the resistance.

# 19. JEWISH PARTISAN FIGHTERS

The Jewish partisans were small, widely scattered bands of fighters that operated mostly as independent entities in isolated regions. Their full history has yet to be written, since Soviet sources are inaccessible, German sources are biased, and Jewish sources, though numerous, are in many different languages.

The groups of partisans were small, woefully underfed, and ill-equipped. They faced all the usual problems confronting guerilla fighters, plus the fact that the local populations were often unfriendly. There were some non-Jewish, anti-Semitic guerilla units which could be as hostile to the Jewish bands as to the Nazi enemy.

Alliances with other non-Jewish guerilla bands enabled the Jews to obtain provisions and weapons, but the Jewish units were unwelcome at first, and had to prove themselves as effective fighters before they were finally admitted into the non-Jewish partisan organizations. During the last years of the war Soviet, Lithuanian, and Polish units included large numbers of Jewish fighters, but even then the Jews suffered discrimination. As Jews, they had no choice but to fight; the others could leave the group and "pass" among the local population. Frequently this led to their being assigned the most dangerous missions.

Partisan activities included sabotage, bombing of enemy installations, ambushes, fighting pro-Nazi collaborators, and using every possible means of obstructing enemy operations. If caught, the partisans were subjected to unspeakable tortures so that their deaths would inspire fear in others.

In France, the Low Countries, and Scandinavia, the situation was different, since the local populations were not so contaminated by Jew-hatred. As a result, the Jews in the resistance organizations of Western

444

Europe fought as equals with their Gentile comrades-in-arms. All told, though Jews constituted less than 1 percent of the total French population, they made up between 15 and 20 percent of the membership of the French partisan movement.[1] Even the French Jewish Boy Scout organization participated, successfully smuggling three thousand adults and one thousand children to safety in Spain and Switzerland.[2]

# The Belski Partisan Group

*First to organize into forest partisan fighters were those Jews who escaped from the doomed ghettos to the sheltering woods of the Ukraine and White Russia. They drew inspiration and courage from the ghetto rebellions of Warsaw, Bialystok, Vilna, and others. When they could, they joined the Soviet partisans. Tuvia Belski defined the distinctiveness of the Jewish fighters . . .*

In March, 1943, we sent ten comrades under the leadership of Avraham Polanski to bring food . . . They completed their assignment, obtained the required supplies that we estimated, and returned. At a distance of five kilometers from Novogrodek they turned off to the farm of Bielus, one of Polanski's acquaintances, and asked him to let them rest for a day . . . Bielus received them in a friendly manner, gave them food and drink, and even offered them places to sleep. Of course they put up sentries, but at midnight the farm was surrounded. Bielus informed (this we found out later) that Partisans were in his home. He sent one of his sons with the information to the police station in Novogrodek. When our friends woke up in surprise, it was too late to fight. They were all shot, except Avraham, who managed to hide in the chicken coop under the stove. When he heard the police and their officers leaving, and the family rejoicing and celebrating its victory, he came out of his hiding place and shouted to Bielus: "The Partisans will take revenge." Suddenly an ax, wielded by one of Bielus' sons, came down on his head. These details became known to us later through the testimony of Bielus' housemaid, who was an eye-witness to these events. The Bielus family thought the matter ended, and that with the death of the only witness, the awful crime was erased.

[1]Leon Poliakov, "Studies on the Epoch of the Jewish Catastrophe, 1933–1945," *YIVO Annual of Social Science* (1953), pp. 252–63.
[2]Yuri Suhl, *They Fought Back*, p. 285.

From *A Tower from the Enemy,* edited by Albert Nirenstein.

We waited a day, two days for the return of our emissaries—and no news. We went out to look for them in the villages. We questioned and investigated until we reached the place and found out all the details, as they were told to the friends and neighbors by the murdering family, and their maidservant who had been present.

We could not allow ourselves to be restrained about this matter. If we did not take revenge against these informers, what would our end be? Every farmer would turn us over to the authorities. The first group that we sent to reconnoiter to investigate this matter came upon a group of Jews in the forest, hiding in a forlorn bunker on a farm. Among the six or seven Jews there was Hirsh Berkovski (who had) heard about the terrible massacre of the ten Jewish Partisans, and also knew that the maidservant of Bielus was present when the crime was committed. The scouts contacted her and questioned her. At first she denied any knowledge, but after she had been convinced that it might be better for her to tell the whole story, she told all. The scouts reported back to us.

Asahel took the men of the first group, the best trained and best armed among us, twenty-five men, and they went out in wagons to bring justice upon the family of Bielus.

I commanded Asahel: "Don't take a thread from the house of Bielus. Everything must go up in smoke." I reminded them of the command of Joshua in his day and the affair of Achan (Joshua Ch. 7).

I said to him: "As our ancestors did." And he promised.

Asahel and his men surrounded the house at midnight. His thunderous pounding on the door frightened them into opening it . . . They came to the point immediately, declaring that they had come to avenge the blood of their ten comrades. Bielus felt what was coming, and resisted. When the four of them aimed their guns at him, he grabbed the barrels and wrestled with them. Even after he had been stabbed several times, he continued to struggle. Asahel shot him and ordered his friends to finish the job. They completed what they had set out to do in the course of a few minutes. The house, the stable, and the barn went up in smoke.

One of the group, Michal Leibovitz, took a coat with Asahel's permission. In the pocket of that coat we found afterwards a letter from Traub, the German Commander of Novogrodek, in which he thanked Bielus for informing on the ten members of our gang, and expressing his hope that all of Bielus' neighbors would follow his example, and help wipe out the Partisans. The letter was translated for us by Dr. Eisler, from German into Russian, and we kept it, presenting it to the Partisans' high command.

On the way back, the punitive expedition went to the house of a farmer, with whom the people of Novogrodek had an unsettled account. In 1941 they bought a pail from him, and there was a dispute concerning the transaction. He told the police that the Jews had robbed him of several items. The police lined up 250 Jews and he identified four of them who were taken out and killed. Our men now repaid him their debt . . .

---

# Saul: A Boy Partisan's Story

*Lena Kichler, who directed a home for DP children in Poland and later in Paris, recounts the story told to her by fourteen-year-old Saul, a native of Lvov (Lemberg), who lived through the hell of war and Nazi occupation and finally became a partisan . . .*

I decided to go to the forest. The forest was only a kilometre from the village, but it was not at all easy to penetrate into it. At that time there were all sorts of people in the forest. There were ordinary robbers, who used to attack passers-by. There were "Bandrov-tzi" (Ukrainian Fascists, under the leadership of Stefan Bandra). It was dangerous to go near them. Once, a woman went out to gather mushrooms and unintentionally approached their camp. They shot and killed her . . . But there were Poles and Jews of all sorts in the forest as well. The farmers were frightened of the forest-dwellers, because if you did not satisfy their demands, they would kill you on the spot, and if you did then the Germans would take it out on you afterwards, or even burn the whole village.

I very much wanted to reach the Russians in the forest, because they had weapons and they were not afraid of the Germans—but how could I find them?

It was the beginning of spring . . . I wandered all through the forest, I must have walked about five kilometres. Suddenly I heard a voice behind me say in Russian, "Where are you going?" . . . I replied I was a Jew who wanted to join them in order to fight the Germans. They accepted me, even though I was small.

I told them everything that had happened to me: how the Germans had taken my father and mother and how I had worked in the village, and how the boys had driven me away.

The Russians behaved well towards me. There were other young boys there but I was the youngest. They told me not to be afraid. If I stayed with them, no one would hurt me. They told me that there used

---

From *The Massacre of European Jewry.*

to be a Jew among them, 26 years old, and they all liked him because he was a good comrade—but he was killed . . .

They were not frightened of the Germans, because they had weapons and the Germans did not enter the forest. They gave me vodka and cigarettes, but I refused to drink or smoke. They cooked for themselves, repaired their own clothes, cleaned their weapons and played cards. Those were the best days I had at that time. I felt that I was a free man. No one called me a "damned Jew". I would not have returned to the village or the town for all the money in the world, even though in the forest we had no roof over our heads and we slept on the bare ground.

There were about 150 of them. There were no women; and I was the only young Jew among them. The following day they began to ask me about the Germans: where I had seen them and on which side of the forest. I told them all I had seen. Then they wanted to know who the rich farmers in the village were. They were planning a "raid".

In the evening, they harnessed two horses to a cart and saddled two others. Two of them were with me in the cart and the other two rode their horses. There was a Russian officer and an ordinary soldier with me. They took a sub-machine gun and grenades with them. They had revolvers in their pockets. They were dressed as civilians and no one would have imagined that they were soldiers. They looked for all the world like farmers returning from market. The sub-machine gun was covered with straw. There were sacks at the side . . .

We left the forest at dark. One of the riders went on ahead. He preceded us in order to see if it was all clear in front of us. After that, he returned and we all moved off. We entered the village and stopped at one of the huts. One of the mounted men guarded us from a short distance away and the other one kept a lookout. I remained in the cart. The two entered the house with their hands in their pockets. They stood in the doorway and demanded foodstuffs.

They did not even have to show their pistols. The farmer quickly understood what his position was and brought butter, a ham, bread, cheese and sausage. He gave us more than we had expected. We put it all in the sacks and quietly returned to the forest. We did not return via the road, but through the fields. That was how my first raid finished. After that, I often went with them, because 150 men had to be fed and it was not easy.

The following day, I was awoken by shots. The Germans had encircled part of the forest, but were afraid to enter it. Only their dogs rushed up to us, but we were not afraid of the dogs. If they came close, we put a bullet in them from a pistol and that was that . . .

The Russians packed up, put the sub-machine gun in the cart and some getting on their horses, moved on into the depths of the forest. It was a large and dark forest and gave us excellent cover. We travelled for about half a day and set up camp in a wilder place which the Germans had not reached. We camped there for about a month and a half. We used to go to the neighboring village every three days to get food, and we always took weapons with us.

The Russians gave me a small horse. He was black and had a tendency to bite. I used to hold his head with both my hands so that he could not move his jaw. The Russians advised me to whip him whenever he tried to bite me, but I could not . . . I pitied him too much. I used to curry him and brush him every day until his coat glistened in the sun. I used to go a long way every day to bring him fresh hay. Often the Russians used to tease me and take his fodder for their horses. I never said a word: I just waited. After a moment they would slap me on the shoulder, grin, and return the fodder. They treated me well and always gave me plenty to eat and drink . . . In the evenings, I used to join them around the fire and listen to their stories about the war, about their homes and wives and children. They used to show me pictures of their children and tell me what they would do when they returned home . . .

The front did not move for three months then . . . After that, the situation became worse. The whole retreating German Army attacked us. The forest was surrounded by tanks and cannon. It was impossible to burst out. If we managed to leave the forest once a week, and that only to get food, it was considered extraordinary. We had no food and we just starved. Often we saw no food for two or three days at a time.

Finally the Russians attacked. The "Katiushas" (batteries of rockets) began to sing and the whole forest shook. Bullets flew over our heads and grenades exploded all the time. The forest went up in flames. The dim forest was lighted like an open field.

The explosions went on the whole night; they approached and retreated, became louder and then softer. There was lightning and thunder; the forest was filled with sound and the ground shook . . .

Two other boys and I were commanded to leave the forest in order to bring food. We had not tasted a thing for two days. My friends went before me and I followed in their tracks. They walked very fast, in order to pass quickly over the dangerous path, and I hardly kept up with them. We left the forest. Now we had to jump over one of the German trenches. The Germans were no longer there. They were retreating and the Russians were advancing. I followed them. I saw how they sprang over the trench. I was supposed to do as they did. Suddenly there was an immense explosion and I was knocked backwards as though by a fist. A pillar of smoke rose and hid everything. I do not know what happened then, because I lost consciousness. I do not know, either, how long I lay there.

When I awoke I felt that my fingers were wet and I could not move them at all. I could not move my head either—it hurt me. I felt that my

449

hands and feet were not part of my body. Everything around me was black and red. I could not distinguish anything clearly. There were black and white patches before my eyes. My ears were ringing and my chest was wet with blood.

I do not know what happened after that. Everything went hazy. I heard voices of my friends and felt that I was being carried somewhere. I was badly wounded.

I was taken to a hut and I lay there all night. I asked about the two boys who had gone before me. The Russians said that both of them had been killed. They had stepped on a German mine, which had blown them to pieces. I had been wounded by fragments from the same mine.

The Germans were no longer there. The Russians captured the village and continued to advance. They bandaged me provisionally, and the following day they sent me to a Russian hospital.

The doctor gave me an injection immediately. I do not remember what happened afterwards very clearly, because I was very ill. I lay in hospital for more than eight months. They performed operation after operation upon me. They extracted one eye. They took off three of my fingers. Pieces of metal entered my lungs. I was very weak and could barely breathe. There was little food and the patients starved. They used to pick green plums and stuff themselves with them—they were so hungry.

Then Jews began to visit me and brought me food and I was not so hungry after that. After eight months they let me out of hospital and the Jews took me to Poland. I came to Cracow. But I did not want to live among strangers, even though they treated me well. I did not want to be a burden to them. I decided to go to an orphanage . . .

I did not want to be in Poland for all the money in the world. It seemed to me that everything there was just as it was in the days when the Germans were there. At every turn I was called names and threatened: "You are a dirty Jew! Get out of here—no one needs you!"

I am in France now. It is not like that here, but I still do not want to stay here. I am tired of wandering around in foreign countries. It will be like Poland everywhere . . .

## Lena Kichler's Postscript to Saul's Story:

Saul had undergone many operations in a Soviet hospital. He had only one eye, an ear had been removed, his face and body were completely scarred, he lacked a few fingers, and, worst of all, he suffered badly from tuberculosis and shrapnel in the lungs.

He was difficult, undisciplined, stubborn and resentful. He had faith in no one; and he was angry with the whole world. He always walked around gloomily with a stick in his hand . . .

I sensed his noble nature and his strong character. I knew that the

450

stick was a residue of the war, while his bitterness and suspicions were the results of his wounds.

He had lost everything: home, family, childhood's warmth, his healthy body, his sight, his mobility. His lungs were peppered with shrapnel . . . We tried to help him. We fitted him with an artificial eye and afterwards his tuberculosis improved too.

When Saul heard that he might travel to Eretz Yisrael, he began to have confidence in me . . . I began to give him responsibility. I let him supervise the small children, the ones he used to hit. The educational miracle took place. Saul grew attached to the children and they to him.

In one matter he did not change: he remained a fighter for freedom, a rebel.

One day he came to me with about twenty other 14-16-year-old boys and girls: our oldest group.

"We are leaving the Home," he announced coldly.

"Why? Is it bad here?"

"We are not leaving because it is bad but because it is too good here. We do not want to live here in Paris and visit the theatre and the cinema while our people are suffering on their way to Eretz Yisrael in ghost ships. We want to fight for Israel too. We do not want to wait any longer. We are going." . . .

They reached our country in the "Exodus, 1947" and in it they received their first baptism of fire in the struggle for freedom and for the establishment of Israel.

Shortly after they arrived in Eretz Yisrael, the War of Independence began. They all joined the army. Saul could not join the fighters because of his bad sight and his missing fingers. To this day it is not clear to me how he managed to persuade the military authorities to take him. He joined the Military Police and was even praised for exemplary conduct in battle.

A few years later he became seriously ill once more; his old wounds reappeared . . .

But Saul won the battle and recovered. Today (1961) he is a sailor in the Israeli Navy.

Saul—stubborn son of a stubborn people.

# A Partisan Group in the White-Russian Forests

The terrible winter began. The German visits to the villages around the forest became more frequent, so we decided to prepare a secret camp immediately. In the thickest part of the forest, we dug a large hole into which eighty men could enter. We made the top of this shelter even with the face of the ground round about so that it would be possible to walk over it without recognizing anything. Instead of a window we put in the roof an old tree—tall and hollow, through which air could reach us and which would rouse no suspicion on the outside.

Inside we made three tiers of shelves. Some tens of yards away we built a regular earthen bunker. This was connected with our shelter by an underground tunnel. The entrance from the bunker into the tunnel was excellently camouflaged.

One of our most important functions now was to get some arms. The Brisk-Warsaw road passed about 22 miles from us. This road was used continuously by the German army, both by day and by night. We decided to ambush the Germans.

In the middle of the night we stole silently to the road, sat at the edge of the forest and waited. Nazi tanks, armored-cars full of soldiers passed before our eyes—convoy after convoy. The entire neighborhood hummed with military activity. We sat and waited, a group of partisans with only a few antiquated rifles which had to be cleaned with steel wool after each shot. Some of us were armed with mock wooden rifles, others held stones or knives in their hands.

The night was dark and a cold autumn rain stung our faces. A bitterly cold wind blew and chilled us to the marrow, as we lay in wait by the road.

One after another columns of Germans passed. After them a belated Nazi car with soldiers came by. The order came: to attack this car.

It approached us and we opened fire. The car stopped and we fell upon it with our wooden rifles, stones and knives. Through the air thundered the shots of the partisan rifle, the "knotziza" with its sawed-off barrel to make it easier to carry under one's coat. It's true the sawed-off barrel causes inaccuracies in aim—but it makes a dreadful noise. A

From *Unsung Heroes* by Hakibbutz Hameuchad.

452

terrible fear fell upon the Germans. They couldn't understand what kind of weapon was being used against them, and they lost control of themselves suddenly. Some of them were killed, some wounded—whoever could flee, fled. They left the car and their arms behind.

We carried the arms and the clothing with us to our shelter. Those who had come with wooden dummy guns, returned with two German rifles each, one for themselves, and one for a comrade. We burned the car. What use had we for a car in our paths through the swamps and forests, the hills and valleys?

The Germans began to use the roads during the day time only—after another car was blown up by a mine which we placed during the night. They sent advance parties on bicycles to reconnoitre the road, and we fell on them and took their weapons. After that they began to send advance parties in armored cars, and we lay in wait for them, and attacked them as well.

With the addition of arms, and those who were fleeing from the Ghettos, we became stronger and stronger.

At day-break, one day, the last group of Jews from the Baranowitcz Ghetto came to us and told us of another slaughter—the worst till then. The Ghetto had been turned into a slaughter-house, the murderers killing with hatchets and with iron bars.

Two of our young chaverim, Itzik Asherovsky, and Moshele, the darling of our group decided by themselves to take vengeance on the three Germans for whom they had formerly worked. Those same Germans had taken part in the slaughter. They asked for permission from the commander to go to the city and bring arms—and received his consent.

It was January with a strong frost and a wind driving the snow. The two youngsters went out on their way alone, promising to act carefully. We parted from them, and they disappeared in the distance.

We awaited their return impatiently.

On the next day Moshele returned, breathing with difficulty, hardly alive. He told: they had reached Baranowitcz at midnight, stolen into a house opposite the dwelling of the three murderers. They had lain under the steps at the entrance, and waited for the morning which delayed its coming.

"We were hungry," Moshele told, "and the cold frost penetrated our bones. I fell asleep, but Itzik waked me. 'Get up Moshele, or you'll freeze in your sleep. Woe betide us if we fail to enter the stall in the yard of the murderers at daybreak.'

"Let me alone!," I was angry at him. I just spoke to my father and mother. They came to me in a dream and spoke to me. I saw my sister, too. She was stretched out on the ground, wounded and groaning. I swore to my parents to avenge their blood, and they listened to me . . .

"We were both silent. Hunger grew stronger, gnawing at us. It was as if the cold wind had agreed with our hunger to torture us. We pressed closer to one another and waited for the light of day. The roosters began to crow, the morning star lighted up. Silently, we left our position under the steps and went into the small stall in the yard of the Germans' house. We saw two of the Germans coming out and locking the door. They placed the key in its usual place, which we already knew. But where was the third? If he were within, why did they lock the door? It must be that he was not there, we decided. Stealthily we left the stall, found the key, opened the door,—and found the third German lying in bed, asleep. Here the murderer was in our hands! Near the wall—his arms. But it was impossible to shoot, lest the sound of the shot betray us. I took my pen-knife from my pocket and cut his throat. It seemed to me that the blood was not red, but grey—like dirty dish water.

"How could we pass through the streets of the city in our torn clothing and with our rifles on our shoulders? We would undoubtedly be stopped. We were just putting on the Fascist uniforms when the door opened and another of the three appeared in the doorway. When he saw us, and his glance fell on the bed, in which the body lay wallowing in its blood, he shot—but missed. At the sound of the shot, the entire neighborhood came running. How I escaped from the hands of the Germans, I don't know—it was a miracle. Actually I fled from their hands. As I ran, I heard the sound of the bullets being shot at us. Then I heard the explosion of a hand grenade. Itzik, who saw no possibility of escape from the murderers who surrounded him, took his grenade out of his pocket and threw it. He himself was torn to bits, and with him two Germans died and several were wounded."

So we lost Itzik. In a later battle Moshele fell.

"May their names be remembered and blessed."

# Sabbath in a Polish Partisan Camp

*A small group of Jews joined Polish partisans. They were led by Bynie, their "rabbi," and Edi, a doctor . . .*

The Jews were twelve, enough, that is, to form a community of prayer. There was no altar, no scrolls of the Torah. What was worse, though, was that in the last few days—and particularly since the fighting in the forest—the men had changed. They oscillated between dumb despair and noisy violence. Many wanted to be like the Poles, to let their own nature disintegrate so that they might seek salvation in a new and foreign one. Those spoke only Polish among themselves and swore as did Skarbek's (the Polish leader) people . . . They tried to make themselves popular with the Poles by giving them presents and telling them jokes: they wanted to do everything which would stop them from being themselves. At night they had to think of their wives and children, now lying in the limepits up by the brickworks behind the town, mown down on the day following the battle in the beech forest. Perhaps we are guilty, they thought. We should have stayed with them, they thought, instead of trying to escape our common destiny. But the next day they ran across to the Poles once more. Yes, they were afraid to live and afraid to die . . .

There were others who were strangely troubled. They did what they were told, they went on guard, they slept, they ate, and they prayed; yet it seemed as though they relapsed into the shadows as soon as they were left alone. Then everything about them became, as it were, rigid. Was it fear that so affected them or was it sorrow for the dead? They no longer expressed any feelings. Only a miracle could restore them to real life, Bynie thought. But he could not perform a miracle, nor might he even attempt to do so. He had strayed from the true path.

The men across the way were no longer singing. Bynie bent his head over his book once again. He read, half aloud: *"So God created man in His own image, in the image of God created He him."*

The commentator asked: *"Why the repetition since in his own image is unequivocal?"* . . .

The answer was: *"When the Creator saw his creation, the first man, He hesitated and considered that now He would no longer be alone, that henceforth, together with His form, He had confided a part of His dignity to a weak creature capable of destroying that dignity by evil deeds. Nevertheless the Almighty did not alter the image. Man thus became His boldest undertaking, and that is what is made plain by the repetition: ". . . in the image of God created He him." This means that man is the sole creature whose duty is to be holy and whose very countenance is a promise."*

"What are you reading, young Rabbi?" Jusek asked.

"I am not reading, I am learning."

"What are you learning?"

"To understand the beginning, the first chapter of the first book."

From *Than a Tear in the Sea* by Manes Sperber.

"You're only learning that now? And they say you Jews can read the Bible even when you're still small children. Well, the devil alone can understand you people! I've come to tell your chief that you're to collect all your rifles and ammunition at once and put them here under the lantern. We're going to keep them with ours. If there's any fighting to be done you'll be given them back. Tell him!"

Bynie called Edi across and told him what the Pole had said.

"First he must bring me a written order, signed Pan Skarbek, and then we'll do what he asks," Edi replied. "Till I get that I'm not giving him even one empty cartridge case."

"Don't translate that!" said one of the men from Wolyna in Yiddish who had overheard Edi's words. "Why make bad blood? After all, we're only here because—"

"I understand what he said. There's no need for you to translate," said Jusek, and his voice was not friendly. "Tell him that Pan Skarbek will not be back before tomorrow or the day after. Until then you must all obey me."

Edi wished to know why and for what purpose Jusek required their weapons. The Pole replied it was for reasons of good order. Anyhow he hadn't come to argue. His voice was unnecessarily loud, and soon some of his comrades appeared.

"I see the Jews are threatening you, Jusek. Tell me which one went for you," one of them demanded.

"No one, Janusz, no one, but it's a good thing you're here. They don't want to hand over their guns. Their leader says he won't give us even one empty cartridge case."

The Poles pressed about Edi. He stepped back as far as the post. They followed him.

"Tell them, Bynie, that I've got a particularly powerful grenade in my pocket. If they so much as touch me I'll set it off. It'll blow me up, but they'll all go too. Translate quickly!"

When they understood they all moved back. Bynie alone remained standing beside him by the post. Jusek cried in broken German:

"But why? Want nothing bad, why not give guns? Then quiet, peace, all good friends!"

One of the Jews came up behind Edi and whispered in his ear:

"He's a good man. Let's give him what he wants, and a gold coin, too, and then he'll leave us in peace."

Edi turned about quickly and stared into the man's heavily bearded face. He seized him by the jacket, pulled him under the light, boxed both his ears, and threw him to the ground. The Poles were closing in again and Edi quickly put his right hand back in his coat pocket. He said loudly:

"I was a lieutenant in the Imperial and Royal Austrian Army, and am not accustomed to accept orders from private soldiers or non-commis-

456

sioned officers. In this gallery I am in command. Let any man who doubts this speak up. I shall allow you, Sergeant Jusek, to remain here, and I order you to send your men away at once. Do you understand?"

"If that is so," Jusek replied, "then I forbid the Jews to leave this gallery. I'll post guards and order them to shoot on sight."

When the Poles had left Edi picked up the man from Wolyna whom he had struck and said loudly, so that all the others might hear:

"I hit you, Mendel Rojzen, because I intend to silence the voice of the ghetto once and for all. We shall not leave this cellar alive if we cannot manage to convince those others that it's dangerous for them to attack us."

"Yes, but they're three hundred and we're twelve," put in Rojzen. There was blood on his chin and his upper lip was swollen. "We must do nothing any more. We—listen carefully—we here are the only free Jews left in the land. We fear nothing, nobody any more. Have you all understood?"

They did not reply. They did not look at him. After a little time Bynie said:

"It is easy and it is hard to understand what you mean. In a few minutes it will be the Sabbath. Tell us what we should do, for it will soon be time to pray."

"What is hard to understand?" Edi asked roughly.

"That we are free. What does it mean to be free? To act in accordance with one's conscience. And what does that mean? It means to behave in a way in which it would be right for everyone to behave. Violence is therefore not freedom."

Edi interrupted him:

"Enough of that. Load your rifles at once. From now on there will be four men on guard all the time, two at each end of the gallery. The guards will give the alarm as soon as anyone comes near. Nobody is to be allowed in without my permission. Relief every two hours."

The men obeyed but still they would not look at him. They understood well enough what it was he wanted, they believed him to be clever. But in the last few days he had come to seem ever more foreign to them. They felt clearly enough that he despised them and that he was only prepared to die with them because he valued his own life so low. He was a Jew, true enough, but only by birth. He could not tell one Hebraic letter from the next, he knew not a single prayer, and he had undoubtedly never paid any attention to what the law demanded and what it forbade. With all his worldly knowledge he was for them an ignorant man. And this was the man who ordered them about, had power over them, and now told them in all seriousness that they were free. They had lost seventeen men, brothers, cousins, and friends, at the forest's edge. Now they were at the mercy of the Poles. What use were these guns? Better to give them to Jusek, if he insisted on it, and avoid a fight. Better still to make a deal with the Poles, to let them see that they regarded themselves more or less as their tenants and were willing to pay a high rent as such. But how should this foreigner know the proper way of coming to an understanding with Poles? A bomb in his pocket, blowing everyone to bits—that was the only sort of thing he thought about. Day and night they were pining away with grief, thinking all the time of the dead and the missing, until a man might wish to tear his own skin. But this Edi thinks only of new deaths.

Half aloud they spoke the joyous chant with which the beginning of the Sabbath must be greeted: *"Come, beloved, towards the bride . . ."* Their eyes kept turning towards Bynie. His father had died a martyr's death; now this boy was the rabbi. It was up to him to lead them. He should decide whether they were to follow the foreigner or shake him off at last.

After the prayer they surrounded him. One said:

"You are our rabbi, the successor of the Zaddik of Wolyna. Tell us now what we should do. We will listen and obey."

"My father has been taken from us before his time. I have not learned enough. I am filled with questions and know no one who will answer them. I do not know the meaning of why the strange Jew came particularly to us, or of why he asked us to take up arms. In his heart he is a good man, and yet so hard, harder than any I have ever seen. What does that prove? It proves that he is acting not in obedience to his own, but to a higher, will. And of all the Jewish communities Wolyna was spared until the last. And it is to us alone that Dr. Rubin Edi has come. In order to save us? I do not believe so. What have we done to deserve that we be spared from death, we particularly? So the meaning is that we are to die in some way different from that in which the rest of our people died. I ask you and command you to obey the foreign Jew in all matters even as do I, the last rabbi of Wolyna. Jews, I wish you a good, a holy, a joyous Sabbath."

For generations in their little town it had been the custom that no one leave the prayer house before the rabbi had pronounced these last words.

The night passed quietly. In the morning Jusek came and asked the guard in a friendly fashion to summon Edi and Bynie.

"You must see, Lieutenant, sir, that I'm in a difficult position. You know, I'm not your enemy, just the opposite, and I'm absolutely determined nothing shall happen. I can keep my men quiet if you'll at least let me have your ammunition. The guns you can keep."

Bynie translated Edi's reply:

"You have not yet explained to me why you wish to disarm us."

"It's only fair. You killed the militiamen and took their rifles, better rifles than we've got. It's thanks to us you did it. So it's not fair, that's what our people are saying."

458

"In that case your people have forgotten the share of the booty we gave you, which cost us seventeen men and you one electric torch. They died covering your withdrawal. Go back, Sergeant, and ask your people if that doesn't make us quits."

Jusek hesitated, was about to leave, and then stopped. He said:

"Well, I think I understand, Lieutenant. But look at it this way. This is our place and everything here belongs to us. I'm only trying to avoid any unpleasantness. So give us your cartridges."

"Tell him, Bynie, that I'll give him one hundred and eighty cartridges, against a signed receipt and his word that they won't ask for anything more."

"Not enough!" said Jusek. There was a bad smile on his lips and he looked as though he were suddenly drunk. "Not enough. We want all your ammunition. And then we'll come and see you haven't any more hidden away. We're not taken in by your Jewish tricks. So give us what belongs to us, or we'll take it by force."

"Bynie, translate my answer word for word: The only way we shall deliver our cartridges will be through the barrels of our rifles. And now tell him to get out . . ."

# We Fought Back in France

*Abraham Raisky was a leader of the Jewish partisans in France. He saved many Jewish lives by smuggling Jewish children into Switzerland and attacking transports to death camps in the east. His resistance group received citations from the general French resistance movement and from the de Gaulle headquarters in London . . .*

On August 14, 1941 German occupation troops marched through the streets of a still docile Paris posting huge placards announcing the execution of three young Frenchmen. These men were the first martyrs of the underground. Two of them, Henri Bekerman and A. Tishelman, were Jews.

Within a few days, the placards were key rallying points for Parisians who had already lived under the Nazi boot for a bleak year. Women stopped foraging the markets for food long enough to make a furtive sign of the cross over the Jewish names. Their husbands stood silently by and, when the police were not looking, scribbled anti-Nazi slogans.

From *Commentary Magazine,* February 1946, by Abraham Raisky.

Thus was the spark of French resistance first fanned, and Jewish names continued to be linked with the story of freedom until the final expulsion of the Germans. (After Bekerman and Tishelman, came thousands of doctors, merchants, working men, young wives and war widows who merged their different backgrounds and beliefs to form a powerful sector in the army of the underground. They fought a war all French patriots will remember with gratitude and which all Jews can remember with pride.)

Bekerman was a shy, slim boy, a medical student, who was captured by the Gestapo while brazenly distributing leaflets calling for a mass demonstration, the first public defiance of the Nazis, on Bastille Day. The demonstration, organized by student groups, went off on schedule, but Bekerman was already in a torture cell.

Hundreds of young men, aware that they were making history, had assembled nervously at the Porte St. Denis. At exactly 4 P.M. they formed orderly lines, unfurled three flags of the Republic and marched down the boulevards singing the *Marseillaise*. On the sidewalks amazed Parisians, ashamed of their first shocked silence, found voice and cheered.

German military police rumbled through the boulevards in crowded trucks and opened fire on both the students and bystanders. The flag-bearer, surrounded by a picked group of guards, slowly fell back along a side street. Among the guards was Tishelman, a seventeen-year-old lad. He had managed to get hold of a rusty World War I revolver, and while the other boys retreated, Tishelman exchanged fire with the well-armed Germans until his bullets were gone. A moment later he was seized.

General von Stuelpnagel, the Nazi occupation boss, realized at once that this demonstration by a handful of ragged students was the beginning of a battle. By publicly announcing the executions of his youthful prisoners, he intended to show the French that the Germans would be ruthless in the face of resistance.

Stuelpnagel committed a historic error in assuming that two Jews could never become heroes to the French. Though the underground then consisted of little more than isolated islands of hatred and hope, small demonstrations began to break out almost every day. Soon Stuelpnagel's troops posted a second placard with another Jewish name on it—Rolnikas, a lawyer and social worker. Again Frenchmen quietly congregated and, peering guardedly into each other's eyes, found the starved look of freedom.

A few days later the Germans methodically cleaned out the Belleville (Jewish) district in the first house-to-house manhunt of Jews. Every Jewish male rounded up was hurled into sealed vans headed for the murder camps of Maidanek and Auschwitz. For them it was the end, but the Germans could not imprison every patriotic Frenchman, nor even every Jew. The early heroism of Bekerman, Tishelman and Rolnikas was the handwriting on the wall for the enemy. Slowly, the French underground began to take shape.

The Jewish army was a vital part of this underground. It participated in every important blow against the Nazis and begged for the most dangerous missions. It was a separate unit, however, because we, the Jews of France, wished to provoke the Nazis by letting them know that a special Jewish army was resisting them. While millions of other Jews throughout Europe, tragically outnumbered and historically isolated, could be herded into death factories in long hopeless lines, we wanted to redeem their dignity by open warfare.

I shall never forget the night on which our decision was reached. It was on August 22, just eight days after the first placards had been posted. A group of Jewish leaders had gathered in a small apartment in the heart of the Belleville district to discuss the latest decree—the death penalty for every form of anti-German activity. The measured, menacing steps of a German patrol floated up to us through the too-still night. Tonight, they passed on.

We had to decide quickly: were the Jews to join in the underground as individuals, lost in the mass, or were they to form independent groups? One of us, a business man who was later to prove his bravery a hundred times, said:

"This is a war for survival between us and the Nazis. Perhaps our first duty is to make certain that some form of Jewish life will continue. Let us not risk total extermination."

Another man spoke. Just an hour before, he had escaped a German detail by climbing over his apartment house roof in the Rue d'Angoulème to a neighboring street that had been "purged" of Jews a few days before. He said:

"When I heard the German boots on my stairs tonight, I realized how ridiculous it would be for me to fall into their hands without a struggle. I couldn't just sit there and wait for them to murder me. You all know that I am not athletic, but that thought gave me strength to jump from roof to roof. I am sure that all Jews will find such strength now."

We knew that in the camp at Drancy more than 3,000 Jews were being "processed" through the first stage of their one-way journey to Auschwitz, Birkenau and Buchenwald. Thousands more would follow them; there was no way of telling which of us might be alive in a month. Still, the course had been set, for we too would leap over roofs, not to escape the Nazi but to ambush him, to drive him insane and to kill him.

Within a year that small group had mushroomed into a complex army of men and women between the ages of 18 and 50 who served as killers, spies, saboteurs, strong-arm units, liaison officers and messengers. We were to derail trains, blast key anti-aircraft batteries, pillage German stores, kill thousands of enemy troops and completely undermine the morale of the enemy. In those first months, however, freedom could not wait for an efficient organization to be developed. Our people went to war using primitive arms and substituting courage for training.

Hersh Zimmerman and Salomon Bat typify this period. They were the first Jews to kill German soldiers, to throw bombs—and to die at their posts. Bat, a violinist, learned to taper his fingers around a revolver. Remembering the American gangster movies, so popular in Paris a decade before, he carried his bombs in his violin case. Zimmerman was a brilliant young chemist and he made the bombs.

It must be realized that these young men began their underground activity long before resistance became an almost public badge of honor in France. They were pioneers who improvised and they went along and hoped that others, afterward, would improve on their crude techniques.

To get the ingredients for explosives, Bat and Zimmerman spent dangerous weeks going from one pharmacy to another and buying a small amount of drugs in each. They armed themselves by waylaying German officers at night and taking their revolvers. Their bombs were tin cans filled with explosives. The wicks had to be lit before the bombs were thrown and the danger of premature explosion was, of course, tremendous.

For their first attack they chose the Porte D'Orleans, a crowded street constantly used by German detachments. The plan was to throw two bombs simultaneously, one at the head of a marching column, and one at its end. When the column approached, the conspirators saw they had a prize, for it was an elite group of Nazis from an officers' school nearby. At the precise moment they lit the wicks with their cigarettes, waited an agonizing few seconds and hurled the homemade bombs. Scores of Germans died in an explosion that made Jewish resistance a reality.

The two men escaped and returned to their clandestine laboratory. Those of us who had known Bat as a sensitive young musician were shocked to see him changing into a fighting man. As time passed, and other young Jews changed in the same manner, I understood what had happened. Like that first man on the roof, Bat had found unexpected strength and stamina. That he was fighting back for the first time in his life made him very happy.

One night, while Bat and Zimmerman were attacking a military target in the Latin Quarter, a violent explosion rocked the entire district. The violinist was found dead, and the chemist, dying. Apparently the crude bombs had gone off prematurely. It was an end they both had expected.

Soon after this the Gestapo made several arrests and discovered that a separate Jewish organization was functioning. We heard of Stuelpna-gel's reaction through a French police commissioner who, posing as a collaborator, was in constant contact with the underground. "What!" shouted the German leader, "those cowardly Jews dare to fight? We'll teach them what it means to attack German soldiers."

On December 15 the papers carried a communiqué from Stuelpna-gel which leveled a billion-franc fine on the Jews of occupied France, ordered new deportations to forced-labor camps and announced the execution of one hundred "Jews, Communists and Anarchists, who have certain connections with the authors of the attacks."

Despite such threats, the Jewish resistance, an army within an army, rapidly expanded. Though all our plans were approved by the General Military Committee, each of our units had to work independently, support itself, find its own arms and choose its own objectives. Jewish fighters were in much greater danger than others—the French, Ital-ians, Spaniards or Poles. They could always hide out among relatives or friends. But since all Jewish homes were subject to raids at any moment our men could never think of spending even one night in a Jewish home or of using a Jewish office as a "front."

Finding a place to live was a constant problem which ended only with liberation. Our next biggest problem was identification papers. Obviously it was impossible for a resistance man to function without forged papers, and as ration cards were issued monthly, it was also necessary for us to print forged cards every month. After some time the authorities learned of what we were doing and complicated the system. Finally we settled the matter by storming the ration offices on the last day of every month and carrying off the cards prepared for the next month. The cards, however, were worthless without money, so we also had to raid tax offices, post offices and brokerage houses.

These raids were carried out only to keep us alive and give us tools for our resistance work, yet hundreds of our people lost their lives in them for eventually the police became able to anticipate the attacks.

The Gestapo, meantime, began flooding Paris with spies who posed as Jews and claimed they wanted to join our organization. An elaborate examination system was set up to guard against such infiltration. The Commission des Cadres had scouts out scrutinizing each applicant, and often their work turned into counter-espionage. Despite all Gestapo ruses, we suffered very few losses through spies.

Once we were certain an applicant was legitimate, a further examina-tion was still necessary. Would the applicant handle himself or herself courageously on missions of great danger? How would he act if caught and tortured? Usually, one of our people would take long walks with an applicant, probing into his background and his motives. One fifteen-year-old boy told the following story:

"My mother, father and two younger sisters were taken away to

463

Germany. When the Nazis came for them I happened to be out, and as I reached home my family was being pushed into the police car. For a moment my youngest sister's eyes fell on me, and I shrank back farther into a corner. To this day I do not know whether I did the right thing in not joining them. At that time I was not yet fifteen. How could I have known what to do? Now I know. I beg you to admit me to your organization."

The boy was accepted, along with musicians without music, housewives without husbands and schoolboys without schools; and by 1943 the Jewish resistance organization in Paris was supporting thirty direct-action groups. There was a military committee coordinating all plans, a political committee training the newcomers, a technical committee setting up laboratories and providing arms and a medical committee operating underground hospitals.

Our three-man military committee met once a week to set in motion orders passed on by the over-all underground organization. If an attack in some general area was ordered, the committee selected the likeliest objectives. Then the scouting committee was told to bring back a detailed report on those objectives, usually German parking lots. This meant that the women and girls who worked as scouts spent many dangerous hours near German buildings, and to pass unnoticed they often changed their clothes two or three times a day. The better dressed they were the less they looked like Jews.

After the scouts had made their report, the men who had been chosen to carry out the attack were given their assignments one day in advance, so they could casually reconnoiter the scene. The technical committee was told to deliver the needed bombs and guns.

The coordinating of these committees had to be done on a split-second schedule. No committee members knew the addresses of the others. They met before an attack at a safe rendezvous and would remain only five minutes. If for any reason one group failed to show up, the action was postponed and the men quickly scattered.

In such a clandestine organization, where an accident or betrayal could have eliminated a key man in a few seconds, disaster was always expected. For example, the technical committee used the apartment of a pretty young woman in the 15th Arrondissement, near the Porte de Versailles, as a laboratory for explosives. This woman dressed with style and furnished her apartment handsomely, making it clear to the neighbors that she cared little for politics and meant to live through the war as comfortably as possible. She also let it be known that the man who visited her regularly was her lover. Actually, he was a resistance scientist who went there to make the explosives.

One night the laboratory table suddenly caught fire and the scientist's face was horribly burned. He threw his coat over his head and raced out of the building. Luckily, the police had not been called and

464

he was able to escape. In a few minutes, however, his suffering was so great that he could no longer walk. Knowing he was lost if he remained in the open, the chemist gambled on the sympathies of a woman passer-by. He explained that he was a patriot and begged her to help him. The woman took him to her home, but he wouldn't let her call a doctor and a few hours later, after resting, he left. Lurching along the blacked-out streets for two hours he at last reached the apartment of a friend. By this time it was too late to call one of the underground doctors, and he had to spend a very painful night.

The doctor did come the next day to remove the chemist to a sanitorium. Even this was only a temporary expedient, for the police had discovered the cause of the explosion and knew that a man with a burned face had fled the apartment. Already detectives were checking all hospitals and institutions. When a sympathetic policeman warned the sanitorium officials that the search was headed their way, the chemist was taken to the near-by home of a schoolteacher. Again his rest was a short one, for a neighbor, suspected of being an informer, had seen the stretcher bring him in and the next day he was transferred to a safer hideout.

The resistance was lucky in this case, and in several months the chemist was making explosives again. Still, many persons exposed themselves to save him, and if he had been captured they all would have been executed. Despite such hazards, some of the most important attacks in Paris during the winter and summer of 1943 were made by Jewish groups. These included throwing hand grenades into a German officers' canteen during a New Year's Day brawl, the killing of scores of Germans as they left the Folies Bergère, an attack on a group of enemy soldiers near the École Militaire and the raiding of a gasoline depot near the Porte de Vincennes.

On February 23 of that same year the Jewish legion carried out the first important attack against enemy positions in the Paris area: the wiping out of powerful anti-aircraft batteries the Nazis had set up just a few days before on the Passy Bridge over the Seine. Our attack group had to pass through a four-block area swarming with secret police who were on a special alert, yet they blew up the batteries and killed some thirty Germans without a single loss to themselves.

Just a month later two Jews managed to steal aboard a Versailles train crowded with German officers returning from the Russian front and dumped grenades into two of the cars which killed or wounded at least sixty Nazis.

The desperate enemy launched new pogroms, but they only brought us new recruits, as even the most timid of our Jews was inspired to join the crusade.

At this time our women volunteers, veterans of communications and medical work, began to beg for front-line missions. In some cases their

465

personal losses at the hands of the Nazis had been such that their pleas could not be denied. Thus we began to produce heroines as well as heroes, and of them, three who will never be forgotten are Helen Kron, Haya Igla and Rega.

Helen Kron, the pretty blonde wife of a prisoner of war, attracted the whistles and winks of the Germans as she walked through the streets carrying a market basket in which revolvers and grenades were hidden. Haya Igla joined us after her husband had been caught and killed by the Germans. Rega, a tiny, chirpy woman who always seemed to be on her way to exchange recipes with some other housewife, hid under her smile a sly technique for slipping through police cordons at strategic points.

These women formed a team that worked in German parking lots. They disguised themselves as peddlers, but carried bombs in their baskets, and each time they moved through a lot the Germans lost six cars. Finally the Gestapo trapped them, and they were tortured with special devices reserved for Jewesses who worked in the underground.

Helen Kron, the prettiest, got the most brutal and humiliating treatment. After the Germans had ravished her they took her with them when they went to search her apartment. Her four-year-old son was there, and she asked the guards to remove her handcuffs so that she could embrace the child for the last time. Confident the woman could not escape, the guards opened the handcuffs. Helen Kron held her son, calmed his frightened cries and gently put him back to bed. Then she plunged through a window to her death. Haya Igla and Rega were murdered a few days later in a camp in Silesia.

It was early in 1944 that the Nazis, realizing at last that the underground could not be crushed by deportations and executions, resurrected one of their oldest propaganda tricks. They launched a nationwide campaign "proving" that the liberation forces were composed entirely of Jews and "other criminals."

The campaign began with the first big public trial of patriots. Ten Jews were among the twenty-four defendants. In the past resisters had been murdered without benefit of judge and jury, but this time the Germans wanted to single out the Jews and make them seem responsible for the miseries of the Occupation. Posters were hung throughout the countryside showing photographs of the Jewish defendants superimposed upon gory shots of wrecked trains and mutilated bodies. Each poster bore such captions as, "I am a Jew from Poland," or "I am a Jew from Russia." There was also a list of the many "innocent Frenchmen" each was supposed to have killed.

At the same time movie houses featured films in which German actors impersonated Jewish fighters. Documentaries were put on showing ruined houses and mangled bodies—allegedly, the work of our people. Actually the films had been taken in Warsaw and other bombed cities.

This clumsy propaganda was a failure. Frenchmen cheered the resisters in the movie houses and wrote sympathetic comments on the extravagant posters. They also laughed.

In the so-called Free Zone, which was not occupied until November 11, 1942, Jewish patriots in the cities quietly supported the more spectacular *maquis,* who were gangs of young people hiding in the woods and hills to escape the slave-labor gangs. After Paris the most powerful underground center was in Lyons, and here again our people were prominent. Located on the hub of two of France's most important highways—Paris-Marseilles and Bordeaux-Toulouse-Geneva—Lyons was an ideal headquarters for the entire underground. Its narrow, winding streets and houses with double exits gave patriots a protection they found nowhere else.

The Lyons Jews became famous throughout France because of their leader, Simon Fried, one of the legendary heroes of the liberation movement. Fried planned and led a number of bold attacks on the Nazis and their collaborators. He finally was wounded and captured during a raid on an office and was sentenced to death by a collaborator judge named Finaly.

After Fried was guillotined the underground, following a grim tradition, condemned the judge to death. The very next morning three Jews, carrying the forged cards of Gestapo agents, rang the bell of Finaly's private apartment. The judge thought they had been assigned to protect him and greeted them cordially. A moment later he was dead.

In such a way did the Jews of France fight back. But by far the largest part of the story is still untold. This is but one chapter.

---

# Kaddish in a Serbian Forest

... That evening at sunset, they buried Zhanka, the partisan. They buried her where she fell above Gorni-Potok, where the Germans and the Ustachi[1] had tried to break through for two days. ...

They dug her grave, placed her in it, and then covered her up. They piled stones above the grave, so that they would be able to find it ... if they should look for it. Drago while standing near Tosho, said (and did not know how it came up in his mind):

"We should say Kaddish."

[1] Yugoslavian collaborators of the Nazis.

From *The Massacre of European Jewry.*

"We should say what?"—asked the Commander. Twenty-two of them stood around the grave.

"The Jewish burial-prayer," said Drago.

"Why a Jewish prayer?"—the Commander was surprised.

"Because she was a Jewess. There are another few Jews here too."

"More Jews? Who else here is a Jew?"

"I am" . . . "and I" . . . "and I," three people answered. The Commander could not get over his surprise.

"And I did not know! I didn't have the faintest idea! Well. all right—pray as you like."

"Do you know how to say Kaddish?" Tosho asked Drago.

"May you say it with only three? I think . . . "

Three Jewish partisans, in the heart of the Lika Forest—where there had never been any Jews in peacetime—decided to say Kaddish for their comrade.

"Say it, Drago, say it!"—and Drago began.

*"Yitgadal veyitkadash . . ."* and stopped suddenly. His forehead became creased and his eyes quickly passed over his friends' faces. Hundreds of times in his life he had said Kaddish by heart and fluently, without thinking and without becoming confused. He knew the words from his childhood—but at this moment he did not know them and could not remember. The rhythm and the tune were still in his memory—but the words were gone. And so, without knowing the rest of the prayer, he fixed his eyes on the grave, bowed his head and said:

"Zhanka, when you stand before Him, before the Judge, tell Him to look at you well and see what they have done to you—what they have done to all of us. Let Him look and see that not enough has remained in us even to be able to say Kaddish according to His laws. Amen."

"Amen" responded the lips of twenty-two partisans.

468

# Have We Cause to be Ashamed?—A Comparative Account

*Ghetto fighter, commander of a guerilla group (named* Nekamah, *"Vengeance"), Haganah member, officer of the Israel Defense force, author, editor and poet, Abba Kovner reflects on the resistance . . . .*

It was a wet, windy miserable night, that evening of September, 1943, when the last groups of fighters from the Vilna Ghetto reached the Rodniky Forest.

During our stay in the forest we met, more than once, various partisan bands. Each group had its own beginnings. One began in a prisoner-of-war camp; one began in a village which had been burnt and its lands temporarily occupied by the invader; another may have taken off from Moscow at midday and parachuted into the forest that evening. The beginning of our division, the Jewish Partisan Division, was in the sewers. Behind us we had left an open mass-grave and ruins and two years of bloody self-defense.

Those who descended into the sewers did not imagine they would be saved. Whoever did not see the long chain of human forms in the depths of the ground has no idea what a nightmare march it was. One hundred and fifty seeming-corpses moving in a tunnel, angry-faced and carrying revolvers, like unextinguished candles in their hands. Three days earlier we had descended into the sewers in order to break a way out of the ghetto. At night we came up in an empty courtyard. After that, we broke out of the city in small groups. Most of the streets were closed off by patrols and suddenly-shining searchlights. Our girls (will someone write a poem about them?) maintained contact between the groups in the dark. On the way, three of our men were taken from us. We afterwards found out that they had come up against a German guard-patrol, shot at it and killed its officer. They were caught and publicly hanged . . . After that, we spent the night in an abandoned palace that had belonged to Pushkin.[1]

---

[1]Famous Russian poet (1799–1837).

From *The Massacre of European Jewry.*

We waited for a messenger from the forest. Our scouts told us that the eastern and northern roads to the forest were blocked by columns of German soldiers moving that way. That was where our base was—two hundred kilometres away. Our first battalions went there earlier, with most of our weapons. There was only one way left—southwards—and none of us were familiar with it. We had no guide either. But we went.

At the twentieth kilometre there was a bridge. On the bridge there was a permanent armed guard, with an army barracks nearby. We had no choice but to cross that bridge, so we prepared ourselves and crossed it. Later on we were told by the farmers that the soldiers ran away and abandoned the bridge that night. The sight of us set them to flight. At the entrance to the forest, we found Teibl's body. She had gone to reconnoitre the way for us and fell into an enemy ambush. She and her companion defended themselves courageously. She fell on the threshold of the forest.

We reached our base and held a parade. We were met by officers of the Soviet Command. The Chief Commissar said: "Now we shall be brothers-in-arms—freedom-fighters—in the forest." That is what he said at the parade. After the parade, questions just poured on to us. There were very many, and they all flowed together and became one great serious question: "Why did your people go to the slaughter like sheep? You yourselves are different. But the masses—millions are spoken of—went like sheep!" The question was not asked merely out of curiosity . . . I do not remember what we answered then.

Two days later we went on our first action. We had no mines and there was no T.N.T. in our stores. With our bare hands we dismantled a section of railway line. Next time we went out to ambush, with a few miserable rifles. The commander had one submachine-gun and his second-in-command had another. Both of them were borrowed. After that we had to blow up a railway. The partisans had a routine way of doing things: when they managed to lay a mine, they would quickly withdraw from the area at once. But we lay down near the lines and waited. We would press our faces into the dust when a guard went by—but we did not move until our eyes saw what we had been waiting for: the enemy train going heavenwards in a cloud! Now and again we would catch the cries of the wounded, and someone would say: "That's for Ponar[2]!"

Perhaps our boys fought so well because there was some question burning within their souls or perhaps because they wanted to remove some weight from their hearts. We would stand and watch as the enemy installations caught fire; we would stand and watch as the flame

[2]Death camp near Vilna.

470

glowed in tens of shades of red. When we were on our way back, someone would turn the group around and gesture: "What redness!— Jews' blood!" Perhaps that is why we fondled and kissed every rifle that we captured, not to speak of machine-guns. Perhaps that is why we waited so expectantly for the aeroplane which supplied us with arms. Finally the Halm Forest became ours and the enemy did not dare to set foot in it. And every farmer and every Lithuanian and every German knew: Jewish partisans are in control there! . . .

Many days went by. During one of those majestic forest nights, we few score partisans were signalling with bonfires to the aeroplane which was supposed to come. It did come—a brave, stumpy-bodied, stub-winged Douglas. It dropped fifteen parachutes, turned on its lights for a few seconds in farewell to us, and flew away. As well as the many arms-filled bags, there was one with reading material. Among the rest, there was a bundle of Polish newspapers. Since they were in Polish, we, the Jews, received them . . . It was a bundle of "Free Polish" newspapers. Within one of the copies, I found an article headed, "Immortal Heroes." I read it and I could not understand who the "Immortal Heroes" were.

I impatiently continued to read it. The author wrote with much feeling; with much feeling, indeed, and with sheer strength, and called those who were murdered in the Katyn Forest[3] "immortal heroes." He finished thus: "When Poland is liberated, when Warsaw is free, the Polish people will establish a Temple of Heroism, and there every one of the sacred martyrs of Katyn will be brought."

What pain and anger seized me then! In our hearts, we had only pity, only tears for the dead of Ponar and of Treblinka. We felt only pain for them—and secretly, the pain was not only because they were no longer with us, but because of the way they had been taken from us. But they—they are proud of Katyn? Which of us is insane—the author of the article or I? No, of course he is sane. Suddenly I felt that something terrible was taking form in some far away place, in some as yet unconquered city; that something was a lie; it was false. I felt that one day the implications of that story could overpower and choke one until the tears started and yet one would not be able to cry.

While I was still shaking, a pamphlet came into my hands, Lithuanian this time. The author (a Jew as it happened) did not describe the German atrocities alone, but went on to describe deeds of heroism which none of us who were living in Lithuania at the time had heard of or had even seen their like. This is how he finished his composition (I

[3]Katyn—Forest near Smolensk where thousands of Polish Officers and soldiers were executed. Nazi propaganda later claimed that the Soviets were responsible for the slaughter (indeed the evidence dug up proved the Soviets guilty).

remember the words perfectly): "The Lithuanian people has never surrendered to the Nazi fiends. The struggle of the Lithuanian worker, peasant and intellectual is a glorious chapter in the history of our homeland's struggle against the Hitlerite invader!"

God in Heaven! That is what is written about a whole nation of traitors! That whole people participated in murder. They began to murder masses of Jews while the Germans were still at their gates; their soldiers, who were trained and equipped by the Red Army were among the first to sabotage that Army when it had to retreat, and they killed Red soldiers mercilessly. Such a nation receives praise like that?!

I dejectedly put the pamphlets aside and took up "Pravda". On the front page there were a number of telegrams, with reports of partisan activities all over Russia. In one of the columns I found similar dates, the same objectives, similar operations carried out to those of our company. One thing only was different: the name "Lithuanian partisans" . . . Lithuanians . . . Lithuanians!

We cannot do likewise. We cannot assume other people's glory. But neither should we maintain silence out of false modesty.

The account is large and terrible. There was the mass volunteering to the Red Army during the dark days of retreat. If the opportunity had been granted, there would have been tens of thousands of Jewish fighters in the ranks. Then there were the national divisions. You have probably heard of the Lithuanian Division. How could you not know of it?—It liberated Lithuania. That division at one stage was made up almost completely of Jews (85%!)—some of the best of our Lithuanian Jews. Even the Russians nicknamed it, "The division with the sixteen Lithuanians." Most of those Jews were tragically killed in the dramatic battles for a hill, the number of which was "N. Zero-zero-something", near Uriol.

You of course know of the defense of Moscow. Perhaps you have heard that at the head of those who broke the German attack there stood the Latvian Brigade—a lion for bravery. Afterwards, as a reward for this bravery it was granted the title, "Gvardskaya."[4] But you most probably do not know that the Latvian Brigade was composed almost exclusively of Jews and that the first battalion which broke through the German wall of steel was composed only of Jews and was commanded by a Jew.

Then they began to organize the Polish Kosciusko[5] Divisions. There was such a flood of Jewish volunteers that finally they refused to accept any more Jews, "so as not to become propaganda targets of the London Government-in-exile which might be tempted to revive the old story of

[4]Heroic brigade.
[5]Polish general who fought in the American Revolution.

472

the connection between Communism and the Jews." I want you to know one more thing—at least in one sentence. There is no area, no forest almost, in Lithuania, White Russia, Poland and the Ukraine where the founders of the Soviet partisan movement, the pioneers of the war in the forest, were not Jews. . . . Like most front-line troops, most of them fell in battle. In those days, partisans did not mark graves. What happened to the remainder? They were dispersed afterwards in all directions.

There must be someone—he has not been found yet—who will describe all that. Because if today nations diseased with treachery and surrender try to tell us of their contributions of blood in the struggle for victory, then we should know that the spilt blood of Jewish fighters, the bloody tithe of our small, isolated, tortured people, was much greater than it should have been.

Today, when I stand on this soil, two years after the last ghetto barricade and one year after we travelled like living skeletons across frontier after frontier, only to find the gates of our country closed insolently in our faces, I want to go back there, to bury my head in the ground and, with a voice choked by angry tears, to shout into it. Perhaps Mordechai and Frumka will hear; perhaps Edek and Yosef and the rest of them will listen; all those hundreds of partisans who crouched amid all the hills of Poland and Lithuania; perhaps my young brother, Michael, will hear it, in the soil of Yerkazan—perhaps the unknown soldiers in the fields of Uriol will hear too?—I want to shout: This tithe was too great! . . .

But our people as a whole went like a flock of sheep. However, we shall be doing the silent victims a great disservice and staining their good name if it is not unequivocally stated here at least: Everyone else went like that too. I cannot but remember the masses of Soviet prisoners. We used to meet them in the streets, and the sight of them made us forget our own terrible plight. The Germans maltreated them to their last breath, and when they were brought to their graves they were just worn-out wrecks. Only a cap here or a button there was evidence that the things before us had been soldiers once. They used to kill those ghastly wrecks—no!—they used to throw themselves into graves which they had prepared for themselves, thousands of them.

I cannot but remember (and no comparison is intended) how they paraded the Lithuanians in their underwear, with upraised hands. The Germans set up a Lithuanian army, which served to slaughter Jews and to fight partisans. When they had completed that job, the Germans wanted to send them, as usual, to the front. The "heroes" refused. It was not to their taste. Then the Germans went into the Lithuanian Army barracks and took away their . . . belts. They commanded them to remove all their trouser-buttons. Then they took them out into the streets, long lines of them, and when the order, "Hands up!" was suddenly heard, their trousers slid down. In this fashion, they traversed the whole city, their capital city. They did not return.

How did the Poles go? One day the last group of young Jews—who had worked there in chains, burning corpses—escaped from Ponar to the forest. I cannot tell their story now. This is what one of those boys told us. Once, when a German officer took them on a tour of inspection and "explained" to them the story of each mass-grave (incidentally, they were forbidden to use the words, "corpses" or "people": only the term, "figures" was permitted), he pointed at one of them and said: "In this grave lie those who sang (he quoted in Polish the words of the Polish national anthem), 'Poland is not yet lost; we shall not go thus'— but they went." No less than three million went! The whole Polish intelligentsia was deported.

In this terrible comparison between the Jewish people and the Goyim we have no cause to be ashamed of the passivity of our millions of slaughtered brethren.

There is no consolation in that. God forbid! The tragedy of the general sheeplike acquiescene is too great for us to be able to derive consolation from the fact that it was general. However, if an account is made, and if any of you feel pained about the passivity of our brothers and sisters, then let the account between us and the other peoples be clear—quite clear . . .

# The Song of the Partisans (abbreviated)

*The* Song of the Partisans *was originally composed in Yiddish by H. Glick, and it was a favorite of the Jewish partisans who fought against the Nazis* . . .

> O never say that you have come to your journey's end,
> When days turn black, and clouds upon our world descend.
> Believe the dark will lift, and freedom yet appear.
> Our marching feet will tell the world that we are here.
>
> . . .
>
> The dawn will break, our world will yet emerge in light,

From the new translation by Ben Zion Bokser.

# Jewish Partisan Fighters

*Our agony will pass, and vanish as the night.*
*But if our hoped for rescue should arrive too late*
*These lines will tell the world the drama that was played.*

*No poet's playful muse has turned my pen to write,*
*I wrote this song amidst our anguish of our plight.*
*We sang it as we watched the flames destroy our world,*
*Our song is a banner of defiance we unfurled.*

*O never say that you have come to your journey's end,*
*When days turn black, and clouds upon our world descend.*
*Believe the dark will lift, and freedom yet appear.*
*Our marching feet will tell the world that we are here.*

# Readings

See also chapter 18, Resistance and Rebellion.

*Blessed Is the Match* by Marie Syrkin (Jew. Pub. Soc., 1947), gives a dramatic presentation of the Jewish parachutists and the life of the survivors of the *Shoah* in Israel.

*The Shadow War: European Resistance 1939-1945* by Henri Michel (Harper and Row, 1972), provides a comprehensive pan-European survey of resistance, sabotage, guerilla warfare, and national uprisings. Includes the facts of Jewish resistance within these rubrics. Translated from the French; authoritative.

*Uncle Misha's Partisans* by Yuri Suhl (Four Winds Press, 1973), is a story, based on fact, about Motele, who is a member of Uncle Misha's Jewish partisans in the forests of the Ukraine.

*The Noble Saboteurs* by Ronald Seth (Hawthorne Books, 1966), depicts the heroism of non-Jews and Jews in the war against the Germans. Above two books are intended for younger readers.

# 20. DEATH MARCHES AND LIBERATION

By early 1945, as the end of the twelve-year nightmare drew near, the "Thousand Year Reich" was beginning to fall apart. But even in defeat the Nazis were determined to carry out their mission of destroying the Jews of Europe. As they retreated before the advancing Allies, the SS often brought their prisoners along, force-marching them to new camps deeper in German-held territory, and shooting those who collapsed along the way from hunger, cold, thirst, or exhaustion.

The German armies had been crushed and were near defeat, however, and as the weeks passed, those still surviving in the camps—about 715,000 men and women[1]—were liberated by Soviet forces in the east and American, British, and French forces in the west. The scene awaiting the victorious Allied troops in the camps was gruesome. The survivors were barely alive. While many were saved by the largest mass administration of blood transfusions, glucose, and anti-typhus injections in history, many were so weakened that they could not regain their strength and died in freedom after having endured years of brutal captivity.[2]

Confusion and chaos prevailed in the ravaged lands of Europe in the days following the liberation. The bombed roads were clogged with millions of slave laborers, displaced persons, and wounded, all surging homeward. Without food, funds, clothing, personal identification, or authorization papers, they pressed through the lines in an effort to return home, propelled by the hope of rejoining kith and kin.

[1]Livia Roth Kircher, "The Final Solution in Its Last Stages," *Yad Vashem Studies,* vol. 8, p. 25.
[2]For a graphic visual descriptive account of the liberation of Bergen-Belsen, amply illustrated with photographs, see *Holocaust and Rebirth* (World Federation of Bergen-Belsen Survivors, 1965).

Jewish survivors of the long, agonizing journey found almost no Jews alive in their hometowns. Moreover, the non-Jewish neighbors, especially in the Slavic and Baltic countries, were hostile. They shrank from recognizing the returnees, and malevolently refused to acknowledge that they had seized the homes, stores, and property of the Jews, plundering their belongings and dispossessing them of their effects. The murder of returning Jews in the pogrom in Kielce, Poland, on July 4, 1946, was a bloody lesson matched only by the crimes of the SS. It became apparent to the Jews that they could never again take up the threads of life at "home." The break was complete and irreversible. Bitter and weary, the remaining Jews left again—this time for good—to find a new home and begin life all over once more.

---

# I Went to Belsen

*On April 24, 1945, the Oxford historian, Patrick Gordon-Walker, BBC commentator and chief editor of Radio Luxembourg, went to the concentration camp at Belsen. Following is his report as broadcast to the United States . . .*

I went to Belsen. It was a vast area surrounded by barbed wire. The whole thing was being guarded by Hungarian guards. They had been in the German Army and are now immediately and without hesitation serving us. They are saving us a large number of men for the time being. Outside the camp, which is amidst bushes, pines, and heather, all fairly recently planted, were great notices in red letters: DANGER—TYPHUS.

We drove into what turned out to be a great training camp, a sort of Aberdeen, where we found the officers and Oxfordshire Yeomanry. They began to tell us about the concentration camp.

It lies south of the training area and is behind its own barbed wire. The Wehrmacht is not allowed near it. It was entirely guarded by SS men and women. This is what I discovered about the release of the camp that happened about the fifteenth. I got this story from Derek Sington, political officer, and from officers and men of Oxfordshire Yeomanry.

Typhus broke out in the camp, and a truce was arranged so that we could take the camp over. The Germans originally had proposed that we should by-pass the camp. In the meanwhile, thousands and thou-

---

From *A Treasury of Great Reporting*, edited by Louis L. Snyder and Richard B. Morris.

sands of people would have died and been shot. We refused these terms, and demanded the withdrawal of the Germans and the disarmament of the SS guards. Some dozen SS men and women were left behind under the command of Higher Sturmführer Kramer, who had been at Auschwitz. Apparently they had been told all sorts of fairy tales about the troops, that they could go on guarding, and that we would let them free and so forth.

We only had a handful of men so far, and the SS stayed there that night. The first night of liberty, many hundreds of people died of joy.

Next day some men of the Yeomanry arrived. The people crowded around them, kissing their hands and feet—and dying from weakness. Corpses in every state of decay were lying around, piled up on top of each other in heaps. There were corpses in the compound in flocks. People were falling dead all around, people who were walking skeletons. One woman came up to a soldier who was guarding the milk store and doling the milk out to children, and begged for milk for her baby. The man took the baby and saw that it had been dead for days, black in the face and shriveled up. The woman went on begging for milk. So he poured some on the dead lips. The mother then started to croon with joy and carried the baby off in triumph. She stumbled and fell dead in a few yards. I have this story and some others on records spoken by the men who saw them.

On the sixteenth, Kramer and the SS were arrested. Kramer was taken off and kept in the icebox with some stinking fish of the officers' home. He is now going back to the rear. The rest, men and women, were kept under guard to save them from the inmates. The men were set to work shoveling up the corpses into lorries.

About thirty-five thousand corpses were reckoned, more actually than the living. Of the living, there were about thirty thousand.

The SS men were driven and pushed along and made to ride on top of the loaded corpses and then shovel them into their great mass open graves. They were so tired that they fell exhausted amongst the corpses. Jeering crowds collected around them, and they had to be kept under strong guard.

Two SS men committed suicide in their cells. Two jumped off the lorry and tried to run away and get lost in the crowd. They were shot down. One jumped into a concrete pool of water and was riddled with bullets. The other was brought to the ground, with a shot in the belly.

The SS women were made to cook and carry heavy loads. One of them tried to commit suicide. The inmates said that they were more cruel and brutal than the men. They are all young, in their twenties. One SS woman tried to hide, disguised as a prisoner. She was denounced and arrested.

The camp was so full because people had been brought here from east and west. Some people were brought from Nordhausen, a five-day

479

journey, without food. Many had marched for two or three days. There was no food at all in the camp, a few piles of roots—amidst the piles of dead bodies. Some of the dead bodies were of people so hungry that though the roots were guarded by SS men they had tried to storm them and had been shot down then and there. There was no water, nothing but these roots and some boiled stinking carrots, enough for a few hundred people.

Men and women had fought for these raw, uncooked roots. Dead bodies, black and blue and bloated, and skeletons had been used as pillows by sick people. The day after we took over, seven block leaders, mostly Poles, were murdered by the inmates. Some were still beating the people. We arrested one woman who had beaten another woman with a board. She quite frankly admitted the offense. We are arresting these people.

An enormous buried dump of personal jewelry and belongings was discovered in suitcases. When I went to the camp five days after its liberation, there were still bodies all around. I saw about a thousand.

In one place, hundreds had been shoveled into a mass grave by bulldozers; in another, Hungarian soldiers were putting corpses into a grave that was sixty feet by sixty feet and thirty feet deep. It was almost half full.

Other and similar pits were being dug. Five thousand people had died since we got into the camp. People died before my eyes, scarcely human, moaning skeletons, many of them gone mad. Bodies were just piled up. Many had gashed wounds and bullet marks and terrible sores. One Englishman, who had lived in Ostend, was picked up half dead. It was found that he had a great bullet wound in his back. He could just speak. He had no idea when he had been shot. He must have been lying half unconscious when some SS man shot him as he was crawling about. This was quite common. I walked about the camp. Everywhere was the smell and odor of death. After a few hours you get used to it and don't notice it any more. People have typhus and dysentery.

In one compound I went, I saw women standing up quite naked, washing among themselves. Near by were piles of corpses. Other women suffering from dysentery were defecating in the open and then staggering back, half dead, to their blocks. Some were lying groaning on the ground. One had reverted to the absolute primitive.

A great job had been done in getting water into the camp. It has been pumped in from the outside and carried by hoses all over the camp with frequent outlet points. There are taps of fresh clean water everywhere. Carts with water move around.

The Royal Army Service Corps has also done a good job in getting food in.

I went into the typhus ward, packed thick with people lying in dirty rags of blankets on the floor, groaning and moaning. By the door sat an

English Tommy talking to the people and cheering them up. They couldn't understand what he said, and he was continually ladling milk out of a caldron. I collected together some women who could speak English and German and began to make records. An amazing thing is the number who managed to keep themselves clean and neat. All of them said that in a day or two more, they would have gone under from hunger and weakness.

There are three main classes in the camp: the healthy, who have managed to keep themselves decent, but nearly all of these had typhus; then there were the sick, who were more or less cared for by their friends; then there was the vast underworld that had lost all self-respect, crawling around in rags, living in abominable squalor, defecating in the compound, often mad or half mad. By the other prisoners they are called Mussulmen. It is these who are still dying like flies. They can hardly walk on their legs. Thousands still of these cannot be saved, and if they were, they would be in lunatic asylums for the short remainder of their pitiful lives.

There were a very large number of girls in the camp, mostly Jewesses from Auschwitz. They have to be healthy to survive. Over and over again I was told the same story. The parades at which people were picked out arbitrarily for the gas chambers and the crematorium, where many were burned alive. Only a person in perfect health survived. Life and death was a question of pure chance.

Rich Jews arrived with their belongings and were able to keep some. There were soap and perfume and fountain pens and watches. All amidst the chance of sudden, arbitrary death, amidst work commandos from which the people returned to this tomb so dead beat that they were sure to be picked for the gas chamber at the next parade, amidst the most horrible death, filth, and squalor that could be imagined.

People at Auschwitz were saved by being moved away to work in towns like Hamburg and were then moved back to Belsen as we advanced. At Auschwitz every woman had her hair shaven absolutely bald.

I met pretty young girls whose hair was one inch long. They all had their numbers tattooed on their left arm, a mark of honor they will wear all their lives.

One of the most extraordinary things was the women and men—there were only a few—who had kept themselves decent and clean.

On the first day many had on powder and lipstick. It seems the SS stores had been located and looted and boots and clothes had been found. Hundreds of people came up to me with letters, which I have taken and am sending back to London to be posted all over the world. Many have lost all their relatives. "My father and mother were burned. My sister was burned." This is what you hear all the time. The British Army is doing what it can. Units are voluntarily giving up blankets.

Fifty thousand arrived while I was there and they are being laundered. Sweets and chocolate and rations have been voluntarily given.

Then we went to the children's hut. The floors had been piled with corpses there had been no time to move. We collected a chorus of Russian girls from twelve to fourteen and Dutch boys and girls from nine to fifteen. They sang songs. The Russian children were very impressive. Clean and quite big children, they had been looked after magnificently amidst starvation. They sang the songs they remembered from before captivity. They looked happy now. The Dutch children had been in camp a long time and were very skinny and pale. We stood with our backs to the corpses, out in the open amidst the pines and the birch trees near the wire fence running round the camp.

Men were hung for hours at a time, suspended by their arms, hands tied behind their back, in Belsen. Beatings in workshops were continuous, and there were many deaths there. Just before I left the camp a crematorium was discovered. A story of Auschwitz was told to me by Helen—and her last name, she didn't remember. She was a Czechoslovak.

When the women were given the chance to go and work elsewhere in the work zones like Hamburg, mothers with children were, in fact, given the choice between their lives and their children's. Children could not be taken along. Many preferred to stay with their children and face certain death. Some decided to leave their children. But it got around amongst the six-year-old children that if they were left there they would at once be gassed. There were terrible scenes between children and their mothers. One child was so angry that though the mother changed her mind and stayed and died, the child would not talk to her.

That night when I got back at about eleven o'clock very exhausted, I saw the Jewish chaplain again and talked to him as he was going to bed. Suddenly, he broke down completely and sobbed.

The next morning I left this hell-hole, this camp. As I left, I had myself deloused and my recording truck as well. To you at home, this is one camp. There are many more. This is what you are fighting. None of this is propaganda. This is the plain and simple truth.

# The Message on Liberation Day: To Remain Human

I remember: April 1945, Buchenwald. Liberated, at last. Twenty thousand inmates on one side, the entire world on the other. When the first American jeeps appeared at the gates, there were no outbursts of joy; the inmates did not have the strength left to rejoice. They looked and looked at their liberators; they looked but they could not see; their eyes still held the image of the 60,000 prisoners taken away the preceding week. Then, something happened: a few Russian POW's grabbed some jeeps and machine-guns and raced to Weimar, the neighboring town, and opened fire at will. That was their first gesture as free men. They needed vengeance before they needed food. And what did the Jewish inmates do to prove they were free? Believe it or not, they held services. To give thanks to God? No, to defy Him! To tell him: listen, as mere mortals, as members of the human society, we know we should seize weapons and use them in every place and in every way and never stop. Because it is our right. But we are Jews, and as such we renounce that right; we choose yes, choose to remain human. And generous.

Is there no message in this tale? Is this not the message of Jewish tradition? To remain human even in the face of inhumanity?

Another example: in setting up their machinery, the Germans cunningly aimed to corrupt the Jewish spirit before exterminating the Jewish people physically. Plans to debase Judaism were charted and carried out faithfully. Hence the establishment of ghettos with their own laws, kings and fools. If the Germans ordered Jewish policemen to help organize the deportation of their fellow-Jews, it was not because they lacked manpower, but because they wanted to prove a point; that Jews could be as vicious, as ruthless as their executioners—even more so, since their cruelty would be directed at their own people. Therefore, from the beginning, the Germans made every effort to enlist the support, not of the Jewish underworld, but on the contrary, of members of the intellectual and moral elite. Do you know who were the first to be corrupted inside the camps? The intellectuals. Not the thieves. Also the professors of literature and philosophy, the courageous liber-

From *The Message on Liberation Day: To Remain Human,* Address delivered at the General Assembly, Council of Jewish Federations and Welfare Funds, by Elie Wiesel.

als and professional humanists. As soon as their universe collapsed, they gave in all the way; they had nothing to hold on to. The moment they realized the fragility, nay, the futility of their own teachings, they couldn't but choose the alternative of sadism and frustrated brutality. Do you know that those who resisted the most and did not falter in any way, were the rabbis. Yes, when the chips were down, when the choice was narrowed simply to this—either you suffer or you cause suffering—there was not a single rabbi who accepted compromise. Most preferred to stay with the victims. To the end.

What does this example teach us? I'll tell you: when all else has failed, the Torah provides a moral shield. That which philosophers and sociologists, politicians and psychologists . . . could not offer to their disciples, the collective consciousness of the Jewish people could, and did, offer to its own.

---

# Liberation Day: The Bitter Reality

*Upon liberation, the Jews in Buchenwald suddenly faced themselves. "Where now? Where to?" . . .*

Those were dreary, endlessly monotonous days, the last days in Buchenwald . . . We exchanged whispers, in passing, whispers in all the languages of the world. For there were people from all lands, there were French, Belgians, Dutch, Hungarians, Russians, Poles, Italians. And also, of course, Jews. But during this last period there was no distinction of race in the concentration camp; all, even the Jews, were treated on the same level. All were hungry, all were oppressed, beaten, degraded . . . The long, gray, hopeless days dragged on. Wraiths of human beings dragged themselves around the camp, or sat against their barrack walls, staring endlessly with vacant eyes, and thinking of nothing. They were broken and apathetic . . .

April 11, 1945. Liberation. An American commander took over the camp. Immediately, there was set up an International Camp Committee; people now grouped themselves according to nationality, and there was a representative of each group on this committee. There were a few Jews on this committee, but not as Jews; they represented the countries of their birth. The entire committee was drawn from the

From *Kibbutz Buchenwald,* translated and edited by Meyer Levin.

484

former underground organization, and its Jewish members were men who had been leaders in the struggle for freedom.

Now, gradually, after the liberation, the inmates of Buchenwald began to live again, to come to themselves. Once apathetic and hopeless, they now nearly went mad with joy. Freedom! Freedom! We lived to see it!

Their faces were ablaze. They began to think, to talk about going home. To their own countries, to father, mother, wife, and child.

And the Jews? Well—the Jews.

The Jews suddenly faced themselves. Where now? Where to? They saw that they were different from all the other inmates of the camp. For them, things were not so simple. To go back to Poland? to Hungary? and they saw visions from old times, visions of Jewish villages . . . a white-bearded Jew, all bloodied . . . little children falling from upstairs' windows into the street . . . masses of Jews streaming into the far unknown. And now, streets empty of Jews, towns empty of Jews, a world without Jews. To wander in those lands, lonely, homeless, always with the tragedy before one's eyes . . . and to meet, again, a former gentile neighbor who would open his eyes wide and smile, remarking with double-meaning, "What! Yankel! You're still alive!"

Yes, the Jews faced themselves. Was our tragedy only beginning? In any case, we now understood that our situation was different from that of all others in the camp. For us, there was no going back where we came from. And now we saw it as a fact, that there were distinct and specific Jewish problems.

A Jewish self-help committee was organized in the camp. Several of the comrades who had previously belonged to the underground, and who had entered the International Camp Committee, now saw the reality of the hour and joined the Jewish committee.

And this was decided: we are Jews. Nothing else. And we must go to the Jewish land, to Palestine.

And then there came an idea: to found, even here in Germany, a kibbutz of young, energetic Jews who wanted to prepare for Palestine.

From that idea sprang Kibbutz Buchenwald.

Comrade Posnansky came out with an idea . . . To build a group of Buchenwald's Jewish youth, and find a farm where we could prepare for Palestine . . . There would be no lack of candidates for the Kibbutz, for energy was re-awakening in the survivors and seeking an outlet.

After several days, the Jewish Committee in Buchenwald came into the possession of a document which gave it the right to make use, for a long term, of the township farm of Eggendorf, near Blankenheim.

*July 3, 1945.*

Here we are, sitting on a truck that is taking us away from Buchenwald. . . We are leaving the place which was such a horror to us, even after liberation . . . Now all the horrible past is really being left behind us. We are also leaving behind us the long, purposeless days of these last months, the endless questioning: to Poland, France, America, Palestine? Now, all this agony and confusion fades behind us, slowly sinking behind the hill . . . On this direct road, which turns neither to right nor to left, we head for our new life . . . this road, and it must take us straight to a place of our own, a Jewish settlement where we can put our energy into something that will belong only to us . . . A place where we can live for the future: this road must take us to Palestine . . .

That day (July 3, 1945) sixteen of us arrived. We settled in a few rooms of the farmhouse, where there was still some furniture . . .

In the first day we were completely occupied with physical work; we had to clean, repair, improve everything. We took the wagons to the smithy; we bought tools; we found furniture for the bedrooms; we worked in the fields, cleaned the barn, cleared the manure out of the stables. We had to go to the village constantly, to clear up problems with the burgomaster; and as the farm began to be productive, there was more work—taking the milk to the creamery, etc. But we divided up the tasks. On the day after our arrival, there were Jewish hands hitching the oxen to the plough and turning over Germany's soil.

Yes, the thought went through all our minds: what are we doing here, working Germany's land? What is the object of this? . . .

Everyone knew that one could live a life of comparative ease in Buchenwald, since liberation. Plenty of food, and nothing to do. And yet, here we were; and there were many who wanted to join us, even though joining our kibbutz meant accepting all the difficulties of providing for ourselves through hard work.

The locomotive whistles, sighs, and we are on our way. At the last moment, a gentile, carrying a package, jumps into the compartment . . .

I move over and ask the man to sit with us. He settles himself and asks, "Are you Polish, too?"

"No," I answer in Polish, since I come from that land. "I am a Jew."

"Where are you going?"

"To Blankenheim."

"Oh. You are from the Kibbutz? I've heard of you people. And I'm glad I've met someone from that Kibbutz. Would you mind if I ask you a few questions?"

"Not at all."

"Is it true that you yourselves are working in the fields?"

"Yes."

"Is it really true that after six such years in the concentration camps you people, of your own free will, went to work at black labor? And are you planting crops so that the Germans won't go hungry next winter?" There was a faint irony in his tone.

486

Death Marches and Liberation

"Yes," I said. "We went to work of our own free will."

He was still puzzled. "Until now," he said, "I've only known Jews who were merchants and speculators. And now, when not a single one of the liberated non-Germans is working, you choose of your own volition to go to black labor?"

"Yes. Precisely now," I answer firmly. "Now, after six years under the Fascists, we know that we Jewish people can only work out a place for ourselves with a plough in our own hands. We are workers, and we will work out our own future. We must learn to love work itself, and bring this love with us to Palestine. Even while we were still in Buchenwald, we volunteered to work in the hospital, to save the few who were still alive. And there were quite a few Poles among them. We did the heavy work, the cleaning and washing, we washed the sick, we didn't run away, even when the typhus epidemic spread. We decided to work until all the sick were on their feet. Then, as soon as it became possible to found our Kibbutz, we did so. We suffered a great deal in the last six years, but we came out with enough strength to understand that only through love of labor can we find a lasting foundation for our future."

The Pole takes a tin of preserves out of his rucksack. I take a roll out of mine. Everyone in the car prepares to eat. But meanwhile the Pole notices some blue cloth in my pack and asks me what it's for. Proudly, I inform him that we are holding a celebration tomorrow, for the founding of our Kibbutz. And I have been to Weimar to secure cloth for a flag.

"Blue?" He is puzzled.

"Yes. Our national flag is blue and white . . . Tomorrow, on the flagpole where the swastika flew only two months ago, we'll hang out our Jewish flag. This will be the first celebration in Germany to be held under the Jewish flag, for six years."

The cars shake, and the train comes slowly to a halt. I want to say goodbye to him but he takes my arm, and we go out together. He asks if it is possible for him to attend our celebration tomorrow. Certainly, I tell him. He leaves me with these words: "I never believed to find such energy and such determination to work as you people have shown—and right out of Buchenwald!"

487

# "Why Don't I Kill You?"

*Moses Moscowitz, an American army officer, whose responsibility was the handling of displaced persons (D.P.'s) recounts a scene he witnessed . . .*

Just as the German masses feel no sense of guilt for the six million Jewish dead in Europe, so the great majority of the surviving Jews feel no particular vindictiveness towards the German people. The day the Landsberg concentration camps were uncovered in April 1945, an incident occurred that was difficult to explain at the time but which, in retrospect, has a symbolic significance. German prisoners of war were on hand to clear the barracks of the dead, to dig graves, burn infested clothes, and do menial labor of every kind. When they lined up for their evening meal, one of the Jewish inmates spotted a pair of shiny boots on the feet of a German soldier. He approached him and forced him to follow him into a vacated barracks. I decided to look.

The half-naked, skeleton-like Jew was stripping the soldier of his boots and in the process ceremoniously addressing him, half in Yiddish and half in German, as follows: "In reality, I should take not only your boots, but your life as well. You and your kind killed my wife and my children, my mother, my aunts and uncles, my cousins, and everybody who was dear to me. You killed all the Jews, burned all the synagogues, and trampled upon everything that was holy to us. Why don't I kill you? Because I only want your boots and not your life. God will take care of you and mete out the punishment you deserve. Who am I to sit in judgment?" The soldier remained seated throughout in stony silence. After the Jew tried on the boots and thought they fitted him, he asked the soldier to step into his worn-out wooden clogs. The soldier obeyed, but his face turned blue with agony.

"They are not very comfortable," the Jew remarked, and launched into another tirade. "In reality," he said, "you don't deserve even these wooden clogs. But what shall I do with you, let you go barefoot? I shall give you a piece of advice. If you want to be more comfortable, pad the inside with some cloth or cotton. Stand up and let me see how you walk. Good, you will get used to them. Now get back to the chow line." With what looked like a pat on the soldier's back, he escorted him to the field kitchen.

If the Jews had been given to vindictiveness, they would have had

From *Commentary Magazine*, July 1946, by Moses Moscowitz.

many opportunities to avenge themselves. But there has been no recorded incident of Jews who took the law into their own hands, unprovoked. Very few Jews regard German property as legitimate booty, even though many suspect that the clothes worn by German men, women, and children were once theirs. To be sure, they deeply resent the freedom enjoyed by those Germans whose rightful place is behind bars, and the comfortable quarters of others who belong in dungeons. But they are careful to distinguish between innocent and guilty, and to think clearly about the Germans as a political and human problem. Among Jewish displaced persons one can hear the most objective discussions on de-Nazification and the political trends of the different German political parties.

The attitude of the Jews towards Germans seems to be guided by an unshaken belief in humanity, a deep sense of justice, plus incurable optimism. A Jewish physician, who, together with his twenty-year-old son, survived six years of the most cruel tortures in Dachau and other concentration camps, once remarked that if it were proven that all the seventy-odd million Germans were capable of committing the crimes perpetrated against him and his thousands of fellow inmates, Jews and minorities in general were threatened everywhere. But he refused to condemn the entire human race by condemning so large a segment of it. In the interest of justice, he preferred to see the million or so Germans who engineered and executed the enormities against the human race hang, rather than to distribute the guilt among seventy million people and reduce their sentences proportionately. Like the Rabbi of Berdichev, the Jews in Germany, native or foreign, bend over backwards to find some goodness in the German so as to justify his existence on this earth.

# At Germany's Defeat: The Death Marches

*A well-known non-Jewish German novelist who fought on the Russian front as a teenager, Michael Horbach, has written novels and documented books on the Nazi survivors whom he interviewed in various parts of the world. Below is the story of one survivor in Israel.*

*Celina Manielewitz, married and living in Israel, was a survivor of the camps in East Prussia. At the beginning of 1945 there were about sixty thousand prisoners in these camps; only 1,500 were saved. All others perished during the death marches to the west and during the so-called Baltic Sea "evacuation."* . . .

So far, Celina had told her story without faltering. But now she was silent; and I could see the tortured memories in her eyes.

I waited. For a while there was silence in the room . . . I scrutinized Celina's face . . . The shade of eternal sadness lay across it, indicating that she had experienced something frightful.

She tried to pull herself together. She murmured desperately, "I've forgotten."

Her husband laid a comforting hand on her arm. He was a customs official at the Mandelbaum Gate, the Israel-Jordan crossing point; a slim, sunburned Polish Jew who, with bitter tenacity, had built a new life here for himself and his family.

"Go on," he said protectively. "Tell him everything. I'm here— remember."

She nodded slowly. Her black eyes wandered from her husband to me. Then she told it . . .

It was the last days of January, 1945. The Germans had started a rumor that at the coast we'd be put on board ship for Hamburg; we didn't believe it. We believed the Germans meant to kill us. We saw the pickets; a guard every five yards with submachine guns pointed at us; and the heavily armed sleds, travelling constantly up and down the column. We didn't believe the evacuation story; we were too exhausted to build up such hopes. We'd stopped thinking. We didn't give a damn.

Suddenly we heard a terrific shooting coming from up front, where the men were marching. Flares flew up and illuminated the whole landscape. It was only later that I heard that, at that moment, a group

---

From *Out of the Night*, edited by Michael Horbach.

of 300 prisoners had gone for the S.S. with their bare hands. They were all shot. We saw their bodies lying in the snow when we passed the spot where they had tried, in their desperation, to get rid of their tormentors.

Then, the rumor: the S.S. are driving us into the sea!

This was true, we knew it at once.

Where were the ships that were waiting for us, then? We were making for a steep headland with dangerous rocks. There was no harbor anywhere, no kind of bay where a big ship could anchor. Besides, there were still over 8,000 of us. What ship could carry these 8,000—here on this desolate coast?

"We've had it," Genia whispered to me. I could only nod. I was so worn out that I was quite indifferent . . . I just stumbled along in my row without looking left or right. I'd lost my clogs long ago; I was just staggering barefoot in the snow.

Again we heard shooting—quite near this time—from up front. This time it didn't stop.

We were getting nearer. Again the flares flew up and we could see it: the coast, lying before us . . . S.S. men with machine-guns stood on the rocks to the left and right of us. They drove the prisoners to the edge of the precipice and shot them down mercilessly. If anyone tried to turn back he was soon grabbed by the armed guards before he could manage a step.

We said our goodbyes.

Those in front of us shrank back horrified from the frightful abyss opening out at their feet; their shrieks ripped the night open. I was so numbed, mentally, that it didn't affect me.

"Get going!" the S.S. chief in charge of the operation shouted. I knew him—Sergeant Stock, a great blond hulk, and a pitiless bully. When he saw us young girls he bounded over to us.

"Get down," he yelled, "down, you Jew bitches." He swung his gun and hit Genia with the butt in the small of the back. She staggered and fell over; an S.S. man pushed her over the cliff edge. Then I was knocked with the butt, too—in the back of my neck—and I reeled. I saw the abyss before me and hurtled over. Then I felt nothing.

When I came to again I was lying half in water and half on an ice-block. There were the great slopes above me, the open sea behind me. People were still falling over the cliff, the machine-guns still barking. All around, in that grey-green sea, corpses were floating, half hanging on the ice blocks. The wounded were moaning; some prayed to God to let them die.

Suddenly it was quiet up there; the last salvoes from the machine-guns died away.

Then: dark figures on the beach, S.S. men who'd climbed down.

"If you're still alive lift up your head!" they screamed. And those

491

poor creatures who were still living lifted their heads in one final, lethargic movement; the sentries sprang from one iceberg to another and finished them off.

Fela Lewcowicz lay at my feet. I heard her moan. I wanted to crawl over to her, but then she raised her arm, shouting:

"I'm still alive, Mr. Guard!"

One of the S.S. turned and shot her in the temple, a few inches from my feet.

"Don't move," a voice behind me whispered. Genia.

I don't know how long we lay there, like that. Icy water gnawed away at our skin and bones. I knew we'd never survive if we had to lie there much longer. Why shouldn't I lift my head, too, and let them shoot me? There was no escape, anyway.

Then suddenly, I started. Genia had been shaking me, waking me up. "They've gone," she whispered.

I propped myself up on my elbows. Far as the eye could reach in that misty dawn, we saw a welter of swirling corpses washed by the current to the open sea or slowly sinking.

The S.S. had vanished. We gazed at the clifftop; no trace of the murderers.

Genia got up. As she stood there, Manja's figure raised itself not far from me. She, too, had survived the massacre. A miracle.

Genia jumped from the ice block; the water was up to her hips. Slowly, she waded ashore. While she tore pieces of clothing and rugs from the corpses floating around us, Manja and I slipped into the water, too, and followed. On the beach she gave us the rugs, and we wrapped them round us. All our limbs were trembling and our teeth chattering. I was shaking with cold and fever. I'd swallowed sea water, and was pretty sick. Laboriously, we clambered to the top of the cliff; there wasn't the slightest trace of S.S.

I could hardly put one foot before the other. Manja was very weak, too; but Genia kept driving us on.

"We can't let up," she said. "If we hold out now, we're saved."

In the distance we heard a rumble, like thunder.

"The front line," whispered Genia, "the Russians. If we can hang on just a few days—if we can hide somewhere—we're all right."

But where could we hide?

After struggling up that cliff we looked around over the flat, pale landscape. Only the misty twilight shielded us.

Our ragged clothes froze solidly to our bodies, and we were soon covered with a white layer of ice. I simply couldn't go on. I wanted to sit down for just a moment, just to rest; but Genia hurried me on.

"If we sit down now we're done for," she insisted. "We must go on."

She kept saying that as we staggered through the snow, the three of us. We must go on. We must go on.

492

We'd been stumbling along like that for about an hour, I suppose, when we saw the dark outline of a small village before us. Smoke rose from the chimneys, forming blue curls in the cold air.

It was very quiet; it was still early in the morning. We approached the houses and knew we had to stake everything on one throw. We couldn't go any further; in bright daylight they'd find us anyway.

But which door to knock at? Germans lived in every house. We were Polish Jewesses who'd escaped the massacre, how could we pick out, instinctively, the home of a German who wouldn't betray us to the murderers right away?

But Genia had made up her mind; she went up to the very first house, a farmhouse with a number of outhouses.

Genia banged on the door.

Dumbly we stood and waited. At last, approaching footsteps; the door opened.

A woman stood in the doorway. She was frightened to death when she saw us. All the color left her face. Without a word, she whirled round and went quickly back into the house. Then a man appeared—a big, uncouth-looking type.

"What d'you want here?" he asked. Pity and fear, repulsion and horror mingled in that face.

"Hide us, please," said Genia. "We're the sole survivors from last night. Don't send us away—please."

The man's face twitched.

"I'll get shot if they find you," he said.

"Please, give us something to eat," whispered Manja.

The man hesitated. His wife shouted something from the kitchen.

"Come on, then." He glanced quickly in all directions. "Did anybody see you?"

We shook our heads.

He pushed the door open and we entered the house. We were conducted to a flight of stairs leading up to the first floor and from there up to the attic.

"Get a move on—and keep quiet!" the farmer ordered.

We scrambled upstairs. There was a pile of straw in one corner; we threw ourselves down, pulled our rugs over our heads and had dropped off to sleep before the farmer could shut the trapdoor again. We were saved.

# "Let Her Cry It Out"

*At fifteen Gerda was caught up in the war; she had spent her teenage years as a slave in the labor camps. At twenty she trudged a thousand miles in the dead of the winter through Europe—one of four thousand slaves. At twenty-one she was one of two hundred survivors who finally reached a Czech border town. On her twenty-first birthday she celebrated Germany's surrender in a hospital. The day before, she had met her savior—an American lieutenant who looked to her like a "young god." A year later they were married . . .*

We went back to the barracks where most of the rest of the girls had gathered. We found chaos: crying, and shouts of joy. The hour had struck at last. Somehow I couldn't grasp it. There were no golden trumpets to proclaim our freedom. There were no liberators in sight.

Liesel was lying on the littered floor. She knew we were free but did not seem elated.

"Where is Suse?" I asked her.

"She went out to get water and hasn't returned. She has been gone a long time."

I went out to look for Suse. She was not at the pump. I found her off a way lying in the mud. Her eyes were glassy, unseeing, but for a moment I did not realize she was dead.

"Suse, we are free!" I called to her. "We are free, the war is over!"

When I touched her, I knew the truth.

I did not tell Liesel. It was too sad for Liberation Day . . .

My mind was so dull, my nerves so worn from waiting, that only an emotionless vacuum remained. Like many of the other girls I just sat and waited for whatever would happen next.

In the afternoon a strange vehicle drove up. In it were two soldiers in strange uniforms, one of whom spoke German.

The German mayor of the town was with them. He was trying to tell the two soldiers that he really was not anti-Semitic. The soldiers were Americans; I knew as soon as I heard them speak to one another . . .

Tears welled from my eyes as they approached us. The German-speaking soldier patted me with his clean hand. "Don't cry, my child," he said with compassion, "it is all over now."

"We must return to headquarters," said the other one in German. "Can you girls wait until morning? We shall return."

---

From *All but My Life* by Gerda Klein.

I remember nothing else happening that day. The next thing I remember was waking up, wrapped snugly and warm in a coat which the SS had left behind . . .

The barracks was bathed in sunshine, and I woke up with the knowledge that I was free. I was eager to go outside, to move about freely. Perhaps I would meet the Americans again. I swayed as I started to walk. My skin was hot and dry. As I reached the door, the first thing I saw was that strange vehicle bouncing toward us through the brilliant May sunshine. I was overcome with joy.

I called to the other girls that some Americans were coming. The soldier on the left made a motion to the driver who stopped the vehicle a few feet from where I was standing. The soldier jumped out and walked toward the barracks. He wasn't the one who had come the day before. Shaking my head, I stared at this man who was to me the embodiment of all heroism and liberty. He greeted me. I must tell him (that we're Jewish) from the start, I resolved, so that he has no illusions about us. Perhaps I had acquired a feeling of shame. After all, for six long years the Nazis had tried to demean us.

"May I see the other ladies?" he asked.

"Ladies!" my brain repeated. He probably doesn't know, I thought. I must tell him.

"We are Jews," I said in a small voice.

"So am I," he answered. Was there a catch in his voice, or did I imagine it?

I could have embraced him but I was aware how dirty and repulsive I must be.

"Won't you come with me?" he asked. He held the door open. I didn't understand at first. I looked at him questioningly but not a muscle in his face moved. He wanted me to feel that he had not seen the dirt or the lice. He saw a lady and I shall be forever grateful to him for his graciousness.

"I want you to see a friend of mine," I remember telling the American, and we started to walk toward Liesel. On the dirty, straw-littered floor Lilli was lying, covered with rags. As we tried to reach Liesel, she looked up, her eyes enormous, burning in their sockets. She looked at my companion and her face lit up with a strange fire. I heard her say something in English, and saw how the American bent down closer and answered her. Her hands were shaking as she gently, unbelievingly touched the sleeve of his jacket. In the exchange that followed, I made out the word "happy." I understood that word. Then she sighed, released his hand and, looking at him, shook her head and whispered, "Too late". . .

I looked back at Lilli; her eyes were fixed on the American, a solitary tear ran down her cheek. An ant was crawling over her chin. Shortly afterward, Lilli died.

I heard the American give commands in English. He seemed furious

495

that things weren't moving fast enough. He explained to me in German that a hospital was being set up for us. Then he asked me:

"Is there anything I can do for you in particular?"

"Yes, there is," I said. "If you would be kind enough, and could find the time. You see, I have an uncle in Turkey. Could you write to him, let him know that I am alive, and that I hope he has news from my parents and my brother?"

He took out a notebook, and removed the sunglasses he had been wearing. I saw tears in his eyes. He wore battle gear with a net over his helmet. And as he wrote, I looked at him and couldn't absorb enough of the wonder that he had fought for my freedom.

He snapped his book shut.

"I would like to ask you a question," he said softly. "But please don't answer if you don't want to. We are aware of what has happened. Tell me, were you girls sterilized?"

I did not answer at once. I was too full of emotion. Why should he, of all people, who looked to me like a young god, inquire about the deepest treasure that I, who must have looked like an animal to him, carried still within me?

"We were spared," I managed to say.

A few moments later, joined by his companion and the mayor, he drove off. Before I had even asked his name—he vanished!

Within an hour, Red Cross trucks arrived. Litter bearers gently but swiftly loaded the ill. Other soldiers carried girls in their arms like babies, speaking to them soothingly in words the girls did not understand. But the gestures of warmth and help were unmistakable. In a trance I walked to a truck and got in . . . Their uniforms, their language, their kindness and concern made it true: we were finally free!

The hospital we were taken to was a converted school. Wounded German soldiers had been moved to the third floor so that we could be installed in the first two floors. How strange—in a matter of one day, the world had changed: Germans were put out to make room for us.

We were taken to a room where huge caldrons of water were being heated on a stove. Round wooden tubs stood steaming on the floor.

A woman in a white coat motioned me to undress.

Doing so, I stepped into one of the tubs. The warm water, reaching to my neck, felt strange: it had been at least three years since last I sat in a tub. Bidding me stand, the nurse soaped my body with quick, invigorating pressure. It was pleasantly painful to sit back in the tub again and let the warm water engulf me.

A young peasant girl came in, her cheeks rosy and shining, her colorful peasant skirt reaching to her ankles . . . When I saw the girl gather up my clothes in a basket, I looked at the nurse with a questioning glance.

"They will be burned," she said.

Only one thought remained. With my wet hand I reached for my ski boots, took the left one and reached under the lining. There was the dirty shapeless package containing the pictures I wanted to save. I pulled the pictures out and laid them on the dry towel beside the tub. And the other packet—the poison I had bought in Grünberg—I gratefully let go to the fire.

I stepped out of the tub; the nurse dried my body and hair. As I stood nude, before a clean blue and white checkered man's shirt was put on me, I realized abruptly that I possessed nothing, not even a stitch of clothing that I could call my own. I owned only the pictures of Papa, Mama, Arthur, and Abek that I had carried for three years.

A blanket was thrown over my shoulders as I was led to a bunk. The sheets were fresh and white. A nurse brought me a drink of milk!—I hadn't had any in three years. As I drank it something tremendous and uncontrollable broke loose within me. My body shook convulsively. I wanted to stop it but I couldn't. I heard my voice and could do nothing about it.

A nurse hurried up; then a doctor. I heard him say, "No, let her cry it out." Long pent-up emotions finally burst out. I cried for Ilse, for Suse, for other friends, and finally for my family too. Deep in my heart I had known they were dead, but dreams about happy reunions with them had kept me going.

When I opened my eyes a night had passed. A nurse was approaching with a breakfast tray. This is the life of a fairy princess, I thought.

As I lay daydreaming after breakfast there was a sudden commotion. Nurses hurried in.

"Germany has capitulated!" they told us. "The war in Europe is over!"

For me, the war had ended with my liberation. I had not realized that the fighting had continued after that.

I looked out the window. Coming down the hilly, winding road was a company of unarmed and bedraggled German soldiers. As they passed my window, I could see their unshaven faces and hollow cheeks. Proud, handsome American soldiers guarded them.

A doctor and a nurse came in. They stopped at each bed. After asking my name and birthplace, the doctor asked for my date of birth.

"May 8, 1924."

"May 8!" the doctor exclaimed. "Why, today is the eighth."

"Happy birthday!" the nurse chanted.

After they left, I repeated to myself, "It's my birthday, my twenty-first birthday, and Germany capitulated!"

I though of Tusia, who had so desperately wanted my assurance that we would both be free on this day. I remembered her lying dead in the snow. Why am I here? I wondered. I am no better.

497

As I lay back on my white clean pillow, lost in thought, I heard someone approach. It was the doctor again. He put something in my hand.

"For your birthday," he said, smiling.

It was a piece of chocolate.

# The Losses Sustained by European Jews

The physical destruction of Jewish lives and property was overwhelming. According to the survey prepared by the Central Jewish Committee in Poland on August 15, 1945, there were altogether 73,955 Jews left in that country including some 13,000 serving in the Polish army and 5,446 recorded in 10 camps in Germany and Austria. This tiny remnant of more than 3,300,000 Jews (in the somewhat larger area of prewar Poland) was distributed over 224 Polish localities, leaving the large majority of the former 2,000 communities devoid of any Jewish population. Germany and Austria likewise had lost the vast majority of their Jews; the small remnant of some 15,000 living in Germany outside the Displaced Persons' camps consisted largely of those who had escaped deportation and death because they had intermarried and had long lost contact with the Jewish community. The Nazi murder program had most severely affected the children. In Bohemia, Moravia, and Silesia, for instance, where, according to the census of 1930, there had lived 117,551 Jews, only 14,489 were registered in October 1945, including only 1,179 children under 15—an abnormally low ratio of 8.6 per cent. There was a low ratio of Jewish children even in countries like Rumania and Hungary, with their relatively large percentage of adult survivors. According to the Jewish health organization OSE, at the end of 1946 there were altogether 130,000 Jewish children in continental Europe outside the Soviet Union, although, like their elders, some children had been saved by escaping into the interior of the Soviet Union and had subsequently returned to their home countries.

It is difficult to be precise about the total Jewish losses in Europe, since the Germans wiped out not only the people but also the docu-

---

From *A Historian's Notebook: European Jewry Before and After Hitler* by Salo W. Baron.

ments on which reasonably correct calculations might have been based. Most statistical estimates converge around a total of six million Jews killed, a figure cited at the trial of the major war criminals at Nuremberg. Gregory Frumkin, who for years edited the *Statistical Year Book* of the League of Nations, writes in his *Population Changes in Europe Since 1939* that the total figure of Jewish dead in all places that had been occupied by the Germans might easily be between six and seven million. The Anglo-American Committee of Inquiry on Palestine in 1946 estimated the loss of Jewish population in Europe between 1939 and 1946 at over 5,700,000. Consequently, the figure of six million that is usually cited is probably close to the actuality.

This enormous loss augured badly for the future of the Jewish community, even though the biological strength of European Jewry had not been entirely broken. The people's regenerative power was shown by the relatively few survivors in the DP camps, whose birth rate was among the highest in Europe. But the children born in those exceptional conditions still are only adolescents today. Together with their elders, they were sooner or later evacuated, for the most part to Israel, and they could not contribute to the reconstruction of the communities from which their parents had come and which they themselves had never seen.

The tragedy was greatest where Jewish communal and cultural life had flourished most—in Poland, Germany, and the bordering countries. Gone were the cultural treasures painfully accumulated over many centuries. The 3,000 *kehillot* with their age-old institutions had vanished, and their place was taken, at best, by some new tentative bodies, making valiant but often futile efforts to start afresh. The great schools of higher learning, the newspapers and magazines, the book publishers, and artistic centers had been stamped out, with no possibility of even a semblance of replacement. Even more than might be indicated by the enormous percentage of Jews who perished during the Catastrophe, their intellectual elite was so depleted that the few struggling remnants were deprived of their traditional rabbinic, literary, scholarly, and informed lay leaders.

The sharp decline is doubly pronounced when compared even with the fate of nations defeated in the war. Germany herself had suffered much retribution. At the time of its surrender many of its cities lay in ruins, certain regions were depopulated, and most of the others suffered from hunger and want. Japan had her Hiroshima and Nagasaki. Nevertheless, today, 16 years after the war, the population of divided Germany has increased substantially and that of Japan is about a third larger than twenty years ago. By contrast, world Jewry still numbers only some 12,000,000, as against the 16,500,000 or more living in 1939.

The extent of the decline becomes manifest when one realizes that, in the 22 years since 1939, the Jewish people should have *increased* by more than 2,500,000, if we assume a continuation of the average growth in the 1930's, namely, 120,000 per annum. If the Jews had participated in the general population growth of the 1940's and 1950's, the average might well have exceeded even the annual growth of the 1920's, 140,000. If that had been so, the world Jewish population now would have reached or exceeded 20,000,000. What is more, the Jewish communities in formerly Nazi-occupied Europe still are crippled, qualitatively even more than quantitatively. That great reservoir of Jewish population and of cultural and religious leadership has dried up, leaving the rest of Jewry, particularly the segments residing in Israel, the New World, and the British Commonwealth, bereaved.

One's imagination is staggered if one considers what might have happened, if during the Franco-German War of 1871 a Hitler, rather than a Bismarck, had guided Germany. If that Hitler of seven decades earlier had succeeded in overrunning the same countries that were overrun between 1939 and 1945, and if he had had the same program of murdering the Jews from the Atlantic to the Russian Pale of Settlement, the genocide of the Jewish people would have been almost total. There would have been no Israel today, and the other present-day largest concentrations of the Jewish people—in the New World, the Soviet Union, and the British Commonwealth—would have consisted, at best, of small, struggling communities.

Through the disappearance of the Jewish communities the European continent has been deprived of an industrious and enterprising population that contributed significantly to economic and cultural progress. Moreover, the Nazis' genocide left behind a permanent precedent and menace for all mankind . . .

Only belatedly, after the war, was the conscience of mankind aroused by the Nazi murder camps. Men began to realize that such wholesale slaughter of the members of one people can serve as a ready precedent for the murder of any group disliked, for whatever reason, by another group in power. The Nazi doctrine of a Master Race remains a threat for all future times.

Death Marches and Liberation

# Readings

*Holocaust and Rebirth: Bergen-Belsen (1945-1965)*, edited by Sam E. Bloch is an oversized album of documentary pictures and text, written by authorities such as Dr. Jacob E. Robinson, dealing with Bergen-Belsen, the martyrs, the survivors, and the activities of the World Federation of the Bergen-Belsen Association. It is trilingual: Hebrew, Yiddish, and English.

*We Survived* by Erich H. Boehm (Yale University Press, 1949), comprises autobiographies of fourteen survivors, members of all classes. Simply and movingly written, they tell of hatred, sadism, courage, self-sacrifice, liberation and its aftermaths, and the autobiographies of survivors whose excerpts are found in this book.

# 21. THE "HOMECOMING"

When the Nazi scourge was over, the peoples of Europe counted their losses while the Jews counted their survivors. The unbelievable toll inflicted on the Jews is shown in Table 3.

Jacob Presser, the historian of Dutch Jewry, cites that the survivors "bore upon them the indelible mark of their terrible ordeal." Many of them felt guilty just because they had survived. "Simply to live," Presser quotes one survivor as reporting, "everyone had been forced to betray someone else . . . Each one had, at a given moment, torn away from his helpless father or brother, from his wife or child." Some committed suicide; the others lived with the gnawing feeling that there was no justice in their own survival.

They had to build their lives anew. And together with their loneliness and mental anguish came the additional agony of the hostility exhibited toward them by the Gentiles of the countries of Eastern and even some parts of Western Europe.

In the USSR and its satellites, there was no relief from persecution. Anti-Semitism persisted as an instrument of official policy and as a weapon to strengthen Communist Russia's control over the countries under its sway. Communism vilified the Zionists, who were accused of posing a grave danger to the future of the Soviet Union. Moscow substituted "Zionism" for the "international Jewry" idea, which was the object of attack in the Nazi period. During the bloody years of Stalin's dictatorship, untold numbers of Jewish intellectuals, artists, and men of science were executed. So-called international Zionist conspiracies were trumped up and trials were held, which were no less shocking than during the days of Hitler.

The Soviet brand of anti-Jewish oppression was evidenced during the final stages of Allied victory; it is an integral part of the aftermath of the Holocaust.

TABLE 3
Jewish Losses in the Holocaust

| Country | Jewish Population in 1939 | Jews Killed | | Survivors |
| | | Number | Percentage of 1939 Population | Percentage of 1939 Population |
| --- | --- | --- | --- | --- |
| Poland | 3,250,000 | 2,850,000 | 87.9 | 12.1 |
| Soviet Russia[a] | 2,100,000 | 1,500,000 | 71.4 | 28.6 |
| Rumania | 850,000 | 425,000 | 50.0 | 50.0 |
| Hungary | 0 | 200,000 | 49.6 | 50.4 |
| France | 300,000 | 90,000 | 30.0 | 70.0 |
| Czechoslovakia | 315,000 | 240,000 | 82.5 | 17.5 |
| Germany | 193,000 | 110,000 | 91.0 | 9.0 |
| Austria | 90,000 | 45,000 | 66.6 | 33.4 |
| Lithuania | 150,000 | 130,000 | 90.0 | 10.0 |
| Latvia | 95,000 | 80,000 | 89.5 | 10.5 |
| Holland | 150,000 | 105,000 | 72.4 | 17.6 |
| Belgium | 90,000 | 40,000 | 44.4 | 55.6 |
| Yugoslavia | 75,000 | 55,000 | 73.3 | 26.7 |
| Greece | 75,000 | 60,000 | 80.0 | 20.0 |
| Italy | 57,000 | 15,000 | 26.3 | 73.7 |
| Bulgaria | 50,000 | 7,000 | 14.0 | 86.0 |
| Miscellaneous[c] | 15,000 | 5,000 | 30.0 | 70.0 |
| Total | | 5,957,000 | 73.4 | 26.6 |

Source: Jacob Lestchinsky, *Crisis, Catastrophe, and Survival: A Jewish Balance Sheet, 1941–1948* (New York: World Jewish Congress, 1948), p. 50. Revised in 1955 (*Yad Vashem Bulletin,* No. 10, April 1961).
[a]Occupied parts only.
[b]Does not include Jewish victims killed between 1933 and 1939, estimated at between 30,000 and 40,000 by Lestchinsky.
[c]Denmark, Estonia, Luxembourg, Norway, Danzig.

# "Homecoming": Lodz, 1945

The realization that the war was over finally penetrated our consciousness. In our innocence and inexperience we really thought that the sun of redemption would soon rise out of the darkness and that we would step straight into the light.

But reality was altogether different . . .

We began our journey in a large wagon drawn by a single horse, jammed together with the girls of the "gang"; they had managed to find a wagoner.

The wagon advanced with difficulty, overloaded as it was with the bundles the "gang" had piled there, leaving little room for passengers.

We spent the first night in a deserted building. When we woke up in the morning we discovered to our amazement that the wagon as well as the whole gang had disappeared. We were left with nothing. Russian soldiers were everywhere and they readily offered us their assistance. Many of our group accepted their offer and by noon most of them had scattered.

The five of us who remained, along with Liuba, a girl who joined us, were completely at a loss. We did not want to go with the Russians who hinted quite plainly at the price they would demand for any help they would extend: "We liberated you!" (You owe us your bodies.)

At night we had to barricade the doors and windows to keep them from getting in.

I really think it was God himself who sent us a messenger in the image of a man who introduced himself to us as a Pole bent on returning to Poland and prepared to help us too.

After he fulfilled his mission of bringing us to the train (this took seven days), we discovered he was actually a German trying to make his escape back to Germany and using us as a cover. (Later the Russians arrested him as soon as they found out his true identity.) When he had offered us the transportation he had only a horse. Then, from a deserted stable (most of the Germans had fled before the approaching Russians) he had taken a wagon and thus we had set out on our journey.

The spirit of war still hovered in the atmosphere and the air was full of the stench of the corpses scattered on the roads we passed. Aban-

From *Mibead Le'halon Beiti* (From the Window of My House): Ghetto Lodz by Sara Selver-Urbach (translated).

doned machine guns and overturned tanks lay strewn at the sides of the road, and beneath them lay the dead. Our stopovers at night were a source of constant fear and before dawn we hastened on so as to avoid being seen by the Russians. One such night was especially bad and only a miracle saved us. We happened to reach a deserted camp, which evidently had served as a camp for Russian prisoners of war; a few of them were still there. As we entered the gate to see whether we could stay there overnight, several soldiers attached themselves to us, particularly one who was very drunk and who seemed very much attracted to Salusha.

We were very miserable. Our gentile leader could not understand our anxiety. "And what," he wondered, "if one of you should join him. We'll have peace; that's all." It seemed to us that our distress amused him and that somehow he was enjoying the situation.

We made use of every trick we knew. We pretended to agree that Salusha go with the Russian soldier. She went with him while one of the girls walked ahead carrying a kerosene lamp to light the path leading to the barracks.

Suddenly, according to plan, the lamp light went out, and it was pitch dark. All of us, including Salusha, started to run in the opposite direction. It was a mad race down hill. A few minutes later we heard the Russian, who in the meantime had realized how he had been fooled, shouting and running drunkenly in our footsteps ... As we ran we came across a building, an abandoned carpentry shop. We forced our way in, locking and barring the gate behind us. We found two boys inside but we drove them out and barred the gate securely again. After a while the infuriated Russian reached the gate.

Crowded in one corner, panting with exhaustion and excitement, we listened to his cursing and banging on the heavy wooden door. We were terrified that he might succeed in breaking it; he was now in a state of insanity. Then we heard additional voices and a cold sweat covered us from head to toe.

At long last, who knows how much time it actually took—to us it seemed like endless hours—his shouts and wails diminished and they all went away. It sounded as if someone were dragging him off.

Before dawn we slipped away. We tied kerchiefs over our heads and faces so as to conceal our youthfulness. We continued our journey, eating food that we found in abandoned homes along the way, and hastening on: with all our hearts we wanted to reach our destination as rapidly as possible.

The sights we saw on the way were horrible. Extermination and destruction were everywhere. At one spot we saw a man hanging from a scaffold. We tried to shut our eyes, not to see, just to keep going; but it was not possible to advance quickly. We were traveling on dirt roads and had to get off frequently and push the wagon. For hours on end we had to go on foot. Poor Blumka suffered dreadfully: she had sores on her feet and they became infected and filled with pus.

Finally we arrived at the railroad station in Nameslau. Needless to say, at war's end the trains were not running on schedule. Whenever a train did appear at last, after many hours of waiting, it was already very crowded and new passengers had to jump and struggle to board it and push their way in. We stayed in the station overnight. There for the first time we met some other Jews, who like ourselves were survivors of concentration camps. Red Cross workers distributed bread and hot tea in the station. As I recall, it was only on the following evening that we succeeded in climbing on to a freight train and, pressed together in the crowded mass, felt the train move off . . .

We had to change trains several times. Each station brought fresh adventures until finally, after traveling for three days, we were at last approaching Lodz. The train was passing through the suburbs. As we got off the train, our hearts were beating wildly and we trembled with emotion. Where should we go? Unanimously we decided to go to the ghetto, straight to our last home, and not into town, where we had lived before the war.

Lodz. We gazed at the city streets through the windows of the crowded street car we were riding. Everyone stared at us with curiosity for it was perfectly obvious who we were and where we had been until now. We heard murmurs around us and then the remark: "Again Jews! Just see how many of them are still left!" That was our first meeting with the post-war world.

We got out near the ghetto. Two of our group remained to watch our meager belongings while the rest turned toward the ghetto. What can I say? Our return to the ghetto was a most trying experience; it was deeply shocking and made us apprehensive as to what would follow. There was not a living soul in the streets; the houses were destroyed and in ruins. Not a sign of life stirred in them. The wind shrieked and howled among the ruins, setting numberless papers flying: they were not ordinary papers but *shemot,* torn fragments of Hebrew pages of sacred books. *Shemot* were everywhere, on all sides, at every step, in the mud, between the rocks and stones, or twirling aloft, as the wind made them dance. It seemed like one huge cemetery with *shemot* and other scraps of paper hovering about like so many lifeless ghosts.

How still and silent were the cobblestones of the streets, those mute witnesses to the tragic life that a year previously had still existed here. Every vestige of life had vanished and the wind was wailing, mourning the emptiness and desolation that reigned in this place of death.

It was dusk when I reached our flat on Melinarska Street.

The wardrobe was standing in its accustomed place; otherwise everything was demolished with bits and pieces lying scattered around. The sacred books, which were the first things we carried with us into the

506

ghetto, lay torn on the wooden floor, the windows and doors were broken and the draught tossed and tumbled the papers endlessly.

I dropped to the floor speechless and dry-eyed. I couldn't make a sound, couldn't shed a single tear. I was numb, paralyzed. I don't know how long I kneeled there. After a while something stirred and flickered in my mind, reminding me that the girls would be waiting for me at the appointed place. I must get up. I dragged myself up with difficulty. Then I rummaged a bit among the *shemot* until I found my mother's *siddur*. On the once beautiful cover the pale remains of the gilt letters of her name could still be discerned: *Malkah Zelver*. Clutching it in my hand I stumbled away suddenly aged and greatly saddened.

When I got to the meeting place, I found all the other girls already there. A number of Jews who had come to the ghetto before us spoke to us and informed us that a Jewish welfare committee was already functioning in the place, assisting Jewish refugees. They told us how to go there . . .

From the committee we received some money to cover basic expenses. We lived in a wretched windowless room, ate anything we could get or not at all. Later we lived in other rooms; we slept on the floor. Then we got a job classifying the cards of the dead for the cemetery files. And we always barricaded the door at night because of the Russian soldiers drifting about the city.

We followed the lists of the survivors from day to day: they were posted on the walls of the building by the committee. As soon as a new list appeared, we crowded up to see: perhaps one had survived? Our entire being yearned to see even one name, one remnant of our families. The days passed and not one of my dear ones appeared, neither in person, nor on the lists.

Only now . . . did we grasp the full significance of the horror, only now did we realize the extent of the work of the devil, the total extermination. Only now did we comprehend the vastness of the hell of Auschwitz, Treblinka and Maidanek as we listened to the tales of those who had experienced them and when we read newspapers, periodicals and saw various exhibits.

Once again the days became nightmares: I was haunted day and night by scenes that only now had become real; by the furnaces of Auschwitz, heretofore vague and only now sharp and clear in my mind. Ceaselessly I could see in my mind's eye the death trains, the gas chambers, people breathing their last, dying. And my loved ones were among them.

We attended the exhibits, arranged so the world might find out and never forget what and how the Nazi machinery of annihilation had done to the Jews. There we saw the shoes, the prayer shawls, the cans of lethal gas and much, much more. There was no end to the gruesome display.

I was particularly affected by a poster that could be seen on many walls around town, showing a mother and her son in the gas chamber. They were two skeletons, one large, the other small. Their agonized faces expressed the fearful cry issuing from the torture chambers of purgatory. To me it seemed that the poster spelled out the words: "Thus they were led to their death." Tortured by these nightmares and thoughts, we wandered around, hoping that someone, at least one, might yet appear.

More than once it happened that as we walked along a street we saw someone on whom the force of our profound yearning bestowed the look of one we loved and longed for. We then ran with pounding heart to the image there ahead of us and came—face to face with a total stranger. Another illusion shattered; another mistake. It was not our dear one but someone else. We continued to walk around and console ourselves with wonderful stories of meeting our loved ones, suddenly, around the corner and how we would fall in each other's arms with unbounded joy. Some lucky people were really blessed with such meetings, but they were very few. Entire families were wiped off the face of the earth and the rare ones who survived were lone remnants, each one the solitary lonely representative of his whole family.

When we first returned to the ghetto we went to the cemetery; everyone had his own dead buried there. I turned up the path that was familiar to me. On the way I saw the huge pits that had been dug to hold the eight-hundred Jews who had remained in the ghetto of Lodz after its liquidation. Fortunately, the Germans were prevented from carrying out their beastly plan of burying the whole group alive: the Russians entered and captured the city and the last Jews of Lodz were saved.

I reached my father's grave. The large stone we had set at the head was still in place but the tin name-plate attached to it was rusty. I threw myself on the grave with my heart full of anguish, but no tears came. Now, years after that day, I am still capable of weeping when he comes to me in memory, but on that day I could not cry. Why, I kept thinking, am I the one who returned? Why am I the only one?

I could not locate my little sister's grave for the tin name-plates had been torn off in her row and it was impossible to identify any of them. The mounds had sunk down deeper into the ground and tall grass covered them with a green blanket that moved gently in the breeze, as if caressing the children's part of the cemetery so they might rest in peace.

My heart wept because my dear ones (who were killed in the camps) had no grave to which I could go. Their dust was scattered to the four winds; not a trace remained of their lives, or of their deaths, except in the memories I cherished in my heart. Thus I lost them a second time: I sensed their agony and their death before they departed and I am tortured by the pain of not having been able to say good-by. We did not even part properly from each other. The most important things were left unspoken and everything was cut off in the middle . . .

I alone remain, only I, to begin a new life.

# "Homecoming": Hamburg, Germany, 1947 (British Occupation Zone)

Of the twenty thousand Jews resident in the city of Hamburg [in 1933] about three hundred are left today. Four or five—all women—succeeded in hiding in the city through the last few ghastly years of the Nazi regime. All the others are survivors from the death-mills of the East . . .

For a few weeks the Russians, the Red Cross officials, and American doctors and nurses took care of them, dressed their wounds, clothed them, tried to lead them back, gently, into normal life. The process of recuperation progressed but slowly; they screamed in their sleep, they couldn't forget; it was hard for them to learn to believe, to trust, to hope. After six to eight weeks the doctors and the Red Cross officials thought it best they return to their German home towns, to their old surroundings, the little comforts of their own little world. They were sent back. About three hundred—of twenty thousand—returned to Hamburg.

There was an old couple by the name of L., a man and a woman, both over sixty, who by some miracle had survived the slaughter. Members of a famous old Jewish family of Hamburg—of bankers, lawyers, philanthropists. They traveled back from Oswiecim by bus, a two-decker, in the upper compartment. They had bathed in warm water, their hair and nails were cut and clean, the man was shaved, they wore clean clothes—not their own, of course, but that didn't matter. It was all a miracle. The woman was almost blind, her eyes swollen and red from too much crying; and the man looked out through the windows and described the passing landscape. I might just as well add

From *Menorah Journal*, Autumn 1947, Victor Bienstock.

at this moment that the home-coming of the particular couple L. is reported not for any sentimental reasons. I have been given scores of similar reports on reactions of German Jews when they came back home.

The old woman said to her husband: "What are we going to do with our big house, we two old people, when we come back? There are sixteen rooms. Maybe we ought to sell the house, and take an apartment somewhere—just for you and me."

"No," the old man said, "I want to stay in the house. It is a big house all right; but we could take in some people who were bombed out. I want to stay in our house, where my father died, and my grandfather, and where I was born."

"Yes," the old woman said, "you are right."

After a while she said: "I wonder where we have to go to get our things back—our woolen underwear, I mean, and the pots and pans, and my jewelry and things. I want the wedding ring, you know—that is what I want most. I think I shall go and get it the first day we'll be back. Day after tomorrow."

"Day after tomorrow is Saturday, Mother," the man said. "We ought to go to *Schul*. We have a lot of things to thank God for." . . .

It was interesting to observe, I was told, that on this trip back to their home towns the Jews either did not talk at all or they never stopped talking. Among the latter was that old couple L., the almost blind woman and her husband; they talked all the time. They talked of the home they were going to live in; they remembered the old little comforts, the carpet in the bedroom and the mirror in the bathroom; they spoke of the changes they were going to make. And suddenly they both stopped; a terrible thought had entered their minds at the same time: maybe the house was bombed, or was burned out, or damaged. They became very quiet. The bus traveled on.

"What do you see now?" the old woman asked when the bus crossed a wooden bridge. He told her. Suddenly the woman said: "It can't be. The house must still be there. After all we've gone through—after all that—oh no, God can't, couldn't permit it. I know the house is still there. . . ."

And Frau L.'s faith proved to be justified. The house, an old comfortable building, sat spaciously in a lovely garden. All around it the houses were razed to the ground, parks burned out, gardens blackened and wild. Only the house of the L.'s was still standing, and the old trees in the garden had never been touched.

Only, unfortunately, a former Nazi with his family lived in the house of the L.'s—the house where Herr L.'s father and grandfather had died, and where Herr L. had been born. I cannot give you all the details of the story, how Herr and Frau L. stood in front of the house when they finally arrived in Hamburg, how they entered it through the back door, and how they were told, amiably but firmly, that the house was not theirs any more. The present owner even took the trouble of showing Herr L. the official paper, that he had bought the house, legally, from the City of Hamburg. Yes, he had been a Nazi, the present owner smiled, and, "We all make mistakes sometimes, don't we?" But he had never participated in any unpleasant activities; Ja he had not even known until a short time ago that they had occurred. He admitted that his case had not been finally decided yet by the Denazification Court; but he had excellent letters of recommendation and a good lawyer, and he had no doubt about the outcome. The house? Of course, the house was his.

The owner looked with hardly suppressed contempt at the shabby, nervous old couple. "And now, if you'll excuse me . . ."

Herr and Frau L. went to a dozen offices and officials: to the police (to the *Wohnungsamt*, to the *Wirtschaftsamt*[1]) to the Committee for the Victims of Nazism; they even went to the office of the Mayor of Hamburg, Herr Brauer, and to the British Military Governor, and to the British Civilian Governor. In the end they returned once more to the people who now lived in their house, the reformed Nazis. With the heavy eyes which had cried themselves blind, they begged to be allowed to live in at least a couple of the rooms in *the* house—or just in one single room. But no, it couldn't be done. They all shook their heads, the Germans and the British, the Mayor and the Governors, the officials and the Nazis . . .

A few months ago Herr L. chose the easiest way out: he died. I spoke with the doctor who attended him, and the doctor shrugged his shoulders, and said: "He was an old man—what do you expect? Neither his body nor his soul could offer resistance; he had no strength left. I had the impression that he did not want to live—and so he died . . ."

I have visited Frau L. in her "emergency quarters" which the *Wohnungsamt* of the City of Hamburg after all arranged for her. It is a dark hole with a single small window high up on the wall leading into the staircase of the apartment house. She has to burn electric light all day— but, unfortunately, electricity is rationed in Germany. Most of the time, if Frau L. does not walk along the streets of Hamburg, she has to sit in the dark. The room is large enough for a bed, a chair and a chest of drawers.

There Frau L. is living now, a German Jewess who was liberated by the democracies. She receives 90 marks a month from a German charity organization—although she is a millionairess in her own right. For it isn't only her house that wasn't returned to her; she hasn't received back her other property either; neither her woolen under-

[1]Housing and property authorities.

wear, her pots and pans, her carpets, her jewelry, her clothes, nor her wedding ring, her blankets and her pillowcases, which the Nazis had confiscated. She didn't get anything back.

The Nazi leaders, the SS men and the Gestapo officials, when discharged from their camps or when they have served their eight-to-twelve-month jail sentences for wholesale murder—they can go to their banks and draw from their frozen bank accounts. But today, over two years after the "liberation," no Jew is permitted to draw a single *pfennig* from the bank accounts confiscated and frozen by the Nazis.

So Frau L. lives on 90 marks a month charity money. And today she receives the same starvation ration food cards as the Germans—although throughout the war years the Germans lived very well indeed on the food robbed from the countries they had conquered, while Frau L. was fed worse than any animal in the death-camps in the East.

And Frau L. is only one of the three hundred Jews in Hamburg. They all are treated like outcasts. As far as their bank accounts and their property are concerned, none of them has received anything back. And—although there are no statistics—we estimate that at the utmost two dozen of the three hundred survivors were permitted to move back into their old homes . . .

## The Jewish Community House

The war is over, and the pitiable survivors have returned. For reasons I find hard to understand the *Juedische Gemeinde* (Jewish Community) was given the small house in the Rothenbaum Chaussee to open its offices. Because the house had been one of the buildings occupied by the Gestapo? When the Jews moved in they found, among hundreds of empty bottles of French champagnes and wines, heavily used instruments of torture. Till today they have kept a rubber truncheon crusted with blood. It is probably Jewish blood. Many a Jew has been "questioned" by the Gestapo in this building—and never left it alive.

That is the house where the offices of the *Juedische Gemeinde* of Hamburg are today, and you may now understand why people say it is haunted.

The first time I saw the house my visit coincided with the monthly food distribution of the American Joint Distribution Committee. Once a month the Joint gives each one a package of five to six pounds of flour, sugar, cereal, coffee, a can of fish, a can of milk, and a few cigarettes. It is the only food help the Jews are getting . . .

They were standing in a long line, and I walked by. The corridor was dimly lit—there are not many light bulbs in Germany. At first I thought I had come to the wrong place. The forty or fifty people there acted—whispering and hardly moving—as if they were waiting for a funeral.

512

When I passed they lifted their eyes, and then I got used to the darkness and I recognized my own fellow-townsmen. Their eyes seemed heavy—and yet, they were empty. They looked at me, but it was as if they saw something far away. One of them recognized me. A few voices rose for a moment and then ebbed away. They didn't smile. Their shoulders sagged. Their eyes, heavy with emptiness, never changed.

"Why have you come back?" somebody asked.

I explained. They shrugged their shoulders. Their eyes fell again. Silently they moved forward.

A man came out with his little parcel, and I recognized him. He used to be a famous lawyer, an authority in international law. He said: "Hello, my friend. Maybe you could give me an answer to a question that has been puzzling me for some time. The point is that I've heard a rumor that this war was fought to suppress terror and injustice, and to proclaim the dignity and the rights of man. Imagine! I've been told that the democratic countries of the world sacrificed millions of their men and billions of their money to avenge the Nazi horror and to establish the four freedoms, decency and justice . . . Well," he concluded, "look around you, my friend. You will find that all this is nonsense. You will find that today the Nazis in Germany—in prison camps or out—are still better off then we Jews . . ."

# Lena Regains Her Son and Her Husband

*Lena and Alexander Donat had arranged for their son, Wlodek, to be smuggled out of the Warsaw Ghetto and hide with a Catholic family; later Wlodek was put into a Catholic orphanage. Father and mother went through the hells of the holocaust in labor camps, resistance, etc. The final chapter is narrated here—one of the extremely rare happy endings of the Tragedy. (The italics are Wlodek's comments; the rest is Lena's story.) The family is now residing in New York . . .*

At daybreak the next day we took the train for Otwock. I still had enough of the money Berlowicz had given me to buy tickets with. When Maria and I walked up the street, there was a big

From *The Holocaust Kingdom* by Alexander Donat.

villa, typical of the country houses around Otwock . . . The superintendent recognized Maria and greeted her warmly. "This is Wlodek's
mother," Maria introduced us. It took them a long time to find Wlodek.

*Miss Olenka called me and said, "Hide in the bushes, Wlodek. Some Jewess
has come for you." I had a couple of potatoes under my jacket which I had taken
from the cart. I ran to the bushes right away but I began to wonder. Who had
come for me? Had they brought something to eat? So I sneaked out to where I
could look, and I saw Auntie Maria with some other lady. I walked over to them
with the other boys.*

When Wlodek finally came, I didn't recognize him. They all stood
there, in dreadful rags, barefoot, with close-cropped heads. They all
looked alike, every face pinched with hunger; I couldn't have picked
my own child from among them. Not until he ran up to Maria and
threw his arms around her did I see the two hollows at his temples, the
marks made by the forceps when he was brought into the world.

"Do you know who this lady is?" Maria asked him.

"I think I know. Let me guess," he replied. He looked me over
apprehensively. His feet were covered with monstrous sores. My experienced eyes immediately diagnosed scabies. Could this little starveling,
this ragged creature, frightened to death and looking like a hunted
animal, could this be the pampered little boy I had longed for night
after terrible night in Auschwitz? My poor baby! How he must have
suffered to be in such a pitiful state. Even Maria had not expected
anything like that, and she burst into sobs.

I did not say anything, I did not cry. After a [while], I went closer to
him and stroked his head lightly. He did not move away. When the
other boys went away, he took a couple of potatoes out from under his
jacket. "Come with me, my little boy," I said, "I'll buy you something to
eat. Do you know where I can get food around here?"

"Of course." He was more animated now and I recognized his voice.
"There's a grocery store just around the corner."

I bought him a big roll. We sat on the empty porch and he began to
eat it, biting off big pieces and swallowing them without chewing. I
could hardly hold back my tears.

"That was good," he said when he had finished. He looked at me
more closely.

I bought him some ice cream. "Do you recognize me now?" I asked
him gently.

"Yes, I do. But Mama had curly hair, now it's straight."

So he had preserved some image of me through those years. I edged
closer to him.

"Wlodek, would you like to come with me and stay with me forever?"

"No, I want to stay with the boys," he said, his eyes glistening with

514

tears. Then something occurred to him. "Mama, if I come with you, will I never be hungry again?"

"I swear to you that never, never as long as you live, will you ever be hungry again."

He huddled closer to me and squeezed me. "Well, then, I suppose I'll come."

I asked Maria to tell the superintendent at once. She got busy, and was going to have his things brought from the laundry. But I didn't want his things; I didn't want to wait. I took him as he was and would not let go of his hand.

The train was crowded and we lost Maria. Only after the train started did I burst into tears, whether from my own happiness, because of the pitiful little creature who was my son, or my own sudden exhaustion. I realized that I had no place to sleep, no money, and no one in the world except this boy to whom I had just solemnly promised that he would never go hungry again. Wlodek was excited, too. He couldn't stop talking for a minute, and soon all our fellow passengers knew that his mother had come back from a camp, that his father had not come back, and that he had just been taken from the orphanage. He looked so miserable that one passenger, with tears in his eyes, thrust a banknote into Wlodek's hand. I came to my senses just in time. Not that, not while I was alive.

I decided to go back to the Berlowiczes, and on my way, ran into Sarenka. When she saw us, she drew back as if frightened, as if she had seen a ghost. She held her head in her hands, and stared goggle-eyed. "You found him!" she cried out. And then she told me that never for a moment had she believed that my son would be alive, nor had any one of the others. They had looked on my faith as harmless madness, to be humored because it helped me to survive.

The Berlowiczes received us warmly, and we spent the night on an armchair. Wlodek could not sleep. Because he was so excited or had eaten too much, he had diarrhea. The next day the Berlowiczes showed great energy. They found me a tiny, dirty room (in Zabkowska Street,) but to me it seemed like a palace. And Dr. Berlowicz also got me a job. I was to organize a pharmacy for the Jewish Committee with the medicines it had received from America, from Palestine and from the Polish government. I had a place to sleep, the Jewish Committee would give me breakfast and dinner, food for Wlodek and a little money as well. My life took on meaning and purpose once more.

It didn't take long to get rid of Wlodek's scabies; cleanliness, better food, and some medical treatment worked wonders. But I had more trouble with his mind, which had become warped. He was a regular guttersnipe who talked the language of the streets. And he had also been infected with rabid anti-Semitism; he hated everything Jewish. I shed bitter tears over this child of mine. I knew it would take all the love and devotion I had to get him straightened out. The greatest tact would be necessary if he was to grow up without serious emotional difficulties. (I had no particular theories on the score; I simply trusted my feelings.)

The day after we moved into my little place, where, under the name of Jakubowska, I occupied one room and an elderly Gentile woman the other, Wlodek said prayers from morning to night, on his knees. I pretended that it didn't bother me, but even my neighbor was surprised by such excessive religious zeal. "Wlodek," she remarked to him, "not even priests pray that much. Just say an 'Our Father,' that's quite enough."

To wipe out the memory of the past few years, I sang the lullabies I used to sing him when he was a child and I was happy when he joined in. "I want you to remember these lullabies," I said to him. "When you grow up and have children of your own, you'll sing them the same songs your mother sang to you."

"I won't have children," he replied, quite serious. "I want to be a priest. But if you want to have grandchildren, try to have a little girl. And do it quickly, before Daddy comes back, so he'll have a surprise."

He would ask me in the middle of the day, "May I pray to the Lord Jesus?" I never said no.

One day when I came home from work—I had to leave Wlodek alone during the day—he handed me a letter he had written which was addressed to "Miss Olenka." "Please put a stamp on it and put it in the mailbox," he said. "But you mustn't read it. It's secret."

The letter read: "Dear Miss Olenka, I am well, Mother is very good to me, and I am never hungry. Mother even bought me a red radish once. And *what we talked about*—it's all right for now." He wrote several such letters. Later, he told me that "what we talked about" referred to his prayers. He had agreed with Miss Olenka that he would run away and go back to her if his mother did not let him pray.

I was not too upset by Wlodek's Catholicism . . . After the ordeal we had lived through, simply for being Jewish, I could not endure the hatred my child had been taught. His was no true Christianity based on love of his fellow man; instead, his mind had been poisoned by a medieval distortion of Christianity, a fanatic version of Catholicism impregnated with hatred for his own people. I was deeply hurt by his anti-Semitic songs and chatter. When he repeated them out of childish spite, they made me wince. "All Jews are thieves and swindlers," he would say, with firm conviction. "They killed the Lord Jesus and now they kill Christian children to mix their blood in the matzos." Sometimes he hummed a song which made fun of Jewish speech and habits, and explained, "You see, Mommy, that's how Jews pray."

One day I had had it. "Look here, Wlodek," I said, "we've got to talk about this once and for all. You're Catholic, I'm Jewish. You may pray to God the way you want to and as often as you want to. I won't tease

516

you about it. But don't you dare to make fun of my religion, or the way I say my prayers."

"But you never pray!"

"I don't have to kneel two hours a day and fold my hands in order to pray. I pray in my mind and God can hear and understand me. I could make fun of you, too, because you have to kneel, and fold your hands, and pray for hours on end. But I don't. And I don't want you to do it either. Then we can be friends."

That stopped him for good.

He often asked me to take him to church, and I would walk with him as far as the door and tell him, "Go in, say your prayers. I'll wait outside."

"Please come in with me."

"No. I'm Jewish. I won't go in, but I promise not to budge from this spot until you come out."

He never went in alone, he was afraid to. For many years he was to be pursued by the fear that he would suddenly find himself deserted by everyone.

Every day at 6 A.M. a woman would come by with milk and I always ran to get some for Wlodek. Once I bought him an egg, hard-boiled it, and sliced an onion into it so he would get the vitamins. When he saw the onion, he burst into tears and bitterly reproached me: "Why did you have to spoil a nice egg like that? Onions stink. Only Jews eat onions." But he couldn't resist the temptation and so he ate the Jewish dish with great relish. "You know," he said, "it's not so bad after all. . . ."

He could be very cruel, with all the cruelty of children. One time he told me that I was not his real mother because otherwise I wouldn't forbid him to do anything he wanted to do.

"Now, what makes you say that?" I asked. "Don't you see that I know all kinds of things about you and I sing your old lullabies for you?"

"That's nothing. You were in camp with my real mother. She told you all about me. And you promised her you'd take care of me. But you're not my real mother."

Though I wept about such things, they grew rarer and he became increasingly attached to me. Once he cuddled up to me and said pensively, as if talking to himself, "All Jews can't be bad. You're Jewish and you're not bad at all . . ."

Wlodek had not been sick for two years, but now his whole organism seemed to be making up for all that time. The moment his scabies disappeared, he had stomach troubles; then bronchitis. Though I had a job, I didn't earn enough to buy him shoes and he went around barefoot. I still wore my heavy ski boots and he had nothing. One day it was raining when I took him to the doctor and that was when a cold became bronchitis. The doctor, a woman, examined him and filled out the usual form. "Name? Address?" When she asked about his father, I said, "His father has not come back yet."

"What do you mean? Have you heard from him?"

"No. I have not heard from him, but he has not yet come back."

The doctor looked at me strangely, but asked no further questions. As for me, I had not the slightest doubt he would come back. My Michal would not disappoint me; he'd be back. I waited for him impassively, just as I had waited for the moment of reunion with Wlodek. Hundreds of people came to the Committee, pored over the records, hoping against hope. Then they turned away, sagging, apathetic, hopeless. I kept very much to myself, putting people off with, "Wait until my husband returns." People around me thought my experiences had unbalanced me, that I was a victim of a kind of madness. My unflinching faith shocked many. How could one be so self-centered in an epoch of universal disaster, and refuse even in one's innermost thoughts to let go of something one had possessed? But I believed in Michal. When people tried to bring the subject up, I would reply, "Until someone comes and tells me that he saw Michal die with his own eyes, Michal is alive as far as I am concerned, and I shall wait for him."

Early in July a stranger who came to the Committee offices suddenly threw himself into my arms and began to kiss me. It was Melcer. "Send someone to the city gates to tell your husband you're alive. He is convinced that you're dead. If he sees you suddenly like this, he'll drop dead on the spot." But I sent no one. And I was not a bit surprised when Michal appeared in the doorway, in an old German uniform, emaciated and white as chalk. I felt strong and calm. I pushed him gently away from me and said over and over again, "Now, now, calm down," but everything in me sang. The dingy Committee offices were suddenly bathed in light. I had my husband back, I had my son. Life had the promise of new happiness. We were not only liberated, we were saved.

Strangers crowded around us. Everyone wept. They wept not only because they had witnessed an incomprehensible miracle, an improbable joy. Their tears were also a terrible lament. They wept for the millions who would never come back, who for all ages will remind us

. . .

# Pogrom in Kielce, Poland

*One hundred twenty-five Jewish survivors returned to Kielce, Poland, where 19,000 Jews (one third of the population) lived before 1939. Forty-three of them were killed in the pogrom after the homecoming . . .*

We arrived in Kielce at seven o'clock, and went straight to the residence of the *wojewoda* (the governor) . . .

While waiting in the house of the *wojewoda,* I asked a soldier who sat in the corridor if he knew what had caused the pogrom. He replied candidly that the massacre had started because "the Jews kidnapped Christian children and hid them in their house at Number 7, Planty Street" . . .

The rumor of the kidnapping of Christian children had been the pretext for the terrible carnage, and even this hard-bitten soldier had accepted the fantastic story as true.

Since the governor was bedridden with a broken leg . . . we had to wake the deputy governor . . . He assured us that he had done everything in his power to calm the enraged mob. Here is his version of the events:

On Wednesday, July 3rd, a Mr. and Mrs. Blaszczyk reported to the police that their nine-year-old son had been missing for three days. Soon thereafter a rumor spread that something was about to happen to the one hundred and fifty Jews who still lived in Kielce, most of them in the large community house.

On the following morning, Thursday July 4th, the same couple returned to the police station, accompanied this time by their boy, Henryk, who had finally come home. Henryk declared that three days before a stranger had asked him to carry a parcel to the house occupied by Jews, and that the Jews had imprisoned him in a cellar. He claimed that he had been starved and maltreated, that he had seen the bodies of murdered Christian children in the cellar, and that only by great luck had he succeeded in escaping from his torture-chamber. This story ran rapidly through the town, and large crowds began to gather in the courtyard of the community house, uttering threats and demanding reprisals.

At ten that morning, said the governor, he received a telephone call from the president of the Jewish community, who informed him that

---

From *Between Fear and Hope* by S. L. Schneiderman.

the house on Planty Street was surrounded by an excited mob of nearly five thousand Poles. The deputy governor immediately led the city militia to the house, but they were unable to break through the mob which was hurling stones at windows and killing every Jew who tried to come out.

"I ordered the fire-brigade to use the hoses," said the deputy governor, "but the mob attacked the fire trucks and tore the hoses to shreds."

Asked why he had not given his men the order to fire, the deputy governor replied that the militia had fired a few shots in the air, but that they had had no effect. He could not, he added, tell his men to fire directly into the mob, because that would have caused many casualties. In concluding his report, the young deputy governor spoke eloquently of the martyrdom of the Polish Jews and exclaimed with passion:

"I want you all to see the place where these terrible events occurred. I want you to be witnesses to the results of that vicious crime. It is high time the world realized that the gangsters who call themselves Polish patriots, and who receive support from abroad, are actually a blight and a misfortune for Poland" . . .

Later, when I talked to eyewitnesses, I heard the full story of the pogrom. These witnesses were the injured Jews in the hospital and those who had been rescued and kept in the police station, to be protected from the mob.

On entering the police station, I saw a number of these survivors in the garden. Still nervous and fearful, with their heads in bandages, they gathered around and all tried to speak at the same time. The narrative of those who could speak more calmly was continually interrupted by the hysterical cries of the women, who rushed about desperately trying to get some scrap of information about their husbands from whom they had been torn in the pogrom. Finally I succeeded in attracting the attention of one man in the crowd by mentioning that I had brought a few bottles of vitamins from (the) president of the Kielce landsmanschaft in New York . . . He immediately led me into the courtyard, where he gave me his account of the disaster.

When the excited crowd began to gather in front of the community house, he related, two uniformed men came inside. Claiming that they represented the military authorities, they ransacked the house. They found a few pistols which they confiscated, together with some money and other valuables. On leaving the house they shouted, "And now we'll settle accounts with you!"

Just after they left, stones came crashing through the windows. An infuriated mob broke into the house, beat the Jews with iron bars and axes, and hurled their victims through the windows to the crowd outside, which trampled them to death. The assassins recognized Dr. Kahane, the president of the community, and attacked him with particular fury. He was instantly killed.

# The "Homecoming"

Dr. Kahane was born in Lwow. Throughout the Nazi occupation he fought in the ranks of the Polish guerillas. At the end of the war he settled in Kielce, where he assumed leadership of the remaining Jews, who numbered one hundred fifty. They were all that was left of more than twenty-five thousand who had lived there before the war. Dr. Kahane died a martyr, appealing with his last breath to the conscience of his murderers . . . During the pogrom, the murderers looted their victims, stealing their purses and tearing rings from women's fingers.

From the police station, we went to the scene of the massacre. The sight of the large, modern apartment house on Planty Street was the ultimate in ruthless havoc . . . The immense courtyard was still littered with blood-stained iron pipes, stones and clubs, which had been used to crush the skulls of Jewish men and women. Blackening puddles of blood still remained. From the window frames hung the rags of the clothes of victims who had struggled with their assassins. Blood-drenched papers were scattered on the ground—sticky with gore, they clung to the earth though a strong wind swept through the yard.

I picked up some of these scraps of paper. There were letters addressed to the victims by their relatives in Palestine, Canada, and the United States. I was apparently free to pick up anything I wanted—the stones, the iron bars, the fragments of wrecked radiators that served as instruments of murder. The guards armed with machine guns who had been assigned to keep watch in the courtyard were utterly indifferent; they just lay on the grass sunning themselves. However, the Gentile superintendent of the house . . . cried bitterly when she told us her story. The assassins had locked her in her room after taking from her kitchen an ax, knives, and other utensils which they used for the butchery. During the Nazi occupation this Gentile woman had hidden a Jew with whom she was in love. She had come with him to Kielce to live in the house that served as a refugee center for several Jews from the surrounding towns and for some from Cracow, Lwow, and even distant Vilno . . . She showed us how she was forced to look on helplessly from her window as the mob slaughtered the Jews in the courtyard . . .

Joel Cang of the *London Times* and I went to see the "hero" of the Kielce tragedy—the boy whose alleged disappearance was used as a pretext for spreading the report of a ritual murder.

The accusation of ritual murder is an old, repeated means of provoking pogroms. But in former times the instigators often produced a dead Gentile child as "evidence." The Polish anti-Semitics, however, had learned from Hitler that no actual "evidence" is needed, and that a big lie is sufficient to produce the desired effect. There was no dead child in Kielce; the rumor was enough.

In a sunny room on the third floor of the police building sat nine-year-old Henryk Blaszczyk, guarded by two soldiers. The boy calmly told us about the diabolical machinations of which he had been the

521

main instrument. He explained how a friend of his parents, Tadeusz Bartoszynski, had met him in the street and taken him to the village ten miles from Kielce.

When I asked the supposedly innocent Henryk how he had gone to the village, whether he had walked or been driven in a car, he answered that he did not remember. I asked him what was the purpose of his trip. "The Bartoszynskis have marvelous cherries," he said. "I went there last year with my parents and I liked the cherries. That's why I went again."

I asked him whether he had told his parents that he was going to the village. He said, "No" and took the trouble to emphasize this several times. Then he told us that after sunset several persons came to the Bartoszynskis and talked for a long time, but he was unable to hear them. He candidly admitted that it was Bartoszynski who had ordered him to tell the story about being kidnapped and kept in the cellar of the Jewish house on Planty Street, threatening to beat him if he refused.

On July 3rd, at night, Henryk unexpectedly returned to his parents' home and told them the story that spread with amazing speed throughout the city. The next morning, Henryk was taken by his parents to the police. On the way he pointed at the house on Planty Street and accused the first Jew he saw of being the culprit who had hidden him in the cellar and maltreated him.

As soon as they reported to the police, a patrol of six militiamen was sent to arrest the accused, Singer, who was thus saved from certain death. Then another group of twelve militiamen was sent to search the cellar. They discovered that the boy's story was false, but in the meantime the mob had assembled and begun to storm the house . . .

The night following the pogrom the leaders of all the parties in Kielce . . . issued an appeal to the population, in which the crime was denounced in the sharpest terms. The appeal referred to the pogrom as "a blot on the entire Polish nation," and branded its organizers as belonging to "the reactionaries of the National Armed Forces." The people were advised not to believe the "alarming rumors spread by the forces of darkness." The diocese of Kielce did not sign this appeal, but issued one of its own . . .

The author of this appeal was worried primarily because the misfortune took place in the presence of children, and ascribed the murders to a "coincidence." In reality, even the children of Kielce, including the nine-year-old Henryk Blaszczyk, knew perfectly well that the pogrom was the result of a diabolical machination. On the same day, a number of other towns and villages witnessed pogroms similar to those of Kielce. Thus, it was only at the last moment that it was possible to check pogroms in Ostrowiec, Lublin, and Czestochowa. The mobs everywhere had been incited by rumors of ritual murders. On July 4th, as a result of the same instigations, thirty Jews were murdered in trains . . .

One of the passengers reported the following facts: When the train was approaching the station, a man wearing an armband with the English inscription, "Poland," suddenly appeared in his car. (Such armbands are worn by the soldiers of General Anders' Army.) The soldier spoke to the passengers, encouraging them to murder all the Jews on the train because fifteen ritual murders had been committed in Kielce. Suddenly the train slowed down, and stopped at some distance from the station. Jews were dragged out of the cars and beaten. Many succeeded in escaping to the woods, but seven were killed.

Subsequent investigation disclosed that the engineer had promised the organizers of the pogrom to stop the train before reaching the station in order to facilitate this crime . . .

# Readings

*Anti-Semitism without Jews; Communist Eastern Europe* by Paul Lendvai (Double-day, 1971), unfolds the official policies of hostility and persecution of the Soviet satellite countries.

*Black Years of Soviet Jewry* by Yehoshua Gilboa (Little Brown, 1971), is a carefully researched and documented book on the persecution of Jews in the U.S.S.R. with special emphasis on Stalinism.

*Jews in Russia* by Jonathan Porath (United Synagogue Commission of Jewish Education, 1973), is a collection of documents which reveal the policies of hostility toward Jews during the czarist and communist periods.

*The Rise and Fall of Stalin* by Robert Payne (Simon and Schuster, 1965), is a fascinating revealing book about one of the most treacherous and terrifying dictators of modern times.

*A Girl Called Judith Strick,* autobiographic materials by Bernard Goldstein, Alexander Donat, Jan Kuper, Gerda W. Klein, and certain titles mentioned in the bibliography, like Rudolf Vraba, Kitty Hart, Sala Pawlowicz, Nathan Shappley, cover the aftermaths of Liberation Day.

# 22. THE SHE'ERIT HAPLETAH

When the war ended, World Jewry, and especially American Jewry, through the JDC, mobilized for the relief and rehabilitation of the approximately 1,400,000 Jewish survivors—the *She'erit Hapletah,* or "Surviving Remnant," who became known as the displaced persons (DPs).

The initial reaction of the Jewish survivors was one of joy, but this was soon replaced by depression, even despair. For many, rescue was but a brief interlude in their suffering. Some were repatriated against their wishes to their countries of origin. Others were moved from concentration camps only to end up in DP camps. These camps, of course, were not death factories, but they were a far cry from home or true freedom. Moreover, while the rescuers had at first shown great sympathy to the victims, they soon got used to them, and, being "camp-keepers" themselves, turned somewhat callous.

Those in the DP camps led a shadow existence while awaiting the opportunity to find a permanent home. The camps were overcrowded and life was spartan, but the DPs nevertheless established elaborate communal structures and organizations for themselves. They were deeply involved in religious, cultural, social, educational, and artistic activities. Many attended adult education courses to prepare for eventual Aliyah to the Promised Land. Political life in the camps also flourished—camp administrations were democratically elected, and the DPs organized numerous political parties often reflecting the political structure of Palestine.

One might expect that the survivors would have dedicated themselves to seeking revenge. On the contrary, however, they felt it was their mission to affirm life and Jewish rebirth. They saw it as their duty to both the living and the dead to help in the establishment of a Jewish state in Palestine—to the living, because without a state Jews would again be endangered, to the dead because only in Zion rebuilt could their martyrdom be memorialized. In the words of one Holocaust survivor, "The eyes of She'erit Hapletah are large and deep, for they have looked on eternity."[1]

Because the Surviving Remnant had been sensitized by their crushing experiences during the Holocaust, they saw themselves as a touchstone, or barometer, of humanity—a "chosen group" within the "chosen people." With this focal point of view, they were a catalyst which quickened and united world Jewry. Indirectly, they helped stimulate the birth of the State of Israel. Their tragedy stirred the formerly passive world to action and ultimately led the society of nations to recognize the need for a Jewish state.

---

# The Strange Case of Sarah E., A Prisoner-of-War

*Karl Frucht is the scarcely concealed "Sergeant Franck" of this story, which plainly falls into the "stranger than fiction" class. It tells one of his experiences as a member of an Army Prisoner-of-War Interrogation team in Europe during the last war . . .*

When the convoys arrived the first truck always carried the women prisoners. The prettiest invariably climbed down from the seat next to the driver. . . .

We seldom bothered with the girls. There was no time. We got all kinds: nurses and auxiliaries of different Wehrmacht branches, now and then an SS girl, and toward the end the CI (counter-intelligence) cases who had been arrested for security reasons, for being Party bosses or just for having married Party bosses. We never expected anything from women's interrogations. They were handled in routine fashion and evacuated as fast as possible.

And yet, our most incredible case of the campaign was a woman

---

[1]Samuel Gringauz, "Jewish Destiny and the DP's As I See It," *Commentary*, December 1947.

---

From *Commentary Magazine*, September 1947, by Karl Frucht.

prisoner shortly before VE Day. We might well have missed her except for Captain Wilkins.

Captain Wilkins was a woman herself, a Wac . . . She asked to be shown around the cage. She said she wanted to study social problems; she was supposed to deal with German women after the war. She knew a little German . . .

Sergeant Franck suggested a look at the girls' cage. A new transport had just arrived and the women were marched over in single file, on a narrow path between concertina barbed wire. Boards had been laid across the mud, but it usually happened that all had to step off the boardwalk to let a detail of stretcher-carriers pass, live PW's carrying dead PW's, blanketed bodies of victims of exposure, exhaustion, disease, suicide, or revenge. There usually was an elderly woman prisoner who would start crying, "He looks like my son—please, let me see him," and lift a corner of a blanket, only to drop it again with a scowl, "Isn't it terrible what's become of Germany?" . . .

A PW brought a box of food. The MP started throwing K-rations to the new ones . . . An SS girl dropped hers and it fell in the mud. She did not stoop to recover it, but stood staring ahead, seeing nothing, as if in a trance. The next girl nudged her and, when nothing happened, pointed her finger at her own forehead and then at her staring friend. Her meaning was clear. The other was out of her mind. That also happened frequently.

Captain Wilkins picked out one of the better dressed women and spoke to her as at a garden party. "My name is Captain Wilkins."

The prisoner seemed delighted: "It's a pleasure to meet you, to meet a lady here." Then she turned up her nose, "I'm Frau Uhl."

Franck, checking papers, noticed that Frau Uhl had omitted her rank . . . With the Nazis she had been the equal of an army colonel. With us she was an automatic arrest.

"Break it up, Uhl," Franck said. "Step over here and keep your trap shut. MP, keep an eye on her."

Captain Wilkins looked helpless. "What's wrong? She seemed to be a fine lady. Though one never knows these days . . ."

"Let me handle that, Captain ma'am," said the sergeant.

He looked again at the stunned SS girl who had dropped her rations and not bothered to pick them up. She and her friend made a strange couple: one slight, dark-haired, dog-tired; the other big, blonde, happy-go-lucky . . .

Their papers did not identify them as SS auxiliaries. They had been issued by the German Labor Front. But the blonde—Gertrude So-and-so, according to the brown document—proudly showed the blood-type tattoo under her left armpit and claimed that they both had served in

527

the same SS prisoner-guard company in charge of an "East-workers" battalion. The dark one nodded confirmation. But her certificate was differently colored, green, and the number had the prefix "A," standing for *Auslaender* and meaning "alien."

"*Ah ça,*" said the sergeant, "a French SS girl. What do you know." He read aloud to the captain, "Rose-Marie Establet from Montauban, Tarn et Garonne, France."

"From Brussels, from Belgium," the dark girl protested weakly.

"What's the difference? Nazis grow everywhere," Franck said. There were fascists from all over Europe in the SS . . . The Belgian Nazis had invented an interrogation method that our prisoner trusties sometimes wanted to apply: stand a man with his face to a wall and rub his nose until the bone shines through. SS-woman Establet was a Belgian? Franck would give her a Belgian . . .

Franck ordered him (a trusty) to get Jacky. Jacky's first name was Jacques-Bernard; he was a Belgian-born corporal . . . he hated Germans like poison. He would tell SS-woman Establet whether or not she was a Belgian.

The dark girl stood staring dumbly. Suddenly she swayed a little. Blonde Gertrude caught her, seated her on an empty K-ration box, kneeled down before her and untied her shoe to lift the tucked-in trouser. A dirty, blood-soaked bandage was wrapped around Rose-Marie Establet's leg. Gertrude tightened the bandage.

"She's wounded," the Wac captain said in a shocked voice.

Gertrude shrugged. "It was her own fault. No one told her to get in the line of fire."

"Whose fire?" Franck asked.

"Oh, when the boys shot those Russians and Jews."

"Where?" Franck asked quickly.

The blonde looked up and shrugged. "I don't know. We just came by. They weren't our Russians."

Franck asked the dark girl, "Where were you wounded?"

Rose-Marie did not answer. Gertrude grinned again, pointing at her forehead. "Shellshocked, you know."

"Poor kid," said Captain Wilkins.

Franck cleared his throat and frowned. After all, these were SS girls. He was about to launch upon an indoctrination lecture when Goetz returned—alone. Jacky, he reported, was out on pass.

"You're lucky," Franck told the girl. She did not seem to hear and he decided to question her himself. A demonstration of our technique might not be bad for Captain Wilkins, either. "Well, Establet," he said, trying to look tough, "why did you get into the line of fire when your boys shot those Russians and Jews?"

The dark girl looked at him. It was the first time she seemed to come

528

out of her apathy. Her eyes were large, hopeful, and terrified at the same time. She said, "I'm Jewish."

"You're—*what?*"

Franck was no interrogator. First, he was soft. Second, he could not control himself. That was why he had been assigned to office work. The point of our job was that the PW's should show their emotions to us, not that we should show ours to PW's.

"You," the sergeant sputtered, "you—an SS girl—you have the nerve to stand there and say you're Jewish?"

"I *am* Jewish," she said.

"That's what she tried to tell me, too," said Gertrude. "I told you she's not quite there."

"Shut up, you!"

Rose-Marie closed her eyes. She was shivering.

Captain Wilkins took over. "Why don't we go into a tent, Sergeant?" she asked. It seemed a good idea. They went into the next compound and entered one of the interrogation tents.

"Couldn't we get her some coffee?" Captain Wilkins asked. Franck went out and sent a trusty for some coffee. When he came back, the motherly Wac had the girl sitting on a chair and was soothing her. "Now," she said, "just calm down." She winked at Franck to keep quiet. "Now tell us your story."

The story took half an hour in the telling. It came out in gasps and sobs and broken, incoherent sentences in German and French.

Her name was Sarah, the girl said. She used to live in Brussels. Her father was a diamond-cutter there, a Jew.

She had been fifteen when the Boche came to Belgium. They had fled to France—her parents, her brother Sammy and she, and the family of her brother's friend. They had a car, but the car did not get them far. All roads were blocked by refugees. They were strafed by planes, too. They came to Compiègne, and then to Paris.

"When did you get to Paris?"

In the first days of June, she said. About a week ahead of the Boche. They had tried in vain to get a train to the South, to get a ride in a car, or to buy bicycles. In the end they had walked.

"Where did you leave the city?"

By the Porte d'Orléans; they had taken the subway to get there. Then they walked for days. They were bombed and strafed at Etampes, and again at Orléans.

"How did you cross the river at Orléans?

There was a bridge. It was blown up just after they crossed—not five minutes later.

"It was? How many days had you been walking from Paris?"

The girl tried to remember. She tried to count. "Four days," she said.

Franck said nothing. The Wac captain asked him in English, "Why do you keep trying to trap her?"

The sergeant did not say that it was his job. Instead he quoted in German, half to the captain and half to the SS woman Establet, from *Summary of Restrictions whose Violations endanger Security, as listed in SHAEF Ordinance No. 1:* "The following capital offense punishable by death: wilful deception of Allied personnel on duty . . ."

"But why should she lie?" asked the Wac captain. "Would it help her if she was Jewish?" . . .

If she was French or Belgian, she was probably headed for a treason trial by her compatriots. If she were Jewish—which she wasn't, of course . . . it might be taken as evidence that she had been forced to join.

Franck turned back to the girl, who sat staring at her feet again. "Go on. Where did you go from Orléans?"

They had gone south, she and her parents. Her brother had been killed at Orléans and they had lost her brother's friend and his family. A few times people let them ride on trucks or cars.

"Did you come through Blois?"

Yes, Blois and Tours.

"Then you must have come through Angoulême?"

Yes—that was where the soldiers had given them bread.

"French soldiers?"

No, not French—Czechoslovakian, Rose-Marie thought.

The sergeant chuckled. Captain Wilkins turned to him and whispered. "Do you really know all that?"

"Sure," he said, "I was there."

"Oh, were you really? What were you doing there?"

"Fighting."

"But we weren't at war then."

"I was."

The SS girl tried to follow them. She seemed to fear that they had found a hole in her story. She tried to be very precise: "We got to Bordeaux at night; there was a bombardment, and the soldiers we had met at Angoulême were getting on a ship."

"So we were," Franck told the captain. "We were embarking for England. That was my outfit." He left the Wac to shake her head in amazement and turned back to Rose-Marie. "Go on."

They had walked on to Agen and then to Montauban, to stand in line for hours at the Préfecture for a permit to stay, to stand outside the Hôtel de Ville whose walls were plastered with "want ads" seeking news of a husband or wife, a mother, father, sister, brother, lover or sweetheart, to scale wooden ladders, because the notices were posted all the way up to the second floor. They slept in the open among people from

Holland, Belgium, and France, among French and Polish and Czech soldiers and deserters and Senegalese and Moroccans. They found a small *auberge* (hotel) where they could stay without papers, until one day the police came for her parents and they did not come back.

Then Rose-Marie made the round of the Vichy internment camps ... When she arrived at the Gurs camp in the Pyrenées, one of the most desolate places in the world, she was detained as a suspect alien. After weeks of cold and hunger and despair she suddenly was released and a man she did not know handed her a railroad ticket and a slip carrying the name of some people she did not know and an address in Montauban. Then he wished her *bon voyage*. Rose-Marie did not understand a word. At the Montauban address, the next day, she asked an old lady for Monsieur and Madame Establet. This was the name on the paper. The lady led her through a courtyard to the rear of the building and up a spiral staircase to the top floor. She knocked—and her mother opened the door.

Then she learned how her parents had managed to bribe the guards on the convoy that was to have taken them to Gurs. They hid on farms until a reliable source gave them the address of an employee of the Montauban Préfecture who issued false identity papers to refugees, a certain Mr. Lefevre.

For what was left of their money, Mr. Lefevre also found out what had happened to the girl, arranged for her rescue, and transformed her into Rose-Marie Establet, a French girl, a defense worker, Catholic, eighteen years old. It was two years more than her real age; she certainly had grown up. Her parents no longer dared to go out on the street—it seemed they could only talk Yiddish—so it fell to Rose-Marie to do the shopping, and when the money ran out to do the working.

She became a salesgirl. Her employer fired all his Jewish employees; but Rose-Marie could stay. She had to stop seeing the few refugees left of the many she had known. She read the posters when all foreign Jews from 18 to 55 years of age were organized into "work battalions" and sent to Germany. She heard of the thousands handed over by the Vichy government, from camps and from the street, of the convoys that no longer passed the "collecting point" at Drancy but went directly to Eastern Europe. She heard of the great Gestapo hunt at Nice that alone netted some 5,000 victims. She also heard of Frenchmen's efforts to help, of the widespread "Aryanization" of Jewish children whose parents had been deported, of secret convoys said to have taken such children to safety—but she did not know if that was true ...

In February 1943 a Vichy law had imposed a labor draft on all men from 18 to 60 and all women from 18 to 45. It did not affect the girl's parents but it affected her, Rose-Marie Establet, a Catholic and now twenty, according to her papers. Failure to register meant loss of food and clothing rations. She registered. She was not called up for a while, though—not until she had heard of one girl from Montauban who hanged herself in a German pig-sty after one beating too many by the woman she was working for. Another girl had her face marred by a blow; from the hospital she only wrote about an accident. Rose-Marie, with papers identifying her as a defense worker, could at least expect a job in industry. She thought it would mean better treatment.

The morning when she and fifty others were herded together on the Place Nationale . . . her mother, for the first time in years, had left the house. In the gray dawn the girl could see the tears on her mother's face and her father leaning out of the window of their top-floor hideout with his white beard flowing in the wind. When they ordered the fifty women to get on the truck and Rose-Marie tore herself away from her mother, she suddenly heard a sound not uttered aloud in years: right on the Place Nationale, amid Vichy police and in front of the German officer supervising the loading, her mother cried out as only those can cry who have been persecuted for centuries: "Aiaiai, Sarale, aiaiai . . ." And looking down from the truck, Sarah—or rather, Rose-Marie Establet—saw her mother crumple at the German's feet before the truck pulled out.

The girl paused a moment. Franck felt a hand on his arm; the gesture contravened military regulations, but at this moment the woman beside him was not an officer in the US Armed Forces. She was a social worker whose heart had been touched by a case the like of which was unknown in Minnesota. "You still think she's lying?" she asked. "You still think she could be lying?"

The sergeant said nothing. He wanted to say that the girl had only to hide the fact, for instance, that she had worked for the German military government in Montauban; there she would have learned all that and more. He wanted to say that only yesterday we had a kid who ate two pages of his pay book, and would have fooled us into taking him for just a Hitler youth employed by the Wehrmacht and entitled to immediate release if PW's had not picked him out as a non-com who shot two men of his platoon when they tried to surrender. We had cases like that every day. Why should the SS girl be different? But Franck said nothing.

The captain seized the girl's hand. It was small but strong, with dirty, bitten fingernails and scars and bloodstains; the captain dropped it again. "Go on," she said.

SS-woman Establet continued. She told a story we had heard a thousand times, from French and Belgian and Dutch and Polish DP's. The stories differed only in degree, and those of the French were not the worst. They all told of riding in cattle cars, without food, of stopping to sleep in barracks, without blankets, of traveling for three days and nights through the bomb-blasted Reich and arriving in

Leipzig or some other city to see a factory near the track still burning, of being unloaded, hardly able to stand, and broken up into smaller groups and marched off as from a slave market." . . . Rose-Marie was in the last group.

She told of getting her residence permit from the police—granted for an indefinite period and accordingly stamped for ten marks, and her work book for five marks. She told of the work, done in two 12-hour shifts under the eyes of about eight Gestapo men and many stool pigeons. She told of having been suspected of sabotage, and having been doubly terrified because of the secret of her true identity. She had seen Russians and Poles among the foreign workers, but no Jews. She never asked what had become of the Jews who had lived here, or elsewhere. She lived in terror, and terror made her work so well that she was officially appointed liaison between the German Labor Front, and her compatriots.

"You mean, a spy," the sergeant corrected her, "a Gestapo informer."

"Yes," the girl said.

"And you did that work, too?"

"Yes," the girl said.

From that day on the others had despised her. When she wanted to share her larger rations they refused, though they were nearly starving. They loathed Rose-Marie Establet more than they loathed the Germans. But the head of the Werkschutz, the Nazi factory protection setup, a bulky SA-man from Dortmund, promised her a furlough home after three reports on her less efficient co-workers. After her third report he beamingly appraised her of something much more honorable than a home leave. She was judged one of the few foreign girls worthy of joining the ranks of the SS. She had only to sign her application to leave for a training camp; it was most fortunate, he said, that he had just been asked to recommend candidates for SS auxiliaries. She really was too able to risk having her damaged by some jealous foreign workers.

Rose-Marie signed. The training camp was a slave-labor camp in Silesia. It was there she met Gertrude. Gertrude was kind, the first person who had been kind to her since Montauban. It was the last cruel winter and at night they lay together under one blanket, and Gertrude somehow managed to prevent the SS-men at the camp from "bothering" Rose-Marie. In the spring, when the Russians overran Silesia, the camp was evacuated. That is to say, the SS guard was evacuated. The workers, Russians and Poles and Jews, were shot. Rose-Marie looked on as the guards mowed them down with machine guns.

That night she told Gertrude that she was Jewish. But Gertrude would not believe her. Their truck convoy, headed for Leipzig, raced the Russians up through Silesia. On the way they passed another labor camp with trucks outside ready to move and the prisoners lined up in a ditch ready to be killed. Their convoy stopped and the SS-men got off to join in the fun. The girls got off too, to watch, and Rose-Marie ran toward the prisoners and was shot in the leg. Gertrude pulled her back and she was lifted into the truck. She did not really know what happened later, until she sat with Gertrude and the other women in our truck and came to our cage.

The story ended abruptly somewhere in the middle. It was finished, though—complete. There was a long pause. SS-woman Establet sat with half-closed eyes as if exhausted by this recital of her own disintegration. Captain Wilkins looked down at her with something like disappointment. Gertrude, the big, happy-go-lucky blonde, stood in a corner watching her friend with an oddly twisted smile. Sergeant Franck reviewed the incredible tale in his mind, searching for a hole in it. He found none. The web was complete. The girl was lying or she was telling the truth; it was an interrogator's job to find out which, but she had not obliged him by making the job easier.

"Well," he finally said in a voice full of sarcasm. "So now you'd like to be Jewish again. Only you aren't."

"It doesn't really matter much, does it?" the Wac broke in, a little sadly.

Franck did not get her meaning. Somehow, for him, there seemed to be more at stake than just the truth or falsehood of a PW statement. He said, "Who d'you think we are, Establet? Think you can fool us that easily?"

The girl looked at him fully. "I know why you won't believe me. You're Jewish, too. You don't want me to be. You're scared of it. Oh, they were right about the Jews—they were right!" she burst out. Then she turned to the motherly woman, "Maybe the lady will believe me."

Franck thought he saw the ghost of a smile on the captain's face. It made him furious. He walked over to the girl, very slowly, coming closer and closer: "So you say you're Jewish, do you? You think you're a smart girl. Well, you won't go through with it, I promise you—not you from the SS. You'll take everything back, understand? Everything."

A giggle came from Gertrude's corner. "Why do you bother with her? She's crazy."

"Shut up," said the sergeant. And to the dark girl, "So you still say you're—"

"I *am* Jewish," she interrupted him, wildly. "I was born in Brussels— my name is Sarah—I am Jewish—*verstehste*, Yiddish—*je suis juive—a yidene—ich, Sarah, bin eine Juedin!*" Then she collapsed on the table.

The grin on Gertrude's dirty face was frozen. She looked at Franck, at the Wac captain, at her friend. Then she shrugged, casually, "I told you she's crazy," and came and stroked the thin shaking shoulders until the whining stopped.

Suddenly Rose-Marie got up from the table. Her voice was louder and stronger than the sergeant's. "My name is Sarah. I am Jewish."

She did not collapse again. Gertrude's smile faded for the first time. Before Franck could say more, the Wac captain stepped in and asked the girl to sit down again. Then she opened the tent door and called out for another cup of coffee.

Rose-Marie's voice had attracted quite an audience. Looking through the window holes into the tent, despite a shower . . . were MP's, trusties, PW's waiting their turn to be interrogated, interrogators, members of the CIC team. It was very quiet. The constant murmur of the cage was no longer noticed.

"Why you *sagen* you are *juedisch?*" the Wac captain resumed the interrogation. "It won't make a difference."

Franck repeated, "You are an SS auxiliary like any other, Jewish or not. You'll be held responsible for every crime committed by your unit."

"I know," she nodded. "I'll take my punishment like Gertrude." But Gertrude did not smile again.

The sergeant still wanted to pin the girl down on the motive for her story. True or not, he had to crack her on that. "Why do you want to convince us if it won't make any difference to you?"

She clenched her teeth and said nothing.

He was stumped for questions, and so he asked her again: "How can you prove you're Jewish? We can't look into your heart."

And the girl all but tore off her blouse, hammering small white breasts with her dirty fists: "Here I'm Jewish, and I can't help it if you can't see it. Here—here—"

Captain Wilkins' eyes begged the sergeant to drop that line of questioning. The captain had thrown a blanket around the girl's shoulders.

In the chow line Franck saw the Belgian-born CIC interpreter he had sent Goetz to get. Jacky had just returned from a three-day pass to Brussels where he had searched vainly for survivors of his family; Jacky was Jewish. The sergeant confided in Jacky. The chow line was surprised when the Belgian gave up his place just outside the mess hall . . . and followed Franck to the cage . . .

The command-post tent was pitch-dark filled with whimpers and snores. "Rose-Marie Establet!" the sergeant shouted.

"Present," came the answer in a timid voice, close by.

No candle was lighted, no flashlight turned on. Jacky started his

535

interrogation in French; Rose-Marie responded without hesitation or difficulty.

"Where would you find the Great Synagogue in Brussels?"

She sounded overjoyed. *"Mais oui, dans la rue aux Laines, près de la Porte de Namur."*

"Check." Jacky shot another question. "Name me a few suburbs of Brussels."

The girl took a long breath and then started off without pause: "Schaerbeck, St. Josse-ten-Noode, Etterbeck, Ixelles, St. Gilles, Andetkecht, Molenbeck, Kockelberg . . ."

"Enough, stop."

He checked on a few more things, on ritual customs at Jewish holidays, on Jewish history, and soon they were not speaking French any more, nor German either, but Yiddish.

When Jacky ran out of questions, he searched in the darkness with his flashlight. And then the incredible happened. When the beam fell on the girl's face, after hardly enough time for recognition, Jacky gasped in surprise: *"Sarahleben, was machste da*—Sarah—you?!"

Franck lighted the candle, and it shone on her weeping face. Jacky took the girl's head firmly in his hands, to reassure himself, and now she knew him, too.

"Jacques-Bernard."

"Where is your brother, Sarah? Tell me about Sammy . . ."

"Sammy was killed on the road, by planes, in summer '40. Sammy is dead. But you'll get me news from *mamele* and *tateleben,* won't you?"

*"Mais oui,* Sarah. Sure. Sure. Now go to sleep. Come, we'll put you up in the hospital tent, on a litter, with a lot of blankets, and we'll bring you chocolate. Don't cry."

"I'm not crying," the girl sobbed. "I'm happy. Now I'm Jewish again . . ."

---

# Desperate Searchings

*Actress Helen Waren, who went overseas with a USO troupe to entertain the American armed forces, was among the first to enter Germany after VE Day. She chose to remain to help in the "illegal" immigration to Palestine . . .*

I awoke my second morning in Nuremberg and pre-

From *The Buried Are Screaming* by Helen Waren.

pared to go out. It had rained the night before and this morning a terrible odor of decay hung about the city. It was very hot and the heat was stirring the dead lying beneath the fallen stone in the streets. The smell of death will stay in Nuremberg for a long time to come and as the wreckage is carted away, more and more will the streets be permeated with the terrible scent of their crimes and self-inflicted death. As I passed the front desk of the hotel, the clerk said, "This message was left for you early this morning."

I took the message and read, "I shall be waiting around the corner to the right whenever you come out. Isaac Papirovitch." I hurried out and at the appointed place, there, sure enough, he stood—small and squat . . .

An intense feeling of irritation passed over me as I caught sight of him. "What are you still doing here!" was my greeting. He looked most uncomfortable, his eyes pleading for understanding while little beads of perspiration gathered around the thin black handles of his glasses which were attached to the frames with dirty bits of adhesive plaster.

"I could not go with the rest though I hope to meet them later."

I was unable to subdue my exasperation as I said, "Three days ago you told me in order to live you must get out of Germany—your one hope is to get to the Palestinian troops in Italy. You insisted that the eight of you must positively leave together; you could not bear to be separated, you were like brothers together. I worked very hard at great risk to myself to make this possible. Illegal permits, transportation, convoy dates to Italy, everything arranged finally—and now you let your comrades leave without you! Were you lying to me? Is it that you are not so desperate as you said? Have I been exhausting myself for a whim?"

Even as I said these things to him I knew I was wrong, but overtired from sleeplessness . . . I had not been able to stop my tirade. He stood there dumbly like a whipped animal and without raising his eyes to mine he finally said, "When the Nazis took my wife from me they told me that she was to be killed, but although it is many years I cannot believe that she is dead. I live with the hope that somewhere sometime I will find her again. This morning just before my comrades and myself were to leave we met a Jew from W———. He described a woman to me who truly appears to be my wife. How could I leave without going first to see? I have the permit you got for me and I shall not trouble you for transportation. With my permit I shall manage to reach Italy and then perhaps Palestine. I did wish very much, however, to know where you will be situated when I come back. I will feel easier if I know where I can find you in case of an emergency." . . .

I marveled at the stoutness of that Jewish heart, after all he had been through, which made him prepare for this walk as though it were just a matter of a few city blocks.

537

"How long do you believe it will take you to go there and back?"

"Perhaps five or six days."

"In that case I will still be right here in the same billet when you return."

An obvious wave of relief crossed his face as he grasped my hand tightly. "I shall see you then when I come back." His eyes were dancing as I bade him Godspeed and wished him success on his mission.

On the sixth day after he started there was a message waiting for me. Instead of finding him in the usual place I found him boldly waiting for me right by the entrance as I stepped outside . . . I saw that he was very tired but at the same time brimming with excitement and nervous tension.

"Did you find her? Was it she?"

"No," he confessed, "it is not my wife. But I found another woman. And—please you must not be angry—I brought *her* with me."

"You brought her here?"

"Yes, she is waiting around the other corner. She is so eager to see you but before she meets you I want to tell you how it was, so that you will understand her better."

He went on before I could say a word. "When I came I went to the neighborhood that had been described to me and I immediately pinned on my little Shield of David, that many of us have made for ourselves, in order to attract Jews to me. I walked up and down pushing out my badge as conspicuously as possible and it was as if from beneath the piles of rubble and garbage littering the destroyed streets that Jews began to appear. Each one greeted me like a long lost brother but none knew of the woman that I sought. After about three hours I began to get discouraged, when I met a man who told me that this woman for whom I was looking had indeed been in that neighborhood but that she had gone. 'Where?' No, he did not know where but perhaps I might find her at the camp not far from there, if she had been admitted by the authorities.

"I followed his directions to the camp and posted myself at the gate with my shield pinned on as before. When I received no response there I began to walk the length of the fence slowly so that the inmates who were taking some air on the inside might see me, and if there were Jews among them surely they would make some sign and perhaps know something of my wife. As I strolled around the enclosure I passed a young woman who stared hard at me and then turned pale as she caught sight of my pin. For a few seconds she seemed to be struggling to maintain command of herself and then she motioned me to a section of the fence which was more or less deserted.

"As we met there she whispered, 'Are you a Jew?'

"'Yes,' I said. She put her hand over mine as tears fell from her eyes.

"'I cannot believe it, I cannot believe it . . . All these months I have been hiding here in the camp among these non-Jews and I believed myself to be the only surviving Jew in Europe. When I saw your little pin I thought at first it might be some kind of cruel joke to catch me . . . But then I could not bear to let you pass without knowing. All these years I have passed myself off as a non-Jew, a Pole. And all these years I have watched the parade of my people to extermination. I have seen their beings soar to the heavens in clouds of black smoke rolling from the stoves and seen their bodies delivered in great mountains of ashes back to the earth.' She broke down weeping convulsively. How could I do else but comfort her by telling her that I was going to Palestine and that if she could manage to steal out of the camp I would be more than happy, honored indeed, if she would come with me?"

Naturally moved by this tale, and more than a little gratified by the demonstration of his renewed feeling of self-sufficiency and responsibility, nevertheless I had some doubts which I voiced.

"How can you be sure that she is not a fraud, that she is not some Nazi now attempting to save her life by getting out of the country without being brought to justice by posing as a Jew? So many are doing this very thing."

"Oh, she speaks Yiddish. We have spoken together even a little Hebrew. It is not very nice to tell you but she was living for some time in a sort of a loose fashion with a Polish storm trooper. But that is really how her life was spared and why she was saved from sterilization, the fate of all the other Jewish women. It is hard to fool a Jew. A Jew knows a Jew. My heart tells me she is Jewish."

A wily smile crossed his face. "What certificate do you have, my dearest friend, that I am not such a fraud?"

What certificate indeed? What guarantee does the heart give? Somehow one knows one's brothers! I took little Papirovitch's arm and together we walked toward the usual corner. "And so you want me to conjure up another permit? Of course I shall. In any case I shall try my best, and if I fail we will find another way to get you both to Italy."

As we rounded the corner a fair-headed woman, looking still quite healthy, came quickly toward us with her hand outstretched. But I did not take it immediately, so great was my surprise. For she was not alone! With her were four men of varying ages and dressed in the usual oddly-assorted bits and pieces of the displaced person. All four were wearing little home-made Shields of David.

I looked at Papirovitch questioningly. His head cast down as if expecting to be chastised, he looked at me from under his glasses and then, breathing a great sigh, he explained, "I neglected to tell you— please, you must not be angry with me—I brought some friends also that I made there. I told them that I was on my way to Palestine. They were all very desirous of going to Palestine also so I promised to take them with me—if you will get them permits, that is . . ."

I think of little Isaac Papirovitch very often. And I pray that he and his friends arrived at their destination with the help of the permits which I did manage to get for them. And I dream that I will meet him in Palestine one day, a very important official in a very important position with the department of mass immigration.

# Berl, the Half-Man

*On p. 390 we read about the role of Jewish chaplains. In the following narrative another episode is related . . .*

My chapel office was rather quiet. It was a cold, crisp day and problems don't seem to flourish on crisp winter days. Suddenly my phone rang. It was the Army psychiatrist at the hospital. "Chaplain, I found another Jew for you. He's not a soldier. In fact, we don't know what he is, but we know he's just half-a-man."

At such times a telephone conversation doesn't clarify, it only frustrates. "Don't explain, I'll be right over," I replied. Then I rushed over to the hospital and met Berl for the first time.

He was locked behind bars in one of the hospital rooms. He paced back and forth in the small room like a mad and utterly terrified dog, his face a mask of distrust and fear. He was tall and, after he had calmed down, rather handsome.

"I speak English," Berl finally said. "I was raised in the Bronx."

"Then you're an American?" I asked.

"No, I was born on the way to America and lived there until I was 12. Then my parents took me to Poland to visit my grandparents. We never got the chance to return to the States. We were caught by the Nazi tide of death that swallowed the Jews of Poland."

"Why didn't you migrate to Israel after the War?" I inquired.

"I couldn't," Berl replied. "I'm a Russian spy."

Even in this serious situation, I couldn't suppress a half smile.

"This is no place for a Russian spy," I said . . .

Berl grabbed my hand and whispered harshly: "No, no, I escaped here. They want to kill me; they want to poison me. I don't want to spy for them, I hate them, but if I stop, they'll kill me."

I mopped my brow. It had suddenly become very warm on this cold winter day . . .

From *Rabbis in Uniform*, edited by Louis Barish. Story by Pincus J. Goodblatt.

I visited the psychiatrist who had called me and who had examined Berl. His first words to me were: "He's mad, you know, or close to it. I checked his story with Counter Intelligence to see if he is a spy, and they know nothing about him. They doubt his entire statement but I do believe that he did live in America and that he is Jewish."

"But why," I asked, "did you call him half-a-man when you phoned me?"

"Didn't he tell you?"

"Tell me what?" I was puzzled.

The psychiatrist lowered his voice and continued.

"He was the subject of a sex experiment in a Nazi concentration camp. He was totally castrated. He has no sex organs whatsoever. Instead of nipples, which they also cut off, he has two ugly jagged slashes across his chest."

I sat there in bitter silence, too shocked even to curse them for what they had done to this miserable distorted shadow of a man. It was then that I began to grieve for Berl. I didn't care who he was or what he had done. I had to help him.

"What can I do to help him?"

"Nothing much," sighed the doctor. "We are not allowed to treat non-Americans, and besides, he has no papers. We'll probably send him away in a day or two."

"Please," I pleaded. "Keep him here a few days longer so I can help him, so I can make arrangements for him before he leaves the hospital."

He promised to keep Berl as long as possible, perhaps a week or so, but no longer than that, he just couldn't. I had one week to untangle the tormented, twisted mind of half-a-man; one week to make whole that which the devil's disciples had torn asunder.

The very next day I drove to Munich, to the office of the Joint Distribution Committee. Before even sitting down I blurted out, "I have come here to seek aid for a DP castrated by the Nazis, a certain Berl . . ." I wasn't permitted to finish.

"Berl Bessing, he's turned up again!"

The official snatched the name out of my mouth. He literally leaped out of his chair to take Berl's case history from the files. It was much fingered. Berl was well known to the JDC. The official explained that without papers, without funds, Berl kept smuggling himself across the borders, weaving back and forth, to appear, disappear and reappear again and again in different places in Western Europe. As his quiet voice droned on, presenting the case history of this human debris floating aimlessly to and fro, I imagined a lost and tormented soul stumbling through Hell, without hope and without end.

"Stop!" I shouted. "Enough! I'm not interested in sucking each tragic fact to the last drop of its bitter gall. How can we help him? He'll be released in a week from the U.S. Army hospital. Can't we arrange something for him before he leaves?"

"Help him?" The official laughed bitterly. "We have tried again and again, and failed. Only he can help himself. Berl has 85,000 marks coming to him in restitution, but we can't get him to sign the necessary papers."

"Give me the papers," I urged. "Perhaps I can get him to sign."

"I wish you all the luck, but don't be too upset if you fail."

I could sense the resigned sympathy he felt for me. I could see he was thinking: "He'll learn. He's new at this but he'll learn."

The next day Berl promised me he would sign the papers I gave him, but he never did, though I'd urge him day after day.

Through certain connections, I managed to get Berl into Valka Lager, a camp for refugees from behind the Iron Curtain. He soon became the favorite of the Jewish inmates there. Amongst his own, and when he wasn't too upset, Berl possessed a child-like charm and displayed an intense desire to help others. He'd come to the chapel office every day. He'd sweep up, help my assistant and try to be useful in every way. I gave him warm clothes, food, some money for expenses. He seemed somewhat better but still he refused to sign the required papers for the 85,000 marks. "That's more than $20,000," I told him. "With it, you can do anything you want. You'll be a king, instead of a poor refugee."

Berl's eyes opened wide. His face became taut and white. "No, I don't want their filthy money. I don't want anything from them. I'll kill them. I killed a Nazi last year in Belgium. That's why they put me in that Belgian insane asylum. If you don't believe me, here are my discharge papers."

His words were flying far too quickly for me to grasp them. "What did you say?" Was this another of Berl's lies? He had insisted he was a Russian spy when I first met him, but neither the American, the French, nor the British Counter Intelligence Corps knew anything about him. I could not fathom why he should falsely accuse himself of so gross a crime. Even the psychiatrist couldn't dig beneath the many layers of sickness that hid the once strong and healthy personality who had been Berl Bessing. Was he simply trying to shock me as does an insecure and frightened little child?

"Here," he shouted, and he waved his hands in nervous agitation as if he sought to drive away old fears and some twinges of terror that still lurked in his twisted mind. "Look, here are my discharge papers!" Even with my meager knowledge of French, I could see that this time Berl had uttered the truth. He had killed an ex-Nazi guard in Belgium and had spent the previous year in an insane asylum.

"You see, I fooled them. I pretended I was crazy to escape punishment. I fooled them good!"

542

I felt I was being sucked into a whirlpool of madness . . . Conflicting feelings of pity and fear wrestled within me as I silently stared at this emotional monstrosity. Neither one of us spoke a word until Berl heaved himself at the door, tore it open and, without a word, slammed it shut behind him . . .

I found I missed Berl. He had taken root in my heart. I sought him in Valka Lager, but he hadn't returned there. The other Jews there hadn't seen him. No, they didn't worry about him . . . I had hoped perhaps he would come on Friday night to help prepare the chapel for the *Oneg Shabbat,* but again I was disappointed. Yet it seems that he had missed the friendly warmth of the Chapel group, for I later discovered that he had come during services, peeped into the Chapel once or twice and then, as if he must always stand on the border of human friendship but never enter, he shuffled sadly away—an eternal stranger in the land of men.

This was not the end of our relationship. That night, about 2 A.M., I was awakened by the persistent ringing of my phone. It was Berl, weeping incoherently and speaking in a torrential stream, trying to cram all his grief into the telephone mouthpiece.

"Calm down, Berl," I begged of him. "I'm sorry if I hurt you. Where are you?"

"I'm drunk," he cried. "I'm drunk, because only with wine can I wash away the dirt that covers my soul."

"Berl," I continued to plead as a father pleads with a child, "we'll get you into Israel. You'll take root there. You'll live a normal life."

"No," he wept again. "You know that can never be. You know that because I was judged insane and left the asylum against the advice of the doctors, Israel won't let me in unless I enter an asylum and someone pays for my upkeep."

I knew what he said was true, that even Israel could no longer absorb the sick unless someone supported them. Emigration to America was out of the question. Berl was a Polish citizen. If he were a normal person, I might find some rich American to sponsor him . . . But in his present mental state this was impossible. Berl would be just another file marked "Rejected." I begged him to come and see me the next day and he promised he would. The next morning I spent several hours discussing him with the Army psychiatrist.

"Chaplain," he sadly shook his head, "it's hopeless. He'll never find himself. He'll drive himself through life like a lost soul caught in the limbo of his own personal hell. In fact, because of what the Nazis did to him . . . I am sure he will eventually kill himself. Unless they have roots somewhere, they always do."

The psychiatrist's words seared my heart. When Berl finally showed up late that night, I begged him to let me help him. Berl, however, had a new plan.

543

"I can't stay, I am going to Hamburg. I've heard that the city officials there need workers and will give anyone working papers, which I can't get here."

I pleaded with him that the laws were the same throughout Germany. "Don't run, Berl, you're only fleeing from yourself. We will find some answer, some way of helping you."

But Berl, with the insight of the half-mad, knew that there was really nothing I could do to help him. Finally, I gave him some warm clothes, an old army coat, 25 marks, and offered him God's blessing. He seemed to shrink as he walked into the endless night.

Only once more did I hear from Berl. It was an official letter from the Jewish community of Hamburg informing me that Berl was in a German prison for some minor offense and had asked them to obtain from me the 2,000 marks he had left with me. I informed them that Berl had never left any money with me; in fact I had given him some small sums from my own pocket. I enclosed 20 marks for Berl and I assured them that no matter what he did, he had suffered and he was no longer responsible for his actions.

Yes, that was my last official news about Berl. But many times in the summer stillness of the night, Berl reappears from the shadowy mists. He gazes at me and his eyes are filled with hopeless misery. After a few moments, he soundlessly shrinks into the silent night of despair, as he did when I last saw him. Then, once more and forever, I grieve for Berl.

# Kol Nidre at a Children's Home

*Survivor Nathan Shapell lived through his teenage years in the hell of Auschwitz. After liberation he, together with his only surviving sister and a group of DP's, succeeded in escaping from the oppressive Russian zone into the American. There he suffered a period of misery until he finally found some American officers who took the group under their care and provided asylum and security. Special concern was shown for the surviving Jewish orphan children who were rounded up by the Shappel group. The children, ages 8–11, were housed in a spacious German castle. Tne United Nations Relief and Rehabilitation Administration (UNRRA) provided their physical needs; the Jewish Welfare Board Chaplains Corps saw to their religious training. The few German Jewish Survivors presented a Sefer Torah and religious objects and the emissaries of the*

# The She'erit Hapletah

*Jewish Agency set up a Hebrew educational program designed along the kibbutz way of life. The children were surrounded with great loving care and every effort was made to blot out their bitter memories.*

*Yom Kippur was approaching. After much soul searching, Mr. and Mrs. Shappel and the committee-in-charge decided to arrange for the children to have their own religious service . . .*

With the approach of the High Holy Days, the JDC shipped in the special food for our widespread communities in the towns, the jail, the kibbutzim, and the Children's Home. With the traditional foods were included Yahrzeit (memorial) candles so meaningful and significant to all of us.

Each year at the High Holy Days in the past we had traditionally lit a memorial candle for each of our dead. For most of us this would be the first time since 1939, seven years, that we had been able to practice our religious rituals openly in our own place of worship and could mourn all those we had lost.

Kol Nidre services were planned for the synagogue in the community center, but I did not know what to do about the Children's Home. I went to talk to the leaders there. "What do you think we ought to do about the High Holy Days. Shall we hold services on Kol Nidre for the children or will it upset them?" I asked. They had already discussed the situation and arrived at a decision. They felt that since the children already knew about the coming Holy Day and were, in fact, looking forward to it, especially the older children who remembered, there was no choice but to go ahead. We could only hope that despite the harrowing effect it would undoubtedly have on the children, it might also prove to be a valuable emotional release. We had deliberately tried to suppress their thoughts of the past until now. We could not expect to do so forever.

I agreed with them, never dreaming the full effect it would finally have. In the late afternoon before Yom Kippur, I was driven alone to Schloss Schauenstein, promising Lilly and our family that I would meet them later at the synagogue for services. At the castle, the children were gathered in one enormous hall, around a gigantic table. At sundown, services began, and I stood to one side, watching, not fully aware for several minutes of what I and the other adults were about to witness. Each child held a Yahrzeit candle, and when the time came each boy and girl lit his or her candle and placed it on the table as each walked by. In a few brief moments hundreds of flickering lights blazed out at me and the children began to cry, softly at first and then in tearing, uncontrollable sobs. The sight of the candles and their faces blinded my eyes, and the sound of their weeping roared in my ears. I felt as if I

---

From *Witness to the Truth* by Nathan Shapell.

had been struck a staggering blow. The sight made by those hundreds of candles and the children who had lit them for their dead parents and families engulfed me. The suffering they had known and everything I had lived through myself lived again in that moment. Each of those lights burned for a mother or father lost forever, to a child doomed to grow up never knowing the love of its parents, to a child who could never completely erase the scars on its body or soul of a childhood too horrible to imagine. My own tears ran scalding down my face, and I could not bear it another moment. I stumbled out of the room and staggered to the door.

# Surveys of American DP Camps

*Ira Hirschmann went to inspect the DP Camps on behalf of UNRRA. He not only visited but also met with the Military, State Department officials, and field workers. Below is a report of three installations . . .*

Kloster Indersdorf, the Displaced Persons Children's Center in the suburbs of Munich, is ten miles from Dachau . . . Ancient, swept by drafts and wind, it is precisely the kind of building one would not choose for children. . . . But it was the only place available when the war ended and UNRRA took it over as the first center for "unattached children". . . . Here, with the help of some Catholic nuns, lived some 300 children, the majority of them Jewish, ranging from infancy to eighteen years. They were to be rehabilitated physically and spiritually and prepared for repatriation or resettlement.

At Indersdorf I was received by Mrs. Jean Henshaw of Canada, its Director. In the course of my tour through the huge monastery, walking down a long corridor I stopped before a closed door and upon impulse turned the knob and walked in, closing the door quietly behind me.

I had no idea what I was getting into. In a small, bare and darkened room I heard weak sobs and then made out a woman seated in a chair, enfolding a moaning child in her arms. I apologized, tiptoed over and

From *The Embers Still Burn* by Ira Hirschmann.

546

looked down at a three-month-old baby whose breathing was labored and whose body was covered with salve and bandages. Death was hovering near. This French Welfare Officer whose name was Miss Yvonne Menny, held the infant close, as if refusing to give it up.

She had been sitting up all night with the child and was winning her fight. She whispered to me that it was suffering from an illness of undernourishment which creates giant lesions on the little bodies and gradually sucks out their strength. . . .

Later, when I interviewed Menny, as everyone affectionately called her, she answered my questions in broken English, but with straightforward dignity. When I commended her for her devotion, she blushed and said modestly that she was only doing her job. Her quiet mien changed, however, when she told me that what was really responsible for saving the child's life was the medicine she had stolen from a German pharmacy.

"It is a shameful thing," she said. "These children need medicine desperately. I cannot go on stealing medicines in the village."

"Why do you have to steal?" I asked, although by now I knew the answer. "Has not Headquarters provided what was needed?"

She shook her head. "Neither medical supplies nor medical men," she replied. "We have not had a doctor here in twenty-four days. In that time I have had five children ill with diphtheria. Two of them died. . . ." I asked her to take me to the infirmary, and there I checked the medical supplies. They were low in dressings, in sulfa, in vaseline, in alcohol, in penicillin—in fact, in everything needed for children. As I was looking through the cupboards, one of the nurses approached me. "We need a baby scale so badly," she said apologetically. "Until now we bought such things from the German doctors in the village, but we no longer have money for it."

Five minutes later I was in Mrs. Henshaw's office. Yes, they were low in supplies. Yes, she had requisitioned them from Headquarters, but Headquarters had ignored her requests.

I immediately directed . . . my aide for this tour to the job of tracing the requisitions. He reported to me in a few days that the requisitions had not been sent in . . .

A Jewish boy of sixteen asked my help in obtaining a job in the camp kitchen. Half a dozen Jewish youths, who were idle and had nothing to occupy their hands, had asked Mrs. Henshaw for such work but had been turned down because Germans from near-by Dachau were employed in the kitchen.

One of our basic regulations stipulated that no German could be employed in an UNRRA installation unless there were no DP's who could do the work.

"Why does she prefer Germans?" I asked.

The youth shrugged his shoulders. "Maybe because they have more experience, or because they are not Jews," he replied. "But it is not such a skilled work, working in a kitchen. We could learn it in a day."

I said I would look into it when the time came.[1]

Funk Caserne is a name to remember.

The first thing you see when you walk into Funk Caserne, once a Luftwaffe base, is a three-story cement garage, a block square. The Germans had found it unfit for human habitation and used it to store coal and lumber.

Now the Germans had left, but what they had found unfit for human beings was offered as shelter to Jewish Displaced Persons because the United States Army did not arrange for adequate space in other areas.

I came to Funk Caserne in a cold, slanting rain, to find 1,800 men and women herded together like cattle in an abattoir; for these 1,800 there were three toilets. These men and women lived, ate, and slept in double-decker beds and cots jammed so closely together that there was no place to put their few clothes and belongings.

Although my first impulse was to run from such a revolting scene, I forced myself to circulate through the narrow spaces between cots and to try to understand how people could remain alive and human when forced by civilization into a subhuman state. As far as the eye could reach stretched this sea of men and women sitting on cots, staring silently at me. It was late afternoon. The rain and wind blew in fitfully through the glassless windows; the odor of heavy, sweat-drenched clothes, of unwashed bodies, of the dankness of cement floors and walls, and above it all the stench of urine and human excrement, was overpowering. The second floor was like the first, and the third like the second. Some of those wretched souls clutched at me as I passed, seeing that I was a stranger; perhaps someone who might help. . . .

At Funk Caserne, I blew up. I was no longer the Inspector General, but an American who felt himself an accessory to this crime of abandoning and condemning human beings to a state of degradation and despair. But I feared I was becoming so emotionally involved that when the time arrived for me to tell my story I would have only indignation and not facts to support me. I was glad I had brought photographers to make an unchallengeable record of what I had seen.

I found myself almost running out of the building and to the near-by office of the UNRRA Camp Director, Laurence A. Dawson.

"I know what you're going to say," he said. "I've done everything in my power, but I'm helpless." A slim, quiet-spoken former welfare

[1] I recommended to Jack Whiting, U.S. Zone Director for UNRRA, that Mrs. Henshaw be dismissed. To my dismay, I learned later that she had been promoted to a position in which she supervised numbers of children's camps!

worker in Ohio, Dawson explained: "Jewish refugees, as you certainly know by now, have been coming here in increasing numbers for the last two months. Now they're pouring in at the rate of 500 a day. Most of them survived the concentration camps; others are refugees come out of hiding and have been traveling on the roads for months.

"Well, you've seen that garage. I had to turn to that." He went on, "You may be interested to know that the three toilets there for nearly two thousand people are in the basement."

He paused. "If you were to move every soul out of that building, flush it and scrub it clean with boiling water from top to bottom, and move the people back, within one hour the place would be as filthy again. If an epidemic should occur, it would be almost impossible to control it."

The Medical Officer added, "The lack of ordinary privacy is hardly less serious than the physical hazards. Among people who have for years suffered deep psychological wounds, such a factor cannot be taken lightly.

"Most of them have fallen into a state of permanent resignation. Their brief interlude of hope when the war ended and they were 'liberated' has turned to deepest dejection under our tender ministrations . . . How much can the human spirit endure, Mr. Hirschmann? I don't know. I can only marvel."

I asked one question: "Did you keep Frankfurt and Arolsen informed about this influx of people?"

Dawson threw up his hands. "Of course I did. Don't think we didn't let them know. They knew these people were on the way. We warned them we'd need more accommodations. But UNRRA has to requisition everything through the Army." . . .

Dawson lit a cigarette and smiled sadly at me. "In these last few weeks I have been on the point of resigning a dozen times a day—but what good would that accomplish? I've let Headquarters know that I shall not receive another refugee. The guards have orders to turn them away at the gates. Any kind of shelter they can find outside the camp— even a cave—can be no worse than what we have to offer them."

Not far away at the gate we saw a group of several hundred bedraggled people, most of them with shabby bundles, coming toward the camp.

"What happens to them?" I asked.

"They will be turned away," said Dawson. "They have probably walked from Poland to get here—and we'll turn them away."

"Let's go out and talk to them," I said. "We can at least do that."

At first Dawson shook his head vehemently. "No," he said, "they will mob us. I can't take it any more." Then, "All right. But what are you going to tell them?"

He had not exaggerated. Men and women surrounded us, pulled at

549

us, and with tears streaming down their faces hysterically begged us to take them in. We were almost swept off our feet, pushed one way, then another. These people also had come from concentration camps; they had met on the road to Vienna; they had walked day and night to Salzburg, to Ainring and then here. Hundreds more were on the roads. Certainly UNRRA or the American Army would take them in!

Then suddenly, an idea, born of desperation, came to Dawson. "There is something we can do—not much, but better than nothing. The train station is about half a mile from here. I saw about twenty boxcars on the siding this morning." He shouted for an aide and, presently, the newcomers, counted off by fours, marched through the oncoming dusk to the station. They climbed into the empty, open boxcars and huddled together in the midnight rain, while Dawson arranged for food to be brought from the Funk Kitchen . . .

Fahrenwald, which housed more than 4,000 Jewish Displaced Persons, had been an I. G. Farben German workers' settlement. I arrived there at noon to find the inmates queued up outside the kitchen for their midday meal, a watery stew. Many of the tins they carried were rusted. They had been waiting nearly two hours because the central electric facilities had failed, as they had many times before.

"Once we had no water for five days," an old man in the line said to me.

"The Germans have fresh milk, eggs and butter," volunteered a haggard-looking woman.

Here, as elsewhere, housing presented an insoluble problem. In one room I found four couples sleeping, each in a single bed, one woman in her ninth month of pregnancy.

Clothing was poor; but when the Displaced Persons, some of whom had been tailors and seamstresses, put up a tailor shop, it had to shut down for lack of needles and thread. Shoes were desperately needed, although I saw a mountain of them outside the supply office. They had arrived from the States through UNRRA, collected in a nation-wide American drive, but they turned out to be mostly odd shoes and I was defied to find two mates in the lot.

Henry Cohen, the Camp Director, said, "We have no materials here for work projects, no trained welfare workers to deal with adolescents, and we lack more than 80 per cent of the medical supplies we should have.

"My greatest job here is to maintain morale. How can I do it under such circumstances?"

His question echoed in my mind as I left his office. Approaching the camp entrance, I saw a group of agitated Displaced Persons. As I came nearer I realized that standing there armed, in full uniform, wearing steel helmets, were two German police. I stared in amazement. Apparently they had attempted to enter the camp and met a solid phalanx of Jewish Displaced Persons. With eyes blazing, these men and women, who saw before them specters of the Nazi horror which they thought they had escaped, seemed ready to destroy them. I would not have given two cents for the lives of the policemen had they not been spirited away.

Several weeks later a riot actually took place between the Jewish Displaced Persons from Fahrenwald and German police, resulting in the death of one and the injuring of several others.

---

# The DPs Celebrate Purim

Purim was celebrated with local variations in 152 halls, schoolrooms and synagogues throughout Germany. For a day the spirit of the people was relaxed and tension let up. How unrestrained and symbolic was the merriment can be illustrated by the unique celebration in the Landsberg center.

This Purim Carnival was planned with a dramatist's instinct for theme and scenery; added to the established features known to history was merriment born of the pent-up feeling among the participants and of the living associations with the surroundings of Landsberg. Within walking distance, Hitler had written *Mein Kampf*. Within hearing range, he had declared in 1943 that the Jews of Europe would not live to celebrate Purim again. Shushan itself could not have presented a more perfect setting for a festival to extol and enjoy the triumph of justice. "On Sunday, March 17, you will prove," announced the camp newspaper, "that in the city where Hitler wrote *Mein Kampf* Jews are celebrating the great historical Purim of the Hebrew Year 5706 – (1946) the Purim of Hitler's downfall." It was not hyperbole when the same paper announced a week later, in bold headlines, that, "A Jewish community in the Diaspora never saw anything like it . . . It demonstrated the desire of our community to transform this first Purim after liberation—here in the land of our bitterest enemies—into a glorious national holiday."

Preparations had begun on Friday. When the sun rose out of a clear blue sky on Sunday morning, Landsberg had a new face. All the walls were adorned and placarded with satirical posters, every building and many windows were decorated with multi-colored bunting, and the

---

From *The Redeemers* by Leo W. Schwarz.

whole camp was a sea of blue-and-white flags. Prizes of Red Cross packages were to be awarded for the building and window adjudged the best decorated by popular acclaim, and so the competitive instinct asserted itself in the colorful and original displays.

Crowds assembled early and moved from poster to poster. Some announced events of the day, like that of the Kibbutz Bnai-Akiba: "At 6:30 P.M. a public burning of *Mein Kampf* will take place in the Square." Others played upon the holiday theme with bright illustrations. In the center of the camp gate a diminutive Hitler held a huge copy of *Mein Kampf* decorated with military and Nazi medals. A window was covered by a poster in the design of a theater ticket, announcing the première of a new play, "Greater Germany," to be produced by the modern sons of Haman, Hitler, Goering, Goebbels, Streicher; admission prices: the head of a Nazi. A neighboring window showed a crowned head in a rope on a gallows, with the legend: "Whoever starts up with us ends like Haman."

By ten o'clock the costumed jesters invaded the streets. They were the poster caricatures come to life. Like circus clowns, they ran through the streets to the delight of the jubilant onlookers. As to the winner there was no question. Who but Berek Gold, dressed as the classic prototype of Hitler?

Meanwhile the carnival committee were shouting themselves hoarse over the loud-speakers in the attempt to assemble all who were to participate in the parade. They withdrew from the revelry with reluctance; but by one o'clock the motorpool that had been designated the assembly point became as tense and vivid as the backstage of a musical show on the eve of its première. The camp blossomed out with slogans, flags, pictures, displays, jesters: police and firemen, trade schools and kibbutzim, sport clubs and fraternal societies, shoemakers and tailors, lumberjacks and hospital orderlies, musicians and actors, were equally represented.

The parade proved to be the *pièce de résistance* of the day's program. It took off from the Sport Arena at two o'clock, with the gaily dressed orchestra and the vivacious drum major in the lead. At the newly erected reviewing stand the bigwigs of the camp and the welfare corps enthusiastically recognized each unit as it marched past.

A troop of motorcyclists in military formation was trailed by a train of motorcars, trucks, tractors, cows and horses. The proud kibbutzim— bearing names like Bnai-Akiba, Benativ, Greifenberg, Hannah Senesch, Negev inscribed on their banners—marched to the music. Between a guard of boxers and soccer players there moved a pageant of political propaganda in the form of a boat—labeled "Immigrants"— which carried determined youth storming the gates of Palestine.

Then, as the crowds surged toward the reviewing stand, Gringauz formally opened the mass meeting. He called on the leader of the

Kibbutz Bnai-Akiba to recite the Scroll of Esther. The man stepped forward, dressed in a concentration camp striped suit and intoned the Biblical narrative. But as he reached the finale of the story, the children rattled their noisemakers and the crowd cried out the name of the ancient tyrant. Finally, a number of speakers talked of the historical significance of the festival and with dedications to liberty and justice brought the formal program to a happy close.

Informal festivities—masked balls, parties, dances, musicales and the like—continued after the burning of Hitler's effigy on the Square that evening, until the early hours of the morning . . .

---

# DPs Meet David Ben Gurion

*Rabbi Judah Nadich of New York City's Park Avenue Synagogue served as chaplain in the U. S. Army during World War II and advisor to General Eisenhower on Jewish affairs. Here he recalls a momentous event . . .*

I took Mr. Ben Gurion in my car to the first DP camp that he would visit, at Zeilsheim. Both for him and for myself, as well as for the many hundreds of Jews in the camp, it was an unforgettable experience. We drove into the camp just a little distance beyond the gates and I parked my car, asking Mr. Ben Gurion to remain inside until I should make the necessary arrangements. Stepping out of my car, I was quickly surrounded by a number of the DPs and several of the members of their Central Committee came up to chat with me . . . Suddenly, one of the Jews in the group happened to peer into my automobile and, recognizing the strong face and white shock of hair, suddenly screamed in an unearthly voice, "Ben Gurion! Ben Gurion!"

Like one man, the entire group turned toward the car and began shrieking, shouting the name of the man who was accepted by all of them as their own political leader. But he was far more than that to them. He was the personal embodiment of all their hopes for the future. During all the many years of their hell, during what had seemed the several lifetimes of their subjection to Nazi debasement and degradation . . . that which had kept them alive, that which had buoyed them up even amidst the darkest days, was the yearning, the longing, the hope for Palestine . . .

Now, after all these many years, here was Palestine right in the midst

---

From *Eisenhower and the Jews* by Judah Nadich.

of their DP camp on German soil! For who better than Ben Gurion personified *Eretz Yisrael* and its fight for freedom and independence? . . .

The shrieks and the cries multiplied and the crowd quickly grew larger and larger until I became frightened of a possible riot. I appealed to the pride of the people and to their desire to show Ben Gurion how well-ordered and self-disciplined they were. I promised them that they all would have the chance to see and hear Ben Gurion if they would follow my instructions. Quickly they gathered together in the camp auditorium and the word was flashed throughout the camp. In a few minutes I led Ben Gurion into the large jammed hall, all the seats occupied, all the aisles filled, every inch of space packed, those unable to enter, standing near the doors and leaning across the window-sills. As I led Ben Gurion into the hall, the people spontaneously burst into song, "Hatikvah," the hope that had never died . . . As Ben Gurion stood on the platform before them, the people broke forth into cheers, into song and, finally, into weeping. At last he began to speak, his voice choked up, his eyes filled. He had to stop as he broke down for a moment. In the sudden quiet one could hear the muffled sobbing from all sides of the auditorium. Very few eyes were dry. For the incredible was true; the impossible had happened. Ben Gurion was in their midst and they had lived despite Hitler . . .

He spoke to them in words of comfort and consolation. He brought them the message of good tidings from their brethren in Palestine who anxiously were awaiting their coming. He assured them they would be welcomed with open arms and that their own people in Palestine were eager to bring balm to their wounds, the healing that comes from love and brotherhood. He promised them that the Jews of Palestine would brave every obstacle in order to transport them to Palestine as quickly as possible.

No newspapers had heralded his coming and his appearance in the camp was, therefore, as totally unexpected as it was thrilling. Nothing that had yet happened had given the displaced persons such a boost in their morale, such a conviction that now it was only a question of waiting a little while longer . . .

# Readings

*The Redeemers* by Leo W. Schwarz (Farrar, Straus and Young, 1953), is a deeply stirring book depicting the heroic saga of the DP's, who smashed their way into Eretz Yisrael, and their redeemers.

*The Buried are Screaming* by Helen Waren (Beechhurst Press, 1948), is the story of a U.S.O. entertainer who helped the DP's find themselves and assisted in their illegal immigration to the Promised Land.

*Eisenhower and the Jews* by Judah Nadich (Twayne Press, 1953), is the record of the American army relations to the Jewish DP's as reported by Eisenhower's Jewish Advisor.

# 23. "ILLEGAL IMMIGRATION" OF DPS TO PALESTINE

According to David Ben-Gurion, the father of the State of Israel, "Behind the dramatic story of Israel's War of Independence [1948] . . . there lies another story—more modest and perhaps less dramatic, but of even deeper moral significance."[1]

He was referring to the story of how the *Yishuv* (the Palestinian Jewish community) kept the gates of the Promised Land open in defiance of the strict immigration quotas enforced by the British mandate.

Struggling to survive as a power in the Middle East and hoping to appease the Arabs, Britain, starting in the 1930s, tried to close off Jewish immigration to Palestine, unswayed by the fate of the Jews in Europe. Despite the British efforts, those who were escaping Hitler, and later the inmates of the DP camps, had no alternative. Palestine was their only option.

In 1937 the *Yishuv* organized *Mossad Aliyah Bet* (Illegal Immigration Organization) to help them. The secret *Mossad* network had been active throughout Europe even during the war itself. Its emissaries, working undercover due to British opposition, sought out refugees and DPs, organized and sustained them, and led them on the long, secret trek to the sea, where they took passage on ramshackle old ships—the only ones available—and prepared to run the British blockade.[2]

Turning the full weight of their military and naval strength against the "illegals," the British intercepted many refugee ships and arrested the

---

[1]Jon Kimche and David Kimche, *The Secret Roads* (New York: Farrar, Straus & Cudahy, 1955), introduction.
[2]Samuel Tolkowsky, in *They Took to the Sea* (Thomas Yoseloff, 1964), gives accounts of sixty-five such vessels that made the attempt in the years 1946–48.

passengers of others after they landed in Palestine, sending them back to Europe or interning them in detention camps in Cyprus or Mauritius. The plight of one such ship, the *Exodus,* gained world attention, and provided the basis for the best-selling novel of the same name by Leon Uris, later made into a popular film.

Another distinguished novel, Ludwig Lewisohn's *Breathe Upon These* (New York: Bobbs-Merrill, 1944), recounts the tragic tale of the *Struma.* With 769 Rumanian "illegals" aboard, the *Struma* was turned back by the British and denied port access at Istanbul, where it sought provisions and repairs. On February 22, 1942, the ship blew up and everyone aboard perished, except for one survivor.

---

# Stealing Across the Alps

---

*The director of B'riha ("Flight") describes his experiences . . .*

As a result of British pressure on the Italian authorities, B'riha was forced to close the Alpine border stations which it had operated for some time. We therefore had to start traveling over remote Alpine passes where we would not be likely to be found out. After studying maps and scouting mountain trails, we decided to set up an "experimental" post in a certain town on the Austrian border. The place was not ideal, but then we did not have much of a choice. During most of the year the mountain trails were blocked by heavy snow. The few passes which we found were criss-crossed by mountain streams so that we had to set up temporary "bridges."

We did not know whether we were justified in exposing old people, or women and children, to the hazards of crossing the snow-bound Alps, especially since each trip had to be made after dark. We therefore planned to use these trails only for moving young people and other individuals who were physically fit for the rigors of clandestine border crossings and for the "illegal" journey by boat to Palestine.

But the DP camps in Germany and Austria were filled to the bursting point. As a result, many camp inmates were crossing into Italy on their own, alone or in little groups without the guidance of B'riha. These unorganized, dare-devil attempts of desperate refugees could have caused the collapse of the entire operation. Something had to be done. . .

Our immediate problem was to find a building—or several build-

---

From *Briha: Flight to the Homeland* by Ephraim Dekel.

ings—near the border which could accommodate our workers and the transient refugees. Exploring the area in question, we discovered an Italian border police outpost. The house was filled with officials wearing every conceivable type of uniform—customs, *carabinieri,* security, and what have you. The commander of B'riha in northern Italy decided to add a sprinkling of American army uniforms. One night—it was after midnight—we turned up at the outpost, after quite a risky journey. All of us, from the Rumanian refugee whose entire English vocabulary consisted of a faltering "Yes," to the emissary who had just arrived from Palestine, were wearing American uniforms. We were stopped several times by policemen, but when they saw our American uniforms they saluted smartly and, in return for some American cigarettes, gave us all the information we wanted about traveling conditions on the highways. We rented two rooms at an inn near the outpost. A sleepy-looking fellow, the officer in charge of the security police, asked us what we were doing there. We showed him an official-looking paper, which apparently impressed him. We explained to him in Italian that we were going to set up a rest camp for American military and civilian personnel stationed in the area. The Italians fell for our story; maybe the canned foods and the American cigarettes we gave them helped persuade them. This is how we set up a B'riha station in the Alps, some 8,200 feet above sea level. The border police officials lived on the upper floor of the house. Our men became friendly with them and were able to get information from them about border patrol movements. They really believed our story; when our refugees came to the house, weary after the long trek over the mountains, the Italians never suspected that they might be anything else but American officers in need of a good rest.

On those nights when we moved refugees across the border we would throw parties, complete with hired bands, for the *carabinieri* and the people of the nearby village of Gazara (which we renamed Manara, after one of our kibbutzim in Eretz Yisrael). While the Italians were busy at our party, we would bring in our refugees. A few of our workers stayed at the shindig to make sure that the Italians were having too good a time to get suspicious.

B'riha did important work also in Merano [a resort town in Tyrol, about 37 miles south of the Austrian border and some 30 miles east of the Swiss border]. That town, which had been used by the Nazi army as a rest and recuperation center during the war, had a population of about 30,000; half of these were Tyrolean Austrians, the rest were Italians. The Jewish Brigade became active in that area almost immediately after the liberation of Italy, transferring thousands of refugees from the British occupation zone in Austria into Italy by way of Villach and San Candido. Our B'riha unit in Merano consisted of 35 people under the command of a Jewish Brigade veteran. In the beginning, between 1945 and 1946, the B'riha group pretended to be a team of American war relief workers and set up headquarters at the Hotel Terminus. Later, B'riha rented a larger house where the staff was stationed and where the refugees stayed until they could proceed to Italy. Originally the property of a Jewish family, the house had been taken over during the war by the Nazis, who had set up a printing press there for the production of counterfeit American dollars. Next to the house, and also in the courtyard, there was ample space for the army trucks which we had inherited from the Jewish Brigade or obtained through other channels.

After 1946, our "official" activities in Italy centered on the borders near Resia, the Alpine passes and the Brenner Pass itself. The most important aspect of our work at the time was the transfer of refugees into Italy from Austria's French occupation zone. Most of these refugees were moved either without documents or with "homemade" identification papers.

We had more than our share of troubles. On particularly cold and snowy nights we were often unable to get the refugees to our shelters and had to put them up at farm houses in the area until the weather cleared up. Sometimes we had to hire sleds to bring the refugees into Italy.

One day in May, 1947, a transport of 390 people, traveling in 15 cars, set out for Italy from Austria. Somehow the British intelligence people found out about it, and when the group got to Nauders, on the Austro-Italian border, it was stopped by British soldiers. First thing, the British got hold of the "documents" we'd used for the transport. Naturally, we didn't want to give the Limeys a chance to read the documents, so our men simply grabbed the papers from the hands of the officer who happened to be holding them. Before the British realized what was happening, our 15 cars had turned tail and were heading straight back into Austria. The refugees hid out for eight days and then crossed into Italy at some other point.

Another time, 216 refugees—including 16 women and nine children—were turned back from Merano after a horrible journey across the Alps. The Italians couldn't stand up against the pressures from the British. The incident got some publicity; the Italian press carried articles protesting against the inhumanity of leaving helpless refugees exposed to the bitter cold, and the refugees let it be known that, despite the five grueling days they had just been through, they would not give up but would try to cross the border at some other place.

The British intelligence people had their headquarters in San Candido, near the town of Cortina d'Ampezzo. There were several dozen British agents—in uniform and in plain clothes—whose main job it was to spy on the "Jewish underground." They didn't get much help from the Italians, though, because they insisted on behaving like conquerors and treating the Italians like the natives in one of their colonies.

According to our records, over 50,000 Jewish refugees entered Italy from Germany and Austria between the end of the war and the establishment of the State of Israel. Most of these got to Palestine aboard the "illegal" boats that sailed from the Mediterranean seaports of Italy.

# The Secret Embarkation and Making of a Film

*The celebrated American writer Meyer Levin recorded for posterity the stirring chapter of illegal immigration in film and story. He reported on the underground transports and the secret embarkations in the dead of night at obscure ports on the Mediterranean . . .*

The contact was with Ada Sereni . . . the widow of one of the greatest Palestine heroes of the war, Enzo Sereni. In past years I had often visited the kibbutz which he had founded not far from Tel Aviv, an immensely successful settlement, Givat Brenner. Sereni was an idealist Zionist, descended from an aristocratic Jewish Italian family. During the war he had served with the Allied propaganda forces in Cairo as the editor of an anti-fascist newspaper. When the British decided to accept Palestinians to work behind enemy lines in Europe, Enzo Sereni, though beyond the age limit, managed to become a parachutist. But he was seized just after his first drop. For a long time his fate remained unknown. His wife, volunteering in the women's forces, reached Italy with the Jewish Brigade and set out to trace him. The last details she discovered only after the liberation of Dachau; there, survivors told how Enzo Sereni had been tortured to death.

Ada Sereni had remained in Italy to carry out her husband's mission—to bring the people home. She worked with Yehuda Arazi[1], organizing the departure of vessel after vessel from the Italian shores.

Engaged in this work for more than two years, she had sent off a score of ships. And yet each vessel was a new agony, to be worried

[1] A leader in the struggle for "illegal immigration."

From *In Search* by Meyer Levin.

through on bare nerves. For in addition to the constant watchfulness of British agents on shore, the British ships and planes at sea, in addition to the difficulties in securing crews and in securing provisions, there was the normal, eternal adversary: the weather. Beachhead embarkations could be carried out only in a calm sea.

We sat with Ada Sereni in the hotel lobby while she waited for a report. Contact with the vessel had been made, but for several days the ship had circled off-shore, due to the heavy weather. Each day spent hovering in Italian waters made discovery more likely. If the British found the vessel they could put pressure on the Italians to impound it; that would mean an immense loss in time, effort, and money.

Presently a typical Palestinian arrived—he had the open, optimistic manner of the sabras. In Hebrew, he reported that there was too much wind today, but there were hopes for tomorrow. Should the ship remain in the vicinity of the beach? It was decided to continue the risk.

As for us, Ada Sereni was of two minds. She had received a call from Paris about us and she too wanted the voyage filmed. But every added moment spent in loading was an added risk. How much of our equipment was essential? I said that if necessary we would leave all of our personal belongings behind, and carry the camera, film, and a minimum of lighting material on our backs . . .

The next morning, Ada Sereni had lost her look of agony. Or rather it had changed to a different sort of agony. The weather now seemed workable. This opened up a whole series of worries—of timing the vessel's approach, timing the arrival of the preparatory shore units so as to cause the least distraction on the beach, of coordinating the arrival of a thousand refugees from a half-dozen scattered camps at a specified hour at the secret beach. All this, without alerting the enemy . . .

At noon, we left with Ada Sereni and a couple of Haganah boys for the beach. Ada Sereni had thought of a way to utilize our presence as cover for contact with the ship. The beach, she explained, had been used during the war for the landing of an OSS[2] unit that had worked behind the German lines. If our car appeared, conspicuously marked "Film Documents," the local inhabitants, should they happen to notice unusual activity, could easily be convinced that we were an American unit making a film about the OSS landing. The presence of the vessel offshore might even be taken as part of the re-enactment.

We set off, with this explanation in readiness . . . On the horizon we made out an approaching vessel. A B'riha car had accompanied us. Now they opened a suitcase containing a shortwave radio, and made contact with the vessel. Presently a dinghy detached itself from the ship and rowed toward us. Ada Sereni and her daughter, a sixteen-year-old sabra, hurried along the beach, waving their scarves. The dinghy

[2]Office of Strategic Services, U.S. secret agency created in 1942.

pulled up to shore and two men climbed out. The first was an old seaman with gray stubbled face, powerful wrinkled hands, and the precise dignity and kindliness of bearing one would have anticipated in a person engaged in this work. With him was a tall, younger man, curly-haired and handsome, the captain of the vessel. There was a brief discussion of prevailing winds. Conditions were fair. The ship would anchor offshore at nine that evening . . .

A Haganah truck had arrived with a crew of lads who were unloading the inflating rubber landing craft. In my absence my eager cameraman had attempted to film this work; since night was falling he had lighted a few flares.

When the torches flamed up, with their ghastly intense yellow light and their sputtering fumes, half the B'riha had leaped on him, taking him for a spy in the act of signalling the English! Only Ada's intervention had prevented a lynching.

In the intense strain and suspense of these last hours, his action had put our entire project in disfavor. We were viewed as dilettantes who would only get in the way and create danger. Ada had practically decided to cancel our trip . . .

And now the immigrants began to arrive. Instead of the usual trucks, a stream of hired busses appeared. They parked in neat rows, with each group of refugees coming out to form around their leader.

As the busses came pouring in on time, and as the refugees were silently ranged, the tension began to relax a trifle . . . We weren't going to miss the boat after all. The beach unit was completing the assembly of a little emergency pier—out of the same prefabricated units that I had seen on that terrible night three years before, in a river crossing during the Battle of the Bulge. At least here was a good use for U.S. Army leftovers.

The night became quite cold. Two units alternated, working in the water. The boys wore only bathing trunks, and gradually their legs turned greenish. A small bonfire was lighted in a well-screened hollow; the off-crew danced and jumped around it until their turn came again.

A sizable swell had arisen, capsizing a dinghy which was being used as a buffer between the pier and the rubber rafts. The watercrew struggled with the dinghy, managed to get it righted. Now the rafts were ready to begin ferrying passengers to the vessel. A cable-line was established.

The first group of refugees was led from the parking lot. They crossed a stretch of sandy waste; occasionally a flashlight showed for an instant. Slowly, tortuously, they came toward the beach.

Now they were burdened with their total possessions. The scenes I had witnessed in the marches through the woods across the borders of Europe were utterly eclipsed. For each individual was bowed nearly to the ground, half-crawling in the effort to carry every bit of his earthly

562

goods. With their gigantic bulging knapsacks, topped with blankets, with suitcases and bundles knotted onto the knapsacks, their shapes, in weirdly glimpsed silhouettes, were of fantastic creatures unrelated to any known living form. And amongst all these, there were an inordinate number of women with babies swathed in shawls, in blankets, slung before them, burdens balancing the sacks the same women carried on their backs.

The people were led down onto the beach and seated on a little rise of sand facing the improvised pier, to wait their turn for the rafts. Slowly their ranks grew until a few hundred were sitting there, utterly silent, immobile, their infants hushed and sleeping. Thus five or six rows of them sat waiting their last wait, staring at the dark sea and at the vague, scarcely discernible blot out there, the ship, their ship, with its tiny lights arching slowly as it rocked on the black water.

To witness this, to have the means at hand and be unable to film it, put us into an agony of frustration that endured most of the night through. I sought out Ada Sereni, who was hovering around the operation whispering instructions, urging speed, speed. But actually there was nothing more that she could do now: the operation would follow its course regardless of prodding. She could now listen to me. "Surely," I pleaded, "a few torches would go unnoticed in this isolated area. They couldn't even be seen as far as the main road. If a ship at sea noticed them, and even if the ship made inquiries, it would be daylight before any search could be started, and by then our vessel would be loaded and on its way." Surely, if she agreed with the usefulness of our project at all, she had to give us a minimum opportunity to carry it out.

"Yes, yes," she said, "it had to be done, but only at the last moment, when everything had been loaded and we could get away quickly . . ."

"It would have to be the last raft-loads that were filmed," she said. And we ourselves would only be taken aboard at the end, for if any had to be left behind, it would be us, rather than immigrants. We could light our torches just before our turn came on the rafts.

There was nothing to do but wait, even uncertain that we would be taken at all. The loading of the rafts was slow and terribly arduous. The crew had to pull each raft to the pier, hold it there against the sea-swell while the immigrants, with their immense burdens and their babies stepped the length of the slippery narrow pier, like soldiers bent under a double-load of equipment. Then, balancing on the overturned boat, they climbed into their raft. The bottoms of the rafts were several inches deep in water. The people piled in, twenty, thirty, and then the crew shoved, and they pulled on the cable, and as their raft moved out, the next one was pulled against the pier.

As the night wore on, some of the boys stumbled out of the water, falling from exhaustion. Volunteers were called from among the immigrants.

Once the pier disintegrated. Loading was suspended for nearly an hour as the numbed lads labored in the water to get it into place again. The refugees sat with fear and despair in their eyes, as though already watching the long-awaited vessel fade in the dark, without them. Ada Sereni stood over the laboring water-crew, devouring herself with impatience. Every moment she asked her daughter for the time. But the pier was put together again at last, and the loading resumed.

But it went so slowly! Watching the little line of refugees coming to the pier, every one of them with two or three times the allotted poundage of baggage, Ada Sereni gave vent to her impatience, scolding, scolding the leaders, the people . . . Oh, why would people never learn discipline, how could anything ever be accomplished!

And at last in an excess of agony she retreated to the car, huddled, not having the heart to make anyone leave a single bundle behind, and demanding every few seconds, "What time is it?"

And each sailing was like this, and the people were whispering tales as of the time when everyone arrived at the beach but the English caught the boat and got the Italians to intern it, and the people had to be taken back to their camps to wait for another chance.

As this rumor spread, they began to crowd to the water's edge. Not all would be taken aboard, it was rumored. There had been a miscalculation. Too many busses had been ordered, too many people had been brought from the camps. Some would have to go back.

Soon there was a pushing desperate jam at the little pier, and a double row of burdened half-hysterical refugees were jostling each other as they tottered along the narrow slippery boards, trying to leap into the next raft. Hoarse, whispered disputes, muted curses and exhortations in all the languages of Europe spread along the beach.

The beach commander angrily ordered them back, threatening to halt the embarkation altogether. But more and more people crowded to the pier, in panic. The group leaders exhorted, pushed. At last the launching crew had to be called out of the water to help push back the crowd, and to get them settled again, and quieted. The order of embarkation was resumed.

And yet they all knew they were going to Cyprus, nine chances out of ten. They all knew there might be a fight on the boat when the British captured it, and some of them might be killed, and in any case they would only go to wait in another camp on a desolate island where food and water were scarce. They knew, and they were in panic that they might be left behind. They could not bear this continued stagnation of remaining yet another while in Europe, returning to yet another DP camp to wait for another vessel. To be on the way—no matter where, but to be on the way.

Thus we waited through the whole night. At last only about a hundred immigrants remained on the beach. The commander gave us permission to light two flares.

I held the torches aloft while hoarsely whispering directions . . . in French, in Yiddish, in English, in Hebrew. Despite the preparatory speech I had made, begging everyone to proceed as though we were not there, the people followed the natural reaction of people everywhere, they grinned into the camera, took attitudes, waved—the flares were burning down and what we were getting was hopeless, useless. My whisper became a desperate throttled shout, I gesticulated with the flaming torches while the sparks fell on my arms, in my hair; the commander was asking nervously if I didn't already have enough; I waved the torch in the face of the worst grimacing offender, exhorted . . . The torch sprayed my neck, my hands, but somehow in the burning time of the flare we filmed the entire crowd on the pier . . . the embarkation, the crew pushing the raft into the sea. The torches were down to my fingers. I flung the ends into the water.

I begged for permission to light two more. Even one. No use.

Then it was our turn for the raft. We staggered out with the sacks of equipment on our backs, the case of negatives grasped between us. I jumped into the raft, and found the water halfway to my knees. The equipment had to be kept out of the sea water. I dumped my personal knapsack on the bottom and began piling equipment on top of it, as the material was passed on to me. Amidst the surging muddle of refugees, we somehow got everything on, and I found myself with the heavy case of negatives perched on my knees while I tried to hold a cameracase and a suitcase of accessories above water. The raft cable ran just under my nose, and as I couldn't free a hand, or budge, I expected to be decapitated by the cable at any moment.

Everyone pulled on the cable, to hurry us toward the vessel . . .

At last we bumped against the ship; the sea was choppy; another raft was maneuvering to get away. Hesse (the photographer) being exceptionally tall, managed to swing himself out and seize hold of a rope ladder; in a second he was on deck ready to film the mounting immigrants . . . Word had been sent ahead to the vessel that a film crew was coming and that we were to be permitted to operate . . .

Just then one of the immigrants who had been trying to help free the unloaded raft lost his balance and fell into the sea. We fished for him. Above, Hesse lit a torch to film this scene. Angry hands snatched it from him and flung it into the water. I tried to shout up explanations in Hebrew, and Mika (an assistant) managed to get up beside Hesse to help him.

The drowning man had been hauled into our raft by then. Mika lighted a torch and Hesse filmed the people from our raft as they grappled their way up the rope ladder, reaching for hands that were stretched down to them, and finally rolled over the rail onto the deck. At least so far, though scantily, we had got the essential movements on film . . .

People began to grumble and curse. Dawn was coming. We were delaying the ship. Someone yelled to heave the damn thing (the case of the film which was being hauled onto the ship) into the sea, and in another second all our negative would have been gone. But Mika grabbed a rope, let it down to us, and the crate was rescued. I went up the ladder at last.

We hadn't been in the final raft after all. Two more arrived in the dawn light. We stood in a drenched, shivering, exhausted little group, near the ladder, shooting in the feeble light, and filled with a crazy elation—after everything, we had got this far, we were on the boat. In our limited way we knew what all the others felt: to us it was a film, to them it was their lives.

# Scuttling of the S.S. Patria: A Desperate Act

*In 1940, refugees were dumped by Eichmann aboard three ships which took them to Palestine. After perilous adventures they reached Haifa, where they were caught by the British and transferred to the S.S. Patria, where they were virtually imprisoned. The British planned to deport them to Mauritius in the Indian Ocean.*

*The Yishuv was horror struck. Strikes, fasting, and demonstrations were held. In desperation, the immigrants, with the aid of the Haganah, scuttled the ship in an attempt to force the hand of the government . . . This was the first attempt to actively and openly oppose the British blockade. Faced by an outraged world the survivors (200 died!) were permitted to stay in Palestine . . .*

Monday morning, November 25, 1940. The 1,800 passengers of the Patria paced the deck in helpless anger. Some jumped overboard in desperation, in broad daylight, only to be forced back on board by the British police. Suddenly a muffled explosion resounded from below decks. The ship began to sway and to list to one side . . . Screams arose on all sides. People began running around in panic and confusion.

From *The Gate Breakers* by Bracha Habas.

# "Illegal Immigration"

Crews of other ships anchored in the harbor, as well as British soldiers and policemen, rushed to give help. The Red Cross and the Red Magen David worked side by side.

One of those who were rescued had the following story to tell:

That day we had to make some sleeping room available for the passengers of the Atlantic, and all the women whose cabins were in a certain section were ordered to leave. One cabin had been occupied by a woman and her baby, who had been born on the Black Sea. The soldiers entered her room while she was breast-feeding the baby and forced her to go up on deck at once. There was a lot of movement, because at that time of day, between eight and ten in the morning, they would clean the inside of the ship and everyone had to go up on deck. I hung around near the cabin where the fellows who jumped overboard were being kept. A soldier came up to me with a broom in his hand, and ordered me to sweep up the passageway. I did it willingly, hoping that I would be allowed to sweep the prisoners' cell too. No sooner had the soldier left than I heard a dull blast. At first I paid no attention and went on sweeping. Then I saw people running around and I heard some shouting:

"An accident! Warning! Air raid! Everyone on the back deck—go below!"

People were screaming for help or just screaming.

Suddenly I realized that the boat was slowly leaning to one side. I dashed to the prisoners' cabin and found two of them trying to break the door open. I did my best to help, but we couldn't budge the door an inch. A guard appeared. We demanded that he open the door, and after he did, we all rushed up the stairs. The left deck was crowded with hundreds of people, with everybody holding on to the next fellow; the right side of the ship was submerging rapidly. Someone gave the order to put on life belts.

I remembered that I had seen life belts in the men's sleeping hall and I dashed below. I met five people who were lost, including a boy who was crying because he didn't know how to put on his life belt. I put it on him, grabbed as many life belts as I could, and went back up on deck. By that time I had to crawl on all fours: I couldn't stand up. Hands reached down to pull me up to the upper deck. A soldier was holding on to the air vent with one hand and his rifle with the other, still determined not to let anybody jump overboard. Suddenly we heard more explosions and we were showered with beams and chunks of wood. One of the beams fell on the soldier. He slipped and fell into the water with his rifle in his hand. Lots of people jumped in after him. There were only a few left on deck, and they clutched at anything that came to hand. I lost my balance and slipped into the water. As I surfaced, I saw that the ship was only two yards above my head. Fragments of masts, lifeboats, and planks were falling all around. I started swimming away as fast as I could. I saw the anchor chain of an oil boat in front of me, swam for it, and grabbed hold.

Looking back to the Patria I saw that it had turned over completely—the bottom of the ship was above the water. There were some people sitting there, trying to help the less fortunate aboard. Others were still swimming around in the sea trying to save their lives. Twenty yards in front of me a small motorboat stopped and began hauling people out of the water. I left the chain and swam over to the boat. Hands reached down and I was pulled aboard, and the boat made for shore. Suddenly we heard a horrible scream: a girl who had been swimming towards us from behind had been caught in the big screw and had been crushed. We lifted her body into the boat. Many more boats came out to rescue the swimmers. Only ten minutes had passed since the explosion and many were already standing on the pier; but many had died. "My baby, my baby!" I heard a voice cry out. I recognized the woman—four days before she had given birth aboard the Patria.

"They saved me at the last minute," she wailed. "My husband took the baby and they both disappeared!"

"I saw him in one of the boats, he was holding something in his arms," I quickly lied to her.

"That's what they all say," she answered, and burst out in tears.

A stretcher was brought in and she was taken outside. No sooner had she left than her husband appeared, with the child. But how different he looked! Then I looked around—and everyone looked different. They looked like ghosts of the people they had been the day before.

# The S.S. Struma: Only One Survivor

*David Stolier, the Struma's sole survivor, tells about the tragedy . . .*

On Sunday, February 2, after weeks of anxious waiting, two telegrams arrived. One was from friends and acquaintances in Palestine, urging the immigrants not to despair, and the other was from Dr. Stephen Wise in New York telling them that two thousand certificates had been set aside and that some of them would be distributed to the Struma's passengers. The immigrants' hopes revived, and in their minds' eye they saw the end of their arduous journey.

The following morning a tugboat approached the ship. The immigrants were worried, but hoped for the best. At 1 P.M. some policemen approached in a boat and said that they had come to unmoor the Struma and move it to a nearby location for disinfection purposes. One policeman casually remarked that they would be returned to the Black Sea, to Burgas in Bulgaria or Constanta in Rumania.

The news spread rapidly throughout the ship, and the whispered conversation between the captain and the head of the police did

From *The Gate Breakers* by Bracha Habas.

568

nothing to alleviate the immigrants' fears. They refused to allow the ship to be unmoored. The few policemen, unable to cope with them, left in the direction that they had come. However, within a short period of time, about eighty more policemen arrived in additional boats and surrounded the ship. The passengers struggled with them for half an hour in an effort to prevent their boarding the Struma, but the police were soon in full control. They lifted the anchor, tied the ship to the tug, and at 4 P.M. the Struma was pulled out to sea. The captain offered no complaints and the immigrants suspected that he had a hand in the plot. At their insistence, he signed a document stating his obligation to bring them to Palestine.

At 10 P.M. they were in the Black Sea, thirty miles from shore. Here the tug detached itself and its crew shouted to the Struma's passengers, "You're going to Burgas!"

The immigrants knew that very little food remained aboard ship. Over a week had passed since the last shipment, from the council of the Jewish community of Istanbul. They also knew that they had no fuel. No one slept that night and no one spoke. On the morrow it became clear that during the night the ship had drifted almost two miles farther away from shore. According to the captain, the ship was still within Turkey's territorial waters. He was careful not to say anything that might anger the passengers. He claimed that the engine was being repaired and that as soon as it should be in working order he would bring the ship to a Turkish port.

The sea was very calm. The ship did not move from its location. Then, suddenly, shortly before nine in the morning a violent explosion shook the ship, and within minutes it sank into the sea.

I was swept overboard by the force of the blast. When I surfaced I saw scores of people struggling in the waves. Screams of terror rose from the sinking ship. Pieces of wood were floating around in the water, and some, including myself, managed to grab hold of them in an attempt to save themselves. But the water was icy cold and the people grew weaker and weaker. One by one, their grips relaxed and they sank beneath the waves. By the time it was noon, I was alone . . . My thick leather jacket warmed me a bit. That saved me.

Stolier recalls how he managed to climb onto the platform to which he was clinging and get his body out of the freezing water. Late in the afternoon he spied a bench floating nearby. He got hold of it, dragged it onto the platform, and sat on it, thus removing his chilled body completely from the water . . .

At sunset he saw a man rowing towards him with difficulty. He soon made out the weary figure of the first mate. He helped the man onto the bench where he rested a bit. When asked what had happened, the

569

man replied that he had seen a torpedo coming at the ship and had alerted the captain at once, but it had been too late. He also said that he had seen the captain swimming for hours, but that he finally froze and drowned. All but the two of them had perished.

They decided not to fall asleep, fearing that they might freeze. They warmed each other as best they could, even though it was extremely difficult to move their limbs. So the night passed. The first mate grew weaker and weaker, and by sunrise it was evident that he was dying. Toward the end he went insane. During his last moments he began to play with fish, and in the process slipped into the sea and drowned.

Now I was left alone (related Stolier). I saw the shore in the distance, and decided to swim for it. I gathered my strength and swam about two hundred yards, but seeing that I would not be able to make it, I returned to the platform. I feared that I would suffer the same fate as the captain's mate and decided to commit suicide. I barely managed to get my penknife out of my pocket, but my fingers were so stiff, I couldn't slash my wrists.

Suddenly a boat appeared. I shouted with all my might, but even though the boat passed a few yards away from me it did not stop. The people on board the boat pointed at something on the horizon but I did not understand what they meant. Then, when I had given up all hope, I saw a boat approaching.

P.S.: The rescue boat was sent from Shilo, a small Turkish village in the vicinity. They removed the mate's body from the water, took Stolier aboard in a stretcher, and administered first aid . . .

# The Island of Cyprus: A "Detour"

*The "internment" on Cyprus began with the arrival of 3,000 DP's on August 14, 1946. The number had increased to 31,344 by January 1948. The erection of additional facilities did not keep pace with the needs. The huts were excessively crowded; more than 23,000 were sheltered in old and often damaged tents. There were about 150 new births each month. Agents of Jewish voluntary relief agencies, chiefly the J.D.C., were permitted to provide supplementary feeding. These agencies raised the average ration to approximately 3,000 calories; and supplementary dried milk, eggs, vegetables, and fruit was provided for children, pregnant and nursing women, and those that were ill . . .*

# "Illegal Immigration"

The immigrant ship approached Cyprus. Immigrants and Palestinians . . . all answered the question, "Your name and address?" with "A Jew from Palestine." Everybody began preparing for a fight. Those with experience, for whom it was not new to fight with the English tyrants on the deck of an immigrant ship, advised the rest to prepare wet towels, to counteract the gas bombs which would undoubtedly be used.

We were exhausted by the trip. Instead of the usual 14 hours from Haifa to Cyprus, the ship had sailed in a stormy sea for 50 hours. Everyone on board, without exception, was sea-sick. We had nothing with which to vomit, since we had been given nothing to eat. Aside from our tiredness, we were all dejected by the failure of the struggle that had taken place on the shore of Haifa.

The night before, while we were being transported, laden on trucks like cattle, from the southern shore of Palestine where we were arrested, we had argued about the camp to which we were being transferred . . . When we were told, in Haifa, that we would be sent to Cyprus, we had refused to get off the automobiles. They (the British) tried to get us out by force—and it was no easy task for them. We were empty-handed, but we held on to one another and attached ourselves to the sides of the truck. The English tried to separate some of the girls by pulling their hair, but clenched fists sprang out of our mass of people and flew like bullets.

By the force of blows of rifle-butts and sticks, the British tore off body by body from the solid mass. Four soldiers were needed to drag each of us to the boat. By force, again, we were brought to the ship's hold. We were tired—an exhaustion that we did not feel when we were busy with the unloading of the immigrants from the boat, or in the fight with the army after the identification, a time when many immigrants were freed because they passed as Palestinians. We were tired from the battle in the port of Haifa and from the sea trip. We were now completely exhausted.

In spite of all this, we were ready for a new battle when we felt the ship anchor. We did not want to come out of the holds. The openings of the hold were closed, from outside, after gas bombs had been thrown in. We were prepared for this. The wet towels protected our eyes and noses; blankets, which had been made ready in advance, were thrown on the bombs.

Smoke filled the hold, becoming thicker from minute to minute. The wet towels no longer protected us. Terrible cries pierced the cavity of the holds.

I lay in a corner, insensitive to what was going on. Before my eyes

---

From *Unsung Heroes* by Hakibbutz Hameuchad.

passed pictures of the fruitful kibbutz in which I was born, raised and educated. I knew, more than at any other moment in my life, that my presence on this boat was an integral part of my being. Next to me, writhing with grimaces of suffering, was a young boy, an immigrant, who had seen Eretz Israel for only a limited number of hours. We shook each other's extended hand . . .

Shmuelik

Shall I tell you how I felt when the ship left the shore? I was thrown against the sides of the hold, deep within the ship, and I realized that we were moving. Perhaps it is strange, but my heart was tranquil and perhaps even happy.

Another trip came to my mind: the sailing to Europe for the invasion. Then, there were with us Jewish soldiers from Palestine and British soldiers. Our ship was bombed and 140 of us were drowned in the depths of the sea. After long hours of floating in the water with the help of life belts, the British navy picked us up . . . A few years have passed since. Now the British sailors are on deck, and we are packed in the hold like criminals. Then, we had a common enemy and together we had fought him.

But my heart was calm. It was good to reflect that I was sailing to Cyprus, and in my place a brother had reached home after all his sufferings.

To me, this was an additional lesson in the cruel proof of reality. The voyage enfeebled and taught. We returned ready to assemble again on the shore.

Shlomo

"Illegal Immigration"

# Readings

*Flight and Rescue: Brihah* by Yehuda Bauer (Jew. Pub. Soc, 1970), is *the* authoritative book on the subject. It presents the story of the escape of Jewish survivors in Eastern Europe from 1944–48 and highlights the rescue work of the J.D.C.

*From Diplomacy to Resistance* by Yehuda Bauer (Jew. Pub. Soc., 1970), presents the story from the angle of Palestine Jewry's heroic efforts to aid the DP's.

*Brihah: Flight to the Homeland* by Ephraim Dekel (Herzl Press, 1973), unfolds the story of the Brihah retold by its participating leaders.

*In Search* by Meyer Levin (Horizon Press, 1950), is the story of Brihah as narrated by the celebrated American writer who filmed this epic chapter.

*The Gate Breakers* by Bracha Habas presents deeply stirring narratives of the emissaries from Eretz Yisrael to help their brethren in Europe and Africa to escape to Israel through the "phantom ships," airplane lifts, etc.

# 24. GRIM END AND JUDGMENT DAY

Berlin—April 1945. Hidden in an underground bunker and cut off from what remained of his armies, Hitler continued playing Fuehrer. With the Russians constantly drawing closer and an almost continuous bombardment in progress, the atmosphere in the bunker was hysterical. Abandoned by Himmler and Goering, Hitler was alone except for Eva Braun, his personal retinue, some SS officers, and the Goebbels family.

Ranting madly at the end, Hitler planned "counter-offensives" with nonexistent troops, and condemned Goering and Himmler to death. On April 28, he dictated his last testament—a document which reflected his final madness. "It is untrue," he wrote, "that I, or anybody else in Germany, wanted war in 1939. It was wanted and provoked exclusively by those international politicians who either came of Jewish stock or worked for Jewish interests." Attributing Germany's defeat to the cowardice and treason of the General Staff, he predicted that the Reich would rise again. "Above all," he wrote, "I charge the leadership of the nation, as well as its followers, to a religious adherence to our racial laws and to a merciless resistance to the poisoner of all peoples—international Jewry."

The next day Hitler and Eva Braun committed suicide. Goebbels and his wife and six children followed suit.[1]

Soon after, on May 8, 1945, the guns fell silent in Europe. According to American and Soviet estimates, nine million Germans had been killed in the war, not including civilians. After twelve years, three months, and eight days, Hitler's Thousand Year Reich had collapsed.

[1]For further details on Hitler's end, read Alan Bullock, *Hitler: A Study in Tyranny* (New York: Harper and Row, 1964).

## JUDGMENT DAY

As early as 1941, the Allies had warned the Germans that they would be punished severely for their many atrocities and war crimes. After the war, nineteen nations joined together to try the Nazi war criminals, with American, British, French, and Soviet jurists serving as official prosecutors.

The international war crimes tribunal at Nuremberg (November 20, 1945–August 31, 1946) was one of the most significant criminal trials in history. Never before had legal proceedings been instituted against the leaders of a conquered enemy nation. For the first time, a criminal state was being brought before an international bar of justice. Twenty-four major Nazi criminals were tried (two in absentia). At its concluding session, the tribunal's president pronounced sentence on the defendants. Many of them, including Goering, Streicher, and Bormann, were sentenced to death. Others were given life or long-term prison sentences, including Rudolf Hess, who, in 1977, was still serving his sentence. In addition to the trials at Nuremberg, many lesser war criminals were tried in the various zones of occupation.[2]

## THE EICHMANN TRIAL

In May 1960, Prime Minister David Ben-Gurion announced to the Israel Knesset that Adolf Eichmann, one of the foremost Nazi war criminals, had been captured and brought to Israel to stand trial.

The world was stunned by the announcement, and Argentina complained that Israel had violated its sovereignty by abducting Eichmann from Buenos Aires. Others challenged Israel's right to try Eichmann. The trial, however, was meticulously fair. Eichmann was represented by the defense counsel of his choice, all the normal judicial procedures were maintained, and the world press was constantly in attendance.

Eichmann's main defense was the claim that he had simply been a cog in a machine which would have functioned without him. He also asserted that the Israelis were incapable of giving him a fair trial. Prosecutor Gideon Hausner, however, conducted his case with dignity and vigor, indicting Eichmann on fifteen counts and, with the aid of numerous survivor-witnesses and documents, amply demonstrated that Eichmann had made policy and acted on his own responsibility.

The trial ended on December 15, 1961. Eichmann was sentenced to death by hanging—the only person ever to be executed under Israeli law.

[2]Space does not permit a full report on the many war-criminal trials. Those interested will find a partial listing of sentences in Gerald Reitlinger, *The Final Solution* (A. S. Barnes Co., 1961), pp. 533 and 553–64. The complete account of the Nuremberg trials is available in eleven thick volumes entitled *International Military Trials, Nuremberg* (Washington: U.S. Government Printing Office, 1946).

His body was cremated, and the ashes were strewn over the sea so as not to defile the soil of Israel.

The Eichmann trial had a major impact on Israel and the world, publicizing the enormity of the Nazi crimes against the Jews and against humanity. In particular, it provided many young West Germans with their first opportunity to learn in detail about the unspeakable crimes perpetrated by their country during World War II.

## OTHER TRIALS

Even today, trials of Nazi war criminals are still taking place. On August 29, 1975, for instance, after a sixteen-year series of trials, the former head of the Gestapo in Warsaw was sentenced to life imprisonment for his involvement in the deaths of 230,000 Jews. In November 1975 Hermine Braunsteiner Ryan, a former SS guard who had begun a new life in Queens, New York, was extradited to West Germany and stood trial for mass murder at the Majdanek camp.

In many instances, however, the West German courts have been lenient in recent years, while many Latin American governments have been reluctant to extradite war criminals who have taken refuge within their jurisdiction. Several accused Nazis are also living securely in the United States.[3]

Though more than three decades have passed since the war, decent people throughout the world still demand that the criminals be punished, and the search for those who escaped still continues. Moreover, a few dedicated individuals have devoted themselves to tracking down the remaining criminals. One of these is Simon Wiesenthal. Another is German-born, non-Jewish Beate Klarsfeld.[4] "The victims of the Nazis," she says, "have a right to expect the prosecution of those responsible. It is not enough for young Germans to go to Israel and plant a tree. . . . The German people must be redeemed."

[3]Some of them are named in *Martyrdom and Resistance,* the newsletter of the American Federation of Jewish Fighters, Camp Inmates, and Nazi Victims (505 Fifth avenue, New York, N.Y. 10017).
[4]For more on her exploits, read her *Wherever They May Be* (New York: Viking Press, 1975).

# Ten Nazi Leaders Pay for Their Crimes, 1946

NUREMBERG, OCTOBER 16 Ex-Reichsmarshall Hermann Wilhelm Goering cheated the gallows of Allied justice by committing suicide in his prison cell . . . The crown prince of Nazidom managed to hide, chew, and swallow a vial of cyanide of potassium.

None of the condemned men had been told that they were to die this morning. How Goering guessed this was to be his day of doom and how he managed to conceal the poison on his person is a mystery that has confounded the security forces.

. . . The ten other condemned princes of Nazidom were hanged in . . . the small gymnasium inside one of the prison yards of the Nuremberg city jail.

The executions took approximately one hour and a half . . .

The only one to make any reference to Nazi ideology was Julius Streicher, the arch Jew-baiter . . . He appeared in the execution hall Saturday night . . . at 12½ minutes after two o'clock.

An American lieutenant colonel . . . entered first . . . followed by Streicher. Inside the door, two American sergeants closed in on each side of him and held his arms while another sergeant removed his manacles and replaced them with a leather cord . . .

(Streicher) glanced at the three wooden scaffolds rising up menacingly in front of him. Two of these were used alternately to execute the condemned men while the third was kept in reserve.

After a quick glance at the gallows, Streicher glared around the room, his eyes resting momentarily upon the small group of American, British, French, and Russian officers on hand to witness the executions.

By this time Streicher's hands were tied securely. Two guards, one to each arm, directed him to the gallows on the left. He walked steadily . . . but his face twitched nervously. As the guards stopped him at the bottom of the steps for official identification, he uttered his piercing scream, "Heil Hitler!"

His shriek sent a shiver down the back of this International News Service correspondent, who is witnessing the executions as sole representative of the American press.

From a United Press International News Service dispatch, October 16, 1946.

As its echo died away, another American colonel standing by the steps said sharply, "Ask the man his name."

In response . . . Streicher shouted, "You know my name well!"

The interpreter repeated his request, and the condemned man yelled, "Julius Streicher!"

As he mounted the platform Streicher cried out, "Now it goes to God!"

After getting up the 13 steps to the eight-foot-high and eight-foot-square black-painted wooden platform, Streicher was pushed two steps to the mortal spot beneath the hangman's rope . . .

Streicher was swung around to face toward the front. He glanced again at the Allied officers and the eight Allied correspondents . . . With burning hatred in his eyes, Streicher looked down upon them and screamed, "Purim Fest, 1946!" [a reference to a Jewish holiday commemorating the hanging of Haman, oppressor of the Jews].

The American officer at the scaffold said, "Ask the man if he has any last words."

When the interpreter had translated, Streicher shouted, "The Bolsheviks will hang *you* one day!"

. . . The trap was sprung with a loud bang. With the rope snapped taut and the body swinging wildly, a groan could be heard distinctly within the dark interior of the scaffold.

It was originally intended to permit the condemned to walk the 70-odd yards from the cells to the execution chamber with their hands free, but they were all manacled in the cells immediately following Goering's suicide.

The weasel-faced Ribbentrop . . . uttered his final words while waiting for the black hood to be placed over his head. Loudly, in firm tones, he said, "God save Germany!" He then asked, "May I say something else?" The interpreter nodded. The former diplomatic wizard of Nazidom . . . then added, "My last wish is that Germany realize its entity and that an understanding be reached between East and West. I wish peace to the world."

The ex-diplomat looked straight ahead as the hood was adjusted. His lips were set tight.

Next in line was Field Marshall Wilhelm Keitel, symbol of Prussian militarism and aristocracy. He was the first military leader to be executed under the new concept of Allied international law—(the principle) that professional soldiers cannot escape responsibility for war crimes by claiming they were merely carrying out orders of their superiors.

Keitel entered the death arena at 1:18 . . . while Ribbentrop was still hanging . . . He could not, of course, see the ex-Foreign Minister, whose body was concealed within the first scaffold and whose rope still hung taut.

Keitel . . . held his head high while his hands were being tied, and walked erect with military bearing to the foot of the second scaffold . . . When asked his name he answered in a loud sharp tone, "Wilhelm Keitel!" He mounted the gallows steps as he might have climbed to a reviewing stand to take the salute of the German Army . . . At the top of the platform, Keitel looked over the crowd with the traditional iron-jawed haughtiness of the proud Prussian officer. Asked if he had anything to say, he looked straight ahead and spoke in a loud voice: "I call on Almighty God to have mercy on the German people. More than two million German soldiers went to their deaths for the Fatherland. Now I follow my sons."

Then, while raising his voice to shout, "All for Germany," Keitel's black-booted uniformed body plunged down with a bang. Observers agreed he had shown more courage on the scaffold than he had in the courtroom . . .

There was a pause in the grim proceedings.

The American colonel directing the executions asked the American general representing the Allied Control Commission if those present could smoke. An affirmative answer brought cigarettes into the hands of almost every one of the 30-odd persons present . . .

The directing colonel turned to the witnesses and said, "Lights out, please, gentlemen," and then to another colonel, "O.K." The latter went out . . . to fetch the next man.

This creature was Ernst Kaltenbrunner, Gestapo chief . . . [This] master killer of Nazidom entered the execution chamber at 1:36 A.M. wearing a sweater beneath his double-breasted coat. With his lean, haggard face furrowed by old dueling scars, the terrible successor of Reinhard Heydrich had a frightening look as he glanced around the room.

He was nervous and he wet his lips as he turned to mount the gallows, but he walked steadily. He answered his name in a calm, low voice. When he turned around on the gallows platform he first faced a U.S. Catholic Army chaplain attired in a Franciscan habit. Asked for his last words, he answered quietly, "I would like to say a word. I have loved my German people and my Fatherland with a warm heart. I have done my duty by the laws of my people and I am sorry my people were led by men who were not soldiers and that crimes were committed of which I have no knowledge."

This was strange talk from a man whose agent, Rudolf Hoess, had confessed at a previous trial that under Kaltenbrunner's orders he gassed 3,000,000 human beings at the Auschwitz concentration camp.

As the black hood was about to be lowered, Kaltenbrunner, still in a low, calm voice, used a German phrase which means, "German good luck."

His trap was sprung at 1:39 A.M. . . . .

579

The scaffold was made ready for Alfred Rosenberg, master mind of the Nazi race theories, who had sought to establish Nazism as a pagan religion.

Rosenberg was dull and sunken-cheeked . . . his complexion a pasty brown. But he did not appear nervous, and walked steadily to the gallows. Apart from giving his name and replying "No" to . . . whether he had anything to say, he did not utter a word. Despite his disbelief in God he was accompanied by a Protestant chaplain, who stood beside him, praying.

Rosenberg looked at the chaplain once, but said nothing. Ninety seconds after he had entered the hall he was swinging from the end of a hangman's rope . . .

Hans Frank, the *Gauleiter* of Poland and former SS general, was next in the parade of death. He was the only one of the condemned to enter with a smile on his lips.

Although nervous and swallowing frequently, this man, who was converted to Catholicism after his arrest, seemed relieved at atoning for his evil deeds. He answered to his name quietly and when asked if he had any last statement replied in almost a whisper, "I am thankful for the kind treatment during my captivity and I ask God to accept me with mercy."

He closed his eyes and swallowed as the black hood went over his head.

The sixth man . . . 69-year-old Wilhelm Frick, former Nazi Minister of the Interior, entered at 2:05 . . . He seemed to be the least steady of any so far and stumbled on the thirteenth step of the gallows. His only words were, "Long live eternal Germany" . . .

Following . . . removal of Frick's corpse at 2:20 A.M., Fritz Sauckel, the slave-labor director and one of the most bloodstained men of Nazidom, faced his doom . . .

Looking wild-eyed, Sauckel proved to be the most defiant of any except Streicher. Here was the man who drove millions into bondage on a scale unknown since the pre-Christian era. Gazing around the room from the gallow's platform, he suddenly screamed, "I am dying innocent. The sentence is wrong. God protect Germany and make Germany great again. God protect my family."

The trap was sprung at 2:26 A.M. and, like Streicher, this hate-filled man groaned loudly as the fatal noose snapped tightly . . .

Ninth was Colonel General Alfred Jodl, Hitler's strategic adviser and close friend. With the black coat-collar of his Wehrmacht uniform turned up at the back as though hurriedly put on, Jodl entered the death house with obvious nervousness.

He wet his lips constantly and his features were drawn and haggard as he walked . . . Yet his voice was calm when he uttered his last six words on earth, "My greetings to you, my Germany."

At 2:34 Jodl plunged into the black hole of the scaffold's death. Both he and Sauckel hung together in the execution chamber until pronounced dead six minutes later.

Czechoslovakian-born Seyss-Inquart was the last actor in the ghastly scene of Allied Justice. He entered the death chamber at 2:38 A.M., wearing the glasses which made his face familiar and despised in all the years he ruled Holland with an iron hand and sent thousands of Dutchmen to Germany for forced labor.

Seyss-Inquart looked around with noticeable signs of unsteadiness and limped on his left clubfoot as he walked to the gallows. He mounted the steps slowly, with the help of guards. When he spoke his last words, his voice was low but intense: "I hope that this execution is the last act of the tragedy of the Second World War and that the lesson taken from this World War will be that there should be peace and understanding between peoples.

"I believe in Germany."

---

# The Eichmann Trial

Shortly after Eichmann was caught in Argentina and brought to my country, I realized he might attempt to plead insanity. To be ready for such a maneuver, I ordered him examined by psychiatrists. One of the many tests given him was the famous one invented by the Hungarian psychologist, L. Szondi. The accused is shown a long series of photographs. In each group are pictures of a convicted murderer and a proven sadist. The subject is asked to select from each group two photographs of people who attract him and two who repel him. Eichmann was given the test 10 times in 40 days . . . a total of 240 times.

The important thing about the test, of course, is the interpretation of the results . . . We decided to have the results sent to the inventor himself, Professor Szondi. It was not revealed who the subject was.

Doctor Szondi's reply astonished me. He started by saying that he never analyzed tests of people who had not been identified for him, but that when he'd glanced briefly at the results, they were so extraordinary that he performed a complete analysis. The subject, he declared, revealed in all phases "a man obsessed with a dangerous and insatiable

From *Eichmann and His Trial* by Gideon Hausner, in the *Saturday Evening Post,* November 3, 1962.

urge to kill, arising out of a desire for power." In every group of photographs he had unerringly picked out the murderer and the sadist as people who appealed to him. According to Doctor Szondi, this had never happened to him in his 24 years of practice as a criminal psychologist, a period in which he'd tested more than 6,000 criminals.

Other psychiatric tests . . . confirmed that we had on our hands a dangerous, perverted, sadistic personality . . . However, they also confirmed he was legally sane and responsible for his actions. Eichmann's feeling about Jews started with anti-Semitism and developed into much more. In the end it was no ordinary hatred. In order to hate, one must feel. It is impossible, for example, to hate a chair or a table. And to Eichmann, Jews were nothing more—in fact, far less. In short, he was the final, undiluted product of the murderous Nazi regime—a man chosen because of his special qualities to perform the grisly task of exterminating 6,000,000 Jews . . . And he did his job so well that he was once able to say that, although Germany had lost the war, nonetheless "I can joyously jump into my grave, knowing my mission has been fulfilled."

Humanity deserves the fullest possible picture of a system of government and of a man able to spread a deadly dragnet over most of Europe and scoop up millions of men, women and children for slaughter in one of the greatest crimes of all time . . .

. . . There were many like him, and he had legions of assistants . . . Many millions of Germans were aware of what was going on. The regime started by indoctrinating the German people with notions of racial superiority and the denial of moral duties toward their fellow men. "Thou shalt not" ceased to exist for them. Next, they instilled hatred and contempt for aliens. Later . . . they were ready to embark on mass slaughter.

. . . Although we were trying a single murderer, we were also exposing the whole Nazi movement and anti-Semitism at large . . .

Prior to that fateful morning when the trial started in Jerusalem, I had never laid eyes on Eichmann. My first glimpse of him, however, was a shocker . . .

I was fully aware of his ruthlessness. I had seen numerous pleas addressed to him to spare the lives of certain Jews. Some had been written even by Nazi big shots who, for reason of bribery or economic policy, wished certain Jews temporarily spared. Eichmann's reply to all such requests had been a resounding "No!" On one occasion, he even bucked Hitler himself. The *Fuehrer,* late in the war, made a concession to the wavering government in Hungary to allow 8,700 Jewish families to leave, provided the rest of the Hungarian Jews—about 400,000— were handed over to the Nazis. Eichmann was so outraged at the possibility of this tiny remnant of Jewry escaping that he actually

582

appealed to Hitler to change his decision, and finally got the *Fuehrer* to do so.

Eichmann frequently came to grips with high officials who felt that winning the war was more important than annihilating Jews. Toward the end . . . military men insisted that Germany needed every man, every rifle and every railroad train. They did not want these diverted to concentration camps. They wanted the Jews to be put to work . . . However, in the teeth of all this pressure, Eichmann stubbornly managed to keep his death juggernaut rolling, killing as many as 18,000 Jews a day. There was no stopping him.

. . . I half expected to encounter some of the arrogance, some of the posture and some of the diabolic strength of this Gestapo leader.

The shocker . . . was that I saw none of these things. In fact, Eichmann looked like nothing much at all. The man facing me was the kind you might rub elbows with in the street any day and never notice. He was nondescript, in his middle 50's, balding, lean, of dark complexion and of medium height. The first unusual thing one noticed was a twitch around his mouth which gave his face a strange, almost grotesque appearance. Only his narrow eyes behind the heavy eyeglasses disclosed his real personality. When he was cornered on some particularly slippery ground, those eyes would light up with bottomless hatred. Once, when this happened, my assistant tugged at my robe and whispered, "Did you notice his eyes? They frightened me."

But such moments were rare. Almost immediately Eichmann was able to revert to his usual, gray, nondescript appearance . . .

According to Israeli law, after the pretrial interrogation, an accused man must be shown *in advance* every piece of evidence, every document, every statement of every witness who will testify at the trial. Unlike American prosecutors, Israeli ones cannot introduce anything the defense doesn't know about.

Eichmann made the most of this situation. He studied the hundreds of things we planned to introduce and memorized most of them . . . He made extensive notes, turning his glass cubicle into a one-man office. He even had a special microphone in his bulletproof "office" by which he could communicate with his counsel, Dr. Robert Servatius.

. . . Eichmann carefully constructed a picture of himself best calculated to save his life. If—as was proved—Jews were segregated, starved, looted, tortured, turned into slave workers and eventually destroyed in camps, Eichmann's portrait of himself never varied: he was a mere clerk arranging train schedules and other minor details . . . He maintained that he never displayed any initiative or made independent decisions; he was always acting under orders.

. . . We proved that Eichmann displayed a lot of initiative and authority. For example, we introduced a handwritten memo from a

German official who said that when he asked Eichmann what to do with the Jews in Belgrade, he got the reply, "Shoot them on the spot!" Another Nazi official wrote that Eichmann had "agreed" to exterminate Jews by poison gas, rather than by shooting. These obviously were not the decisions of a mere train scheduler.

We also introduced Eichmann orders showing how he diabolically lulled his victims into a feeling of confidence that nothing would happen to them if they only "behaved themselves"—that is, wore the yellow badge proclaiming their Jewishness, turned over their property to the state and quietly took the special trains to the "work camps," which were actually extermination camps. We showed how Eichmann's orders were so skillfully thought out that most Jews were unaware of what was really happening to them until they were on the point of being gassed. Even at the entrance to the death chambers, the victims were told they were merely to be disinfected. Small children were handed pieces of candy to keep them quiet.

All these things were done at Eichmann's behest. Nonetheless, he insisted that in everything he was merely acting under orders. When a document proved that he was acting on his own authority, he took the last retreat: he branded it as a forgery!

Knowing the evidence that we had, Eichmann still half expected somehow to escape with his life. In fact, just before the cross-examination he said to one of his guards, "So long as Mr. Hausner sticks to the documents, I am on safe ground." But when particularly damaging admissions were elicited from him in questioning, he remarked that he never expected cross-examination to be like this, adding, "I don't like the attorney general."

The portrait Eichmann presented in court rarely brought out his total lack of remorse. Four years prior to the trial, when Eichmann had a long discussion in Argentina with the Dutch journalist, Willem A. Sassen, he declared, "There is nothing I have to regret. Had we killed the eleven million Jews as contemplated, however, I would have been happier." (The figure of 11,000,000 referred to the total European Jewish population, including those in Russia, Great Britain, Ireland, Switzerland, Turkey and other countries which the Nazis optimistically expected to get their hands on when they won the war.) . . .

It became increasingly clear that the only things that really mattered to Eichmann were the formalities. The true significance of his unbelievable acts never bothered him . . . We had a striking example of this . . .

One evening . . . we were previewing in the courtroom some films we wished to introduce as evidence. Some depicted shattering scenes of helpless victims being loaded on trains like cattle. Others, surreptitiously shot inside the camps, showed all the ghastly details of mass slaughter. There were pictures of naked men, women and children being lined up before the Nazi execution squads . . . We witnessed one wave of writhing corpses after another fall into the deep open grave dug beforehand by the victims themselves.

Finally came scenes of the liberation when thousands of bodies had to be shoveled by bulldozers into mass graves for fear of infection. They were pictures of unspeakable horror—the kind that turn one's stomach . . .

The courtroom was almost empty at the time. The judges were not there, nor was the general public admitted. The defense counsel, Doctor Servatius, and the accused were in their usual places. Suddenly, Eichmann, who had been watching the films calmly and unperturbed, never lowering his gaze or missing a scene, started an agitated argument with his guards. Everybody expected an objection as to the truthfulness of the pictures . . . However, the reason was quite different. He had noticed people sitting in the seats reserved for the public, and on being told that they were journalists, he protested against having been brought to the courtroom in slacks and a sweater instead of the dark-blue suit provided him for the trial.

Another incident underlined the man's unusual concern with externals.

One evening he developed a rheumatic pain in his right arm. It hampered the putting on of his earphones to get the simultaneous translation of the proceedings in German. He asked the doctor for medicine to relieve the pain at once so that he could put on the earphones in the usual way. "I don't want to appear clumsy in my movements," he explained. The doctor complied . . .

I doubt whether Eichmann ever entered the courtroom without first neatly adjusting his tie or patting his hair in order . . .

In all this, Eichmann was true to the Gestapo type, which Dr. G. M. Gilbert, the Long Island University professor who was the prison psychologist at the Nuremberg trials of the Nazi war criminals, summed up: "An inhuman, murderous robot, quiet and correct in military bearing, functioning intellectually on a high level of mechanical efficiency, utterly devoid of human empathy."

Eichmann gave a droll illustration of the way this mechanical man operates. One morning he was given by mistake six slices of bread for breakfast, instead of the usual two. He ate all six. When the guard asked whether he'd like six in the future, he replied: "Oh, no. Two are quite enough. But when you give me six, I have to eat them." On another occasion he asked that a portion of onions be removed from his tray because the particles got in his dentures. It never occurred to him simply to leave the onions uneaten.

Eichmann's mask was so impassive that it was only such things as his eating habits that occasionally gave us a glimpse of how the evidence was affecting him . . . Before the trial, he was questioned about a secret Berlin meeting in 1939 . . . to arrange that all Polish Jews be concen-

585

trated in ghettos near railroad junctions . . . for the "final solution." Eichmann . . . denied that he was there . . . But when we produced a document showing that he was one of the 16 high-ranking Nazis at the conference, he replied, "Of course, it cannot be denied anymore that I was there." That day Eichmann . . . asked if he might be excused from having lunch or dinner.

. . . Eichmann remained fanatically hostile to religion . . . He admitted that he became so infuriated when his wife read a Bible that he snatched it away and tore it to pieces. He refused to take an oath on the Bible, saying that he did not belong to any church . . . He died as he lived—a pagan. He had a kind of mystic belief in the unity of the universe and in man's being solely a biological product.

. . . We found him one of the most garrulous prisoners on record. His pretrial statement, recorded on tape, covered 3,564 typewritten pages—the equivalent of six long novels. And this did not include his extensive personal notes, memoirs, observations on documents, charts, etc.

He revealed . . . an astonishing memory. He could remember in smallest detail the books he had read in the '20's, the name of the German consul who had given him a visa in Linz in 1933, the names of all the persons he met on a trip to Egypt in 1937, the price of a meal and a glass of beer at a military canteen 25 years before. "A roll was given extra without charge," he recalled.

It was only in matters relating to Jews that he had a lapse of memory. He couldn't remember what he'd seen at extermination camps . . . He couldn't remember when he had first ordered Jews to their death. And he couldn't remember why it was necessary for him to send three retroactive orders to Poland to "cover" the execution of 750,000 human beings that had already taken place, killings over and beyond the quota prescribed by Berlin. It was, of course, needed to make the Nazi records "legal." His earlier feats of memory had been so stunning that no one could seriously believe he was capable of such monumental lapses.

Time and again I asked Eichmann in court what made him consider the Jews, who were less than one percent of the population of Germany, the main "disaster" of the country. His reply was that the Jews were "opponents." Opponents had to be combated . . .

At the height of his career Eichmann was a man of towering arrogance. During the war he strutted across Europe in his smart uniform, topped with the SS cap complete with skull and crossbones. In winter he wore a long leather overcoat on which, according to his own evidence, the brain of a baby was once spilled when he came too near an execution squad liquidating the Jewish population of Minsk in 1941.

His name was whispered in horror throughout the ghettos of Europe. As supreme head of the Gestapo department dealing with

586

Jews, Eichmann had offices in Berlin, Vienna, Prague, Paris, Oslo, The Hague and other capitals . . . He operated so deftly that Gestapo chief Müller was once moved to say, "If Germany had had fifty Eichmanns, we would have won the war!" . . .

In court we saw a totally subdued Eichmann . . . He knew that creating a picture of a small man, forced . . . into doing things he did not like, gave him his best chance for saving his neck.

. . . I knew that Eichmann was a sly, cunning opponent . . . clever enough to elude his trackers for 15 long years—in which he'd had ample time to prepare for a trial . . . Because he destroyed all records of his Gestapo office and because he knew in advance of our documents and witnesses, he had the advantage of being able to allege or deny facts that we could not refute except by general questioning. It was clear, too, that the court of Israel would insist on strict compliance with the rules of procedure and evidence.

Consequently . . . when Eichmann—looking and acting like an insignificant clerk with a faulty memory—appeared before me for the first time that spring morning in Jerusalem, I realized it would not be easy to convince the court that he was indeed the archmonster who presided over the liquidation of 6,000,000 Jews in the shooting pits and gas ovens of the Nazi overlords.

# A Judge Recalls Paul Blobel's Trial

*Justice Michael A. Mussman was the prosecutor of the trials of Otto Ohlendorf, who had been responsible for the murder of 60,000 Jews and Gypsies, and Paul Blobel, leader of an SS unit which was involved in sixteen mass murders including the massacre of 30,000 Jews in Kiev. They were hanged at Landsberg on June 17, 1951. Judge Musmanno recalls the trial . . .*

Next to Ohlendorf, Paul Blobel was perhaps the defendant who excited the most notice among the visitors . . . Nuremberg from late 1945 to 1948 was a Mecca to historians, writers, dramatists, journalists and diplomats who recognized in the proceedings unfolding in the Palace of Justice the serious attempt being made to establish international responsibility to law by individuals, as well as

From *The Eichmann Commandos* by Michael A. Mussman.

nations. While Ohlendorf arrested attention because of his good looks, Blobel drew awed glances for the opposite reason . . . His eyes glared with the penetrating intensity of a wild animal at bay. It was hard to believe that this ferocious-looking creature was once an architect handling weapons no more lethal than a sliding rule and colored pencils.

The Einsatzgruppen reports showed that Sonderkommando 4A, which Blobel commanded from January, 1941 to June, 1942, killed over sixty thousand persons. His attorney, Dr. Willi Heim . . . claimed they were not accurate. The truth of the matter was, he said, that Blobel could not have been responsible for the killing of more than fifteen thousand!

As Blobel strode from the defendants' dock to the witness stand . . . his whole expression shouted that it was absurd he should be charged with crime. He was fighting a war; the reports were wrong; he did not kill as many people as they charged him with. Moreover, all cases were investigated before executions took place. And then he asserted that he committed no crime since his shootings were authorized by international law.

When the Prosecutor asked him: "Did you not have any moral scruples about carrying out executions—that is, did you regard the carrying out of these executions as in agreement with international law and in agreement with humanitarian impulses?" his beard bristled with the resentment of one who has just listened to a preposterous as well as insulting question.

Why, the executions of "agents, partisans, saboteurs, suspicious people, indulging in espionage and sabotage, and those who were of a detrimental effect to the German Army," he stridently rejoined, "were, in my opinion, completely in accordance with the Hague Convention."[1]

He did not stop to name any article of the Convention which authorized the killing of "suspicious people." Nor did he manifest the slightest awareness of the terrible reality that killing on mere suspicion is the very essence of first degree murder . . .

When his attorney asked him if he had any moral scruples against the execution of women and children, Blobel replied that he did not, because "every spy and saboteur knew what he had to expect when he was arrested." He did not specify in what manner women and children were spies and saboteurs.

Another explanation he offered for executions was that they were in the nature of reprisals. He believed that the killing of ten of the enemy for one German soldier "murdered" was not disproportionate because "other countries also carried out reprisal measures, and have given orders for such reprisals, about one to two hundred according to the well-known order of General Eisenhower."

[1]International Agreement Respecting the Laws of War (1907).

Surprised to hear this statement, I asked, "You say there is a well known order of General Eisenhower that two hundred were to be executed to one?"

Testily he replied, "All the German people know, your Honor, that an order was given by General Eisenhower that for every one American who was killed, two hundred Germans are to be shot." The defendant had become a prosecutor.

The courtroom was filled with people, many of them obviously German. I swept my hand from left to right to encompass the entire audience. "In this courtroom there must be, undoubtedly, many Germans. Can you point out one who knew of this order which you have just stated?"

The bearded accuser sat rigidly in his chair and made no answer. I inquired of Blobel's attorney if he knew of such an order. Bowing low, his robe scraping the floor, Dr. Heim said, "No, your Honor."

I asked the defendant whether he had personal knowledge of the order, and when he said that he had not read it himself, I inquired if any attorney in the courtroom knew about the order . . .

Blobel shot out, "Yes."

"Which one?"

"Dr. Heim, for example, read about it."

"Dr. Heim has already denied knowing about any such order. Mention the next person."

"I don't know the other gentlemen as well. I said I presume that people knew it."

He suggested that perhaps Ohlendorf was acquainted with the order, but Ohlendorf was now allowing himself one of his rare smiles. He hated Blobel because he regarded him as a liar and enjoyed seeing him, as he told others later, "stewing in his own juice."

To my question as to whether he could point to one defendant "who can state that he saw this announcement," Blobel replied, "I'd have to ask each one individually."

I faced the dock: "The Tribunal will direct a question to all of the defendants . . . Did any of the defendants here in this court ever see such an announcement? If any one did, he will please raise his hand."

Passing up Ohlendorf, Blobel turned the fiercely burning candle power of his eyes on the defendants, one after another, seeking by sheer ocular strength to lift one hand out of the two score available to confirm his utterance. But not a finger lifted or turned. The whole defendants' dock had turned to stone. I waited for a minute or two and then addressed the glowering Blobel: "No defendant has raised his hand, so now we come back to your original statement, that all of Germany knew of this announcement. Do you want to withdraw that statement?"

The bold and haughty beard had drooped to its owner's chest. The flaunting mustache had also wilted. Through the whiskery jungle came a mumble: "Under those circumstances, I have to beg your pardon."

Blobel was the evil genius of the notorious Kiev massacre ... So expertly did the ex-builder organize the truck service, the firing squads, and the burial teams that at the end of the second day 33,771 persons had been killed and entombed. And in the meantime every item of the "resettled" people's property had been gathered and catalogued ... The official report stated that "Money, valuables, underwear and clothing were secured and placed partly at the disposal of the NSV (Nazi Party Public Welfare Organization) for use of the racial Germans, partly given to the city administration for use of the needy population." ...

In Zhitomir ... Blobel continued his intensive drive in behalf of charity. The clothes taken from his victims in these latter operations required the service of numerous auto-cars. A report dated November 12, 1941, announced that "137 trucks full of clothes, made available in connection with the campaign against Jews at Zhitomir and Kiev, were put at the disposal of the NSV."

Blobel willingly described just how he conducted executions. He related how he divided his extermination unit into shooting squads of thirty men each, after the long ditches had been dug. "Out of the total number of the persons designated for the execution, fifteen men were led in each case to the brink of the mass grave where they had to kneel down, their faces turned toward the grave. When the men were ready for the execution one of my leaders who was in charge of this execution squad gave the order to shoot. Since they were kneeling on the brink of the mass grave, the victims fell, as a rule, at once into the mass grave.

"I have always used rather large execution squads, since I declined to use men who were specialists for shots in the neck. Each squad shot for about one hour and was then replaced. The persons which still had to be shot were assembled near the place of the execution, and were guarded by members of those squads, which at that moment did not take part in the executions." ...

I asked Blobel if he attached any type of marker or sign to the victims in order to guide the aim of the riflemen. If my voice was firm, Blobel's was as steady as a howitzer as he replied that the men of his unit were expert shots.

Nevertheless, I had misgivings, so I went on. "Striking a vital spot in the body requires a very steady hand, a very good eye and perfect control of the nervous system. Would you say that all these riflemen were so well-trained that they could bring home their shot to a vital spot in the victim's body at all times?"

An audible shudder ran through the spectators in the courtroom for they could visualize as well as I the possibility that a person only slightly wounded could be buried alive. But Blobel said that this was impossible. "After each firing order, when the shots were addressed, somebody looked at the victims, because the victims were then put into the grave when they did not fall into the graves themselves, and these tasks were in the field of tasks of the men of the individual kommandos. The edge of the grave had to be cleaned, for instance. Two men who had spades dealt with this. They had to clean it up and then the next group was led there."

I still worried about the possibility of a conscious person seeing the coffin lid of earth closing over him. "Since this was all done rapidly, might it not be possible that a victim would be buried, even though not actually dead?"

"No, that is quite impossible, your Honor."

"You exclude that possibility?"

"Yes, for the simple reason that if it was ascertained that the shots which had been aimed at the head had not actually hit the head, one of the men of the firing squad was called in, who fired again [with rifle] from a distance of three to four paces. He shot again and thus it was made absolutely certain that the person concerned was dead." . . .

Although Blobel asserted that he acted legally at all times, he was concerned about the evidence he left of his executions. He flew back to Berlin and called on his chief Adolf Eichmann in his office. From him he obtained an order authorizing the opening of graves and burning of corpses. The burning process, however, was not as satisfactory as Blobel had hoped, so he resorted to other means. He tried dynamiting. Rudolf Hoess, commandant of the Auschwitz concentration camp, who supervised this operation, stated that this evidence-destroying method did not measure up to expectations. "Blobel constructed several experimental ovens and used wood and gasoline as fuel. He tried to destroy the corpses by means of dynamiting them, too; this method was rather unsuccessful." Hence other means were used . . .

A witness, Albert Hartel, testified regarding his association with Blobel in Kiev in the month of March, 1942. One day Hartel drove into the country accompanied by Blobel who called his attention to various points of interest. Suddenly Hartel was frightened by a terrestrial phenomenon—the earth was exploding. Under the questioning of Dr. Heim, Blobel's own lawyer, as to additional information, Hartel said, "I cannot give any further details of this drive because it made a shattering impression on me at the time. It was snowy, and on one particular spot we touched the spot, the earth still exploded. There were some kind of eruptions, a kind of explosion, and I asked Blobel what that was, and he said, 'Here my Jews are buried.'"

Blobel knew his worth. When Prosecutor Horlik-Hochwald, reading aloud from a document which contained Blobel's name, asked him if his name was Paul Blobel, the bearded and mustached dignitary stood up as well as he could while still sitting down, and declared, "My name is Hermann Wilhelm Paul Blobel."

Regardless of their mode of procedure, the executioners com-

591

mended themselves on the magnanimous methods they observed in accomplishing their missions. Defendant after defendant emphasized to the Tribunal that the requirements of militariness and humaneness were fastidiously complied with in all killing parties. Of course, occasionally, as Otto Ohlendorf described it, "the manner in which the executions were carried out caused excitement and disobedience among the victims, so that the Kommandos were forced to restore order by means of violence," that is to say, the victims were beaten.

The defendant SS-Brigadier General Erwin Schulz also assured us that "useless tortures" were avoided.

How did the people destined to die react to their fate once they became aware of its irrevocable finality? According to the defendant Paul Blobel, most of them were silent. Some of the prisoners, who were to be shot in the back, turned around at that last moment and bravely faced the riflemen, but still they said nothing . . .

# Seven Nazis Were Hanged

*On April 14, 1949, twenty-six Nazi murderers were condemned to hang by the United States Military Government in Germany. One was Oswald Pohl, who had administered the concentration camps and played a chief role in the destruction of the Warsaw ghetto. He had converted to Catholicism and became very devout. Another was Otto Ohlendorf, who by his own testimony had killed tens of thousands of Jews and Gypsies. A third was Paul Blobel (see above). Appeals for clemency poured in and public reaction in Germany was vehement. In the end the death sentences of seven men were confirmed.*

*Arthur Settel, an American Jew, who was chief of the Public Relations Division of the High Commissioner's (John J. McCloy) office, was the official witness to the executions. He arrived in Landsberg the evening before the executions were to take place, April 7, 1951. The diary's schedule follows the European method of recording time. Thus we begin here with 2110 or 9:10 P.M. In the excerpt that follows we report the proceedings up to 0326 or 3:26 A.M. a little over six hours . . .*

Col. Walter Graham, the prison commander, shows me a great heap of letters and telegrams from German sympathizers offering comfort to the criminals. Most of them are biblical quotations,

From *Commentary Magazine,* May 1960, by Arthur Settel.

others enclose pressed flowers. There is a batch from German nationals offering to die in place of the condemned. One telegram to Graham pleads for the privilege of hanging in place of Pohl. Graham says: "I ought to accept this offer; that guy's been begging to be executed."

(There are 513 prisoners in Landsberg as of 2120 hours on June 6. A total of 265 have been hanged since the end of the war.)

2140: Graham receives confirmation from Heidelberg: proceed with executions.

2147: Alexander Bickel, officer of the General Counsel, receives confirmation from Frankfort: proceed with executions . . .

2200: No newsmen will be admitted to the executions . . . Although preparations have been a strictly guarded secret, the news that the seven will be hanged has leaked out—principally via the wives of the condemned, their defense counsel, and the prison grapevine.

The CIC agents tell us that the newspaper reporters, some of them Germans, have been interviewing the wives of the seven. The latter have invented stories about how their husbands are being mistreated. In fact, Landsberg is one of the best operated prisons in Europe, and its inmates receive civilized treatment . . .

2229: A German Evangelical chaplain named Ermann, employed for two years by the prison, was intercepted smuggling mail out for the prisoners, and was sacked. Graham shakes his head. "Those damned Germans. And the way we treat *them*."

2235: Graham is discussing the business of last rites. He says this takes considerable time. Each chaplain is allowed all the time he needs in the cell with the condemned man before he is led to the gallows. "You can't hurry them, you know," says the Colonel philosophically.

2242: The army executioner, Mr. Britt, suddenly puts in an appearance, trim and neat in his tight-fitting uniform. How are you feeling? I ask. Fine, he says. His hand is moist, clammy. He shakes hands also with Bickel when I introduce them. Bickel studies Britt's face. For some reason, Warrant Officer Britt seems just right for his job. Though short, he is athletic, wiry and powerful. I wonder how he can sleep with himself. He has executed scores of criminals and has been flown from Texas to perform his job again . . .

2249: Bickel says he will not be a witness. He will take phone calls in Graham's office. This leaves me the only witness for the State Department. There's no backing out now.

593

2250: Warrant Officer Britt is discussing hangings with the medical officer. Describes how the neck is broken in the fall, how the stomach bulges . . . how it requires 15 to 19 minutes in some cases for final consummation. He says he once had a "case" with a bad heart—it took that one only ten minutes! . . .

2300: Bickel calls Frankfort. He says, we're all set; we'll call you right after the first one is pronounced dead, and after the last . . .

2346: Graham addresses us briefly. He says we must realize the seriousness of the occasion. It will be without levity, emotion, or demonstrations of any kind. We are to stand at attention during the hangings. We may be seated and smoke after each "drop." The queasy feeling in the pit of my stomach comes back.
  We follow Graham to the Death House.

2350: I look into the telephone shack to see exactly where I have to call Bickel after the first drop. There is a staff sergeant, stout and unsmiling, unarmed, standing at the door. His face is yellow in the lamplight. I tell him I will be down to make a call after the first drop. I remember that I must dial "22," which is Bickel's extension in Graham's office. Will I be able to perform this simple act? I have photographs of the seven men in my hands. I am to identify them before certifying.

2353: I return to the Death House, climb up the last stairway, see the gallows for the first time. Now I don't think I can stick it out . . .
  I look around. I see Warrant Officer Britt efficiently rubbing the noose with wax, and his assistant, a sergeant, is busying himself with the black hoods which have been stored in an ordinary army foot locker. I feel as though I am moving in a weird dream as I watch these macabre figures around me, figures in the khaki of the U.S. Army uniform. They seem collected and self-controlled, and I make an effort to get a grip on myself.

2354: Nine minutes left. I wonder what the architect Blobel is thinking down in his cell as he waits to be led out. It is cold up here in the loft of the prison workshop which has now been temporarily outfitted for this unusual purpose. I notice on the other side of the loft a neatly piled stack of white pine coffins which presumably were made for the war criminals whose sentences have been commuted. I wonder what they will be using these for now . . .

2355: I watch the preparations. Mr. Britt is testing the rope now; he lifts and then lowers himself on the closed trap.

594

2357: Hard wood benches line the sides of the loft. It is a small room; I am sitting within ten feet of the gallows. There is a fire extinguisher resting on a stone ledge at the end of the wall. There is an emergency lamp, and a field telephone within reach of Colonel Graham. A few extra folding chairs have been set up. Two cameramen, both GI non-coms, are fooling with their apparatus. The commandant, Colonel Graham, cigar between his teeth, is darting about, a sheaf of papers in one hand.

2359: One minute before midnight. Will there be another reprieve? It is still remotely possible. That sick feeling comes over me again. I shake it off with difficulty. The colonel takes the center of the floor. He repeats his caution against frivolity, although for the life of me I can't imagine how or why anyone would become frivolous. He adds one thought, that none of us likes this business but we've got to go through with it.

2400: Now we hear footsteps and the voice of a chaplain praying in sonorous German. The footsteps have a hollow sound on the wooden stairway leading up into the loft.

*June 7, 1951*
0001: Two soldiers wearing neatly pressed olive drab uniforms are first to arrive in the loft. They are followed by the chaplain, wearing a white tunic and reading from his prayer book. Behind him is Paul Blobel whose Sonderkommando SS unit was involved in sixteen instances of mass murder, including the killing of 33,000 Jews in the Kiev massacre alone. Then two GI guards, unarmed, follow.

Blobel is dressed for death. He wears black shirt, black trousers, leather belt and sandals. His wrists are tied behind him. He is clean shaven now and looks older than his 57 years. I study his photograph, compare it with the man. His face is that of a storekeeper or a teacher. I look for signs of the desperate hater, the ruthless killer, but I don't find any.

The routine, carefully prepared in advance, is followed to the letter.

Graham calls out: "Attention!" All in the room stand. Warrant Officer Britt then places the prisoner on the trap door. He straps prisoner's ankles and steps back. The official cameramen photograph the prisoner after one of the GI assistants places the nameplate across the condemned man's chest. The GI interpreter asks: "Have you any last words?" The prisoner replies: *"Jawohl!"*

0002: There is no wavering in voice or manner, never a sign of fear. Blobel speaks in a detached, remote voice. He says, whatever I have done, I did as a soldier who obeyed orders. I have committed no crime. I will be vindicated by God and history. God have mercy on those who murder me.

0003: The chaplain reads a prayer. He closes with a soft "amen." Britt throws the black hood over Blobel's head. There is a slight "fluff" in the air pocket. Britt adjusts the noose over the man's hooded head. The rope doesn't fit correctly. Britt removes it, places it back on the man's head for the second time, tightens it with the knot at the nape of the neck. Blobel's muffled voice is heard, but what he says is a mystery to those of us in the second circle.

0003½: Britt steps back, glances at Graham. Graham nods.

0004: Britt springs the trap. There is a slight crackle. The rope dangles slightly, then suddenly is very still.

0005: I recoil back into my seat. I light a cigarette. The others are relaxed now, smoking. The JAG lieutenant colonel seated next to me whispers, there but for the grace of God go I. His pipe is fragrant. We wait. My eyes are fixed on the rope. I am quite sick now, my hands are cold as ice. Britt is fooling with the second noose. He is amazingly efficient and cold-blooded. The sergeant aide is looking into the pit where architect Blobel is hanging. How silent it has become.

0007: (Lieut. Colonel) Borom says he wishes there were a seven-man gallows. I agree. I am glad to talk. He talks about his law practice in Alabama, tells me how he once saved a man from the gallows. I keep my eyes away from that rope.

0014: The sergeant pulls up the body while from the floor below someone disentangles the rope. We hear a murmur, then the soft voice of the medical officer. The cameraman's flash goes off in a sudden stab of light. Then there is another sound, the sound of the cover being nailed onto the coffin.

0015: I make my way down the steps to call Bickel. I tell him Blobel has been pronounced dead at 0014½, June 7.

0236: Seven times I have watched, compared the face of the condemned man with his official prison photograph. Seven times I have listened as they swore, in their dying words, that they had merely carried out orders; that they had been fighting for their country; that the Americans were their enemies. First Blobel, then the jurist Braune; Naumann, the SS General; Ohlendorf, the economist and lawyer who murdered 90,000; Pohl and Schallermair and Schmidt—each in his turn. Seven times I secretly murmured *kaddish,* the prayer for the dead, not for the executed man but in memory of their victims. We left the death chamber after Schmidt, of Buchenwald infamy, had been pronounced dead and after I had signed the affidavits as the government's official witness.

I returned to Graham's office. Across the corridor, the GI service unit was still listening to the ball game being broadcast from Ebbets Field, Brooklyn. I took a cup of coffee and a couple of the doughnuts being handed out by the mess sergeant, and sat down to listen to the game.

# Dr. Alina Brewda Accuses Dr. Dering

*In his world-renowned book EXODUS, Leon Uris accused a certain Dr. Wladislaw Alexander Dering as one of the doctors who performed criminal experiments in surgery. The Polish doctor, who after the war had become a British subject, achieving distinction and honors, brought charges of libel against the author, publisher, and printers. The trial was covered by the world press, radio and television, ending with a sensational verdict. Uris fictionalized the trial in his famous book QBV11. Below is the testimony of one of the accusers: Dr. Alina Brewda . . .*

The next witness whose appearance in the witness box had been anticipated from the first day, was Dr. Alina Brewda, a short, middle-aged woman. Born in Warsaw in 1905 of Polish-Jewish parents, she now lived in London.

She had met Dr. Dering when she was a medical student and he was houseman at the Warsaw University Clinic. They were quite friendly. He had married her fellow student some time after 1930. Dr. Brewda had also met him from time to time when they were about the business of the Jewish and Polish Students' Associations, though there were not many social contacts between the two bodies. At that time she had been a member of the Democratic Party, "the party in the middle."

*Mr. Hirst:* Are you now a member of any political party?

From *Auschwitz in England* by Mavis M. Hill and L. Norman Williams.

597

*Dr. Brewda:* No.

*Mr. Hirst:* Have you ever at any time been a member of the Communist Party?

*Dr. Brewda:* Never.

After she qualified in 1930 she specialized in gynaecology and obstetrics and went to Paris. In September 1940 the Nazis had sent her to the Warsaw Ghetto where she lived until the uprising in April 1943. Then she had been taken as an ordinary prisoner to Maidanek with about 8,000 women. She had "appointed herself" to work as a doctor; and, when she was sent to Block 10 at Auschwitz on 24 September it had been "the same story." She just started to examine patients. Her tattooed number was 62761 . . .

*Mr. Hirst:* Who gave you your day-to-day orders?

*Dr. Brewda:* Nobody told me. I was not such a young doctor . . .

She had examined all the women in the block, upstairs and downstairs, and found that about 150 were being used for experiments in sterility by Wirths, and by Clauberg, who injected caustic fluid into the womb. Some of the women were bleeding.

*Mr. Hirst:* What religion did the women profess?

*Dr. Brewda:* They were all Jewesses of about fourteen nationalities.

She spoke Polish, Russian, German and French and so managed to communicate with most of them. She spoke to the Greek girls in very simple French; they were the youngest, some of them "really only children." It had always taken her a long time to get round to see the girls who were on the first floor because they were "terribly afraid of any grown-up person," having by that time already been examined by the S.S. doctors—Wirths, Schumann and Clauberg.

*Mr. Hirst:* When did you first hear that Dr. Dering was in Auschwitz?

*Dr. Brewda:* Not very long after my arrival—and to my astonishment.

When she heard that Dr. Dering was the senior prisoner-doctor in the camp she was sure that he would help her to get drugs for her patients, and she tried to contact him by sending a message through the men who brought their food; but "Dr. Dering did not come." She sent a second message. Then he came. She had met him in the corridor of Block 10. He was smartly dressed and clean-shaven, and wore leather shoes in good condition.

She started the conversation in Polish by asking about getting some milk for three young children. He said it was quite impossible. Then she asked him for white bread for patients recently arrived from Poland bringing an epidemic of scarlet fever. He offered her one diet only, for herself; but she was already on a diet, having had pneumonia.

*Mr. Hirst:* Did Dr. Dering tell you what he was doing in the camp?

*Dr. Brewda:* Yes. He told me that he was a general surgeon and was operating.

*Mr. Hirst:* Did he mention any number of operations he had done?

*Dr. Brewda:* Yes. Thousands—16,000 or 17,000. I asked him what kind of operations . . .

He told her the operations were gastrectomies, ovariectomies (removal of female ovaries), appendicectomies, removal of testicles, and gynaecological. She asked him about his wife, and he said that she was still in Warsaw, probably in prison.

"I was surprised that it was possible, in a camp, to perform such a lot of operations, and I asked him whether the patients survived. He said that they did."

After she had seen him operate on the ten Greek girls she concluded that probably the 17,000 operations were all unnecessary and, therefore, experimental, as were the ten she watched. She had never gone to Block 21 before those operations. She was not allowed to leave Block 10 without an escort. She had never seen the register in Auschwitz. Dr. Dering did not show it to her in the operating room. She had never seen the book at any time before this case and even now had seen only photographic copies of extracts . . .

*Mr. Hirst:* It has been suggested by Dr. Dering that the only thing you ever asked him for was some extra rations for yourself. Is that correct?

*Dr. Brewda:* It is not correct.

The Greek girls had been on the first floor of Block 10. "About twenty-five of those girls we used to call 'Schumann's girls.' The others belonged to Clauberg." She had first examined them for scabies, but found that their skin was covered with suppurating blisters and realized straight away that they were the after-effects of irradiation—"a pretty big dose" and done by people without much knowledge of irradiation . . .

*Mr. Hirst:* Did you ever, at any time, participate in any experimental operations?

*Dr. Brewda:* Never.

Before the operations on the Greek girls, Dr. Schumann had asked her how long it would take her to organize a proper operating room in Block 10. She did not know what to say, and simply said, "I don't know. About three months." In October, he had asked her whether she could remove ovaries, and how long it would take her to perform such an operation. "I said about one and a half hours; and he said I was lying."

*Mr. Hirst:* Were you ever asked by Dr. Schumann actually to perform any specific operation?

*Dr. Brewda:* No. He did not ask me just straight to do this operation.

On the day of the Greek girls' operations in November she had met Schumann in the corridor. He told her that she must go with him "to calm the girls." He was in a "furious state." She went with him. Until then she had never been into Block 21. The first thing she heard in the corridor as she entered was screaming. "I entered into the annexe. I

599

saw two men holding a screaming girl sitting on a couch, and a second one crying. I saw two men and two girls. Dr. Dering was washing his hands in the annexe." The door of the theatre was open and she could see everything. A girl was lying strapped to the table. In the annexe Schumann told her that she was to "calm the girls."

*The Judge:* Could Dr. Dering have heard what Schumann was saying to you?

*Dr. Brewda:* I presume, Yes. It was quite a small room.

She had tried to tell Dr. Dering that the girls had been irradiated. He said that he knew it. She asked him what he was doing. He said "ovariectomies." . . . The girl on the table was screaming and crying and trying to release herself. She took up a position at the head of the table, nearest to the door. Dr. Dering then started to operate.

*Mr. Hirst:* From their appearance—the two Greek girls in the anteroom and the one on the table—did you think that they had had any kind of morphia injection before they were taken to Block 21?

*Dr. Brewda:* Of course not.

She had not given them any premedication and had not been asked to do so. Until Dr. Schumann came over no one had told her that these operations were going to take place. She tried to calm the girl on the table by saying the simplest words in French.

As to the manner of the operation, she said that the incision was abnormally small. The stitching afterwards was done roughly and "at terrific speed." "I told him there would be hemorrhage or péritonitis, and what should I do? He said I should not worry. The operation took about twelve minutes. I had never seen one of this kind done so quickly. I had a very good view, and I did understand what was being done." The normal time would be about thirty minutes.

Dr. Dering then went out of the theatre to the annexe and gave the second girl a spinal injection . . . There had been a couple of minutes between the injection and the operation. The girl was struggling all the time.

*Mr. Hirst:* Did Dr. Dering wash his hands between the first and second operation?

*Dr. Brewda:* Not so far as I remember.

*Mr. Hirst:* Were the instruments sterilized between operations as far as you remember?

*Dr. Brewda:* I don't think so.

After the second injection Dr. Brewda went back . . . The girl on the table was screaming and trying to escape. "We had a common language. I kissed her and comforted her as much as I could. I tried to tell Dr. Dering I had not seen anything like this. It was as though he was operating on corpses . . ."

When the hearing in open court was resumed, Dr. Brewda said that the mode of performance of the second to the eighth operation had not

600

been materially different from the first; and she had done exactly the same thing during and between each operation.

*Mr. Hirst:* Do you remember which two girls came last of the ten?

Yes, she remembered them particularly—"Marta" and Bella—because they were almost the youngest and had already had one operation with a horizontal scar . . . and also they had unhealed irradiation wounds in the lumbar (lower part of back) region so that lying on the hard table was terribly painful and they had been screaming. She also remembered telling Dr. Dering that "Marta" had already had one ovary removed, and "If you remove the second she will be like a eunuch."

*Mr. Hirst:* What did Dr. Dering say to that?

*Dr. Brewda:* Nothing.

From the way in which Dr. Dering had performed those ten operations, she had drawn the conclusion that it was "just a shame to the medical profession" that such things could happen, and also—because it was a very highly organized procedure with everything going very smoothly and at terrific speed, ten girls done in two and a half to three hours in the afternoon—that Dr. Dering had done previous operations of this kind . . . Dr. Dering was in charge of these operations and he performed them all.

After the operations, Dr. Brewda said, the girls' condition had been "terrible." She had had nothing to treat them with during the night. She had had to steal some morphia from Professor Clauberg's rooms—he always had a supply of six morphia injections—but she had exhausted that supply quickly.

*Mr. Hirst:* What happened to Bella during the night?

*Dr. Brewda:* Bella died.

She and Dr. Lorska had been with the girls, and they had both examined Bella. One did not need to be a very old doctor to diagnose internal hemorrhage. She had moved Bella out into the corridor and Bella died soon after. She also remembered Buena, who had died two or three days later—from "shock after operation." She admitted that when she was asked to charge her memory about these events for the purposes of this case she had recollected three girls dying and twelve operations; but now that she had heard the girls giving evidence and had seen the page of the register, she was saying that two out of ten had died after operation. The third Greek girl, who died about the same time, might have died of typhus. She had not discussed this case with the girls at all.

Two or three days after the operations, the girls' wounds started to open. No one in the block had anything but paper bandages. The wounds had also started to smell, and she could not move the other girls from the room. She had tried to send messages to Dr. Dering through the porters, asking him for some sulphonamide drugs.

601

He came eventually—once—about the fifth day. She met him in the corridor and told him that she had had two deaths, and that no wounds were healing, and asked if he could help her in some way. He said nothing, but went with her into the ward.

*Mr. Hirst:* What did he do?

*Dr. Brewda:* He just passed by and looked at them.

"Possibly" he examined some of the girls, but a careful inspection was hardly necessary; by that time she had them all on the lower bunks, and they were close together . . . So far as she knew, he never came to see the girls again. Some of them were in bed for months—"nearly until the spring."

*Mr. Hirst:* Do you remember seeing anything through the window of Block 10 in January 1944?

*Dr. Brewda:* Yes. I saw Dering leaving the camp . . .

She said that she was liberated on 8 May 1945, and returned to Poland in July.

*Mr. Hirst:* It has been suggested by Dr. Dering that you had a post in the N.K.V.D.[1] with either the Russian or the Polish secret police in Warsaw in 1945. Is that correct?

*Dr. Brewda:* It is not correct.

*Mr. Hirst:* Did you have any connection at all with any secret police at any time?

*Dr. Brewda:* Never. I was not a Communist and no one suggested to me to take such a job.

*Mr. Hirst:* It has been suggested that during that period you conducted a sort of personal vendetta (vengeance) to destroy Dr. Dering. Did you?

*Dr. Brewda:* Never.

In February 1947 she had left Poland for England where she had lived ever since . . .

[1] Soviet Secret Police.

# Readings

*Justice in Jerusalem* by Gideon Hausner (Schocken Books, 1968), is a notable work by the prosecuting attorney of Israel, containing the evidence, an analysis of Eichmann, how he was captured, the case for the defense, the legal involvements, the sentence, and its aftermath.

*The Trial of the Germans* by Eugene Davidson (Collier-Macmillan, 1966), is a study of the twenty-two defendants before the International Military Trial at Nuremberg. As each case-history is unfolded the story of Nazi Germany is laid open.

*Tyranny On Trial: The Evidence at Nuremberg* by Whitney R. Harris (Southern Methodist University Press, 1954), uses the Nuremberg Trials, in which the author represented the United States in the International Military Tribunal, as a springboard to document the Nazi atrocities.

*Auschwitz in England* by Mavis M. Hill and L. Norman Williams (Stein and Day, 1965), is the story of the court proceedings of the celebrated libel case in London brought by Dr. Wladislaw A. Dering against the American author Leon Uris.

*The Record* by Lord Russell of Liverpool (Knopf, 1963), is a report of the Eichmann trial.

*The Murderers Among Us* (McGraw-Hill, 1967), contains the memoirs of Simon Wiesenthal as told to Joseph Wechsberg. Wiesenthal is the Nazi criminal hunter par excellence; the living symbol of world justice for the martyred dead. His search and identification of Eichmann is the highlight of the book.

*The Capture of Adolf Eichmann* by Moshe Pearlman (Weidenfeld and Nicholson, 1961), is an authentic documentary account and presents the international legal aspects involved.

*Last Days of Adolf Hitler* by H. R. Trevor-Roper (Macmillan, 1947), is a vivid reconstruction of the drama of Hitler's suicide by a famous British historian.

# 25. POSTWAR GERMANY AND THE JEWS

After the war, most Germans seemed indifferent to the Holocaust. Few were bothered by pangs of conscience, and with the notable exception of philosopher Karl Jaspers, there were no public expressions of guilt or horror. Once ardent Nazis now said that they had joined the party as a result of pressure, ignorance, blackmail, deception, and fear, and many Germans claimed that much as the Jews had been victimized by the Nazis, so had they. The German people rejected Nazism as zealously as they had once espoused it—one might have thought from their protestations that there had never been any real Nazis in Germany.

In the first few postwar years, the German press and radio shied away from discussing the crimes of the Third Reich. The masses instinctively shrank from the idea of collective guilt and persuaded themselves that they were innocent. But the continued presence of the DPs was disturbing. Many Germans lived in terror, fearful that they would be brought to the bar of justice or would be forced to give up the Jewish property they had expropriated during the Nazi years.

The Eichmann trial had a traumatic effect on the Germans. More than any other event, it led many people to look deeply into themselves and to search their consciences. While some Germans still refused to acknowledge their responsibility, and some even boasted of their SS exploits, many accepted their guilt and avowed their collective shame. West German Chancellor Konrad Adenauer expressed the majority sentiment when he declared: "The whole truth must be brought out in the open."

604

## REPARATIONS: THE BITTER DILEMMA

According to the conservative estimate of historian Jacob Robinson, the Nazi regime robbed the Jews of Europe of more than twelve billion dollars worth of public and private property. In the words of Dr. Nahum Goldmann, "Who can deny the moral right of the Jews to make every effort to get back as much of this property as is humanly possible? . . . To deny this right, to take the position that we don't want our own property returned to us by the Germans, would be, in my opinion, absolutely immoral" (*Zionist Quarterly*, Spring 1952).

Despite Goldmann's view, the question of German reparations divided the Jewish world and still does. Many felt a deep revulsion at the idea that money might "make good" the crimes perpetrated by the Nazis. German money, they said, was bloody and filthy—they could not defile themselves by accepting it. Furthermore, no matter how much Germany paid, it would still be but a fraction of the loss. And how could money compensate for the degradation and extermination of two-thirds of the Jewry of Europe, and for the suffering experienced by those who survived?

The German government also debated the question. On September 27, 1951, Adenauer told the West German Bundestag, "Unspeakable crimes were perpetrated in the name of the German people which impose upon them the obligation to make moral and material amends, both as regards the individual damage the Jews have suffered and as regards Jewish property for which there are no longer individual claimants . . ."

West Germany proposed that the new State of Israel be recognized as the legal successor to all the heirless property and claims against Germany. Cautiously and gradually, a feeling of readiness was created in Israel, partly stimulated by the desperate plight of the DPs and the pressing economic needs of the young Israeli state.

In October 1951 representatives of twenty Jewish national and international bodies established the Conference of Jewish Material Claims Against Germany which, along with the Israeli government, proceeded to negotiate with the West Germans, meeting at the Hague since the Israeli representatives, for obvious reasons, would not go to Germany. The following points were accepted by the Bonn government: (1) Jewish material losses were so staggering that they could never be repaid in full; (2) Germany must pay a billion dollars to cover the expenses of integrating the surviving half-million German Jews into Israeli society; (3) the satisfaction of Jewish material claims must in no way be interpreted as expiating or atoning for the millions murdered by the Nazis; (4) five hundred million dollars must be paid for the relief and assistance of Nazi victims living outside Israel.

In addition to making the payments specified in items (2) and (4), the West Germans, over the next decade, allocated millions of dollars in

605

German goods and foreign currency to the State of Israel. These helped the overstrained Israeli economy in many fields. German reparations have also been utilized for such purposes as providing medical care, vocational training, and other services to displaced persons and refugees, as well as to support academic research on the Holocaust and on the destroyed Jewish communities of Europe.

Regrettably, Austria, Italy, and the other Axis countries did not follow Germany's example. While the reparations payments can only be viewed as minimal in the light of the tragedy the Germans inflicted, they represent a gesture in the right direction. Through the reparations program, Germany acknowledged the enormity of its guilt and its obligations, and took a step toward its reinstatement in the society of nations.

# The "Innocents"

*Distinguished correspondent and radio broadcaster, Henry J. Taylor, covered events in Germany up to the invasion of Poland (1939), the war in Europe and North Africa, and the aftermaths. He met with the highest ranking generals and political leaders, as well as Marshal Petain and Pope Pius VII. He was an on-the-spot reporter at the liberation of Bergen-Belsen. In a chapter entitled "The Germans Know the Answers," in his book* Men and Power *he reports on the attitudes of the Germans to Hitler, the Nazi regime and Germany's defeat . . .*

The day Hitler's death was reported, a blond German woman, standing on the doorstep of her bombed-out house, was beaming and blowing kisses to us as we passed. I asked her when she had turned against her country's leadership. "When I learned of the terrible conditions in the concentration camps," she replied, with an odd grimace. Then she looked glum . . .

At first blush her statement sounded impressive, and it seemed to impress some of our G.I.'s standing near by. But what did it mean? Even if true, her statement was a tacit admission that she had been for the Nazis to the end . . .

A waiter in the Baden-Baden Casino . . . told me how glad he was to see the French occupation troops arrive. Now, any German who is glad

---

From *Men and Power* by Henry J. Taylor.

to see French troops arrive any place is a strange German indeed. But the waiter thought such expressions would bring him better treatment, so he did not hesitate to spin his yarn of welcome to the Allies.

A postman in Frankfurt told some other newspapermen and myself that he had moments when "he did not want to deliver a letter because it had Hitler's picture on the stamp." But he admitted that he had been a Nazi Party Member for eleven years. "I had to be, you know," he said, "but not by choice." His son? Yes, he was a Party Member, too. He had joined three years ago. "The Youth Movement was important," explained the father. "He couldn't help it."

But my interview with a famous industrialist at Essen was in many ways the most revealing. Here was the Teutonic mentality again—in the raw. Edward Houdremont, hale and hearty, was managing director of the Krupp armament works. Now, with Germany kaput, Herr Houdremont had his problems.

"This war is very sad for us here at Krupp's," he said, "for Mr. Krupp did not want to make armaments at all. In fact, we did not make armaments here. We were never your enemies. We only made what the government ordered."

Asked what the government might be expected to order from a concern so completely equipped for Germany's war, Herr Houdremont mentioned casually some production of armor plate, artillery, Luftwaffe bombs, and hulls for tanks.

Good Mr. Krupp . . . to say nothing of all the little Krupps, would have preferred to make farm machinery and pleasure automobiles . . . Hitler kept giving them orders they could not politely refuse. And now what is the result? Essen was bombed twenty-eight times. The vast plants were a tangled mass of twisted steel and concrete.

"This," said Herr Houdremont, without batting an eye "is a deep misfortune for Mr. Krupp, for myself, and for the 50,000 workmen here."

In the long run, he maintained, with a decided show of animation, it would have been better if Allied bombers had not ruined this place. We could have trusted Mr. Krupp and all the little Krupps to start making farm machinery as soon as possible—although they never have made any in Krupp's long history.

Then the Allies would have spared themselves any worry about the prosperity of these 50,000 Essen men and women now unemployed, Herr Houdremont implied. And America would not have to consider sending farm machinery to Germany to help the German's feed themselves, because Krupp would be making all the farm machinery needed . . .

"This concern," Herr Houdremont insisted, with a note of irritation in his voice, "was never controlled by the Nazis. It was a private concern. Krupp's made only what the German government ordered, no more, no less, and how can the Allies expect a peaceful Europe after they have bombed such great plants out of existence?"

Asked for his solution, the managing director shrugged and said he had none.

"Perhaps we will need loans from America to build up Krupp's again," he said. "Mr. Krupp is now paying the workmen out of his own pocket, you know, and that cannot go on forever."

Herr Houdremont said now is the time to forget the past and look to the future. Mr. Krupp and all the little Krupps hold no bitterness against anyone. They are ready to start rebuilding tomorrow. All they ask, Herr Houdremont stated, is America's helping hand.

"You would be surprised," he said, "how quickly we could get this place going again."

This is the kind of mentality the world is dealing with there.

Even so, it was not all milk and honey. As our occupation began to settle down, you heard the Germans' idea of truth every now and then; Germany had been right after all in going to war, some said, and her defeat itself proved it.

Consider an interview I had with the Nazi mayor of a small German town. He asked me not to use his name or tell the name of the place . . . and since he had heard that the Burgomaster of Aachen was murdered for collaborating with Americans, he had some fear of reprisals.

The town's population was 10,000. The bland-eyed little man, jug-eared and stocky, came to see General Devers when the General set up his command post there. The mayor stated that as we approached it was he who ordered his townspeople to hang out white flags, or anything white they could lay their hands on, as tokens of surrender . . . Here, as in many towns, the Germans had overdone their compliance a little. As soon as we hove in sight, most of them made their houses look like sailboats. They did not take any chances; bed sheets, pillow cases or towels out front, shirts and handkerchiefs on the beams, quilts flapping in the rear.

Folding his arms and looking warily at General Devers, the round little mayor explained that his official pronunciamento somehow made him responsible, as mayor, for the Americans' good behavior, and he had come to satisfy himself that the American commander was going to back him up. What guarantee could this Nazi make to his people?

General Devers told the German in no uncertain terms that hereafter it was our army that would issue any guarantee to the population and not a Nazi mayor. Devers said he was firing him at once as mayor, although the army might use him temporarily as long as tactically necessary. He knew mayors of German towns represented most of the remaining authority and that where some were ordering populations to resist—as at Ashauffenburg—unnecessary bloodshed was occurring.

Our soldiers were being forced to shoot and kill men and women who were firing from alleys and windows in obedience to mayors' resistance orders.

After this meeting I went with the mayor to his house, sat in the dining room with him, and asked him to tell me what was what. I wanted to know how Nazi mayors still controlled the townspeople so completely.

He said he had been mayor for twenty-four years, or since 1921; he was elected twice, each term running ten years. Then, in 1941, his election was carried over for the duration of the war by a decree from Nazi Party headquarters in Munich.

He distributed most government relief money, which was the root of his local influence . . . "If they want anything," he said, "they must come to me."

He would not say he was a Nazi by choice, for few Germans were admitting that . . . but he did admit he joined the party in 1933 and, naturally, no one could remain burgomaster and have all the powers which went with this office unless he was an obedient Nazi.

Now, however, he told me he was glad the Nazis were out. To hear the Herr Burgomaster talk you would think he liked us better than he ever liked his own people . . .

The mayor, like so many others, nevertheless, said he thought Hitler was a "good man" who had Germany's interest at heart. Hitler had done the best he could, trying to help Germany against the attacks by Russia, England, and the United States. The trouble came from others, chiefly Goebbels, who were unworthy of Hitler's confidence and support. "Der Führer himself is not a bad man," was the universal idea. "It's those around him." . . .

The mayor expressed it exactly. "Our young people," he said, "may not know why or how the last or this war came, but they had fathers or brothers killed in the last war, or they have lost everything, and they know it is terrible to have Germany beaten. What German would not rather die than have this happen again? If it was Hitler who led us, we had to make the best of our leaders just as you made the best of yours. We could expect no loyalty outside Germany. We can expect nothing from outside Germany. No one ever helps us who is not German. We Germans always must save ourselves by ourselves. Hitler tried. He failed, but he tried!

"Hitler always said Germany was being 'encircled' and that the freedom and lives of every man and woman in Germany were at stake. Germany wanted nothing that was not her due. But other countries wanted Germany.

"Hitler always said, did he not, that the long sacrifices he called on Germans to make before the war were necessary because Germany's enemies were so strong? The strength of Germany's enemies only

609

proved how right Hitler was in his demands for sacrifice and privations. Perhaps if we German people had given up even more in those pre-war years we might have stood against the world after all—at least until Hitler's new secret weapons saved us from the massive weight of outside powers. Hitler always predicted the danger of invasion. Well, this is invasion. This is what Hitler tried to spare the German people."

Remembering that the German nature looks on power as a glory, that in their new weakness they will yearn for their old strength, and that an easy precedent for their future attitude is established by the French attitude towards the Man of Power who brought more sadness and pain to France than any Frenchman who ever lived—Napoleon— the chances are overwhelming that in the long run the German people will end up making a martyr of Hitler.

---

# Feelings of Collective Guilt and Shame: A German Writer Bares His Soul

*Gerhard Schoenberner, a German writer, is author of* The Yellow Star, *which documents the Holocaust from 1933 to 1945 with photographs, descriptions, and records. He is unsparing. It is a powerful and moving book. Following are his introductory remarks . . .*

I remember when I saw the Auschwitz Museum for the first time: the store-rooms stacked to the ceiling with clothes and shoes; the wagon-loads of women's hair, tooth-brushes, spectacles, artificial limbs and suitcases displayed behind great glass windows. I found myself then desperately hoping that this was only a bad dream; that the astronomical figures given to us by our guide were based on miscalculations; that it was an optical illusion that made the overwhelming mountains of evidence—those mute, damning witnesses—seem to be heaped up to such a dreadful height. Yet I knew that this storehouse held only an infinitesimal part of the victims' personal belongings, the remnants that were left behind at the end of the war because they could no longer be carted away. And Auschwitz was only one of those death

---

From *The Yellow Star* by Gerhard Schoenberner.

factories that killed and burned human beings, mechanically, by the wagon-load, in the same way that goods are turned out in other industries . . .

The appalling thing about the photographs in this book is that here for the first time a State-planned crime, committed millionfold, is captured phase by phase in the pictures. And most monstrous of all, it is the murderers who photographed themselves at work.

Imagine a professional thief and murderer asking a friend to photograph him as he selected his victims, lured them into the trap and killed them, and then to stick the photographs in an album as souvenirs. That is precisely what did happen. The photographs are almost without exception drawn from German sources. The majority were taken by official Press photographers for the regime and, to a lesser extent, by amateurs in German uniform.

Actual photograph albums were in fact compiled which recorded deportations and executions as if they were holidays spent at the seaside or in the mountains . . . There are the official ones, which may have been intended for the archives of the Third Reich, and there are the private ones, which Hitler's warriors wanted to take home as souvenirs of the heroic deeds that earned them special rations of *schnaps* and cigarettes and even medals . . . It is always the small men— the henchmen, the slave-drivers and the killers—who are seen here. There are no photographs that adequately depict the activity of the top men . . . They remained at their desks and did not show themselves in the places where their plans were carried out . . .

The people shown here had no choice but to have their photographs taken. As they went to certain death, and often knowing that they must die, they saw the enemy's camera turned on them. Their eyes, as they look into the camera lens, meet ours as we look at these photographs some 25 years later and put us into the position of the murderers. There are looks of fearful expectation and hopeless despair, of utter terror and acceptance of their fate. Many of the faces have a distrustful, withdrawn expression. Others attempt a pitiful smile of fear to put the German master in a merciful mood. Yes, many fell on their knees and kissed the hands of the strangers in their uniforms with the death's-head insignia, begging for mercy. They still looked on them as human and thought they would be able to move them to pity. But the soldiers repeated to themselves that these were mere vermin, as they had been taught in their barracks and SS training centers, and carried out the orders of their superiors. They saw themselves in the role of the hero and their defenseless victims as *Untermenschen*—subhuman. The photographs they took are an attempt to record these relative roles. The photographers took pains to photograph their subjects in as unfavorable a light as possible . . . They always selected the physical characteristics that were, to their way of thinking, particularly unattractive and

611

that came nearest to the distorted caricature of the Jew instilled by Nazi anti-Semitic propaganda.

It is moving to see how the truth, despite everything, comes through again and again in these photographs: how much human dignity the victims preserve in utmost degradation and helplessness. The vainly swaggering brutality and violence, on the other hand, become contemptible and vile in comparison. Be they round-faced little children or wasted old men, the thought that they were murdered brings them close to us, and convinces us of the right to live of every one of them. Whether the men in uniform have the hard, pinched faces of cruelty or the soft features of youth, in this situation and condemned by these acts, they stand before us as murderers.

On the other hand, the photographs attempt to conceal the savage and bloody character of the events, to prevent the slightest stirrings of human sympathy. That is why the pictures of life in the Warsaw Ghetto and of its destruction, and also the photographs that came out of the death camps, are, compared to what we know from official and private accounts and from secret film records, almost unreal in their stylisation. The reality was that much worse . . . It was thought proper for women to be forced to undress in front of the men of a firing squad bristling with weapons, that mothers should carry their babies with them into the gas chamber, and that children had to look on while their parents were butchered. The pictures in this book reveal what the murderers considered fit to be photographed.

The documentation is necessarily incomplete. A lot has been left out. Photographs of the manufacture of soap from the corpses of murdered people, of men whose bodies were mutilated by the SS doctors, of lampshades made from tattooed human skin, and scalps processed in the manner of head-hunters were deliberately not included in this collection . . .

There is little available photographic material on the wholesale executions of the Jewish population in the occupied areas of the Soviet Union. By 1941 a general ban was imposed on the photographing of executions. An attempt was also made to confiscate all the photographs already in existence because it was feared that they might fall into enemy hands through the soldiers who had been taken prisoner. The available photographs give only an inadequate idea of the bestial brutality and the immense scale of this slaughter of a whole section of the population. Also, the camera leads us no further than the threshold of the gas chamber. What happened there, when the great bunker doors were bolted, was seen only by the SS, who followed the progress of the slow suffocation through small observation windows, and by the unfortunate prisoners in the special squads who had to clear away the corpses of the murdered people and put them into the ovens. This last station remains hidden from us, we are spared the sight . . .

"Bury the past," demand those who have something to hide. "Do not sully Germany's name," cry those who besmirched it with their bloody hands. "Let bygones be bygones," the murderers advise us. And there are many people who thoughtlessly repeat their words. They forget that outside Germany there is a much sharper memory of those years and that the facts which here often still meet with stubborn silence or with incredulous surprise are common knowledge. Those who kept silent when it was time to speak out talk loudly of forgiving and forgetting. Even well-meaning people speak at the most of shame. But there remains a shared guilt which one cannot easily buy oneself out of, and which cannot be "made good." No one can bring the dead back to life. What is done cannot be undone.

Belated moral condemnation and humane regret are not enough. The historical facts must be made known, the social causes that made them possible must be understood, and we must become aware of our own responsibility for what goes on around us. We do not escape the past by thrusting it to the back of our minds. Only if we come to terms with it and understand the lessons of those years, can we free ourselves of the legacy of Hitlerite barbarism . . .

# "Tell Them the Truth . . . We Will Not—We Must Not Forget . . ."

*Earlier (p. 293) we read about the three rabbis of Warsaw who were offered a chance to save their lives and refused. Only one survived, Rabbi David Shapiro. (His own brother, a U.S. chaplain, was among his liberators in Dachau.) Rabbi Shapiro chose to stay in Fürth (Germany) where he has been the spiritual leader of a small synagogue with a membership of some 130 Orthodox Jews. Irving Halperin, an American professor, visited him for advice on what to say about the Holocaust to German students at a lecture in Frankfort, to which he was invited. . . .*

       I sat beside (Rabbi David Shapiro) in his study. Full and entirely gray, his beard has an elegantly patriarchal cast. He is in

From *Here I Am: A Jew in Today's Germany* by Irving Halperin.

his sixties. His eyes are tremendously alert, and he moves with force and decisiveness. Over his short sturdy figure he wears a black caftan-like robe.

The study is on the second floor of an old tenementlike building hidden away in a bleak street of Fürth. Since the city's main synagogue was destroyed by the SS in 1939, the spiritual needs of the present congregation are served by a small synagogue in the tenementlike building, whose residents are almost entirely composed of the Rabbi's following . . .

I told him about what I had been hearing from some young Germans in Nuremberg. "Rabbi, what shall I say to these young people?" I asked. His reply was immediate, blunt. "Tell them the truth. Tell them—boys, your fathers murdered my fathers. And this we will not—must not—forget!" He paused, reflected. "Yes, tear away the scales from their eyes."

In my lifetime I have heard hundreds of people use the word "murdered." But when this man uttered the words "your fathers murdered my fathers," they slashed through my consciousness like a knife.

Yet there wasn't hate in his voice or face but rather only the passionate conviction of a man who has suffered, who has earned the right to be absolutely blunt.

I related that some of my students at the university had spoken to me about their sense of horror and shame over the destruction of European Jewry.

"I know what they say with their mouths," he said quickly, pointing to his lips. "But what do they feel here?" He touched his breast.

"Rabbi, some Jews I know say we must hate the Germans for what happened—that we must never forgive them." And here I cited a passage from an article, "An Assignment with Hate," by one of the most important writers and prophets of our time, Elie Wiesel:

> I cry out with all my heart against forgiveness, against forgetting, against silence. Every Jew, somewhere in his being, should set apart a zone of hate—healthy, virile hate—for what the German personifies and for what persists in the German. To do otherwise would be a betrayal of the dead. (*Commentary*, December, 1962, p. 476.)

He shook his head. "The Torah bids us to *remember* Amalek, not to hate it." And then he added, citing the words of Ezekiel: "The son shall not suffer for the iniquity of the father." A moment later, as though in an afterthought, he broke out, "We must lift up *Menschen*. Lift up."

When he speaks you believe him. When he says "lift up," you can imagine him going from barracks to barracks in the camps, buoying up the spirits of others . . .

"Rabbi, some people say that the Jews in the camps should have risen against the guards, that they should have gone to their deaths fighting back."

"How do you fight back against such a monster when you are without weapons? Even so, when Jews went with upraised heads to the gas chambers, singing *Ani Maamin*, 'I Believe,' this was like a lead pipe against the Nazis. It was the same as striking them. This is how a Jew should die—with his head high, back straight . . . Faith—this is important. In the camps some would ask, 'Rabbi, do you really believe that one day we shall walk out beyond that barbed wire?' 'Yes,' I said, 'I believe it.'"

"'I believe it!'" he repeated, his face flaming. "And it has come to pass. Later I met one who had been with me in Dachau and he said, 'Rabbi, you were right!'" He paused, and his voice seemed to search, to reach far back into the darkness of the past. "I saw some of them who did not believe," he said quietly, slowly. "They fell away," he gestured, as though describing a falling movement.

Again he paused, and his eyes took on a distant look. "On the days of hard labor, there would be blackness in their faces. I see them . . ." He paused, shook his head slightly. "Then someone would tell them to sing and suddenly they would be singing with all their hearts. For a little while they would forget their troubles."

He was smiling, faintly, as though he were trying to convey something without words. My God, I thought, he has come out of such a hell, has lost a wife and four children, and can still smile! And I wondered—is *that* what I should say at Frankfurt? To lift up their heads and be *worthy* of their spiritual distress? If the Jewish people could rise up out of the charnel houses, it should be no less possible for them (the Germans) to carry their burden of collective shame with *consent* and with dignity.

As I was leaving, the Rabbi said, referring to the coming Frankfurt talk, "Let what passes from your lips come from your heart."

Going through the streets of Fürth, I heard his voice—"Lift up!" And on returning home, I said to my wife, "Well, now I have seen what faith is."

615

# No Statute of Limitations for the Murderers!

*Karl Jaspers is one of the great figures in contemporary philosophy. For many years he taught at the University of Heidelberg. He is the leading, perhaps the sole, exponent advocating clearly the idea of personal and collective guilt of the Germans and collaborating non-Germans for the crimes of the Holocaust. Moreover, he is a strong proponent of the policy that there shall be no "Statute of Limitations" (i.e. that after a certain date the criminals may not be brought to court) . . .*

I doubt if there has ever been this crime in its unique sense before. I know of no instance. It may be that it is being committed in Tibet; I don't know. But I do think we must recognize that we are here dealing with an essentially unprecedented crime before we can make a judgment on the question of the Statute of Limitations. The answer to this question will become quite obvious if we have a clear view of four closely connected questions. The first one is this: What kind of crime? Administrative mass murder, a crime without precedent in history. The crime presupposes a new kind of state—the criminal state. The second question: According to what law is a judgment made? According to international law, the law that binds all men together. The third question: What is the legitimate instrument for the application of this law? As long as humanity does not have the proper legal institution for handling it, the proper authority are the courts of those states that recognize the validity of international law in their own jurisprudence. The fourth question is this: What punishment? The punishment in keeping with this unique crime against humanity is capital punishment, an exceptional punishment reinstated in this exceptional case even after its abolition. These questions have not been cleared up to this day. To a large degree we are still using ideas from an earlier period in dealing with them.

From *Midstream Magazine*, February, 1966.

# Wiedergutmachung (Reparations)

*Yehiel de-Nur, better known as Katzetnik (concentration camp inmate) 135633 (the number tattooed on his arm), is the author of* House of Dolls, *a gruesome book on the Holocaust which sold over five million copies in twenty-two languages. Here, he pours forth his feelings in gripping moving prose poetry . . .*

My mother was—my mother.

How can I describe you—mother?

My mother was—the most beautiful of all mothers in the world.

My mother said:

"No! My little boy didn't do this naughty thing . . ." Lovingly she pressed the profiles of my head between her open palms, her fingers long and parted. Her eyes plumbed the depths of my own as she said: "I—I did the naughty thing! Because I am my little boy!"

Afterwards, I was always very careful to behave, because I couldn't bear for my mother to do a naughty thing.

My mother!

Of all mothers in the world mine was the most beautiful.

On her way to the crematorium my mother saw my face. I know it. Because I too, on my way to the crematorium, saw my mother's face.

Mother, now they want to give me money to make up for you.

I still can't figure out how many German marks a burnt mother comes to.

"My little boy couldn't have done this naughty thing . . ."

Mother, I feel your open palms touching the profiles of my head, my eyes sink into yours: Isn't it true, mother, you wouldn't take money for your little one, burnt?

My sister's hair was long and curly, the color of ripe gold. Mother's hands vanished in white-gold foam every time she washed it. Whenever she rinsed it, sheer gold cascaded down my sister's nape like a waterfall all the way to the bottom of the tub.

My mother loved to plait ribbons into her tiny daughter's hair. She would sort them out, singing soft to herself as she did:

From *Star Eternal* by Yehiel de-Nur (Katzetnik 135633).

> *"Ribbon green for hair's gold sheen,*
> *Ribbon pink for chocolate skin,*
> *Ribbon blue for the eyes . . ."*

My sister's eyes were blue like sky.

Sabbath morning, in front of the house, when the sun met my sister's hair, neighbors at their windows would call:
"Whose hair is that, little goldilocks?"
"My mother's," answered my sister.
I loved my sister's hair. She never lifted scissors to it. She said, "My mother's . . ."

Before my sister was burned in the crematorium of Auschwitz, they shaved off her hair. Seventeen years the golden locks lengthened on my sister's head. Long locks of gold. Seventeen years.

In a shipment of hair, in sacks, or in rectangular bales, tight-pressed like cotton from rich plantations, my sister's hair was sent to Germany. It was unloaded at a factory, to make:
blankets—
    soft club-chairs—
       upholstery—
Somewhere, in Germany, a young Fräulein now covers herself with a blanket. A single hair of gold, unprocessed, thrusts out of the blanket's weave. The Fräulein stretches out a bare arm, pulls, pulls—
"Fräulein! Give me back that hair! It's out of my sister's golden locks—"
My sister, now they want to give me money for you. But I don't know how many German marks your curls should bring.
"Whose hair is it, little goldilocks?"
"My mother's . . ."
"Mother, Mother, what do you say—how much is your little goldilock's hair worth?" . . .

> *"Ribbon green for hair's gold sheen*
> *Ribbon pink for chocolate skin,*
> *Ribbon blue for the eyes . . ."*

Among tens of thousands of shoes I'd recognize a shoe of yours, father!
Your heels were never crooked.
Father, your step was always straight.

Each day a new mountain of shoes piles up on the compound of the crematorium. Remember when I was little? The first time you let me shine your shoes, I polished them tops and bottoms. Oh how you laughed at me then:

"There is, sonny, a dirty side as well, on which a man must tread. When you're big you'll understand."

Father, I'm big now.

The sun bends over the slope of the tall shoe-mountain, illuminating it for me as with a flashlight:

Shoes!
Shoes without end!

A torn baby-shoe—like an infant's open mouth, eager for the full spoon in mother's hand; a torn baby-shoe—an infant's head, eyes bugging from the shoe-mountain to the sun shining on earth.

Nearby—

A narrow delicate woman's shoe, high and slender heeled, brown-scaled. Open on all sides. Several entwined leather straps on top. The gold imprint on the steep arch glitters in the face of the sun.

Nearby—

A lime-spattered workman's shoe. The sun peers into it as into the mouth of a cavern hacked into barren mountain rock.

Nearby . . .

A leg with a shoe on its foot—prosthesis to the groin . . .

Shoes!
Shoes beyond count!
Father, among tens of thousands of shoes I would recognize yours!
Your heels were never crooked—
Father, your step was straight.

How can I take money for my sister the "Field Whore" from you—
and not be a pimp?
Give me—
Give me back one single hair of my sister's golden curls!
Give me back one shoe of my father's;
A broken wheel from my little brother's skates; . . .

619

# Readings

*Post-Mortem: The Jews in Germany Today* by Leo Katcher (Delacorte Press, 1968), is a report of interviews with a representative sampling of Jews from West and East Germany who express their hopes, fears, feelings of guilt, and melancholia.

*The Mark of the Swastika* by Louis Hagen (Bantam Books, 1965), contains true stories of nine Germans (most of them members of the SA, SS, and Gestapo) in the Nazi and post-Hitler period.

Frederick Forsyth: *The Odessa File* (Viking Press, 1972), is a best-seller about the SS underground escape route of postwar Germany. While the book is a suspenseful fictionalized novel, it is based on valid historical data and real people, many of whom are named.

*Konrad Adenauer* by Terence Prittie. (Cowles Book Co., 1971), a biography.

*After Hitler, A Report on Today's Germans* by Jurgen Neveu-DuMont (Pantheon Books, 1970). Intensive interviews with forty-two West Germans.

*The New Germany and the Nazis* by T. H. Tetens (Random House, 1961), presents a rather pessimistic insight into West Germany's citizenry and ideologies.

*Postscript: A Collective Account of the Lives of Jews in West Germany since the Second World War* by Karen Gershon (Victor Gollancz, 1969), the author of *We Came As Children.* The contents of this book is well summarized by its subtitle.

*West Germany* by Michael Balfour (Praeger, 1968), one of a series entitled *Nations of the World,* is a comprehensive view of Germany, its beginnings and the First Reich, to the present. It touches on anti-Semitism and the Final Solution.

*The Sunflower* by Simon Wiesenthal (Schocken, 1976), is a story about a Nazi killer, terrified of dying without absolution, who seeks forgiveness from one of his Jewish victims. The latter does not respond. The author then presents a symposium of opinions by Jewish and non-Jewish intellectuals who were invited by him to express their views on the moral issue posed in the story.

# 26. IN ETERNAL REMEMBRANCE

In an effort to ensure that the Holocaust is never forgotten, hundreds of monuments to the "victims of tyranny," both Jewish and non-Jewish, have been established throughout Europe.[1] Some have been erected on the very ground hallowed by the martyrs of the *Shoah:* the Warsaw Ghetto, the camps at Treblinka and Auschwitz, Anne Frank's home in Amsterdam, and many others.

The world center of remembrance is Yad Vashem in Jerusalem. Its aims are to eternalize the memories of the victims, communities, institutions, heroes, and fighters; to study and publish the history of the *Shoah;* and to oversee the observance of Remembrance Day (*Yom Hashoah*—Nissan 27 in the Hebrew calendar). Located on the Mount of Remembrance near Mount Herzl, Yad Vashem includes a Pillar of Heroism honoring the resistance fighters, a Hall of Remembrance, a museum, a synagogue, exhibition rooms, and vast archives containing information on the Holocaust.

The Hall of Remembrance was designed to resemble a bunker. Its floor contains ceramic panels inscribed with the names of twenty death camps; an eternal light burns in the middle, and beneath it, in a pit, are the ashes of martyrs. Leading up to Yad Vashem is the "Avenue of the Righteous Among the Gentiles," lined by hundreds of trees planted in honor of those who risked their lives to save Jews.

The Yad Vashem archives contain some thirty-three thousand eyewitness accounts, diaries, books, letters, and copies of underground newspa-

---

[1] For photographs and descriptive accounts, see Adolf Rieth, *Monuments to the Victims of Tyranny* (New York: Praeger, 1969). Further information will be found in *In Everlasting Remembrance: A Guide to Monuments and Memorials Honoring the Martyred Six Million* (New York: American Jewish Congress, 1969).

pers. Regular exhibits on the *Shoah* are organized, evidence is still gathered on Nazi war criminals, educational materials on the Holocaust are prepared, and a program of research and publishing is conducted. Indeed, many of the selections in this book come from Yad Vashem publications.

Another major *Shoah* archive, library, and museum in Israel is found at Kibbutz Lohamei Haghettaot ("Ghetto Fighters"), founded by survivors of twenty-nine ghettos and eighty-nine concentration camps.

In New York City, the Yiddish Scientific Institute (YIVO) houses a major library on the Holocaust; so does the Wiener Library, formerly in London and now in Tel Aviv University. Impressive scholarly works on German Jewry are published by the Leo Baeck Institute in London, and several libraries in West Germany also provide research facilities on the *Shoah*.

There are, in addition, various organizations of Holocaust survivors.[2] Outstanding among these is the World Federation of the Survivors of Bergen-Belsen, which has been active in publicizing the Holocaust through its own publications in Hebrew, Yiddish, and English. Another active survivors' group is the Warsaw Ghetto Resistance Association (WAGRA), which arranges annual memorial meetings on *Yom Hashoah* and also publishes materials on the Holocaust. In Israel and elsewhere, moving *Yizkor* (memorial) books on hundreds of individual towns have been published through the efforts of survivors.

In Israel, on the eve of *Yom Hashoah,* the street lights are dimmed and all places of entertainment are closed. The *shofar* is blown, and a short period of silence follows. Throughout the country assemblies are held. The radio broadcasts songs of resistance and talks on the *Shoah*. Many families pluck flowers in memory of the Six Million and light memorial candles.

Some families and communities outside Israel have also instituted similar ceremonies. Many people recall the martyrdom of the Nazi victims at the Passover *Seder,* perhaps by setting an empty chair at the table to symbolize their absence or by special readings. Unless Remembrance Day ceremonies are accepted as an integral part of the cycle of the Jewish year, the *Shoah* may be forgotten. Just as an elaborate liturgy has been developed for *Tisha B'Av,* which commemorates the destruction of the Temple nearly two thousand years ago, so *Yom Hashoah* should be marked by solemn ceremonies and prayers in the synagogue, in community meetings, and in Jewish homes.

---

[2]For a list of survivors and fighters organizations in the United States and Canada, see *The Holocaust and American Jewish Youth* (New York: American Zionist Foundation).

# Albert Einstein's Dedication of the Monument to the Martyred Jews of the Warsaw Ghetto (1948)

The monument before which you have gathered today was built to stand as a concrete symbol of our grief over the irreparable loss our martyred Jewish nation has suffered. It shall also serve as a reminder for us who have survived to remain loyal to our people and to the moral principles cherished by our fathers. Only through such loyalty may we hope to survive this age of moral decay.

The more cruel the wrong that men commit against an individual or a people, the deeper their hatred and contempt for their victim. Conceit and false pride on the part of a nation prevent the rise of remorse for its crime. Those who have had no part in the crime, however, have no sympathy for the sufferings of the innocent victims of persecution and no awareness of human solidarity. That is why the remnants of European Jewry are languishing in concentration camps and the sparsely populated lands of this earth close their gates against them. Even our right, so solemnly pledged, to a national homeland in Palestine is being betrayed. In this era of moral degradation in which we live, the voice of justice no longer has any power over men.

Let us clearly recognize and never forget this: That mutual cooperation and the furtherance of living ties between the Jews of all lands is our sole physical and moral protection in the present situation. But for the future our hope lies in overcoming the general moral abasement which today gravely menaces the very existence of mankind. Let us labor with all our powers, however feeble, to the end that mankind recover from its present moral degradation and gain a new vitality and a new strength in its striving for right and justice as well as for a harmonious society.

From *Out of My Later Years* by Albert Einstein.

# Seder Ritual of Remembrance

On this night of the Seder we remember with reverence and love the six million of our people of the European exile who perished at the hands of a tyrant more wicked than the Pharaoh who enslaved our fathers in Egypt. Come, said he to his minions, let us cut them off from being a people, that the name of Israel may be remembered no more. And they slew the blameless and pure, men and women and little ones, with vapors of poison and burned them with fire. But we abstain from dwelling on the deeds of the evil ones lest we defame the image of God in which man was created.

Now, the remnants of our people who were left in the ghettos and camps of annihilation rose up against the wicked ones for the sanctification of the Name, and slew many of them before they died. On the first day of Passover the remnants in the Ghetto of Warsaw rose up against the adversary, even as in the days of Judah the Maccabee. They were lovely and pleasant in their lives, and in their death they were not divided, and they brought redemption to the name of Israel through all the world.

And from the depths of their affliction the martyrs lifted their voices in a song of faith in the coming of the Messiah, when justice and brotherhood will reign among men.

*All sing* Ani Maamin *("I Believe"),*
*the song of the martyrs in the ghettos and liquidation camps:*

I believe with perfect faith in the coming of the Messiah:
  And though he tarry, none the less do I believe!

From the Seder Ritual Committee, American Jewish Congress, New York, N.Y.

# Remember Us

*In Auschwitz*
*The earth has grown*
*A fresh layer of green*
*To conceal the bloodstains.*
*The smoke from the ovens now dismantled*
*Has vanished in the sky.*
*The cries of anguish have grown silent.*
*God has kept*
*His covenant with man*
*That life shall have rebirth.*
*But piercing the silence*
*I hear God's lament*
*For His children*
*Slain by their brother Cain,*
*And I hear the blood of the innocent*
*Crying out from earth and sky,*
*Remember us,*
*Remember us.*

*Dr. Ben Zion Bokser, Rabbi*

From *Forest Hills Jewish Center Bulletin,* March 31, 1972.

# Readings

In addition to the two books mentioned in the introduction to this chapter, *Monuments to the Victims of Tyranny* and *In Everlasting Remembrance,* read the ongoing publications of Yad Vashem, Jerusalem; Ghetto Fighters' House, Kibbutz Lohamei Hegettaot; Israel; World Federation of Bergen-Belsen Survivors, the Warsaw Ghetto Rebellion Association (WAGRA), and other institutions listed in the introduction.

# 27. THE LESSONS FOR MANKIND

As we come to the end of this book, one word repeatedly pounds in our minds: *unbelievable*. The poisoning of people's minds, the lies, the assault on civilization, the indescribable suffering—it all seems unbelievable. Equally unbelievable was the rekindling of the flame of life from the ashes, the rebirth, the compulsion to start anew.

Has the world learned anything from the bitter Holocaust experience? Could it happen again? Yes. Given the necessary circumstances, it could, God forfend, happen again—and the next time, perhaps, with even more ominous consequences.

Today we stand appalled at what our scientific achievements and advanced technology make possible. It is now possible to destroy the world—something even Hitler could not do. This should shock us into recognizing that the peoples of the earth may yet achieve a Final Solution, the annihilators together with those they wish to destroy.

As they contemplate the dilemmas confronting our civilization, many people become cynical. They see no future for the world or themselves. Their frustration drives them to self-destruction through drugs, or to angry protests and willful violence. If we are to survive, we must each find a constructive solution, a positive way of life, a positive program of action. What elements should be considered?

The Nazi lesson sensitized the world to the lethal power of prejudice and race-hatred. Anti-Semitism and racism were the secret weapons the Nazis used in their assault on civilization. They also destroyed all who disagreed with them, all dissidents of whatever shade.

As citizens of a democracy, we must cultivate our powers of political judgment and critical insight, and must ever be on the alert against beguiling catchwords and slogans like those utilized by the Nazis in their rise to power. We must guard the freedom of the press and must protect the basic rights of all; at the same time, we must make sure that freedom is not turned to license and used against us. The history of Nazism is a blueprint for those who seek to inflict totalitarianism on others and a warning to those who seek to defend their freedom.

On the world scene, the United Nations was set up after the war to prevent aggression by future Hitlers. The UN Genocide Convention and Declaration of Human Rights were intended to crystallize the universal determination that the Nazi experience should never recur, yet for various reasons, both the United States and the Soviet Union have vitiated the Genocide Convention; the United States by failing to ratify it, and the Soviets by insisting that if charged with genocide, they will not be answerable to the International Court at the Hague.

It goes without saying that laws and declarations alone cannot prevent persecution and genocide, but they nonetheless give voice to mankind's highest ideals, and set a standard for both individual and national conduct.

## THE HOLOCAUST AND FAITH

How can we live with the knowledge of the Holocaust and keep our faith in God and humanity in the post-*Shoah* era?

After more than three decades, the tormenting questions posed by the *Shoah* are still fresh: Where was God in Auschwitz? Why is evil so often unpunished? These agonizing questions have left many sapped of faith. Some, declaring there is no God, have given up. Some have viewed the sufferings of the Jews, and of the other victims, as sacrifices for the sins of mankind. Many struggle to believe, but are full of doubts. Others explain that God's plan is still unfolding and that it is His purpose to further purify mankind.

Victor E. Frankl reported that many came out of the tragedy with the feeling "of having learned to fear nothing except God." K. Shabbatai tells of a conversation with the Hassidic Rabbi Halberstam of Klausenburg, who lost his wife and eleven children in Auschwitz. Shabbatai asked the rabbi whether he still believed the Jews were the Chosen People. "Precisely then, after all that had happened to him and the Jewish people, was Rabbi Halberstam confirmed in his belief in the choseness of his people, because it was not the Jews who had committed the acts of horror, but the gentiles."

The establishment of the State of Israel has helped restore faith in the people of Israel and in God. Elie Wiesel, the most eloquent spokesman for the victims of the *Shoah*, quotes an intriguing thought uttered by another Hassidic rabbi: "For the faithful, there are no questions; for the non-believer, there are no answers."

Emil Fackenheim, an outstanding Jewish philosopher, asserts that the survivors lived and remained sane because they believed life was holy and had to be preserved, and that "life and love, not death and hate, shall prevail." Many reached the "breaking point," but their belief in God was not wholly broken, and they did not assimilate and lose themselves "among such good people as the Danes" when they were liberated, but rather flocked to the State of Israel, where they faced new dangers. This gave proof to their credo, *Am Yisrael Hai*—"the people of Israel lives on."

To mankind in general, Fackenheim says that "civilization must struggle with the memory of the Holocaust because it cannot afford to bury it." For the Jewish people, he maintains, the "command from Auschwitz" (the symbol of Jewish suffering) affirms that we would not deserve to exist if we ignored Auschwitz. The voice coming out of Auschwitz unites all Jews—the religious, the pious, the humanists, and the secular. It is an inescapable fact that Jews died because they were part of the unbroken chain of Jewish identity, and because they chose to continue to forge new links in that chain.

As a result, for many members of the present generation, the lesson of the *Shoah* has led to a reaffirmation of Judaism. Mordecai Bar-On, Israeli educator, youth leader, and group worker, has declared, "I belong to the generation which was born without faith. When I read the literature about the *Shoah*, my reaction is, 'I shall not die, but live.' (Ps. 118:17)."

As stressed in various sections of this work, Jews who were committed to Jewish ideas, whether religious, Zionist, or culturalist, withstood the pressure and the tragedy better than those who had lost their ties with their people. This is a lesson that possesses meaning for us all. Who knows what tests we may face in the future? These are precious possessions—to be cultivated, not to be discarded. The implications are manifold, reaching deep into our psyche.

# The Death of My Father

The anniversary of the death of a certain Shlomo ben Nissel falls on the eighteenth day of the month of *Shvat*. He was my father, the day is tomorrow; and this year, as every year since the event, I do not know how to link myself to it.

Yet, in the *Shulchan Aruch,* the great book of precepts by Rabbi Joseph Karo, the astonishing visionary-lawmaker of the sixteenth century, precise, rigorous rules on the subject do exist. I could and should simply conform to them. Obey tradition. Follow in the footsteps. Do what everyone does on such a day: go to the synagogue three times, officiate at the service, study a chapter of *Mishna,* say the orphan's *Kaddish* and, in the presence of the living community of Israel, proclaim the holiness of God as well as his greatness. For his ways are tortuous but just, his grace heavy to bear but indispensable, here on earth and beyond, today and forever. May his will be done. Amen.

This is undoubtedly what I would do had my father died of old age, of sickness, or even of despair. But such is not the case. His death did not even belong to him. I do not know to what cause to attribute it, in what book to inscribe it. No link between it and the life he had led. His death, lost among all the rest, had nothing to do with the person he had been. It could just as easily have brushed him in passing and spared him. It took him inadvertently, absent-mindedly. By mistake. Without knowing that it was he; he was robbed of his death.

Stretched out on a plank of wood amid a multitude of blood-covered corpses, fear frozen in his eyes, a mask of suffering on the bearded, stricken mask that was his face, my father gave back his soul at Buchenwald. A soul useless in that place, and one he seemed to want to give back. But, he gave it up, not to the God of his fathers, but rather to the impostor, cruel and insatiable, to the enemy God. They had killed his God, they had exchanged him for another. How, then, could I enter the sanctuary of the synagogue tomorrow and lose myself in the sacred repetition of the ritual without lying to myself, without lying to him? How could I act or think like everyone else, pretend that the death of my father holds a meaning calling for grief or indignation?

Perhaps, after all, I should go to the synagogue to praise the God of dead children, if only to provoke him by my own submission.

Tomorrow is the anniversary of the death of my father and I am

---

From *Legends of Our Time* by Elie Wiesel

630

seeking a new law that prescribes for me what vows to make and no longer to make, what words to say and no longer to say.

In truth, I would know what to do had my father, while alive, been deeply pious, possessed by fervor or anguish of a religious nature. I then would say: it is my duty to commemorate this date according to Jewish law and custom, for such was his wish.

But, though he observed tradition, my father was in no way fanatic. On the contrary, he preached an open spirit toward the world. He was a man of his time. He refused to sacrifice the present to an unforeseeable future, whatever it might be. He enjoyed simple everyday pleasures and did not consider his body an enemy . . . My father's ambition was to make a man of me rather than a saint. "Your duty is to fight solitude, not to cultivate or glorify it," he used to tell me. And he would add: "God, perhaps, has need of saints; as for men, they can do without them."

My mother taught me love of God. As for my father, he scarcely spoke to me about the laws governing the relations between man and his creator. In our conversations, the *Kaddish* was never mentioned. Not even in camp. Especially not in camp.

So I do not know what he would have hoped to see me do tomorrow, the anniversary of his death. If only, in his lifetime, he had been a man intoxicated with eternity and redemption.

But that is not the problem. Even if Shlomo ben Nissel had been a faithful servant of the fierce God of Abraham, a just man, of demanding and immaculate soul, immune against weakness and doubt, even then I would not know how to interpret his death.

For I am ignorant of the essentials: what he felt, what he believed, in that final moment of his hopeless struggle, when his very being was already fading, already withdrawing toward that place where the dead are no longer tormented, where they are permitted at last to rest in peace, or in nothingness—what difference does it make?

His face swollen, frightful, bloodless, he agonized in silence. His cracked lips moved imperceptibly. I caught the sounds, but not the words of his incoherent memory. No doubt, he was carrying out his duty as father by transmitting his last wishes to me, perhaps he was also entrusting me with his final views on history, knowledge, the world's misery, his life, mine. I shall never know. I shall never know if he had the name of the Eternal on his lips to praise him—in spite of everything—or, on the contrary, because of everything, to free himself from him.

Through puffy, half-closed eyelids, he looked at me and, at times, I thought with pity. He was leaving and it pained him to leave me behind, alone, helpless, in a world he had hoped would be different for me, for himself, for all men like him and me.

At other times, my memory rejects this image and goes its own way. I think I recognize the shadow of a smile on his lips: the restrained joy of a father who is leaving with the hope that his son, at least, will remain alive one more minute, one more day, one more week, that perhaps his son will see the liberating angel, the messenger of peace. The certitude of a father that his son will survive him.

In reality, however, I do not hesitate to believe that the truth could be entirely different. In dying, my father looked at me, and in his eyes where night was gathering, there was nothing but animal terror, the demented terror of one who, because he wished to understand too much, no longer understands anything. His gaze fixed on me, empty of meaning. I do not even know if he saw me, if it was me he saw . . .

I know only that that day the orphan I became did not respect tradition: I did not say *Kaddish*. First, because no one there would have heard and responded "Amen." Also because I did not yet know that beautiful and solemn prayer. And because I felt empty, barren: a useless object, a thing without imagination. Besides there was nothing more to say, nothing more to hope for. To say *Kaddish* in that stifling barracks, in the very heart of the kingdom of death, would have been the worst of blasphemies. And I lacked even the strength to blaspheme.

Will I find the strength tomorrow? Whatever the answer, it will be wrong, at best incomplete. Nothing to do with the death of my father.

The impact of the holocaust on believers as well as unbelievers, on Jews as well as Christians, has not yet been evaluated. Not deeply, not enough. That is no surprise. Those who lived through it lack objectivity: they will always take the side of man confronted with the Absolute. As for the scholars and philosophers of every genre who have had the opportunity to observe the tragedy, they will—if they are capable of sincerity and humility—withdraw without daring to enter into the heart of the matter; and if they are not, well, who cares about their grandiloquent conclusions? Auschwitz, by definition, is beyond their vocabulary.

The survivors, more realistic if not more honest, are aware of the fact that God's presence at Treblinka or Maidanek—or, for that matter, his absence—poses a problem which will remain forever insoluble.

I once knew a deeply religious man who, on the Day of Atonement, in despair, took heaven to task, crying out like a wounded beast, "What do you want from me, God? What have I done to you? I want to serve you and crown you ruler of the universe, but you prevent me. I want to sing of your mercy, and you ridicule me. I want to place my faith in you, dedicate my thought to you, and you do not let me. Why? Why?"

I also knew a free-thinker, who, one evening, after a selection, suddenly began to pray, sobbing like a whipped child. He beat his breast, became a martyr. He had need of support, and, even more, of certitude: if he suffered, it was because he had sinned; if he endured torment, it was because he had deserved it.

Loss of faith for some equaled discovery of God for others. Both

632

answered to the same need to take a stand, the same impulse to rebel. In both cases, it was an accusation. Perhaps some day someone will explain how, on the level of man, Auschwitz was possible; but on the level of God, it will forever remain the most disturbing of mysteries.

Many years have passed since I saw my father die. I have grown up and the candles I light several times a year in memory of departed members of my family have become more and more numerous. I should have acquired the habit, but I cannot. And each time the eighteenth day of the month of *Shvat* approaches, I am overcome by desolation and futility: I still do not know how to commemorate the death of my father, Shlomo ben Nissel, a death which took him as if by mistake.

Yes, a voice tells me that in reality it should suffice, as in previous years, to follow the trodden path: to study a chapter of *Mishna* and to say *Kaddish* once again, that beautiful and moving prayer dedicated to the departed, yet in which death itself figures not at all. Why not yield? It would be in keeping with the custom of countless generations of sages and orphans. By studying the sacred texts, we offer the dead continuity if not peace. It was thus that my father commemorated the death of his father.

But that would be too easy. The holocaust defies reference, analogy. Between the death of my father and that of his, no comparison is possible. It would be inadequate, indeed unjust, to imitate my father. I should have to invent other prayers, other acts. And I am afraid of not being capable or worthy.

All things considered, I think that tomorrow I shall go to the synagogue after all. I will light the candles, I will say *Kaddish,* and it will be for me a further proof of my impotence.

# A Survivor Ponders: Where Was God in Buchenwald?

*"I shall not die, but live, and recount the works of the Lord."*

*(Psalm 118,17)*

The muted whispers of the 2,500 prisoners in barrack number 4 of Buchenwald sounded in my ears like a distant buzzing.

From *The Jewish Spectator Magazine*, October 1969, by Simon Friedman

From time to time they were silenced by a voice coming over the loud-speaker, always beginning: "Listen, you herd of swine!" With the night the sounds gradually fainted away and died. I fell asleep, exhausted . . .

Angry voices woke me up. "Leave the old and take the young!" someone was shouting. A group was taken outside. There were horrible screams; then silence. The storm troopers returned for additional victims . . . Again and again the murderers returned. The nightmarish drama seemed to stretch into eternity. Some of the prisoners lost their minds. They jumped down from their tiers and ran into the arms of their tormentors. One was a man from my congregation. I buried my head between my knees and prayed. I repeated and repeated Psalm 118. And then it happened! When I recited the words: *anah adonai hoshee-ah nah* ("Save, we beseech Thee, O Lord"), the storm troopers began to quarrel among themselves. One said: "I cannot continue with this." Another replied: "This is the command of the Fuehrer." To which the first replied: "I cannot believe that the Fuehrer commanded this." Fighting broke out. The rebel was subdued. The nightmare continued. I realized only the next day that this "mutiny" had been staged deliberately. The storm troopers expected that the prisoners would come to the support of the mutineer. Then the machine guns would have gone into action. But that night I was certain that the Lord had responded to my prayer. I felt secure and fell asleep . . . On that night I made the promise, if "I shall not die . . . I shall recount the works of the Lord" (Psalm 118). Yet, in spite of this religious experience, I would have lost belief if I had not reinterpreted my God concept. This made it possible for me to reconcile the reality of evil with the existence of God . . .

I have often meditated on the question: Why did God not answer the prayers of so many saintly martyrs? Was God "dead?" Gradually and painfully I arrived at these conclusions:

"And God created man in His image . . ." (Genesis 1:27) is a fundamental statement of the Hebrew Bible about the nature of man. Man is both human and divine; human as a physical being and divine in his spiritual endowment. Judaism regards man as "the partner of God in the work of creation." This partnership is mutual and necessary. In His omniscience God created man as an amalgam of the material and the spiritual so as to transform nature into a moral universe.

When we say God is merciful and forgiving it means that He wants man to be merciful and forgiving, endowing him with the potential to do justice and love mercy. God, without man, His partner, does not act goodly, lovingly, or mercifully. The Psalmist proclaims: "The heavens are the heavens of the Lord; but the earth has He given to the children of men." God does not interfere in the events on earth *after* creation. Just as the fertilized ovum contains the features and characteristics of the future person, thus the first living cell contained all the physical, mental, and spiritual potentials of present and future men. To assume divine intervention in the evolutionary process through direct action or revelation *initiated* by God would entail defectiveness in creation and doubt in God's omnipotence and omniscience.

There is a second and perhaps more compelling reason why God does not interfere with the affairs of men. During the War I heard one of my teachers, a distinguished rabbi, exclaim: "How great must be the Lord; He sees all the suffering on earth; He could interfere; but His strength of will enables Him to control His mercy and to suffer with the tormented." I cannot accept this view. As goodness, justice and peace depend upon the decision of man, God cannot interfere in human suffering. This principle is built into the blueprint of the world. God has to limit His power—or there would be no freedom for man. Man, created in God's image, is endowed with His creative spirit.

Man is the "crown of creation" because his spirit lifts him above the causality of nature. He has the potential of making the spirit triumph over matter. In man, evolution has reached its divine goal. Man can sanctify the world of matter. He can accomplish what God cannot do: He can redeem the world from evil. In man, God created the instrument to reach beyond Himself. For only through man is a world of love and goodness possible. God would destroy the purpose of creation, if He were to interfere with the divinely ordained evolutionary process.

# What the Shoah Meant to an Israeli Parachutist

I cannot say that I feel what they felt, they, the doomed who lived without hope in the shadow of earth, but I sense it in all the hell and the terror that shows in their Jewish eyes, the wise eyes that know so much suffering behind the electrified fence. I can never forget it! We visited the building in Kibbutz Lohamei Hagettaot (Kibbutz of the Ghetto Fighters) erected in memory of the Holocaust. I looked at the pictures and understood. Others did not understand; they did not grasp it. And afterwards, I grasped it, and I knew that one must not forget!

From a letter, written on May 1, 1963, by Opher Feniger, parachutist and member of Kibbutz Givat Haim, who fell in the Six Day War in Jerusalem.

I remember that while still in Czechoslovakia, in Prague, a foolish Gentile nursemaid took us to a film about the Nazi atrocities in Czech villages, and already then I was so shaken by terror as to be unable to understand. But it became engraved in me. On the eve of the Holocaust, I sit and look into the eyes of those who were there, and everyone of them completely helpless.

I have the feeling that out of all the horror and the hopelessness there rises and grows up in me an enormous force to be strong, strong even to tears, strong and sharp as a knife, silent and threatening—that is how I want to be. I want to be sure that no longer will sunken eyes look out from electrified fences. Only when I am strong will that look disappear! If we will all be strong! Strong and proud Jews! No longer will we be led to the slaughter.

When I see a trembling Jew, witness a scene or hear a word that recalls all that, I regret every moment I may have wasted in the army, during which I could have striven to become more efficient, more dangerous.

On patrol we moved rapidly, silently and with strength, like devils. Through long nights we moved on strong legs. We climbed mountains and felt we could prevail over them. We accomplished everything that previously we have not believed was possible for us. We were confident of our strength. Is there anything better for a soldier than to be confident, alert and dangerous? Through inhabited areas, hills, and fields, we passed like shadows, unnoticed, and disappeared.

# In Germany: The End of Assimilation

I think of myself as an assimilated Jew. I say that without any particular pride or passion, but merely to provide a perspective for what follows. It was because I consider myself assimilated that I was able to plan a business trip to West Germany last fall without ever thinking twice. It was a trip of more than 2,000 miles through much of the country and I can honestly say that I regarded it as just another job. I left New York on the first night of Rosh Hashanah, 5732.

From *The New York Times*, September 3, 1972, by Stephen Birnbaum.

# The Lessons for Mankind

A flight that leaves New York in the early evening lands in Frankfurt am Main at dawn. Dulled though one's senses might be so early in the day, the impression the Frankfurt airport makes is strong and irresistible. Miles of rubber-clad corridors, with large windows and chrome and aluminum walls and railings, present a strikingly austere and sterile appearance, like something out of Stanley Kubrick's "2001." The poured-concrete buildings are starkly simple, and at dawn there are few signs of activity.

I was surprised by the informality of German immigration and customs procedures, which were, I thought, rather atypical for a country known for strict adherence to rules and discipline. Passports weren't checked or stamped; luggage wasn't inspected. This struck me as odd, but not quite as odd as the fact that I was entering Germany on the second day of the Jewish New Year.

At the exit gate a West German corporate executive who would serve as my driver and guide throughout my stay in Germany was waiting. We would be together constantly for the next 10 days. He was tall and erect, an imposing figure of about 60. Subtract 32, I suddenly thought, and that would make him about 28 at the start of World War II. I found myself wondering what military unit he'd been a part of, and my attitude became hostile. It was an automatic and unreasoning response, yet one I wouldn't shake for most of my stay in Germany. For whatever reason, I perceived my guide-to-be as an instant enemy, and my reaction to him surprised me. After all, I'm a thoughtful and reasonable man. I don't judge people irrationally, and besides, I'm a totally assimilated Jew.

The guide—I'll call him Hans—didn't help things much with his greeting. "Birnbaum," he said, "that's a German name, isn't it? Means pear tree. Tell me, do your people come from Germany?"

It didn't seem worthwhile to explain that while my father's roots were undeniably German, my ancestors had joined a 13th-century Jewish migration to Poland. After all, the move, though made seven centuries before, hadn't saved my father's parents and five sisters from Hitler. So I replied, "Yes, they came from Germany."

"It must have been *difficult* for them during the war," said Hans in clipped, crisp tones.

I nodded, at a loss for an answer. Suddenly my grandparents, my aunts and their husbands, their unknown numbers of children, were real to me. I had been about 6 years old when my parents learned of their deaths and I had never seen any of them. I had never even thought about them before but now I was trying to imagine what they had been like. It had taken two steps onto German soil and just a few words from the first German I had met to evoke this reaction. Talk about consciousness raising . . .

My musings were interrupted by Hans. "But that is all over now," he said, "it is all forgotten. It is all in the past, and we must live for today. Let us now concentrate on enjoying the beauty of today's Germany."

My ears heard and my mind actually agreed. This was, after all, supposed to be a rather pleasant business trip. But there was something rumbling in the pit of my stomach, something I couldn't control.

The uneasiness I experienced in that first conversation with Hans was shunted to the back of my mind once I got involved in my work, for business in West Germany is conducted in much the same way as in Akron or Atlanta. And in Frankfurt, a totally rebuilt, modern city, generally indistinguishable from most major American cities, everyone I met spoke English.

From Frankfurt my schedule took Hans and me through the beautiful Rhine valley. Medieval castles, high above steep vineyards and the bustling river, made the stretch of road from Mainz to Cologne a more than pleasant interlude.

Once in Cologne, I was off to the mammoth ANUGA Fair, a biannual event that caters to West Germany's thriving hotel and restaurant business. For nine days the good burghers of Hamburg and the beer barons of Bavaria inspect every conceivable type of sausage, strüdel and sauerkraut. For me the fair was a long series of meetings.

The meetings were fine but my local interpreter gave me a bit of a jolt. He resembled nothing so much as a character from the cast of an English drawing room comedy, the one who bounds in from stage left, handsome and blond, wearing impeccable whites, racquet in hand, and asks, "Tennis anyone?" The interpreter was blond and wore a perfectly pressed white suit and though a little past the age of male ingenue, was no less enthusiastic. "I am Guntar," he exclaimed. "I speak perfect English. I learned it in a prisoner of war camp." His smile was dazzling.

I shook my head in disbelief. How is it possible to make that statement out loud, I wondered, much less with obvious pride? He actually seemed proud to have been a prisoner; after all, hadn't he learned English? Why wasn't he even a little bit ashamed or self-conscious? I didn't expect breast beating and the rendings of his garments, but did he have to come on this way? I ended up being embarrassed, and I didn't understand the feeling at all.

From Cologne we rode through the Ruhr valley with its huge factories and mills whose predecessors had once fueled the German war machine. From there we traveled along the rolling plains of Westphalia, passing an endless succession of spotless farms, all with austere red brick farmhouses. Then north to Emsland, to a small village not far from the cold North Sea coast, where I was invited for my first meal in a German home.

The home could hardly have been called typical. Though very much

638

in the regional style of architecture, it was more than 500 years old. It was, however, fully restored, for restoration was a great hobby of my host. Long hallways led to large, drafty chambers, and if I had heard the cry of "Off with his head!" it would not have seemed the least incongruous. Dinner was formal and restrained, with somber servants bringing course after course. Cigars and lethally strong brandy followed, and they in turn were followed by a tour of the house.

As we walked along, old suits of armor stood rigidly at attention. Coats of arms and ancient standards hung forlornly from the walls and ceilings. We made our way through a narrow passageway and finally entered a long hall hung with large oil paintings. "This was my great-great-grandfather," said my host, pointing to a portrait of an archduke of somewhere or other. Next came a couple of counts, a baron or two and some miscellaneous civil dignitaries of apparently unquestioned importance. Then he pointed over my shoulder. "And that," he said, with obvious pride, "is my father."

The portrait was not as large as some of the others but it was no less impressive. The father stared out at his son with steely blue eyes and a fiercely determined jaw. His resoluteness was what the artist had primarily attempted to capture, and he had succeeded. Here was a man of bearing and purpose. The artist had missed nothing, right down to the highlights on the lacquered brim of the black military cap and the shining silver SS initials on the collar.

I felt my dinner rising and uttered silent, grateful thanks that I was able to keep it down. I was speechless. What am I doing here? I thought. What am I doing calmly breaking bread with the son of a Gestapo officer and then casually taking a tour of the "family album?" I found it absolutely impossible to remain in the house a moment longer.

My exit was clumsy and confusing. I'm sure my host still thinks that all Americans are quite mad, but my need for air was such that I gave no thought to good manners. Once out of the house, I shook with anger. It was uncontrollable. Five days in Germany had uncovered an identity I had labored a lifetime to minimize. I was a Jew; there was no getting away from it. And I felt a Jew's anger, a Jew's frustration. Assimilation or not, I was in a rage.

Until that night I had been focusing all my undefined belligerence on Hans. A nice man by any objective standard, he nevertheless evoked my initial uneasiness at the airport, and so I had directed my hostility at him. Nothing downright mean, mind you, but I just was not very friendly. Fortunately our driving sessions between stops were relatively short, and conversational necessities were few. But he tended to aggravate the strained atmosphere by laughingly referring to himself every so often as an "old militarist."

I felt so disquieted after the painting episode that I decided to eliminate scheduled visits to Hamburg and Berlin. They were stops that were not essential to my trip and I had neither the heart nor the stomach for them. But passing them up meant a 375-mile drive from the northwesternmost area of West Germany to Regensburg in the southeast, and a full day in the car with Hans.

The trip itself was pleasant enough; the West German autobahns are among the best roads in Europe. And the conversation, surprisingly, was equally pleasant. Hans was something of a local historian, and he spoke knowledgeably about the towns and cities through which we passed. He also spoke happily about his job and proudly about his wife and children.

After a while our conversation shifted to politics and suddenly Hans did not sound quite so much like an "old militarist." Though Eastern European Communism seemed a real threat to him, he turned out to be not the least interested in having West Germany raise a larger army. In fact, the notion of a larger German Army seemed to worry him more than the Communists.

"Have you read Albert Speer's book about the war?" I asked, apropos of nothing. He hadn't. He had, however, heard of the book, written by Hitler's personal architect and later Minister of Armaments, and was anxious to read it. "I knew Speer," he said pensively, "and I liked him very much. He was a very able man." Then he paused a moment, reflected, and added, "He saved my life."

Hans had been working in a factory during *Kristallnacht,* in November, 1938, when an orgy of window smashing, arson, property destruction and murder victimized Jews all over Germany. Hans's maternal grandmother was Jewish, and under German law Hans was, therefore, a Jew. He was among thousands arrested that night, and was slated to go to a labor camp, and probably a concentration camp and gas chamber later on. Speer personally intervened and undoubtedly saved his life, not out of any particular compassion for Jews but because Hans's technological expertise was too valuable for the fatherland to lose. Speer protected Hans all through the war by destroying the evidence of his Semitic forbears.

Some "old militarist!" My surprise was total. Suddenly I had what almost seemed like a coreligionist riding next to me, and the saying about feeling more comfortable with your "own" proved to be quite accurate. Hans had probably never seen a Jewish service in his life, or spoken to more than two Jews, but to me he was now a kindred soul. In the space of three minutes my whole attitude had changed. I now felt I could ask him to help me with a project I'd been considering since early morning.

"Tomorrow we'll be in Regensburg," I said, "and it is Yom Kippur."

He nodded, and apparently I didn't need to explain the meaning of the holiday to him—that it was the Day of Atonement. "There is a temple in Regensburg," he said, anticipating my next question. "Do you wish to go?"

"Yes," I said. "Can you arrange it for me?" He nodded, then fell silent until we reached Regensburg some hours later.

We arrived in the city shortly before sundown, and Hans barely had time to call and ask permission to attend the services and to get directions. They were more than happy to have me. Regensburg is old, with ruins dating back more than 2,000 years, and its position at the point where the Danube River becomes navigable has made it a center of commerce for centuries. The streets are narrow and winding, and there are many dark alleyways. We decided to try to find the temple before going to bed that night, anticipating some difficulty. But we found it barely a block from the city's main commercial thoroughfare.

I hadn't been in a synagogue for more than 18 years, and in the morning, with the services scheduled for 9:30, I presented myself promptly at 9:25. The only other person in the synagogue was the cleaning woman. She looked at me and I returned her stare. We said nothing. After a few moments she tucked her dust cloth into an apron pocket, lifted her broom and left the room. Now I was totally alone.

The synagogue was very small and appeared to be fairly new. It was simplicity itself, its clear rectangular lines broken only by a raised platform at the front. On the front wall was the enclosure that held the rolled scriptures. The only decorations in the room were two velvet and brocade cloths on the side walls, rescued from the ruins of synagogues built over a century ago. Beside each were small cards attesting to their origin. There were perhaps a hundred folding chairs arranged neatly in rows, with a small section at the back of the room separated from the rest by a low, movable screen. Apparently the Jewish Orthodox tradition of separating the sexes was still being observed in spirit.

For about 15 minutes I remained alone. Then two old men entered and nodded to me. Between their halting English and my nearly nonexistent German I was able to determine that one of them had taken Hans's call the night before, and that they were expecting me. They seemed unusually glad that I had come. Their happiness, however, did not preclude a reproving look as they handed me a black paper skullcap and indicated the top of my head. I put it on a little ashamedly.

The two men moved to the front row and each put down a paper parcel he had been carrying. Each parcel contained slippers and an embroidered velvet bag. The men unlaced their shoes, placed them neatly under their chairs and put on the slippers. Then they placed the small velvet bags on their laps. I knew those bags well, and for an instant I was an 8-year-old boy again, sitting beside my father in temple.

His velvet bag had been blue with gold embroidery and it had held the prayer shawl he had received from his father as a boy in Poland.

One of the old men was looking at me. Without warning or comment, he pushed up his left sleeve. There, on his forearm, was a concentration camp tattoo consisting of indelible blue numbers, a mark of horrors seen and survived. His companion also rolled up a sleeve, revealing his own tragic souvenir. When they were sure I had seen, they let their sleeves fall back into place, and in the same matter-of-fact manner unzipped their velvet bags and took out their prayer shawls.

Now a bent old man shuffled slowly into the room, much older even than the two who had preceded him. They all exchanged holiday greetings, and then the old man was introduced to me. He, too, rolled up his sleeve to reveal his own blue numbers, then moved to the other side of the hall where he took a long white cotton caftan from a paper parcel and slipped it over his worn blue suit. He also changed from street shoes to slippers.

It was now 10 o'clock, and there were but four of us in the temple. Then an old woman arrived, followed by another. They exchanged greetings and retired to their prescribed section at the back of the hall. Neither of them greeted any of the men, and the men did not acknowledge them.

Ten minutes later a single man arrived, followed by another with his teen-age son. The son and I were the only persons in the room under the age of 60. Each new arrival was introduced to me, and every one (with the exception of the teen-age boy) went through the sleeve-rolling ritual. The tattoos seemed to be a bond between them, a symbol of tragedy shared.

At 10:25 two more men arrived, one of whom was introduced as the rabbi. He was a shopkeeper in the city. Conversation had switched from German to Yiddish, becoming animated with the entrance of each new arrival. But after a while the talk ceased and the old men stood around toeing the carpet. It was an hour after the services had been scheduled to begin. Then something suddenly dawned on me: They didn't have a *minyan,* the quorum of 10 men needed to hold a Jewish service. On Yom Kippur morning, the holiest day in the Jewish calendar, they couldn't find 10 men for a service. No wonder they had been glad to hear from Hans that I would be coming.

Names were mentioned as those assembled searched their minds for someone to summon so the service could be held. Then came a collective sigh of relief as a figure appeared in the doorway. Enter the 10th man.

Unlike the others, who wore navy blue suits, the new arrival was dressed in brown. His suit was of British cut, with a nipped-in waist and flared trousers. He must have been the same age as the rest, but his

642

deep tan contrasted sharply with their sallow complexions. He wore highly polished brown boots, a pink shirt and a wide red tie. Large gold links shone at his cuffs, and a star sapphire sparkled on his pinky. The rabbi rushed to greet him warmly. They were obviously not strangers. After they had exchanged greetings in Yiddish, the rabbi brought him over to me. "From America," said the rabbi, pointing first to one of us, then the other. The new arrival sat down beside me.

The rabbi reached over to one of the chairs and picked up a prayer book. Already the bent old man in the caftan had gone to the lectern and was beginning to pray. The rabbi opened the prayer book to the proper page, pointed to a passage, then handed the book to me. He then moved onto the raised platform at the front of the room.

"Ben Mandel, Plainfield, New Jersey," said the man sitting beside me. We shook hands. As the service droned on around us, we spoke and it seemed that Ben, like myself, was there more to be present than to pray. He told me about his new home in Plainfield, his business, and about the hotel he owned not far from where I once lived on the West Side of Manhattan. We talked about why he had left Manhattan for the suburbs: the dirt, the violence, Mayor Lindsay. Then I asked, "How do you happen to be in Regensburg?"

"I was liberated here," he replied. Then he rolled up his suit and shirt sleeve to reveal his own set of numbers on his left arm. They stood out starkly despite his tan. "I come from a small town not far from here," he said. "First my brother and I were sent to a labor camp. That was in the late thirties. When Hitler decided that he didn't even want Jews as laborers in his precious Germany, we were shipped to Auschwitz. The two of us were sent there with our sister. She died in the camp."

He paused for a moment. It appeared he hadn't told this story in a long time and it was hard for him.

"We were just lucky. If the Allies had arrived a few days later, I would be fertilizing the fields. They liberated us in Regensburg, and we lived here for a while. Then my brother decided to go to Israel, and I went to America. I can't complain. I've done very well. So every year I visit my brother in Tel Aviv for Rosh Hashanah and spend a week there with him and his family. Then I come here for Yom Kippur.

"It helps me remember how lucky I've been. It makes me remember how it was. Besides, there aren't many Jews left here, just these few old men. Once 10,000 Jews lived in the area, now they can hardly make a minyan on Yom Kippur. Imagine."

The bent old man held firmly to his lectern as he rocked back and forth. The other members of the congregation, all wrapped in silk prayer shawls with long fringes, rocked with him, reciting the ancient prayers.

I closed my prayer book, sat back and cried.

Germany is not the place for an assimilated Jew to visit if he expects to stay assimilated.

---

# Alexander Donat Writes to His Grandson (June, 1970)

My dear grandson, my son's firstborn:

Your father, and my son, was exactly your age on that spring of 1945 when returning from a long journey through Hitler's night via the Warsaw ghetto, Maidanek, Dachau, Ravensbrück, Natzweiler, Auschwitz, we found him emaciated and covered with sores, but miraculously alive, in a Catholic orphanage near Warsaw . . . You will have by now already read my book *The Holocaust Kingdom* in which our family saga is told in detail, and you will know that this book tells also your story, because if not for its "happy ending" you wouldn't be here . . . In April, 1943 we handed our only son, Wlodek, to our Christian friends over the Warsaw ghetto wall. This was the only way we could hope to save his life. He was then five years and four months old . . .

Should I try to describe our last night? Could I? In the morning Maria (a Christian friend) took Wlodek's hand and walked briskly away. His mother did not shed a tear, this was the time of the assassin and the time of the hero. It was April 5, 1943, two weeks before the end of the ghetto. We gave away our son, for agony and for survival . . .

We survived, against hope and against the rules. It was an incredible miracle of survival. We left behind a graveyard of our people. And your father Wlodek, now William, at present thirty-two years old, is father of three children, of whom you are the first-born. You are now seven years old, exactly the age your father was when we found him at the end of the war.

You may ask: Aren't twenty-five years sufficient to dull the pain? Why not forget the past and enjoy life now?

The answer is very simple: Those things are unforgettable. The scars can never be erased. There is no escape from the past except into the future. The guilt of having survived would be unbearable were it not for the mission to convey a message.

---

From *Midstream Magazine,* July 1970, by Alexander Donat

# The Lessons for Mankind

The most dreadful aspect of the Holocaust was that it turned what we regarded as impossible into a commonplace . . . Nobody can delude himself any longer that "it cannot happen here." It can happen here and any place, now and at any time, against Jews, Biafrans, Vietnamese, Russians, or Americans . . .

Had I considered our Holocaust a tragic but closed episode, I would have recommended that it be consigned to oblivion, as one of the many cyclical catastrophes in our history. But it is my firm conviction that the Holocaust was the beginning of an era, not its end—an era of turmoil and upheaval, of irrationality and madness, an era of Auschwitz. We are now in the 29th year of this era, and it may last for centuries if the Bomb will let mankind live that long. A new apocalyptic calendar may well start with a new Genesis: "In the beginning there was Auschwitz . . ."

In a world haunted by the memory of six million unvindicated victims behind us, and a cataclysmic perspective of an atomic doom ahead, with youth devoid of any ideal worth living for and wallowing in the satiated sterility of our affluent futility, what legacy do we leave you? Can I offer you the soothing belief in a good God watching and protecting us? I cannot even tell you that crime doesn't pay for it does. I am ashamed of the world our generation is leaving to you. I cannot assure you that there will be no more Anne Franks, as her father wishfully thinks. I cannot assure you that Auschwitz's chimneys will never smoke again.

What then can I say to you now? Only that I love you. You are my promised immortality.

But there are some aspects of the Holocaust that I wish to communicate to you in simple and unequivocal words.

*Religious aspects:* The Holocaust was for every survivor a crucial religious experience. Day-in and day-out we cried out for a sign of God's presence. In the ghettoes and in the death camps, before gallows and the doors of gas chambers, when confronted with ultimate incredible evil, we cried: "Lord, where art Thou?" We sought Him, and we didn't find Him. The acute awareness of God's puzzling and humiliating absence was always with us. Memory of this experience is always with us . . .

The far-reaching religious implications of the Holocaust have by no means been explored, nor has the process of coming to grips with its meaning been completed. It implies a profound revolution in the basic tenets of Judaism, and the rise of a new set of Judaic values.

*The Germans:* I do not consider every individual a Nazi or subjectively guilty of the Nazi crimes . . .

Yes, postwar Germany made a gesture of repentance. But it was dictated by the head not by the heart. It was not an act of moral atonement, a *catharsis;* it was rather a decision of calculated political

645

necessity. The denazification programs, the Nazi trials, the reparation payments were both insufficient and a travesty of justice. Instead of a summary surgical operation that would have extirpated the Nazi cancer and clearly separated the clean from the contaminated, the Germans chose to live with "the murderers among us" and never came to grips with the horrors of the past. That is why I would never shake hands with a German in his forties until and unless I ascertained beyond reasonable doubt that he wasn't a Nazi, or why the sound of spoken German evokes within me the image of a storm trooper.

*Israel:* The creation of Israel was undoubtedly a consequence of the Holocaust, but we cannot accept Israel as the consolation for the Holocaust. The conscience of the world was momentarily shocked by the enormity of the crime perpetrated on the Jews in the wake of the war. But it soon recovered from the initial shock and cynical opportunistic considerations soon overshadowed the moral impulse.

But whatever the initial impulse for the creation of Israel, it is now a fact that can no longer be erased from Jewish life. The continuing existence of the Jewish people stands and falls with Israel. Without Israel there is nothing but inevitable extinction.

Moreover, Israel is our national and historical insurance policy, our ultimate haven from new Holocausts, from whatever direction they may threaten next.

We are betrothed to Israel by ties stronger than life, stronger than death . . .

*The legacy of the Warsaw Ghetto:* The message of the Warsaw Ghetto can be epitomized in two words: "Never again!" Never again ghetto, never again Treblinka and Auschwitz, never again defenseless martyrdom. But also: no more naive delusions, no more faith in hollow terms like humanity, culture, conscience of the world, proletarian solidarity. Our only security is our own strength. A tragic conclusion for Isaiah's people!

Resistance was not the supreme virtue of the hunted, it was the only impossible choice. It ran against our nature and against our whole philosophy of life but it became the only alternative for us. Our national and historical ambition had always been to be the spiritual and intellectual inspirers of mankind, and not champions of military prowess. But the price they demanded was our very life and we refused to accept annihilation. The *Yishuv* underground, the soldiers of 1967, the frontier guards of 1970 faced the same merciless choice and reached the same ultimate conclusion: "Never again!"

In June, 1967, twelve million Jewish hearts stopped beating. We knew: "Here comes Act II of the Holocaust!" We won this round. But we are all tragically aware that more rounds are coming, whether from the sands of Sinai or from the snowy steppes of Europe's East, or from other places our timid imagination is too frightened to visualize. We, the most peace-loving people of the world, whose very greeting and farewell is "peace," *shalom*—what a cruel and tragic irony of history that our enemies have turned us into stern warriors. The flabbergasted world suddenly saw the Jew as a warrior rather than as the learned *nebbich,* to which it was used for centuries. And so we are now labelled "aggressors," while those who strive to complete Hitler's job have adopted the garment of the underdog.

In the past we had illusions, but no arms. Now we are doubly strong: no illusions and plenty of arms. Our standards are lower now but so much more realistic: we don't ask for love, we will settle for the Sixth Commandment. Don't love us, just stop killing us; just leave us alone in peaceful existence. We have been forced to trade our faith in God and Man for trust in military hardware. This is our strength and hope, and this is our greatest historical tragedy.

# Kol Nidre in Bergen-Belsen

> twice murdered shadows
> rising slowly
> out of deserted
> almost forgotten
> massgraves
> walking naked
> through smoke
> no longer breathable air
> death fog
> in the stone covered silence
> of mankind's forever frozen
> ashes
> nameless
> faceless
> holier than God
> unprayed to

From *Jewish Heritage,* Fall/Winter 1972, by Menachem Z. Rosensaft.

# Chronology

**1920:** Nazi Party founded
**1923:** *November 8:* Munich Putsch
**1924:** Hitler in Landsberg Prison: Writes *Mein Kampf*
**1933**
*January 30:* Hitler named Chancellor by President Von Hindenburg
*April 1:* Boycott Day against the Jews
**1935**
*September 15:* The Nuremberg racial laws are passed by the German Reichstag
**1938**
*March 12:* Austria invaded and annexed
*July 6–15:* Evian Conference, comprised of thirty-two nations
*September 29:* The Munich Agreement; Czechoslovakia is abandoned by the Western powers
*November 9–10:* Kristallnacht Pogroms
**1939**
*March 15:* Czechoslovakia wiped off as an independent nation
*August 23:* Nazi-Soviet Non-Aggression Pact signed
*September 1:* Poland invaded; World War II begins
*September 27:* Warsaw surrenders
**1940**
*April 9:* Denmark and Norway invaded
*April 30:* First Nazi ghetto established, in Lodz, Poland
*May 10:* Netherlands, Belgium, and Luxemburg invaded
*June 10:* Italy enters the war
*June 14:* Paris falls and France is overrun by Germany
*June 28:* Rumania gives up Bessarabia and Bukovina to the Soviet Union
*October 16:* Warsaw Ghetto set up
*October 28:* Greece is overrun by Italy
**1941**
*January:* War in Africa
*February–March:* Bulgaria and Rumania invaded
*April 6:* Yugoslavia invaded
*June 22:* Germany attacks the Soviet Union; the total destruction of the Jewish people (Final Solution) begins in full force
*July 31:* Heydrich charged to proceed with total extermination of European Jewry
*Autumn:* Mass massacre of Jews in U.S.S.R. territories conquered by Germany

*November 30:* Russian counter offensive begins
*December 7:* Japan attacks Pearl Harbor
*December 8:* The United States and England declare war on Japan
*December 11:* Germany and Italy declare war on the United States
**1942**
*January 15:* Allies pledge to punish war criminals
*December 17:* United Nations' declaration of punishment for extermination of Jews
**1943**
*January 14:* At Casablanca, Churchill, Roosevelt, and Stalin issue an "Unconditional Surrender Statement"
*February 2:* Collapse of German troops at Stalingrad; retreat from Russia begins
*April 19–May 16:* Warsaw Ghetto Rebellion and Liquidation
*July 10:* Allies land in Sicily
*July 25:* Fall of Italy's Facist government
**1944**
*March 19:* German troops enter Budapest. Liquidation of the Jews in Hungary, Rumania, and Yugoslavia intensified and accelerated
*June 4:* The Allies enter Rome
*June 6:* The Allies land in Normandy
*July 20:* Plot to kill Hitler fails
*August 25:* Paris is liberated
*September 1:* Budapest is liberated
*September 2:* American troops reach the Rhine
*September 3:* Brussels and Antwerp are liberated
*September 11:* British enter Holland
*November 26:* Himmler begins to wipe out the evidence of the crematoria
**1945**
*February 4:* Conference of the Big Three in Yalta
*March 7:* Allies cross the Rhine
*April 15:* Russian troops in Vienna
*April 21:* Russian troops in Berlin
*April 29:* The Germans in northern Italy surrender
*April 29:* Hitler kills himself
*April:* Concentration camps liberated
*May 7:* Unconditional surrender of Germany signed at Eisenhower headquarters at Reims, France